THE HANDBOOK
OF FORECASTING

A Manager's Guide

THE HANDBOOK OF FORECASTING

A Manager's Guide

Second Edition

Edited by
SPYROS MAKRIDAKIS
INSEAD, Fontainebleau, France
and
STEVEN C. WHEELWRIGHT
Stanford University, Stanford, California

A Wiley-Interscience Publication
JOHN WILEY & SONS
New York   Chichester   Brisbane   Toronto   Singapore

Library of Congress Cataloging-in-Publication Data:

The handbook of forecasting.

  "A Wiley-Interscience publication."
  Includes bibliographies and index.
  1. Business forecasting. I. Makridakis, Spyros G.
II. Wheelwright, Steven C., 1943–

HD30.27.H36   1987   658.4'0355   86-28137
ISBN 0-471-83903-5

Printed in the United States of America

10 9 8 7 6 5 4 3 2 1

PREFACE

The past few decades have seen some major developments in the field of forecasting. These have included an increasing number of sophisticated methodologies for preparing forecasts, experience in using such methodologies in a broader range of planning situations, and a deeper understanding of the psychological and organizational considerations that determine forecasting's impact on planning, strategy, and decision making.

In addition, the events and environmental changes of the 1970s and 1980s have presented managers with both significant challenges and significant opportunities in the field of forecasting. Critical challenges have included:

1. Economic uncertainty, not just in relation to basic factors like growth, inflation, interest rates, and unemployment but also about the underlying relationships among economic factors.

2. Organizational uncertainty in the forecasting of future events (e.g., sales, costs, revenues, competitive behavior) or relationships between various factors (e.g., demand and prices, advertising and sales, R & D and profitability).

3. Complexity of econometric and time series forecasting techniques, leading to requirements for more data, better expertise, and more computations for their application.

4. Recognition of the limitations of management judgment and the fact that it must be matched with analytical skills if forecasting is to be effective.

Significant opportunities for dealing with these challenges have included:

1. Increasing numbers of management students trained in the analytical techniques of forecasting and eager and willing to work with experienced managers in forecasting and planning jobs.

2. Better and cheaper access to computing power through mainframe, minicomputers, and microcomputers.

3. More and better computer programs to apply forecasting methods and thus deal more effectively with the prediction of future events.

4. Technical and data communication advances that provide better access to improved data bases in several areas important to forecasting.

In forecasting, as in most fields of endeavor, practical applications have lagged behind theoretical developments. In recent years, however, a number of organizations and managers have gained solid experience of what seems to work and why. The purpose of this book is to bring together this experience with current theory in a manner that will be most helpful to managers.

We have used three main guidelines in preparing this volume. First, it is intended to be a handbook; that is, it is meant to serve as a reference book— to provide broad coverage, to be up to date, to be easy to read, and to be organized in a manner that makes it easy for the reader to find information. The glossary, the detailed subject index, and the basic structure of the book were developed with this "handbook" concept in mind.

A second major aspect of the book, highlighted by the title, is its intended audience. Not only have chapters been planned and included on the basis of what managers need, but the individual orientation, topic coverage, and presentation of materials have all been geared to a management audience. The style of writing, the coverage of organizational issues and decision-making processes as they interact with forecasting, and the use of numerous practical illustrations, for example, are all in keeping with the needs of managers.

This updated edition includes new chapters on forecasting in the electric utility industry, state and local government revenue forecasting, population forecasting, price forecasting using experience curves and the product life-cycle concept, and forecasting the long-run trend of raw material availability.

Finally, as the title makes clear, the book is about forecasting. However, in keeping with both its handbook role and the needs of its management audience, we have defined forecasting in much broader terms than is done in most books on the subject. It is our view that forecasting is not solely a staff function: Instead it should be seen as an integral part of the manager's job. Although forecasting often involves the use of staff to complement the manager's time and abilities, its successful impact is in fact directly related to the manager's involvement, understanding, and need for the forecast. Unless managers are directly involved in preparing the forecast, the chance that the forecast will be incorporated into planning or decision making is slim. Thus, several chapters in this book highlight the context within which forecasting must be applied, and show what both the manager and forecaster need to understand about each other's roles in order for forecasting to make the greatest impact on the organization's performance.

We would like to give special thanks to the many writers who have contributed to this handbook both in their individual chapters and in the overall structure and philosophy of the book. We also appreciate the work of many managers who were willing to make suggestions for and criticize material included in the handbook, and we hope that their efforts will make the book more useful to its intended audience.

SPYROS MAKRIDAKIS
STEVEN C. WHEELWRIGHT

Fontainebleau, France
Stanford, California
March 1987

CHAPTER TITLES

PART 1. ROLE AND APPLICATION OF FORECASTING IN ORGANIZATIONS

PART 2. APPROACHES TO FORECASTING

PART 3. FORECASTING CHALLENGES

PART 4. MANAGING THE FORECASTING FUNCTION

INDEX

CONTENTS

Techniques · Political, Organizational, and Procedural
Considerations · Model of Revenue Forecast Accuracy ·
Actual Forecasting Accuracy

PART 2. APPROACHES TO FORECASTING

PART 3. FORECASTING CHALLENGES

Michael J. Showalter, *Assistant Professor, Florida State University, Tallahassee*

The Service Environment · Service Forecasting Requirements · Forecasting Service Products · Long-Range Forecasting · Short-Range Forecasting · Forecasting Systems

PART 4. MANAGING THE FORECASTING FUNCTION

1

ROLE AND APPLICATION OF FORECASTING IN ORGANIZATIONS

CHAPTER

1

INTRODUCTION TO MANAGEMENT FORECASTING

SPYROS MAKRIDAKIS
INSEAD, Fontainebleau, France

STEVEN C. WHEELWRIGHT
Graduate School of Business, Stanford University, Stanford, California

While forecasting has always been an integral part of virtually all types of management decision making, as a discipline it has only existed for a few decades. Now, in the late 1980s, forecasting has become a fully fledged academic and practical field, as its importance to planning and decision making has become apparent in such diverse areas as business, government, nonprofit institutions, and military organizations.

Forecasting is not just a technical or statistical area, but the domain of psychology, sociology, politics, management science, economics, and other related disciplines. A major goal of this handbook is to provide an up-to-date summary of these perspectives of forecasting, the progress that has been made in recent years, and the various areas in which forecasting has been applied successfully. Progress in the field of forecasting has been impressive, and the consequences for organizational decision making are significant to managers and forecasters alike.

This introductory chapter has a dual purpose. First, it provides an overview of some of the major perspectives on forecasting that have appeared in the literature in the past two decades. These perspectives can serve as useful reference points for practitioners seeking to broaden their understanding of available approaches to forecasting and the challenges and issues being addressed at the present time. Second, it gives an overview of the various sections of this handbook and suggests their interrelationships.

ALTERNATIVE PERSPECTIVES ON FORECASTING

During the 1960s, when economic and political conditions were relatively stable for the industrialized countries of the world, there was little interest in forecasting. In contrast, in the turbulent environment of the 1970s and early 1980s, the need for forecasting became widely recognized. The irony of this is that when forecasting can be fairly accurate, the need for it is limited and few praise its successes. During times when forecasting can only be inaccurate, everyone complains about its inaccuracy but perceives it as highly useful.

Formal forecasting started as a technical process, dominated by statistical methods applied solely to historical data. In recent years this emphasis has shifted, and while statistical models and quantitative data still play important roles (see Chapters 11 through 14), the psychological and organizational aspects of forecasting have become increasingly important (see Chapters 30, 31 and 32). In addition, it has become clear that many standard methodologies are not adequate for dealing fully with such areas as political forecasting (Chapter 22), new product forecasting (Chapter 24), and long-term forecasting (Chapters 23 and 27). Practitioners seeking sound advice about which methods might give best results for their specific needs often cannot be given a single answer (see Chapter 28). However, an understanding of the basic principles of forecasting and the increasing knowledge and experience of those working in the field can help managers apply forecasting better in their own organizations.

Chart 1-1 summarizes four dimensions of forecasting possibilities. Understanding the pros and cons of each of these helps in developing a reference point for planning forecasting applications. Let us first examine the rows in Chart 1-1. "Intuitive" forecasting refers to processes that are internal to the planner(s) or decision maker(s). Thus, while the person who does the forecasting may have useful inside knowledge and experience, he or she may be subject to many of the biases reported in the psychological literature with regard to such subjective and judgmental estimating procedures (see Chapter

CHART 1-1. Categorizing Forecasting Possibilities

	Implicit	Explicit
Intuitive	Estimating the sales of Product A for the coming month in an intuitive, ad hoc manner	Using a monthly meeting of senior management to develop forecasts for Product A for the next month
Formal	Predicting the sales of Product A for the coming month using a statistical forecasting method	Obtaining monthly forecasts for each major product on a specified date for use in production planning

30). This literature also suggests that intuitive forecasting may be less accurate than simple, statistical methods.

The "formal" forecasting methods referred to in Chart 1-1 are those whose steps can be written down and which, when applied by different individuals, provide similar forecasts. Thus, an important distinction between the intuitive and formal approaches is the degree in which the forecast can be replicated.

The major characteristic of "implicit" forecasts (see first column in chart 1-1) is that they are not integrated into plans and decisions being made. Thus, even if a formal forecasting procedure were used with an implicit approach, the forecast would not be systematically recorded or incorporated into a specific plan of action or decision. "Explicit" forecasting procedures, on the other hand, seek to delineate clearly the value of the forecast and the time at which it is obtained, and to use the forecast directly (possibly after having applied some consistent adjustment process) for planning or decision-making purposes.

As suggested in the final section of this chapter, most forecasting applications start out being intuitive and implicit in nature. However, research in the field of forecasting indicates that moving toward more explicitness and eventually to formal explicit procedures leads to significant improvements in forecasting performance[5] (see Chapter 32). How to manage the movement from the upper left-hand corner of Chart 1-1 to the lower right-hand corner is discussed further in Chapters 32 and 33.

A second perspective on forecasting is that practicing managers need to understand what existing techniques can and cannot do, so that they have realistic expectations when evaluating performance.[8] Many of the major problems currently attributed to forecasting can be tied directly to inappropriate expectations.

What a manager can expect from forecasting depends in large part on the type of method being used and the time horizon of the forecast. Chart 1-2 summarizes formal forecasting methods and shows their major advantages and drawbacks. It distinguishes three major approaches: judgmental, quantitative, and technological. Within the judgmental category, forecasts can be made by individuals or groups or can be aggregated from many individuals. The technological approach is classified as extrapolative or normative. The quantitative category (a major preoccupation of this handbook) comprises two major types of methods: time series and explanatory.

The time series techniques simply seek to extrapolate past data patterns into the future. The basis for the methods is that momentum exists in the event being forecasted and that this momentum will carry the series in the same direction independently of external factors. In one sense, the time series approaches can be viewed as "fatalistic," because they assume that things will not change and that history will repeat itself.

The explanatory (i.e., causal) techniques include regression and econometric models. They attempt to discover explanatory factors that link two or

CHART 1-2. A Taxonomy of Forecasting Approaches/Methods

Forecasting Approaches	Major Categories	Major Forecasting Methods	Short Description	Uniqueness/ Advantages	Disadvantages
Judgmental (major ingredient of forecasting is human judgment)	Individual (forecasts made by single person)	Individual judgment; Multiple-attribute decision making	Intuitive, ad hoc ways of making forecasts; Formalization of forecasting by making explicit subjective probabilities, preferences, and decision process	Changes can be quickly identified and their influence on future assessed	Expensive; Influenced from politics, personal considerations
	Group (forecasts made by groups)	Committees	Forecasts made in groups, meeting face to face and discussing future	Can incorporate into forecasts inside knowledge and past experience	Possible biases caused by over-optimism (or conservatism) inconsistencies and other judgmental shortcomings
		Sales force estimates	Bottom-up approach aggregating sales persons' forecasts	Prerequisite of any quantitative forecasting method whose results must be adjusted judgmentally	
		Juries of executive opinion	Marketing, production, and finance executives meet and jointly prepare forecasts		

	Method	Description	Advantages	Disadvantages
Aggregation (forecasts based on information aggregated from many individuals)	Anticipatory surveys	Intentions of potential customers learned through sampling surveys		
	Market Research	Customer's preferences discovered through pretesting of new products	Can be used when no historical information is available	Cannot deal with changes in established patterns or relationships
Time series (history repeats itself, thus future will be some continuation of past)	Naïve	Simple rules such as forecast equals most recent actual value, or equals last years' same month + 5%	Cheap, Objective	
	Decomposition	Data "broken" down into trend, seasonability, cyclicality, and randomness	Can optimally identify and extrapolate past patterns/relationships	Requires data and usually computer
	Simple time series	Forecasts obtained by averaging (smoothing) past actual values	Can provide information for understanding present	Forecasts could be black boxes
Quantitative (forecasts based on quantitative data)	Advanced time series	Forecasts obtained as combinations of past actual values and/or errors	Can deal with "what if" questions	Always requires human supervision and dealing with exceptions

7

CHART 1-2. (*Continued*)

Forecasting Approaches	Major Categories	Major Forecasting Methods	Short Description	Uniqueness/ Advantages	Disadvantages
	Explanatory (future can be predicted by understanding factors that explain why some variable of interest varies)	Simple regression	Variations in variable to be forecasted explained by variations in another variable	Can monitor for nonrandom changes	
		Multiple regression	Variations in variable to be forecasted explained by variations among more than one other variable	Can be used when large numbers of forecasts are required	
		Econometric models	Systems of simultaneous equations which take into account interdependence among variables		
		Multivariate methods	Statistical approaches allowing predictions through analysis of multivariate data		

Type	Approach	Method	Description	Advantages	Disadvantages
Technological (long-term forecasts of a technological, social, economic, or political nature)	Extrapolative (today's assured basis of knowledge is used to assess conditions of future)	Monitoring			
		Tracking signals	Nonrandom fluctuations identified so that a warning signal can be given		
		Delphi	Systematic and rational way of obtaining intuitive insights of experts, which avoids some problems of group meeting	Provides systematic framework for looking at long term	Expensive
				Allows pooling of experts' opinions	Accuracy of predictions cannot be checked
		Trend extrapolations	Extrapolation of prevailing tendency of series (after it has been modified for possible changes)		Limited range of applications
	Normative (future goals, objectives, and needs are assessed so that their effects and influences can be used as basis of forecasting)	Morphological research	Enumeration of all possibilities in way that could facilitate selecting promising future alternatives	Can incorporate future goals, objectives, and needs into forecasts	
		Cross impact	Interdependence among important future developments is found and used to predict occurrence of those developments that appear most often		

9

CHART 1-2. (*Continued*)

Forecasting Approaches	Major Categories	Major Forecasting Methods	Short Description	Uniqueness/ Advantages	Disadvantages
		PATTERN	Systematic way of incorporating preferences a way of forecasting future events		
		"La Perspective"	Approach to long term based on belief that future is created partly by human actions and partly through uncontrollable events		

more variables together and seek to answer questions like, "What will happen to B if A occurs?" This approach is popular in the natural sciences, and it has inherent appeal to managers. An important aspect of these techniques is an understanding of the relationship(s) between various factors and how the factors interact with each other. For example, if it can be determined that the price increases cause decreased sales, then a planned price increase can be linked to sales forecasts.

One of the problems with both the time series and the explanatory approaches is that the patterns or relationships on which they are based are determined from historical data. However, in most business and economic environments, such patterns and relationships change continually; only the rate of change varies. The higher the rate of change, the less accurate a forecast is likely to be.

This fluidity of patterns and relationships is further accentuated by the goals and actions of managers that influence the future course of events. As with self-fulfilling prophecies, the goals that management seeks to accomplish often becomes determinants of changes in the environment and thus affect the accuracy of forecasting methods. For example, when several companies in an industry forecast a certain business cycle for their product, or forecast the market potential for a new technology, the result for the entire industry may be changed simply because of those expectations and projections.

Thus it is particularly important for manages to be aware of existing goals and expectations, because these influence the future environment as well as their own organizations. Generally speaking, it is of little value to talk about forecasting accuracy without first understanding the complex factors that determine the future and the role of management in affecting those factors. Unfortunately, achieving such understanding raises many of the same problems as extrapolating historical data to predict the future. Relationships do not remain constant, and our ability to understand complex phenomena is limited. Furthermore, the existence of a relationship does not necessarily imply causality. On the other hand, identifying the factors that affect change and the direction of causality can be very helpful in planning and decision making.

A third perspective on forecasting relates to the issue of future uncertainty and its consequences for planning and decision making. The ability of forecasting to reduce future uncertainty is often limited, either because uncertainty may exist independent of what planners and decision makers do, or because the perception of uncertainty changes with the amount of forecasting. Managers would obviously prefer that the more forecasting that is done, the lower the future uncertainty. However, in many situations, spending more time on forecasting has the opposite effect. That is, the very process of exploring the future opens up new possibilities and leads to the consideration of more alternatives (and thus more uncertainty).

From this perspective, an important purpose of forecasting is to enable decision makers and policy makers to understand the uncertainties of the future and to force decisions about the level of risk that managers are willing to accept. Planners and decision makers have a number of choices in dealing with future uncertainty. One choice is to buy insurance against possible undesirable events, for example, fire insurance. Another choice is to develop guidelines to prevent the organization from venturing into situations involving high risk. However, high returns are often associated with high risks, so this choice poses a dilemma. A major role of forecasting is to aid managers in assessing various future alternatives and the levels of risk and return associated with each of them.

A fourth perspective centers on forecasting accuracy. The basic reference point here is the performance of forecasts made in the past[1,3,9,10] and then extrapolation of that performance into the future. Although many factors affect forecasting accuracy,[2,8] the time horizon of the forecast has been shown to be the most critical. Thus, its influence is briefly discussed here.

LONG-RANGE FORECASTING

Forecasts that cover a period of two years or more can be inaccurate. After examining the accuracy of forecasting in such fields as population, economics, energy, transportation, and technology, Ascher[4] reached pessimistic conclusions. He found systematic biases as well as errors that varied from a few to a few hundred percentage points. He concluded that one could not specify beforehand which forecasting approach or forecaster would be right or wrong. Furthermore, because policymakers tend to be supplied with so many different forecasts, the problem of choosing the "best" forecast appears to be as difficult as preparing one's own forecast. Since the fields examined by Ascher tend to be characterized by substantial experience and expertise in forecasting and to have readily available data, one might well postulate that in other fields in which data are less suitable for forecasting (less aggregation and greater fluctuations) and in which there is less forecasting experience, the results will be even worse.

Ascher's conclusions are echoed in the long-term forecasting literature (e.g., Gold[7]). It is difficult to assess beforehand the size of forecasting errors—unforeseen changes in trend can occur, discontinuities can arise, and new events or conditions can emerge. Moreover, past data can provide contradictory clues to future trends.[6] For instance, while certain products in an industry can grow in one way, others may follow very different patterns. Furthermore, even in the early 1970s few imagined the possibility of an oil embargo, oil prices as high as $39 a barrel, severe shortages of raw materials, stagflation, high unemployment accompanied by high inflation and high interest rates, a near collapse of the stock market, and two recessions in less than five years. Moreover, even fewer could have predicted the turnaround, with a drop in oil prices to less than $10 a barrel in 1986, a booming stock market, a fall in raw material prices, and low inflation and interest rates. Long-term forecasts thus tend to be inaccurate, although some basic patterns do seem to hold true (see Chapters 18, 19, and 23). Despite their inaccuracy long-term forecasts are necessary for capital budgeting and strategy formulation. The inherent uncertainty in them, however, can create serious problems that must be faced rather than ignored.

MEDIUM-TERM FORECASTING

Forecasts covering three months to two years are typically derived from long-term forecasts and from a buildup of short-term ones. A number of misconceptions exist about the ability of economists and business forecasters to predict important changes, either in the general level of economic activity or in the level of such activity for a specific industry, firm, or product, over the medium term. Turning points in the business cycle, in particular, are difficult to forecast (see Chapters 20 and 21) with any degree of accuracy.

Medium-term forecasting problems faced by economists and forecasters are twofold: unanticipated recessions and predicted recessions and accelerations that fail to materialize. Finally, with medium-term as with long-term forecasts, numerous approaches and resulting forecasts are available, and most managers tend to choose those that best fit their preconceptions and personal biases.

Medium-term forecasts are indispensable for budgeting purposes and for resource allocation decisions. However, managers must accept their limited ability to forecast recessions and booms in the economy (or in their industry) and develop flexible plans capable of allowing their organizations to adjust in case of cyclical turns.

SHORT-TERM FORECASTING

Because there is considerable inertia in most economic and natural phenomena, the current status of many variables is a good predictor of their near-term future status. This is especially true when the time horizon is three months or less. Mechanistic methods such as time series forecasting techniques can often make relatively accurate short-term forecasts and can even outperform more theoretically elegant and elaborate approaches such as econometric techniques.[1]

Short-term forecasting and planning are an integral part of several operations essential to the basic functions of a business. These include establishment of schedules for production, distribution, and employment; the development of cash management budgets; and the allocation of sales and promotion budgets. For such short-term needs, forecasting tends to be reasonably accurate, and the gains achievable from going from the intuitive/implicit to the formal/explicit mode of forecasting are consistently positive. However, because the management procedures typically used to cope with short-term planning decisions are an integral part of the business, these applications often receive less forecasting attention than they probably deserve. Short-term forecasting is in fact the area where the highest gains can be made.

JUDGMENTAL VERSUS QUANTITATIVE FORECASTS

Judgment is needed in all forms of forecasting. However, information-processing limitations, judgmental biases, and personal/political influences can seriously affect the accuracy of predictions. The advantages and limitations of human judgment versus statistical models thus need to be better understood (see Chapters 30, 31, and 32; also Chart 1-2) and effective ways of combining judgmental and quantitative forecasts (see Chapter 15) found. Managers should not expect or try to eliminate inaccuracies or uncertainties from forecasts. Although this is particularly true in the long term, it also applies in the medium term. Rather, they should seek to understand the limits of their judgment and the forecasting approaches being used. It is important to realize that whatever the problems and difficulties associated with formal forecasting methods, all other alternatives (notably intuitive, judgmentally based forecasts) usually produce results that are even worse. At the same time, obtaining judgmental forecasts can be substantially more expensive.

HANDBOOK OVERVIEW

In developing the outline and contents of this handbook, the editors sought to provide a comprehensive, practical guide for managers. They decided that four major areas needed coverage to accomplish this goal.

Part 1, "Role and Application of Forecasting in Organizations," considers the perspective of the manager in the business organization and his or her view of forecasting needs. The chapters in this section are organized around management planning and decision-making concerns from a functional point of view. Thus, sales and marketing operations and control, capacity and facilities, finance, strategy, population, and operational planning are all included. In addition, general management concerns with medium- and long-term issues, and particularly with long-range and strategic planning, are covered. The final chapter in this part addresses the relationship of forecasting methodologies to management issues and concerns.

In Part 1 the manager should be able to find personal needs and interests represented in the chapter structures and learn from the forecasting applications described. The forecaster, on the other hand, will recognize many of the individual applications, yet find the broad discussion of management concerns of primary benefit. These chapters form a reference base for managers and forecasters to enhance their communication and understanding of each other's perspectives.

Part 2, "Approaches to Forecasting," covers all major forecasting methods, ranging from smoothing to decomposition methods to regression and econometric models. This part also describes some of the more subjective approaches, such as Bayesian techniques, that can be used to complement the more statistical quantitative methods. While the chapters are structured in a manner familiar to forecasters, their contents include numerous applications and highlight the limitations and concerns most likely to be on the minds of practitioners. Chapter 11 ("Smoothing Methods") presents a class of techniques with high managerial potential in particular for short-term forecasting.

Part 3, "Forecasting Challenges," takes a topical view of several critical issues facing forecasting, planning, and decision making for the 1980s and 1990s. Thus, rather than taking the traditional view of either the manager or the forecaster, the chapters in Part 3 are organized around topics that are of mutual concern. Such special problems as forecasting in a rapidly changing environment, life-cycle and price forecasting, dealing with recessions, and the uncertain macroeconomic outlook are addressed. These issues have been of concern during the past couple of decades, and they have yet to be put to rest. A number of issues addressed in this part have come of age only in the last 10 years. These include the forecasting of political risks and of raw material prices. Part 3 concludes by considering other classes of problems that are likely to receive increased attention in the coming decade. Such topics as special events, new products, industrial and service products, and the overall long-term environment are covered.

Part 4, "Managing the Forecasting Function," looks at the task of applying forecasting to organizations. In contrast to the first three parts, which should be of concern to anyone having a specific forecasting requirement, the final part is focused on those who must handle forecasting applications.

Part 4 includes chapters dealing with the evaluation of forecasting models, the selection and maintenance of external data sources, and the use of third-party forecasting services. In addition, internal issues of concern to those charged with improving organizational forecasting are covered in chapters dealing with determining what needs to be forecast, integrating forecasting with decision making, and auditing and evaluating the forecasting function. The final chapter summarizes major concerns of both forecasters and decision makers and discusses future developments for both the theory and practice of forecasting.

REFERENCES

1. Armstrong, J. Scott, "Forecasting with Econometric Methods: Folklore versus Fact," *Journal of Business,* vol. 51, no. 4, pp. 549–564, 1978.

2. Armstrong, J. Scott, *Long Range Forecasting: From Crystal Ball to Computer,* 2nd Ed., Wiley-Interscience, New York, 1985.

3. Armstrong, J. Scott, "Research on Forecasting: A Quarter-Century Review," *Interfaces,* vol. 16, 1986, pp. 89–109.

4. Ascher, W., *Forecasting: An Appraisal for Policy Makers and Planners,* Johns Hopkins University Press, Baltimore, 1978.

5. Dawes, R., "Forecasting One's Own Preferences," *International Journal of Forecasting,* vol. 2, no. 1, 1986, pp. 5–15.

6. Dhalla, N. K., and S. Yuspeh, "Forget the Product Life Cycle Concept," *Harvard Business Review,* vol. 54, no. 1, 1976, pp. 102–112.

7. Gold, B., "From Backcasting Towards Forecasting," *OMEGA,* vol. 2, no. 2, 1974, pp. 209–224.

8. Makridakis, S., "The Art and Science of Forecasting: An Assessment and Future Directions," *International Journal of Forecasting,* vol. 2, no. 1, 1986, pp. 17–42.

9. Makridakis, S., and M. Hibon, "Accuracy of Forecasting: An Empirical Investigation," *Journal of the Royal Statistical Society,* Series A, vol. 142, part 2, 1979, pp. 97–125.

10. Makridakis, S., et al., "The Accuracy of Extrapolation (Time Series) Methods: Results of a Forecasting Competition," *Journal of Forecasting,* vol. 1, no. 2, 1982, pp. 111–153.

CHAPTER

2

SALES FORECASTING REQUIREMENTS*

G. DAVID HUGHES

School of Business Administration, University of North Carolina, Chapel Hill

A company considering the development of sales forecasts will need to answer a variety of questions before it can design a sales forecasting method to meet its needs. Who needs a sales forecast? What should we forecast? What are the determinants of sales? How do we determine the functional relationships between these determinants and sales? What are the sources of data for these determinants? Which direction do we forecast? From the aggregate to the small unit—the breakdown method? Or from the smallest unit to the aggregate—the buildup method? Who participates in the forecast? How do we evaluate a forecast? This chapter will help executives answer these questions when they are developing a sales forecasting procedure. It will also show how microcomputers can aid in implementing forecasting procedures.

WHO NEEDS A SALES FORECAST?

Strategic corporate planning operates in an environment of uncertainty. Sales forecasting attempts to reduce some of this uncertainty by predicting

* An expanded version of this discussion may be found in G. David Hughes and Charles H. Singler, *Strategic Sales Management* (Reading, MA: Addison-Wesley Publishing Co., 1983). Chapter 17.

what will be sold *to whom* and *when*. This information regarding what (products and services), to whom (market segments), and when (time patterns) is necessary input for planning in all functional areas of the firm. It is useful to classify these needs as long-run and short-run needs for sales forecasts.

Long-Run Needs

Chart 2-1 shows graphically where the long-run sales forecast fits into the corporate strategic planning process. This forecast is needed for organizational changes such as divisional decentralization, changing the sales force organization, opening new territories, acquiring new companies, developing new channels, and changing advertising agencies. Adding new products, extending product lines, and dropping old products require long-run sales forecasts. The capital budgeting process and changes in the production facilities will require a long-run sales forecast.

Short-Run Needs

The left-hand side of Chart 2-1 shows how the annual sales forecast is used in the short-run planning process. First, a forecast for next year may help to evaluate the current strategy. The success or failure of the present strategy may be explained as the forecaster examines the trends in the determinants of sales. What looked like an outstanding strategy may have been simply that we underestimated the growth of the market last year. Conversely, a great strategy may have been buried in a declining market.

The short-run forecast is needed for each of the elements in the marketing mix. *Product planning* requires a forecast for estimating inventories that will be required at various times throughout the year and at geographic locations. Timing of *price* changes, channel discounts, and promotional deals require good sales forecasts. Estimates of sales potential for market segments are a prerequisite for the *advertising* decisions that include copy themes and media strategies. A sales forecast may reveal the need for expanding the *sales force,* which will require plans for recruiting, hiring, training, and deployment. A change in the location of potential sales may require altering the *channel* strategy. All of these marketing strategies will appear in the cash budget as marketing expense items.

The sales forecast is needed for planning the production of a product. Scheduling, purchasing of raw materials, inventory planning, hiring and training of personnel, and estimation of overhead charges require estimates of the timing and magnitudes of company sales.

In summary, virtually all departments have some need for the annual sales forecast. Production, finance, personnel, accounting, and all of the marketing functions use the sales forecast in their planning activities.

CHART 2-1. The Role of the Sales Forecast in Corporate Strategic Planning

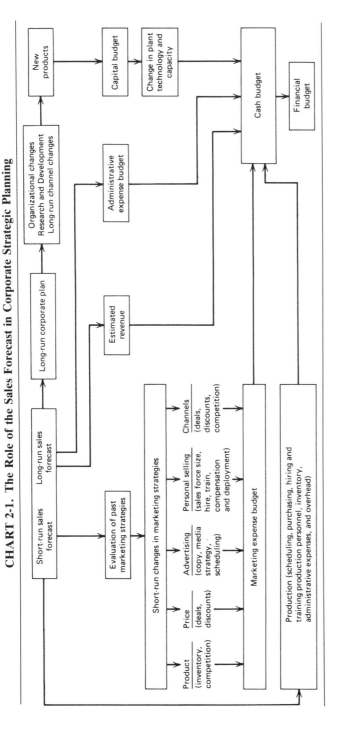

WHAT SHOULD WE FORECAST?

Because the term "sales" can have different meanings, there can be many different kinds of sales forecasts. To prevent confusion, the terms "market capacity," "market potential," "company potential," "company forecast," "sales goals," and "sales quota" will be defined in this section. The next section will explain how each of these forecasts requires a different set of variables.

Market Capacity

Market capacity is the number of *units* of a product or service that could be absorbed by a market at a given time irrespective of prices of products or the marketing strategies of suppliers. Capacity includes unmet needs for which a product or service does not exist. Thus, an analysis of market capacity could be the first step in developing a new product.

Market capacities could be expressed in terms of the total market or disaggregated segments of the market that have similar needs or buying styles. For example, we may forecast the total need for automobiles, or we may forecast the economy segment, the sporty segment, the luxury segment, and the fleet segment. Each segment would have different demographic, economic, and educational, and social–psychological profiles. The needs of a person within one segment would be similar to those of others within the segment, but quite different from those of persons in other segments. The capacity of each of these segments is the *market segment capacity*. The total market capacity is simply the sum of all of these market segment capacities.

Market Potential

Market potential is the sales, expressed in the number of products and the dollar volume, that an entire industry expects, given a known mix of products, prices, and market strategies. Thus, a sales forecast for the automobile industry may be stated in the number of luxury, compact, sporty, and economy cars that will be sold next year, given estimates of manufacturers' prices and their usual marketing strategies. The market potential differs from the market capacity because it speaks in terms of products instead of needs. Potential also introduces the concept of the *ability to buy a product* by introducing price and income. The term "potential" also recognizes the effect that the total industry marketing strategy can have on translating a capacity into a potential. Potentials may be expressed in terms of segments and industry totals.

Company Potential

A *company potential* is the *maximum* that a company could sell at a given price, irrespective of the capacities of its production and marketing facilities. This measure of company potential would be used to decide whether to add production and marketing capacities, whether to subcontract for production and perhaps marketing capacities, or whether to let some of the market go to competitors.

Company Forecast

The *company forecast* is a company's estimated sales, in units and dollars, for a brand, given a price and a marketing strategy. The forecast will reflect the capacity limitations of the firm, so generally it will be *lower* than the company potential.

Company forecasts are frequently expressed in absolute units and dollars and in the industry *share* of these units and dollars. Share estimates must consider competitive efforts regarding product attributes, pricing, promotion, and channel strategies.

Sales Goals

Sales goals are a hoped-for sales level for a company, a division, or a product. They are generally *higher* than a forecast to provide motivation, especially for the sales force. Goals must be within reach, however, or they will be discouraging and therefore demotivating.

Sales Quotas

A *sales quota* is a goal that has been broken down into smaller units, such as a region, a district, or a specific representative's territory, to provide a management objective. The quota is generally part of a motivation plan that is linked to compensation plans for sales managers and representatives.

WHAT DETERMINES SALES?

After the two previous questions have been answered, the sales forecaster must identify those variables that determine sales. Note again that we face the problem of how we want to define sales. For this section we shall examine what variables are needed to forecast market capacity, market potential, and company sales. By examining these three definitions of sales we shall see how each forecast requires different variables.

Variables to Forecast Market Capacity

Market capacity represents the total number of units that could be absorbed, regardless of ability to pay. For many products and services there are limitations. There is a limit to how much one can eat. One haircut per person per week may be the upper limit for that service. One automobile per person may be the market capacity for that industry.

Identifying this capacity is necessary before making a commitment to a product. But there have been classic cases in underestimating the market. When the first adding machine was developed, the market capacity was estimated to be 9000 units—one for each bank branch in the United States and Canada. Fifty years later the computer industry made a similar underestimate when it estimated that the capacity for computers was one for each major university and governmental agency.

Market capacities are based on the needs of individual consumers and firms. The needs of individuals may be defined in broad terms such as the need for food, shelter, safety, clothing, socialization, self-esteem, and self-actualization. A company has needs associated with its basic mission. For example, a manufacturing company will need machinery, materials, capital, trained labor, and management.

The magnitude of a need is measured by variables that are known as *market factors*, which are variables that either cause or are associated with the magnitude of the need. For example, a consumer's age will be related to food, clothing, and social needs. By knowing the number of persons in different age groups we can estimate the market capacity for baby food, soft drinks, and geriatric foods. Additional market factors for individual consumers include birth rates, marriage rates, education, geographic location, and the ages of children in the family. Sources of data for these market factors include the U.S. Census of Population and the *Survey of Buying Power*, published annually by Sales and Marketing Management (see Chapter 29).

Market factors for a manufacturer may be the number of units sold, the dollar volume of services delivered, the number of employees in a company, or value added. The U.S. Censuses of Manufacturing, Transportation, Retail Trade and Wholesale Trade and the *Survey of Industrial Buying Power*, published annually by Sales and Marketing Management, provide data for estimates of industrial market capacity.

Variables to Forecast Market Potential

The market potential forecast is a refinement of the market capacity forecast because it includes the additional variables of price, economic capacity to buy, and the effect of the marketing strategies within the industry. Here we are trying to answer questions such as, "How much would sales increase if we lowered price 1%?" or "How much will sales drop if disposable personal income drops 1%?'' These are concepts of price and income elasticity, as developed by economists.

Market factors for the ability to buy include not only income levels, but employment rates, the availability of credit, inflation rates, and consumers' expectations for the future. Market factors for a firm's ability to buy include the gross national product, inflation, the availability of capital, government policies, and executives' expectations for the future. Consumers and business executives' expectations for the future are reported by The Conference Board, *Business Week,* and the Survey Research Center of the University of Michigan.

Additional variables will be needed to forecast potentials for specific market segments. These variables reflect psychological needs and life styles. Market factor variables that are used to identify market segments include beliefs, attitudes, heavy use/light use, concern for style, worrisome, economical, and sporty. These variables are not generally collected by public sources, so the researcher will need to conduct primary research using survey research methods.

Variables to Forecast Company Sales

The forecast of a company's sales reflects the variables that go into a forecast of the market potential, the capacities of the company, and the effectiveness of its marketing strategy relative to its competitors. Thus, to forecast company sales we need to know the comparative advantages and disadvantages of the company's product, its relative price, and the relative effectiveness of its advertising, personal selling, and channel strategies.

One approach to forecasting company sales is to forecast the market potential and then multiply this potential by a forecast of the percentage of this potential that will be captured by the company. This percentage, known as the *market share,* will be determined by the cumulative effect of previous marketing strategies for the company and the industry as well as planned changes in strategy by the company and other companies in the industry. This approach is known as the *breakdown method* of forecasting company sales.

Three frequently used approaches for forecasting company share are econometric models, brand preference models, and brand switching models. Each of these will be explained in nontechnical terms.

Econometric models reflect several relationships simultaneously. The forecaster may have one equation that predicts the market potential for a product. This market potential equation would have demographic and economic variables. A second equation, to forecast market shares, would have variables that reflect product attributes and marketing strategies relative to the entire industry. The share equation may also reflect the cumulative effect of previous promotions or the carryover effect of a previous advertising blitz. This system of equations would be solved to estimate the effect of a change in a company's marketing strategy. (See Chapters 14 and 21.)

Brand preference models are based on the fact that people do not buy products; they buy a bundle of attributes that will meet their needs. Some needs are more important than others, which is reflected in a choice model by weighting procedures. Buyers perceive brands as possessing different amounts of these attributes. These perceptions are measured as attitudes toward the brands. Various metric and nonmetric methods have been devised for measuring these attitudes. These measures are reported in the form of attitude profiles, brand maps, and models. One of the difficulties with brand preference models is the fact that they are weak predictors of behavior. Their strength would seem to be as a diagnostic tool for developing better strategies. For instance, misperceptions regarding product attributes may be corrected with an advertising strategy. Correctly perceived product weaknesses may require further product research and development.

Brand switching models are based on the assumption that behavior patterns will be repeated. A matrix of the proportion of the market that has switched among brands can be multiplied using matrix multiplication to predict market shares in the future if certain mathematical assumptions have been met. One of the most difficult assumptions to meet is that people are homogeneous with regard to their probabilities of switching. One market segment may be loyal to a single breakfast cereal, for example, while another segment may be loyal to three or four cereals, switching for the sake of variety. This loyalty to a group of brands makes it difficult to identify switching patterns. Another limitation is that the basic model does not fully describe consumer behavior. Refinements in the basic switching model must be made to include the effects of learning that may occur from using a brand or from advertising.

The brand switching model is a better predictor of market shares than the brand preference model because it uses behavioral variables, those of brand switching, to predict behavior. The switching model is inferior to the preference model in diagnosing problems and developing better promotional strategies because it does not explain why consumers behaved as they did.

HOW DO WE DETERMINE THE FUNCTIONAL RELATIONSHIPS?

After we have decided who needs the forecast, defined the kind of sales that we want to forecast, and identified the variables that either cause or are associated with these sales, we are ready for the next forecasting question, "How do we determine the functional relationships between these variables and sales?" Generally we depend on empirical answers to this question.

In the strict definition of the philosophy of science, there are no theories of consumer or buyer behavior, but some empirical regulatories have been so labeled. *Price theory,* for example, states that generally more products will be sold as the price is lowered, except in those cases where there is a snob appeal for high-priced products. Price theory, therefore states only that the sign of the price–sales relationship is generally negative–that as one goes down the other goes up. The degree of change is an empirical question.

Some relationships can be described in terms of empirical probabilities. For example, market capacity (MC) may be defined as the product of the number (N) of persons who have given need, their probability (P) of using the product in question to meet the need, and the rate (R) at which they use the product during the time period t. This relationship may be expressed algebraically as follows:

$$MC_t = N_t P_t R_t$$

For example, if there are 50,000 fans at a football game, N equals 50,000. If the product category is soft drinks, we need an estimate of the probability that a fan will drink at least one cup of a soft drink during the game. We may express this event as either a probability for a single fan or the proportion of the total fans; the outcome is identical. This probability will vary according to the date of the game and its geographic location, both of which will determine the temperature. If it is cold weather, soft drinks may not sell well. Let's assume that this probability is 0.20. Finally, we need to know the rate or number of cups of soda that will be consumed during an average game, given the expected temperature. If we assume that the average number of cups per consumer is 2.25, we may calculate the market capacity for all soft drinks during the game as follows:

$$MC = 50,000 \times 0.20 \times 2.25$$
$$= 22,500 \text{ cups of soft drinks}$$

The *market potential,* however, may be considerably less than this number because of the price charged and the distribution system. Perhaps the price is too high. Perhaps the vendors working the isles of the stadium are more interested in the game than in selling soda. Thus, estimates of price elasticity and salespersons' motivation are needed to forecast the market potential.

What will be the market share for a given brand of soft drink? That will depend on consumers' past buying patterns, which reflect the cumulative effect of past strategies and current marketing strategies. Perhaps we generally get a share of 0.15, but we sold the vendor on using our cups, which show our brand name on one side of the cup and the name of the home team on the other side. From previous experience we have found that this increases the share to 0.20. Thus, in this case we may expect a market brand potential of 4500 cups (0.20 × 22,500).

Empirical relationships may be established with existing data, which is frequently the case with econometric models, or controlled experiments may be used to establish cause and effect relationships. Experimental data are scientifically more acceptable and generally more expensive to collect.

IN WHICH DIRECTION DO WE FORECAST?

The two basic approaches to sales forecasting are the breakdown method and the buildup method. The breakdown approach, as we have already seen, begins with an estimate of the market potential and breaks it first into a company potential that may be divided further into district, region, and territory potentials.

RCA uses the breakdown approach to forecast color television sales (ref. 1, pp. 119–25). It begins with an econometric model that forecasts gross national product (GNP) in constant dollars by using variables to reflect the current supply of money, government expenditures during periods of full employment, a price deflator, and dummy variables to reflect seasonality and periods when strikes occur. The color television model uses this forecasted estimate of GNP in constant dollars as one input along with estimates of the money supply in constant dollars (which would reflect the availability of consumer credit), a dummy variable for strike conditions (segments that would be temporarily off of the market for major purchases), and the position of color television in its product life cycle, expressed as an S-shaped curve. The total model includes 85 variables. (See Chapter 19 for another example of forecasting color television).

The Timken Company makes bearings for railroad freight cars. It forecasts its sales using the breakdown method (ref. 1, pp. 110–14). Timken uses two equations to derive the demand for new and rebuilt freight cars. The first equation derives the demand for railroad ton-miles per day by first estimating the total intercity ton-miles for the next year. This estimate is multiplied by railroads' estimated share of the market to produce the railroad ton-miles for the coming year. This yearly estimate is divided by 365 to produce a daily demand.

The second Timken Company equation estimates the supply of freight service that is available, expressed in terms of ton-miles per serviceable freight car. The size of the fleet that will be required during the coming year is derived by dividing the projected railroad ton-miles per day by the ton-miles per serviceable freight car. Because only 85% of the cars are available for service at one time, this estimated fleet size must be divided by 0.85 to yield the total fleet that is required for the forecasted year. To this figure the Timken Company adds the number of cars that will be retired next year and subtracts the size of the fleet at the end of the previous year. The net result of this computation is the market capacity for new and rebuilt freight cars.

The Cummins Engine Company uses a breakdown and a buildup approach to forecast the sales of its diesel truck engines (ref. 1, pp. 114–19). The breakdown approach uses an econometric model and an estimate of

Cummins's market share to derive a company forecast. The buildup forecast is based on a detailed study of the needs of each Cummins account. This analysis includes market factors such as the account's present engine inventory and back orders as well as the account's marketing program that may increase its truck sales. The resulting forecast is reported by account, model, and month. These individual account forecasts are added to produce a company forecast, which is then reconciled with the company forecast that is derived by the breakdown method.

Which is better, the breakdown or the buildup method? There are no theoretical answers to this question. The breakdown method tends to be less expensive when it can use aggregate forecasts that have been made by others, such as the government, universities, or consulting firms. The buildup method generally requires the forecaster to collect more data. With regard to reliability, Cummins reports that the breakdown method is more reliable for six months and beyond, while the buildup method tends to be more reliable for shorter periods. Thus, the planning horizon seems to determine the appropriateness of the sales forecasting method.

The introduction of the planning horizon requires that we ask, "How far into the future are we forecasting?" If we are making a one-year forecast, variables such as birth rates and geographic shifts in populations are not important because there would be only slight changes. If however, we are making a 10-year forecast, these demographic variables become extremely important.

FORECASTING WITH MICROCOMPUTERS

The rapid development of microcomputers has made it possible for sales and marketing managers to make sophisticated forecasts that were previously the domain of staff statisticians. The greatest advantage of this is that managers can introduce subjective inputs into the forecast and immediately test their effects.

In the last three years many sophisticated forecasting models have been rewritten for personal computers (PCs). It is unlikely that sales managers will want to learn to use these complex models. Instead, they are more likely to use one of the popular spreadsheet programs, such as Lotus 1-2-3(TM), for several reasons. Managers may be familiar with a spreadsheet package, and so do not need to learn new commands; or others in the company may be familiar with spreadsheets, so that help is available. The results from a spreadsheet forecast can be loaded easily into another planning spreadsheet for applications such as projecting the size of the sales force needed to meet forecast, making recruiting and training plans, designing territories, and creating sales budgets. Finally, forecasting models that use a spread sheet structure can be developed within the firm or purchased for less than $100. In contrast, free-standing forecasting models start at about $500.

Do-It-Yourself Forecasting by Segments

To forecast demand by segments, it is necessary to estimate N, PR, and R for each segment for each time period. Chart 2-2 illustrates a forecasting model using Lotus 1-2-3. The chart was created in May 1983 for a decay prevention toothpaste.

Developing such a spreadsheet model, known as *template*, takes less than one hour. One can build in features, such as listing assumptions that went into the forecast. These assumptions can be easily reconsidered as time passes, and the forecast can be modified accordingly. In this case, when 1985 arrived it was obvious that inflation and unemployment rates were much lower than anticipated, and Crest had announced a new product to fight tooth plaque.

N, the number of persons in each segment, can be estimated from census data. The probability of these persons using decay prevention toothpastes, PR, is estimated by studying past trends and estimating the effect of generic educational campaigns. The market share will require continuous evaluations of company marketing strategies and those of competitors. By changing numbers in key cells, the sales manager can estimate the effect of changes in strategies.

The sales manager may purchase sophisticated but easy to use templates for Lotus 1-2-3. Two excellent models that were available in late 1985 are MicroCast$^{(TM)}$ and 1,2,3 Forecast!* The features of each of these templates will be discussed briefly. We may anticipate even more sophisticated forecasting templates after Lotus 1-2-3 releases its new version, which will do matrix multiplication and multiple regression with up to five independent variables.

MicroCast

MicroCast is a Lotus 1-2-3 forecasting template designed for sales managers. It is easy to use and gives graphs that sales managers will understand easily. It allows for judgment inputs of trends, which it calls eyeballing, and it permits bends in the trend line, called doglegging, when unique events occur. The goal of the program is to help the sales manager manage better, with little knowledge of forecasting.

Comments, such as "Competitor lowered price this month," can be added easily. A wild month can be ignored when calculating the trend and season by a simple ignore command.

Charts 2-3 and 2-4 illustrate two of the nine charts that are easily printed. Chart 2-3 tracks monthly sales for four years. Chart 2-4 shows the actual

---

* MicroCast$^{(TM)}$ was developed by CompuCast Software, 5328 Fulton Street, San Francisco, California 94121. 1,2,3 Forecast!$^{(TM)}$ was developed by Bruce L. Gates, PO Box 12582, Salem, Oregon 97309.

CHART 2-2. Estimating Demand By Segments Estimated in May 1983, for 1985 and 1995. Estimate $N(T)$, PR (T), $R(T)$ for each Age Segments 14–24 and 25–34[a]

Product Category: Decay Prevention Toothpaste

Assumptions:	1985	1995
1.	Inflation 7%	Inflation 6%
2.	Unemployment 9%	Unemployment 6%
3.	No new technology	New dental technology

Forecast Period	1985 Age Segments		1995 Age Segments		Change	
Demand Elements	14–24	25–34	14–24	25–34	14–24	25–34
$N(T)$ (000)	43,438	41,781	37,755	40,489	−13.08%	−3.09%
PR(T) category	0.55	0.65	0.60	0.70	9.09%	7.69%
Users N*PR (000)	23,891	27,158	22,653	28,342	−5.18%	4.36%
R (tubes/year)	1.35	1.92	1.55	2.02	14.81%	5.21%
Total tubes/year	32,253	52,143	35,112	57,251	8.87%	9.80%
M, share/segment	0.2	0.27	0.17	0.29	−15.00%	7.41%
Our units est.	6,451	14,079	5,969	16,603	−7.46%	17.93%
Ours, all segments		20,520		22,572		9.95%

[a] Here N = number of persons in each segment, PR = probability of using decay prevention toothpaste, R = number of tubes consumed per year, and M = the market share per segment.
© 1985 G. David Hughes

sales, the straight-line trend, and the forecast that results from the trend and seasonal index.

1,2,3 Forecast!

The 1,2,3 Forecast! template presents sophisticated forecasting concepts in amazingly clear fashion. The manual walks the reader through the real-world experience of forecasting air passenger miles. This template could easily be used as a short course on forecasting, because the appendix clearly explains the concepts behind forecasting techniques.

This template begins with a simple linear regression model, which is graphed nicely in Chart 2-5. The template also graphs residuals. Chart 2-6 shows seasonal and curvilinear influences in the residuals. The example takes the novice through the steps for refining the forecast, which include the following: deseasonalization of the data, an exponential trend of seasonally adjusted values, a quadratic trend of these values, a dummy variable for the effect of the Arab oil embargo, multiple regression with a lagged independent variable, short-term projections using simple moving averages, single and linear exponential smoothing models, and multiplicative linear decomposition analysis (including an estimate of a cycle, which is not found in most forecasting models). All of these discussions are supported by clear

CHART 2-3. Year to Year Sales History, Using Microcast

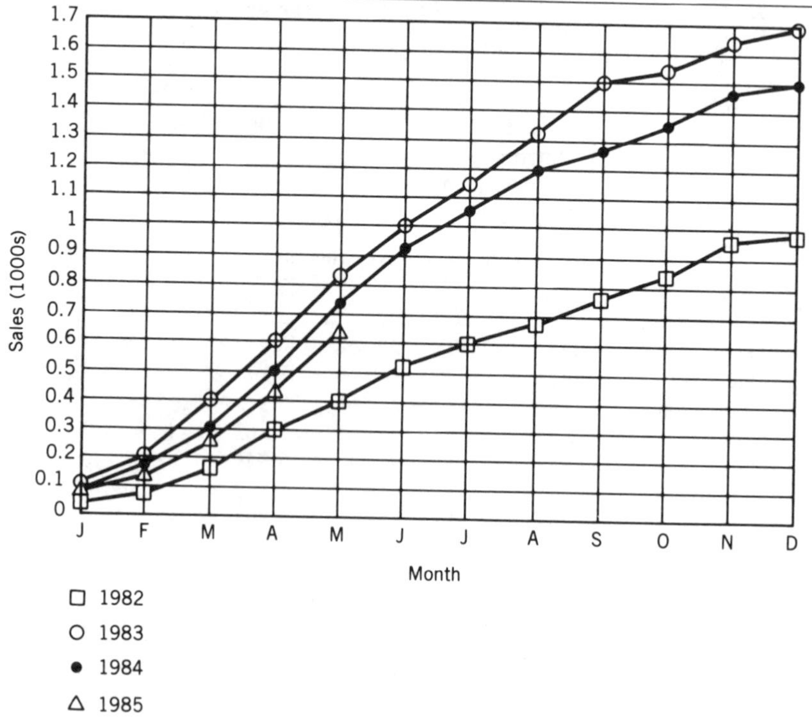

Month

□ 1982
○ 1983
● 1984
△ 1985

graphs and a technical appendix. The author manages to accomplish all of this in a manual of less than 60 pages.

Expert Systems

Expert systems models, which are part of the growing developments in computer artificial intelligence systems, "learn" the model that the expert used in making a decision. These models could be useful when judgment is an important part of the forecast. Human Edge Software, of Palo Alto, California, has developed a personal computer software program that combines the Box-Jenkins model with an expert system. The program is called The Forecasting Edge.

WHO PARTICIPATES IN SALES FORECASTING?

The broadening of the base for strategic marketing planning has also broadened the base for forecasting. Individual sales representatives are frequently involved in forecasting the needs for specific accounts, as illustrated in the

CHART 2-4. Last 24+ Next 18 Months, Using Microcast

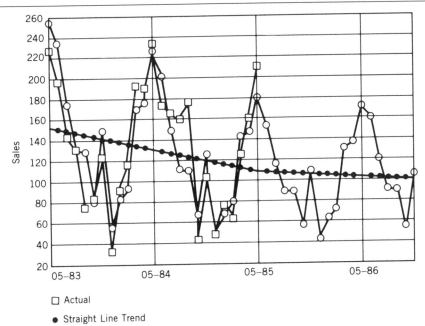

□ Actual

● Straight Line Trend

○ Forecast

CHART 2-5. Air Pass-Miles (MM), Using 1,2,3 Forecast!

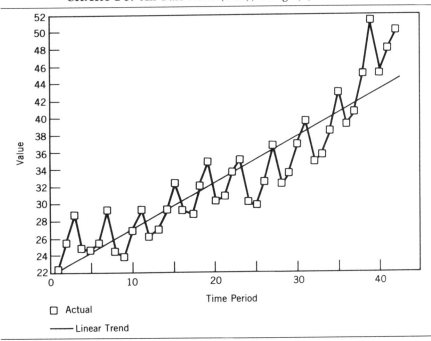

□ Actual

—— Linear Trend

31

CHART 2-6. Air Pass-Miles (MM), Using 1,2,3 Forecast!

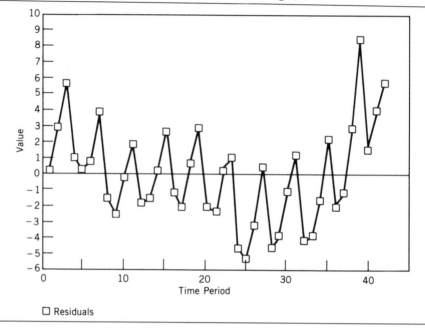

Cummins Engine Company example. Market and product planners will provide input for changes in the general market, changes in competitive activities, and changes in the company's marketing strategies. The legal and government relations departments will provide estimates of regulatory and legislative changes that will affect sales. The Jones & Laughlin Steel Corporation has broad involvement in sales forecasting, including the sales managers, marketing managers, operations personnel, market planners, economics and sales analysts, and a general manager for steel planning (ref. 1, pp. 35–39).

HOW DO WE EVALUATE A SALES FORECAST?

It is harder to answer this question than it is to answer the question, "How do we evaluate a weather forecast?" Because we cannot control the weather, we can evaluate weather forecasting methods according to their reliability and validity. Realiability means, simply, will the method give similar results over time? Validity, in this case, means did it rain as predicted?

To understand the problem of validating a sales forecast, we must consider the concepts of self-fulfilling forecasts and non-self-fulfilling forecasts. A rumor of a run on a bank may produce a run on a bank, which is a self-fulfilling forecast. In contrast, a sales forecast for a bad year may provide a motivation for creating better marketing strategies, and it may stimulate higher selling productivity, thereby increasing sales and invalidating the forecast. This is a happy ending for the company, but it ruins the forecaster's record. Thus, the ultimate test of a sales forecast is whether it made the marketing strategy a better strategy.

CONCLUSION

The sales forecasting requirements of a company will be unique to each company. To design a forecasting system, the company must answer the questions that are asked in this chapter. Subsequent chapters will provide more detail and techniques for answering these questions and for developing an operational forecasting system.

REFERENCE

1. Hurwood, David L. Elliot S. Grossman, and Earl L. Bailey, *Sales Forecasting*, Report No. 730, The Conference Board, New York, 1978.

3

FORECASTING REQUIREMENTS FOR OPERATIONS PLANNING AND CONTROL

BAYARD E. WYNNE

Principal and Director of Modeling and Quantitative Techniques Arthur Andersen & Co.

DAVID A. HALL

Graduate School of Management Northwestern University, Evanston, Illinois

THE OPERATIONS FUNCTION

The fundamental issues in operations planning and control (OP&C) are what to make, how much to make, and when to make it. Marketing presumably converts its assorted customer and competitive intelligence into some form of estimated demand. Facilities management decisions on physical capacity limits are similarly defined externally for OP&C. All these factors are integrated into the financial program, which will be one of the measures used to evaluate OP&C performance.

Within those limits, OP&C has the task of balancing the many tradeoffs among material availability, labor efficiency, capacity utilization, and finished goods inventory balance or customer service.

This chapter treats both the inputs and outputs of a typical OP&C model, their sources, screening, and application. This chapter's references are a good source for more detailed information on OP&C systems and the associated forecasts. In addition, *Journal of the American Production and Inventory Control Society* provides a wealth of applications articles.

MODEL INPUTS

General Requirements

OP&C models are demand driven, receiving their key inputs in the form of demand forecasts from the marketing department and order backlog status reports from the order entry system. This demand for gross products is then exploded[5,10] into indivisible net subcomponent, labor, capital, facilities, and transportation requirements. In turn these are compared against exogenously given working constraints: capital availability, plant capacity, personnel availability, raw materials inventory, and order lead times and finished goods storage and transportation constraints in order to determine desired feasible production and product mix.

Chart 3-1 illustrates this context for forecasting as related to the OP&C function. Implicit in the interrelationships shown in Chart 3-1 is the critical necessity of ensuring that a complete adaptive management information system[2] is in operation to deal with all issues, regardless of the particular organization structure that exists.

Screening

All incoming data should be screened for three key factors: *timeliness, accuracy,* and *sensitivity*. Timely data are both current and available early enough to allow production changes to meet the new projections.

Screening for accuracy is a three-part test. First, is the variable correct? For example, has nominal plant capacity been substituted for peak capacity, and so on? Second, are the data consistent? Have data been correctly entered and do the projected inputs and outputs seem appropriate? Third, have the inputs been intentionally altered, misprojected, or skewed? An example of this inaccuracy occurs when a marketing department with a compensation plan based on exceeding quotas is allowed to set sales forecasts.

Finally, the sensitivity of both inputs and outputs should be considered. How sensitive are current projections for sales or labor costs to changes in competitive strategies, the environment, or anticipated wage increases? How sensitive is the resulting production schedule to variations in these inputs? Output sensitivity to input parameters will highlight those variables requiring the most screening for management purposes.

In actual practice several problems usually must be dealt with as tasks related to the top cluster of elements in Chart 3-1 are defined. Perhaps new potential data sources must be formalized to improve accuracy, to reduce bias, or to synchronize data in time. It is vital that a methodical approach be

CHART 3-1. OP&C Forecasting Context

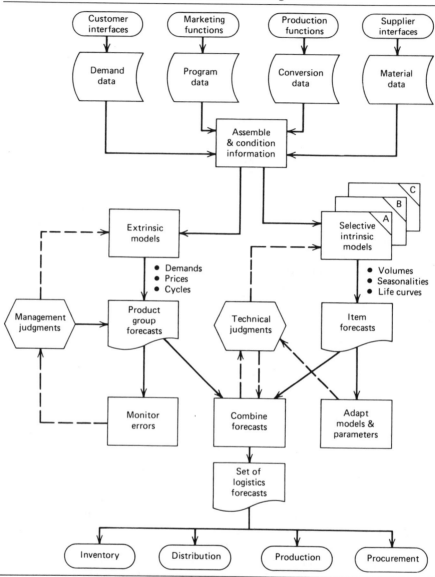

taken in this design of data screening. For example, clear user manuals are required if this foundation of the target OP&C system is to be accomplished successfully.

Specific Input Requirements

Demand Information Treatment

Real demand is not merely backlogged orders and sales forecasts. Rather, it is the required number of shippable units by expected need dates. The discrepancy between orders and real demand can be traced to several key factors.

Order cancellations are a primary cause of this difference and can play a major role in production misscheduling in the face of an economic downturn or in a capital-intensive technological market. While backlogged orders can be aged and weighted to better approximate demand, inappropriate production allocation can arise as a result of customer volatility. This volatility is often a function of how expensive a product is and how technologically sensitive the market for a firm's product is. Witness IBM's dilemma during the introduction of its 3300 series as the market failed to buy and cancelled standing orders in anticipation of the introduction of its 4300 series computer.[9]

In actual practice, the forecaster frequently has to take competitors' behavior into account. Imagine the difficulty of attaining useful demand forecasts if IBM's competitors failed to include data about IBM actions in making their own forecasts. The left side of Chart 3-1 encompasses such issues.

Promotional activities contribute unpredictably to the divergence between orders and demand. Sales promotions can provide both an unpredictable increase in sales and an increase in order cancellations rates because of indecisive marginal trial customers.

Disasters, whether they be natural or economic, that affect the market can further influence this divergence. Examples of these factors would include the near collapse of the construction market in 1980 caused by spiraling interest rates, and the shift to imported economy automobiles in the period 1973–1980 in response to OPEC-generated energy price increases.

Finally, the relationship between orders placed and demand may be seasonal in nature. Parker-Hannifin Corporation has successfully used a pragmatic cycle forecasting technique[8] to approximate demand well enough with sufficient lead time to program integrated sales and production activities by product line in advance of swings in the segments of the economy that affect its business.

Motivational differences further complicate demand forecasts. Marketing targets that include sales objectives, quotas, and executive bias due to compensation plans all motivate one group, while OP&C is driven primarily by shipping requirements. The costs of associated errors in demand estimation also differ between the two functional areas, where stockout costs or carrying costs can far exceed marketing's cost of error.

This difference between motivation- and error-associated costs requires a clarification of cross-functional demand estimation. Who is to make the estimates, and how are those people motivated? How are errors tracked and utilized in updating flexible budgets and testing model accuracy? And, finally, how well do extrinsic and intrinsic demand estimates track real demand?[7] A forecasting system must have systematic feedback if organizational learning is to take place and performance is to improve.[7]

Capacity Information Issues

Physical plant capacity, both nominal and peak as defined by plant engineering, is a basic given to the OP&C manager. While plant capacity is usually assumed to be fixed, it must be subject to periodic updating because of the effects of capital expenditures, replacement or overhaul of equipment, increase in downtime due to plant aging, changes in product production, and the impact of moving along the learning curve.

Manning levels and shifts are one decision variable to the OP&C manager. Shift decisions are long run in nature. Manning levels within a shift are used to "fine tune" production and provide flexibility to meet discrepancies between forecast and actual demand. (See Chapter 11 for an example of one approach to these issues.)

Varying final production mix by scheduling is another decision variable. By changing the number of shifts, the staffing level of shifts, or responsibilities within shifts, product mix within the physical plant capacities can be adjusted.

Key questions concerning capacity constraints include: How are shift changes planned? What constraints are imposed by the union? How much flexibility is provided within shifts by responsibility reassignment with the constraints of the union? Should peak periods be handled by overtime or an additional shift? Who varies manning levels? How much power should be vested in the foreman? Which product should be run when, and in what quantity, taking into consideration demand, capacity, and setup or additional tooling costs?

In actual practice, the forecaster will want to include these production planning/scheduling algorithms and heuristics in the systems analysis diagram. They would appear in conjunction with the bottom cluster of elements in Chart 3-1. The practical reason for including them in the detailed version of Chart 3-1 is to ensure provision for any desirable feedbacks between the several schedules and their predecessor forecasts.

Financial Planning Matters

Marketing shipments are the driving force of OP&C models, and both additions to accounts receivable and marketing expenses are implicit in the model. By assuming inventory buffers as a safety factor, the stockpiling of both raw materials and finished goods to satisfy demand, and the minimization of costs via forward buys and given a targeted customer service level or aggregate inventory level, fluctuation should be plannable. These anticipated fluctuations in inventory, in coordination with marketing expenses and additions to accounts receivable, allow the forecasting of financial requirements. These requirements will be on a cash basis, enabling the firm to quickly assess the feasibility of various production strategies with respect to cash demands and funding requirements. These production demands assist the firm in capital budgeting by providing a calendar of net cash flows with respect to operations covering both expenses and capital outlays.

Operating budgets represent combined functional decisions and are cross-functional agreements concerning allocation of a firm's limited financial resources. The cash flow calendar provided by the OP&C model enables the manager to identify readily those future periods of cash flow problems; it also may suggest replanning of capital expenditures or reallocation rather than budget cuts as an emergency procedure.

These links between the OP&C forecasting system, the derivative planning systems, and the trailing financial planning tools are not shown in Chart 3-1. However, they will be an integral part of the bottom symbol cluster of a detailed version of Chart 3-1.

OUTPUTS

Efficient production planning is the basic goal of all OP&C models, including material requirement planning, machine/work center loading, and shop floor control.[3]

Material procurement is one derivative of the OP&C model. By exploding finished goods demand to yield raw material requirements, and analyzing each input by quantity discount factors and order lead times, the forecaster can derive an economic order quantity (EOQ). This EOQ will minimize total costs by balancing stockout costs, carrying costs, quantity order discounts, desired buffer stocks, anticipated demand, and order placement costs. While no one EOQ method is universally best, the dynamic silver-meal algorithm[6] has had a demonstrated widespread success. A family of forecasts is produced by the model:

Procurement Lead Times. When orders of size EOQ must be placed to maintain buffer and satisfy demand.

In-Process Lead Times. When production must begin and in what quantity to satisfy anticipated demand.

Uncertainty. The buffer level that should be maintained to be sure of satisfying demand at the confidence interval stipulated by the desired level of customer service.

Stockpiles. When and to what levels inventory is allowed to increase for the firm to satisfy demand when demand is anticipated to be greater than production capacity.

Forward Buys. The amount and timing of advance buying against expected consumption levels. Decision rules have been constructed that attain expected returns on investments from investment in commodity futures for consuming organization.

Labor Productivities. Depending on the labor content leverage, learning curve forecasts, for example, can have a major impact both on product costs—and therefore demand—and on effective production capacity.

Process Yields. Long-term drift in mean process yields has high impact on all cost elements as well as on saleable output capacity.

Shipping Times. Time lost in outbound transit is a severe restraint on higher market share and production economies through more stable product mixes that might otherwise be obtained.

These illustrative forecasts, as they relate in a comprehensive OP&C model, are shown in Chart 3-2.

The particular linkages, of course, depend on the business situation. Chart 3-2 should be regarded as a graphic checklist to be specifically structured into the design context.

FORECASTING SYSTEM MANAGEMENT

Three primary issues exist in managing the development and use of forecasting systems. These are (1) careful mutual consideration of the criteria to be satisfied, (2) a focus on systems rather than techniques, and (3) the conduct of forecasting implementation studies or projects.

Management's Forecast Criteria

General management seeks a combination of benefits from an OP&C forecasting system. The particular relative importance attached to each component benefit will vary among organizations. The importance of each will also vary in time within an organization.

Therefore, a good forecasting system will be constructed so that expected tradeoffs among these benefits in response to policy variable changes can

**CHART 3-2. Linkages Among Operations
and Control Forecasts**

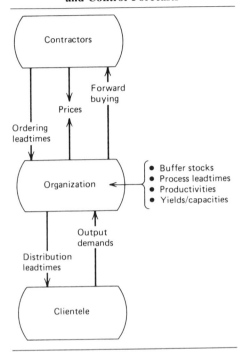

readily be portrayed. As a corollary, a good forecasting system will also be driven by settable parameters through which management can "tune" the forecast system to its desired benefit mix.

The three major component benefits are:

Reasonable customer service

Inventories controllable to targets

Attainment of procurement, conversion, and delivery economics

These benefits have been listed in order of generally perceived importance. It is fundamental to the business organization's survival that it be aware of and potentially responsive to customer service requirements. Within that constraint there must be a capability to control aggregate inventory investments. Then, it is also necessary to be cost efficient.

Brown[1] has codified one good approach (his indifference curve analyses) to providing general management control over the tradeoffs among these benefits. Peterson and Silver[6] provided excellent coverage of the cost-efficiency techniques. Some combination of both objectives (each offers such) is required in the good OP&C forecasting system.

Selection of specific techniques to use to meet the management criteria leads to a consideration of the technical criteria of forecasting systems. An important trio of criteria are

Forecast accuracy

Forecasting cost

Forecast comprehensibility

Generally, the more forecast accuracy, the better. However, small forecast inaccuracies make essentially no difference in the complex aggregate operation of a typical industrial organization. Too many time lags and buffers as well as countervailing pressures exist to enable small forecast errors to have significant impact. Increased forecast accuracy is normally attained only at higher expense.

Therefore, what is usually sought is a robust forecasting technique that operates at reasonable cost with tolerable errors. The technical design issue therefore is to structure the forecasting system so that it effectively uses adequate techniques.

This design perspective will usually satisfy the third technical criterion, that forecasts be comprehensible to the user. System forecasts must be intuitively acceptable to the user or an alternative informal forecasting system will evolve. Again, a well-structured combination of robust techniques with periodic human judgmental interaction, coupled with adaptive or learning feedbacks for both the model and the humans, is appropriate most often.[11]

Systems Versus Techniques

The preceding section emphasized that good forecasting systems are those in which the architectural design specifys the techniques, rather than the "best" forecasting techniques dictating the system design. This theme and related topics are covered in Chapter 32, "The Forecasting Audit." Only some basic reminders are given here:

Even the most accurate forecasts can be wrong.

Error feedback and exception handling are keys to results.

Forecast frequency, period, and horizon are system design variables.

Incorporation of human judgment in the forecasting process is vital.

Technical simplicity is most desirable.

Behavior aspects of forecast users are crucial and can be dealt with only at the system level.

Managing Forecast Studies

The last four chapters of this handbook deal with managing the forecasting function. In contrast, we deal here simply with the management of forecast studies—a development project and the ensuing maintenance task. In the interest of brevity, however, this material is presented as a checklist. Expanded discussion of the context and implications are to be found in the chapters in Part 4.

Specifying the Task

Three steps are involved in project definition and preliminary design. Each is essentially concerned with an external interface with the organization.

1. *Situation Diagnosis.* What is the problem to be overcome or opportunity to be systematically exploited?
2. *Forecasting Strategy.* What inputs are to be converted to what outputs for use in what way and how often?
3. *Acceptance Criteria.* What target standards are to be met by the as yet unknown system?

Organizational Participation

Successful forecasting systems are the product of joint technical and user/management development. How is this joint development attained?

1. *Working Assignments.* Which specific individuals are to do each task? How do these tasks interrelate in time and sequence or dependence?
2. *Steering Committee Role.* Who is on the steering committee? How is task coordination accomplished? Where does system design authority rest?
3. *User Endorsement/Ownership.* Are there programmed milestones or checkpoints at which (a) technicians must attain user sign-off, (b) users must attain technician sign-off, and (c) the study team must obtain management sign-off or redirection?

"Annual Physicals" for Forecasts

This concept is not farfetched. Forecasting systems must be like living things in the sense that they must cope with change and adapt or evolve. To some extent and at some expense this adaptability can be built in, but never to the extent necessary under current technology at affordable prices. Therefore, the question is how to assist externally in attaining adequate adaptation.

1. *Continuous Reading of "Vital Signs."* As shown in Chart 3-1, both management and technical judgment points are contained in the general OP&C forecasting system design. An automatic part of the forecasting system should be the tracking of mean average deviation (MAD) signals on system operation at a number of levels. And this (or comparable indices) should be monitored on both technical and managerial judgments.

2. *Control System Error Propagation.* After some experience is gained with the system, periodic physicals should be given. That is, a study should be made of the impact of the forecasting system on adjacent organization systems as a result of various levels of forecast errors. Simulation is often helpful here. A frequent result is further training of the humans whose judgment is an integral part of the forecasting system so that they can better understand how to interact constructively as a contributing portion of the overall system.

REFERENCES

1. Brown, Robert G., *Materials Management Systems,* John Wiley, New York, 1977.

2. Chambers, John C., Satinder Mullick, and Donald Smith, "How to Choose the Right Forecasting Technique," *Harvard Business Review,* July–August, 1971, pp. 45–74.

3. Johnson, R. A., *Operations Management: A Systems Concept,* Houghton Mifflin, Boston, 1972.

4. Linstone, Harold A., and Murray Turoff, eds., *The Delphi Method,* Addison-Wesley, Reading, MA, 1975.

5. Orlicky, Joseph, *Material Requirements Planning,* McGraw-Hill, New York, 1975.

6. Peterson, Rein, and Edward A. Silver, *Decision Systems for Inventory Management and Production Planning,* John Wiley, New York, 1979.

7. Smith, Bernard T., *Focus Forecasting: Computer Techniques for Inventory Control,* CBI Publishing, Boston, 1978.

8. Sommer, Dale W., "Cycle Forecasting Spots Trends," *Industry Week,* April 25, 1977, pp. 25+.

9. *The Wall Street Journal* 1/31/79, 2:2, "IBM Introduces . . . "; 5/17/79, 47:3, "Amerada Hess . . . "; 9/10/79, 21:1, "Uncalculated Risk . . . ."

10. Wight, Olvier W., *Production & Inventory Management in the Computer Age,* Cahners Books, Boston, 1974

11. Woolsey, Robert E. D., and Huntington S. Swanson, *Operations Research for Immediate Applications: A Quick & Dirty Manual,* Harper & Row, New York, 1975

BIBLIOGRAPHY

Anderson, O.D., *Time Series Analysis and Forecasting,* Butterworths, London, 1976.

Armstrong, J. Scott, *Long-Range Forecasting,* 2nd ed., John Wiley, New York, 1985.

Gilchrist, Warren, *Statistical Forecasting,* John Wiley, New York, 1976.

Makridakis, Spyros, Steven C. Wheelwright, and Victor E. McGee, *Forecasting Methods and Applications,* 2nd ed., John Wiley, New York, 1982.

Montgomery, Douglas C., and Lynwood A. Johnson, *Forecasting and Time Series Analysis,* McGraw-Hill, New York, 1976.

Nelson, Charles R., *Applied Time Series Analysis,* Holden-Day, San Francisco, 1973.

Plossl, G. W., and O. W. Wight, *Production and Inventory Control,* Prentice-Hall, Englewood Cliffs, NJ, 1969.

Sullivan, William G., and W. Wayne Claycombe, *Fundamentals of Forecasting,* Reston Publishing, Reston, VA, 1977.

4

CAPACITY PLANNING FORECASTING REQUIREMENTS

STEVEN C. WHEELWRIGHT

Graduate School of Business, Stanford University, Stanford, California

Planning for capacity requirements is one of the most important decision areas addressed by all but the most stable of organizations. This is especially true when such planning involves new facilities or major changes in existing facilities, as is common in both service and manufacturing industries.

As will be discussed in this chapter, forecasting plays an important role in such capacity decisions for a number of reasons. One of these is simply the lead time needed to alter the physical assets and resources associated with capacity. Another reason is that the cost of such assets is usually a major portion of a company's balance sheet. Finally, the fact that most organizations must live with their capacity decisions for several decades makes the development of accurate forecasts for the amount, type, and location of capacity extremely important.

This chapter is divided into three main sections. The first deals with a general framework for capacity planning and its tie to other forms of both short- and long-range planning. This section also examines the process by which forecasts are incorporated into typical capacity planning procedures and some of the key issues that arise in connection with those forecast requirements. The second section looks at some of the specific forecasting tasks and the approaches that have been found useful in handling them in a variety of settings. This section includes three examples, illustrating how forecasting for capacity planning purposes requires a combination of knowledge of forecasting methodologies, knowledge of the specific problem being addressed, and the judgment needed to appropriately fit existing methodologies to situation requirements. The third section of this chapter addresses the task of integrating forecasting into capacity planning and provides specific guidelines for doing that effectively.

A GENERAL FRAMEWORK FOR CAPACITY PLANNING AND DECISION MAKING

While every situation is somewhat different, a nine-step procedure for tackling capacity planning and facilities decisions has been observed to have practical application in a wide range of situations. These nine steps, outlined in Chart 4-1, can serve as a checklist to guide capacity planning and to reduce the chances of major opportunities being missed.

In thinking about the forecasting requirements for capacity planning, a cursory review of Chart 4-1 might suggest that the forecaster really need only be involved in step 3, estimating required capacity. While that is clearly a major focal point for integrating forecasting into capacity planning, almost every other step of the process also involves significant requirements for forecasting. For example, in the first step of assessing the company's situation and environment, the forecaster can play a very useful role in forecasting the economic environment and its impact on demand for the company's products and services. That first step might also involve the "forecasting" of the competitive environment and the likely capacity plans of other competitors.

In the second step, determining available capacity, the forecaster can contribute by preparing estimates of usable capacity and the relationship of cost to capacity utilization. The concept of capacity is not a precise scientific measure, but involves estimating sustainable levels of output that fall within the cost constraints set by management and the market.

In the fourth step, developing alternative plans for matching required and available capacity, forecasting can contribute by estimating the costs of each

CHART 4-1. Capacity Planning: Nine-Step Procedure

1. Assessment of company situation and environment
2. Audit and analysis of existing capacity
3. Forecast and analysis of required capacity
4. Definition of alternatives to achieve required capacity
5. Quantitative and financial analysis of alternatives
6. Analysis of qualitative issues for each alternative
7. Selection of alternative to be pursued
8. Implementation of chosen alternative
9. Audit and review of actual results

option. This links directly to the fifth step and the thorough quantitative evaluation of the alternatives. This would include forecasting lead times for new construction and relocations, as well as predicting major cost elements such as construction costs, interest rates, and operating costs.

While the remaining four steps of this procedure involve significant amounts of management judgment, a forecaster who understands the capacity issues facing the firm and who has been involved in the first five steps of the planning process can make significant contributions to management in these remaining steps.

In the final step, auditing and reviewing the results of the selected plan, the forecaster has the opportunity to upgrade existing forecasting procedures for capacity planning purposes, as well as to develop personal skills and knowledge with regard to the company's needs in this important area.

Expanding the View of Capacity Planning

In the nine-step procedure outlined in Chart 4-1, the implicit assumption is that the firm has recognized a specific need for a project that will alter its capacity. While such project formats are the normal approach for approving capital appropriations for capacity expansions, alterations, or contractions, in most organizations capacity planning is also given annual or periodic attention as well. In this context, capacity planning can be viewed as a major subsegment of a company's long-range business plan and annual budget plan. Charts 4-2 and 4-3 summarize capacity planning in this context as it commonly arises in both manufacturing and service businesses.

As illustrated in Chart 4-2, capacity planning is often broken into a long-range segment (covering more than one year) and an annual segment which becomes a major part of the budget. There are then two short-term aspects of planning related to overall capacity, but these are generally referred to as scheduling (covering 1 to 12 months) and dispatching (covering the very near-term horizon). As also suggested in Chart 4-2, capacity planning must provide not only for physical space and equipment but also for the human resources and materials required by the organization. A final aspect of Chart 4-2 is the level of the organization taking primary responsibility for each of the various segments of capacity planning. Levels are shown on the left-hand side of the chart and overlap to ensure that shorter-term plans in the operating area are integrated with longer-term plans in the other functions and for the total business.

Many of the decisions associated with the primary resources of physical space and equipment, people, and materials are aligned in Chart 4-3 with the time horizon or major subsegment of capacity planning. The appropriate decision (e.g., building inventory, adding a shift, subcontracting, adding equipment, etc.) depends on the uncertainty in the forecasting situation and

CHART 4-2. Capacity Planning and the Time Horizon in Operations[a]

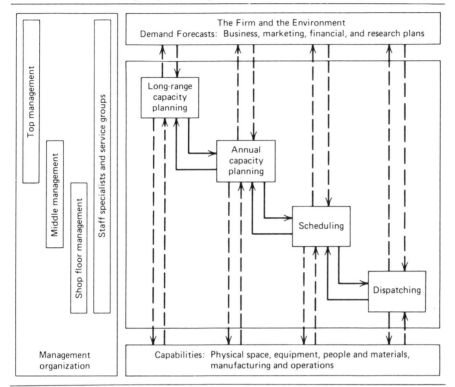

[a] See "Note on Capacity Planning" (9-674-081), Harvard Business School, Boston, 1974. *Capacity Planning and Facilities Choice* (5-979-001), by S. C. Wheelwright, Harvard Business School, Boston, 1979.

the economic realities of the decision options. When forecasters consider their inputs broadly enough to recognize the interaction of the various levels, functions, and resources, they can greatly leverage their contribution to capacity planning.

The remainder of this chapter emphasizes long-range capacity planning and annual capacity planning, but not the two shorter time horizon categories. These are covered in Chapters 3 and 11. There are, however, several other chapters in this handbook that relate directly to the topic of capacity planning forecasting requirements. In Chapter 17, some of the environmental issues related to picking the right forecasting approach and recognizing the assumptions inherent in that approach are reviewed. In Chapters 18 and 19, the impacts of product and market life cycles on demand forecasting and capacity planning are outlined. Finally, Chapter 2 details what is shown in Chart 4-2 as demand (sales) forecasts.

CHART 4-3. Capacity Planning Decisions in Operations[a]

Capacity-Determining Resources	Types of Decisions—by Time Horizon			
	Long-Range Capacity Planning	Annual Capacity Planning	Scheduling	Dispatching
Physical space and capital equipment	Selection of capabilities Location decisions Timing decisions Quantity Capital spending	Minor additions Subcontracting Product mix	Allocation of facilities to products in specific time periods	
Human resources	Hiring and layoff policies Skill requirements Timing Quantity Training and development	Number of shifts Overtime Hire-fire policy Line balancing	Overtime, allocation of manpower to products (jobs) in specific time periods	Rescheduling Expediting and detailed coordination of all three factors of production
Materials	Material requirements Long-term contracts Vendor selection Warehouse requirements Timing Quantity	Short-term purchase commitments Shipping schedules Inventory planning	Ordering materials Marshalling materials Inventory control Allocation of materials	

[a] See "Note on Capacity Planning" (9-674-081), Harvard Business School, Boston, 1974. *Capacity Planning and Facilities Choice* (5-979-001) by S. C. Wheelwright, Harvard Business School, Boston, 1979.

TOOLS AND TECHNIQUES FOR HANDLING THE SPECIFIC FORECASTING REQUIREMENTS ASSOCIATED WITH CAPACITY PLANNING

In the previous section, the topic of capacity planning was viewed from an overall perspective. However, in most companies, when the issue of capacity planning arises, it is split up into a number of separate decisions. These include: How much capacity? When to alter capacity? Where to alter capacity? What form of capacity is required? How to accomplish the capacity plan?

One way to view the forecasting requirements associated with capacity decisions is to take each of these questions and examine the tools and techniques commonly used in answering them. Chart 4-4 summarizes these, and the bibliography at the end of this chapter provides sources of additional detail on each.

As illustrations of how these techniques can be applied, the reference publication *Capacity Planning and Facilities Choice* contains detailed descriptions of six capacity planning situations. Since the forecasting task in capacity planning is often very situation-specific, each of these is reviewed briefly here, with comments on the specific nature of the key forecasting inputs.

1. *Litton Microwave Cooking Products.* In this situation the Microwave Oven Division of Litton Industries must decide how best to expand its capacity in a very uncertain but rapidly growing market. An analysis indicates that the cost of carrying excess capacity is relatively low compared with the cost of having insufficient capacity. As a result, the forecasting task is to estimate the likelihood of a wide range of capacity requirements and to use a technique, such as decision analysis (see Chapter 15), to arrive at an optimal capacity plan.

CHART 4-4. Tools and Techniques for Capacity Decisions

Management Decisions	Tools and Techniques for Forecasting, Analysis, and Planning
1. How much capacity?	Demand forecasting, economics of scale, learning curves, and decision analysis
2. When to alter capacity?	Economic cycle forecasting, competitive analysis, economics of over vs. under capacity
3. Where to alter capacity?	Transportation analysis, site selection
4. What form of capacity to develop?	Technological forecasting, production planning, facilities focus
5. How to accomplish the capacity plan?	Project management

2. *Distrigas Corporation.* A firm is being established in the Boston area to distribute liquefied natural gas, brought in by large ships, to help cover peak load requirements in the winter months. The seasonality of demand for such gas during the winter and the arrival rates of the ships are key factors in determining the appropriate mix of storage tanks and the best operating plan for conveying the gas from the storage farm to the local utilities.

3. *Town of Belmont Payson Park School.* This application is set in the public environment but involves many of the same capacity planning issues found in the private sector. In this particular instance, an elementary school district must determine how best to plan its long-term classroom needs in the face of declining school enrollments. The forecast of school-age children by elementary grade for the next two decades is not only a critical input to the development of the community's school capacity plan, but also becomes the focal point for many political arguments and pressures from special-interest groups. Thus, in this instance, the forecaster is in the middle of a very heated debate that intertwines both the issues of the forecast and how best to cope with declining enrollments.

4. *FMC Crane and Excavator Division.* This business unit manufactures heavy equipment and is faced with long-term expansion needs to maintain its existing market position and support the aggressive marketing and business strategies recently developed within the corporation. The major forecasting requirement is of the long-term operating and investment costs associated with a variety of alternatives ranging from expanding an existing facility to building a completely new facility in a "green field" site. Thus, while marketing has provided some basic demand forecasts, the options open to manufacturing, which is doing the basic capacity planning, are very diverse in their cost implications and the resulting profitability of the integrated business plan.

5. *Carborundum Inc.* In this application, capacity planning takes on a major competitive strategy role because as the market leader, Carborundum may be able to preempt other competitors by picking a particular site for a new facility and carefully timing the announcement of that site. The major forecasting requirements in this situation are twofold. One involves predicting the costs associated with various capacity alternatives and relating those to the likely actions and reactions of competitors in terms of prices and their capacity changes. The other deals with integrating all of the cost elements into an overall projection of delivered cost for each of the possible capacity alternatives. Such things as material cost, operating cost, and transportation cost all have to be forecast to meet this second requirement.

6. *Trus Joist Corporation.* In this company, the major capacity planning situation involves expanding the components end of the business and timing that to fit with an upturn in the depressed housing and construction market. The forecasting task includes predicting the construction industry turnaround and its speed. In addition, the impact of that turnaround on sales mix

(commercial vs. residential), service levels, production capacity requirements, and working capital needs must be forecast.

In each of these situations, the specifics of the environment, the business
strategy, the existing capacities, and the opportunities for improved performance must be factored into the forecaster's task. In recent years several
new concepts relating to operations strategy have also emerged, requiring
ongoing adaptation of management and forecasting methods. For example,
the use of time fences to reduce "order churn" (fluctuations that are self-
induced, not market driven) and of just-in-time production systems to cut
response time has major implications for capacity forecasting.

The foregoing examples illustrate the range of situations for which capacity planning forecasting is required. It is also useful to consider the range of
approaches that can be used effectively in such situations. As suggested
previously, these often require the modification of existing techniques in
order to fit the available data and circumstances of the given situation. Three
very different forecasting approaches, each associated with a different situation, are described in the following.

Forecasting for Capacity Planning When the Learning Curve Applies

In many situations, it has been observed empirically that labor hours per unit
and even operating costs per unit often follow what is referred to as the
learning curve. When the rate of growth is rapid, and the rate of learning is
also fairly rapid, the effect of the learning curve on capacity planning can be
dramatic—the labor required per unit produced declines significantly as additional cumulative production experience is gained. The result is that, over
several years, the labor input per unit may become only a fraction of what it
was initially. Thus, in forecasting equipment, facilities, and floor space requirements as well as human resource requirements, forecasting the learning
curve may be extremely important.

In one major industrial products firm, the approach integrated forecasting, the learning curve concept, competitive price pressures, and the desire
for continued cost reductions into the six-step planning effort summarized in
Chart 4-5. The starting point is analysis of historical price and cost patterns,
as shown in step 1. Marketing must then forecast future prices (in constant
dollars) and volumes over a five-year time horizon as step 2.

In step 3, manufacturing uses marketing's volume projections to develop
alternative cost improvement curves, representing different assumptions
about capital investment and the allocation of other manufacturing resources. In step 4, manufacturing commits to a specific set of assumptions,
resource allocations, and the cost improvements they imply. Thus, by the
end of step 4 the organization has projected the experience and price curves
for the business five years into the future.

In step 5, a set of projects that will provide the promised annual reductions in cost is selected from the project portfolio. These may span a wide

CHART 4-5. Six Steps for Developing a Cost-Reduction Program for a Planning Unit.

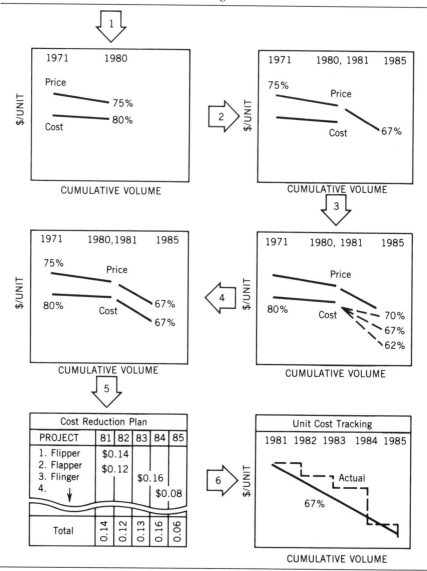

Product ABC—Cost Reduction Program Based on Learning Curve Analysis

Year	Annual Volume	Cumulative Annual Volume	Deflation Index, 1980 = 100	Selling Price/Unit Current $	Selling Price/Unit Constant 1980 $	Production Cost, Current $	Cost/Unit Constant 1980 $
Actuals							
1971	7294	7294	54.6	$33.00	60.43	$20.60	37.72
1972	685	7979	57.3	34.30	59.86	19.60	34.21
1973	1035	9014	60.4	35.20	58.28	20.10	33.28
1974	1725	0739	63.2	35.63	56.38	20.20	31.96
1975	3201	13940	65.3	37.50	57.43	14.30	21.90
1976	3805	17745	68.8	39.10	56.83	14.90	21.66
1977	3852	21597	76.0	40.90	53.82	14.50	19.08
1978	2750	24373	82.6	49.00	59.33	17.40	21.06
1979	2550	26923	90.9	51.40	56.55	17.40	19.14
1980	2831	29754	100.0	52.70	52.70	18.10	18.10
					96.4% (1A)		70.5% (1B)
Projections							
1981	3255	33009	110.0	55.30	50.27	18.46	16.78
1982	3278	36287	120.8	58.10	48.10	19.75	16.35
1983	3378	39665	133.0	61.00	45.86	20.74	15.59
1984	3494	43159	146.3	64.10	43.81	21.84	14.93
1985	3605	46764	159.1	67.40	42.36	23.01	14.46
1981–1985 experience curve slope				139%	69.6% (2)	139%	69.6% (3 and 4)

Source: Hayes & Wheelwright (1984).

range of activities involving, say, direct labor efficiency, production process changes, product design changes, and scale economies. Finally, step 6 consists of tracking actual costs and comparing them with the projections. This makes it possible to identify additional cost improvement projects that need to be pursued.

The lower half of Chart 4-5 illustrates the application of this approach for product ABC. On the basis of the historical data, step 1 identifies the product's historical (constant dollars) price and cost curves as having slopes of 96.4% and 70.5%, respectively. This chart also shows the price, volume, and cost projections (agreed to by management) for 1981 through 1985. These were arrived at through application of Steps 2 through 5. (Step 6, follow-up tracking, will be carried out in subsequent years.) Several observations can be made that highlight the role of forecasting in this situation.

The slope of the expected selling price (in constant dollars) curve is 69.6%, and the cost curve committed to by manufacturing as the basis for its five-year cost reduction program for that product also has a slope of 69.6%. In this example, manufacturing and marketing have projected different future price and cost patterns for the product from those experienced before 1980. Marketing anticipates that constant dollar prices will drop dramatically from their levels of the previous eight years, and production has responded by agreeing to achieve cost improvements equal to the expected price declines, slightly better than those achieved in the past. Another important observation is that despite the absence of significant price pressure on product ABC during most of the 1970s, manufacturing continued to achieve significant cost improvements; as a result, the company's profit margins grew steadily. The goal for 1981–1985 is to maintain that margin (in percentage terms), implying parallel price and cost curves.

Forecasting for Capacity Planning at a Capital-Intensive Electric Utility

An important dimension that has a major impact on the forecasting requirements for capacity planning is the capital intensity of the business. While the preceding example dealt with a parts assembly and fabrication business, in the case of Duke Power, an electric utility, the economics of capacity were very different. Like other major process industries (steel, paper, oil, and food processing), electric utilities deal with significant capital requirements any time they consider capacity expansion.

In this particular application, Duke Power had historically found itself on what is described in Chart 4-6 as the left-hand side of the U-shaped cost curve. That is, prior to the early 1970s, the characteristics of new capacity in the electric utility business were that the capital cost per unit of capacity, the average cost per unit of electricity, and the marginal cost per unit of electricity all had been decreasing.

Since marginal cost was lower than average cost, and since rate setting agencies had traditionally set rates (prices) on the basis of average cost, it

CHART 4-6. U-Shaped Cost Curves. Source: Leone and Meyer (1980)

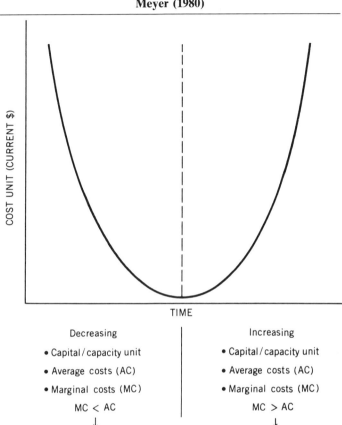

Decreasing | Increasing

- Capital/capacity unit
- Average costs (AC)
- Marginal costs (MC)

MC < AC

↓

Expand

- Capital/capacity unit
- Average costs (AC)
- Marginal costs (MC)

MC > AC

↓

Hold back expansion

Source: Leone and Meyer (1980).

was in the utilities' best interest to continually expand demand and capacity. As a consequence of this environment, the emphasis in forecasting for capacity planning at Duke Power (and most other major utilities) had generally been on avoiding mistakes that would result in not enough capacity. This tended to bias forecasts toward the high side.

As a result of several environmental changes in the 1970s—rapidly increasing oil prices, increased government regulation, and spiraling increases in construction costs—the characteristics of capacity expansion in the utility industry changed dramatically. As shown in the right-hand side of Chart 4-6, utilities like Duke Power found that the capital cost per unit of capacity was increasing (new capacity was more expensive than old capacity), average cost was increasing, and marginal cost was increasing. With marginal cost exceeding average cost and rates based on average cost, the utility and its stockholders seemed to be the losers. As a consequence, the emphasis in capacity planning started to shift toward holding back expansion and waiting as long as possible before providing new generating capacity. This shift dramatically changed the role of the forecaster, putting a premium on accuracy and a more objective recognition of the trade-offs associated with overcapacity versus undercapacity. Increasingly, forecasters found themselves on the witness stand during rate-setting hearings in which increasing pressure was being brought to bear by special-interest groups to cut down on excess capacity while still providing adequate levels of service to all customers.

Some of the implications of this type of a shift from a declining to an increasing cost capacity planning environment are highlighted in Chart 4-7. These implications are not only for management but for forecasters and planners as well. Leone and Meyer (1980) provided further details on the forecasting and planning requirements associated with this shift in capital-intensive, maturing industries.

Forecasting for Tennis Court Capacity at Sea Pines Racquet Club

While the public utility just discussed is an example of a service business, it has many of the same characteristics as capital-intensive manufacturing businesses. However, at Sea Pines Racquet Club, many of the more typical characteristics of capacity planning in the service environment were highlighted during the development of a capacity plan for tennis courts. Like many of the major resort locations in the southeastern United States, Sea Pines started as primarily a real estate venture. Such amenities as golf and

---

CHART 4-7. Implications of U-Shaped Cost Curves

Implications for Management Strategy and Policy

Past	*Future*
Build large scale	Build small scale
Build before demand	Built to match (or lag) demand
Use new capacity first	Use new capacity last
Promote demand	Manage (limit) demand
Avoid stockout	Avoid excess capacity
Compete on price	Compete on service
Expand with new capacity	Expand by revising old capacity

Implications for Staff Forecasters/Planners

Forecasting accuracy required
Forecasting accuracy available
Basic data for forecasting
Cost of over/under errors
Time horizon for planning
Relating forecasting to actions

tennis were viewed as ways to attract potential real estate investors. However, as the company approached the need for capacity planning in terms of tennis courts in later years, it quickly found that even rough forecasts indicated that eventually half the property might be covered by tennis courts if all peak demands were to be met. At that point, a much more systematic approach to forecasting tennis capacity requirements and fitting that with overall business plans was developed.

As a starting point, the manager of the tennis facilities followed the procedure outlined in Chart 4-1. It was determined that during the peak months (July and August), the total daylight hours available for any single tennis court were 319. However, it was felt that only about 80% of those hours were actually "usable" because of the high humidity and heat during midday. In addition, the tennis manager had estimates of total guest nights for three years based on overall business plans for the resort. Finally, records had been kept indicating the court hours required per guest night in the two preceding years. This information is summarized in Chart 4-8.

From this information, a forecast of court hours needed could be prepared, as shown in Chart 4-8. That could then be converted into courts required, initially assuming that 100% of the time was usable and that year 1 usage rates per guest night applied. With this as a base point, an adjustment could be made to reflect the fact that court usage (per guest night) was running 62% higher in year 2 than in year 1. Finally, an additional adjustment could be made to reflect the manager's estimate that only 80% of the available court time was usable.

At that point, the manager of the tennis facilities determined that there was such a wide range of potential court requirements that it made more

CHART 4-8. Forecasting for Tennis Capacity Planning at Sea Pines Racquet Club

	Court Hours/Guest Night		
	Year 1	Year 2	Year 2/Year 1
March	0.040	0.068	1.70
April	0.061	0.082	1.34
May	0.046	0.084	1.83
			Average 1.62

	Hours Available per Court	Guest Nights (in 1000s)	Court Hours per Guest Night (Year 1)	Court Hours Needed	Courts Required		
					Base	1.62 Adj.	÷ 0.80
July year 2	319	83.9	0.056	4700	15	24	30
August year 2	319	86.5	0.056	4840	15	25	37
July year 3	319	130.7	0.056	7320	23	37	46
August year 3	319	129.1	0.056	7230	23	37	46
July year 4	319	168.8	0.056	9450	30	48	60
August year 4	319	166.3	0.056	9310	29	47	59

sense to think about managing demand in this service business rather than simply trying to provide capacity for all possible demand. This was further reinforced by an economic analysis of the cost of a tennis court that is used in only one or two peak months of the year. As a result of this, the facilities manager decided to plan for an intermediate level of capacity and to work with some of the other amenities (golf, swimming, hiking, sailing, etc.) to provide ample opportunity for all guests, but not necessarily to provide tennis for any guest who happened to desire to play at the peak hour in the peak month.

This situation illustrates what is often the case not only in service businesses but in many manufacturing businesses: Seasonal peaks not only need to be forecast, but the possibilities for managing those peaks and spreading them need to be studied.

INTEGRATING FORECASTING, CAPACITY PLANNING, AND BUSINESS PLANNING

As suggested at the outset of this chapter, one of the overriding considerations in forecasting for capacity planning is understanding the context in which that capacity plan is being prepared and the issues that it must address. One approach for thinking about the levels of activity involved in business planning, and the corresponding levels involved in capacity planning, is summarized in Chart 4-9.

CHART 4-9. Integrating Capacity Planning and Business Planning

Operations strategy	Corporate strategy
Capacity strategy	Business strategy
Capacity plan	Business plan
Capital project requests	Capital plan
Department budgets	Budget

Forecasting Inputs to a Capacity Plan or Project

Unit volume requirements
Space requirements
Manpower requirements
Material requirements
Capital requirements
Operating cost requirements
Technology requirements

As highlighted in Chart 4-9, a number of specific types of forecasting inputs can be made at various levels of capacity planning. While Chart 4-1 highlighted the capital project request level of such capacity plans, the subsequent sections have indicated the role that forecasting can and should play at higher levels. Other chapters in this handbook, as well as the bibliography at the end of this chapter, should enable the forecaster to more effectively contribute to capacity plans and strategies.

BIBLIOGRAPHY

"Duke Power Company Revised," (9-677-147). Intercollegiate Case Clearing House, Harvard Business School, Boston, 1977.

Erlenkotter, Donald, "Preinvestment Planning for Capacity Expansion: A Multi-Location Dynamic Model," Stanford University, Ph.D. Dissertation, 1970.

Hayes, Robert H., and Steven C. Wheelwright, *Restoring Our Competitive Edge—Competing Through Manufacturing,* John Wiley, New York, 1984.

Holloway, Charles, *Decision Making Under Uncertainty,* Prentice-Hall, Englewood Cliffs, NJ, 1979.

Leone, Robert A., and John R. Meyer, "Capacity Strategies for the 1980's," *Harvard Business Review,* November–December, 1980.

Makridakis, Spyros, Steven C. Wheelwright, and Victor E. McGee, *Forecasting: Methods and Applications,* 2nd ed., John Wiley, New York, 1983.

Manne, Alan S., ed., *Investments for Capacity Expansion: Size, Location, and Time-Phasing,* George Allen & Unwin, London, 1967.

"Note on Capacity Planning," (9-674-081), Intercollegiate Case Clearing House, Harvard Business School, Boston, 1974.

Riggs, Henry E., *Managing High Technology Companies,* Van Nostrand-Reinhold, New York, 1983.

Sasser, W. Earl, "Match Supply and Demand in Service Industries," *Harvard Business Review,* November–December, 1976.

Scherer, F. M., and A. Beckenstein, *The Economics of Multiplant Operation,* Harvard University Press, Cambridge, MA, 1975.

Schmenner, Roger, "Before You Build a Big Factory," *Harvard Business Review,* July–August, 1976.

Schmenner, Roger, *Making Business Location Decisions,* Prentice-Hall, Englewood Cliffs, NJ, 1982.

Schmenner, Roger, *Production/Operations Management,* 2nd ed., SRA, Chicago, 1984.

Schonberger, Richard J., *Japanese Manufacturing Techniques,* Free Press, New York, 1982.

Skinner, Wickham, *Manufacturing: The Formidable Competitive Weapon,* John Wiley, New York, 1985.

Wheelwright, Steven C., "Manufacturing Strategy—Defining the Missing Link," *Strategic Management Journal,* vol. 5, 1984, pp. 77–91.

Wheelwright, Steven C., *Capacity Planning and Facilities Choice,* Division of Research, Harvard Business School, Cambridge, MA, 1979.

Wheelwright, Steven C., and Spyros Makridakis, *Forecasting Methods for Management.* 4th ed., John Wiley, New York, 1985.

5

FINANCIAL FORECASTING

LAWRENCE D. BROWN

School of Management, State University of New York, Buffalo

It is widely believed that forecasts of firms' future corporate earnings are important for valuing their common shares.* When the capital markets "err" in predicting a firm's earnings, the firm's stock price typically moves in the direction of the "error,"[6] and the magnitude of the stock movement is related to the size of the "error."[2] For example, if the capital market expects a firm's earnings to be $X and reported earnings are actually $Y, the firm's stock price typically decreases (increases) if $X exceeds (falls short of) $Y, and the magnitude of the price movement depends on $|\$X - \$Y| \div |\$X|$.†

Estimates of future earnings numbers can be derived from time series models. Alternatively, they can be obtained from managers or security analysts. This chapter discusses (1) forecasts of annual earnings by time series models, (2) forecasts of quarterly earnings by time series models, (3) forecasts of earnings by financial analysts, and (4) forecasts of earnings by managers. It also briefly discusses forecasts of systematic risk, bankruptcy, and bond ratings.

FORECASTS OF ANNUAL EARNINGS BY TIME SERIES MODELS

Little[60] and Rayner and Little[70] conducted the first systematic analyses of the behavior of reported earnings. These studies concluded that annual earnings of United Kingdom firms follow a random walk. In other words, earnings

---

* Literature on this subject dates back to (at least) 1938 (see Williams[81]).
† The analysis is based on the assumption that the difference between X and Y is due to real economic factors, not to accounting manipulations. For evidence that capital markets "see through" accounting manipulations, see Ball[5] and Beaver and Dukes.[13]

changes are largely unsystematic, or simply a matter of chance. Similar results were obtained by Brealey,[17] Lintner and Glauber,[59] Watts,[77] Albrecht and colleagues,[3] and Watts and Leftwich,[80] who examined reported earnings of U.S. firms.

Other studies only partially corroborated the random-walk result. Beaver[11] concluded that measures of accounting income tend to converge to a long-run value. Ball and Watts[7] suggested that the optimal forecast of next year's earnings is this year's earnings adjusted by a small portion of this year's earnings forecast error (since a fraction of the forecast error is considered transitory). Similar to Beaver and to Ball and Watts, Lieber and colleagues[58] found that a substantial number of firms exhibit a significant transitory noise component of earnings. Beaver and co-workers[15] showed that security prices do *not* act as if earnings follow a random walk. Evidence was provided that a price-based model was a superior forecaster to a random-walk-with-drift model. And Freeman and colleagues[44] hypothesized and provided evidence that a modest enlargement of the predictive information set leads to a rejection of the random-walk model.

Several studies have evaluated whether past quarterly and annual earnings yield superior forecasts of earnings compared with past annual earnings alone. Green and Segall[46,47] concluded that quarterly earnings are not useful for improving forecasts of annual earnings. However, several later investigators concluded the opposite—interim reports do have predictive content for forecasting annual earnings.[26,30,32,49,51,61,62,71] For example, Hopwood and colleagues,[51] in a sample of 267 firms during 1975 to 1979, found that quarterly data reduced the prediction error variance based on past annual data alone by 15% to 21%.

Another approach is to evaluate segmental disclosures. Kinney,[57] Collins,[33] and Silhan[76] compared the accuracy of forecasting models using segmented income and sales data with the accuracy of models using only consolidated figures. Kinney concluded that significantly better forecasts can be obtained with disaggregated data. Collins found considerable overlap in segment sales and profit data, and concluded that segmented data are of limited usefulness for predictive purposes. Silhan adopted a simulated merger approach, found no significant difference in predictive ability between segmented and consolidated earnings data, and concluded that segmented earnings are of limited usefulness in predicting enterprise profits.

Hopwood and McKeown[50] introduced a transfer function model that utilized the time series properties of both annual earnings numbers and earnings of the "economy" (defined as the average of the sample firms' annual earnings). They concluded that the transfer function model was able to generate more accurate predictions of annual earnings than could the quarterly models used by Hopwood and colleagues,[51] as previously discussed. Contrary evidence was provided by Manegold,[64] who compared the predictive ability of models based on components such as operating income before depreciation, depreciation expense, and interest expense with that of models based on only past earnings numbers. Manegold did not find the component-based model to be more accurate than the univariate time series model.

In sum, annual earnings are reasonably well approximated by a random walk, but certain enlargements of the predictive information set (e.g., share prices, book rates of return, earnings of the "economy") lead to improved forecasts. Quarterly reports are useful for improving forecasts of annual earnings numbers, but segmental disclosures (i.e., line of business reporting) and component-based models are not especially useful for this purpose.

FORECASTS OF QUARTERLY EARNINGS BY TIME SERIES MODELS

Early studies of the time series properties of quarterly earnings assumed that the earnings-generating process was either a seasonal submartingale or a nonseasonal submartingale (see, for example, Brown and Kennelly[25] and Brown and Niederhoffer[26]). If quarterly earnings are generated according to a seasonal submartingale process, predicted earnings for quarter q in year t equal earnings for quarter q in year $t - 1$ plus a "drift."* If quarterly earnings follow a nonseasonal submartingale, predicted earnings for quarter q in year t equal earnings for quarter $q - 1$ in year t (for $q = 2, 3, 4$) or earnings for quarter 4 in year $t - 1$ (for $q = 1$).

Foster,[43] Watts,[78] Griffin,[48] and Brown and Rozeff[30] used the Box and Jenkins[16] autoregressive moving average (ARIMA) technique to develop quarterly earnings-generating models. Each of the ARIMA models removed a portion of transitory error from past changes in quarterly earnings that would otherwise affect forecasts of future quarterly earnings numbers. Foster argued in favor of a single autoregressive parameter; Watts and Griffin suggested two moving average parameters—a seasonal and a nonseasonal one; and Brown and Rozeff maintained that the appropriate model utilized the autoregressive parameter suggested by Foster and the seasonal moving average parameter introduced by Watts and Griffin.

The evidence regarding which of these three single-form ARIMA models best describes the quarterly earnings-generating process is mixed. Watts[79] argued in favor of the Foster model; Lorek[61] provided evidence supporting the Watts–Griffin model; and Collins and Hopwood[34] and Bathke and Lorek[9] maintained that the Brown and Rozeff model generates the most accurate predictions of future quarterly earnings numbers.

Dharan[38] has argued that the quarterly earnings-generating process is more complex than can be represented by a single-firm ARIMA model, and has cautioned that a theory of the firm is needed to identify and estimate earnings models. Lorek and Bathke[62] showed that none of the three models is especially good at forecasting nonseasonal quarterly earnings data, and

---

* If the "drift" equals zero, the model is said to be a martingale.

they suggested a nonseasonal ARIMA model as an alternative. Although the evidence regarding the most accurate single-form model is mixed, ample evidence exists that single-form models perform at least as well as the more costly (and more subjective) individually identified ARIMA models.* Thus, single-form models can be used instead of individually identified ARIMA models when a time series forecast of earnings is required.

Foster[43] argued that an alternative (preferable) way to evaluate a predictive model is to examine the relationship between "earnings surprise," conditional on the earnings expectation model, and "abnormal share price movements." More specifically, first define earnings surprise as the difference between actual earnings and expectation of earnings according to a specific predictive model, and abnormal share price movements as the difference between actual share price movement and expectation of movement, according to a return-generating model,† and then correlate earnings surprise with abnormal share price movements. According to Foster, the predictive model whose forecast errors (i.e., earnings surprises) are most highly correlated with abnormal share price movements is the best predictive model. Foster concluded that ARIMA models are better than (seasonal and nonseasonal) submartingale models in two ways: (1) more accurate predictions of future quarterly earnings numbers and (2) higher correlation with abnormal share price movements.

Bathke and Lorek[9] used this dual procedure to evaluate the single-form ARIMA models suggested by Watts,[78] Griffin,[48] Foster,[43] and Brown and Rozeff.[29] They concluded that the Brown and Rozeff model was "best." However, forecasts by financial analysts and/or managers may be "better" than forecasts by time series models. If so, even the "best" single-form ARIMA model will be inferior to an expert (e.g., financial analyst) as a proxy for the capital market's expectation of future earnings numbers.

In sum, the following pertains to forecasts of quarterly earnings by time series models. Three ARIMA models that remove a portion of transitory error from past changes in quarterly earnings have been suggested as generating quarterly earnings per share numbers. The evidence regarding the most accurate single-form model is mixed, but the evidence agrees that single-form models perform at least as well as the more costly individually identified ARIMA models. An alternative way to evaluate earnings-generating models has been proposed: relating share price movements to earnings surprise. This technique has been applied to both time series models and finan-

---

* The difference between a single-form model and an individually identified model is that with the single-form model the model is known and the parameters are estimated, while with the individually identified model both the model and its parameters are estimated.

† It is beyond the scope of this chapter to evaluate return-generating models. Most studies (e.g., Foster[43]) assume that the return on a firm's stock bears a linear relationship to the return on the market. The "market model" was developed by Sharpe.[75]

cial analysts. The time series evidence has been presented in this section; the analyst forecast evidence is presented in the next section.

FORECASTS OF EARNINGS BY FINANCIAL ANALYSTS

Early studies comparing analysts' earnings forecasts with those of time series models concluded that analysts' earnings forecasts are not more accurate.[36,41] More recent studies, using more refined methodologies, have concluded in favor of analyst forecast superiority.[22,28,34] For example, Brown and colleagues[22] showed that security analyst forecast superiority is not an artifact of particular time periods, forecast horizons, forecast error definitions, treatment of outliers, or quarter of forecast initiation. Moreover, these investigators examined two potential sources of analyst superiority: (1) better utilization of information existing at the forecast initiation date of the time series model, a contemporaneous advantage,* and (2) acquisition and use of information since the time series model forecast initiation date, a timing advantage. Their evidence suggested that analyst forecast superiority is attributable to both of these factors.

Brown and co-workers[27] examined the attributes of the analyst's information environment that enable him or her to outperform time series models. They developed and tested a Bayesian model that related analyst superiority to three attributes of the analyst's information environment: (1) its dimensionality, (2) the variance of information observations, and (3) the covariance among information observations. Their test results suggest that an information interpretation provides a partial explanation of analysts' predictive superiority.

Analysts appear to pay attention to quarterly earnings in revising their forecasts of future annual and quarterly earnings (see Abdel-khalik and Espejo[1] and Brown et al.[24] respectively). Analysts also appear to consider changes in accounting methods. Brown[18] showed that unless firms provide pro forma adjustments when they change their accounting methods, analysts' earnings forecast accuracy is impeded. Baldwin[4] concluded that analysts' earnings forecast accuracy is enhanced when firms report segmented earnings. Castenias and Griffin[31] examined whether the FASB (Financial Accounting Standard Board) adoption and initial financial statement disclosure of SFAS (Statement of Financial Accounting Standard) No. 52 (foreign currency accounting) data impacted on security analysts' forecasts of earnings per share. They found that (1) analysts revised their forecasts proportionately more at this time than during other periods and (2) the dispersion of analysts' forecasts of future earnings numbers is greater during this period.

In a manner similar to that of Bathke and Lorek,[9] Fried and Givoly[45] used

---

* Time series model forecasts can be initiated on the date that the firm's earnings are released in *The Wall Street Journal*.

the dual procedure introduced by Foster[43] to compare analysts' earnings forecasts vis à vis those generated by time series models. Finding analysts' forecasts to be more accurate than the time series-based forecasts, and errors conditional on analysts' forecasts to be more closely related to abnormal share price movements than forecasts generated by time series models, Fried and Givoly concluded in favor of analysts' forecasts. Brown and colleagues[23] analyzed the relationship between cumulative two-day excess returns and unexpected quarterly earnings, using as alternative expectations measures forecasts by analysts and forecasts by time series models. Similar to Fried and Givoly's conclusion regarding analysts' annual forecasts, Brown and co-workers concluded in favor of analysts' quarterly forecasts.

In sum, analysts' earnings forecasts are more accurate than forecasts by time series models. Analysts appear to better utilize information available at the forecast date of the time series models, a contemporaneous advantage, and to acquire and use information available after the time series model forecast initiation date, a timing advantage. The relevant attributes of the analyst's information set that allow for his or her predictive superiority appear to be (1) the amount of information available, (2) the variance of the information observations, and (3) the covariance among information observations. Analysts appear to pay attention to reported earnings numbers and to the impact of changes in accounting principles on the reported earnings numbers. Finally, analysts' forecasts appear to be more closely related to abnormal share price movements than are forecasts generated by time series models.

FORECASTS OF EARNINGS BY MANAGERS*

Two types of studies regarding management forecasts have been conducted: (1) the comparative accuracy of management forecasts and (2) the capital market reaction to management forecasts. Green and Segall[47] examined forecasts by 12 managers and found them to be more accurate than those of naive models. These investigators recognized that the results might be attributable to the managers' "timing advantage."† Copeland and Marioni[35] obtained similar results using 50 management forecasts. However, Lorek and colleagues[63] compared the predictive accuracy of firm-specific Box and Jenkins[16] models with the accuracy of 40 management forecasts and found no significant difference between the two.

Management forecasts of earnings have also been compared with forecasts of earnings by financial analysts. Basi and co-workers,[8] Imhoff,[53] Imhoff and Paré,[54] Ruland,[73] and Schreuder and Klaassen[74] found no significant

---

* Much of the following draws upon Brown[19] and Brown and Griffin.[21]
† Recall that Brown and colleagues[22] showed that analysts' comparative advantage is due in part to their timing advantage.

difference in managers' versus analysts' forecasting performance. Jaggi,[55] however, supported the hypothesis that management forecasts were more accurate, especially when published after analysts' forecasts.

Patell[67] examined the "information content" of management forecasts and found forecast disclosure to be accompanied by significant share price adjustments. He concluded that either the data contained in a management forecast, the act of voluntary disclosure, or both, convey information that is then reflected in stock price. Patell was aware that his sample possessed a self-selection bias (i.e., only firms whose managers voluntarily disclosed earnings forecasts were included), so he argued that his results offered little guidance regarding the question of whether firms should be required to issue earnings forecasts.

Patell[67] and Penman[68] found that managers are more likely to disclose "good news" than "bad news" and that investors also react favorably to bad news.* Ajinkya and Gift[2] showed that by using a "better" measure of good news and bad news, managers are equally likely to make bad news and good news forecasts, and that the market responds symmetrically to the direction and magnitude of these forecast signals.

Patell did not examine why managers make earnings forecasts. Several theories exist, including signaling good news in advance of reporting earnings[68] and insider trading by managers in advance of disclosing their forecasts.[69] On the other hand, the motivation for security analysts' earnings forecasts is clear: Analysts sell their forecasts or use them as inputs into their investment decisions and advice, or both.

In sum, management earnings forecasts are at least as accurate as forecasts by time series models and analysts. Managers' forecasts are informative in the sense that the capital markets respond favorably or unfavorably to their good or bad news forecasts. However, managers' forecasts are not readily available for most firms. In contrast, analysts' forecasts are readily available, they are nearly as accurate as managers' forecasts, and they are both more accurate and more informative than forecasts by time series models.†

FORECASTS OF SYSTEMATIC RISK, BANKRUPTCY, AND BOND RATINGS

Drawing on the portfolio model of Markowitz[65] and the diagonal model of Sharpe,[75] Beaver and colleagues[14] proposed that the role of accounting infor-

---

* News is said to be good (bad) if management's earnings forecast exceeds (falls short of) the forecast that prevails in the capital markets immediately prior to the announcement of the news.

† At least three sources of machine-readable analysts' earnings forecasts exist: *IBES* by Lynch, Jones, & Ryan; *ICARUS* by Zacks Investment Research; and *The Value Line Data Base* by Value Line, Inc.

mation is to aid investors' assessments of systematic risk (market beta). These investigators examined the ability of accounting-determined risk measures to predict market-determined risk measures. More specifically, they examined the explanatory power of seven accounting risk measures and found four variables to be significant: earnings variability, dividend payout, accounting beta,* and financial leverage. They concluded that accounting-determined risk measures are useful for predicting systematic risk. Rosenberg and Marathe[72] and Eskew[42] provided corroborative evidence: They concluded that accounting data contributed to better assessing market risk. Other studies, however, have concluded that accounting data do not improve prediction of market-based risk measures[39] and that the results are sensitive to the choice of market index and definition of forecast error.[40]

Beaver[10] examined the ability of six financial ratios to predict firm failure (bankruptcy). He found the ratio distributions of *nonfailed* firms to be quite stable during the five years before failure. The ratio distributions of the *failed* firms, however, exhibited a marked deterioration as failure approached. In fact, as much as five years before failure, the cash flow/total debt ratio correctly classified both failed and nonfailed firms to a much greater extent than would be possible through random prediction. Deakin[37] obtained results similar to those of Beaver. More particularly, using discriminant analysis, he showed that accounting data can be used to predict business failures fairly accurately as much as three years in advance. Ohlson[66] showed that the predictive power of bankruptcy models depends on the information assumed to be available, and that the predictive power of linear transformations of financial ratios is robust across estimation procedures.

Horrigan[52] found accounting data and financial ratios to be useful for determining corporate bond ratings. Total assets, a long-term solvency ratio, a short-term capital turnover ratio, a long-term capital turnover ratio, and a profit margin ratio, plus a dummy legal status variable, correctly predicted over one half of the bond ratings samples. Kaplan and Urwitz[56] developed a simple linear model and applied it to samples of seasoned and newly issued bonds. The model, which used a subordination dummy variable, total assets, the long-term debt/total assets ratio, and systematic risk, classified two thirds of a holdout sample of newly issued bonds. Moreover, on the basis of market yields, the model measured systematic risk better than did the Moody's bond ratings.

In sum, accounting data and financial ratios are useful for predicting systematic risk, firm failure, and bond ratings. Thus, the use of accounting data is not confined to enhancing of earnings forecasts by time series models, financial analysts, and managers.

---

* Brown and Ball[20] introduced the concept of the accounting beta. It is defined as the slope coefficient in the regression analysis of a firm's earnings to the earnings of the market.

REFERENCES

1. Abdel-khalik, A. R., and J. Espejo, "Expectations Data and the Predictive Value of Interim Reporting," *Journal of Accounting Research,* Spring 1978, pp. 1–13.

2. Ajinkya, B. B., and M. J. Gift, "Corporate Managers' Earnings Forecasts and Symmetrical Adjustments of Market Expectations," *Journal of Accounting Research,* Autumn 1984, pp. 425–444.

3. Albrecht, W. S., L. L. Lookabill, and J. C. McKeown, "The Time Series Properties of Annual Earnings," *Journal of Accounting Research,* Autumn 1977, pp. 226–244.

4. Baldwin, B. A., "Segment Earnings Disclosure and the Ability of Security Analysts to Forecast Earnings Per Share," *The Accounting Review,* July 1984, pp. 376–389.

5. Ball, R., "Changes in Accounting Techniques and Stock Prices," *Journal of Accounting Research,* Supplement 1972, pp. 1–38.

6. Ball, R., and P. Brown, "An Empirical Evaluation of Accounting Income Numbers," *Journal of Accounting Research,* Autumn 1968, pp. 159–178.

7. Ball, R., and R. Watts, "Some Time Series Properties of Accounting Income," *The Journal of Finance,* June 1972, pp. 663–681.

8. Basi, B. A., K. J. Carey, and R. D. Twark, "A Comparison of the Accuracy of Corporate and Security Analysts' Forecasts of Earnings," *The Accounting Review,* April 1976, pp. 244–254.

9. Bathke, A. W., and K. S. Lorek, "A Time-Series Analysis of Nonseasonal Quarterly Earnings Data," *The Accounting Review,* April 1984, pp. 163–176.

10. Beaver, W. H., "Financial Ratios as Predictors of Failure," *Journal of Accounting Research,* Supplement 1966, pp. 71–111.

11. Beaver, W. H., "The Time Series Behavior of Earnings," *Journal of Accounting Research,* Supplement 1970, pp. 62–99.

12. Beaver, W. H., R. Clarke, and W. F. Wright, "The Association Between Unsystematic Security Returns and the Magnitude of Earnings Forecast Errors," *Journal of Accounting Research,* Autumn 1979, pp. 316–340.

13. Beaver, W. H., and R. E. Dukes, "Interperiod Tax Allocation and Delta-Depreciation Methods: Some Empirical Results," *The Accounting Review,* July 1973, pp. 549–559.

14. Beaver, W. H., P. Kettler, and M. Scholes, "The Association Between Market Determined and Accounting Determined Risk Measures," *The Accounting Review,* October 1970, pp. 654–682.

15. Beaver, W. H., R. Lambert, and D. Morse. "The Information Content of Security Prices." *Journal of Accounting and Economics,* March 1980, pp. 3–28.

16. Box, G. E. P., and G. M. Jenkins, *Time Series Analysis: Forecasting and Control,* Holden-Day, San Francisco, 1976.

17. Brealey, R., "Some Implications of the Comovement of Company Earnings," paper presented at Seminar on Analysis of Security Prices, November 15, 1968, University of Chicago.

18. Brown, L. D., "Accounting Changes and Analyst Earnings Forecast Accuracy," *Journal of Accounting Research,* Autumn 1983, pp. 432–443.

19. Brown, L. D., *The Modern Theory of Financial Reporting,* Business Publications, Plano, Texas, 1986.

20. Brown, P., and R. Ball, "Some Preliminary Findings on the Association Between the Earnings of a Firm, Its Industry, and the Economy," *Journal of Accounting Research,* Supplement 1967, pp. 55–77.

21. Brown, L. D., and P. A. Griffin, "Evidence on the Properties of Reported Accounting Numbers," *Usefulness to Investors and Creditors of Information Provided by Financial Reporting*, Financial Accounting Standards Board, Stamford, CT, 1986.

22. Brown, L. D., P. A. Griffin, R. L. Hagerman, and M. E. Zmijewski, "Security Analyst Superiority Relative to Univariate Time-Series Models in Forecasting Earnings," *Journal of Accounting and Economics* (forthcoming 1987).

23. Brown, L. D., P. A. Griffin, R. L. Hagerman, and M. E. Zmijewski, "An Evaluation of Alternative Proxies for the Market's Expectation of Earnings," *Journal of Accounting and Economics* (forthcoming 1987).

24. Brown, L. D., J. S. Hughes, M. S. Rozeff, and J. H. Vanderweide, "Expectations Data and the Predictive Value of Interim Reporting: A Comment," *Journal of Accounting Research*, Spring 1980, pp. 278–288.

25. Brown, P., and J. W. Kennelly, "The Information Content of Quarterly Earnings: An Extension and Some Further Evidence," *The Journal of Business*, July 1972, pp. 403–415.

26. Brown, P., and V. Niederhoffer, "The Predictive Content of Quarterly Earnings," *The Journal of Business*, October 1968, pp. 488–497.

27. Brown, L. D., G. D. Richardson, and S. G. Schwager, "An Information Interpretation of Financial Analyst Superiority in Forecasting Earnings," *Journal of Accounting Research* (forthcoming 1987).

28. Brown, L. D., and M. S. Rozeff, "The Superiority of Analyst Forecasts as Measures of Expectations: Evidence from Earnings," *The Journal of Finance*, March 1978, pp. 1–16.

29. Brown, L. D., and M. S. Rozeff, "Univariate Time-Series Models of Quarterly Accounting Earnings Per Share: A Proposed Model," *Journal of Accounting Research*, Spring 1979, pp. 179–189.

30. Brown, L. D., and M. S. Rozeff, "The Predictive Value of Interim Reports for Improving Forecasts of Future Quarterly Earnings," *The Accounting Review*, July 1979, pp. 585–591.

31. Castenias II, R. P., and P. A. Griffin, "The Effects of Foreign Currency Translation Accounting on Security Analysts' Forecasts," research paper, Graduate School of Administration, University of California at Davis, March 1985.

32. Coates, R., "The Predictive Content of Interim Reports—A Time Series Analysis," *Journal of Accounting Research*, Supplement 1972, pp. 132–144.

33. Collins, D. W., "Predicting Earnings with Sub-Entity Data: Some Further Evidence," *Journal of Accounting Research*, Spring 1976, pp. 163–177.

34. Collins, W. A., and W. S. Hopwood, "A Multivariate Analysis of Annual Earnings Forecasts Generated from Quarterly Forecasts of Financial Analysts and Univariate Time-Series Models," *Journal of Accounting Research*, Autumn 1980, pp. 390–406.

35. Copeland, R. M., and R. J. Marioni, "Executives' Forecasts of Earnings Per Share Versus Forecasts of Naive Models," *The Journal of Business*, October 1972, pp. 497–512.

36. Cragg, J. G., and B. G. Malkiel, "The Consensus and Accuracy of Some Predictions of the Growth of Corporate Earnings," *The Journal of Finance*, March 1968, pp. 67–84.

37. Deakin, E. B., "A Discriminant Analysis of Predictors of Business Failure," *Journal of Accounting Research*, Supplement 1972, pp. 167–179.

38. Dharan, B. G., "Identification and Estimation Issues for a Causal Earnings Model," *Journal of Accounting Research*, Spring 1983, pp. 18–41.

39. Elgers, P. T., "Accounting-Based Risk Predictions: A Re-Examination," *The Accounting Review*, July 1980, pp. 389–408.

40. Elgers, P. T., and D. Murray, "The Impact of the Choice of Market Index on the Empirical Evaluation of Accounting Risk Measures," *The Accounting Review*, April 1982, pp. 358–375.

41. Elton, E. J., and M. J. Gruber, "Earnings Estimates and the Accuracy of Expectational Data," *Management Science,* April 1972, pp. B409–B424.

42. Eskew, R. K., "The Forecasting Ability of Accounting Risk Measures: Some Additional Evidence," *The Accounting Review,* January 1979, pp. 107–118.

43. Foster, G., "Quarterly Accounting Data: Time-Series Properties and Predictive-Ability Results," *The Accounting Review,* January 1977, pp. 1–21.

44. Freeman, R. N., J. A. Ohlson, and S. H. Penman, "Book Rate-of-Return and Prediction of Earnings Changes: An Empirical Investigation," *Journal of Accounting Research,* Autumn 1982, pp. 639–653.

45. Fried, D., and D. Givoly, "Financial Analysts' Forecasts of Earnings: A Better Surrogate for Market Expectations," *Journal of Accounting and Economics,* October 1982, pp. 85–107.

46. Green Jr., D., and J. Segall, "The Predictive Power of First-Quarter Earnings Reports: A Replication," *Journal of Accounting Research,* Supplement, 1966, pp. 21–36.

47. Green Jr., D., and J. Segall, "The Predictive Power of First-Quarter Earnings Reports," *The Journal of Business,* January 1967, pp. 44–55.

48. Griffin, P. A., "The Time-Series Behavior of Quarterly Earnings: Preliminary Evidence," *Journal of Accounting Research,* Spring 1977, pp. 71–83.

49. Hillison, W. A., W. S. Hopwood, and K. S. Lorek, "Quarterly GPPA Earnings Data: Time-Series Properties and Predictive Ability Results in the Airlines Industry," *Journal of Forecasting,* October–December 1983, pp. 363–375.

50. Hopwood, W. S., and J. C. McKeown, "An Evaluation of Univariate Time-Series Models and Their Generalization to a Single Input Transfer Function," *Journal of Accounting Research,* Autumn 1981, pp. 313–322.

51. Hopwood, W. S., J. C. McKeown, and P. Newbold, "The Additional Information Content of Quarterly Earnings Reports: Intertemporal Disaggregation," *Journal of Accounting Research,* Autumn 1982, pp. 724–732.

52. Horrigan, J. O., "The Determination of Long-Term Credit Standing with Financial Ratios," *Journal of Accounting Research,* Supplement 1966, pp. 44–62.

53. Imhoff Jr., E. A., "The Representativeness of Management Earnings Forecasts," *The Accounting Review,* October 1978, pp. 836–850.

54. Imhoff Jr., E. A., and P. V. Paré, "Analysis and Comparison of Earnings Forecast Agents," *Journal of Accounting Research,* Autumn 1982, pp. 429–439.

55. Jaggi, B., "Further Evidence on the Accuracy of Management Forecasts Vis-à-Vis Analysts' Forecasts," *The Accounting Review,* January 1980, pp. 96–101.

56. Kaplan, R. S., and G. Urwitz, "Statistical Models of Bond Ratings: A Methodological Inquiry," *The Journal of Business,* April 1979, pp. 231–261.

57. Kinney Jr., W. R., "Predicting Earnings: Entity Versus Subentity Data," *Journal of Accounting Research,* Spring 1971, pp. 127–136.

58. Lieber, Z., E. I. Melnick, and J. Ronen, "The Filtering of Transitory Noise in Earnings Numbers," *Journal of Forecasting,* October–December 1983, pp. 331–350.

59. Lintner, J., and R. Glauber, "Higgledy-Piggledy Growth in America," research paper, Harvard Business School, Harvard University, Cambridge, 1969.

60. Little, I. M. D., "Higgledy Piggledy Growth," *Bulletin of the Oxford Institute of Economics and Statistics,* November 1962, pp. 389–412.

61. Lorek, K. S., "Predicting Annual Net Earnings with Quarterly Earnings Time-Series Models," *Journal of Accounting Research,* Spring 1979, pp. 190–204.

62. Lorek, K. S., and A. W. Bathke, "A Time-Series Analysis of Nonseasonal Quarterly Earnings Data," *Journal of Accounting Research,* Spring 1984, pp. 369–379.

63. Lorek, K. S., C. L. McDonald, and D. H. Patz, "A Comparative Examination of Management Forecasts and Box-Jenkins Forecasts of Earnings," *The Accounting Review,* April 1976, pp. 321–330.

64. Manegold, J. G., "Time-Series Properties of Earnings: A Comparison of Extrapolative and Component Models," *Journal of Accounting Research,* Autumn 1981, pp. 360–373.

65. Markowitz, H., *Portfolio Selection: Efficient Diversification of Investments,* John Wiley, New York, 1959.

66. Ohlson, J. A., "Financial Ratios and the Probabilistic Prediction of Bankruptcy," *Journal of Accounting Research,* Spring 1980, pp. 109–131.

67. Patell, J. M., "Corporate Forecasts of Stock Price Behavior," *Journal of Accounting Research,* Autumn 1976, pp. 246–276.

68. Penman, S. H., "An Empirical Investigation of the Voluntary Disclosure of Corporate Earnings Forecasts," *Journal of Accounting Research,* Spring 1980, pp. 132–160.

69. Penman, S. H., "Insider Trading and the Dissemination of Firms' Forecast Information," *The Journal of Business,* October 1982, pp. 479–503.

70. Rayner, A. C., and I. M. D. Little, *Higgledy-Piggledy Growth Again,* Basil Blackwell, Oxford, England, 1966.

71. Reilly, F. K., D. L. Morgenson, and M. West, "The Predictive Ability of Alternative Parts of Interim Financial Statements," *Journal of Accounting Research,* Supplement 1972, pp. 105–124.

72. Rosenberg, B., and V. Marathe, "The Prediction of Investment Risk: Systematic and Residual Risk," *Proceedings of the Seminar in Analysis of Security Prices,* University of Chicago, November 1975.

73. Ruland, W., "The Accuracy of Forecasts by Management and by Financial Analysts," *The Accounting Review,* April 1978, pp. 439–447.

74. Schreuder, H., and J. Klaassen, "Confidential Revenue and Profit Forecasts by Management and Financial Analysts: Evidence from the Netherlands," *The Accounting Review,* January 1984, pp. 64–77.

75. Sharpe, W. F., "Capital Asset Prices: A Theory of Market Equilibrium Under Condition of Risk," *The Journal of Finance,* September 1964, pp. 425–442.

76. Silhan, P. A., "Simulated Mergers of Existent Autonomous Firms: A New Approach to Segmentation Research," *Journal of Accounting Research,* Spring 1982, pp. 255–262.

77. Watts, R. L., "The Time Series of Accounting Earnings," in "The Information Content of Dividends," Ph.D. Dissertation, University of Chicago, 1970, Appendix A.

78. Watts, R. L., "The Time Series Behavior of Quarterly Earnings," research paper, Department of Commerce, University of Newcastle, New South Wales, April 1975.

79. Watts, R. L., "Systematic 'Abnormal' Returns After Quarterly Earnings Announcements," *Journal of Financial Economics,* June/September, 1978, pp. 127–150.

80. Watts, R. L., and R. W. Leftwich, "The Time Series of Annual Accounting Earnings," *Journal of Accounting Research,* Autumn 1977, pp. 253–271.

81. Williams, J. B., *The Theory of Investment Value,* MIT Press, Cambridge, MA, 1938.

6

FORECASTING AND STRATEGIC PLANNING

NOEL CAPON
JAMES M. HULBERT
Graduate School of Business, Columbia University, New York

In this chapter we outline the forecasting requirements for a firm that practices strategic planning. In the first section we draw a distinction between strategic planning and other forms of planning, and identify the critical dimensions of strategic planning. We then briefly review the forecasting literature and look critically at its relationship to strategic planning. In the third section a normative approach to the relationship between firm performance, environmental change, forecasting requirements, and strategy development is discussed. In the final section the characteristics of a strategic forecasting system are outlined.

STRATEGIC PLANNING

Over the past 10 to 15 years an enormous amount has been written about formal planning systems—their characteristics, the extent of their adoption, and the relationship between their adoption and performance (for a review see Lorange[22]). Whereas most authors agree on what is meant by "formal"—a set of planning activities assigned to specific individuals, scheduled at specific times, using standardized methodologies, and producing a written plan output (see, for example, Henry[13,14])—there has been much less concern with the type of planning involved.

The type of planning involved in a formal planning system can range from one in which the basic unit of analysis is considered fixed, in which case the planning task may be more extrapolative with a heavy emphasis on future firm performance, to one in which the basic unit of analysis is considered variable, in which case the potential for change of the unit becomes important. Change at the product line level implies addition and deletion of product offerings and entry and exit from market segments; change at the business level may imply addition and deletion of both product lines and markets; while at the corporate level, change may mean the addition and deletion of businesses with consequent major change in the nature of the corporation.

The focus of earlier writing on formal planning[30,31] seemed generally to lean toward the fixed unit of analysis, so that the emphasis was often on simple extrapolative forecasting of future firm performance. However, in part due to a shift from the comparatively benign environments of the 1960s to the more turbulent environments of the 1970s and 1980s; in part due to the development of planning concepts and models such as portfolio and policy analytic techniques,[8,16] at the heart of which is the notion of active management of the firm's portfolio of products, markets, and businesses; and finally in part due to increased interest in strategy per se, the literature on planning has begun to shift focus and is increasingly characterized by the adjective "strategic" being appended to the practice of planning—hence "strategic planning."

Despite extensive literature on strategic planning, there is only limited agreement among authors as to what constitutes "strategic."[7] Presumably the term was appended to indicate that planning activities should focus on development of strategy. Certainly, the concern that formal planning per se does not necessarily improve strategy is legitimate. Nonetheless, on the basis of a literature review and some empirical work, we concluded that gathering environmental information and adapting to environmental change are the primary distinguishing characteristics of planning that is "strategic." Clearly, then, forecasting takes a central role in strategic planning, for forecasting is the only means to develop an information base about the future environment. We shall argue in the next section, however, that company forecasting systems are often misaligned with the needs created by strategic planning.

FORECASTING

Traditional forecasting literature has focused mainly on the development and testing of new quantitative forecasting methodologies, and the solution of short-term operating problems.[6,24] The unit of analysis in such problems is typically a product or product line and the concern is accurately to forecast sales so that inventory and production scheduling decisions can be made.

A number of authors have more recently begun to address the question of the relationship between forecasting and planning that has a longer time horizon than is typically considered for the inventory and scheduling problem.[4,15,21,23,28,36] The concern with this relationship has undoubtedly increased as a result of the turbulent world environment[11] and the difficulty of forecasting the impact of a set of environmental changes on the firm.

Most writers view the changing environment as hostile and something that the firm must defend against. Nonetheless, they generally take the view that to the extent that the firm is able to improve forecasts of its environment, it will be better able to respond to environmental changes and thus perform more effectively. However, rarely do writers clearly identify critical environmental dimensions, although they place major emphasis on the current demand environment and occasionally show some concern for the technological environment.* Furthermore, similar to those who write about forecasting, planning authors typically focus on a firm operating in a single industry and are frequently concerned with a single product line.

Some authors writing in the forecasting field have noted the relevance of such concepts as portfolio and policy matrices[21] and strategy matrices[28] to strategic planning, but have failed to develop relationships between use of these techniques and forecasting requirements.

Thus, the critical underlying assumptions of literature that attempts to integrate strategic planning and forecasting appear to be:

- The firm operates in an increasingly turbulent environment (but the key aspects of that environment are typically not described).

- To survive and prosper the firm should predict future environmental trends and react to them.

- The appropriate level of analysis for the firm is at the product or product line level.

We believe that these assumptions are fundamentally incorrect. First, for a given product line it is insufficient to view the firm as operating in a single environment, frequently identified as the demand environment. Rather, that single environment has many aspects or dimensions, each of which may be more or less important in its effect on the firm. For example, the demand environment can be disaggregated in a number of different ways—geographically, by application, by customer type, and so forth. Other important environmental dimensions are governmental, purchased materials and components, human resources, financial markets, competition, technological, and so forth. Theory appears to be inadequate to guide selection of initial environmental variables, and two classes of consequences can be discerned:

---

* Armstrong[4] does also consider environmental forecasting, but the major focus is on economic trends and cycles that are seen as an input into developing the sales forecast.

Certain environmental factors might affect the level of aggregate industry demand in markets, and other factors might change the existing competitive equilibrium within the industry. Some of these factors will be more important than others, and some may be more predictable whereas others may be very turbulent.

Second, the increasing turbulence of the environment should not necessarily be viewed as something to be feared, for it may facilitate changing the firm's product-market domain, and thus the broader environment to which the firm is exposed. The extent to which managers should be fearful of changing product-market scope should arguably be a function of the firm's current and prospective strategic position in a particular product market, and of its ability to change. Herein may lie the Achilles' heel of success, however, for if a firm has developed a successful strategy and is high profitable, it may well become complacent or even rigid.[1] Such a firm is likely to prefer a stable environment so that it can continue to implement successfully its current strategy and to reap profits. Indeed, Tushman and Romanelli[35] have developed a whole theory of company evolution based on punctuated equilibrium, wherein long convergent periods are postulated for successful firms. However, when marked changes occur in critical environmental sectors, the factors necessary for success also are likely to change. Thus, because of the inertia often (although not always) associated with large organizations, a firm with large investments in an existing strategy may find it difficult successfully to change course and develop a new strategy to take account of these sectoral environmental changes.

Conversely, managers of other firms may view a turbulent or potentially turbulent environment differently. Indeed, in many cases changes may work to the advantage of competitors of the leader, for to the extent that the environment is stable, it may be difficult to compete successfully with the dominant firm. A marked change or potential for change in critical environmental factors may represent the wedge that a follower firm can use to improve its strategic position. Thus, a turbulent environmental sector may well be seen as a positive, and not a negative, state of affairs, as previously foreclosed opportunities become available. Clearly, managers' views of environmental changes should be a function of their firm's current strategic position and its key strengths and capabilities.

Third, the assumption that the firm must react to environmental changes is not necessarily correct. Many environmental factors may be beyond the firm's control, but the firm may be able actively to change critical factors to its advantage by various strategic moves; in other words, it may be able to shift from a passive to an active posture with respect to its environment. Indeed, it can be argued that a key purpose of strategy is to destabilize the environment, for example, to develop new technology, to lobby for changes in regulation, to develop new sources of supply, to weaken the grip of unions, to effectively constrain competitor's actions, and so forth, in an attempt to gain competitive advantage.*

Further, not only is the assumption that the firm can only react to environmental changes incorrect but so also is the unidimensional level of analysis of the firm as a single product or at least highly specialized entity, which leads to the implicit and incorrect assumption that the firm is stuck with the current environment. Nothing could be further from the truth, for a firm may choose to diversify along a number of dimensions—geographically, technologically, customer type, product application, industry, and so forth. In such diversification moves, the firm in effect selects the environment within which it will conduct its business. Indeed, the experience of major U.S. companies over the past 30 years, both in geographic expansion to become multinational organizations and in diversification away from the single business organization, is testimony to a selection (by design or default) of new environments in which to operate, albeit with mixed success.[33] Furthermore, by divestiture, abandonment, or other means the firm can exit from those environments which it deems to be too hostile and in which it fails to achieve an acceptable level of profitability.†

We believe that a new set of assumptions must be developed with which to address the strategic planning/forecasting problem:

- The environment faced even by a particular product is multifaceted. Changes in some environmental sectors are more likely to occur than in others and may be more critical in some than in others as regards their impact on the success of the firm.

- The impact of environmental turbulence on the firm is not necessarily negative. Rather, the impact of environmental change is a function of the firm's strategic position and ability to change.

- Many environmental factors may be beyond the firm's control. However, the firm may, through its various strategic moves, actively be able to affect and manage certain key environmental sectors.‡

- The firm is able to select the environment in which it operates. By various forms of diversification it can choose to operate with new envi-

---

* See, for example, Harley Davidson's success in persuading the U.S. government to raise import tariffs on large motorcycles, and Ford and Chrysler's efforts to block the GM/Toyota manufacturing agreement.

† See, for example, National Industries exit from the steel industry, Banker's Trust's Trust's sale of its consumer banking operations, and the recent withdrawal of both Northwest Industries and Gould Inc. from those businesses that previously formed their corporate raison d'être, the railroad and battery businesses, respectively.

‡ The concept of environmental control resembles Ackoff's[2] notion of "interactive planning," which he distinguishes from "preactive planning," whose focus is on predicting the future environment.

ronmental imperatives, and by divestiture, abandonment, and so forth it can exit from current environments.

STRATEGIC PLANNING AND FORECASTING

In this section we take a much broader view of forecasting than is usual. We view forecasting as an activity that provides information about the future, both the future of the firm (sales forecasts, etc.) and the future of various environmental sectors, futures both that we expect to happen, ceteris paribus, and futures that we expect to occur given various strategic actions, "what if" futures. Indeed, the inclusion of "what if" forecasts distinguishes forecasting important for strategic planning from more typical operational forecasting. (For an excellent case history, see Wack.[37]) In operational forecasting, strategic moves are typically assumed away—they have already been set and the forecasting job is to determine the expected future. In strategic planning, one of the key activities is the generation and examination of various alternative strategies and the forecasting of the likely results of those actions.

To explore the relationship between strategic planning and forecasting, we focus first on a single-product firm and later aggregate to a multiproduct, diversified organization. Our basic model is that of a multifaceted single-product firm interacting with a multifaceted environment. We define strategy as that set of decisions that relate to the allocation of resources, ultimately to sustain or improve competitive position in the marketplace.

As a first step, the strategic planner must identify which environmental sectors are most important to influencing the performance of the firm. Of all the various relationships between the firm and its environment, some subsets will typically have a more important impact than others. Typically such environmental sectors as customers, competitors, suppliers, and so forth are critical, but legal, regulatory, unions, stockholders, and others may at some time enter the critical set.*

Obviously, the ability to forecast which of these aspects will be critical over the planning horizon would be highly desirable. Thus, the strategic forecasting problem here is to forecast the future of the various aspects of the environment. Such forecasting may be highly quantitative, such as industry demand or numbers of customers, or it may be highly qualitative, such as identifying the future political or regulatory environment. Often particularly important is a forecast of the presence of future competitors and their actions. Given that strategy exists to maintain or gain competitive advantage, an ability to forecast competitive moves better enables management to develop an acceptable strategy.

---

* See Jemison[17] for a review of that aspect of strategic management research that deals with the relationship of an organization to its environment.

In developing its own strategy, the firm must address the anticipated environmental changes that its forecasts have identified. Of course, within any environmental sector, the forecaster may believe that particular futures will occur with probabilities that can be assigned. In such cases contingent strategies should be developed. In cases where forecasts of the environment predict stability, however, the planning effort must focus on strategy development, which might include attempts to destabilize the environment (an option that may at times suit either leader or follower). While strategic options are being actively explored conditional forecasting retains an important role, a role that we would view as strategic, but from this point forward the forecasting tasks become operational and more conventional.

When critical environmental sectors are forecast to be destabilized, the strategic forecasting task is both more complex and more important. A destabilized critical environment sector implies that continuation of the current strategy may not produce satisfactory performance. The firm has to address these changes with new strategic actions. These actions themselves will result in a different set of environmental factors than those prevailing had the firm continued with its present strategies. However, the firm must identify a set of strategic options and investigate the results of implementing a feasible subset of them. The forecasting job here is again of the "what if" variety, but involves both environmental and strategic changes. As the planners test feasible actions designed to counteract the destabilizing effect of exogenous environmental factors, they must move to identify those actions whose forecast results best enable the firm to defend or improve its current position.

If a forecast has not identified destabilized environmental sectors, the firm may seek to destabilize the environment itself. By doing so, it may be able to corner a key source of supply, effect a key regulatory change, reposition a key product, acquire a firm with key technology, and so forth. The intent of such aggressive destabilizing moves would be to bring about disequilibrium such that when the dust eventually settles, the instigator has gained ground and improved its performance at the expense of its competitive targets. The forecasting problem here is again of the "what if" variety, for a firm that has the ability to destabilize critical environmental sectors will have a number of options. The results of implementation of each must be forecast before a course of action can be chosen. (For further discussion of industry experience with scenarios and contingency planning, see O'Connor.[29])

The implementation of a forecasting system that requires (1) identification of key environmental sectors, (2) forecasting of key environmental sectors, and (3) conditional forecasting for alternative strategic options, addresses the strategic planning/forecasting problem at the business or product-line level. However, whereas strategic planning at these lower levels within the organization implicitly assumes a narrow scope of resource allocation, at the corporate level a much broader scope is appropriate. At lower levels, those environmental sectors that the firm addresses are established by the scope of the subunits' mission, and changes at these levels are likely to be highly related to the current environment. More extreme changes might include geographic expansion to different national environments; siting of new production facilities; or the use of different production facilities. Any of these requires interaction with different union environments, but nonetheless the degree of relationship between any such modification and the original business is typically likely to be very high.

At the corporate level there are more degrees of freedom, for given its broader mission focus than that of any individual subunit, the firm has much greater ability to select the set of environmental sectors with which it deals. If overall anticipated corporate performance from the set of subunits does not meet corporate objectives, the firm may seek to diversify or divest, usually within the scope of its existing mission. Such diversification, whether internally generated or arrived at by acquisition, we argue, must be planned, for the record of scattershot changes in corporate portfolios is not encouraging. The firm will need to develop an environmental scanning ability to identify opportunities,[3] a forecasting capability to predict the future of the set of key environmental factors surrounding each opportunity, and a "what if" forecasting capability, given that the firm accepts the opportunity and makes alternative strategic moves.

At the corporate level, then, an extra environmental forecasting resource is needed—a scanning mechanism to identify options. The environmental forecasting and "what if" forecasting capabilities are no different in concept from those required at the product-line level, but they are different in nature, since the firm has less information on new areas of opportunity than it does when planning for its existing subunits.

THE CONCEPT OF STRATEGIC FORECASTING

Our argument to this point can be simply summarized as follows: The bulk of existing forecasting efforts is devoted to predicting the results of a set of predetermined strategic actions in an existing environmental structure. The purpose of such forecasting is to enable better operating decisions to be made; we might call these efforts "operational forecasting." While this approach may be sufficient for firms successfully positioned in slow-changing or uncompetitive environments, it is certain to be both ineffective and inefficient in the fast-changing and competitive environments characterized by high degrees of oligopolistic concentration that are common in many sectors today. Under these conditions, forecasting efforts must focus much greater attention on changes in the very elements that, in the past, have been treated as unchanging. In other words, *strategic* planning needs strategic (not operational) forecasting. Furthermore, concern must be given not only to forecasting those areas in which the signals are strong, but also those areas in which environmental signals are either weak or nonexistent,[27] for it may be that in these latter domains significant potential for competitive advantage lies. Such forecasting is quite different from operational forecasting. In this section we build on our previous discussion to develop the key elements of a strategic forecasting system.

Environmental Emphasis

A major preoccupation of a strategic forecasting system must be prediction of the structural environment within which the industry's business will be conducted. Strategic forecasters must identify critical environmental elements, those in which any change would upset the competitive equilibrium. It is on these structural elements that the strategic forecasting emphasis must be placed.* This emphasis must far outstrip a focus on the economic forecasts that are routinely included in long-range plans, and include such areas as technological, social, political, cultural, and so forth. Such forecasting is highly complex, often interactive, and frequently today not systematically included in the strategy formulation process.

Long-Term Time Horizons

Strategic decisions are concerned with changing the nature of the business, and often its environment, so that relatively long periods are involved. Such a long-term focus contrasts sharply with short-term operational forecasting efforts. What is "long term" is a function of the individual business, but can be thought of as that period during which all assets may be varied, a time span varying from just a few months for some service businesses to as long as 15 years for a major capital goods manufacturer.

Conditional Forecasting

Strategic decisions involve the allocation of significant quantities of resources, and thus corporations should investigate the results of alternative strategic actions before committing those resources. Since strategic actions may influence critical environmental factors, the firm must be able to forecast the future of those factors as well as the ultimate results that the firm itself will achieve. These forecasts are "what if" forecasts—not futures that the firm expects to happen but futures that the firm would expect to happen conditional on some set of strategic actions. It is the critical importance of "what if" forecasts in strategic planning that renders strategic forecasting neither an input to nor an output from, but rather an integral part of, the strategic planning process.

* See Klein[18,19] for a discussion of selection of the environmental variables to forecast and Klein[20] for results of a study that indicate an increased investment by major corporations in resources to perform environmental assessments.

Data Base Requirements

The data bases required for strategic forecasting are qualitatively and quantitatively different from those of most companies' forecasting systems. Few companies are committed to such areas as social forecasting or technological forecasting, yet we argue that it is forecasting of just this type, dealing with structural parameters of the industry, that is central to much of the job of strategic forecasting. Thus, the firm perhaps should develop a data base of key social or technological indicators which it may use as the basis for making social or technological forecasts. However, just forecasting a set of indicators is insufficient, for it is the *effects* of trends and events that are more important both to understand and to predict than the primary changes themselves.[36]

Alternatively, the firm may be able to forecast such areas as the impact of government regulation in a particular national environment by analogy with similar changes in some other national environment. This implies that the firm may wish to build up a multination data base for some particular environmental areas. Indeed, some experts argue that time series forecasts have limited usefulness for strategic planning and that greater insight into feasible strategic actions can be obtained by cross-sectional forecasting, the use of analogy from similar historic strategic situations.[34]

Forecast Methodologies

No doubt some of the advanced quantitative techniques that have been developed for the operational forecasting problem will prove to be useful in the environmental forecasting area. However, other techniques such as delphi[32] and the nominal group method[9] will probably prove to be more attuned to the strategic forecasting problem than to operational ones. (See Martino[26] for a broad coverage of techniques.)

Forecast Accuracy

Whereas in the operational forecasting problem a heavy premium is typically set on forecast accuracy, high degrees of accuracy in forecasting for strategic planning are both unlikely and unnecessary.[5] What matters is that the broad thrust of the forecast is in the right direction, for strategy formulation is concerned with setting the appropriate general course, not in deciding the fine details, which are the concern of tactical planning. Furthermore, rather than focus on the development of single point estimates, strategic forecasting should focus on the development of a range of possible outcomes, such that the decision maker can ultimately make the risk/return tradeoffs.

Forecast Availability

The prototypical large organization today is a multibusiness activity typically organized in some form of divisionalized structure. Irrespective of the degree of diversity in technologies and markets across the corporation, there will doubtless be areas of overlap of critical environmental factors. In this area, then, it is particularly important that the firm develop a library and access system so that forecasting performed at lower levels in the organization can be made available across departmental and divisional lines. No doubt some forms of global environmental forecasting will be performed at the corporate level and made available to the various divisions, perhaps as part of the corporate planning effort, but it is for forecasts at the lower level that transorganizational access is important. Such dissemination applies both to forecasts themselves and to models or approaches to solving particular environmental forecasting problems.

SUMMARY AND CONCLUSIONS

In this chapter we have addressed the issue of integration of forecasting with strategic planning. We first distinguished strategic planning from other forms of planning. We then noted that much of the effort in forecasting is concerned not with strategic planning but rather with operational planning. Furthermore, to the extent that researchers have addressed the problem of the interrelationship of forecasting with strategic planning, a set of questionable assumptions is typically employed. Rather than viewing the firm as a specialized entity reacting to a set of environmental changes, we identified strategy as involving major shifts of competitive equilibrium, such that the ability to cope with structural change is a crucial requirement of the forecasting system. Furthermore, we believe that the generation of "what if" forecasts is a crucial part of the development of strategy. We have dubbed such a system a strategic forecasting system, and we suggested a number of ways in which it would differ from typical operational forecasting systems.

We doubt that many organizations have yet developed fully a strategic forecasting system, though without question some are further ahead than others.[10] Indeed, it might easily be argued that unless a strategic orientation is firmly embedded in organization—perhaps akin to Glueck and colleagues[12] notion of strategic management—attempts to upgrade forecasting efforts will be foredoomed. The shift of outlook necessary at a number of organizational levels involves not so much *forecasting* methodology as it does *management* methodology. Thus, we do not believe that such a system can be built up overnight; rather a sustained effort over a period of time will be necessary. However, though the development of a strategic forecasting capability is clearly an expensive proposition for a corporation, since the ultimate purpose of strategy is to reconfigure the competitive equilibrium in such a way that the firm has the advantage, it is our belief that the investment of resources in developing better forecasting capabilities to achieve this end is justified. Forecasters, planners, and managers alike share an interest in broadening the narrow context within which forecasting has traditionally been viewed, so that it might better serve the strategic needs of the firm.

REFERENCES

1. Abernathy, Ralph, and Kenneth Wayne, "Limits of the Learning Curve," *Harvard Business Review,* vol. 52, September–October 1974, pp. 109–119.

2. Ackoff, Russell L., *Creating the Corporate Future,* John Wiley, New York, 1981.

3. Aguilar, F. J., *Scanning the Business Environment,* Macmillan, New York, 1967.

4. Armstrong, J. Scott, "Strategic Planning and Forecasting Fundamentals," in Kenneth Albert, ed., *The Strategic Management Handbook,* McGraw-Hill, New York, 1983, pp. 2-1–2-32.

5. Beck, Peter W., "Forecasts, Models—The Opiate of Decision Makers," paper delivered at Third International Symposium on Forecasting, Philadelphia, June 5–8, 1983.

6. Brown, Robert Goodell, "The Balance of Effort in Forecasting," *Journal of Forecasting,* vol. 1, 1982, pp. 49–53.

7. Capon, Noel, John U. Farley, and James Hulbert, *Corporate Strategic Planning,* Columbia University Press, New York (in press), 1986.

8. Day, George S., "Diagnosing the Product Portfolio," *Journal of Forecasting,* vol. 1, 1977, pp. 29–38.

9. Delbecq, A., A. Van de Ven, and D. Rustafson, *Group Techniques for Program Planning,* Scott Foresman, Glenville, IL, 1975.

10. Dino, Richard N., Donald E. Riley, and Pan G. Yatrakis, "The Role of Forecasting in Corporate Strategy: The Xerox Experience," *Journal of Forecasting,* vol. 1, 1982, pp. 335–348.

11. Drucker, Peter E., *Managing in Turbulent Times,* Harper & Row, New York, 1980.

12. Glueck, F. W., S. P. Kaufman, and A. S. Welleck, "Strategic Management for Competitive Advantage," *Harvard Business Review,* July–August 1980, pp. 154–161.

13. Henry, Harold W., "Formal Planning in Major U.S. Corporations," *Long Range Planning,* vol. 10, 1977, pp. 40–45.

14. Henry, Harold W., "Commentary on Formal Planning Systems: Their Roles in Strategy Formulation and Implementation," in D. E. Schendel and C. W. Hofer, eds., *Strategic Management,* Little Brown, Cambridge, MA, 1979.

15. Hogarth, Robin, and Spyros Makridakis, "Forecasting and Planning: An Evaluation," *Management Science,* vol. 27, 1981, pp. 115–138.

16. Hussey, David, "Portfolio Analysis: Practical Experience with the Directional Policy Matrix," *Long Range Planning,* vol. 11, 1978, pp. 2–8.

17. Jemison, David B., "The Contributions of Administrative Behavior to Strategic Management," *Academy of Management Review,* vol. 6, 1981, pp. 663–642.

18. Klein, Harold E., *Incorporating Environmental Examination Into the Corporate Strategic Planning Process,* Ph.D. Dissertation, Columbia University, 1973.

19. Klein, Harold E., "Commentary on Utterback," in D. E. Schendel and C. W. Hofer, eds., *Strategic Management,* Little Brown, Cambridge, MA, 1979.

20. Klein, Harold E., "The Role of Environmental Forecasting/Assessment in Formal Corporate Planning Processes—An International Study of Corporate Practice, paper delivered at Third International Symposium on Forecasting, Philadelphia, June 5–8, 1983.

21. Lasserre, Philippe, and Heinz T. Thanheiser, "Forecasting in Strategic Planning," in Spy-

ros Makridakis and Steven C. Wheelwright, eds., *The Handbook of Forecasting: A Manager's Guide,* New York, Wiley, Ch. 6, pp. 69–82, 1982.

22. Lorange, Peter, "Formal Planning Systems: Their Role In Strategy Formulation and Implementation," in D. E. Schendel and C. W. Hofer, eds., *Strategic Management,* Little Brown, Cambridge, MA, 1979.

23. Makridakis, Spyros, "If We Cannot Forecast How Can We Plan?," *Long Range Planning,* vol. 14, 1981, pp. 10–20.

24. Makridakis, Spyros, and Steven C. Wheelwright, "Forecasting: Framework and Overview," *TIMS Studies in the Management Sciences,* vol. 12, 1979, pp. 1–15.

25. Makridakis, Spyros, and Steven C. Wheelwright, "Forecasting in the Future and the Future of Forecasting," *TIMS Studies in Management Sciences,* vol. 12, 1979, pp. 329–352.

26. Martino, J., *Technological Forecasting for Decision Making,* Elsevier North-Holland, New York, 1983.

27. Milutinovich, Jugoslav S., and John M. Mankelewicz, "Identification of Environmental Problems When Signals are Weak or Non-Existent," paper delivered at Third International Symposium on Forecasting, Philadelphia, June 5–8, 1983.

28. Naylor, T. H., "Strategic Planning and Forecasting," *Journal of Forecasting,* vol. 2, 1983, pp. 109–118.

29. O'Connor, Rochelle, *Planning Under Uncertainty: Multiple Scenarios and Contingency Planning,* The Conference Board, New York, 1978.

30. Ringbaak, Kjell-Arne, *Organized Corporate Planning Systems—An Empirical Study of Planning Practices and Experiences in American Big Business,* Ph.D. Dissertation, University of Wisconsin, 1968.

31. Ringbaak, Kjell-Arne, "The Corporate Planning Life Cycle—An International Point of View," *Long Range Planning,* vol. 5, 1972, pp. 10–20.

32. Roman, D. D., "Technological Forecasting in the Decision Process," *Academy of Management Journal,* vol. 13, 1970, pp. 127–138.

33. Rumelt, Richard, *Strategy, Structure and Economic Performance,* Harvard University Press, Cambridge, MA, 1974.

34. Schoeffler, Sidney, Remarks in panel discussion, *Forecasting for Strategic Planning,* S. Makridakis, Chair, at Third International Symposium on Forecasting, Philadelphia, June 5–8, 1983.

35. Tushman, Michael L., and Elaine Romanelli, "Organizational Evolution: A Metamorphosis Model of Convergence and Reorientation," in L. L. Cummings and B. Staw, eds., *Research in Organizational Behavior,* vol. 7, JAI Press, Greenwich, Conn., 1985, pp. 171–222.

36. Utterback, James M., "Environmental Analysis and Forecasting," in D. E. Schendel and C. W. Hofer, *Strategic Management,* Little Brown, Cambridge, MA, 1979.

37. Wack, Pierre, "Scenarios: Uncharted Water Ahead," *Harvard Business Review,* September–October 1985, pp. 73–89.

7

FORECASTING IN THE ELECTRIC UTILITY INDUSTRY

WILLIAM R. HUSS

Xenergy, Inc., Burlington, Massachusetts

WHY FORECAST?

The prime directive of any regulated electric utility is to provide adequate and reliable electricity supplies to the consuming public at reasonable cost. Over time, the demand for electricity is constantly changing, as are construction and fuel costs. To meet these fluctuations in demand, a utility must constantly add new capacity, retire inefficient plants, and expand existing ones. New plant construction normally requires 5 to 10 years; in the case of nuclear it can be even longer. Proposed sites must be selected and evaluated, financing must be obtained, and approval from the regulatory body must be received. Because of a lead time that may extend to several years, capacity expansion must be based on a forecast of future demand. The ability of a utility to minimize the cost of electricity depends directly on the ability of the load forecast to predict the level of energy sales and peak demand over time. Overbuilding causes unnecessary cost to consumers, while underbuilding can result in brownouts and reduced reliability of service.

Utilities also use forecasts for financial planning, operational planning, market research, and meeting of federal and state regulatory data requirements. Increasingly, utilities are using forecasts to test the effect of time-of-day rates, conservation programs, new technologies, advertising, severe weather conditions, and so on. Forecasts of total sales (kilowatt hours), total output including losses, winter and summer peak loads (kilowatts), and load shapes are all necessary. Total sales forecasts are used primarily to drive financial models and for rate design. Peak forecasts are also used in rate design but are the primary input to the utility's construction plans, while load shape forecasts are useful for evaluating various demand-side management alternatives, such as time-of-day rates.

Utilities and their stockholders suffer penalties both when forecasts are too high and when they are too low. High forecasts encourage overbuilding. These added construction costs result in large rate increases and, due to the effect of price elasticities, lower electricity use as well. As the use of electricity decreases, the higher costs must be passed on to a smaller group of customers, which compounds the problem. In addition, regulatory agencies may not allow all of the extra costs to be passed on to the customer; instead the utility's rate of return may be reduced.

A low forecast, on the other hand, causes undercapacity. Brownouts and blackouts are likely. Expensive peaking units must be run as base load and high-priced off-system power must be purchased. If customers do not have adequate electricity supplies, increased regulatory pressure is a certain result.

Typically, utility forecasts are disaggregated into residential, commercial, industrial, and sometimes agricultural sectors. In general, electricity consumption is distributed almost equally among sectors. The residential sector is characterized by a fairly homogeneous population and a large number of customers. Thus, no one individual greatly affects consumption. Sampling procedures are often useful in obtaining data. The commercial sector also has many customers, but they are of a more heterogeneous nature. Certainly electricity use in a warehouse is quite different from electricity use in a grocery store. Thus, commercial sector forecasts are often further disaggregated by building type.

The industrial sector has a heterogeneous population and is relatively small. In fact, the top 10 industrial customers in a service area often account for over 50% of the industrial electricity sales. Therefore, a single customer who unexpectedly goes out of business or relocates to another service area can drastically affect the accuracy of the forecast. For this reason, actual customer surveys are often used as a forecasting tool in the industrial sector. In addition, industrial forecasts are often disaggregated to at least the two-digit standard industrial classification (SIC) level in an attempt to minimize the heterogeneous population problem.

In early 1985, the author conducted an extensive survey of the 75 largest utilities in the United States on the basis of 1982 sales. Fifty-eight utilities with combined sales comprising roughly 70% of total U.S. sales chose to participate. The survey addressed such critical issues as forecast uses, criteria used to select or evaluate forecasts, the level of effort devoted to forecasting, and the techniques used to forecast each sector. The survey also collected a number of historical forecasts to see how accurate they have been. Recommendations could subsequently be made to assure that the best possible approaches are being used by the industry. In addition to the 58 utilities, 50 state regulatory commissions plus the District of Columbia were contacted to provide similar information. Thirty-eight of these chose to participate. A list of all respondents appears in Chart 7-1. The remainder of this

CHART 7-1. Survey Participants: 58 Utilities (Top) and 38 State Commissions (Bottom)

Alabama Power	Minnesota P&L
Allegheny Power	Mississippi Power
American Electric Power	Mississippi P&L
Arizona Public Service	Montana Power
Arkansas P&L	NEPOOL
Baltimore G&E	New York Electric & Gas
Boston Edison	New York Power Pool
Carolina Power	Niagara Mohawk
Central Illinois P&L	Northern States Power
Central P&L	Northwest Power Plan
Commonwealth Edison	Ohio Edison
Consolidated Edison	Oklahoma G&E
Consumers Power	Pacific G&E
Dayton P&L	Pacific P&L
Delmarva Power	Pennsylvania Electric
Detroit Edison	Philadelphia Electric
Duke Power	Portland G&E
Dusquene	Public Service Colorado
Florida Power	Public Service Oklahoma
Georgia Power	San Diego G&E
Gulf States Power	SoCal Edison
Houston Lighting	South Carolina Electric
Illinois Power	Southwest Electric
Kansas G&E	Tampa Electric
Long Island Light	Toledo Edison
Los Angeles DWP	Union Electric
Louisiana P&L	Virginia Electric
Massachusetts Electric	Washington Water Power
Mid-South Services	Wisconsin Electric

Alabama	Minnesota
Alaska	Mississippi
Arizona	Missouri
Arkansas	Nevada
California	New Hampshire
Colorado	New Jersey
Connecticut	New York
Delaware	North Dakota
District of Columbia	Ohio
Florida	Oklahoma
Idaho	Pennsylvania
Illinois	Rhode Island
Indiana	Texas
Iowa	Utah
Kansas	Virginia
Kentucky	Washington
Maine	West Virginia
Maryland	Wisconsin
Michigan	Wyoming

chapter discusses the results of this study and characterizes the history and current status of load forecasting in the electric utility industry.

FORECAST USES

One of the key questions in the survey requested information on forecast uses. Chart 7-2 shows the responses of utility analysts and senior managers to certain uses. Both managers and analysts agreed that the most important use of forecasting at a utility is for generation planning. Other important uses are satisfaction of state and federal filing requirements, financial planning, rate design, and to a lesser extent evaluation of marketing programs.

CRITERIA FOR FORECAST SELECTION AND EVALUATION

The survey also addressed the use of the best criteria for selecting and evaluating an electric utility load forecast.

All respondents were provided with a list of 18 criteria (Chart 7-3) that were developed through various interviews and structured group meetings with utility and regulatory personnel. Respondents were asked to add any relevant criteria and then to select the eight most important criteria from the list. Next, respondents ranked these eight criteria in order of importance, from the most important to the least important. A weighted, normalized score was calculated on the basis of the number of times each criterion received a given ranking. For example, suppose out of 20 respondents, five gave a particular criterion a score of 8, five gave it a score of 1, and the remaining 10 gave it no score. The weighted average of the ranks would be $5(8) + 5(1) = 45$. This weighted average would then be normalized by dividing it by the number of respondents and then multiplying by 100 to remove the need for decimal points. Thus, the weighted, normalized score in this example would be:

$$\frac{4500}{20} = 225$$

Chart 7-4 ranks the top 10 criteria weighted score for each of the three client groups, namely, large utility managers, large utility analysts, and commissions. All three groups felt that the most important criterion was "Does the forecast make sense?" In addition, the historical performance of the model and data availability ranked in the top four of all groups. The high ranking of data availability may imply that the theoretical development of models has surpassed the industry's ability to collect the required data.

Perhaps the most interesting result is that both utility analysts and managers ranked explainability and acceptability to the commission in the top

CHART 7-2. Forecast Uses (Large Utility Respondents)

		Percent of Respondents					Number of Respondents
		Not Applicable	Minor Importance	Important	Very Important	Critical	
Generation planning	Mgr	0.0	0.0	2.3	34.9	62.8	43
	Anal	0.0	0.0	1.8	28.1	70.2	57
State/federal filing requests	Mgr	2.3	2.3	23.3	46.5	25.6	43
	Anal	1.8	5.3	24.6	38.6	29.8	57
Rate design	Mgr	0.0	14.0	44.2	32.6	9.3	43
	Anal	7.3	20.0	32.7	30.9	9.1	55
Financial planning	Mgr	0.0	2.3	4.7	65.1	27.9	43
	Anal	5.3	0.0	10.5	45.6	38.6	57
Marketing programs	Mgr	0.0	16.3	32.6	48.8	2.3	43
	Anal	5.3	21.1	29.8	38.6	5.3	57
Short-term operational planning	Mgr	—	—	—	—	—	—
	Anal	8.8	10.5	26.3	36.8	17.5	53
Environmental planning	Mgr	—	—	—	—	—	—
	Anal	35.8	35.8	18.9	7.5	1.9	53
Rate cases	Mgr	—	—	—	—	—	—
	Anal	5.3	3.5	12.3	35.1	43.9	56

CHART 7-3. Criteria Definitions

A. Historical Performance of Model

For well-developed modeling approaches, this includes the model's ability to fore-cast accurately as measured by mean absolute percentage error, mean square error, or other error measures. For new models, it means a validity check where the fore-caster uses the model structure as if it had been formulated several years in the past and measures the difference between model forecasts and actual consumption or peak load.

B. Consistency Between Forecast Assumptions and Drivers

The variables such as price, income or employment that drive the model should reflect the assumptions that the forecaster intuitively believes about the forecast environment.

C. Inclusion of Statistical Tests

Includes various goodness of fit tests such as R^2 and Theil's U, Chi-squared, t-tests, and F tests.

D. Does the Final Forecast Make Sense Given Input Assumptions?

Does the forecast seem within reasonable bounds and reflect the forecaster's intui-tive judgment of the future? Does the approach seem logical and account for all key factors or influences?

E. Explainability to Regulators and Managers

Can the forecasting approach be described to managers and regulators in a simple, logical, and intuitive fashion which does not require extensive familiarity with statis-tics, computer programming, or the associated jargon?

F. Cost to Design and Update

Includes time spent to collect data, design and implement modeling approach, purchase or write appropriate software, and produce model updates. Cost should be considered relative to the magnitude of the decision affected so that more money would be spent on forecast, to improve a more significant decision.

G. Availability of Data

Can the proper data be obtained in a simple, cost-effective manner and will the data continue to be available throughout the lifetime of the model?

H. Reproducibility

Can the approach, data sources, etc., be described in such a manner that an inde-pendent individual or organization can reproduce and understand the forecast? Is the forecasting approach well documented?

I. Ability to Evaluate Fundamental Structural Changes

Can the model capture fundamental changes such as the increased conservation ethic, the decline of heavy manufacturing industries, and the growth in service and information industries? Can the model help evaluate market environments (e.g., heat pumps or other new technologies) and deregulation?

J. Clear Statement of Purpose

Has the forecaster described why a forecast is needed and how it is to be used? Is the approach consistent with the purpose?

K. Acceptability of Method in Published Literature and from Peer Reviews

Do the academic and professional journals support the technique used? Is the approach consistent with what is employed by other utilities or by the Electric Power Research Institute (EPRI)?

CHART 7-3. (*Continued*)

L. Consistent Inclusion of Both National and Local Economic Variables

Does the model reflect both national *and* local economic conditions as well as the relationship between the two? Both the national and local forecasts of economic conditions must be based on the same set of assumptions.

M. Stability of Method/Results Over Time

If the forecast results undergo drastic changes from year to year or even from month to month, confidence in the forecast suffers. The same can be said for a forecast model or approach that shows no consistency over time.

N. Reasonable Sensitivity Analysis Using Alternative Input Assumptions and Alternate Techniques

Is the forecast relatively stable regardless of the technique used? Have the forecasters tested the effect of errors or changes in the input variables? Have these sensitivities included the development of a "scenario" or consistent set of alternative input assumptions (rather than taking the extreme of all input assumptions)?

O. Inclusion of Fuel Prices and Price Elasticities

How well does the model incorporate the effect of price or other key variables into the process?

P. Ability to Analyze Marketing Strategies

Can the model measure the effect on load of utility demand-side management activities including load management, time of day rates, electrification, advertising, conservation or home energy audit programs, etc.?

Q. Acceptability to Commission, Administration, and Other Political Organizations

Will the approach and resulting forecast meet the requirements of the various public organizations that will not only scrutinize the forecast technically but reflect public perceptions or political motivations as well?

R. Level of Disaggregation

Does the model have the proper level of disaggregation? Models that are not adequately detailed do not permit managers to address individual customer classes. Models that are too disaggregated are expensive and cannot be adequately supported by available data.

10, while the commission group ranked explainability 14th out of 18 and acceptability to the commission 18th and last. Obviously the utilities feel that they have suffered enough in the way of rate cases and rigorous cross-examination and critique, and that forecast acceptability to the commission is a key factor in model development. The commissions, on the other hand, feel that their role is one of guidance and that the best forecasting model is one that meets the utility's needs in a theoretically appropriate manner.

As expected, the analysts who must understand and work with the internal details of the system are more concerned with statistical tests than are senior managers, who are more concerned with the political issues such as explainability and acceptability to the commission. Commissions seemed much more concerned with a clear statement of the purpose of the forecast, sensitivity analysis, and the cost of the forecast.

CHART 7-4. Top 10 Criteria by Client Group Using Weighted Score

Large Utility Managers	Score	Large Utility Analysts	Score	State Commissions	Score
D. Does the forecast make sense?	484	D. Does the forecast make sense?	527	D. Does the forecast make sense?	482
A. Historical performance of model	419	G. Data availability	375	G. Data availability	403
E. Explainability to regulators	274	A. Historical performance of model	373	A. Historical performance of model	364
G. Data availability	267	C. Inclusion of statistical tests	278	I. Evaluates structural change	332
I. Evaluates structural change	263	E. Explainability to regulators	265	N. Sensitivity analysis	268
Q. Acceptability to commission	249	M. Stability over time	220	J. Clear statement of purpose	226
B. Consistency between assumptions/drivers	209	I. Evaluates structural change	202	F. Cost	226
O. Inclusion of prices/elasticities	205	B. Consistency between assumptions/drivers	200	C. Inclusion of statistical tests	218
M. Stability over time	202	Q. Acceptability to commission	194	O. Inclusion of prices/elasticities	168
N. Sensitivity analysis	191	O. Inclusion of prices/elasticities	192	R. Level of disaggregation	166

FORECASTING TECHNIQUES USED BY THE ELECTRIC UTILITY INDUSTRY

Prior to 1973, most industries, including utilities, forecasted growth using a rather straightforward time trend approach. Fitting of a curve to historical data, however, did not capture the underlying causes of load growth, and therefore was unable to predict sudden changes in the growth rate. Chart 7-5 shows how the annual growth rate in electricity sales dropped from the 6% to 9% range that was in effect from 1934 to 1972 to less than 3% in the years following the 1973–1974 Arab oil embargo. When trend extrapolation methods were unable to capture this change, newer more sophisticated econometric and end-use models were developed. The following gives a general description of the primary approaches used in electric utility forecasting.

CHART 7-5. History of Electric Load Forecasting

Span of Years	Average Annual Growth-%	R^2
1921–1928	10.1	.987
1928–1934	0.0	—
1934–1944	7.6	.986
1945–1955	8.9	.994
1955–1964	6.0	.993
1964–1972	8.8	.990
1972–1980	2.9	.938
1920–1980	6.7	.993

LOG PEAK LOADS 1921–1928

LOG PEAK LOADS 1964–1972

LOG PEAK LOADS 1928–1934

LOG PEAK LOADS 1972–1980

The history of the development and use of these techniques will be described later.

Trend Extrapolation. These methods include straight line, polynomial, and logarithmic extrapolations in which the best fit of historical data is obtained using techniques such as least squares minimization. In the 1970s it was quite common for utilities to first extrapolate historical sales and then make judgmental adjustments on the basis of special insights gained from experience and knowledge of customer behavior.

Aggregate Single Equation Econometric. This method consists of a linear or log–log formulation of sales or peak load versus independent variables such as gross national product (GNP), price, degree days, month of year, and so on. This method uses at most one equation per sector. Sectors are typically residential, commercial, industrial, miscellaneous, and in some cases agricultural.

Disaggregate Single Equation Econometric. This method is the same as the one just described except that the sectors are disaggregated (e.g., residential by location or income, commercial by building type, and industrial by SIC code).

Multiequation Econometric. This method includes fuel share and flexible functional-form models as well as models that estimate the factors of production using factor price and factor outputs. The method generally involves several equations per sector which are solved simultaneously or in sequence, the results of one equation being fed into another.

End-Use/Equipment. In the residential sector, this method is characterized by forecasts by appliance, where the number of households times the appliance saturation times the use per appliance results in consumption per appliance. In the commercial or industrial sector, the forecasts are generally structured by equipment type such as heaters, boilers, furnaces, and so on.

Process Model. Used almost exclusively in the industrial sector, this model defines and optimizes the actual process flow of products as they are manufactured. At each stage of production, choices are made as to what equipment and fuel to use on the basis of minimization of life-cycle costs. The model is often constructed at the three- or four-digit SIC level rather than at the two-digit level. It often involves linear programming techniques to develop an optimal solution.

Advanced Time Series. This method includes techniques such as Box–Jenkins, moving average, exponential smoothing, adaptive estimation, window moving average regression, and many others. The method is based only on a time dimension, but can incorporate trends, seasonals, and cycles as well.

Expert Judgment. This technique includes interviews with utility personnel, consultants, and government experts to gather opinions of future sales and peak loads.

Customer Survey. This method includes mail, phone, and in-person interviews with customers to obtain their expectations of future electric consumption for their household, plant, or establishment.

Load Factor Analysis. This method is used exclusively in forecasting peak load. It is based on forecasting a load factor from historical data and then applying the load factor to the forecasted energy. In other words

$$\text{Load factor} = \frac{\text{annual energy}}{(\text{peak hour load} \times 8760)}$$

$$\text{Peak hour forecast} = \frac{\text{annual energy forecast}}{(\text{load factor forecast} \times 8760)}$$

HISTORY OF FORECASTING TECHNIQUES

The forecasting techniques used in the utility industry have undergone considerable change over the past 10 to 15 years. In the residential sector, econometric techniques began penetrating the market in 1976 (see Chart 7-6) and were the predominant technique by 1980. End-use techniques began taking hold at about the same time and now control a larger market share than econometric techniques.

Commercial forecasting continued to involve primarily trend extrapolation until 1978, when econometrics became the predominant technique and remains so today. End-use techniques, however, seem to be increasing in market share (see Chart 7-7).

In the industrial sector (see Chart 7-8) there is a very similar pattern in that econometrics began to replace trend extrapolation about 1976 and became the major technique by 1980. The one difference, however, is that since 1972 customer surveys have played an important although not dominant role in industrial sector forecasting. Surveys, of course, are often used because the industrial sector is typically dominated by a few large companies which, at least in the short term, have a pretty good idea of future energy use.

Trend extrapolation was also the number one technique for peak forecasting in 1972. The market share for econometric techniques began to grow by 1976, and by 1980 these were the ones used most often. Their growth has

CHART 7-6. History of Large Electric Utility Residential Load Forecasting

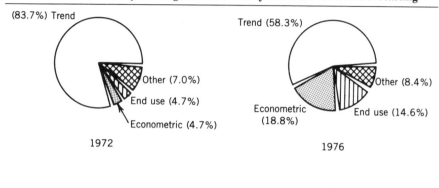

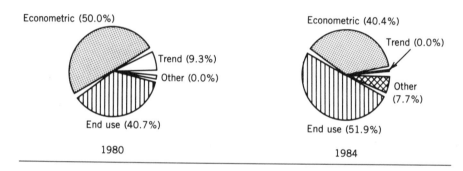

been insignificant since then. Load factor analysis has continued to be an important technique, although its market share is only about half what it was in 1972. Although still very minor, the use of end-use techniques in peak forecasting seems to be increasing. The history of peak forecasting is shown in Chart 7-9.

KEY VARIABLES USED IN FORECASTING

In the next section of the survey, utilities were given a list of 22 variables often used in utility forecasting and were asked to rate them as either not used, used judgmentally, used but not considered a significant factor, used and considered a key factor, or used and considered critical at the respondent's utility. Respondents were also encouraged to include additional variables, although few did so. Chart 7-10 shows the percentage of utility respondents rating each variable at each of the respective levels of use.

CHART 7-7. History of Large Electric Utility Commercial Load Forecasting

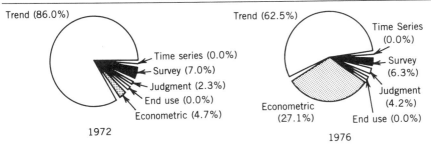

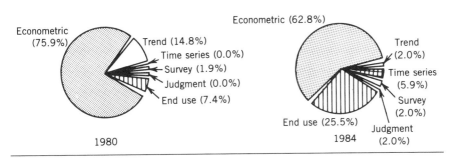

THE UTILITY FORECASTING ORGANIZATION

In this section of the survey, utilities were asked to provide a history of the forecasting organization and the time they devoted to forecasting. For the utilities that responded, the average number of person-months devoted to forecasting grew from 11.37 in 1972 to 41.83 in 1984, reflecting the ever-increasing emphasis being placed on forecasting by senior utility management.

The majority (54.4%) of the large utilities have central forecasting departments, with the average age of these departments being 11.64 years and the median age 8.50 years.

ANALYSES OF TOTAL ENERGY FORECASTS

Each of the participating utilities also submitted historical company forecasts back to 1972 as well as explanations of what techniques were used to

CHART 7-8. History of Large Electric Utility Industrial Load Forecasting

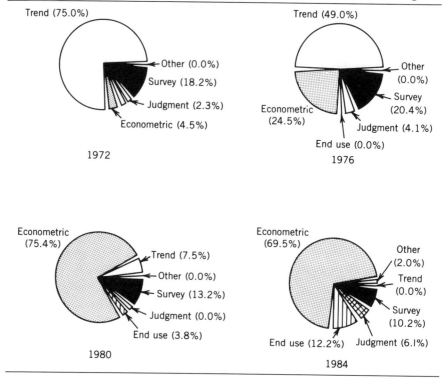

produce them. These forecasts were for total energy sales as well as for sales by sector, namely residential, commercial, and industrial.

Charts 7-11 and 7-12 present the historical accuracy data for total energy forecasts. The results are disaggregated by technique as well as by vintage and horizon. The mean absolute percentage error (MAPE) and its standard deviation along with the median absolute percentage error (MedAPE) and the number of responses are also presented.

Forecasts made using (1) a combination of trend extrapolation and judgment, (2) econometrics, and (3) end-use models were compared. Since most total energy forecasts are calculated as the sum of the residential, commercial, industrial, and miscellaneous sector forecasts, one must be careful in placing a forecast in one of the three categories. Whichever technique predominated tended to define the category.

Complex econometric models (those having multiple equations for each sector) seemed to outperform simple models in the short term (two-year horizon) with 90% to 95% significance (based on the standard paired t-test) but did only slightly better (60%–65% significance) for the four-year horizon.

CHART 7-9. History of Large Electric Utility Peak Load Forecasting

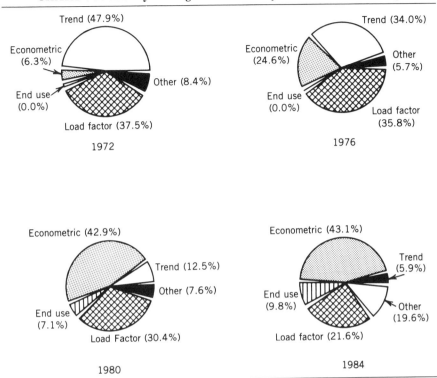

Simple econometric models, on the other hand, did better in the longer six-year horizon at an 85% to 90% significance level. These results are consistent with the philosophy that complicated techniques provide a better fit to the data and therefore do better in the short term, while simple techniques tend to capture the long-term trend and miss short-term fluctuations.

End-use models seemed to be the big winner, outperforming econometric techniques for all horizons at a minimum 90% confidence level. End-use techniques also did better than trend approaches, although the difference was insignificant in the two-year horizon tests. The fact that trend approaches include judgment gained as a result of considerable customer contact perhaps can explain the strong performance of trend/judgment techniques in the short term. In the long term, however, these techniques must rely less on judgment and more on identifying the long-term trend through extrapolation.

Finally, when trend/judgment techniques were compared with econometrics, results showed that the trend approach was better in the short term with little or no difference apparent for the six-year horizon.

CHART 7-10. Variables Used in Forecasting (Large Utility Respondents)

	Not Used	Used Judgmentally	Used But Not Significant	Used and Key Factor	Used and Critical	Number of Respondents
			Percent of Respondents			
Appliance saturations	1.8	5.4	5.4	51.8	35.7	56
Electricity price	0.0	8.8	1.8	57.9	31.6	57
Gas price	11.1	22.2	16.7	33.3	16.7	54
Oil price	25.9	22.2	11.1	25.9	14.8	54
U.S. GNP	44.4	18.5	7.4	24.1	5.6	54
Local GNP	45.3	11.3	9.4	22.6	11.3	53
National employment	43.6	14.5	14.5	25.5	1.8	55
Local employment	8.8	8.8	1.8	56.1	24.6	57
Sq-Foot commercial	58.9	5.4	5.4	17.9	12.5	56
Sq-Foot residential	78.2	5.5	7.3	5.5	3.6	55
Heating degree days	9.1	5.5	10.9	50.9	23.6	55
Cooling degree days	10.9	5.5	10.9	47.3	25.5	55
Industrial output by SIC	18.2	14.5	5.5	38.2	23.6	55
Energy intensity	45.5	9.1	7.3	21.8	16.4	55
Technology choice	40.7	31.5	7.4	9.3	11.1	54
Fuel choice	20.4	33.3	11.1	25.9	9.3	54
Appliance efficiency	5.5	29.1	7.3	36.4	21.8	55
People per household	21.8	21.8	10.9	25.5	20.0	55
Residential housing construction	27.8	20.4	9.3	31.5	11.1	54
Number of customers	5.3	1.8	3.5	42.1	47.4	57
Population	2.1	10.6	17.0	38.3	31.9	47
Income	8.9	5.4	5.4	51.8	28.6	56

CHART 7-11. Mean and Median Absolute Percentage Errors for Energy Forecasts by Large Utilities

Vintage: Horizon

Technique		72:73	76:77	78:79	80:81	82:83	72:75	76:79	78:81	80:83	72:77	76:81	78:83	72:82
All techniques	Mean	2.72	4.54	3.73	4.82	5.60	16.75	8.14	10.65	11.70	22.24	17.35	23.55	65.34
	Std. Dev.	3.048	7.807	4.167	5.594	5.144	7.518	5.362	7.405	10.397	11.183	10.783	23.001	20.378
	Median	1.37	3.28	2.72	3.48	4.49	17.50	7.08	9.725	8.54	22.47	16.99	19.70	63.52
	No. Resps.	21	42	44	47	49	22	42	44	48	21	42	44	17
Trend/ judgment	Mean	2.48	4.93	3.96	3.07	3.75	15.92	8.07	10.69	9.27	20.68	16.50	29.16	62.90
	Std. Dev.	2.854	8.983	5.249	1.721	1.308	6.890	5.204	7.198	6.741	10.561	10.903	31.984	21.426
	Median	1.37	3.37	2.53	2.84	4.49	17.51	7.22	9.72	6.50	22.42	15.57	23.96	60.625
	No. Resps.	18	31	19	8	3	18	31	19	8	18	31	19	14
Simple econometric	Mean	9.18	3.55	3.53	8.80	10.71	32.94	6.94	10.60	16.88	44.17	16.24	16.51	73.91
	Std. Dev.	—	2.387	4.361	9.839	9.125	—	4.622	6.170	15.617	—	9.186	7.248	—
	Median	9.18	2.50	1.03	5.94	6.13	32.94	5.96	12.20	10.14	44.17	15.97	18.01	73.91
	No. Resps.	1	5	8	8	6	1	5	8	9	1	5	8	1
Complex econometric	Mean	2.65	3.17	4.12	5.12	5.27	16.37	11.15	11.51	13.03	30.85	22.26	22.66	68.43
	Std. Dev.	—	3.469	2.903	4.941	3.996	10.239	8.549	9.088	10.016	—	13.92	13.777	—
	Median	2.65	0.63	3.83	3.85	5.34	16.37	8.23	8.96	9.20	30.85	22.89	18.38	68.43
	No. Resps.	1	4	12	19	25	2	4	12	20	1	4	12	1
All econometric	Mean	5.91	3.38	3.89	6.21	6.32	21.89	8.81	11.14	14.23	37.51	18.91	20.20	71.17
	Std. Dev.	4.617	2.721	3.460	6.775	5.606	11.997	6.559	7.877	11.876	9.419	11.179	11.782	3.875
	Median	5.91	2.50	3.65	5.56	5.34	23.61	6.93	10.09	10.14	37.51	20.23	18.38	71.17
	No. Resps.	2	9	20	27	31	3	9	20	29	2	9	20	2
End-use	Mean	—	3.20	2.10	2.85	5.08	—	8.65	5.86	6.81	—	17.08	12.66	—
	Std. Dev.	—	—	1.838	3.210	4.516	—	—	4.965	5.637	—	—	11.336	—
	Median	—	3.20	0.93	1.27	3.28	—	8.65	3.67	5.52	—	17.08	11.51	—
	No. Resps.	—	1	4	11	13	—	1	4	11	—	1	4	—

103

CHART 7-12. Mean and Median Absolute Percentage Errors for Two, Four, and Six Years Ahead for Energy Forecasts by Large Utilities

Technique		Horizon		
		2-Yr	4-Yr	6-Yr
All techniques	Mean	4.50	11.16	20.86
	Std. Dev.	5.569	8.031	16.989
	Median	3.30	9.74	19.18
	No. Resps.	203	156	107
Trend/judgment	Mean	3.91	10.71	21.14
	Std. Dev.	6.451	6.314	19.166
	Median	2.70	10.21	19.73
	No. Resps.	79	76	68
All econometric	Mean	5.43	12.79	20.94
	Std. Dev.	5.394	10.053	11.536
	Median	4.75	10.31	20.15
	No. Resps.	89	61	31
End-use	Mean	3.76	6.69	13.54
	Std. Dev.	3.945	5.489	11.336
	Median	2.19	5.25	12.62
	No. Resps.	29	16	5
Simple econometric	Mean	6.78	13.23	18.39
	Std. Dev.	7.217	11.010	8.007
	Median	4.08	10.94	19.15
	No. Resps.	28	23	14
Complex econometric	Mean	4.82	12.53	23.05
	Std. Dev.	4.086	9.608	13.808
	Median	4.23	9.40	20.17
	No. Resps.	61	38	17

The superiority of the end-use approach seemed to be confirmed when median absolute percentage errors were compared. Since one conclusion of this study was that end-use techniques seem to improve forecasting accuracy, the key issue becomes how much this additional accuracy is worth to the utility in the way of increased development and data collection costs.

ANALYSES OF RESIDENTIAL SECTOR FORECASTS

For the residential sector, statistical analyses compared end-use, econometric, and trend/judgment techniques for two-, four-, and six-year forecast horizons. Data were available for the 11-year horizon, but the sample size was too small for much in the way of statistical analysis. Data for the residential analyses are presented in Charts 7-13 and 7-14, with the statistical analyses appearing in Chart 7-15.

CHART 7-13. Mean and Median Absolute Percentage Errors for Residential Energy Forecasts by Large Utilities

Vintage: Horizon

Technique		72:73	76:77	78:79	80:81	82:83	72:75	76:79	78:71	80:83	72:77	76:81	78:83	72:82
All techniques	Mean	3.07	3.46	5.47	3.35	3.15	14.24	10.97	11.05	6.27	21.20	19.30	17.04	62.64
	Std. Dev.	2.056	2.228	3.460	3.216	2.534	4.572	7.183	7.067	6.079	9.022	10.365	10.994	14.853
	Median	3.16	3.46	5.14	1.86	2.67	12.87	9.82	10.77	5.34	21.58	18.82	16.31	61.38
	No. Resps.	11	22	24	27	27	10	21	22	27	10	21	21	7
Trend/ judgment	Mean	2.57	3.83	6.61	2.04	—	14.83	11.26	11.26	4.48	20.37	17.71	15.83	62.72
	Std. Dev.	2.191	2.135	2.896	2.503	—	4.041	7.627	4.833	3.974	9.918	11.757	11.442	11.135
	Median	1.62	3.51	7.22	2.04	—	13.75	8.46	9.68	4.48	18.74	16.14	13.66	58.37
	No. Resps.	8	12	5	2	—	7	11	4	2	8	11	4	4
Econometric	Mean	4.57	3.20	6.35	4.01	2.41	19.32	12.16	12.72	7.29	27.40	24.23	19.00	47.23
	Std. Dev.	—	2.573	3.792	4.503	1.918	—	9.439	7.966	6.670	—	10.627	11.67	—
	Median	4.57	1.75	6.73	1.82	2.49	19.32	12.00	13.85	5.38	27.40	25.09	16.76	47.23
	No. Resps.	1	4	12	9	11	1	4	12	10	1	4	12	1
End-use	Mean	3.44	2.88	3.15	2.80	3.47	6.51	9.65	7.55	4.61	21.58	18.92	13.31	62.42
	Std. Dev.	—	2.463	2.247	2.162	2.823	—	5.759	5.893	4.068	—	7.771	10.056	—
	Median	3.44	1.41	3.40	1.86	2.68	6.51	6.50	4.23	3.58	21.58	17.51	11.96	62.42
	No. Resps.	1	6	7	15	15	1	6	6	14	1	6	5	1

105

CHART 7-14. Mean and Median Absolute
Percentage Errors for Two, Four, and Six Years Ahead for
Residential Energy Forecasts by Large Utilities

Technique		Horizon		
		2-Yr	4-Yr	6-Yr
All techniques	Mean	3.75	9.81	18.75
	Std. Dev.	2.845	6.519	10.399
	Median	3.21	8.95	18.34
	No. Resps.	111	80	52
Trend/judgment	Mean	3.84	11.74	18.31
	Std. Dev.	2.318	6.187	11.099
	Median	3.53	9.87	16.61
	No. Resps.	27	24	23
All econometric	Mean	4.22	10.87	20.72
	Std. Dev.	3.433	7.706	11.066
	Median	3.68	10.64	19.35
	No. Resps.	37	27	17
End-use	Mean	3.11	6.45	16.80
	Std. Dev.	2.468	4.911	8.860
	Median	2.36	4.48	15.54
	No. Resps.	44	27	12

Again, the end-use method shows considerably lower mean absolute percentage errors (MAPE) with respect to all techniques for all horizons. For the two-year horizon, end-use MAPE (MedAPE) was 3.11 (2.36) compared with 3.84 (3.53) for trend/judgment and 4.22 (3.68) for econometrics. These differences were significant at the 95% level in all cases. For the six-year horizon, end use also was the strongest performer, with MAPE (MedAPE) of 16.80 (15.54) compared with 18.31 (16.61) for trend/judgment and 20.72 (19.35) for econometrics. These differences were significant only at the 65% level.

No significant differences above the 65% level were shown between trend/judgment and econometrics at any forecast horizon.

ANALYSES OF COMMERCIAL SECTOR FORECASTS

For the commercial sector (Charts 7-16 and 7-17), large utility forecasts employing trend/judgment and econometrics were compared. End-use models are just beginning to be used by the electric utility industry, and not enough data were available to compare end-use models.

Although all of the resulting differences were significant in the range of only 60% to 80%, the trend/judgment techniques did better in the two- and six-year horizons, while econometrics was slightly more accurate for the four-year horizon. (The result was virtually identical for the residential sector.) These results may lend some support to the philosophy that trend/judgment is strong in the short term because it relies on judgment gained from close association between the utilities and their customers, and that it is strong in the long term because it captures the long-term trend and is not affected by sudden changes, as more adaptive techniques might be. Its weakness is perhaps in the middle term of three- to five-year horizons. Obviously, however, the evidence is inconclusive.

ANALYSES OF INDUSTRIAL SECTOR FORECASTS

For the industrial sector (Charts 7-18 and 7-19), comparisons were made between large utility forecasts using either trend/judgment, econometrics, or customer surveys. Since the industrial sector tends to be dominated by a few large customers, utilities often rely on these customers' estimates of future electricity consumption. The customers are better able to evaluate the economic conditions affecting their industry and may also have insights concerning plant additions/shutdowns and the introduction of new technologies. End-use techniques are used only by a few utilities, because obtaining the necessary inventory of equipment and associated use patterns is prohibitively expensive and often customers are sensitive about releasing such information.

The results showed that customer surveys do extremely well in the short term (two-year horizon) with a MAPE (MedAPE) of 2.32 (1.55) compared with 4.50 (3.68) for trend/judgment and 7.44 (3.90) for econometrics, significant at the 90% level or above. For the longer forecast horizons, there was no significant difference between any of the three approaches. For the reasons stated earlier, it is not surprising that in the short term, customer surveys seem to produce good industrial sector forecasts. Plant managers usually have a pretty good idea at least two years ahead about what plant additions (and sometimes closings) and new equipment may be needed. Their forecasts, however, deteriorate when the forecast horizon is extended.

Trend/judgment techniques seemed to perform better than econometrics for the two- and four-year forecast horizons. Trend/judgment showed a MAPE (MedAPE) of 4.50 (3.68) for the two-year horizon compared with 7.44 (3.90) for econometric methods. For the four-year horizon, trend/judgment showed a MAPE (MedAPE) of 13.26 (12.71) compared with 22.73 (20.37) for econometrics. The fact that judgment results from knowledge of customer plans for electricity use may explain the short-term superiority of trend/judgment over econometrics. Econometric models in the utility industry are for the most part calibrated using data from the 1950–1975 time frame (some more recent data for the recent forecasts). In general this time frame does not show the volatility currently experienced in the economy as shown by the recessions of 1974–1975, 1979–1980, and 1982–1983. Therefore, these

CHART 7-15. Statistical Analyses of Historical Forecast Errors

Sector	Comparison	Horizon (yr)	Pooled Variance (S^2)	Sample Variance of Difference in Sample Means (S_d^2)	t^a	P
Total energy	Large utility Simple econometric vs. complex econometric	2	27.678	1.442	−1.63	0.90–0.95
		4	103.092	7.195	−0.26	0.60–0.65
		6	133.932	17.445	+1.12	0.85–0.90
Total energy	Large utility Econometric vs. end-use	2	25.829	1.181	−1.54	0.90–0.95
		4	86.876	6.854	−2.33	0.97–0.99
		6	132.541	30.784	−1.33	0.90–0.95
Total energy	Large utility Econometric vs. trend/judgment	2	34.978	0.836	−1.66	0.95–0.97
		4	67.065	1.982	−1.48	0.95–0.95
		6	294.885	13.849	+0.05	0.50–0.55
Total energy	Large utility Trend/judgment vs. end-use	2	34.734	1.637	−0.11	0.50–0.55
		4	38.244	2.893	−2.36	0.97–0.99
		6	353.880	75.98	−0.87	0.80–0.85
Residential	Large utility Econometric vs. end-use	2	8.686	0.432	−1.69	0.95–0.97
		4	41.750	3.093	−2.51	0.99–0.995
		6	104.548	14.862	−1.02	0.80–0.85
Residential	Large utility Trend/judgment vs. econometric	2	9.096	0.583	+0.50	0.65–0.70
		4	49.477	3.894	−0.44	0.65–0.70
		6	122.880	12.571	+0.68	0.70–0.75

Residential	Large utility					
	Trend/judgment vs.	2	5.821	0.348	-1.24	0.95-0.97
	end-use	4	30.765	2.421	-3.40	0.995-0.9995
		6	108.292	13.733	-0.41	0.65-0.70
Commercial	Large utility					
	Trend/judgment vs.	2	6.681	0.308	+0.27	0.60-0.65
	econometric	4	32.546	1.852	-0.72	0.75-0.80
		6	106.363	9.156	+0.44	0.65-0.70
Industrial	Large utility					
	Econometric vs.	2	56.824	3.585	-1.55	0.90-0.95
	trend/judgment	4	312.530	23.972	-1.93	0.95-0.97
		6	389.428	44.835	-0.19	0.55-0.60
Industrial	Large utility					
	Econometric vs.	2	61.714	6.820	-1.96	0.95-0.97
	survey	4	407.200	63.625	-1.23	0.85-0.90
		6	266.161	69.867	+0.21	0.55-0.60
Industrial	Large utility					
	Trend/judgment vs.	2	16.829	2.262	-1.45	0.90-0.95
	survey	4	59.084	10.071	-0.10	0.50-0.55
		6	388.964	117.713	+0.28	0.60-0.65
Peak	Large utility					
	Trend/judgment vs.	2	22.055	0.803	-0.69	0.75-0.80
	econometric	4	55.593	2.472	-0.59	0.70-0.75
		6	142.031	9.560	+0.85	0.80-0.85
Peak	Large utility					
	Trend/judgment vs.	2	33.591	1.181	-0.96	0.80-0.85
	load factor analysis	4	73.520	3.012	-0.54	0.70-0.75
		6	139.659	7.162	+0.11	0.50-0.55
Peak	Large utility					
	Econometric vs.	2	27.486	0.867	-0.46	0.65-0.70
	load factor analysis	4	71.155	2.986	-0.01	0.50-0.55
		6	186.434	12.548	-0.66	0.70-0.75

[a] Negative sign means better performance for second group listed.

CHART 7-16. Mean and Median Absolute Percentage Errors for Commercial Energy Forecasts by Large Utilities

Technique		Vintage: Horizon												
		72:73	76:77	78:79	80:81	82:83	72:75	76:79	78:81	80:83	72:77	76:81	78:83	72:82
All techniques	Mean	3.78	3.36	4.76	2.54	2.70	12.52	10.71	10.18	5.09	19.83	18.44	15.91	66.56
	Std. Dev.	4.145	2.617	3.292	1.991	1.952	9.167	7.235	5.471	4.132	11.525	11.525	8.622	18.709
	Median	1.99	3.04	5.04	2.44	2.22	12.11	9.97	10.43	4.39	17.75	18.11	15.91	68.24
	No. Resps.	9	20	23	26	25	8	19	21	25	9	19	20	7
Trend/ judgment	Mean	2.43	2.91	4.54	2.76	1.18	11.69	10.44	8.80	6.37	17.60	18.54	14.22	61.29
	Std. Dev.	1.797	2.364	2.754	2.298	—	5.401	6.027	4.048	4.874	9.652	10.605	6.543	20.04
	Median	1.48	2.94	5.79	1.57	1.18	12.11	9.98	10.07	5.99	17.75	12.86	14.13	53.34
	No. Resps.	7	13	9	5	1	6	12	8	5	7	12	7	5
Econometric	Mean	3.00	4.19	4.90	2.50	2.51	29.61	11.18	11.03	4.71	40.8	18.27	16.83	81.58
	Std. Dev.	—	3.045	3.690	2.195	2.052	—	9.489	6.187	4.216	—	13.991	9.681	—
	Median	3.00	3.27	4.53	2.79	1.68	29.61	9.97	10.47	3.25	40.8	18.11	16.27	81.58
	No. Resps.	1	7	14	17	18	1	7	13	18	1	7	13	1
End-use	Mean	—	—	—	2.26	4.03	—	—	—	5.30	—	—	—	—
	Std. Dev.	—	—	—	0.266	1.077	—	—	—	1.287	—	—	—	—
	Median	—	—	—	2.13	4.63	—	—	—	5.30	—	—	—	—
	No. Resps.	—	—	—	3	5	—	—	—	2	—	—	—	—

CHART 7-17. Mean and Weighted Absolute Percentage Errors for Two, Four, and Six Years Ahead for Commercial Energy Forecasts by Large Utilities

Technique		Horizon		
		2-Yr	4-Yr	6-Yr
Both techniques	Mean	3.34	8.83	17.64
	Std. Dev.	2.666	6.110	10.421
	Median	3.04	8.43	17.13
	No. Resps.	103	73	48
Trend/judgment	Mean	3.16	9.60	17.12
	Std. Dev.	2.368	5.289	9.448
	Median	3.13	9.77	14.52
	No. Resps.	35	31	26
Econometric	Mean	3.31	8.62	18.45
	Std. Dev.	2.708	6.013	11.302
	Median	2.93	7.54	18.05
	No. Resps.	57	39	21

models are apparently less able to capture downturns in the economy than forecasters using expert judgment and trend approaches. In addition, these methods often miss the current emphasis on conservation.

ANALYSES OF PEAK LOAD FORECASTS

Peak load forecasts were compared for trend/judgment, econometric, and load factor techniques (see Charts 7-20 and 7-21). (Again, not enough utilities are using end-use techniques for these to be included in the analyses.) Load factor analysis is somewhat different from the other approaches in that it derives from the energy forecast. In fact, for the most part the forecast is obtained by estimating a constant multiplier (the "load factor"), which is then applied to the energy forecast.

Although no differences between the three techniques were significant above the 80% level, load factor analysis held a slight edge in MAPE for the two- and four-year horizons and a slight edge in the MedAPE for all horizons. There is some evidence that trend/judgment improves its performance over longer horizons, but unlike in the commercial and industrial sectors, it fails to perform well for the two-year horizon peak energy forecasts.

COMPARISON OF SECTOR FORECASTS

Chart 7-22 shows the results of *t*-test comparisons between large utility forecasts of the residential, commercial, and industrial sectors. Commercial

CHART 7-18. Mean and Median Absolute Percentage Errors for Industrial Energy Forecasts by Large Utilities

Vintage: Horizon

Technique		72:73	76:77	78:79	80:81	82:83	72:75	76:79	78:81	80:83	72:77	76:81	78:83	72:82
All techniques	Mean	2.69	5.33	3.25	6.62	13.53	21.16	10.41	14.17	30.34	22.70	20.42	38.14	92.59
	Std Dev	2.193	5.304	3.712	6.418	13.822	8.935	7.405	11.427	25.529	14.199	14.660	24.427	30.338
	Median	2.35	2.73	2.08	4.45	6.55	25.14	8.60	9.16	26.39	22.06	19.42	32.50	98.87
	No. of Resps.	10	18	21	24	21	9	17	19	21	10	17	16	7
Trend/judgment	Mean	3.39	6.28	1.54	4.63	11.49	15.89	11.89	7.20	31.02	14.70	23.94	52.14	75.35
	Std Dev	2.673	6.234	1.128	5.664	—	8.724	8.474	4.912	6.555	11.627	14.842	40.120	30.255
	Median	3.36	4.21	1.55	4.63	11.49	14.79	11.14	7.23	31.02	9.56	24.97	37.14	80.42
	No. of Resps.	5	9	6	2	1	5	9	6	2	6	9	4	3
Econometric	Mean	2.30	4.19	4.20	6.28	12.07	25.86	7.56	19.40	30.02	28.71	14.03	35.27	73.51
	Std Dev	—	4.576	4.65	6.311	12.295	—	5.376	12.153	29.262	—	17.099	17.896	—
	Median	2.30	1.39	1.64	4.14	6.11	25.86	6.90	22.09	23.24	28.71	3.15	33.00	73.51
	No. of Resps.	1	5	12	16	17	1	5	11	15	1	5	10	1
Survey	Mean	1.47	2.71	2.74	3.58	0.38	27.04	8.82	10.62	18.56	41.14	22.01	23.71	118.31
	Std Dev	1.915	3.390	1.442	3.550	—	2.687	10.239	—	8.704	3.649	13.322	—	27.238
	Median	0.44	0.92	2.74	3.58	0.38	27.04	8.82	10.62	18.56	41.14	22.01	23.71	118.13
	No. of Resps.	3	3	2	2	1	2	2	1	2	2	2	1	2

CHART 7-19. Mean and Median Absolute Percentage Errors for Two, Four, and Six Years Ahead for Industrial Energy Forecasts by Large Utilities

Technique		Horizon		
		2-Yr	4-Yr	6-Yr
All techniques	Mean	6.82	19.30	27.54
	Std. Dev.	7.953	16.510	18.844
	Median	3.88	16.68	24.90
	No. Resps.	93	66	43
Trend/judgment	Mean	4.50	13.26	26.96
	Std. Dev.	4.590	7.610	21.312
	Median	3.68	12.71	22.67
	No. Resps.	23	22	19
All econometric	Mean	7.44	22.73	28.22
	Std. Dev.	8.518	22.023	17.655
	Median	3.90	20.37	23.40
	No. Resps.	51	32	16
Survey	Mean	2.32	12.93	30.00
	Std. Dev.	2.739	7.912	9.767
	Median	1.55	10.29	30.00
	No. Resps.	11	8	5

sector forecasts seemed to be slightly more accurate than residential forecasts for the two-, four-, and six-year horizons; however, the difference was insignificant except perhaps for the two-year horizon, with a significance level between 85% and 90%. Residential forecasts did slightly better for the 11-year horizon, although the sample size was small and the significance low at 65% to 70%.

Both the residential and commercial sector forecasts did *considerably* better than industrial sector forecasts, with significance levels well in excess of 99% for the two-, four-, and six-year horizons. Even for the 11-year horizon with its small sample size, the significance level was greater than 95%. Since the residential, commercial, and industrial sectors each comprise roughly one third of electricity consumption, there seems to be room for improvement in the industrial sector. This observation may justify utilities spending more time and money to improve performance of industrial sector models than they spend for residential and commercial sector approaches.

FORECASTING ACCURACY OVER TIME

Although no statistical analysis was conducted, direct observation shows little or no evidence that utility forecasting has improved over time. The one-year horizon MAPEs for 1972, 1976, 1978, 1980, and 1982 forecasts respectively are 2.72, 4.54, 3.73, 4.82, and 5.60. Except for the 1978 forecast for

CHART 7-20. Mean and Median Absolute Percentage Errors for Peak Energy Forecasts by Large Utilities

Vintage: Horizon

Technique		72:73	76:77	78:79	80:81	82:83	72:75	76:79	78:81	80:83	72:77	76:81	78:83	72:82
All techniques	Mean	4.70	5.15	6.00	7.40	5.34	14.79	12.96	9.95	10.36	20.93	20.24	18.26	59.75
	Std. Dev.	3.873	4.542	4.130	6.745	5.431	8.575	8.219	6.259	9.327	10.835	12.540	12.656	24.014
	Median	3.46	3.78	5.13	5.37	3.90	13.19	11.01	9.04	9.28	19.86	20.46	14.22	63.18
	No. Resps.	22	40	41	44	42	22	41	42	43	21	41	41	17
Trend/ judgment	Mean	5.63	4.90	7.07	11.42	6.04	15.30	13.15	8.70	12.10	22.13	19.32	14.83	59.63
	Std. Dev.	4.187	3.263	4.685	11.431	4.024	7.721	8.264	7.220	8.499	10.858	10.998	7.961	21.680
	Median	3.53	3.78	7.90	5.82	6.48	14.66	11.73	8.87	10.89	19.94	21.86	12.40	63.18
	No. Resps.	12	17	11	6	4	12	17	11	6	12	16	11	9
Econometric	Mean	2.16	5.10	6.48	7.13	4.69	10.45	11.94	12.82	10.67	14.15	20.29	23.83	69.74
	Std. Dev.	2.835	3.177	4.084	5.146	3.481	3.005	7.731	6.912	7.392	3.946	11.353	16.858	—
	Median	2.16	5.43	6.64	5.73	3.58	10.45	10.68	13.30	9.60	14.15	19.28	24.35	69.74
	No. Resps.	2	9	13	19	18	2	10	13	19	2	10	12	1
Load factor	Mean	3.31	5.48	4.79	6.27	6.07	17.01	13.46	8.79	10.30	20.82	21.20	16.80	58.47
	Std. Dev.	3.253	6.509	3.848	6.779	7.787	10.113	9.017	4.687	12.845	12.424	15.330	11.438	29.874
	Median	2.87	3.31	3.71	3.81	2.85	15.05	9.34	7.98	4.15	16.91	17.82	13.25	53.06
	No. Resps.	7	14	16	14	15	7	14	17	14	7	15	17	7

CHART 7-21. Mean and Median Absolute Percentage Error for Two, Four, and Six Years Ahead Peak Energy Forecasts by Large Utilities

Technique		Horizon		
		2-Yr	4-Yr	6-Yr
All techniques	Mean	5.85	11.62	19.59
	Std. Dev.	5.196	8.125	12.266
	Median	4.43	10.27	17.85
	No. Resps.	189	148	103
Trend/judgment	Mean	6.43	12.51	18.92
	Std. Dev.	5.343	7.646	10.199
	Median	5.09	11.68	18.60
	No. Resps.	50	46	39
Econometric	Mean	5.81	11.58	21.55
	Std. Dev.	4.093	7.252	14.312
	Median	5.13	10.98	21.39
	No. Resps.	61	44	24
Load factor	Mean	5.38	11.56	19.21
	Std. Dev.	6.115	9.317	13.240
	Median	3.36	8.27	18.51
	No. Resps.	66	52	39

1979, increasing rather than decreasing errors are observed. Although the 1972 three-year forecast shows the highest MAPE, with a drop to 8.14 in 1976, errors begin to grow again with a three-year MAPE of 10.65 for the 1978 forecast and 11.70 for the 1980 forecast. The five-year forecasts show a MAPE of 22.24 for the 1972 forecast, falling to 17.35 for the 1976 forecast, but rising again to 23.55 for the 1978 forecast.

CONCLUSIONS AND RECOMMENDATIONS

The results described in this chapter support a number of conclusions.

1. The accuracy of utility forecasting has apparently not improved over time. New techniques are being developed all the time, and many recently developed techniques have not been around long enough to be tested, especially over the longer term. But utilities should be somewhat skeptical of spending tremendous amounts of time and money on new techniques and data collection in the hope of improved forecast accuracy. Detailed models should be justified by their ability to provide special insights into relationships between and among variables and into the behavior of specific customer segments.

CHART 7-22. Statistical Analysis of Historical Forecast Errors By Sector for Large Utilities

Comparison	Horizon (yr)	Pooled Variance (S^2)	Sample Variance of Difference in Sample Means (S_d^2)	t^a	P
Residential vs. commercial	2	7.619	0.143	−1.15	0.85–0.90
	4	213.097	5.583	−0.41	0.65–0.70
	6	108.359	4.341	−0.41	0.65–0.70
	11	245.260	70.074	+0.47	0.65–0.70
Residential vs. industrial	2	33.732	0.690	+4.19	>0.999
	4	148.946	4.297	+5.05	>0.999
	6	224.923	9.917	+3.14	0.995–0.999
	11	635.210	211.737	+1.79	0.95–0.97
Commercial vs. industrial	2	33.215	0.656	+3.79	>0.999
	4	145.345	4.019	+4.73	>0.999
	6	219.668	9.333	+2.88	0.995–0.999
	11	530.444	176.815	+2.25	0.97–0.99

[a]Negative sign means better performance for second group listed.

2. In the residential sector, end-use techniques outperform all other techniques. Utilities possessing end-use analysis capabilities also seem to do better when forecasting overall energy use as well.

3. In all sectors, econometric techniques fail to outperform trend extrapolation/judgment techniques. Unless econometric modeling can provide needed insights, sensitivities, or a level of disaggregation unavailable from other methods, its use in utility forecasting must be questioned.

4. Very little difference is apparent between the forecast accuracy of the residential sector versus that of the commercial sector; however, forecasts for both of these sectors have been considerably more accurate than those made for the industrial sector.

5. Customer survey forecasts seem to be by far the best technique for forecasting the industrial sector up to about a two- to four-year forecast horizon.

6. Utilities and commissions stress somewhat different criteria for the selection and evaluation of forecasting approaches. These differences bring into focus the need for commissions and utilities to improve communication. Meetings should be held early in the annual forecasting cycle so that the criteria can be discussed and disagreements identified.

8

STATE AND LOCAL GOVERNMENT REVENUE FORECASTING

STUART I. BRETSCHNEIDER
Maxwell School of Citizenship and Public Affairs
Syracuse University, Syracuse, New York

WILPEN L. GORR
School of Urban and Public Affairs,
Carnegie-Mellon University, Pittsburgh, Pennsylvania

INTRODUCTION

The budget process is to the public-sector manager what profit maximization is to the private-sector manager. All of the budget process innovations of the last 25 years (e.g., program budgeting, planning programming budgeting system, management by objectives, and zero-based budgeting) have the major goal of maintaining efficiency and economy in the provision of public goods and services.

Since budgeting is concerned with making financial provisions for future activities, it depends on accurate forecasts of revenues and expenditures. Classical budgeting theory attempts to limit uncertainties in financial forecasting by foreshortening the forecast horizon to one or two years and by maintaining strict controls on expenditures. In practice, budgeters have guarded against surprises by informal strategies of underestimating revenues, overestimating expenditures, and limiting spending in the first part of the year.[5]

Recently increased importance has been placed on financial forecasting in state and local governments due to fiscal stress. Politicians, responding to the perceived mood of the public, put tax relief and lower budgets near the top of their priorities, restricting expenditure growth to the rate of inflation or below. However, there is no compensating decrease in demand for public goods and services, and the demand is expected to rise in the future. In part, demand is rising at state and local levels due to the efforts of the Reagan administration to shrink the role of the federal government. There has been, and continues to be, a transfer of program and fiscal responsibility to the state and municipality.

State and local governments preceded the federal government in establishing systematic budgeting practices in the United States. No formal federal budget was established until the Budget and Accounting Act of 1921, which provided a legislative check on federal expenditures. Since then, however, the federal government has been the center of attention in budgeting and financial forecasting, so that relatively little is now known about state and local government counterparts. This chapter helps to fill this void. First, it describes the problems and current practices of financial forecasting in state and local governments as related to the budget process. Second, it provides a new model and the first empirical results, we believe, on factors impacting revenue forecasting accuracy by state governments. This leads to recommendations to improve accuracy through organizational designs, procedures, and techniques for financial forecasting.

BUDGET-RELATED FINANCIAL FORECASTS

As shown in Chart 8-1, in government a number of financial forecasts are made, all with different purposes and horizons but all in support of the

CHART 8-1. Typology of Government Financial Forecasting Problems

Forecast Horizon	Horizon Length	Purpose	Management Issues
Long-range	2 to 5 years	Gap and policy impact analysis	Identify long-range trends and predict the impacts of policy interventions for strategic planning
Medium-term	1 to 2 years	Budget process	Forecast expenses and revenues to limit totals used in budget design
Short-term	1 month to 1 year	Budget monitoring	Identify deficits or surpluses for corrective action
Immediate	1 day to 3 months	Cash management	Balance liquidity needs with desire to invest in higher interest, longer term instruments

budget process. Long-range forecasts on revenue and expenditure streams are made for three to five years into the future for two purposes—gap analysis and impact analysis. Such forecasts are used to identify trends that might lead to revenue shortfalls, "gaps," in operating and capital budgets. Bahl and Schroeder[3] stated that ". . . gap analysis allows policymakers to consider the magnitude of revenue and expenditure adjustments which will be required under various economic scenarios." Impact analysis predicts the fiscal impacts of alternative policy decisions. Here, as with gap analysis, it is desirable to use multiple regression or econometric models for forecasting, to allow the use of various economic scenarios and investigation of "what if" questions in regard to policy alternatives. With the severe financial outlook facing city governments today, strategic planning and multiyear forecasts are of growing importance. Over 100 cities now have the capability to conduct gap and impact analyses.[12] In the next section we describe a software package for such analyses developed jointly by the Greater Pittsburgh Chamber of Commerce and Carnegie-Mellon University.

Medium-range financial forecasts are tied directly to the budget process. Two thirds of the states operate on an annual budget cycle, while the remainder have a two-year (biennial) cycle. Legislatures approve budgets six months in advance of the start of the fiscal year, so the needed forecasts must be made with the same lead time.

Short-run financial forecasts of a year or less are used for monitoring the budget. For example, revenue forecasts originally made six months before the beginning of a budget cycle are revised on the basis of current receipts and other variables. In a 1985 survey by the Public Policy Institute,[20] an arm of the New York Business Council, 72% of the 33 states responding reevaluate their original revenue forecasts on an as-needed, monthly, quarterly, or semiannual basis. Monitoring provides early warnings of budget-year shortfalls or surpluses, thereby triggering corrective actions.

Though most government units other than the federal government have strict balanced-budget laws, it is nevertheless possible for both deficits and surpluses to occur. For example, in New York City operating deficits have been covered by bond financing. Other less blatant examples of "creative accounting" have been used to cover deficits or surpluses across budget years. Balanced-budget laws, however, do prevent long-term growth of deficits or surpluses and make state and local government forecasters strive for realistic and accurate forecasts. In contrast, American business firms often use unrealistic forecasts designed to motivate managers and workers toward increased productivity or other goals.[18,23]

Finally, immediate-term forecasts are only indirectly related to the budget process. Increasingly, state and local governments are becoming more sophisticated in cash management and are investing cash balances in repurchase agreements, treasury notes, and so on to provide additional revenue. This calls for daily, weekly, and monthly expenditure and revenue forecasts, and the problem is to balance liquidity needs with the desire to invest in higher interest and therefore longer-term instruments.

Generally, expenditure forecasting is less well developed than revenue forecasting in government. For example, Bahl and Schroeder[3] found that local governments that attempted to forecast expenditures did so with "accounting models" that applied various factors to the previous year's expenditures to arrive at the forecast. Expenditure projections are open to negotiation and preference, so accounting models are appropriate, but some components could probably be improved via objective forecasting. Revenues are much less controlled on a year-to-year basis, and require genuine forecasts. A typical state or local government forecasts revenues derived from a variety of sources, as few as 10 to as many as 100. These may be grouped, nevertheless, into eight categories—personal income tax, corporate income tax, property tax, sales tax, severance tax, gift and death tax, licenses, and intergovernmental transfers (Chart 8-2).[21] Major differences are evident in this chart between state and local sources of revenue. Major sources for the states are sales tax (28% of total receipts), personal income tax (17%), and intergovernmental grants (25%). In contrast, major sources for local governments are intergovernmental grants (43%), nearly twice the level of state governments, and local governments use property taxes according to historical agreements between these two levels of government.

It is especially difficult to forecast intergovernmental grants, because they are the result of higher-level government decisions; and this causes problems for both state and local governments, but especially the latter because of the

CHART 8-2. Relative Importance of State and Local Government Revenue Instruments

Revenue Source	Grand Total Revenues Collected in the U.S. ($ millions)	
	State Level	Local Level
Personal income tax	498 (17)	55 (2)
Corporate income tax	131 (4)	9 (0)
Property tax	33 (1)	882 (32)
Sales of gross receipt tax	389 (28)	165 (6)
Severence tax	74 (3)	— (0)
Gift and death tax	25 (1)	— (0)
Licenses	107 (4)	248 (9)
Intergovernmental grants	727 (25)	1,186 (43)
Others	522 (18)	220 (8)
	2,956 (100%)	2,765 (100%)
Percent of GNP	9%	8%

Source: State Government Finance, Bureau of the Census, 1983.

high percentage of their revenue being in this category. Recently there have been reductions in grants-in-aid, block grants, and revenue sharing; and this has contributed to the fiscal stress of state and local governments. Sales, personal income, and corporate taxes follow business cycles in the regional and national economies and therefore present the attendant uncertainties to forecasts.[2] For example, the 1982 budget crisis in Ohio was exacerbated by an econometric forecast of personal income that missed a downturn. Licenses and fees behave somewhat like market prices. In part, these are attempts by government to have individuals pay directly for public goods and services that they consume, such as trash collection and city water.

In the long term, and sometimes in the medium and short terms as well, controllable factors can be used to influence government revenues. Tax rates, valuation of tax bases, extension of tax bases, collection procedures, and other factors can be changed. Some of the recent work in this area has focused on the effects of taxpayer revolts and the politics of rolling back current levels of taxation.[14] Not only do revenue forecast models need to be segmented by revenue source, but several segments need also to be decomposed into tax rate and tax base components. Such components can be set or projected separately and then multiplied together. It is more difficult to identify control variables for intergovernmental transfers, though lobbying efforts of local governments and individual agencies or client groups attempt to influence federal policies and state formulas for distribution of federal grants to local governments.

FINANCIAL FORECASTING TECHNIQUES

At the local government level, extensive research on revenue and expense forecasting was carried out in the late 1970s and early 1980s by the Metropolitan Studies Program at Syracuse University. The research consisted primarily of case studies of large cities including Memphis, New Orleans, Washington, DC, New York City, Dallas, San Antonio, Kansas City, and San Diego (Occasional Papers 48 through 52 and 59, Metropolitan Studies Program). As mentioned earlier, researchers found expenditures forecasting to be limited to "accounting" models that apply factors to the previous year's expenditures to arrive at forecasts. Techniques used for revenue forecasting were qualitative best guess, simple trend extrapolation, and some multiple regression models. The researchers felt that limited resources and lack of forecasting expertise led to a high reliance on qualitative techniques.

More recently, local governments have taken greater interest in long-term financial forecasting. As stated earlier, over 100 cities now have the ability to conduct gap and impact analyses. In January 1985, the Greater Pittsburgh Chamber of Commerce, under the direction of S. Kiely, and Carnegie-Mellon University, with research conducted by P. Larkey, finished a long-range forecasting computer package for gap and impact analyses, Systems Program for Interactive Financial Forecasting (SPIFF[22]). Forecasting techniques included the simple "accounting" model of factor adjustment, simple trend extrapolation, and econometric forecasting. The motivation to develop this package came from the serious financial problems of Pittsburgh and the need for long-term solutions. These problems included widening gaps between revenues and expenditures, a growing percentage of tax-exempt property, increasing worker's compensation and pension liabilities, declining population, weakening employment bases, decaying infrastructure, and diminishing federal aid. SPIFF has been implemented in the City of Pittsburgh, in the County of Allegheny (in which Pittsburgh lies), and by the Pittsburgh Board of Education. One of the immediate benefits has been that Moody's Investors Services raised Allegheny County's bond rating from Baa1 to A1 in part because of the county's new in-house financial forecasting system.*

SPIFF runs on a Vax minicomputer under VMS. Currently under development or already available are a number of microcomputer packages for local government financial forecasting. One likely to be used widely is the Financial Trend Monitoring System (FTMS) developed by the International City Management Association in 1984.† This is another package intended for long-range forecasting, but it includes only time-based curve fitting for extrapolation and so is limited to a restricted kind of gap analysis. The package, which runs on IBM PCs or PC/XTs, has seven predefined work sheets with a total of 36 economic, demographic, and financial indicators—plus the capability to add user-defined variables. One of the work sheets is for expenses and another is for revenues. Up to 20 years of annual data can be stored and 10-year forecasts can be made. This package focuses attention on important variables, provides convenient data handling, and produces useful graphic and tabular displays. On the negative side, its forecasting capabilities are quite limited.

At the state level, several surveys have shown a growing sophistication in techniques. Gambill[8] in 1978 found that 45% of responding states made use of econometric models to do some or all of their revenue forecasting. The number of equations used in these models ranged from 2 to 400. Of those using econometric models, 60% hired outside consultants to develop or maintain their models. In the 1980 survey by Klay and Zingale,[13] each of the 33 responding states described the revenue forecasting techniques in use by their executive branch agencies. We conducted a content analysis on these descriptions using four categories of techniques—qualitative, time series, simple econometric (multiple regression models), and complex econometric (simultaneous equation models). The results showed that 88% of the

* More information on SPIFF can be obtained from the Greater Pittsburgh Chamber of Commerce.
† Available from Community Systems and Services, Inc., 8300 Greensboro Drive, McLean, VA 22101.

states used simple econometric models, 40% used qualitative methods, 48% used time series techniques, and 30% used complex econometric models. These results are consistent with expectations. Simple econometric models are appealing because they are understandable, yet can include the impacts of economic and other indicators whose effects on many revenue sources are well known.

POLITICAL, ORGANIZATIONAL, AND PROCEDURAL CONSIDERATIONS

The government setting for revenue forecasting has many factors at work affecting forecast accuracy. Some of these are forces that push in the direction of biased forecasts, while others—laws, organizational designs, and procedure—pull in the direction of realistic and accurate forecasts.

One obvious factor is politics: Democrats versus Republicans, conservatives versus liberals, and so on. To the extent that the balance of power goes to one side, we can expect forecasts to be predictably biased. For example, Klay and Zingale[13] in their 1980 survey found that in 74% of the states sampled, legislatures were more likely to challenge or debate the executive branch's revenue forecasts if the governor was a member of the opposition party. At the federal level, several investigators (e.g., Kamlet and Mowery[11] and Ellwood[7] have found evidence that macroeconomic forecasts used in both the executive and congressional budget processes have become more politicized in recent years. In particular, there is suspicion that forecasts of exogenous variables used in econometric models are treated as policy variables, that is, modified strategically to further political goals.

As discussed briefly earlier in this chapter, budget officers have a strong preference for surpluses over deficits. For example, one state secretary of revenue, who must remain anonymous, wrote of his revenue forecaster, ''. . . [he] follows a prudent forecasting strategy, resulting in small forecast errors in three of the last four fiscal years with greater than expected surpluses.'' It is more difficult to cut back appropriations for approved, in-process activities than it is to find uses for additional funds. This is a part of human nature explained by prospect theory.[10] Simply stated, people overreact to losses and underreact to gains relative to the status quo. Faced with a potential loss, a person often becomes risk taking to avoid the loss; faced with a gain, the same person becomes risk averse.

All states have some form of balanced-budget law, and as mentioned earlier, this encourages realistic revenue and expense forecasts. Also, government budgets often take the form of formal legislation which, once enacted, may be adjusted only through complex and formal procedures. In Ohio, for example, a special review board made up of state legislators must pass on specific revisions of the state budget. This inflexibility of government budgets encourages forecast accuracy.

All governments in the United States have the separation-of-powers design of the executive, legislative, and judiciary branches. The impact of this is that quite often the executive and legislative branches make independent revenue forecasts, which are combined to make the final forecast. For example, in 1980 Klay and Zingale[13] found that 41 state legislatures (82%) either made or commissioned independent revenue estimates and that 15 (30%) had developed a consensus approach to reconciling the executive and legislative forecasts. In the 1985 survey by the Public Policy Institute[4] it was found that 64% of 33 responding states identified a legislative agency responsible for developing revenue forecasts independent of those made by the executive branch, while 51% reported that either an informal or formal procedure was used to develop a consensus revenue forecast. Chart 8-3 provides further details on these results.

The production of independent forecasts should improve forecast accuracy by challenging assumptions and exposing political positions for debate. A procedure for combining forecasts should further improve forecast accuracy, since there is a growing literature supporting the idea that combining forecasts improves accuracy (e.g., see Newbold and Granger[19] and Makridakis and Winkler[17]). The Public Policy Institute's 1985 survey also showed that 30% of the 33 responding states have a Council of Economic Advisors. We hypothesize that these states have, as a result, lower forecast accuracy, since a great deal of evidence suggests that experts, such as economists, provide biased forecasts (e.g., see Armstrong's review of the literature on this subject[1]).

A last aspect of government summarized here is sometimes referred to as "life in a fishbowl." Many of the internal activities of government revenue

CHART 8-3. Survey Results on States Using Independent and Combined Revenue Forecasts

Location of agencies with responsibility for revenue forecasting	Number of States
Executive only	8 (24)
Executive and legislative	21 (64)
Other	4 (12)
	33 (100%)

Consensus Process for Final Forecasts	Number of States
None	16 (49)
Informal	10 (30)
Formal	7 (21)
	33 (100%)

Source: An Analysis of State Revenue Forecasting Systems, The Public Policy Institute of New York, 1985.

forecasters are highly visible to external groups, including the public at large. For example, Klay and Zingale[13] found that 26 states (50%) had their deliberations leading to final revenue forecasts open to members of the press. This provides another force for accurate and realistic forecasts.

MODEL OF REVENUE FORECAST ACCURACY

Chart 8-4 shows our proposed causal model for explaining government revenue forecast accuracy. As explained earlier, state budgets are approved six months prior to the start of the fiscal year, so the forecasts under study are total revenues for the year made six months in advance of the start of the year. To allow comparisons between different states and different vintage forecasts, we use the absolute percentage forecast error = 100|actual − forecast|/actual as the measure of accuracy. It is also desirable for the percentage forecast errors to be signed, so that biases can be investigated.

There is a large and growing literature on the impact of forecasting tech-

CHART 8-4. Theoretical Model of Government Revenue Forecast Accuracy Over an 18 Month Forecast Horizon

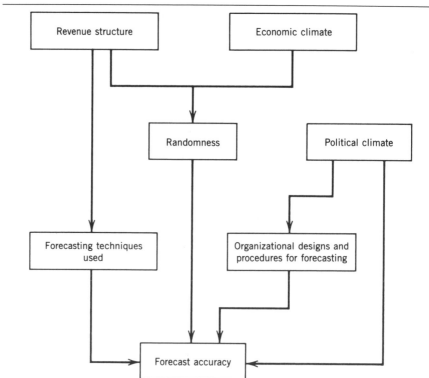

niques used on forecast accuracy (e.g., see Makridakis and Hibon,[16] Makridakis et al,[15] and in general the *Journal of Forecasting* and the *International Journal of Forecasting*). From our reading of this literature, we would rank time series techniques as the most accurate for these one-step-ahead forecasts, simple econometric models next, and qualitative and complex econometric techniques least accurate.

The previous section discussed at length the impacts of organizational designs and procedures for forecasting. We expect states using independent executive and legislative branch forecasts to have better accuracy than those using a single forecasting agency. Furthermore, those who also have consensus procedures for combining independent forecasts should have even better accuracy.

By randomness (Chart 8-4) we have in mind a measure such as the percentage of total variation that is in the error term as obtained from classical decomposition. This measure was used successfully by Makridakis and Hibon[16] in their model of forecast accuracy for general univariate series. As explained earlier in this chapter, some revenue sources, such as intergovernmental grants, are more difficult to forecast. Revenue structure, or the particular mix of the eight or so major categories of revenue sources, therefore has an impact on randomness. For example, Illinois has changed some of its tax laws to smooth out the flow of revenue receipts and make them more predictable.* Similarly, economic climate impacts randomness, since many revenue sources are directly dependent on economic activities. Regional as well as national business cycles and trends affect revenue predictability.

Randomness, then, impacts forecast accuracy. We speculate further that the more difficult revenue is to predict, the more complex will be the forecasting techniques used and the greater the pressure for independent forecasts and consensus procedures in organizational designs and procedures for forecasting.

Finally, in Chart 8-4 the greater the conflict in the political climate of a state, the more likely independent forecasts will be made. We speculate, however, that conservatives will provide more accurate forecasts than liberals, on the basis of the stereotype that the latter are more likely to increase expenditures and let policies influence forecasts.

ACTUAL FORECASTING ACCURACY

The Public Policy Institute of New York collected valuable and unique data on state government revenue forecasting in its 1985 survey.[20] We have used these survey data for the Forecast Accuracy, Forecasting Techniques, and Organizational Designs and Procedures for Forecasting components of our

---

* Private communication, January 1984, with Richard Kolhauser. Deputy Director, Illinois Bureau of the Budget, Springfield.

model in Chart 8-4. Additional data sources were used for other components.

First, the 1985 survey contains absolute percentage forecast errors but no signed percentage errors, so we can investigate accuracy but not bias. It would have been interesting to see, for example, if econometric models, with their independent variables available for manipulations, "explain" surpluses. The available data are for 29 of the 33 responding states and include from one to seven consecutive years' observations for each state (from 1978 to 1984), yielding a total of 85 data points. Order statistics on these absolute percentage forecast errors are

Upper extreme	24.7%
Upper quartile	6.0%
Median	3.0%
Lower quartile	1.7%
Lower extreme	0.1%

The mean absolute percentage error (MAPE) is 4.7%, which compares favorably with results obtained in the M-competition.[15] The competition has 20 yearly data series, each of which has one-step-ahead (and other) forecasts calculated by 24 time series techniques. The forecast MAPE is averaged over all series and forecasts. The competition also has 35 macroeconomic time series, and the MAPE over all series and techniques is 5.7%, still worse than the revenue forecasts.

Indicator data on forecasting techniques used are from the content analysis of the 1985 survey, as discussed earlier. "QUALIT," "TIME," "ECONSIMP," and "ECONCOMP" are defined in Chart 8-5. Indicator data on organizational designs and procedures, "MIX," "ECONADV," and "CONSEN" are also from the 1985 survey and defined in Chart 8-5.

Annual data on revenue receipts by source were obtained for each state for 1979 through 1984 as published by the Bureau of the Census.[21] The resulting six data points are insufficient for use of classical decomposition to determine randomness, so we calculated "COEFVAR," the coefficient of variation (sample standard deviation divided by sample mean) as a crude measure of randomness. No data were prepared for revenue structure, nor were data obtained for economic climate, because of the recursive structure of the model in Chart 8-4. The coefficient of variation is sufficient to estimate the model.

Two measures were obtained for the political climate of a state. The first, "PIDEO," is a measure of political ideology. Each state was scored between -1 (liberal) and $+1$ (conservative) by aggregating results from various political poles run between 1974 and 1982, as provided by Wright and colleagues,[24] who included results supporting the validity and reliability of this measure. We expect PIDEO to be negative according to an earlier-stated hypothesis. A second political variable indicates which party, Democratic or

CHART 8-5. Summary of Independent Variables

Variables	Measurement	Mean	Standard Deviation
QUALIT	0 = No qualitative techniques 1 = Qualitative techniques	.39	.50
TIME	0 = No time series 1 = Time series	.48	.51
ECONSIMP	0 = No simple econometric models 1 = Simple econometric models	.88	.33
ECONCOMP	0 = No complex econometric models 1 = Complex econometric models	.30	.47
MIX	Agencies producing revenue forecasts 0 = Executive agencies 1 = Executive and legislative groups	.64	.49
ECONADV	0 = No council of advisors 1 = Council of economic advisors	.30	.47
CONSEN	Procedures for combining executive and legislative forecasts -1 = No consensus process 0 = An informal process 1 = A formal process	$-.27$	.80
COEFVAR	Measure of variability in revenue structure	.19	.06
DEMCONTROL	Measure of democratic control 0 = no houses $\frac{1}{3}$ = 1 house $\frac{2}{3}$ = 2 houses 1 = 3 houses	.50	.25
PIDEO	Ratio measure of political ideology -1 = Liberal $+1$ = Conservative	.15	.09

Republican, controls the Senate, House, and executive branches of a state government. "DEMCONTROL" is 0 if the Republicans control all three, $\frac{1}{3}$ if the Democrats control one, $\frac{2}{3}$ if they control two, and 1 if they control all three. A 50% majority rule for each house of the state legislature was used as an indicator of party control, while the mean proportion of years the governorship was held by a party over the same time period was used to determine control of the executive branch. We expect DEMCONTROL's to be positive.

A limitation of our independent data is that we have only one observation per state, while we have from one to seven observations of the dependent variable (the absolute percentage error of the one-year-ahead forecast). We assumed, therefore, that the independent variable values persisted over the time interval of observations for a state's dependent variable data, and we used a repeated-runs design for the multiple regression model of the next section (e.g., see Draper and Smith[6]). Each year's forecast for a given state is viewed as a separate, independent trial, with all conditions determined by the independent variables as fixed. Some of our independent variables are averages calculated over several years' data—COEFVAR (1979–1984). PIDEO (1976–1982), and DEMCONTROL (1980–1984)—and therefore are compatible with the assumption. Data from the 1985 survey an organizational designs and procedures are compatible in the aggregate with results of earlier surveys in 1978 and 1980. Also here, and in forecast techniques used, we can always rely on the fact that things change slowly in bureaucracies.

RESULTS

There are 85 state-year observations on revenue forecast accuracy, but due to missing values for independent variables, the final data set for testing the model of Chart 8-4 has 74 complete observations. Chart 8-6 presents ordinary least squares estimates of a simple linear specification for this model. The adjusted R-square value is .34, so there is substantial unexplained variation. Nevertheless, the overall F test for the regression and the majority of the individual coefficient t-tests are significant at the .05 level or better, so the model has explanatory value. A standard diagnostic test for multicolinearity (see Belsley et al.[4]) indicated no problems in this area.

The results largely support our hypotheses, although there are a few surprises. To get started, if we set COEFVAR, DEMCONTROL, and PIDEO to their mean values from Chart 8-5, multiply them times their coeffi-

CHART 8-6. Estimates for Model on Government Forecast Accuracy

Variables	Coefficient	t-Statistics	P-Value
Intercept	10.4	1.96	.05
COEFVAR	11.2	0.78	.44
MIX	−5.6	−3.56	.00
ECONADV	2.36	1.88	.06
CONSEN	−2.8	−3.29	.00
DEMCONTROL	1.9	1.81	.07
PIDEO	−8.2	−1.01	.32
QUALIT	−2.3	−1.96	.05
TIME	5.4	4.09	.00
ECONSIMP	−5.7	−2.39	.02
ECONCOMP	3.5	2.26	.03

Adjusted R-square = .34
Root mean squared error = 4.09
F-Statistic = 4.79

cients from Chart 8-6, and add the intercept, we get a 13.5% MAPE for forecast accuracy. The remaining variables are dummys and so we can find their impacts by simply adding estimated coefficients from Chart 8-6 to 13.5%. Recall that the forecast MAPE is 4.7% (i.e., the average of the dependent variable is 4.7%), so the remaining dummy variables typically combine to reduce the 13.5% value, reflecting often-good current practices.

First, all of the coefficients for the forecasting techniques indicators are significant at the .05 level or higher. The use of simple econometric models typically reduces forecast errors by subtracting 5.7% from the MAPE, while the use of complex econometric models does the opposite by adding 3.5%. This is consistent with our hypotheses.

Inconsistent are the results on qualitative and time series techniques. We expected the former to produce larger errors than the latter, but qualitative techniques subtracted 2.3% while time series techniques added 5.4% to the MAPE, on average. We can speculate on the reasons. First, since revenue forecasts are generally only one-step-ahead annual forecasts, states may have near-term inside information on some revenue sources that enter forecasts as qualitative adjustments. Recently, Huss[9] found that electric utility forecasts of demand for one-year ahead were superior to all independently run objective forecasts that he produced (from a number of univariate and simple econometric models). For two years and beyond, however, many objective techniques provided forecasts superior to the utilities' forecasts. Huss speculated that the one-year-ahead forecasts benefitted from inside information on large customers' plans for electricity use. Second, with time series techniques, we suspect that state revenue forecasters are using simple trend extrapolation via simple time-based regression analysis. This technique had the poorest forecast accuracy of the 24 time series techniques used in the M-competition.[15] So it may be that revenue forecasters should use better univariate techniques.

To summarize the impacts of forecast techniques, if a state revenue forecaster uses qualitative and simple econometric techniques, the net result is to decrease the forecast MAPE by 8%. If a forecaster uses time series and complex econometric techniques, the forecast MAPE increases by nearly 10%.

Perhaps the most important results of the study are the new ones on organizational designs and procedures for forecasting, which are highly significant in the cases of the use of independent forecasts and consensus procedures. If a state has independent forecasts by the executive and legislative branches (i.e., MIX = 1), the forecast MAPE is reduced by 5.7%. In addition, the use of formal consensus procedures (i.e., CONSEN = 1) subtracts another 5.6% relative to use of no procedure. The use of informal procedures subtracts 2.3%. The total reduction using both factors is as high as 11.3%. Apparently the separation of powers improves forecast accuracy, as we hypothesized. Significant at the .10 level (P-Value = .06) is ECONADV. If a state has a council of economic advisors, the forecast

MAPE typically increases by 2.4%, which is consistent with our hypothesis that experts such as economists detract from forecast accuracy.

The coefficient for COEFVAR, our measure of randomness, is not significant. Randomness was such an important explanatory variable in the forecast accuracy model of Makridakis and Hibon[16] on time series techniques, that we suspect that COEFVAR is not a good enough measure of randomness. Future work on revenue forecast accuracy should include a better measure of this variable.

On the political climate variables, PIDEO (political ideology) is not significant, and DEMCONTROL is significant at the .10 level (*P*-Value = .07). The results for the latter suggest that when Democrats are in control, the forecast MAPE increases by 1.9%. This is consistent with the view that Republicans are generally more conservative.

CONCLUSION

This chapter has described the forecast problems and current practices surrounding the budget process in state and local governments. Furthermore, it has provided new results on the determinants of forecast accuracy in state revenue forecasting. An important finding is that the separation-of-powers design of U.S. governments is a major force for accurate and realistic forecasts. The executive branch has responsibility to prepare revenue and expense forecasts for budgeting, but in 64% to 82% of the states (depending on which survey results we use) the legislative branch also independently generates forecasts. This exposes political positions and assumptions to debate and, on the average, reduces revenue forecast MAPEs by 5.7 percentage points. Furthermore, for states with independent forecasts that also have an informal or formal process to arrive at consensus forecasts, forecast MAPEs are reduced another 2.8 or 5.6 points, respectively.

The forecast techniques used also make a significant difference in forecast accuracy. Qualitative and simple econometric techniques typically reduce forecast MAPEs by 2.3 points and 5.7 points, respectively, while time series and complex econometric techniques add 5.4 and 3.5 points, respectively. The result on time series techniques is surprising; we thought on the basis of the literature that these techniques would reduce errors. We are suspicious, however, that state revenue forecasters have used time-based regression models for trend fitting and extrapolation, and this model is one of the least accurate time series techniques. Politics was not a major force in determining forecast accuracy. There is some evidence that when Democrats are in power, forecast errors are slightly higher.

Local governments are most in need of better financial forecasting due to fiscal stress. In the past they received an average of 43% of their revenues from intergovernmental transfers (from federal and state governments), but the amount is being cut back. At the same time, the shrinking federal government has transferred programs and fiscal responsibility to the local levels, while the mood of the public is for tax relief. As a result, local governments have become sharply interested in long-range fiscal forecasting to carry out gap and policy impact analyses. Microcomputer packages now being produced explicitly for local governments are, we fear, overly simplistic. They tend to provide only the inaccurate time-based regression models for trend fitting and extrapolation. Moreover, multiple regression models are necessary to test the impacts of alternative economic scenarios and policy options. Many masters graduates of public administration and public policy and management schools are now taking forecasting courses. We recommend hiring an appropriately schooled graduate and using a general-purpose forecasting package such as FUTURCAST or Sybil-Runner on microcomputers. SPIFF, available from the Pittsburgh Chamber of Commerce, is a worthy package for Vax computers running under VMS.

REFERENCES

1. Armstrong, J. Scott, *Long-Range Forecasting: From Crystal Ball to Computer,* 2nd ed., McGraw-Hill, New York, 1985.

2. Bahl, Roy, Bernard Jump Jr., and L. Schroeder, "The Impact of Business Cycles and Inflation on the Finances of State and Local Governments," Occasional Paper No. 91, Metropolitan Studies Program, Syracuse University, Syracuse, NY, 1985.

3. Bahl, Roy, and Larry Schroeder, "Forecasting Local Government Budgets," Occasional Paper No. 38, Metropolitan Studies Program, Syracuse University, Syracuse, NY, 1985.

4. Belsley, D., E. Kuh, and R. Welsch, *Regression Diagnostics Identifying Influential Data and Sources of Collinearity,* John Wiley, New York, 1985.

5. Caiden, Naomi, "Public Budgeting Amidst Uncertainty and Instability," in F. S. Lane, ed., *Current Issues in Public Administration,* 2nd ed., St. Martin's Press, New York, 1982.

6. Draper, N. R., and H. Smith, *Applied Regression Analysis,* John Wiley, New York, 1966.

7. Ellwood, J. W., "The Great Exception: The Congressional Budget Process in an Age of Decentralization," in L. C. Dodd and B. J. Oppenheimer, eds., *Congress Reconsidered,* 3rd ed., Congressional Quarterly Press, Washington, DC, 1983.

8. Gambill, J., "State Use of Econometric Models for Revenue Estimating: A Report on a Survey," *Proceedings of NATA Revenue Estimating Procedures Conference,* Federation of Tax Administrators, Washington, DC, 1978.

9. Huss, William R., "Comparative Analysis of Company Forecasts and Advanced Time Series Techniques Using Annual Electric Utility Energy Sales Data," *International Journal of Forecasting,* vol. 1, no. 3, 1985, pp. 217–239.

10. Kahneman, D., and A. Tverskey, "Prospect Theory: An Analysis of Decisions Under Risk," *Econometrica,* vol. 47, 1979, pp. 263–291.

11. Kamlet, M. S., and D. C. Mowery, "The First Decade of the Congressional Budget Act: Legislative Imitation and Adaptation in Budgeting," *Policy Sciences,* vol. 18, 1985, pp. 313–334.

12. Kiely, E. S., et al., *Local Government Financing Project, Final Report,* Greater Pittsburgh Chamber of Commerce, Pittsburgh, PA, 1985.

13. Klay, E., and J. Zingale, "Revenue Estimation as Seen from the Administrative Process," *Proceedings of NATA Revenue Estimating Procedures Conference,* Federation of Tax Administrators, Washington, DC, 1980.

14. Lowery, David, and Lee Sigelman, "Understanding the Tax Revolt: Eight Explanations," *American Political Science Review,* vol. 75, 1981, pp. 963–974.

15. Makridakis, S., et al., "The Accuracy of Extrapolation (Time Series) Methods," *Journal of Forecasting,* vol. 1, no. 2, 1982, pp. 111–153.

16. Makridakis, A., and M. Hibon, "Accuracy of Forecasting: An Empirical Investigation," *Journal of the Royal Statistical Society,* Series A, vol. 142, part 2, 1979, pp. 97–145.

17. Makridakis, S., and R. L. Winkler, "Averages of Forecasts: Some Empirical Results," *Management Science,* vol. 29, no. 9, 1983, pp. 987–996.

18. Majani, Bernard E., "Decomposition Methods for Medium-Term Planning and Budgeting," in S. Makridakis and S. Wheelwright, eds., *The Handbook of Forecasting: A Manager's Guide,* John Wiley, New York, 1982.

19. Newbold, P., and C. W. J. Granger, "Experience With Forecasting and the Combination of Forecasts," *Journal of the Royal Statistical Society,* Series A, vol. 137, part 2, 1974, pp. 131–146.

20. Public Policy Institute of New York, "An Analysis of State Revenue Forecasting Systems," Albany, NY, 1985.

21. *State Government Finance,* annual publication of the Bureau of the Census, U.S. Department of Commerce, Washington, DC, 1979–1984.

22. *Systems Program for Interactive Financial Forecasting, Users Manual,* Greater Pittsburgh Chamber of Commerce, Pittsburgh, PA 1985.

23. Wildavsky, Aaron B., "Budgeting as a Political Process," in F. S. Lane, ed., *Current Issues in Public Administration,* 2nd ed., St. Martin's Press, New York, 1982.

24. Wright, G., R. Erikson, and J. McGuire, "Measuring State Partisanship and Ideology with Survey Date," *Journal of Politics,* vol. 47, no. 2, 1985, pp. 469–489.

CHAPTER

9

POPULATION FORECASTING

DENNIS A. AHLBURG

Industrial Relations Center, University of Minnesota, Minneapolis

Population forecasting is concerned with estimating the future number of individuals in a population. The population may be the total population of a nation or that population disaggregated by age, sex, race, region, marital status, household status, labor force status, and/or other socioeconomic characteristics such as educational attainment or income. In contrast to most other forecasts, population forecasts generally have a relatively long time horizon. Because many demographic processes take a long time to work themselves out and because a long lead time is needed to design and construct public works, horizons of 50 or more years are common. With such a long-run focus, many forecasting agencies ignore current information that may affect the forecast.

Population forecasts have inherent interest but also are a critical input to many other forecasts. For example, they are used in forecasting demand for air travel, medical care, schoolteachers, energy, water treatment facilities, and the like. Accuracy in population forecasting is necessary, for errors in these forecasts will introduce errors of similar magnitude into population-dependent forecasts, unless offsetting errors occur elsewhere in the forecasts. For example, a 1965 study showed that differences in total energy consumption forecasts arose more from differences in underlying population forecasts than from differences in the assumptions about individual energy use.[3]

This chapter is concerned with methods for making population forecasts and the accuracy of the resulting forecasts. Because the field of population forecasting is dominated by official agencies, such as the Bureau of the Census in this country and the Office of Population Censuses and Surveys in the United Kingdom, particular attention is paid to the production and accuracy of "official" forecasts.

PROJECTIONS OR FORECASTS?

At the outset, the distinction between "projections" and "forecasts" must be addressed. Demographers claim to produce population projections, that is, the correctly computed numerical outcome of a specified algorithm whose form, controlling parameter or transition values, and initial values are specified by the analyst. By definition, a projection must be correct unless arithmetical or other errors are made. However, users of population projections require population "forecasts," that is, "a population projection selected as a likely outcome for the purposes of planning."[19] Thus, a demographer makes a projection, and his or her reader uses it as a forecast. This distinction between projection and forecast breaks down, however, when one realizes that demographers present only one of many possible projections. On what basis do they choose it? On the basis that they judge the projection to be the most likely to occur. Therefore, population projections may be treated as population forecasts.

POPULATION FORECASTING METHODS

The models used to produce population forecasts may be classified into four major groups: cohort-component models, trend models, structural models, and time series models.

Cohort-Component Models

The cohort-component model is used by most national government agencies to produce official population forecasts. The model is basically a demographic accounting framework that allows the forecaster to work through the implications of a set of *assumed* cohort-specific fertility, mortality, and migration rates. The fertility rate assumption involves further assumptions about levels of cohort fertility, mean age at childbearing, and timing pattern of births. The mortality rate assumption is based on extrapolations of changes in age–sex specific mortality by cause of death. The migration rate assumption is a constant based on historical trends. Even though this set of assumptions may appear complex, it often reduces to a simpler form. For example, Lee[13] argued that the "principal input to [U.S. Bureau of the Census] population projections is an implicit uncritical input of a simple and implausible autoregressive structure to the time series of fertility," that is, future fertility is simply a continuation of fertility in the recent past. (For more detail on the cohort-component methodology, see Land[11] and Long and McMillen.[15] The assumptions on which forecasts are based are often not explicitly stated in the forecast publication, and the user typically ends up choosing the middle forecast.

The cohort-component method is also used to produce population forecasts for states. Centrally produced state forecasts usually assume that the national forecast is correct and sum the state forecasts to the national total. State fertility and mortality rates may be assumed to converge to national levels or to remain a constant percentage of the national rate. The most troublesome component of subnational forecasts is migration. Alternative assumptions, such as a continuation of the rate observed in the past 5 or 10 years, or zero migration, are often made. Recently the U.S. Bureau of the Census has experimented with using time series and structural models to forecast migration.

State and local authorities also produce population forecasts, and these may not agree with those of the central agency. While the central agency may lack adequate knowledge of local conditions, a bias may be present in locally produced forecasts. For example, funding for federally funded projects may be tied to future population, leading to an incentive for "optimistic" population forecasts. The U.S. Environmental Protection Agency collected state-generated population projections for use in allocating sewerage treatment construction grants. The sum of the state-generated forecasts exceeded the 1990 U.S. population forecast by tens of millions.[7] When forecasts are available from government sources at different levels, the user is advised to check the past accuracy of each agency's forecast and the purpose for which the forecast was prepared.

While official population projections are the primary output of government forecasting agencies, these agencies also commonly provide other demographic forecasts based on the population forecasts. Chart 9-1 shows types of forecasts provided by the U.S. Bureau of the Census and associated agencies.[14] The household forecasts are extrapolations of past household/population ratios based on log-linear regressions. The labor force forecasts are also extrapolations but with a significant amount of forecaster judgment. The school enrollment and educational attainment forecasts use a mixture of judgment, regression lines, logistic curves, exponential smoothing, and structural models. (See Long[14] for further details.) A basic problem with this group of official forecasts is the lack of a mechanism for assuring consistency among forecasted series and the apparent arbitrariness of many of the assumptions used.

Trend Models

Trend models are of the general form

$$p_t = f(t, \beta) \tag{9-1}$$

where p_t is population, t is time, and β is some set of parameters. In stochastic models, an error term, ε_t, is added.

CHART 9-1. Typical Official Population Forecasts. Adapted with permission from Long[14]

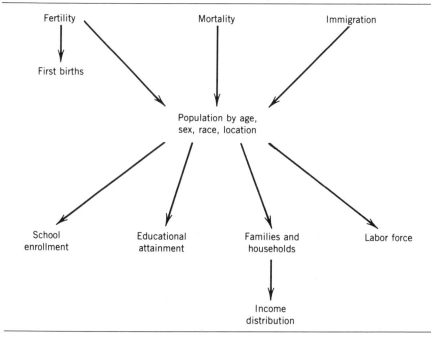

Trend models rely either on the historical pattern of population growth to indicate its future path or on a particular theory of population growth to point to a particular functional form for Equation 9-1.

The rationale for atheoretic trend extrapolation is that the processes underlying population growth are not well understood, strong historical inertia is evident, and no compelling reasons for expecting the trend to change exist. Therefore, the existing trend is the most reliable indication of the future path of population. Modified versions of this approach are often used as simple rules of thumb, such as assuming that the recent growth rate will continue. This approach is used by the U.S. Bureau of the Census to forecast the population of countries with a population of less than 300,000. It is also used by the Bureau to produce some of the forecasts in Chart 9-1 and also by some state and local agencies to set the fertility, mortality, and migration assumptions within the cohort-component method.

The decision rule about which rate of increase to apply is critical and relies solely on forecaster judgment. Isserman[8] illustrated this point with forecasts of the population of Madison County, Iowa, in the year 2000, using exponential extrapolation. If the average annual rate of population growth for 1850–1980 is assumed to continue, then the population will be 11,569; if, however, the postwar (1950–1980) rate is assumed to continue, the population will be 18,136; and if the rate observed between 1970 and 1980 continues, the population will be 14,941. Which assumption is correct has significant implications for planners.

1. *Linear Trend Model.*

$$p_t = a + bt$$

where p is population, t is time, and a and b are parameters to be estimated. This model assumes a constant amount of growth but a declining rate of growth as population increases.

2. *Exponential Growth Model.*

$$p_t = p_o \cdot \exp(rt)$$

where r is the rate of growth and p_o the size of the population at the origin ($t = 0$). This model is a linear trend model in the transformed variable $p_t^* = \ln p_t$:

$$\ln p_t = \ln p_o + rt$$
$$p_t^* = p_o^* + rt$$

The growth rate is constant at r.

3. *Geometric Growth Model.*

$$p_t = p_o g^t$$

where g is the growth ratio and p_o is the initial size of the population. This model is a linear trend model in the transformed variable $p_t^* = \ln p_t$:

$$\ln p_t = \ln p_o + (\ln g)t$$
$$p_t^* = p_o^* + g^* t$$

The growth rate is constant at $\ln g$.

4. *Logistic Growth Model.*

$$p_t = \frac{k}{1 + \exp(a + b^t)}$$

where k is the maximum size the population can attain and a is the difference between the population size at the origin (p_o) and the value of k. The growth rate decreases with population and ultimately reaches an asymptotic value, k. The logistic is useful when a self-correcting mechanism is assumed, that is, when a high rate of growth will bring forth intervention to reduce it and when low growth will bring forth intervention to increase it.

   5. *Gompertz Growth Model.*

$$p_t = ka^{bt}$$

   This is a modified geometric growth model in the transformed variable $p_t^* = \ln p_t$

$$\ln p_t = \ln k + \ln a \ b^t$$

$$p_t^* = k^* + a^* b^t$$

   The rate of change of the population, $[\ln b \cdot \ln(p_t/k)]$ decreases as the population increases (see Granger[6] and Willekens[23] for further details).

   When should these curves be used? Granger[6] suggested the following:

1. When growth (decline) is rapid and increasing, use the exponential model with $r > 0$ $(r < 0)$; add an extra term, ct^2, to the linear model (parabolic) with b and $c > 0$ (b and $c < 0$).

2. When growth is strongly up (or down), use the linear model with $b > 0$ $(b < 0)$.

3. When growth is rising but easing off (falling, but at a slower rate), use the parabolic model with $c < 0$, $b > 0$ ($c > 0$, $b < 0$); the Gompertz model with $a^* > 0$ ($a^* < 0$); or the logistic model with $b > 0$ ($b < 0$).

   For some of these curves, for example the linear, exponential, and geometric, parameter values may be derived by regression analysis. For other methods of estimating the parameters of these and the other models, see Granger.[6]

   Several curves may be appropriate for a particular case of population growth or decline. In this case, all possible curves should be fitted and then criteria applied to choose the best (for example, those given on page 146) or an average of the forecasts of the curves may be made. Makridakis and colleagues[16] found that overall forecast accuracy can be improved by combining forecasts from different methods.

   Subnational population forecasts often involve the extrapolation of population shares, population differentials, and population densities in addition to population levels. That is, p_t in Equation 9-1 may be the ratio of the population of city i to the population of its county. Share extrapolation extends past trends of a city's share of its county's population; differential extrapolation extends past trends of the difference between the city's growth rate and its county's growth rate; and density extrapolation projects a city's population density relative to a predetermined maximum density. Given an exogenous forecast of county population, city population can be derived, for example, by multiplying a population share forecast by the exogenous forecast of county population.

Structural Models

Structural models express population as a function of variables that are thought to explain the temporal variation in population. These variables are of the general form

$$p_t = f(X_t, \beta) + \varepsilon_t \tag{9-2}$$

where X is a vector of explanatory variables.

Population, or its components fertility, mortality, and migration, may be specified as a single equation or embedded in an economic model to form an economic-demographic model. These formal models allow the investigator to evaluate the consequences of alternative demographic and nondemographic policies, to illuminate the interaction between population and other variables, and to aid in achieving consistency in policy formation, planning, and implementation. Many formal models also have the advantage that their underlying assumptions are made explicit.

Major developments in this approach have been the modeling of household formation, income distribution, and the components of population. For example, the U.S. Bureau of the Census forecasts household formation as a ratio of its purely demographic population forecast. This approach implicitly assumes an infinitely elastic supply of housing at acceptable cost. These assumptions have been responsible for forecast errors of over 20% for two- to five-year forecasts.[21] In contrast, economic-demographic models specify household formation as a function of demographic variables and real disposable income and cost factors such as interest rates. These models have the advantage that they can simulate the effect of inflation, rising interest rates, and changes in tax provisions on household formation. This is important for forecasts of housing starts and the demand for consumer durables, in which the consumption unit is the household rather than the individual. (See Ahlburg[2] for a survey of these models.)

Data Resources Inc. (DRI) has developed a model that provides income and cell size forecasts for up to 10 years for selected consumer segments of the U.S. population. The model estimates the number of households and families that fall within each of the selected demographic cells and future income as influenced by work, marriage, divorce, and inflation. This linkage of economic and demographic models is important, for economic changes are generally selective, and modeling of each population segment increases the probability of correctly identifying the demographic impact of economic change. Also, particular consumer behavior, such as home purchase, differs significantly across demographic categories. To understand and forecast this behavior it is necessary to examine the effect of economic conditions on the specific demographic subgroups of interest.

Other advances have occurred in the Wharton and other models in which births, marriages, divorces, school enrollments, household formations, and other outcomes are modeled as a function of demographic and economic variables. A significant development is the construction of an endogenous population model in which the population components of fertility, mortality, and migration are specified as a function of economic and demographic variables.

Paralleling the development of national economic-demographic models has been the development of regional economic-demographic models. These models have been used to study the impact of large-scale projects, of various broad-based industrial policies, and of slower national growth on regions. In the U.S. Bureau of the Census' ECESIS model, migration was a function of economic conditions in each state. In simulations this model was found to be 20% more accurate than a purely demographic model in estimating net migration by state. (See Ahlburg[2] for a survey of these regional models.)

Structural models are also being used to forecast subnational populations. For example, Mandell and Tayman[17] forecasted the population of Florida counties as a function of past population, sales tax revenue, and owner-occupied dwelling units. Bierrens and Hoever[4] forecasted population of Dutch cities and villages as a function of the size and age distribution of population and various characteristics of the stock of dwellings. These models have performed quite well and can be of simple specification, making them an attractive forecasting approach for many users.

Time Series Models

Time series models, like trend models, are generally atheoretic and assume that the best source of information for a forecast is past values of the series itself, although a recent innovation has been the use of multivariate rather than univariate models. Time series models are of the general form

$$\phi(B) \, \Delta^d p_t = \delta + \theta(B) \, \varepsilon_t \qquad (9\text{-}3)$$

where δ = constant term that relates to the mean of the stochastic process,
$\phi(B)$ = autoregressive operator, and
$\theta(B)$ = moving average operator.

The operators basically generate lagged values of p_t and ε_t. (See Chapter 12 of this volume, and Granger[6] for a discussion of these models.)

Time series models are increasingly being applied to population forecasting, and therefore it is important for the user to be aware of the characteristics of these models. Univariate time series models are based on the series being forecast and are thus sophisticated forms of extrapolation. They assume that the population series has been generated by a stochastic (or random) process with a structure that can be characterized and described. Time series models can also generate confidence intervals around the forecast, which allow the user to evaluate the forecast. However, more than 50 observations are needed to get good estimates of the parameters of the models and they appear to be useful only for short-run forecasts. In forecasting annual population, point estimates tend to flatten either to constant levels or converge to constant oscillations after four to six years. In addition, the confidence bands produced tend to be quite broad. Time series models are not "automatic." Use of this approach often produces several alternative models among which it is impossible to discriminate on grounds of empirical performance. Judgment is required at this and other points in the process.

THE ACCURACY OF POPULATION FORECASTS

Confidence in the accuracy of population forecasts varies widely. Writing in 1930, O. E. Baker claimed that "the population of the United States ten, twenty or even fifty years hence, can be predicted with a greater degree of assurance than any other economic or social fact" (quoted in Dorn[5]). Twenty years later J. S. Davis remarked that "it is disheartening to have to assert that the best population forecasts deserve little credence even for five years ahead, and none at all for twenty to fifty years ahead . . . available techniques do *not* permit reliable predictions to be made for five, ten, twenty or fifty years ahead. Planning for food, agriculture, industry, schools, etc. cannot be safely done on the basis of supposedly expert population forecasts."[5]

Given this diversity of opinion and the importance of population forecasts, "one might have thought that population forecasters would be obsessed with eagerness to see how well they have done in the past, and that users would insistently demand reports on the error of current forecasts." However, "no such obsession or demand is to be seen."[10]

How, then, can one judge the accuracy of population forecasts? Two methods have been suggested: a comparison of forecasts to actual figures and confidence intervals generated as part of forecasts.

Measures of Ex-Ante Forecast Error

A number of measures of forecast error are commonly used to evaluate forecast accuracy, for example, mean absolute percentage error (MAPE) and root mean square error (RMSE). (See Ahlburg[1] and Chapter 28 of this volume for a discussion of these measures.)

Cohort-Component Forecasts

Keyfitz[10] studied over 1100 forecasts of population generated over the past 30 years. He found that the RMSE for current forecasts was 0.4%. In the 1950s, the RMSE of forecasts was 0.56%. Keyfitz also found that the RMSE of population forecasts did not increase as the horizon of the forecast increased. For countries growing at less than 1.8% per year, the RMSE was 0.29%, for those growing at between at between 1.8% and 2.6% percent it was 0.48%, and for those growing at greater than 2.6% the RMSE was 0.60%. For subnational estimates, for example, those of states, the RMSEs were larger. For the 50 U.S. states, the pre-Census projections had a RMSE of 1.164%, that is, more than double that of the national forecast.

From this study Keyfitz concluded that:

1. Relatively short-run forecasts (5–20 years) do tell something about the likely population but we know nothing about the population 50 years hence.

2. The larger the unit of aggregation, for example, nation versus state, the smaller the error.

3. The more rapidly growing the unit being forecast, the larger the error.

To illustrate these findings, consider the U.S. population. This population is officially forecasted to rise from 226.50 million (1980) to 267.99 million (2000), implying an average annual rate of increase of 0.84%. The two-thirds confidence bounds would be ±0.29%, or 0.55% to 1.13%. That means we could bet 2 to 1 odds that the population in the year 2000 would be between $226.5 (1.0055)^{20}$ and $226.5 (1.0113)^{20}$, or between 252.76 and 283.58 million. The official low and high population projections are 255.64 and 282.34, respectively. These are reasonably close to those of the two-thirds confidence intervals, and the probability that the official variants will straddle the actual population is about two thirds.

For faster growing countries, Keyfitz suggested using a RMSE of 0.48%, or for most developing countries, 0.59%. For subnational forecasts, one would presumably use a RMSE of 1.0%.

Keyfitz[10] chose a subsample of 810 United Nation population forecasts made in the late 1950s and compared these forecasts with those based on two simple assumptions: (1) that the observed rate of increase from 1950–1955 prevails in the future and (2) that the rate of increase implied by the U.N. forecast for the first five years holds into the future. The official forecasts were superior to those based on assumption one but were quite close to those based on assumption two. He concluded that official demographic forecasts were more accurate than those based on the simple assumptions, but what counts most is the direction of the initial takeoff.

Ahlburg[1] analyzed 5-, 10-, and 15-year forecasts of total live births published by the U.S. Bureau of the Census between 1948 and 1975 and found that with only a few exceptions these forecasts were less accurate than the simple rules of thumb of "assume no change" or "assume a constant rate of change." Ascher[3] found that for U.S. population forecasts over the period 1891 to 1972, the Bureau's more sophisticated techniques generally produced forecasts less accurate than those produced by earlier approaches. One encouraging sign noted by Ahlburg[1] was that the cohort-component methodology adopted by the Bureau of the Census in 1964 produced more accurate forecasts vis-à-vis the simple rules of thumb than did the period methodology used earlier.

Trend Models

Comparing simple trend models and the official forecasts for the United States, United Kingdom, France, and Sweden over forecast horizons of from 10 to 100 years, Murphy[18] found that the most accurate model was the asymptotic model (a modification of the logistic model). The RMSE from this model was about half that of the official forecasts. Using these models, he claimed that half of the forecasts 50 years ahead might be expected to be within 10% of the true value.

Leach[12] used the logistic model to forecast the population of Great Britain, Scotland, and the United States and concluded that it provided an acceptable model of growth and was superior to the cohort-component method.

In an extensive study of population projections of subcounty areas, Isserman[7] found that extrapolation gave forecasts at least as accurate as complex demographic and structural models. He found that in forecasts of population 10 years ahead, the exponential model was most accurate for towns growing by more than 25% or declining by less than 25%; the linear model was best for towns growing by less than 25%; and the double-log model best for towns declining by more than 25%. The MAPEs for these models were around 10%. For other methods, errors of 13% to 26% have been noted. Rapidly growing areas were hardest to forecast. Towns growing in excess of 25% had MAPEs of over 15%, with less than 40% of populations being predicted within 10% of the actual. For populations growing by less than 10%, MAPEs were 8.5%, and for towns with growth below 25%, 60% to 70% were forecast within 10% of their actual population.

Isserman[7] suggested a hybrid approach to forecasting the population of areas composed of subareas growing at different rates. If the forecaster can predict the approximate magnitude of growth and select the appropriate extrapolation model, for example, a linear model for moderately growing towns, forecast errors can be reduced below the 10% average. He also found that direct forecasting of the population, rather than using a ratio, differential, or density approach, was most accurate.

Time Series and Structural Models

A recent study by Long and McMillen[15] compared the accuracy of several methods in forecasting U.S. total live births from 1977 to 1984. The MAPEs for the ARIMA (autoregressive moving average) time series models were 7.96% to 9.06%; for the cohort-component model, assuming constant vital rates, 3.34%; for a structural economic-demographic model, 3.44%; and for the official forecast, 3.54%. The official projection was considerably more accurate than previous Bureau of the Census forecasts and was only slightly less accurate than the economic-demographic model. The forecasts also showed the tendency for ARIMA model forecasts to flatten out and the superiority of ARIMA over structural model forecasts over a one- or two-year horizon, but the superiority of the structural model thereafter. In a study of time series models, Murphy[18] found that these models of British births for the 1970s had a RMSE half that of the official forecast and a third lower than that of an assumption of no change.

Structural models appear to offer a useful approach to forecasting small-area population. Mandell and Tayman[17] found MAPEs for 10-year forecasts for small counties of between 5% and 7% and of 2.6% to 5.2% for large counties. Bierrens and Hoever[4] found MAPEs of 2% to 3% for an eight-year forecast of city population. Both of these studies showed the usefulness of information on housing in forecasting small-area population.

For selecting among regression-based models, Mandell and Tayman[17] suggested the following criteria: (1) lowest MAPE, (2) random pattern of residuals, (3) lowest value of the stability measure (an F statistic based on Chow's test of structural change), and (4) largest adjusted R^2. Criterion 3 was found to be strongly related to estimate accuracy. One additional point to note about regression-based structural models is that they are of little use if the independent variable (X_t) is harder to forecast than the population variable. Land[11] concluded that if the mean square error (MSE) of forecasts of X_t are not substantially less than the variance of the observed values of X_t, little reduction in the MSE of population forecasts can be expected from using X_t. It is for this reason that many demographers reject structural models.

Confidence Intervals

Time series models generate confidence intervals that allow the user to ascertain the degree of uncertainty in the forecast, as Keyfitz has done in building confidence intervals based on past errors. Land[11] found that the confidence bands on time series model forecasts of annual population have been "appallingly broad": Within five years the 95% interval may be ±30% of the point forecast; within 15 years, ±50%. Pittenger[19] claimed that the exercise of forecaster judgment at various points in time series models makes the confidence intervals generated judgmental.

Sets of official population forecasts commonly have a high, medium, and low variant. Users commonly pick the medium variant. There is disagreement over the interpretation of these variants. Keyfitz[9] claimed that "without some probability statement, high and low estimates are useless to indicate in what degree one can rely on the medium figure, or when one ought to use the low or the high." However, Siegel[21] indicated that the high and low variants were "in a sense, a reflection on the analysts' confidence in the medium series of projections," while the British Central Policy Review Staff[18] claimed that "there is no way of assigning measures of probability to the variant projections. Rather they illuminate the magnitude of uncertainty which attaches to the central projections."

It is, however, possible to interpret the variants in a probabalistic sense. Murphy[18] found that the range in variants of official British forecasts is similar to a 50% confidence interval of a statistical forecasting model, and Stoto[22] and Keyfitz[10] showed that the U.S. Bureau of the Census' high and low variants correspond roughly to an empirically based two-thirds confidence interval around the medium series.

Have the variants of the official forecasts actually bounded the actual series? Ahlburg[1] found that the upper and lower bounds of Bureau of the Census birth forecasts had not bounded actual births, except for the first three years in the 1972 and the first five years in the 1967 and 1975 forecasts. In addition, the official forecasts failed to predict a single turning point in the series. Turning point errors may be of interest if special costs are associated with missing the direction of change. In a study of population and household forecasts, Siegel[21] found that all forecasts made before 1958 failed to bound the actual series, while those in the 1960s did so.

CONCLUSION

Population projections produced by various governmental agencies are commonly used by planners and decision makers as official forecasts of population. However, the accuracy of these forecasts and their usefulness has been questioned. Forecast errors in excess of 20% after 5 or 10 years are not uncommon for national population forecasts. For populations growing less than 1.8%, a two-thirds confidence interval of ±0.3% has been proposed. For moderately growing (1.8% to 2.6%) and rapidly growing (in excess of 2.6%) populations, confidence intervals of ±0.5% and ±0.6%, respectively, are indicated.

Most users of official population forecasts choose the medium forecast. While this is understandable, it is not recommended. Of six 5-year birth forecasts made between 1950 and 1975, the medium forecast was most accurate on only one occasion. For four 10-year birth forecasts, it was less accurate than an alternative on each occasion.[1] Research has shown that the high and low variant population forecasts form a two-thirds confidence interval around the medium forecast in the United States and a 50% interval in the United Kingdom.

Decision makers and planners need not place sole reliance on official forecasts of population. Reasonably simple trend models have been shown to be at least as accurate as more complex cohort-component models in forecasting national and subnational populations. Similarly, relatively simple single- or multiple-equation structural models have produced population forecasts with accuracy at least equal to that of official forecasts. Time series models, while more complex, may produce quite accurate forecasts for one or two years (and for monthly forecasts and seasonal patterns).[11]

However, accuracy is not the sole measure of forecast value. Population forecasts are also useful because they can indicate (1) that policy intervention is necessary to prevent a forecast from coming true and (2) the degree of uncertainty underlying a forecast, and therefore can suggest that contingency planning is desirable.

Since official forecasts generally assume no intervention by public or private agents, they give an indication of what will occur *unless* something is done to affect the future. Thus, a forecast of declining population may stimulate government policy to create new economic opportunities or manufacturers to diversify their product line. These responses, if effective, may cause a population forecast to be inaccurate.

A population forecast with broad bands around a medium forecast may similarly stimulate planning activity to accommodate the degree of uncertainty. Where sustained population growth is uncertain, and the costs of overbuilding exceed those of expanding a facility later on, school districts may build or lease temporary buildings or a manufacturer may put on an extra shift rather than build extra capacity.

The user of population forecasts should be aware that assumptions involving judgment are critical in all methods used for the forecasts. Therefore, the user should critically evaluate the assumptions underlying a forecast to see if he or she agrees with them, should compare the forecast with forecasts from other models to see if and why it departs from these forecasts, and should investigate the costs of the chosen forecast being wrong and plan accordingly.

REFERENCES

1. Ahlburg, Dennis A., "How Accurate Are the U.S. Bureau of the Census Projections of Total Live Births?," *Journal of Forecasting,* vol. 1, 1982, pp. 365–374.
2. Ahlburg, Dennis A., "Modelling Macro Economic-Demographic Linkages: A Study of National and Regional Economies," in K. Land and S. Schneider, eds., *Forecasting in the Natural and Social Sciences,* in press.
3. Ascher, William, *Forecasting: An Appraisal for Policy-Makers and Planners,* Johns Hopkins University, Baltimore, 1978.

4. Bierens, Herman J., and Roy Hoever, "Population Forecasting at the City Level: An Econometric Approach," *Urban Studies,* vol. 22, 1985, pp. 83–90.

5. Dorn, Harold F., "Pitfalls in Population Forecasts and Projections," *Journal of the American Statistical Association,* vol. 45, 1950, pp. 311–334.

6. Granger, Clive W. J., *Forecasting in Business and Economics,* Academic Press, New York, 1980.

7. Isserman, Andrew M., "The Accuracy of Population Projections for Subcounty Regions," *Journal of the American Institute of Planners,* vol. 43, 1977, pp. 247–259.

8. Isserman, Andrew M., "Projection, Forecast, and Plan: On the Future of Population Forecasting," *Journal of the American Planning Association,* vol. 50, 1984, pp. 208–211.

9. Keyfitz, Nathan, "On Future Population," *Journal of the American Statistical Association,* vol. 67, 1972, pp. 347–363.

10. Keyfitz, Nathan, "The Limits of Population Forecasting," *Population and Development Review,* vol. 7, 1981, pp. 579–593.

11. Land, Kenneth C., "Methods for National Population Forecasts: A Critical Review," Working Paper No. 7.001, Population Research Center, University of Texas at Austin, 1985.

12. Leach, Donald, "Re-evaluation of the Logistic Curve for Human Populations," *Journal of the Royal Statistical Association,* vol. 144, 1981, pp. 94–103.

13. Lee, Ronald D., "Forecasting Births in Post-Transition Populations: Stochastic Renewal with Serially Correlated Fertility," *Journal of the American Statistical Association,* vol. 69, 1974, pp. 607–617.

14. Long, John F., "Survey of Federally Produced National Level Demographic Projections," *Review of Public Data Use,* vol. 9, 1981, pp. 309–319.

15. Long, John F., and David B. McMillen, "A Survey of Census Bureau Population Projection Methods," in K. Land and S. Schneider, eds., *Forecasting in the Natural and Social Sciences,* in press.

16. Makridakis, Spyros, et al., "The Accuracy of Extrapolation (Time Series) Methods," *Journal of Forecasting,* vol. 1, 1982, pp. 111–153.

17. Mandell, Marylou, and Jeffrey Tayman, "Measuring Stability in Regression Models of Population Estimation," *Demography,* vol. 10, 1982, pp. 135–146.

18. Murphy, Michael J., "Population Forecasting: Alternative Approaches," Office of Population Censuses and Surveys Occasional Papers, 1984.

19. Pittenger, Donald B., "The Role of Judgment, Assumptions, Techniques, and Confidence Limits in Forecasting Population," *Socio-economic Planning Science,* vol. 22, 1978, pp. 271–276.

20. Pittenger, Donald B., "Some Problems in Forecasting Population for Government Planning Purposes," *American Statistician,* vol. 34, 1980, pp. 135–139.

21. Siegel, Jacob S., "Development and Accuracy of Projections of Population and Households in the United States," *Demography,* vol. 9, 1972, pp. 51–68.

22. Stoto, Michael A., "The Accuracy of Population Projections," *Journal of the American Statistical Association,* vol. 78, 1983, pp. 13–20.

23. Willekens, Frans, "Population Forecasting," Working Paper, Netherlands Interuniversity Demographic Institute, 1984.

CHAPTER

10

FORECASTING: THE ISSUES

ROBERT FILDES

Manchester Business School, University of Manchester, England

This chapter argues that an organization must be concerned with a much wider set of issues than just the technical problem of selecting a forecasting procedure when it examines its forecasting performances. An overview of the wider aspects of forecasting is presented in a preliminary discussion of the Forecasting Framework. This is not to say that the problem of selecting an appropriate procedure should be neglected. The various commonly used methods of forecasting are described here and an evaluation offered of their strengths and weaknesses. In many important applications, however, even the most accurate of methods leaves a high level of residual uncertainty. Organizations have to develop ways of limiting the impact of forecast error, and some possible approaches are described here. Unfortunately, most of the alternatives to forecasting cost money. The chapter concludes that all aspects of forecasting—the technical, the organizational, the information-gathering system on which the forecasts are based—require careful evaluation in terms of improvement, and that the major benefits will accrue from improvements in design of the organization's information-gathering system about its environment.

A FORECASTING FRAMEWORK

Who makes forecasts? Who needs forecasts? How are they used? What is the best forecasting method to use? The first part of this chapter highlights the areas of forecasting that demand attention by the practical forecaster.

R. Michael Jalland was particularly helpful in commenting on this chapter as it appeared in the first edition of this book, while Scott Armstrong was his usual acerbic self in trying to improve the chapter in this edition.

The aspect that has been best researched is the forecasting methods themselves. The second part of the chapter examines the methods most widely used, concentrating on their advantages and disadvantages. The aim is to show where resources can best be employed by the organization intending to improve its forecasting performance. It turns out that forecasting techniques can be improved quite easily. Of more importance, however, is the context in which forecasting takes place, the information on which it is based, and the organization's response to a forecast.

Chart 10-1 presents a framework for understanding the process of organizational forecasting and the issues it covers. In this model the forecaster is advising the decision maker on the predicted consequences of a proposed set of plans. To do this he or she uses selected information about the environment. The information might be available through a formal management information system (MIS)—but as likely as not it will be collected on an ad hoc informal basis. The forecaster adopts a particular forecasting procedure on the basis of cost, the time available before the forecast is needed, and the likely accuracy of the methods he or she is competent to perform. The forecaster also takes into account the value of improving forecast accuracy.

These criteria are not defined in a vacuum. The forecaster has the professional expertise that has taken so long to develop and his or her personal career goals (labeled the forecaster's values in chart 10-1). But the forecaster's organizational masters, the decision makers of Chart 10-1, have their values too, and the two sets may not match. The forecaster is influenced by the decision-maker's values, but does not necessarily share them. In fact, as Wheelwright and Clarke[26] showed, the forecaster's and decision-maker's views of the problem are often in substantial conflict. The forecaster is too technical, does not understand the manager's problems, and is rarely perceived as performing cost effectively. To the forecaster, the decision maker understands little if anything about the technical aspects of forecasting.

However, the forecaster will do his or her best. And if, after carrying through a chosen approach, the forecaster does not like the result, he or she will modify it; so too will the decision maker, when the forecast is delivered, this time using alternative sources of information. The resulting forecast (the "working forecast" in Chart 10-1) may still not please when measured by its conformity to the decision-maker's initial values and objectives. In this case the planning guidelines and assumptions used for the initial set of forecasts have to be revised. Round one of the planning process has been unsuccessfully completed.

Perhaps the most obvious omission from this model of the interrelationship between the forecaster and the decision maker is that it fails to include the organizational framework in which the two protagonists (or participants) work. Hidden assumptions in different parts of the organization will influence what variables are considered crucial and what modifications will take place. Also, forecasting of the same variables may well be done in different

CHART 10-1. The Forecasting System[a]

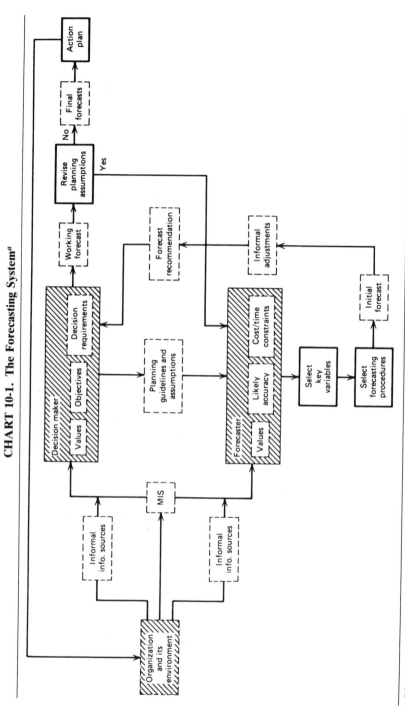

[a] Direct influences or flows. The shaded boxes represent the major components of the forecasting system. The bold-outlined boxes represent actions taken by the participants—the forecaster and the decision maker. The broken boxes represent informtion and assumptions.

parts of the organization and is therefore subject to differing pressures toward bias and inaccuracy, depending on the organizational source. Thus it is often argued that marketing staff tend to produce optimistic forecasts, due to their need to believe sales are likely to improve from a better marketing effort. Likewise, accountants' sales forecasts are often seen as pessimistic, for this allows them to argue either "I told you so" or "We've done better than expected." They thus protect themselves from criticism. These two examples lead to contrasting sales forecasts, each with different errors.

The next sections examine the forecasting system with a view to establishing priorities.

Links between the Forecasting and Decision-Making Systems

The links between the forecasting and decision-making function are weak in many organizations, because decision makers and forecasters differ in their priorities. What are the most productive organizational designs that link the two? Fildes and colleagues[10] and Wheelwright and Clarke[26] suggested some solutions. The key to evaluating the organization's forecasting performance is to examine how forecasts are used, not just how they are produced.

The Quality of the Management Information System (MIS)

Most forecasting procedures are premised on the assumption that information useful to the organization is readily available. However, many firms do not keep adequate records, nor has a consistent approach to collected information been thought through; thus, for example, volume and price figures for homogeneous product groups are often not available. It is true that before advanced techniques can be used, suitable information must be collected over a number of years. However, forecasting should not be delayed until a suitable data base is developed. Instead the data base should be designed with a number of alternative forecasting procedures in mind.

It might be objected that the MIS should not be the concern of an article surveying forecasting problems. However, the slow adoption of quantitative forecasting techniques can perhaps be explained only by reference to an often ill-developed MIS. The routine collection of data is an elementary aid to decision making. Good forecasting demands a good data base and a good data base management system.

Selecting Key Variables

There are two ways of looking at the selection of key variables—how it is done and how it should be done. Casual empirical evidence collected by Jalland and Fildes and reported in Fildes and colleagues[10] suggests that many managers are confused by the differences among forecasts, budgets, plans, and targets. The effect of this confusion is that items that should be treated as variable and subjected to forecasting are assumed to be constant. Consider, for example, an item such as "time taken by a debtor to pay," which is an input into a monthly cash flow forecast. Historically this may well have been treated as fixed. For debtors, however, the time taken to pay creditors depends on their cash flow position; in a recession the time is likely to lengthen. Thus, just when it is most important to be realistic about cash flow, the assumption that "the time taken by a debtor to pay is fixed" is least likely to be valid.

A related issue is when two interdependent items, for example, sales volume and margin on sales, are treated separately. While margin on sales *may* be decided by the administrative fiat of the finance director as an input into the annual corporate plan, to neglect the effect of this assumption on sales volume would very likely undermine the revenue forecasts in the plan.

These two simple examples point to the importance of identifying items that should be treated as variable. The interrelationships of the planning assumptions and the variables that are forecast also need to be systematically considered, as the second example shows. This is a particularly dangerous problem when a new planning system is introduced.

One approach to establishing the firm's forecasting needs is shown in Chart 10-2. For an organization operating in a competitive environment, buying and transforming resources such as labor, finance, and raw materials into a supply of products, particular forecasts are needed to support the operating and strategic decisions that need to be made. In the short term, most variables can be regarded as fixed. As the time scale of decision making lengthens, it becomes increasingly necessary to consider slowly changing variables in the social, legislative, and technological spheres that can reasonably be ignored in operational decision making.

CHART 10-2. The Firm's Forecasting Needs

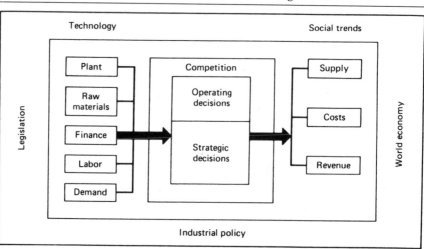

By considering a checklist of variables and their likely impact on the decisions being currently contemplated, it becomes possible to identify those that most require attention. The sensitivity of the decisions to forecast error also places an upper limit to expenditures on forecasting. For example, if an error of 10% in a product sales forecast leads to increased costs (or loss of revenue) of $100,000, it is worth spending up to $100,000 to eliminate that 10% forecast error.

Cost and Benefits of Improving Forecasting

The value of eliminating forecasting error is only one consideration in evaluating forecasting procedures. A second aspect requires the forecaster to take a view on likely improvement in accuracy as a function of expenditure on forecasting. Put more formally, improved accuracy is a function of expenditure on forecasting (possibly increasing), while the benefit from forecasting is a function of improved accuracy. This argument leads us to the truism that there is an upper limit on *profitable* expenditures on forecasting. It also highlights what we would like to know—the relationships between expenditure and accuracy and between accuracy and benefits. Fortunately, the cost of forecasting is relatively simple to calculate for any chosen approach. (Later in this chapter what is known about the accuracy of various methods employed in forecasting is examined in some detail.) The remaining element in the equation is the estimation of likely benefits derivable from improvements in accuracy. This estimation is made by calculating the consequences of various levels of forecast error and comparing the results with what would have obtained if perfectly accurate information had been available.

The foregoing paragraphs describe the economic costs and benefits of improved forecasting. But these are not the only considerations—the forecaster and the decision maker each have their preferences for one particular approach or another. Often enough these preferences seem to dominate the economic arguments and lead to the neglect of the more rational analysis just described, as Fildes and Lusk[11] have shown. Such neglect can be costly. It is important that organizations estimate the economic consequences of inaccurate forecasting and, when necessary, try to move toward a more cost-effective forecasting system.

Selecting a Forecasting Procedure

Earlier writers on forecasting have speculated on which methods are most accurate. If one turns to these works, one finds that the evaluations offered boil down to the principle, "increased sophistication is good," and they leave aside questions of cost.

Even in their own terms this begs the question: If we want to forecast a particular variable, how do the various methods perform? Since these early publications, the prescriptions offered have been subject to empirical criticism which, in particular circumstances, showed them to be misleading.[9,21] Armstrong,[2] however, summarizing the empirical evidence, offered some simple rules for selecting among the various methods. Nevertheless, support for any particular rule is weak, and the forecaster will rarely be able to select a method (within the cost constraints) confident of its accuracy compared with that of competing approaches.

Nor will the analyst usually search through all alternative methods, comparing and evaluating, although such a systematic search would help. This approach is ruled out for any except the most important project because of time/cost considerations. Instead, choices are made on the basis of a range of considerations, as follows:

Prior Beliefs of the Forecaster. If only one method is known, that is the one that will be used. If a long time has been spent learning a complicated method, that effort is likely to influence unduly the choice. Previous experience and related research by the forecaster will also be important influences. (See Fildes and Lusk[11] for further discussion of this.)

How the Forecast Is to Be Used. If the decision maker requires an evaluation of the impact of, say, advertising as a part of the market forecast, the approach selected will have to answer that question.

Complexity and Comprehensiveness. If a model is too complex for the decision maker to understand, it is unlikely to be used. On the other hand, if a model fails to include those elements the decision maker regards as important, the model again will be rejected.

Comparative Testing. If the job of selection is being taken seriously, a few of the more plausible methods will be developed in parallel and tested for their forecasting performance.

Important decisions sensitive to forecast inaccuracy require a careful search through a range of alternatives. The all too likely mistake is to limit consideration to a narrow range of forecasting methods. Armstrong[2] has persuasively argued that there are invariably advantages to trying more than one approach, the more disparate the approaches the better. Organizations therefore need a forecasting procedure that for important problems permits easy comparison of a range of alternatives. This means that the MIS should be well developed and that records of previous forecasting performance should be kept. The ongoing costs of such record keeping are small and, once the system is complete, time can be spent on forecasting rather than data collection. A wide range of alternative statistical, economic, and marketing models should also be available for easy use with the data base. The recent development of user-friendly software has facilitated the comparison of forecasting methods. The likely effect of implementing these improvements is more accurate forecasts, based on the effective use of a wide variety of methods and information sources.

Adjusting the Forecasts

Both forecaster and decision maker allow themselves to alter the forecast to suit their own beliefs. Armstrong comments on this practice in Chapter 32 of this handbook. The adjustments take place for a number of reasons: to make the results more "plausible," to better meet the expectations of the decision maker, and to comply with some prespecified target. In general, this practice does not improve the final forecast. But the evidence is not strong.

Three alternatives exist for integrating prior beliefs into a forecasting procedure: (1) as formal input into the model, (2) as adjustments of the type just discussed, and (3) interactively, in which the forecaster is able to examine the effects on the forecast of adopting a particular viewpoint.

Macroeconomic forecasters regularly constrain their forecasts to accord with the latest information they have on the economy, as Young[27] has discussed. Such constraints seem to improve forecast accuracy (Fildes[7]). In contrast to this approach to the incorporation of subjective information, decision support systems in marketing require the user to specify a number of parameters, such as "advertising effectiveness." The model can then be adjusted until the forecaster is happy both with the chosen parameter and the resulting forecast.

Unfortunately, we just do not know which of these procedures for judgmental adjustment is likely to produce the better forecast. Both forecasters and decision makers typically believe such adjustments are necessary. It is therefore important to monitor performance both with and without the adjustments. Computer software should be designed to implement such monitoring.

Revising Plans

The final stage of the planning round arises if the conditional forecasts derived from a particular business plan are at odds with the objectives set by the decision maker. The decision maker or planner will then search for alternative courses of action that are likely to bring about the forecasts when revised into line with his or her set objectives. Discussion of this topic is left to the planners, however.

A PROBLEM IN ORGANIZATION DESIGN?

What are the important issues in forecasting? The previous section has shown that the technical aspects of forecasting are just a small part of the problem of generating cost-effective forecast information and acting on it. Distortions and inefficiencies creep in from a variety of sources. Leaving aside the technical issues for the moment, the major weakness of the system just described is the system itself: an information system set up by accountants and therefore unconcerned with markets and not future oriented, a forecaster entranced with the sophisticated statistical hardware of the profession, and a decision maker whose primary concern is saying what his or her bosses want to hear (a caricature certainly and only one of many possible). However, it underscores the major theme of this chapter: Because we do not know how best to improve the information flow from the environment to the decision maker, we have to experiment. To experiment means to evaluate and measure. Information systems can be improved, and (in the British companies we have examined) there is major scope for such improvement. Technical staff can be deployed so that they understand the manager's problems but are not subject to the same political pressures. Decision makers can distinguish between an objective forecast and the political actions they wish to take for their own or their organization's success.

No single solution to the behavioral problems in forecasting can be applied across all organizations. With experimentation and monitoring of the results of the experiments, it is not unreasonable to hope for major improvements in the effective generation and use of forecast information. Analysis of such experiments by researchers should result in a better understanding of how forecasting and information systems best fit with an organization's needs and how the recommended improvements should be implemented. We could then more reasonably move on to worry about the issues most familiar, the technical.

APPROACHES TO FORECASTING

The Methods

Of all the aspects of forecasting, the one most studied is the technicalities of the various forecasting methods. The methods can be broken down into three classes:

Judgmental. Individual opinions are processed, perhaps in a complicated fashion.

Extrapolative. Forecasts are made for a particular variable using only that variable's history. The patterns identified in the past are assumed to hold into the future.

Causal (or structural). An attempt is made to identify relationships between variables that have held in the past, for example, volume of brand sales and that product's relative price. The relationships are then assumed to hold into the future.

Most forecasters use more than one of these approaches. But before going into how these approaches fit in with the general questions already raised, this section describes some of the more common methods under the foregoing headings and evaluates them.

Charts 10-3, 10-4, and 10-5 give brief definitions of the most important methods in each class. Later chapters in this handbook discuss how they are used in more detail. For the moment these definitions will suffice.

Judgmental Forecasting

Chart 10-3 describes the standard judgmental methods of forecasting.

Extrapolative Forecasting

A number of useful surveys exist. Although a little dated now, Makridakis[17] (with further comment by Anderson[1] and Makridakis[18]) and Fildes[6] offered interesting insights, while Makridakis and colleagues[21] offer up-to-date descriptions of a wide variety of methods, as well as a comparative analysis of their performance.

Extrapolative methods only work for quantitative variables, and in the remainder of this section Y_t is used to denote the variable to be forecasted, measured at time t. Chart 10-4 gives a brief description of the most well-known methods. Mentzer and Cox[23] have examined the use of extrapolative models, and Fildes and Lusk[11] have considered the important question of how a particular extrapolation model is selected for use.

Causal (Structural) Models

The aim of these models is to link the variable being forecast to the causes that historically have influenced it and to use their established relationship to forecast. Chart 10-5 lists the well-known approaches and offers a brief definition. Fildes[7] recently reviewed the subject.

CHART 10-3. Judgmental Methods—Definitions

Method	Definition
J1 Individual (subjective)	Individual makes a judgment about the future without reference to any other set of forecasts.
J2 Committee/survey	Committee aspects are all too familiar. A variant, the "sales force composite," aggregates the opinions of the sales force or "experts" on future prospects. Alternatively, customers can be surveyed as to prospective purchases.
J3 Delphi	Delphi has three attributes that distinguish it from the committee method: anonymity, feedback, and group response. Typically, participants are unknown to each other. The forecasting exercise is conducted in a series of rounds with each participant offered a summary of the opinions expressed earlier.

CHART 10-4. Extrapolative Methods—Definitions

Method	Definition
E1 Trend curves	Past observations are described as a function of time, and the identified pattern is then used to forecast ahead. Typical functions are the straight line, the exponential, and the S-shaped curve. Available computer software provides a number of alternative curves. The method is often used for long-term forecasting. Meade[22] gave a recent evaluation.
E2 Decomposition	Time series is thought of as having four components, trend (long-term behavior), cyclical (longer-term swings around the trend), seasonal, and a random component left over. Once the systematic components are identified they can be reintegrated to generate forecasts.
E3 Exponential smoothing	Forecast is based on a weighted sum of past observations. The weights depend on so-called smoothing parameters, which have to be chosen either by the user or through statistical techniques. The method can be easily adapted to take into account trend and seasonal factors. Gardner[12] offered a recent survey.
E4 Box–Jenkins (or ARIMA)	Like exponential smoothing, forecasts are based on a weighted sum of previous observations. However, the choice of weights is much more complex. ARIMA models offer the analyst a range of different models, and the most appropriate is selected for the particular application (Jenkins[15]).
E5 Bayesian	In normal applications, Bayesian forecasting is similar to exponential smoothing. However, sudden changes in series behavior can take place that are essentially unpredictable, for example, a strike at a competitor's plant. Regular extrapolative forecasting methods require human intervention to recalibrate after such a change. Bayesian forecasting attempts to allow for these changes by evaluating each new data point to see whether any change has occurred. Once change is recognized, the forecasts are adjusted automatically. The method can also incorporate subjective information. Fildes in Makridakis and colleagues[21] gave a description.

CHART 10-5. Causal (Structural) Models—Definitions

Method	Definition
C1 Single equation regression	Dependent variable Y_t is thought of as determined by a number of "causes," or "exogenous factors," as well as past values of the dependent variable itself. The relationships between Y and its causes are identified by examining past data. To forecast, either assumptions need to be made concerning the values of the exogenous factors in the future or these values have to be forecasted. Fildes[7] offered an evaluation.
C2 Simultaneous system	These have a structure similar to the single equation regression models but have more than one dependent variable. The dependent (or endogenous) variables are forecasted by making assumptions about the future values of the exogenous variables.
C3 Simulation	Like simultaneous system models, simulation models are concerned with a large number of variables and their interrelationships with exogenous factors. Simulation modelers stress model structure (rather than the linear structures of the regression and simultaneous system models). Typically they include a lot more detail of the system being modeled, for example, information flows. Identifying the model is usually much more ad hoc than with the rigorous statistical models C1 and C2.
C4 Input–output models	Input–output models are based on the idea that to obtain a given output of goods or services requires a fixed set of inputs. Once forecasts are made of consumer demand, input–output techniques allow calculation of the amount of a particular product needed to sustain that level of demand (Blin et al[5]).
C5 Cross-impact analysis	A list of events likely to have an impact on the system being analyzed is generated. The probabilities of each of these events happening are then estimated. The conditional probability of event A happening given that event B has happened, for all possible events A and B, is also estimated. From these assumptions it is possible to define scenarios made up of a mixture of these various events and to calculate the associated probability of each scenario. Those sets of events with low probability are eliminated. (Helmer[13]).

Other Approaches

The foregoing list of forecasting methods is not all-embracing. It neglects in particular a range of adaptive extrapolative methods (Fildes[6]), leading indicator methods (McLaughlin[16]), and the wide range of ideas that go under the heading of social and technological forecasting. Any method can be employed either badly or well, and a careful analysis of how the organization uses its chosen procedures should usually lead to improvement. However, the major technical issue is how to choose among the competing approaches.

EVALUATION OF FORECASTING METHODS

No one method can be relied on to produce the "best" forecasts in all circumstances. Each of the methods has its strengths and weaknesses, and these are summarized in Chart 10-6.

Each of the methods discussed in Chart 10-6 has been evaluated on a set of criteria, and the results are summarized in Chart 10-7. (Armstrong's[2] Exhibit 14-1 takes a similar approach. See also Makridakis and Wheelwright.[20]) The conclusion that stands out from Chart 10-7 is that the problem of selecting a forecasting procedure is far from straightforward. No one method is better than the others on all the dimensions considered.

SELECTING A FORECASTING PROCEDURE REVISITED

An earlier section briefly considered some of the issues involved in selecting a forecasting procedure. Here the information that would help a forecaster select the appropriate procedure for the problem in hand is reviewed.

Ideally the forecaster would be able to describe the problem to be forecasted on a series of dimensions, for example, certain simple statistical characteristics of the variable, the forecast lead time, the level of aggregation in the data (are the data firm, market, or macroeconomic data?), the type of economic or social system in which the forecasted variable is generated, and so on. With a stable relationship established among these problem categories the performance of the various methods the choice only depends on the returns from forecast accuracy. In essence, a forecasting model of forecast performance would exist to guide the choice of model.

If this sounds too fanciful, certain authors have attempted to do exactly this (Makridakis and Hibon[19]), although with only limited success. Armstrong[2] has also evaluated a wide range of forecasting cases and has attempted to generalize about when to use which method, while Makridakis and colleagues,[21] through a large-scale forecasting competition, have attempted to develop guidelines for selecting among extrapolative models. Fildes and colleagues[8] accepted the difficulties of developing a quantitative model to explain forecasting success and produced a large-scale bibliogra-

CHART 10-6. Advantages and Disadvantages of the Forecasting Methods

Method	Advantages	Disadvantages
Judgmental		
J1 *Individual (subjective)*	Can be inexpensive; flexible, can forecast anything; anybody can do it	Accuracy suspect (Armstrong[2]), although perhaps quality of judgments can be improved by evaluating forecaster's accuracy; skills are embodied in person rather than organization; subject to all problems of human judgment (Hogarth and Makridakis[14] provided survey)
J2 *Committee/survey*	Brings different perspectives to bear on problem, plus has advantages listed for J1	One loudmouth can dominate, and this person might not be best forecaster; no one wants to disagree with boss; needs human judgment; more expensive than individual method; problems in selecting participants and organizing meeting (Armstrong[2,pp. 90–96,108–132]). A survey may say more about people's *current* attitudes and expectations than about future activities
J3 *Delphi*	As J1 and J2, but attempts through anonymity to eliminate effects of authority and group domination	Complex; pressure toward consensus as rounds progress; no necessary convergence to agreed forecast; not necessarily improvement on more straightforward committee (Sackman expanded on these[25])
Extrapolative		
E1 *Trend Curves*	Easy to learn, to use, and to understand	Too easy and therefore encourages thoughtlessness; particularly in long term why should curve depending only on time provide suitable description of distant future? (Meade[22] expanded on associated statistical problems)

CHART 10-6. (*Continued*)

Method	Advantages	Disadvantages
E2 Decomposition	Intuitively plausible	Limited statistical rationale; not ideally suited to forecasting, and suffers from same problems as trend curves; useful method of identifying trend, seasonal, and cyclical factors
E3 Exponential smoothing	Easy to computerize for large number of products; very cheap to operate; easy to set up monitoring schemes; easily understood; good performance in forecasting competitions	Misses turning points
E4 Box–Jenkins (or ARIMA)	Choice of weights is wide, allowing user to identify much more subtle patterns in data than with previous methods; offers philosophy of modeling based on principal of parsimony: simpler the model the better, so long as it passes range of suitable diagnostic checks	Complex and difficult to understand; for many users it promises more than it delivers
E5 Bayesian	Attempts to include probability of structural change; includes subjective information; can be used with very few data points	Complex; performance in forecasting competitions disappointing

Causal (structural)

C1 *Single equation regression*	Sufficiently reliable models typically outperform alternatives (Fildes[1]); are ideal in that they answer question, "How does company influence sales?"; can be control as well as forecasting models	Models difficult to develop, requiring expert staff and large amounts of data that organization often fails to collect; problem in forecasting exogenous factors (see Ashley[4])
C2 *Simultaneous system*	Many systems do not naturally fall into format of single equation model, for example, sales and advertising may be jointly determined; simultaneous system models capture these interrelationships	Large data requirements; hard to understand, statistically complex; difficult to define model; expensive; no evidence simultaneous approach better than single equation models in forecasting
C3 *Simulation*	If properly implemented, can offer decision maker substantial help; can be designed to be simple to use and understand; can also solve "right" problem	Expensive; often large data requirements; no clear rationale behind construction; requires careful validation
C4 *Input–output*	Unlike many techniques described, are ideally suited for forecasting industrial products	Governmental input–output tables seldom contain sufficient detail for company concerned with specific product classes; tend to be out of date; usually assumes constant proportionality between input and output; expensive to prepare; forecasts depend on accuracy of initial forecasts of consumer demand
C5 *Cross-impact Analysis*	Can deal with unlikely events that have major impact; can deal with both quantitative and qualitative events	Probabilities usually have to be estimated through various judgmental methods, which may affect which scenarios are given full consideration; choice of which events to include is potentially crucial; is evidence available that cross-impact has predictive value?

FORECASTING: THE ISSUES

CHART 10-7. Evaluation of Various Forecasting Procedures

METHOD	Data requirements	Statistical basis	Staff Expertise — To set up	Staff Expertise — To use	Comprehensibility	Assessability[a]	Reported effectiveness[b]
Judgmental							
Individual	0[b]	0	0	0	0	4	2
Committee/survey	0	1	4	1	0	4	1
Delphi	0	2	4	2	0	4	1
Extrapolative							
Trend curves	2	1	1	1	1	4	4
Decomposition	2	1	1	2	1	3	4
Exponential smoothing	1	1	1	1	1	3	4
Box–Jenkins	3	2	1	3	2	1	4
Bayesian	1	3	1	3	2	1	4
Causal							
Single equation	3	2	2	3	2	2	4
Simultaneous system	4	4	4	4	4	1	4
Simulation	2–4	4	4	4	2	2	2
Input-output	4	4	4	4	2	1	4
Cross-impact	1	4	4	4	3	2	1

The heading *Criteria for Evaluating Forecasting Procedures* spans the criteria columns.

[a] "Assessability" denotes the ease with which the procedure under discussion can be evaluated. It measures whether the procedure is completely specific or not.

[b] In the scoring system, 0 is equivalent to "low" or "easy" and 4 to "high" or "hard."

phy that describes the success analysts have had in forecasting in a wide range of circumstances. Asher[3] has attempted an evaluation of forecasting success (and failure) for a number of situations, for example, energy, population, and transport. These various studies have increased our knowledge of predictability and have changed our views on the likely success of the alternative methods. Unfortunately, the residual uncertainty is very high, and as we move from the short to the medium term, the situation in which increased accuracy probably has the highest payoff, our knowledge decreases to almost zero. For me, the major issue in selecting a forecasting procedure remains how to link simple measures of the forecasting problem to forecast accuracy. Without substantial further progress, decision makers and their organizations will have to give more attention to the final topic here, the avoidance of forecasting.

AVOIDING FORECASTING

If forecasting with validity is impossible, what alternatives exist? Of all the issues in forecasting, this remains perhaps the least researched. Most forecasting research has concentrated on the short term. In rough-and-ready terms, forecasting for the short term may be described as (1) choose a plausible forecasting procedure, (2) modify it a little, (3) estimate the likely magnitude of the error, and (4) carry enough stocks or do whatever else is necessary to reduce the impact of forecast uncertainty. We are used to responding to uncertainty in our decision making. Any inaccuracy in our estimate of the error is blamed on God, and for a brief period the forecasting department is inundated by irate telephone calls. But the system settles down after this period of chaos. Stability is restored.

Contrast with this the long-term forecaster's problem. His or her misestimate of the forecast error can lead to under- (or over-) employed factories. Such poor performance can even lead to bankruptcy or opportunities missed forever. Unlike the inventory control example, the mistake will not quickly go away.

A number of answers have been developed that can help the long-term decision maker avoid the consequences of very poor forecasts.

Insurance

In contrast to the stock control example, covering the residual uncertainty in long-term forecasts and riding out the consequences may sometimes be regarded as too dangerous. Instead the risk is reduced by sharing the consequences of any disaster with an insurance company. The effect, of course, is a reduced return in that insurance always costs money.

A subtler variation of this idea has been described by Quinn[24] as "logical incrementalism." Simply described, it is the recommendation that where uncertainty is high, only those decisions are contemplated that are viable over a wide range of possible futures. For example, in planning a power station, the decision on which fuel to use may be postponed, plans being based on either coal or oil as the power source. While costly, such duplications overcomes the very high uncertainty in fuel price forecasts. As the forecasting (and planning) lead time reduces, uncertainty is also reduced and more definite choices can be made. Decisions here are seen as sequential rather than taken only once. The cost, more limited than the straightforward "insure" option, derives from the alternative courses of action being kept open for a longer period than if the decision had been made once and for all. Such an approach also demands sophisticated planning departments.

Portfolio Procedures

It has long been known that if two alternative investments can be found with similar returns but with outcomes negatively correlated, a portfolio investment in both decreases the risk level, leaving the return unchanged. The same idea can be used in examining whether diversification (of products or businesses) can lead to decreased risk. In effect, the forecaster needs to forecast not just the returns from different projects but their interrelationships as well. Although in some contexts improvements necessarily derive from considering a portfolio rather than its individual components, the problem remains one of identifying alternative investments that are negatively correlated with one's own. The difficulties associated with the portfolio approach do not negate the usefulness of seeking out countercyclical investments. It is a solution that should prove profitable.

Organizational Flexibility

The time horizon of a forecast is made up of a number of distinct times: the time to gain information (the information lead time), the time to plan and execute a course of action (the planning lead time), and the time during which the action reaps its consequences (the action lead time). The first two of these are under the control of the organization. By increasing the speed at which internal information is made available and by increasing the organization's responsiveness to a problem, the need to forecast is minimized. For research-based organizations, however, this is only of limited help, in that the action lead time is considerably longer than the other two.

Leverage (Gearing)

Forecasting attempts to reduce risk at only a limited cost. But there are a number of alternative structural solutions that the organization can sometimes adopt. For firms funded by both debt and equity, an increased proportion of funds deriving from equity (reducing the leverage) has the effect of lowering the degree to which fluctuations in pre-interest profits are amplified in terms of post-interest profit. Low leverage also reduces exposure to interest rate fluctuations.

Leverage is a concept primarily associated with finance, but it also applies to functions such as purchasing, production, and sales. For example, raw materials (and foreign currency) can be purchased through a futures market so that the amount to be paid for a future need is known now. In marketing, long-term contracts can be made with large purchasers. Although all of these devices cost money (even though the cost is sometimes hidden as an opportunity cost), they do meet the aim of lessening the need to forecast.

FORECASTING—WE STILL CANNOT DO AWAY WITH IT

The ideas just discussed do not eliminate the need for forecasting long term. Portfolio procedures shift the emphasis from forecasting for one business to forecasting for joint performance of businesses. Insurance shifts the problem to the insurer, but at some cost. Organizational flexibility and leverage have only limited applicability. No means is thus available that allows an organization to avoid forecasting altogether. Instead, two simple questions have to be squarely faced:

How best to forecast?

How to estimate the likely forecast error reliably?

As argued here, the answers are both technical and organizational. The latter has received little attention, and in the longer term it seems to hold the most promise for helping avoid the worst consequences of what often seems to be an increasingly malevolent future.

REFERENCES

1. Anderson, O. D., "A Commentary on 'A Survey of Time Series'," *International Statistical Review,* vol. 45, 1977, pp. 273–297.

2. Armstrong, J. S., *Long Range Forecasting: From Crystal Ball to Computer,* 2nd ed., John Wiley, New York, 1985.

3. Asher, W., *Forecasting: An Appraisal for Policy Makers and Planners,* Johns Hopkins University Press, Baltimore, 1978.

4. Ashley, R., "On the Usefulness of Macroeconomic Forecasts as Inputs to Forecasting Models," *Journal of Forecasting,* vol. 2, 1983, pp. 211–223.

5. Blin, J. M., E. A. Stohr, and B. Bagamery, "Input–Output Techniques in Forecasting," in S. Makridakis and S. C. Wheelwright, eds., *Forecasting,* TIMS Studies in the Management Sciences, vol. 12, North-Holland, Amsterdam, 1979.

6. Fildes, R., "Quantitative Forecasting—the State of the Art: Extrapolative Models," *Journal of the Operational Research Society,* vol. 30, 1979, pp. 691–710.

7. Fildes, R., "Quantitative Forecasting—the State of the Art: Causal Models," *Journal of the Operational Research Society,* vol. 36, 1985, pp. 691–710.

8. Fildes, R., D. Dews, and S. Howell, *A Bibliography of Business and Economic Forecasting,* Gower, Farnborough, H.nts., Great Britain, 1981. (First supplement 1984.)

9. Fildes, R., and S. Howell, "On Selecting a Forecasting Model," in S. Makridakis and S. C. Wheelwright, eds., *Forecasting,* TIMS Studies in the Management Sciences, vol. 12, North-Holland, Amsterdam, 1979.

10. Fildes, R., R. M. Jalland, and D. Wood, "Forecasting in Conditions of Uncertainty," *Long Range Planning,* vol. 11, August 1978, pp. 29–38.

11. Fildes, R., and Lusk, E. J., "The Choice of a Forecasting Model," *Omega,* vol. 12, 1984, pp. 427–435.

12. Gardner, E. S. Jr., "Exponential Smoothing: The State of The Art," with discussion, *Journal of Forecasting,* vol. 4, 1984, pp. 1–38.

13. Helmer, O., "Problems in Futures Research—Delphi and Causal Cross-Impact Analysis," *Futures,* vol. 9, 1977, pp. 71+.

14. Hogarth, R., and S. Makridakis, "Forecasting and Planning—An Evaluation," *Management Science,* vol. 27, no. 2, 1981, pp. 115+.

15. Jenkins, G. M., *Practical Experiences with Modelling and Forecasting Time Series*, GPJ Publications, Jersey, Channel Islands, 1979.

16. McLaughlin, R. L., "Leading Indicators: A New Approach for Corporate Planning," *Business Economics*, vol. 6, no. 3, 1971, pp. 7–12.

17. Makridakis, S., "A Survey of Times Series," *International Statistical Review*, vol. 44, 1976, pp. 29–70.

18. Makridakis, S., "Time Series Analysis and Forecasting: An Update and an Evaluation," *International Statistical Review*, vol. 46, 1978, pp. 255–278.

19. Makridakis, S., and M. Hibon, "Forecasting Accuracy and Its Causes: An Empirical Investigation," *Journal of the Royal Statistical Society*, Series A, vol. 142, 1979, pp. 97–145.

20. Makridakis, S., and S. C. Wheelwright, "Forecasting: Framework and Overview," in S. Makridakis and S. C. Wheelwright, eds., *Forecasting*, TIMS Studies in the Management Sciences, vol. 12, North-Holland, Amsterdam, 1979.

21. Makridakis, S., et al., *The Forecasting Accuracy of Major Time Series Methods*, Wiley, Chichester, 1984.

22. Meade, N., "The Use of Growth Curves in Forecasting Market Development—A Review and Appraisal," *Journal of Forecasting*, vol. 3, 1984, pp. 429–451.

23. Mentzer, J. T., and J. E. Cox, "Familiarity, Application, and Performance of Sales Forecasting Techniques," *Journal of Forecasting*, vol. 3, 1984, pp. 27–36.

24. Quinn, J. B., "Strategic Change: Logical Incrementialism," *Sloan Management Review*, Fall 1978, pp. 7–21.

25. Sackman, H., *Delphi Critique: Expert Opinion, Forecasting and Group Process*, Lexington Books, Lexington, MA, 1975.

26. Wheelwright, S.C., and D. G. Clarke, "Corporate Forecasting: Promise and Reality," *Harvard Business Review*, vol. 54, 1976, pp. 40+.

27. Young, R. M., "Forecasting with an Econometric Model: The Issue of Judgemental Adjustment," *Journal of Forecasting*, vol. 1, 1984, pp. 189–204.

PART

2

APPROACHES TO FORECASTING

11

SMOOTHING METHODS FOR SHORT-TERM PLANNING AND CONTROL

EVERETTE S. GARDNER, JR.
College of Business Administration, University of Houston, Houston, Texas

INTRODUCTION

Exponential smoothing is a forecasting method that extrapolates historical data patterns such as trends and seasonal cycles into the future. Forecasts are computed by averaging (smoothing) the data, to isolate true patterns from purely random fluctuations. The fundamental principle underlying exponential smoothing is nothing more than common sense: Recent data contain more information than do older data. Thus the averages are weighted, with the greatest weight assigned to recent data. As the data get older, the weights decline in an exponential pattern, which gives exponential smoothing its name.

Smoothing was invented during World War II, although widespread applications did not occur until the computer revolution of the 1960s. The father of smoothing is Robert G. Brown, who developed the idea when he worked for the U.S. Navy's Operations Evaluation Group near the end of World War II. One of his assignments involved the design of a tracking system for fire-control information on the location of enemy submarines. This information was used in an ingenious mechanical computer (a ball-disk integrator) to estimate target velocity and the lead angle for dropping depth charges. Brown's tracking model was essentially exponential smoothing of continuous data, an idea still used in modern fire-control equipment.

In the early 1950s, Brown developed the principles of exponential smoothing for business data. One of his early applications was in forecasting the demand for spare parts in Navy inventories. The improvements in accuracy and savings in data storage over previous ad hoc forecasting methods led to the adoption of smoothing throughout the Navy's inventory systems in the late 1950s. Brown's first book[1] presented a set of simple models for inventory applications. His second book[2] developed a complete methodology for time series forecasting with smoothing methods.

Another scientist, C. C. Holt, worked independently of Brown in the 1950s to develop similar smoothing models for business applications. Holt's early work was sponsored by the Office of Naval Research. Peter Winters assisted in the development of Holt's methods, which were completed in 1960.[5,8]

Since 1960, smoothing methods have become widely used in practice, especially for short-term planning and control in operations management. For example, almost every computer-based inventory system today includes some form of smoothing to update demand forecasts on a periodic schedule and to set safety stocks. The popularity of exponential smoothing is due to several practical considerations. Smoothing models are relatively simple. Thus the components of the models, for example, the average trend and seasonal cycle, have intuitive meaning to the user. Only limited data storage and computational effort are required. Tracking signal tests for forecast monitoring are easy to apply.

Empirical studies demonstrate that smoothing is quite accurate compared with more complex forecasting methods. For example, two large-scale studies found little difference in mean forecast accuracy between smoothing and Box–Jenkins models (see Makridakis and Hibon[6] and Makridakis et al.[7]). The robustness of smoothing is the reason that it performed so well in these studies. By robustness is meant the fact that smoothing is generally insensitive to particular data patterns or to the occasional extreme observations (known as outliers) that occur in business data.

This chapter is a working reference on exponential smoothing. The following section is an overview of the types of models available. Then calculations are reviewed in detail for the most popular models. The last section presents an objective procedure for selecting the best smoothing model for a time series.

The emphasis throughout the chapter is on practice rather than theory. For more information on the theory of exponential smoothing, consult Gardner.[3,4]

TYPES OF SMOOTHING MODELS

Smoothing models can be classified by forecast profiles or plots showing the general pattern of the forecasts over time. A variety of forecast profiles are presented in Chart 11-1: four trend patterns, each coupled with three seasonal patterns. The constant-level models assume no trend at all in the data.

CHART 11-1. Forecast Profiles from Exponential Smoothing Models

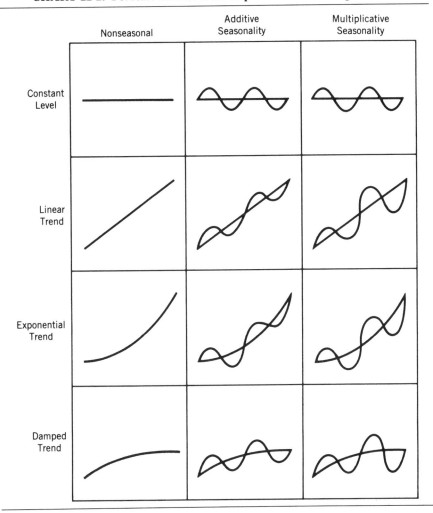

The time series is assumed to have a relatively constant mean and the forecast is a horizontal straight line for any period in the future. The constant-level models are widely used for one-step-ahead forecasting or when time series contain a great deal of noise or randomness.

A linear trend is the most popular assumption in practice. The forecasts simply call for straight-line growth for any period in the future. Early in the life cycle of a product, growth may increase continuously, making an exponential trend the best assumption. In empirical studies, both linear and exponential trends were too optimistic and tended to overshoot the data if extrapolated too far into the future. For longer-range forecasting, the damped trend

CHART 11-2. Notation for Exponential Smoothing

Symbol	Definition
X_t	Observed value of the series in period t
$\hat{X}_t(m)$	Forecast made at the end of t for m steps ahead
e_t	Forecast error in t
S_t	Level (mean) of the series at the end of t
T_t	Trend at the end of t
I_t	Seasonal index for t
h_1	Smoothing parameter for the level of the series
h_2	Smoothing parameter for the trend
h_3	Smoothing parameter for the seasonal index
ϕ	Trend modification parameter
p	Number of periods in one season

was shown to be a better choice.[4] As the name implies, a damped trend produces a gradual decline in the amount of growth each period.

The additive seasonal pattern in Chart 11-1 assumes that the range of seasonal fluctuations is constant, independent of any growth in the data. The multiplicative seasonal pattern assumes that the seasonal fluctuations are proportional to the data. As a trend increases, multiplicative seasonal fluctuations get larger.

Charts 11-2 through 11-5 summarize the exponential smoothing models corresponding to these forecast profiles. All notation used in this chapter is given in Chart 11-2. Nonseasonal models are shown in Chart 11-3. Additive and multiplicative seasonal models are shown in Charts 11-4 and 11-5, respectively.

CHART 11-3. Nonseasonal Models

Constant level

$$e_t = X_t - \hat{X}_{t-1}(1)$$
$$S_t = S_{t-1} + h_1 e_t$$
$$\hat{X}_t(m) = S_t$$

Linear trend

$$e_t = X_t - \hat{X}_{t-1}(1)$$
$$S_t = S_{t-1} + T_{t-1} + h_1 e_t$$
$$T_t = T_{t-1} + h_2 e_t$$
$$\hat{X}_t(m) = S_t + m T_t$$

Nonlinear trend

$$e_t = X_t - \hat{X}_{t-1}(1)$$
$$S_t = S_{t-1} + \phi T_{t-1} + h_1 e_t$$
$$T_t = \phi T_{t-1} + h_2 e_t$$
$$\hat{X}_t(m) = S_t + \sum_{i=1}^{m} \phi^i T_t$$

CHART 11-4. Additive Seasonal Models

Constant level

$$e_t = X_t - \hat{X}_{t-1}(1)$$
$$S_t = S_{t-1} + h_1 e_t$$
$$I_t = I_{t-p} + h_3 e_t$$
$$\hat{X}_t(m) = S_t + I_{t-p+m}$$

Linear trend

$$e_t = X_t - \hat{X}_{t-1}(1)$$
$$S_t = S_{t-1} + T_{t-1} + h_1 e_t$$
$$T_t = T_{t-1} + h_2 e_t$$
$$I_t = I_{t-p} + h_3 e_t$$
$$\hat{X}_t(m) = S_t + mT_t + I_{t-p+m}$$

Nonlinear trend

$$e_t = X_t - \hat{X}_{t-1}(1)$$
$$S_t = S_{t-1} + \phi T_{t-1} + h_1 e_t$$
$$T_t = \phi T_{t-1} + h_2 e_t$$
$$I_t = I_{t-p} + h_3 e_t$$
$$\hat{X}_t(m) = S_t + \Sigma_{i=1}^{m} \phi^i T_t + I_{t-p+m}$$

CHART 11-5. Multiplicative Seasonal Models

Constant level

$$e_t = X_t - \hat{X}_{t-1}(1)$$
$$S_t = S_{t-1} + h_1 e_t / I_{t-p}$$
$$I_t = I_{t-p} + h_3 e_t / S_t$$
$$\hat{X}_t(m) = S_t I_{t-p+m}$$

Linear trend

$$e_t = X_t - \hat{X}_{t-1}(1)$$
$$S_t = S_{t-1} + T_{t-1} + h_1 e_t / I_{t-p}$$
$$T_t = T_{t-1} + h_2 e_t / I_{t-p}$$
$$I_t = I_{t-p} + h_3 e_t / S_t$$
$$\hat{X}_t(m) = (S_t + mT_t) I_{t-p+m}$$

Nonlinear trend

$$e_t = X_t - \hat{X}_{t-1}(1)$$
$$S_t = S_{t-1} + \phi T_{t-1} + h_1 e_t / I_{t-p}$$
$$T_t = \phi T_{t-1} + h_2 e_t / I_{t-p}$$
$$I_t = I_{t-p} + h_3 e_t / S_t$$
$$\hat{X}_t(m) = (S_t + \Sigma_{i=1}^{m} \phi^i T_t) I_{t-p+m}$$

THE CONSTANT-LEVEL MODEL

To explain how these models work, let us start with the constant-level, nonseasonal model, also called simple exponential smoothing (refer to Charts 11-2 and 11-3):

$$e_t = X_t - \hat{X}_{t-1}(1) \qquad\qquad (11\text{-}1)$$

$$S_t = S_{t-1} + h_1 e_t \qquad\qquad (11\text{-}2)$$

$$\hat{X}_t(m) = S_t \qquad\qquad (11\text{-}3)$$

In Equation 11-1, we compute the forecast error e_t, defined as actual data minus the forecast. The letter t refers to the time period. The current period, for example the month, is t, while the last period is t-1. S_t is the new level, or the weighted average of the time series at the end of t. The new level is equal to the level at the end of $t-1$ plus a fraction of the error. The fraction h_1 is called the smoothing parameter and lies between 0 and 1.

$\hat{X}_t(m)$ is the forecast made at the end of t, for m steps ahead. This notation may seem cumbersome but, as we shall see in the more complex models, it is important to keep track of when a forecast was made and to what period in the future it applies. In this case, since we assume a constant level, the forecast is just S_t for any period in the future.

The constant-level model behaves much like an automatic pilot or thermostat. As each data point in the time series is observed, we compute the forecast error. If the error is positive (the last forecast was too low), we increase the forecast. If the error is negative (the last forecast was too high), we reduce the forecast. Thus the errors are used to steer the forecasts toward a target: the true level of the time series.

Chart 11-6 is an example of the calculations for simple smoothing. The time series is the annual number of passenger embarkations in thousands at the Carrboro, North Carolina, International Airport for the 12-year period 1974–1985. To get started, a value for h_1 and a forecast for period 1 have to be supplied (more about how to choose these later). After that the model runs automatically.

Suppose we use $h_1 = 0.1$. The starting level is $S_0 = 29.0$ and is recorded in row 0 of Chart 11-6. Next we move S_0 down to row 1 and use it as the forecast for period 1, that is

$$\hat{X}_0(1) = S_0 = 29.0$$

Then we compute the forecast error at the end of period 1

$$e_1 = X_1 - \hat{X}_0(1) = 28.0 - 29.0 = -1.0$$

Now we can update the level at the end of period 1

$$S_1 = S_0 + h_1 e_1 = 29.0 + 0.1(-1.0) = 28.9$$

CHART 11-6. Constant-Level Model, Nonseasonal, $h_1 = 0.10$

Time t	Data X_t	Forecast $\hat{X}_{t-1}(1)$	Error e_t	Level at End of t $S_t = S_{t-1} + h_1 e_t$
0				$S_0 = $ 29.0
1	28.0	29.0	-1.0	$S_1 = 29.0 + 0.1(-1.0) = 28.9$
2	27.0	28.9	-1.9	$S_2 = 28.9 + 0.1(-1.9) = 28.7$
3	34.0	28.7	5.3	$S_3 + 28.7 + 0.1(5.3) = 29.2$
4	26.0	29.2	-3.2	$S_4 + 29.2 + 0.1(-3.2) = 28.9$
5	32.0	28.9	3.1	$S_5 + 28.9 + 0.1(3.1) = 29.2$
6	33.0	29.2	3.8	$S_6 = 29.2 + 0.1(3.8) = 29.6$
7	27.0	29.6	-2.6	$S_7 = 29.6 + 0.1(-2.6) = 29.3$
8	30.0	29.3	0.7	$S_8 = 29.3 + 0.1(0.7) = 29.4$
9	27.0	29.4	-2.4	$S_9 = 29.4 + 0.1(-2.4) = 29.2$
10	34.0	29.2	4.8	$S_{10} = 29.2 + 0.1(4.8) = 29.7$
11	25.0	29.7	-4.7	$S_{11} = 29.7 + 0.1(-4.7) = 29.2$
12	33.0	29.2	3.8	$S_{12} = 29.2 + 0.1(3.8) = 29.6$
13		29.6		

S_1 is now the forecast for period 2

$$\hat{X}_1(1) = S_1 = 28.9$$

This forecast is moved down to row 2, the error is computed, and the level at the end of period 2 is updated

$$e_1 = X_2 - \hat{X}_1(1) = 27.0 - 28.9 = -1.9$$
$$S_2 = S_1 + h_1 e_2 = 28.9 + 0.1(-1.9) = 28.7.$$

The level is moved down to row 3 and used as the forecast

$$\hat{X}_2(1) = S_2 = 28.7$$

The remaining calculations follow in a similar manner. Each period we compute the error, update the level, and move it down to the next period as the forecast. At the end of period 12, the forecast is 29.6 for any period in the future.

In this example, the first forecast and the smoothing parameter were selected to keep the arithmetic simple. In practice, these values must be chosen carefully. If the first forecast is not representative of the data, later forecasts will be distorted. Furthermore, the first forecast has a great deal of influence on the choice of smoothing parameter. For example, in Chart 11-6 suppose we start with a forecast of 20. This forces us to use a smoothing parameter of 1.0 to catch up to the data. To avoid this danger, the mean of the data should always be used as the first forecast.

To choose the smoothing parameter h_1, a range of trial values must be tested. The parameter is usually chosen to minimize the mean squared error (MSE). Minimum absolute error or percentage error could also be used. An efficient routine to locate the best-fitting parameter is as follows. First, compute the MSE at two values of h_1, 0.33 and 0.67. Choose the best h_1. Then compute the MSE at a range of ±0.17 around the best h_1. Update the best h_1 if necessary. Continue the search from that point with progressively smaller ranges (±0.08, 0.04, 0.02, 0.015, 0.0005) until the change in MSE is less than some arbitrary percentage, say 1%.

It is a good idea to set a floor on h_1 of at least 0.1 to allow for some response to future changes in the time series. If h_1 is allowed to reach zero, this means that the first forecast is never changed. To see why, look at Equation 11-2 again. If $h_1 = 0$, the equation reduces to $S_t = S_{t-1}$.

Two factors interact with each other to determine the best smoothing parameter. One is the amount of noise in the series. The greater the noise, the smaller the parameter will be to avoid overreaction to the noise. The second factor is the stability of the mean of the time series. If the mean is relatively constant, the parameter will be small. If the mean is changing, the parameter will be large to keep up with the changes. In the limit, the parameter will reach 1.0, which means that the new forecast is equal to the last data point.

Chart 11-7 shows how the smoothing parameter affects the stability of the forecasts. The data are the same as in Chart 11-6. With $h_1 = 0.1$, the fore-

CHART 11-7. Effects of the Smoothing Parameter

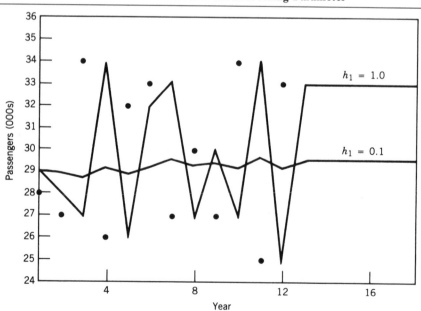

casts are stable, which is what we want with this time series because the mean is relatively constant. But with $h_1 = 1.0$, the forecasts fluctuate wildly and the errors are much larger.

The value of the smoothing parameter also controls the weights assigned to past data. The weights can be found with an equation equivalent to Equation 11-2:

$$S_t = h_1 X_t + h_1(1 - h_1)X_{t-1} + h_1(1 - h_1)^2 X_{t-2}$$
$$+ h_1(1 - h_1)^3 X_{t-3} + h_1(1 - h_1)^4 X_{t-4} \qquad (11\text{-}4)$$
$$+ \qquad \cdots \qquad + h_1(1 - h_1)^k X_{t-k}$$

Every data point gets some weight, although the weights for older data quickly become very small.

THE LINEAR-TREND MODEL

The smoothing model for a linear trend is an extension of a regression model with time (a consecutive series of integers) as the independent variable. The regression equation is $X = a + bt$. The intercept of the trend line is a and the slope is b. Both a and b are averaged over all the data and are treated as constants.

In smoothing a linear trend, the intercept and slope are not constants but are updated each period, giving more weight to recent data. Empirical studies (see Makridakis et al.[7]) show that smoothed estimates of the intercept and slope are far more accurate than the constant estimates used in regression.

The smoothing model for a linear trend is (refer to Charts 11-2 and 11-3)

$$e_t = X_t - \hat{X}_{t-1}(1) \qquad (11\text{-}1)$$

$$S_t = S_{t-1} + T_{t-1} + h_1 e_t \qquad (11\text{-}5)$$

$$T_t = T_{t-1} + h_2 e_t \qquad (11\text{-}6)$$

$$\hat{X}_t(m) = S_t + mT_t \qquad (11\text{-}7)$$

The first step is to compute the forecast error using the same equation (11-1) as in the constant-level model. Next we update the level of the series in Equation 11-5. This equation is similar to the constant-level model except that we add in the previous trend. The level in the linear-trend model is the intercept of a trend line that originates at the current period. Contrast this idea with the regression model. In regression, the intercept is fixed at period 0, but in smoothing, the intercept is adjusted with each data point. The slope of the trend line is called the smoothed trend, T_t, and is analogous to the slope b in regression. Notice that we have separate smoothing parameters, h_1 and h_2, for the level and trend.

Chart 11-8 is an example of the calculations for the linear-trend model. The time series is the annual number of paid subscriptions to *Creative Computing* magazine for the 12-year period ending in 1985. To get started, the following elements must be specified: S_0, T_0, h_1, and h_2. How these are selected is discussed later in this section. To demonstrate the model, we will use $S_0 = 54.0$, $T_0 = 2.0$, $h_1 = 0.2$, and $h_2 = 0.1$.

Chart 11-8 is organized as follows. First, we record S_0 and T_0 in row 0. The forecast for period 1 is computed in the last column of row 0:

$$\hat{X}_0(1) = S_0 + T_0 = 54.0 + 2.0 = 56.0$$

The forecast is moved down to the forecast column of row 1. Next we compute the error in period 1:

$$e_1 = X_1 - \hat{X}_0(1) = 54.0 - 56.0 = -2.0$$

Now we continue working in row 1 and update the level and trend as of the end of period 1:

$$S_1 = S_0 + T_0 + h_1 e_1 = 54.0 + 2.0 + 0.2(-2.0) = 55.6$$
$$T_1 = T_0 + h_2 e_1 = 2.0 + 0.1(-2.0) = 1.8$$

The last step in row 1 is to compute the forecast for period 2:

$$\hat{X}_1(1) = S_1 + T_1 = 55.6 + 1.8 = 57.4$$

This result is moved down to the forecast column in row 2.

Let's reflect for a moment on what we have accomplished. The beginning level and trend, S_0 and T_0, define an initial trend line. This line starts at 54.0, the value of S_0, and increases at a rate of 2.0 units per period, the value of T_0. But at the end of period 1, we have an updated trend line. This line starts at 55.6, the value of S_1, and increases at a rate of 1.8 units per period.

In period 2, the error is

$$e_2 = X_2 - \hat{X}_1(1) = 55.0 - 57.4 = -2.4$$

Next we update the level and trend using this error:

$$S_2 = S_1 + T_1 + h_1 e_2 = 55.6 + 1.8 + 0.2(-2.4) = 56.9$$
$$T_2 = T_1 + h_2 e_2 = 1.8 + 0.1(-2.4) = 1.6$$

Now we can compute the forecast for period 3:

$$\hat{X}_2(1) = 56.9 + 1.6 = 58.5$$

CHART 11-8. Linear-Trend Model, Nonseasonal, $h_1 = 0.20$, $h_2 = 0.10$

Time t	Data X_t	Forecast $X_{t-1}(1)$	Error e_t	Level at End of t $S_t = S_{t-1} + T_{t-1} + h_1 e_t$	Trend at End of t $T_t = T_{t-1} + h_2 e_t$	Forecast for $t+1$ $\hat{X}_t(1) = S_t + T_t$
0				$S_0 = 54.0$	$T_0 = 2.0$	$\hat{X}_0(1) = 54.0 + 2.0 = 56.0$
1	54.0	56.0	−2.0	$S_1 = 54.0 + 2.0 + 0.2(-2.0) = 55.6$	$T_1 = 2.0 + 0.1(-2.0) = 1.8$	$\hat{X}_1(1) = 55.6 + 1.8 = 57.4$
2	55.0	57.4	−2.4	$S_2 = 55.6 + 1.8 + 0.2(-2.4) = 56.9$	$T_2 = 1.8 + 0.1(-2.4) = 1.6$	$\hat{X}_2(1) = 56.9 + 1.6 = 58.5$
3	57.0	58.5	−1.5	$S_3 = 56.9 + 1.6 + 0.2(-1.5) = 58.2$	$T_3 = 1.6 + 0.1(-1.5) = 1.5$	$\hat{X}_3(1) = 58.2 + 1.5 = 59.7$
4	60.0	59.7	0.3	$S_4 = 58.2 + 1.5 + 0.2(0.3) = 59.8$	$T_4 = 1.5 + 0.1(0.3) = 1.5$	$\hat{X}_4(1) = 59.8 + 1.5 = 61.3$
5	66.0	61.3	4.7	$S_5 = 59.8 + 1.5 + 0.2(4.7) = 62.2$	$T_5 = 1.5 + 0.1(4.7) = 2.0$	$\hat{X}_5(1) = 62.2 + 2.0 = 64.2$
6	62.0	64.2	−2.2	$S_6 = 62.2 + 2.0 + 0.2(-2.2) = 63.8$	$T_6 = 2.0 + 0.1(-2.2) = 1.8$	$\hat{X}_6(1) = 63.8 + 1.8 = 65.6$
7	59.0	65.6	−6.6	$S_7 = 63.8 + 1.8 + 0.2(-6.6) = 64.3$	$T_7 = 1.8 + 0.1(-6.6) = 1.1$	$\hat{X}_7(1) = 64.3 + 1.1 = 65.4$
8	65.0	65.4	−0.4	$S_8 = 64.3 + 1.1 + 0.2(-0.4) = 65.3$	$T_8 = 1.1 + 0.1(-0.4) = 1.1$	$\hat{X}_8(1) = 65.3 + 1.1 = 66.4$
9	69.0	66.4	2.6	$S_9 = 65.3 + 1.1 + 0.2(2.6) = 66.9$	$T_9 = 1.1 + 0.1(2.6) = 1.4$	$\hat{X}_9(1) = 66.9 + 1.4 = 68.3$
10	70.0	68.3	1.7	$S_{10} = 66.9 + 1.4 + 0.2(1.7) = 68.6$	$T_{10} = 1.4 + 0.1(1.7) = 1.6$	$\hat{X}_{10}(1) = 68.6 + 1.6 = 70.2$
11	63.0	70.2	−7.2	$S_{11} = 68.6 + 1.6 + 0.2(-7.2) = 68.8$	$T_{11} = 1.6 + 0.1(-7.2) = 0.9$	$\hat{X}_{11}(1) = 68.8 + 0.9 = 69.7$
12	75.0	69.7	5.3	$S_{12} = 68.8 + 0.9 + 0.2(5.3) = 70.8$	$T_{12} = 0.9 + 0.1(5.3) = 1.4$	$\hat{X}_{12}(1) = 70.8 + 1.4 = 72.2$
13		72.2				

This result is moved down to the forecast column in period 3. Again there is a new trend line. This time it starts at 56.9, the value of S_2. The slope of the new line is 1.6.

The remaining calculations follow in a similar manner. Every period a new trend line is produced. The final trend line starts at 70.8, the value of S_{12}, and increases by 1.4 units per period.

So far all we have done is to forecast one step ahead (for $m = 1$). But at any time forecasts can be made for longer horizons. At the end of period 12, suppose a forecast is needed for six steps ahead ($m = 6$). The equation is

$$\hat{X}_{12}(6) = S_{12} + (6)T_{12} = 70.8 + (6)1.4 = 79.2$$

As with the constant-level model, caution is required in initializing the linear-trend model. The recommended procedure to obtain the starting level and trend is to perform a linear regression with time as the independent variable. Set S_0 equal to the regression intercept a and set T_0 equal to the regression slope b.

The smoothing parameters are found by a grid search. Begin by computing the MSE (or other error measure) for four combinations of parameters: $h_1 = 0.33, 0.67$ and $h_2 = 0.33, 0.67$. Next compute the MSE at points ± 0.17 around the best combination of parameters and adjust the best combination if necessary. Continue with progressively smaller ranges ($\pm 0.08, 0.04, 0.02, 0.015, 0.0005$) until the change in MSE is less than 1%. The best h_2 parameter for the trend is usually found to be less than h_1 for the level. The reason is that the amount of trend each period is usually very small compared with the level. If we add the same fraction of the error to both level and trend, the forecasts may be unstable. As with the constant-level model, it is a good idea to set a floor on the parameters. Minimum values of $h_1 = 0.10$ and $h_2 = 0.01$ are recommended.

NONLINEAR-TREND MODELS

The linear-trend model can be modified to accommodate the nonlinear trends illustrated in Chart 11-1. The trick is to add a new parameter to control the rate of growth in the forecasts. This is ϕ, called the trend-modification parameter. The nonlinear-trend model is

$$e_t = X_t - \hat{X}_{t-1}(1) \tag{11-1}$$

$$S_t = S_{t-1} + \phi T_{t-1} + h_1 e_t \tag{11-8}$$

$$T_t = \phi T_{t-1} + h_2 e_t \tag{11-9}$$

$$\hat{X}_t(m) = S_t + \sum_{i=1}^{m} \phi^i T_t \tag{11-10}$$

Again, we use Equation 11-1 for the forecast error. Except for the trend modification, the other equations are the same as in the previous section. In the level equation (11-8) and the trend equation (11-9), notice that the old trend is multiplied by ϕ. In the forecast equation (11-10), the new trend is multiplied by ϕ. What is the effect of ϕ? If ϕ is greater than 1, we have an exponential trend, and the amount of growth in the forecasts increases each period. If ϕ is less than 1, we have a damped trend, and the amount of growth in the forecasts decreases each period.

Chart 11-9 is an example of the calculations for the nonlinear trend model. The time series is the same as the one in Chart 11-8. To simplify comparisons with Chart 11-8, the level and trend parameters are also the same. A ϕ value of 0.8 is used to demonstrate the model. Since ϕ is less than 1, we will refer to the model as the damped-trend model. The calculations are similar to those in the linear-trend model, so we will not discuss them in detail except for the forecast equation for $m > 1$, which may be confusing.

The final level and trend in Chart 11-9 are $S_{12} = 68.8$ and $T_{12} = 1.3$. These are used to build up forecasts as follows. For a one-step-ahead forecast ($m = 1$), we have

$$\hat{X}_{12}(1) = S_{12} + \phi^1 T_{12} = 68.8 + (0.8)^1 1.3 = 69.8$$

This is the same as the forecast for period 13 in the table. For two steps ahead ($m = 2$), the forecast is

$$\hat{X}_{12}(2) = S_{12} + \sum_{i=1}^{2} \phi^i T_{12} = 68.8 + (0.8)^1 1.3 + (0.8)^2 1.3 = 70.7$$

For three steps ahead ($m = 3$), the forecast is

$$\hat{X}_{12}(3) = S_{12} + \sum_{i=1}^{3} \phi^i T_{12} = 68.8 + (0.8)^1 1.3 + (0.8)^2 1.3 + (0.8)^3 1.3 = 71.3$$

Thus, as the forecast horizon increases, ϕ^i decreases, eventually approaching zero.

Chart 11-10 is a comparison of the linear and damped-trend models. The linear forecasts are taken from the example in Chart 11-8. In one-step-ahead forecasting through period 12, the behavior of the two models is similar. This is what we should expect, because the level and trend parameters are the same. The effect of the trend modification parameter is to hold the damped forecasts slightly below the linear forecasts until period 12 is reached. Beyond period 13, as we forecast two through six steps ahead, the damping has a stronger effect and the two models diverge.

The procedure for obtaining starting values for the nonlinear model is similar to that for the linear model. A linear regression is used to obtain the

CHART 11-9. Linear-Trend Model, Nonseasonal, $h_1 = 0.20$, $h_2 = 0.10$, $\phi = 0.80$

Time t	Data X_t	Forecast $X_{t-1}(1)$	Error e_t	Level at End of t $S_t = S_{t-1} + \phi T_{t-1} + h_1 e_t$	Trend at End of t $T_t = \phi T_{t-1} + h_2 e_t$	Forecast for $t+1$ $\hat{X}_t(1) = S_t + \phi T_t$
0				$S_0 = 54.0$	$T_0 = 2.0$	$\hat{X}_0(1) = 54.0 + 0.8(2.0) = 55.6$
1	54.0	55.6	-1.6	$S_1 = 54.0 + 0.8(2.0) + 0.2(-1.6) = 55.3$	$T_1 = 0.8(2.0) + 0.1(-1.6) = 1.4$	$\hat{X}_1(1) = 55.3 + 0.8(1.4) = 56.4$
2	55.0	56.4	-1.4	$S_2 = 55.3 + 0.8(1.4) + 0.2(-1.4) = 56.1$	$T_2 = 0.8(1.4) + 0.1(-1.4) = 1.0$	$\hat{X}_2(1) = 56.1 + 0.8(1.0) = 56.9$
3	57.0	56.9	0.1	$S_3 = 56.1 + 0.8(1.0) + 0.2(0.1) = 56.9$	$T_3 = 0.8(1.0) + 0.1(0.1) = 0.8$	$\hat{X}_3(1) = 56.9 + 0.8(0.8) = 57.5$
4	60.0	57.5	2.5	$S_4 = 56.9 + 0.8(0.8) + 0.2(2.5) = 58.0$	$T_4 = 0.8(0.8) + 0.1(2.5) = 0.9$	$\hat{X}_4(1) = 58.0 + 0.8(0.9) = 58.7$
5	66.0	58.7	7.3	$S_5 = 58.0 + 0.8(0.9) + 0.2(7.3) = 60.2$	$T_5 = 0.8(0.9) + 0.1(7.3) = 1.5$	$\hat{X}_5(1) = 60.2 + 0.8(1.5) = 61.4$
6	62.0	61.4	0.6	$S_6 = 60.2 + 0.8(1.5) + 0.2(0.6) = 61.5$	$T_6 = 0.8(1.5) + 0.1(0.6) = 1.3$	$\hat{X}_6(1) = 61.5 + 0.8(1.3) = 62.5$
7	59.0	62.5	-3.5	$S_7 = 61.5 + 0.8(1.3) + 0.1(-3.5) = 61.8$	$T_7 = 0.8(1.3) + 0.1(-3.5) = 0.7$	$\hat{X}_7(1) = 61.8 + 0.8(0.7) = 62.4$
8	65.0	62.4	2.6	$S_8 = 61.8 + 0.8(0.7) + 0.2(2.6) = 62.9$	$T_8 = 0.8(0.7) + 0.1(2.6) = 0.8$	$\hat{X}_8(1) = 62.9 + 0.8(0.8) = 63.5$
9	69.0	63.5	5.5	$S_9 = 62.9 + 0.8(0.8) + 0.2(5.5) = 64.6$	$T_9 = 0.8(0.8) + 0.1(5.5) = 1.2$	$\hat{X}_9(1) = 64.6 + 0.8(1.2) = 65.6$
10	70.0	65.6	4.4	$S_{10} = 64.6 + 0.8(1.2) + 0.2(4.4) = 66.5$	$T_{10} = 0.8(1.2) + 0.1(4.4) = 1.4$	$\hat{X}_{10}(1) = 66.5 + 0.8(1.4) = 67.6$
11	63.0	67.6	-4.6	$S_{11} = 66.5 + 0.8(1.4) + 0.2(-4.6) = 66.7$	$T_{11} = 0.8(1.4) + 0.1(-4.6) = 0.7$	$\hat{X}_{11}(1) = 66.7 + 0.8(0.7) = 67.3$
12	75.0	67.3	7.7	$S_{12} = 66.7 + 0.8(0.7) + 0.2(7.7) = 68.8$	$T_{12} = 0.8(0.7) + 0.1(7.7) = 1.3$	$\hat{X}_{12}(1) = 68.8 + 0.8(1.3) = 69.8$
13		69.8				

CHART 11-10. Alternative Trend Models

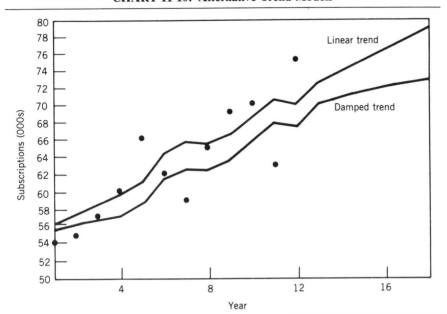

beginning slope and intercept, S_0 and T_0. Although an exponential or a damped regression could be done, it is tedious and a linear regression is adequate. A grid search is conducted for the three parameters h_1, h_2, and ϕ. The procedure for the search is the same as the one for the linear trend except that 20 combinations of parameters are tested initially: $\phi = 0.33$, 0.67, 1.00, 1.33, and 1.67; $h_1 = 0.33$, 0.67; and $h_2 = 0.33$, 0.67. The best combination is chosen from this set. Thereafter, progressively smaller ranges of values (the same as for the linear trend) are tested around each parameter.

It may be surprising to learn that the nonlinear model often produces forecasts that are approximately the same as those produced by either the constant-level or the linear model. For example, if the nonlinear model is applied to a set of data in which there is no trend, a grid search for ϕ will yield a value near zero and the forecasts will approximate the constant-level model. To see why, set $\phi = 0$ in the nonlinear model and compare the results with those of the constant-level model. The two models are identical.

If the trend in a set of data is actually linear, the search for ϕ will yield a value near 1 and the forecasts will approximate the linear model. To see why, set $\phi = 1$ in the nonlinear model and compare the results with those of the linear model. The two models are identical.

Thus the nonlinear model can be used as an automatic forecaster for any nonseasonal time series. One of four forecast profiles will be obtained from a grid search for the model parameters:

1. $\phi \approx 0$, a constant level
2. $\phi < 1$, a damped trend
3. $\phi \approx 1$, a linear trend
4. $\phi > 1$, an exponential trend

An exponential trend may be dangerous in an automatic forecasting system. This type of trend can be ruled out by restricting the parameter search so that ϕ will lie between 0 and 1. In the search procedure just described, the initial ϕ values to accomplish this would be 0.33, 0.67.

Empirical results on the use of the nonlinear model as an automatic forecaster are given in Gardner and McKenzie.[4] Forecasting accuracy for the nonlinear model is significantly better than that obtained with the common practice of using a linear trend in every time series. Of course this modeling scheme is not foolproof, and the nonlinear model will sometimes identify the wrong trend. But, on average, the nonlinear model works well in applications where it is not possible to choose an individual model for each time series.

The need for an automatic forecasting model is critical in large inventory control systems. For example, in U.S. Navy inventory systems, more than 1.5 million forecasts of repair parts demand are needed each quarter. The best strategy in such applications is to use the nonlinear model for all series, especially if the inventory lead times are greater than one period. Forecasts are usually needed for an entire lead time, and if this is more than one period, the advantage of the nonlinear model over the other models becomes more significant.[4]

SEASONAL SMOOTHING

So far, all the models we have discussed are nonseasonal and deal only with trend patterns in the data. If a seasonal pattern exists, the nonseasonal models are extended by adding a smoothed seasonal index for each period of the year. The index is used to adjust the forecasts according to the expected seasonal fluctuation. If the seasonality is additive, the index is defined as the difference between each data point and the data average for the year. The additive index can be used to obtain deseasonalized data (in which the seasonal pattern has been removed): actual data − index = deseasonalized data. We can also reseasonalize or put the seasonality back: deseasonalized data + index = actual data.

If the seasonal pattern is multiplicative, the index is defined as the ratio of each data point to the data average for the year. To deseasonalize, we use:

actual data ÷ index = deseasonalized data. To reseasonalize, we use: deseasonalized data × index = actual data.

To explain how smoothed seasonal indices work, we will demonstrate the constant-level model with multiplicative seasonality (refer to Charts 11-2 and 11-5):

$$e_t = X_t - \hat{X}_{t-1}(1) \tag{11-1}$$

$$S_t = S_{t-1} + h_1 e_t / I_{t-p} \tag{11-11}$$

$$I_t = I_{t-p} + h_3 e_t / S_t \tag{11-12}$$

$$\hat{X}_t(m) = S_t I_{t-p+m} \tag{11-13}$$

In this model, I is the smoothed seasonal index and there are p indices per year, one for each period. The notation I_t refers to the index for period t. The notation I_{t-p} refers to the index p periods, or one year ago.

Again, we use Equation 11-1 for the forecast error. In Equation 11-11, the level of the series, S_t, is in deseasonalized terms and is updated with a fraction of the deseasonalized error. In Equation 11-12, I_t is updated by a fraction of the ratio of the error to the current deseasonalized level and has its own smoothing parameter, h_3. In Equation 11-13, the forecast is the product of the deseasonalized level and the appropriate index for the future period. The time subscript in Equation 11-13 is critical. Pay particular attention to the subscript of I. Also keep in mind that this subscript works only for one complete season or year into the future, up to the point where $m = p$. To forecast any period during the second year ahead, the subscript of I is $t - 2p + m$.

Chart 11-11 is an example of the calculations for the constant-level model with multiplicative seasonality. The data include 20 quarterly sales figures in thousands of units of gas-powered barbecue grills, manufactured by Georgia Natural Gas, Inc. The sales cover the years 1983–1985. As might be expected, sales peak in the third (summer) quarter and fall off to a trough in the first quarter of the year.

Chart 11-11 is an example of the calculations for the constant-level model with multiplicative seasonality. The data include 20 quarterly sales figures in thousands of units of gas-powered barbecue grills, manufactured by Georgia Natural Gas, Inc. The sales cover the years 1983–1985. As might be expected, sales peak in the third (summer) quarter and fall off to a trough in the first quarter of the year.

To get started, an index for each period of the year must be specified, and these are recorded in rows −3 through 0 of the chart (the reason for these subscripts will be evident in a moment). A beginning level in deseasonalized terms, S_0, must also be specified and is recorded in row 0. Two smoothing parameters, $h_1 = 0.1$ and $h_2 = 0.01$, are provided.

The first calculation in the chart occurs in row 0, where we obtain the forecast for period 1. This is done by multiplying the index for the first

CHART 11-11. Constant Level Model, Multiplicative Seasonality, $h_1 = 0.10$, $h_3 = 0.01$

Time t	Data X_t	Forecast $\hat{X}_{t-1}(1)$	Error e_t	Deseasonalized Level at End of t $S_t = S_{t-1} + h_1 e_t / I_{t-p}$	Seasonal Index at End of t $I_t = I_{t-p} + h_3 e_t / S_t$	Forecast for $t+1$ $\hat{X}_t(1) = S_t(I_{t-p+1})$
-3					$I_{-3} = 0.6122$	
-2					$I_{-2} = 1.0086$	
-1					$I_{-1} = 1.3303$	
0				$S_0 = 74.3$	$I_0 = 1.0489$	$\hat{X}_0(1) = 74.3(0.6122) = 45.5$
1	53.0	45.5	7.5	$S_1 = 74.3 + 0.1(\ 7.5)/\ 0.6122 = 75.5$	$I_1 = 0.6122 + 0.01(\ 7.5)/75.5 = 0.6132$	$\hat{X}_1(1) = 75.5(1.0086) = 76.2$
2	85.0	76.2	8.8	$S_2 = 75.5 + 0.1(\ 8.8)/\ 1.0086 = 76.4$	$I_2 = 1.0086 + 0.01(\ 8.8)/76.4 = 1.0098$	$\hat{X}_2(1) = 76.4(1.3303) = 101.6$
3	92.0	101.6	-9.6	$S_3 = 76.4 + 0.1(-9.6)/\ 1.3303 = 75.7$	$I_3 = 1.3303 + 0.01(-9.6)/75.7 = 1.3290$	$\hat{X}_3(1) = 75.7(1.0489) = 79.4$
4	78.0	79.4	-1.4	$S_4 = 75.7 + 0.1(-1.4)/\ 1.0489 = 75.5$	$I_4 = 1.0489 + 0.01(-1.4)/75.5 = 1.0487$	$\hat{X}_4(1) = 75.5(0.6132) = 46.3$
5	44.0	46.3	-2.3	$S_5 = 75.5 + 0.1(-2.3)/\ 0.6132 = 75.2$	$I_5 = 0.6132 + 0.01(-2.3)/75.2 = 0.6129$	$\hat{X}_5 = 5.2(1.0098) = 75.9$
6	75.0	75.9	-0.9	$S_6 = 75.2 + 0.1(-0.9)/\ 1.0098 = 75.1$	$I_6 = 1.0098 + 0.01(-0.9)/75.1 = 1.0096$	$\hat{X}_6(1) = 75.1(1.3290) = 99.8$
7	102.0	99.8	2.2	$S_7 = 75.1 + 0.1(\ 2.2)/\ 1.3290 = 75.2$	$I_7 = 1.3290 + 0.01(\ 2.2)/75.2 = 1.3293$	$\hat{X}_7(1) = 75.2(1.0487) = 78.9$
8	60.0	78.9	-18.9	$S_8 = 75.2 + 0.1(-18.9)/\ 1.0487 = 73.4$	$I_8 = 1.0487 + 0.01(-18.9)/73.4 = 1.0461$	$\hat{X}_8(1) = 73.4(0.6129) = 45.0$
9	55.0	45.0	10.0	$S_9 = 73.4 + 0.1(\ 10.0)/\ 0.6129 = 75.1$	$I_9 = 0.6129 + 0.01(\ 10.0)/75.1 = 0.6142$	$\hat{X}_9(1) = 75.1(1.0096) = 75.8$
10	88.0	75.8	12.2	$S_{10} = 75.1 + 0.1(\ 12.2)/\ 1.0096 = 76.3$	$I_{10} = 1.0096 + 0.01(\ 12.2)/76.3 = 1.0112$	$\hat{X}_{10}(1) = 76.3(1.3293) = 101.4$
11	108.0	101.4	6.6	$S_{11} = 76.3 + 0.1(\ 6.6)/\ 1.3293 = 76.8$	$I_{11} = 1.3293 + 0.01(\ 6.6)/76.8 = 1.3302$	$\hat{X}_{11}(1) = 76.8(1.0461) = 80.3$
12	59.0	80.3	-21.3	$S_{12} = 76.8 + 0.1(-21.3)/\ 1.0461 = 74.7$	$I_{12} = 1.0461 + 0.01(-21.3)/74.7 = 1.0433$	$\hat{X}_{12}(1) = 74.7(0.6142) = 45.9$
13		45.9				

190

quarter of the year by the deseasonalized level S_0. At time 0, the subscript of I is $t - p + 1$ or $0 - 4 + 1 = -3$. Thus, I_{-3} is the index for the first quarter and the calculation is

$$\hat{X}_0(1) = S_0 I_{-3} = 74.3(0.6122) = 45.5$$

In period 1, the first step is to compute the error:

$$e_1 = X_1 - \hat{X}_0(1) = 53.0 - 45.5 = 7.5$$

Then we update the level using the deseasonalized error:

$$S_1 = S_0 + h_1 e_1 / I_{-3} = 74.3 + 0.1(7.5)/0.6122 = 75.5$$

Notice the subscript of I, which is $t - p = 1 - 4 = -3$. Now we can update the index for the first quarter:

$$I_1 = I_{-3} + h_3 e_1 / S_1 = 0.6122 + 0.01\ (7.5)/75.5 = 0.6132$$

Again, the ratio of the error to the new level is used to update the index. The forecast for period 2 is the product of the new level and the index for period 2. The time subscript of I that we want is $t - p + 1$ or $1 - 4 + 1 = -2$. Thus we use I_{-2}

$$\hat{X}_1(1) = S_1 I_{-2} = 75.5(1.0086) = 76.2$$

The error in period 2 and the level at the end of 2 are

$$e_2 = X_2 - \hat{X}_1(0) = 85.0 - 76.2 = 8.8$$
$$S_2 = S_1 + h_1 e_2 / I_{-2} = 75.5 + 0.1(8.8)/1.0086 = 76.4$$

The new index for the second quarter is then

$$I_2 = I_{-2} + h_3 e_2 / S_2 = 1.0086 + 0.01(8.8)/76.4 = 1.0098$$

The forecast for period 3 is the product of the new level and the index for period 3.

$$\hat{X}_2(1) = S_2 I_{-1} = 76.4(1.3303) = 101.6$$

The remaining calculations follow in a similar manner. At the end of period 12, the forecasts for the next four quarters can be computed as follows:

$$\hat{X}_{12}(1) = S_{12}I_9 = 74.7(0.6142) = 45.9$$

$$\hat{X}_{12}(2) = S_{12}I_{10} = 74.7(1.0112) = 75.5$$

$$\hat{X}_{12}(3) = S_{12}I_{11} = 74.7(1.3302) = 99.4$$

$$\hat{X}_{12}(4) = S_{12}I_{12} = 74.7(1.0433) = 77.9$$

The same level, S_{12}, is used in all the forecasts, while the seasonal index is incremented according to the forecast horizon. Chart 11-12 plots the forecasts versus the data. At the end of quarter 12, forecasts are made through eight quarters ahead. Since the model parameters are small, the forecasts change very little from the initial values.

Calculations for the other seasonal models are similar to those in this example. Each seasonal model follows directly from the nonseasonal case by adding a smoothed index. To apply the seasonal models, the first step is to compute starting indices. There are many ad hoc methods that could be used, but the safest procedure is to use a decomposition method (see the discussion of decomposition in Chapter 13) to get starting indices. The second step is to compute S_0 and/or T_0. This is done using deseasonalized data. The mean of the deseasonalized data is taken as S_0 in the constant-level model. A linear regression on the deseasonalized data is used to obtain S_0 and T_0 for the trend models. Finally, a grid search is conducted for the smoothing parameters. Usually, the smoothing parameter h_3 for the seasonal

CHART 11-12. Smoothing Seasonal Data

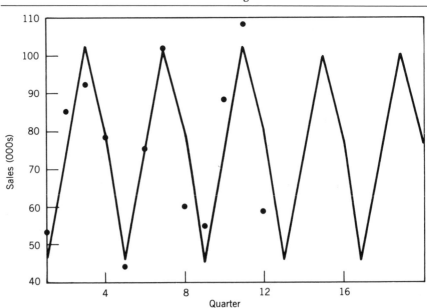

indices is found to be quite small, in the range of 0.01 to 0.10. A floor on h_3 of 0.01 is recommended.

The seasonal versions of the nonlinear trend model may be cumbersome because they require four parameters: h_1, h_2, h_3, and ϕ. These models can be simplified by making h_1 and h_2 a function of a single smoothing parameter, α. The expressions for h_1 and h_2 then are

$$h_1 = \alpha(2 - \alpha), \qquad h_2 = \alpha(\alpha - \phi + 1)$$

As discussed in Gardner and McKenzie,[4] constraining h_1 and h_2 in this manner results in some loss of accuracy but the parameter search is much faster.

MODEL SELECTION

In forecasting systems for large numbers of time series, there may be no alternative to the use of a single model for all series. As discussed previously, for nonseasonal data the nonlinear-trend model is recommended, perhaps constrained to avoid exponential trends. If the data are seasonal, the nonlinear trend with multiplicative seasonality is recommended. The multiplicative seasonal pattern appears to be more robust than the additive.

In smaller applications, there are several alternative approaches to model selection. One is to analyze the autocorrelations of the data to identify an ARIMA (autoregressive integrated moving average) model equivalent to the exponential smoothing model. This approach has limited practical value, because many exponential smoothing models do not have ARIMA equivalents.[3] For example, the linear-trend model with multiplicative seasonality has no ARIMA equivalent. Another idea is to plot the data and choose the most likely forecast profile form Chart 11-1. But graphic analysis is tedious and can be misleading.

A simple, objective way to select a model is to analyze the variances of the differences of the data. In this approach we restrict our attention to three possibilities for trend: constant-level, damped, or linear. Recall that the damped trend is the nonlinear-trend model with ϕ restricted to lie between 0 and 1 in the parameter search.

As an example, consider the data from Chart 11-6. The first step in model selection is to compute the variance of the original data. The result is shown in Chart 11-13. The second step is to compute the variance of the differences of order 1, a new time series composed of the differences between consecutive observations of the original data. If there is a trend in the data, in most cases it should be removed by the operation of differencing. Thus the variance of the differences of order 1 should be smaller than the variance of the original data. If there is no trend, the variance of the differences of order 1 should be larger, as in Chart 11-13. Since these data have a constant mean,

CHART 11-13. Variance Analysis

Time t	Original Data	Difference: Order 1	Difference: Order 2
1	28		
2	27	27 − 28 = −1	
3	34	34 − 27 = 7	7 − (−1) = 8
4	26	26 − 34 = −8	−8 − 7 = −15
5	32	32 − 26 = 6	6 − (−8) = 14
6	33	33 − 32 = 1	1 − 6 = −5
7	27	27 − 33 = −6	−6 − 1 = −7
8	30	30 − 27 = 3	3 − (−6) = 9
9	27	27 − 30 = −3	−3 − 3 = −6
10	34	34 − 27 = 7	7 − (−3) = 10
11	25	25 − 34 = −9	−9 − 7 = −16
12	33	33 − 25 = 8	8 − (−9) = 17
Variance	10.4	36.1	131.3

differencing increases the variance. We conclude that there is no trend and the best model is the constant-level model.

But what if a difference of order 1 should reduce the variance? Is the trend damped or linear? To answer this question, we difference again. Using the series of differences we just computed, we take another difference of order 1. This yields the differences of order 2 (shown in the last column of Chart 11-13). If there is a trend, and the variance of the differences of order 1 is smaller than that of order 2, this indicates a damped trend. If the variance of the differences of order 2 is smaller than that of order 1, the trend is quite strong and we should use the linear-trend model.

What about seasonality? At this point, we know the series that yields the minimum variance: original data, differences of order 1, or differences of order 2. Using the series with minimum variance, we take a seasonal difference, defined as the difference between observations separated by p periods. Then we compute the variance of the seasonal differences and compare it with the earlier results. If the seasonal difference further reduces the variance, the time series is seasonal. It is difficult to determine whether the seasonality is additive or multiplicative. The multiplicative pattern should be used as a matter of course unless there is some evidence that the additive pattern applies. One problem with seasonality is that at least three seasons of data are needed to analyze the differences. If there are fewer data, the decision is subjective.

To sum up, the procedure for model selection is to compute the variances of three times series: the original data, the differences of order 1, and the differences of order 2. The minimum-variance series indicates a constant-level model, a damped trend, or a linear trend. Then we take a seasonal difference of the minimum-variance series. If the variance is further reduced, we use a multiplicative seasonal model, unless there is contrary evidence.

REFERENCES

1. Brown, R. G., *Statistical Forecasting for Inventory Control,* McGraw-Hill, New York, 1959.

2. Brown, R. G., *Smoothing, Forecasting, and Prediction of Discrete Time Series,* Prentice-Hall, Englewood Cliffs, NJ, 1963.

3. Gardner, E. S., "Exponential Smoothing: The State of the Art" (with commentary), *Journal of Forecasting,* vol. 4, 1985, pp. 1–38.

4. Gardner, E. S., and E. McKenzie, "Forecasting Trends in Time Series," *Management Science,* vol. 31, 1985, pp. 1237–1246.

5. Holt, C. C., et al., *Planning Production, Inventories, and Work Force,* Prentice-Hall, Englewood Cliffs, NJ, 1960, chapter 14.

6. Makridakis, S., and M. Hibon, "Forecasting Accuracy and Its Causes: An Empirical Investigation," *Journal of the Royal Statistical Society A,* vol. 142, 1979, pp. 97–145.

7. Makridakis, S., et al., "The Accuracy of Extrapolation (Time Series) Methods: Results of a Forecasting Competition," *Journal of Forecasting,* vol. 1, 1982, pp. 111–153.

8. Winters, P. R., "Forecasting Sales by Exponentially Weighted Moving Averages," *Management Science,* vol. 6, 1960, pp. 324–342.

CHAPTER

12

A PRACTICAL OVERVIEW OF ARIMA MODELS FOR TIME SERIES FORECASTING

DAVID J. PACK
Miami University, Oxford, Ohio

IN THE BEGINNING

Let us define a *time series* as an ordered sequence of values of a variable observed at equally spaced time intervals. Chart 12-1 illustrates the monthly time series of U.S. government three-month treasury bills interest rates from January, 1956, through December, 1978.* Chart 12-2 pictures the highly seasonal monthly time series of the number of enplanements of international airline passengers on U.S. air carriers from January, 1961, through December, 1978.†

Time series forecasting is based on a time series model (implicit or explicit, depending on the approach) that expresses the relationship of current data to historical data. Having seen the enplanements series of Chart 12-2, one might well believe that later values in the series could readily be forecasted solely on the basis of earlier values in the series. In other words, a single series model may be quite adequate. The interest rate series of Chart 12-1 does not look very describable by its own history (graphs may, of course, not reveal all)—perhaps motivating one to seek other time series, such as money supply, that may help, and thus a multiple series model. So

---

* Obtained from the *Survey of Current Business.*
† Obtained from the monthly *Civil Aeronautics Board Air Carrier Traffic Statistics.* This series is similar in behavior to an older series used by Box and Jenkins,[2] but it is not from the same source as their series (no longer available) and is apparently differently defined in some way.

CHART 12-1. Interest Rate Time Series

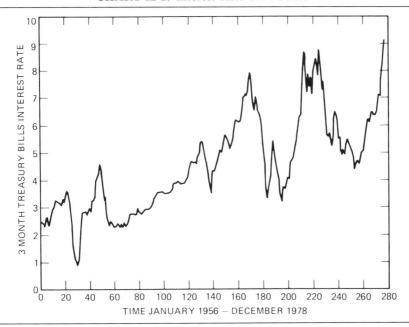

CHART 12-2. Enplanements Time Series

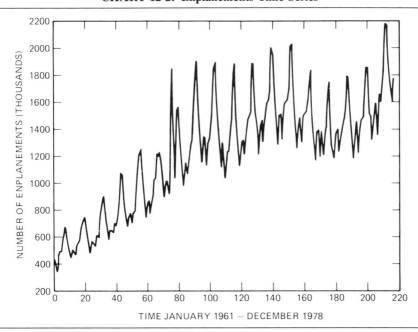

be it. In principle, time series forecasting (or time series models, or time series analysis) need *not* be limited to a single series environment.

The last 15 years have seen significant growth of a time series forecasting philosophy and methodology formulated by Box and Jenkins[2] based on autoregressive integrated moving average (ARIMA) time series models. This chapter first illustrates the single series methodology by describing its application to the forecasting of the interest rate data in Chart 12-1 and the enplanements data in Chart 12-2. In both cases, 21 months of data from January, 1979, through September, 1980, have been held in reserve for forecast evaluation. The following commentary then summarizes the Box–Jenkins philosophy and the ARIMA model structure and gives particular emphasis to

Practical aspects of application

Forecast interpretation, strengths, weaknesses

Comparison with other time series forecasting approaches

The chapter concludes with a brief but strong emphasis on the fact that both the Box–Jenkins philosophy and ARIMA models extend into the multiple series domain. In terms of Chart 12-3, you need not limit your time series forecasting perspective for forecasting the variable Z_1 at time t to the first row of available data, but may employ other variables $Z_2, Z_3, \ldots$ at times $t, t - 1, t - 2, \ldots$. Recent research has provided practical (admittedly still developing) methodologies for building true multiple series ARIMA models—multiple equation models structurally comparable to the typical econometric model—that produce simultaneous forecasts of multiple time series. One can conceive of a long-term ideal in the forecasting discipline where econometric forecasting, which has focused rather heavily on the first column (or two) of available data in Chart 12-3, and time series forecasting, which has focused rather heavily on the first row of available data in Chart 12-3, will merge to become one.

CHART 12-3. Available Data Matrix

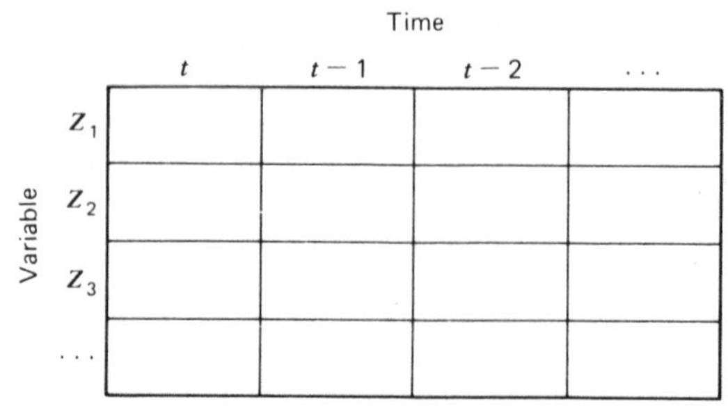

THE INTEREST RATES EXAMPLE

What is the best model (i.e., description) of the relationship of a value of the three-month treasury bills interest rate to the values before it? The philosophy of Box and Jenkins says that this model leads immediately to the logical forecasts of future rates, given that information is limited to the forecast series' history. It further says that this model should be built up with the aid of simple summary statistics from the data on hand, rather than be simply assumed on the basis of abstract theory, or arrived at via relatively uninformed trial and error.

One set of summary statistics is the observed data's autocorrelation function—simply the correlation of the data with itself at time lags 1, 2, 3, ... Chart 12-4 shows the autocorrelation function for lags 1 through 36 of the logarithm* of the 276 observed interest rates in Chart 12-2. Thus, .97 is the correlation between the value at time t, say Z_t, and the value at time $t - 1$, say Z_{t-1}, calculated over pairs of times (2, 1), (3, 2), . . . , exactly as one would calculate the correlation of two distinct variables X and Y.

The crux of the Box and Jenkins methodology is to be able to identify patterns in summary statistics such as those in Chart 12-4 as being indicative of a particular model. The analysis in this case proceeds as follows:

Chart 12-4 suggests the time series is nonstationary (has no mean), and any model should focus on the first difference series $W_t = Z_t - Z_{t-1}$.

Similar summary statistics for the first difference series given in Chart 12-5 suggest a regression of W_t on some previous W's , although the exact lags to be used are not clearly revealed (combinations of 1 and 2, or 1 and 6, are most likely).

Partial autocorrelations for the first difference series (essentially the estimated coefficients of W_{t-k} in regressions of W_t on $W_{t-1}, . . . , W_{t-k}$ for lags $k = 1, 2, . . .$) given in Chart 12-6 suggest a regression of W_t on W_{t-1} followed by (compounded by, or multiplied by) a regression of lag 6.

The identified model may be written in terms of W_t as

$$W_t - \phi_1 W_{t-1} - \phi_6' W_{t-6} + \phi_6' \phi_1 W_{t-7} = a_t$$

an autoregression of W_t on W_{t-1}, W_{t-6}, and W_{t-7} involving parameters ϕ_1 and ϕ_6'. The a_t represents the model error term in period t, assumed to follow

---

* Note that the interest rate data in Chart 12-1 evidence increasing variability with increasing level—the typical motivation for using logarithms. Actually, the logarithmic transformation has little impact on the analysis in this case, as was seen through use of the Box–Cox choice of transformation procedure in Pack's computer program (see footnote on page 208).

CHART 12-4. Interest Rates Autocorrelations

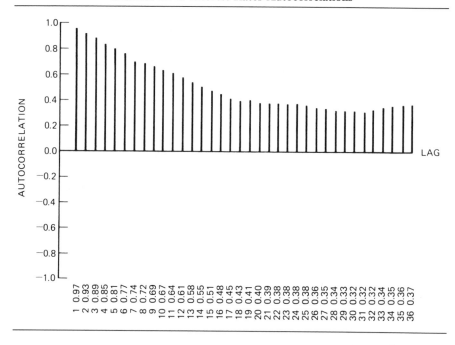

CHART 12-5. Differenced Rates Autocorrelations

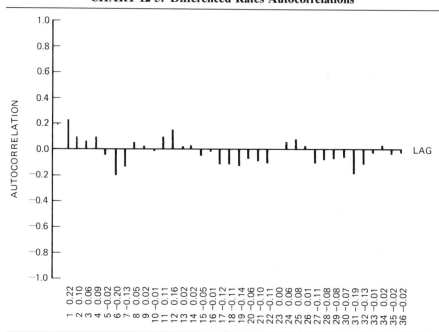

200

CHART 12-6. Differenced Rates Partial Autocorrelations

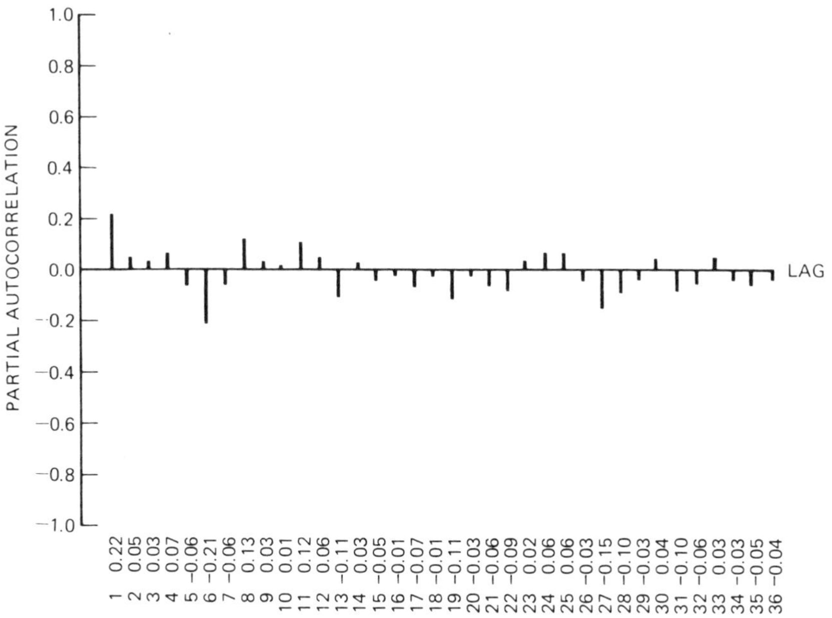

the usual error term assumptions of zero mean, independence between observations, and so on.

Estimation of the parameters ϕ_1 and ϕ_6' is the next task, and it is accomplished by general-purpose minimization of squared error techniques. Given the parameter estimates, an estimated set of errors (a_t's) can be calculated. The Box–Jenkins philosophy strongly emphasizes a lengthy examination of these estimated errors, and this examination is termed *diagnostic checking*. One asks if the errors appear to be unrelated to each other (i.e., independent), with an average value of zero, constant absolute size regardless of time, and so on. A primary tool is the determination of the autocorrelation function of the estimated errors, in the same spirit as Charts 12-4 and 12-5, but it is hoped in this case containing patternless correlation that is not significantly different from zero. Diagnostic check failures lead iteratively to reidentification, reestimation, and rechecking.

An estimated model that has passed all diagnostic checks is easily turned into a forecasting model. In the estimated interest rates model, the rate at time t is described by

$$Z_t = 1.36Z_{t-1} - 0.36Z_{t-2} + 0.24Z_{t-6} - 0.3264Z_{t-7} + 0.0864Z_{t-8} + a_t$$

using the estimated $\hat{\phi}_1$ of 0.36 and the estimated $\hat{\phi}_6'$ of -0.24. Forecasts for $t = 277, 278, \ldots$, follow by recursive application of this equation, using observed Z's on the right when subscripts are 276 or less, previously calculated forecasts for Z's on the right when subscripts are 277 or more, and the expected value zero for a_t in all cases, since it will always represent future error.

Forecasts for January, 1979, through September, 1980, are shown against the actual three-month treasury bills interest rates in Chart 12-7 (both unlogged). The results are, of course, a disaster! There is no need to calculate mean squared errors here to confirm failure! What happened to the interest rate during this period of time *was unprecedented in its history.* Unfortunately, this history was the information on which we based the forecasts.

THE ENPLANEMENTS EXAMPLE

The international airline passenger enplanements data of Chart 12-2 present a very optimistic picture for the time series forecaster in that the time series has followed a highly seasonal historical precedent reasonably faithfully for 216 months.

Working with the logarithms of the data,* we can identify a model through the autocorrelation function summary statistics, as follows:

Chart 12-8, like Chart 12-4, suggests that one change focus from the nonstationary Z_t values to the what is hoped to be a stationary first difference $W_t = Z_t - Z_{t-1}$.

The autocorrelation function for the W_t series in Chart 12-9 implies a further nonstationarity at a 12-period lag, suggesting one focus on the further difference $W_t - W_{t-12}$, or, redefining W_t, $W_t = Z_t - Z_{t-1} - Z_{t-12} + Z_{t-13}$.

The autocorrelation function for the latest W_t series in Chart 12-10 contains isolated correlations at lags 1 and 12. This correlation may be most efficiently represented in a model by suggesting that, if W_t is affected by random error a_t, W_t also contains parts of the previous errors a_{t-1} and a_{t-12}.

One experienced with the methodology would probably go slightly beyond this discussion and identify the model in terms of W_t as

$$W_t = a_t - \theta_1 a_{t-1} - \theta'_{12} a_{t-12} + \theta_1 \theta'_{12} a_{t-13}$$

---

* Logarithms are again introduced, following the line of discussion in the previous footnote. In the case of the enplanements data, the Box–Cox choice of transformation procedure strongly predisposes to use of the logarithmic transformation over the original metric.

CHART 12-7. Forecast (Solid) Versus Actual (Dashed)

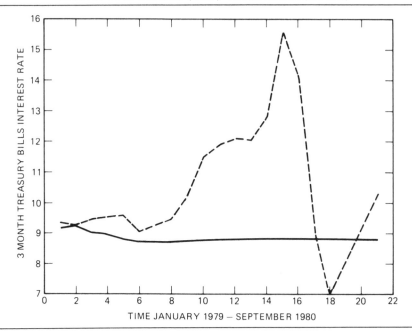

CHART 12-8. Enplanements Autocorrelations

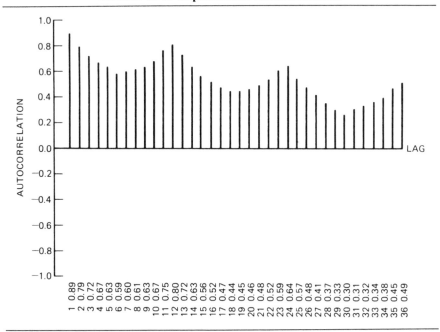

CHART 12-9. Differenced Enplanements Autocorrelations

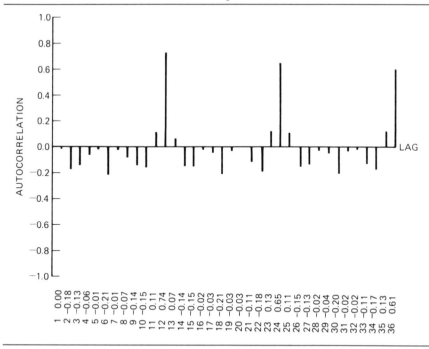

CHART 12-10. Further Differenced Enplanements Autocorrelations

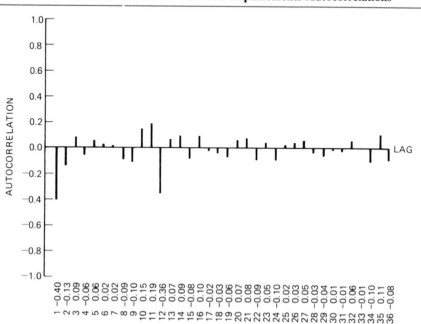

CHART 12-11. Forecast (Solid) Versus Actual (Dashed)

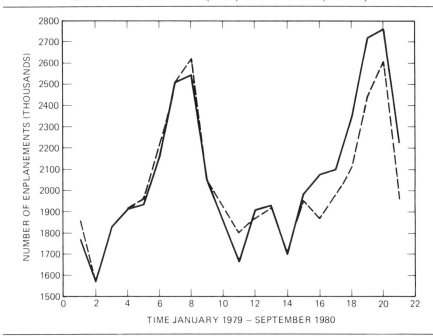

TIME JANUARY 1979 – SEPTEMBER 1980

that is, basically using a product of lag 1 and lag 12 terms with parameters θ_1 and θ_{12}' rather than a simple addition.* The series of W_t's described is loosely seen to be a "moving average" of the random errors.

Having estimated the parameters θ_1 and θ_{12}' in the identified model, having diagnostically checked the implied random errors via their autocorrelation function, and so on, and having found no problems, we see that the identified model becomes the forecasting model. The number of enplaned passengers in month t (logged) is described by

$$Z_t = Z_{t-1} + Z_{t-12} - Z_{t-13} + a_t - 0.57a_{t-1} - 0.96a_{t-12} + 0.5472a_{t-13}$$

using the estimated $\hat{\theta}_1$ of 0.57 and the estimated $\hat{\theta}_{12}'$ of 0.96.

Forecasts for January, 1979, through September, 1980, follow from the forecasting model when $t = 217, 218, \ldots, 237$, as described in the previous example (adding the fact that a's on the right are replaced by calculated errors from the estimation process when the subscripts are 216 or less). Chart 12-11 graphs these forecasts and the actual enplanements (both un-

---

* The product form is known to produce theoretical autocorrelations for W_t at lags 1, 11, 12, and 13, with the lag 11 and 13 autocorrelations being equal to the product of the lag 1 and 12 autocorrelations. Chart 12-10 agrees reasonably well with this theoretical pattern.

CHART 12-12. Steps in the Iterative Approach to Model Building

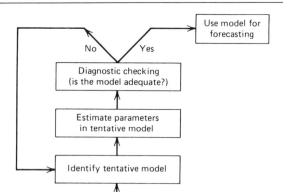

logged). In this case the strong historical precedent continued, and the time series forecasts are quite successful. The absolute percent error in the forecasts is 2% over the first 12 months and 4% over the entire 21-month span.

PHILOSOPHY AND STRUCTURE

The Box–Jenkins philosophy of model building for time series forecasting has been demonstrated through the interest rates and enplanements examples. This philosophy is expressed generally in Chart 12-12*:

Identify a tentative model using summary statistics (autocorrelations, partial autocorrelations) calculated from available data.

Estimate parameters in the tentative model via minimization of squared error.

Diagnostically check the estimated errors (via their autocorrelation function, etc.). Reidentify, reestimate, and recheck when checks indicate a problem. When the model is adequate, proceed to forecasting.

Chart 12-12 further suggests that the philosophy of model building must be supported by a structure of potential models. Box and Jenkins have employed the general class of autoregressive integrated moving average (ARIMA) models in the building of a forecasting model for a single time

* Taken from Box and Jenkins.[2]

series variable. The examples of the previous sections have suggested the three major elements of the ARIMA model:

If the original times series, represented by Z_t in period t, is nonstationary, it may be differenced, say d times, to obtain a new time series, say W_t in period t. This is the integrated element—Z_t may be recreated from W_t by a process of "integration" (actually summation is our discrete environment).

The W series (if Z was stationary, define W as the deviation of Z from a mean) value at period t may be autoregressed on W_{t-1}, W_{t-2}, . . . , W_{t-p}, that is, have a pth order autoregressive element.

The W series value at period t may be a moving average of random errors a_t, a_{t-1}, . . . , a_{t-q}, that is, have a qth order moving average element.

If all three elements are simultaneously present, the model would then be expressed as

$$W_t - \phi_1 W_{t-1} - \cdots - \phi_p W_{t-p} = a_t - \theta_1 a_{t-1} - \cdots - \theta_q a_{t-q}$$

where the ϕ_j represent autoregressive parameters and the θ_j represent moving average parameters. This is the ARIMA (p, d, q) model.

The structure represented by the previous equation is readily expanded, or limited, in some meaningful ways that should be noted briefly:

Expanded to deal fully with seasonal behavior, essentially by saying the as from the previous equation would follow their own ARIMA (sp', sd', sq') model, with s representing the basic seasonality. The interest rates and enplanements examples both involved this expansion [the former ARIMA $(6, 0, 0)$ where $s = 6$, and the later ARIMA $(0, 12, 12)$ where $s = 12$].

Expanded to imply deterministic trend by insertion of a constant term on the right.

Limited to purely autoregressive models (i.e., $q = 0$). Many people find moving average models nonintuitive, and they can in principle always be reexpressed in a purely autoregressive form. This reexpression, however, often requires additional parameters. Box and Jenkins employ the moving average form because their philosophy emphasizes minimizing the number of model parameters (i.e., seeking parsimony).

PRACTICAL ASPECTS OF APPLICATION

The practical problem of applying the time series forecasting approach discussed in this chapter focuses on the suggestion that the user should itera-

**CHART 12-13. Practical Requirements for the ARIMA Model Building Time
Series Forecasting Approach**

ARIMA model building computer software	M.S. statistician or a mathematical equal
50 observations per series minimum; 100 observations desirable	100 or fewer separate series to forecast in a short period

tively build up a forecasting model based on substantial user interpretation of summary statistics from the data—particularly autocorrelation and partial autocorrelation functions like those in Charts 12-4 through 12-6 and Charts 12-8 through 12-10.

The practical requirements imposed by ARIMA model building are summarized in Chart 12-13—with certain qualifications. First, it is perhaps obvious that this forecasting approach cannot be undertaken without appropriate computer software. Such software is widely available for in-house installation, either as a separate package* or as a component of the latest versions of the major statistical packages (BMDP, SAS, SPSS). Computationally, this time series forecasting approach is more demanding than a number of alternatives, but the demands are very ordinary in terms of today's computers and the broad range of mathematical demands made of these computers.

The ARIMA model-building requirement that should be emphasized most strongly is that of having an observed time series of 50 or more observations. Thus, one will rarely use the approach on yearly data—demanding instead observations on at least a quarterly basis. This requirement is motivated by the identification process (*not* the estimation process, where something less would suffice)—getting estimates of autocorrelations and partial autocorrelations of sufficient quality to maintain the integrity of patterns such as those in Charts 12-4, 12-5, 12-6, 12-8, 12-9, and 12-10.

What need one require of the actual forecaster as an individual analyst? Subjectivity abounds in answering this question, but it is clear that this time series forecasting approach does contain a need for the analyst's interpretation of a number of calculated statistics, focusing on, but not limited to, autocorrelations and partial autocorrelations. Certainly the approach is not

---

* David J. Pack, "A Computer Program for the Analysis of Time Series Models Using the Box–Jenkins Philosophy," available through Automatic Forecasting Systems, P.O. Box 563, Hatboro, PA 19040 (May, 1978). This computer program has capabilities in multiple series transfer function modeling and intervention modeling, which are discussed later in the chapter, as well as in single series modeling. Automatic Forecasting Systems also sells its own personal computer (PC) software for ARIMA model building.

for the mathematically naive. Neither does it require a Ph.D. statistician. The description in Chart 12-13 serves as a good compromise.

Another practical concern is for the manager or organization that must produce forecasts for numerous products, regions, and so on in a short period of time. ARIMA model building properly done does take time. It is not realistic to think that one can apply the methodology fully to hundreds of time series in a short period of time—unless the series are really very similar (i.e., follow the same ARIMA model).

There is an important qualification to be added to the requirements suggested by the last two paragraphs (the right side of Chart 12-13), beyond the subjectivity already implied. In principle, the process of identification, that is, interpretation of autocorrelation and partial autocorrelation functions, can be turned over to the computer, lessening the demands for the analyst's training and time. "Automatic" modeling computer software internalizing the identification process does exist.* While this "checking your brains at the door and letting the computer do it" philosophy is strongly disavowed by Box and Jenkins, it has clear practical value for the manager or organization that hopes to produce forecasts for numerous *similar* products, regions, and so on in a short period of time.

Finally, the practical manager is wisely cautioned to be sure that he or she sees the trees as well as the forest in this time series forecasting approach. The initial graphing and calculation of autocorrelation and partial autocorrelation summaries of available time series data are simple and informative— whether or not followed by the full-blown ARIMA model-building effort. Simply structured autocorrelation might suggest a less sophisticated time series forecasting approach to a manager worried about the complexities of ARIMA model building. Total lack of autocorrelation implies that no time series forecasting approach (at least not a single series approach) will produce useful forecasts, and thus it directs the forecaster to other methods.

FORECAST INTERPRETATION, STRENGTHS, AND WEAKNESSES

How does one interpret the time series forecasts produced by the ARIMA model-building approach? Let us discuss the forecasts and the models that produced them, with the understanding that, until otherwise noted, the discussion concerns a series of forecasts like those in Charts 12-7 and 12-11, a series of forecasts from *one* time origin that involves no known data beyond that time origin.

The interest rates forecasting model suggested that

$$Z_t = 1.36Z_{t-1} - 0.36Z_{t-2} + 0.24Z_{t-6} - 0.3264Z_{t-7} + 0.0864Z_{t-8} + a_t$$

* Available from David P. Reilly, Automatic Forecasting Systems, P.O. Box 563, Hatboro, PA 19040.

Mathematically, the forecasted value at time t is strongly related to the forecast (or observed) value at time $t - 1$, mildly related to values at times $t - 2$, $t - 6$, and $t - 7$, and weakly related to the value at time $t - 8$. The autoregressions present in this model, a "regular" autoregression through the estimated $\hat{\phi}_1 = 0.36$ and a "seasonal" autoregression through the estimated $\hat{\phi}_6' = -0.24$, are both relatively weak.* Thus, the model is dominated by the first difference $W_t = Z_t - Z_{t-1}$, and the primary influence in the time t value is the time $t - 1$ value. Chart 12-7 showed one property of a first difference forecasting model—the forecasts aproach a constant level for longer lead times. This pattern obviously bears little resemblance to the observed interest rate behavior.

The enplanements forecasting model described the number of enplanements in period t as

$$Z_t = Z_{t-1} + Z_{t-12} - Z_{t-13} + a_t - 0.57a_{t-1} - 0.96a_{t-12} + 0.5472a_{t-13}$$

This model includes an extremely strong monthly seasonal component through two elements—differencing between the same month in consecutive years, and the strong seasonal moving average element represented by the estimated $\hat{\theta}_{12}' = 0.96$. The first 13 forecasts from a given time origin are influenced by one or more of the random error terms on the right. Thereafter, one can see (by subtracting Z_{t-12} from both sides) that this month's change from last year is forecast to be the same as last month's change from last year. In essence, each month is forecast by a trend line with an intercept equal to the first forecast of that month and a slope that is the same for all months equal to the difference between the 13-period-ahead forecast and the one-period-ahead forecast. As demonstrated in Chart 12-11, this pattern matches the observed enplanements behavior very closely.

The forecast models for ARIMA model time series forecasting should not be interpreted as saying that observations at time t are *caused by* previous observations and/or random errors. The time series history serves as a surrogate for exogenous variables that one might include in a model to represent a cause for changes in the forecast variable (cause can never really be proven in an uncontrolled environment). The potential strength of this removal of exogenous variables is that no forecasts are required for these variables to produce a forecast for the one variable of interest. The weaknesses of this removal are potentially that (1) the surrogate simply contains little or no information and (2) the exogenous variable patterns change so that the time series history is no longer the meaningful surrogate it might once have been. The interest rate forecasts certainly suffer the first weakness, and there is evidence that they suffer the second weakness as well. On the other hand, the enplanements forecasts are derived from a strong and unchanging surrogate.

---

* Each autoregressive parameter in the model is restricted to be less than 1 in absolute value to guarantee a stationary system. Absolute values of the estimated parameters close to 1 would be indicative of strong autoregression.

ARIMA model time series forecasting is particularly suited to short-term forecasting and to forecasting highly seasonal variables. The utilization of quarterly or more frequent observations in model building tends to dictate the short-term nature of the approach. Even in the interest rates example, if one focused on one- or two-month lead times the forecasts would be reasonably good (if uninteresting because they were not too different from the last observation). The enplanements example was highly seasonal. The ARIMA approach captures not only what the eye sees—the 12-month cyclical upward trend of Chart 12-2 described by $Z_t = Z_{t-1} + Z_{t-12} - Z_{t-13}$—but the potential for momentary change in the trend also present in Chart 12-2 and allowed for in the model by the moving average elements. Almost by definition, the surrogate (time series history) contains substantial information in highly seasonal situations and may allow us to extend the "short term" to three or four years.

A final set of strengths and weaknesses focuses on the fact that this time series forecasting approach is based on a statistical model. Assuming the estimated model is the true model, one is readily led to the following:

A strength in one's ability to calculate justifiable ranges within which the observed values will fall with a particular certainty (i.e., confidence limits). These limits are presumably conservative in that the estimated model is assumed to be the true model.

A weakness in the fact that forecast errors are often significantly correlated, usually in the positive direction.* Thus, one sees the pattern of Chart 12-11 where the forecasts go above (below) the observations and stay above (below) them for a sequence of lead times (lead times 15–21 in Chart 12-11).

A strength in one's ability to easily and meaningfully update the original forecasts when one or more new observations become available. New observations give information on random errors (as) that were originally set equal to their expected value of zero. Chart 12-14 shows the September, 1980, enplanements forecast made based on data through December, 1978, and the sequence of *updated* forecasts as each new month of data becomes available. There is little change for about 12 months. Then the updates begin to trend down toward the finally observed value.

COMPARISON WITH OTHER TIME SERIES FORECASTING APPROACHES

The previous section's discussion of ARIMA model time series forecasts' interpretation, strengths, and weaknesses should provide some indirect

---

* Box and Jenkins[2] discussed correlation of forecast errors in forecasts of various lead times from the same time origin. See p. 129 and pp. 159–160.

CHART 12-14. Updated Forecasts of September 1980 Enplanements

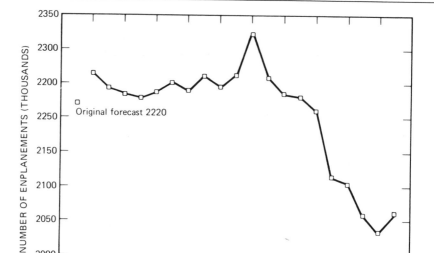

guidance in the choice of a forecasting methodology. This choice would be further aided by more direct general comparisons of the ARIMA model approach with other specific approaches. This section provides brief general comparisons with a few general time series forecasting approaches.

Exponential Smoothing, Census II Method, and Other Approaches

There are innumerable time series forecasting approaches, simple exponential smoothing and the census II method* being only two of the more common ones, in which forecasts are produced by exactly the same sequence of mathematical steps on *every* forecasting problem. This is equivalent to the implicit assumption of the *same* "model" (explicit models are usually ignored in these approaches) for *all* forecasting problems irrespective of the evidence in the data. The very appealing logic of the ARIMA approach model identification—that the model should be built up with the aid of simple summary statistics from the data on hand—is ignored in all of these approaches.

* See the book by Makridakis and Wheelwright.[9] It contains summaries of the two methods explicitly mentioned and many others of the same spirit in terms of the discussion at this point.

Function of Time

Expressing observations as functions of time, such as linear trends, polynomials, sine and cosine curves, and so on, is an often-employed time series forecasting approach. Some have termed such a model "deterministic." While from one viewpoint the model can still be called "stochastic" (i.e., it includes an error term), the forecasts produced by the model are deterministic in nature as compared with the adaptable ARIMA model forecasts.

Consider the enplanements example. The original ARIMA model forecasts of Chart 12-11 follow the pattern diagrammed by solid lines in Chart 12-15—individual month trend lines with common slope but individual intercepts. One or more new observations lead to updated forecasts (as discussed at the end of the previous section), which follow a similar overall pattern but have a potentially different common slope and a potentially different set of individual month intercepts—as suggested by the dotted lines in Chart 12-15. Alternatively, if enplanements were forecast by some sine–cosine curve combination, new observations could not change the forecasts unless one elected to totally reestimate the curve parameters (and even this change would typically be very small in the face of very much historical data).

Regression Analysis

One frequently encounters applications of regression analysis to time series forecasting problems. While regression analysis as usually defined involves two or more variables, and thus is not comparable with the ARIMA model approach as discussed to this point in an overall sense, there is one point of contrast that must be emphasized here.

The ARIMA model approach is directed toward fully dealing with any

CHART 12-15. Original and Updated Enplanements Forecast Pattern

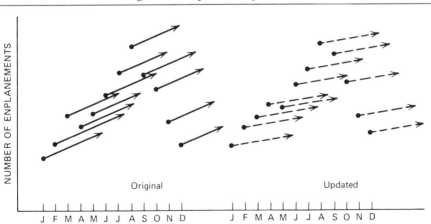

pattern of autocorrelation (i.e., dependence) that may exist in a set of time series observations. Regression analysis in its raw form does *not* permit *any* dependence between observations of the dependent variable—a dependence that usually exists in time series observations. This dependence leads to autocorrelated errors. Particular procedures, such as applying differencing or autoregression to the observations, have been used to deal with particular autocorrelation patterns. However, general patterns of observation dependence are not well dealt with in a regression analysis framework.*

MULTIPLE SERIES ARIMA MODELS FOR TIME SERIES FORECASTING

The principle emphasis of time series forecasting is on the reasoned utilization of time lagged data in the forecasting process. Those who practice time series forecasting have no inherent desire to deal with a single series, and certainly they do not believe that they can always produce a successful forecast in a single series environment.

Just as the discipline of regression analysis developed over the years through a logical progression of research from simple regression to multiple regression to dummy variables to nonlinear forms to simultaneous linear relationships to today's complex econometric models, so is the discipline of time series analysis and forecasting developing. Speaking of ARIMA model building specifically, published practical methodology dates from 1970—the publication date for the Box–Jenkins time series analysis book.[2] Logically, published applied research in the 1970s focused primarily on single series applications. Several additional books have limited themselves to single series methodology.[1,10,12] However, research in the late 1970s and early 1980s has produced significant practical methodology beyond the single series case, and continued research is constantly expanding the ARIMA model building scope.

ARIMA models for time series forecasting beyond the single series model exist under the following labels:

Transfer function models

Intervention models

Calendar variation models

Multiple time series models

---

* There are those who suggest doing a full ARIMA model analysis on the residuals of the raw form regression analysis. (See Pindyck and Rubinfeld.[13]) This would in principle speak to the problem under discussion but it leaves other problems not under discussion here untouched (choice of time lags on independent variables).

While all four of these models involve "multiple" time series, that is, more than one time series, note that the title "multiple time series models" is reserved for a particular model form that is in fact a generalization of the other three forms.

Transfer function models are comparable to simple or multiple regression models in that the model focuses on one dependent (or endogenous, or output) time series to be forecast as a function of one or more independent (or exogenous, or input) time series. The dependent time series' history may naturally also play a part in the forecast. The model form, however, presumes that the dependent series does not influence subsequent values of the independent series—thus permitting a single equation representation. The 1970 Box–Jenkins book provided practical methodology for the one input case. This methodology follows the identification, estimation, and diagnostic checking philosophy of Chart 12-12. Identification must logically focus on cross correlation of series with each other, care being exercised to adjust what is cross correlated to avoid confusion of within-series dependence and between-series dependence. A tutorial on the methodology[11] may be observed as applied to a sales-advertising relationship in an article by Helmer and Johansson.[3]

Intervention models allow one to represent the effects of identifiable isolated events such as strikes, wars, boycotts, price changes, and so on within the overall ARIMA model structure. Could the slope changes in the enplanements data of Chart 12-2 be associated with airline industry decisions? Could some of the interest rate movements of Chart 12-1 be associated with specific monetary policy decisions? The event is represented by a "dummy" time series assuming 0–1 values corresponding to times of nonoccurrence or occurrence of the event. Structurally, the model is a transfer function model with a dummy input series. The single series model identification, estimation, and diagnostic checking methodology is still employed in principle. However, model identification is complicated in proportion to the magnitude of the effects of events represented, and identification and representation of specific event effects in the model largely rest on graphic or theoretical hypotheses. Wichern and Jones[15] provided a practical illustration in their assessment of the impact of the American Dental Association's 1960 endorsement of Crest toothpaste on the Crest toothpaste market share.

Calendar variation models deal particularly with monthly time series and the possible influence of calendar construction on the recorded monthly values. The dates of holidays such as Easter change from year to year. Many monthly series are affected by the number of working days, or even the number of individual days of the week. These calendar variation effects can significantly impact forecast accuracy. Such effects may be estimated and then extrapolated during forecasting using a model that is structurally like a transfer function model, in which the input series summarize calendar characteristics (for example, number of Mondays, number of Tuesdays, . . .).

Hillmer[5] provided an example of calendar variation model development on a monthly time series of telephone disconnections.

It should be noted that extension of the Box–Jenkins philosophy of model identification through the use of one or another correlation function derived from the data encounters some difficulty in the areas of multiple input transfer function, intervention, and calendar variation models. In all of these models is a presumption of the presence of two or more possibly important elements in the dependent time series to be forecast. These elements may all significantly impact the chosen correlation functions, and thus often the correlation functions cannot accurately reflect the individual nature of the different elements. Liu and Hanssens[7] have developed a procedure for identification that deemphasizes correlation analysis as an identification device, using instead a preliminary least squares estimation form of identification. This identification procedure is applicable to intervention and calendar variation models as well as to the multiple input transfer function model discussed in the cited reference, because the first two models are just special cases of the last model. The procedure is available as one option in Liu and Hudak's[8] ARIMA time series modeling computer software.

Multiple series models that involve a simultaneous equation structure are placed under the "multiple time series model" label. Suppose, for example, that having seen the failure of the single series interest rate model in this chapter, one determined that a money supply time series might help. Further presume that one wanted the ARIMA model to permit each series' past behavior to affect the other series, that is, to treat both series as dependent (or endogenous, or output). If Z_1 and Z_2 represent the two series, with W_1 and W_2 being respective stationary differences, a model allowing this joint dependence representing an expansion of a single series model with an autoregressive element of order 1 (i.e., $p = 1$) would look like

$$W_{1t} = \phi_{11} W_{1,t-1} + \phi_{12} W_{2,t-1} + a_{1t}$$
$$W_{2t} = \phi_{21} W_{1,t-1} + \phi_{22} W_{2,t-1} + a_{2t}$$

These equations clearly express the dependence of current values of each series on past values of the other series (as well as its own past values) using the arbitrarily assumed order 1 autoregressive element. If $\phi_{12} = 0$ or $\phi_{21} = 0$, there is a one-directional relationship between the two series; this special case has been discussed under the label "transfer function model."

Extending the class of ARIMA models into the simultaneous equation domain is much easier than extending the philosophy of identification, estimation, and diagnostic checking into that domain. While the latter extensions are still active research subjects, two practical methodologies do exist. Jenkins illustrated his methodology in a 1979 book[6] that contains two extensive examples as part of a sequence of examples of single series, transfer function, intervention, and multiple time series model building. Tiao and Box illustrated their methodology in a 1981 article[14] containing two interesting examples. Heyse and Wei[4] gave a further demonstration in a case study of advertising–sales relationships. The Tiao–Box methodology is fully incorporated in computer software by Liu and Hudak.[8] The Jenkins methodology and the Tiao–Box methodology differ most clearly in what they elect to cross correlate during the identification stage of the analysis.

CONCLUSION

In conclusion, let us simply and briefly enumerate the major highlights of our practical overview of ARIMA models for time series forecasting:

The single series methodology was seen to work well on one example and poorly on another. No one methodology always works.

ARIMA model building for time series forecasting is supported by a very logical philosophy and structure. It possesses a degree of generality and a potential beyond that of many other time series forecasting approaches— but it can look just as bad as much simpler approaches when applied to informationless time series.

The ARIMA model has certain practical requirements (Chart 12-13).

The approach allows simple and informative graphing of time series data, and calculation of their autocorrelation and partial autocorrelation summaries—whether or not a full-blown ARIMA modeling effort is to follow.

ARIMA model time series forecasting is particularly suited to short-term forecasting and to forecasting highly seasonal variables.

Because the approach is based on an explicit statistical model, one can determine justifiable confidence limits for forecasts, and the forecasts are readily adapted to new data; on the same basis, one knows that forecasts for various lead times from the same time origin are correlated.

The absence of exogenous variables in the single series methodology is a weakness in that patterns in these variables may never have been captured in the surrogate history, or may change at some point. It is also a strength because these exogenous variables do not have to be forecast themselves.

ARIMA models are not limited to a single series horizon (nor is time series forecasting). Practical methodology exists for building transfer function, intervention, calendar variation, and full multiple time series models.

REFERENCES

1. Anderson, Oliver D., *Time Series Analysis and Forecasting—The Box–Jenkins Approach*, Butterworth, London, 1975.

2. Box, George E. P., and Gwilym M. Jenkins, *Time Series Analysis, Forecasting and Control,* Holden-Day, San Francisco, 1970.

3. Helmer, Richard M., and Johny K. Johansson, "An Exposition of the Box–Jenkins Transfer Function Analysis with Application to the Advertising-Sales Relationship," *Journal of Marketing Research,* vol. 14, May 1977, pp. 227–239.

4. Heyse, Joseph F., and William W. S. Wei, "Modelling the Advertising–Sales Relationship Through Use of Multiple Time Series Techniques," *Journal of Forecasting,* vol. 4, April–June 1985, pp. 165–181.

5. Hillmer, Steven C., "Forecasting Time Series with Trading Day Variation," *Journal of Forecasting,* vol. 1, October–December 1982, pp. 385–395.

6. Jenkins, Gwilym M., *Practical Experiences with Modeling and Forecasting Time Series,* Gwilym Jenkins & Partners (Overseas) Ltd., St. Helier, Jersey, Channel Islands, 1979.

7. Liu, Lon-Mu, and Dominique M. Hanssens, "Identification of Multiple Input Transfer Function Models," *Communications in Statistics—Theory and Methods,* vol. 11, no. 3, 1982, pp. 297–314.

8. Liu, Lon-Mu, and Gregory B. Hudak, *The SCA Statistical System, Version III,* Scientific Computing Associates, DeKalb, IL, 1985.

9. Makridakis, Spyros, and Steven C. Wheelwright, *Forecasting Methods and Applications,* John Wiley, New York, 1978.

10. Nelson, Charles R., *Applied Time Series Analysis for Managerial Forecasting,* Holden-Day, San Francisco, 1973.

11. Pack, David J., "Revealing Time Series Interrelationships," *Decision Sciences,* vol. 8, April 1977, pp. 377–402.

12. Pankratz, Alan, *Forecasting with Univariate Box–Jenkins Models,* John Wiley, New York, 1983.

13. Pindyck, R. S., and D. L. Rubinfeld, *Econometric Models and Economic Forecasts,* McGraw-Hill, New York, 1976.

14. Tiao, George C., and George E. P. Box, "Modeling Multiple Time Series with Applications," *Journal of the American Statistical Association,* vol. 76, December 1981, pp. 802–816.

15. Wichern, Dean W., and Richard H. Jones, "Assessing the Impact of Market Disturbances Using Intervention Analysis," *Management Science,* vol. 24, November 1977, pp. 329–337.

CHAPTER

13

DECOMPOSITION METHODS FOR MEDIUM-TERM PLANNING AND BUDGETING

BERNARD E. MAJANI

Director of Corporate Planning
Aussedat-Rey, Villacoublay,
France

INTRODUCTION

Decomposition methods represent the oldest and most commonly used approach to forecasting. They employ simple mathematical formulas to separate the four components of a time series: seasonality, cycle, trend, and randomness. Removing seasonality and randomness gives the trend-cycle curve which, in my opinion, is the most important element in business forecasting. The popularity of the methods is reflected in the fact that they are widely used in the business world today.

The trend-cycle curve not only allows the present situation to be visualized within a historical perspective, but it also extends to the user the facility of incorporating his or her own knowledge and intuition into the formulation of a forecast. Other methods may in fact be more accurate; but they tend not to be used by management because their results are difficult to interpret and integrate into the decision-making process.

Several publications[1-6] describe in detail the various methods available to decompose a time series. The classical decomposition method is very simple, and all calculations can be carried out manually by a hand calculator. The census II method (and its many variations[7-9]) is much more elaborate, requiring a computer, and is used on a wide scale by governmental and business organizations.

THE CLASSICAL DECOMPOSITION METHOD

To separate a time series into its four components, the simplest procedure is as follows:

1. Calculate a moving average based on the length of seasonality: 12 terms moving average for yearly seasonality, three terms for quarterly data, and so on.

2. Divide the actual data by the corresponding moving average value. This provides the seasonality ratios.

3. Remove randomness from the seasonality ratios by averaging corresponding values. Thus, all January ratios are averaged together, all February ratios are averaged together, and so on. These averages represent the coefficients of seasonality.

4. Divide the original data by the coefficient of seasonality to obtain the deseasonalized series. Such series still include the three other components: trend, cycle, and randomness.

5. Remove randomness. This is accomplished by computing a three or five terms moving average of the deseasonalized values. This moving average series is called the *trend-cycle series*.

These few steps suffice to obtain a fairly smooth curve of the trend-cycle components. Two additional operations will improve it:

1. Center the moving average (i.e., put it in the middle of the averaged N data values) in the foregoing step 1, when the number of average terms is even. When the length of seasonality is odd, the average is automatically "centered."

2. Use a medial average ratio in step 3. This is done simply by removing the highest and the lowest value before averaging the ratio of seasonality. Removing the outliers will result in greater stability of the seasonality coefficient.

THE CENSUS II METHOD

The census II method was developed in 1955 by the Bureau of Census of the U.S. Department of Commerce. Drawing on the empirical evidence accumulated through tens of thousands of deseasonalized series, the Bureau of Census has greatly improved the classical decomposition method, designing tests to verify the accuracy of the decomposition process.

To improve on the classical method, the Bureau of Census discovered a means of separating one by one the four components of a time series—seasonality, trend, cycle, and randomness—and recommended a method of correcting the original series for trading days.

Trading Days Adjustment

Excluding the month of February, any month can have as many as five, or as few as four, Saturdays and Sundays. This can represent an additional variation in the data of up to 10% and has to be corrected prior to deseasonalization. To adjust for trading days, the original data are multiplied by the ratio between the number of trading days corresponding to each month, and the average of trading days is found for the same month throughout the years.

Removal of Randomness

The deseasonalized series include trend, cycle, and some randomness. To avoid removing randomness at this stage, the census method calculates a very smooth trend-cycle series from the deseasonalized values. This is generally achieved using a Henderson weighted moving average. The original data are subsequently divided by the Henderson series. This operation removes the trend-cycle component from the original series, leaving only seasonality and randomness in the data. Randomness can, at this point, be removed with greater accuracy, as the data are not encumbered by the presence of the trend-cycle component.

Other Improvements

Several other steps are incorporated in the census method to secure better seasonality coefficients. These include a procedure to replace extreme values in the ratio of actual to moving average values and a method to replace the lost data at the beginning and end of the series.

Testing the Accuracy of Decomposition

To determine whether the decomposition process has been successful, the Bureau of Census has devised three tests: the adjacent month test, the January test, and the equality test.

The Adjacent Month Test

The census method calculates the ratio between the deseasonalized values and their adjacent months' average. Empirical evidence shows that the overall average of these ratios for a given month should be between 95 and 105 for the deseasonalization process to be adequate.

The January Test

This test, which was conceived to ensure that the deseasonalized data do not include any intrayear seasonality, involves computing the ratio between each month of any given year and the corresponding January value. A plot of these monthly ratios will reveal that there is no seasonality if the ratios are random. If there is a pattern in the ratios, it will be shown from one year to the next, as is the case in Chart 13-1. This graph represents the January test values for the years 1974 and 1975 for electricity consumption in France. This widely used time series experienced a major seasonality change after the 1973 oil price rise, which was easily detected by the January test (see Chart 13-1).

The Equality Test

The purpose of this test is to detect any overadjustment arising from the census process itself. Such a discrepancy may occur in the final deseasonalized series. A ratio of the final to the preliminary deseasonalized series will reveal whether the data were overadjusted. Experience has shown that these ratios should neither fall below 90 nor rise above 110.

Statistics

The census II method of decomposition provides many interesting and useful statistics, of which the percentage change figures are of particular benefit to the forecaster. The monthly percentage change is calculated for the four major series: the original, deseasonalized, trend-cycle, and randomness series. A browse through these percentage change series will reveal the largest percentage changes, which can then be rectified after detection of the reason for the discrepancy. The overall percentage changes for these four series, which measure the magnitude of each component, are also available.

For the French printing paper series shown in Chart 13-4, these average percentage changes are:

Original series, 25.13%

Seasonally adjusted series, 5.96%

Randomness component, 5.71%

The percentage change in randomness (5.71%) indicates the maximum accuracy to be anticipated with this series. The percentage change difference between the seasonally adjusted series (5.96%) and the original one (25.13%) measures the improvement derived from deseasonalization. This difference is 19.17% (25.13% − 5.96%); thus the seasonality factor represents 76.3% of all variations in the data. The trend-cycle variations represent 0.25% (5.96% − 5.71%). Seasonality is therefore the most important factor. It explains the significance and appropriateness of decomposition, as well as the interest of practitioners in this approach.

Months for Cyclical Dominance Trend-Cycle Curve

As the number of terms included in a moving average series increases, the curve obtained becomes smoother. Conversely, if more terms are included

CHART 13-1. French Consumption of Electricity—Ratios to Preceding January

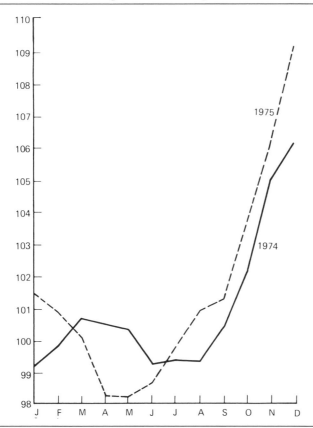

in a moving average series, a corresponding number of terms are lost at the end of the series.

According to the census method, the number of terms in the moving average trend-cycle series should be the minimum required to permit the trend-cycle to "dominate" the randomness component. The number of months for cyclical dominance (MCD) is obtained simply by dividing the percentage change average of the Henderson weighted moving average series by the percentage change average of the randomness component. More often than not, the number of months for cyclical dominance will be between three and five, and only one or two terms will have to be filled in at the end of most series.

TREND AND CYCLE ANALYSIS

Past events are in fact recorded in time series, but most of them are fleeting changes linked to seasonality and randomness. These must be removed from the series to analyze the recent past. When this has been accomplished, the trend cycle and trend curve are obtained. These curves, together with a thorough cycle analysis, provide a sound basis for forecasting.

The Trend Cycle

The trend-cycle curve, obtained from decomposition methods, is a great improvement over the original series, as original data do not provide a good description of the actual state of business. The reason for this is that they are affected by such factors as seasonality and randomness, which thus makes their interpretation difficult. In Chart 13-2, the original monthly values of newsprint consumption in France have been plotted. Seasonality and randomness dominate the pattern and render it incomprehensible. Chart 13-3, on the other hand, exhibits the trend-cycle series that was obtained from the same data used to plot Chart 13-2. Such a curve illustrates the evolution of the business, and it can become the basis for forecasting the cycle of newsprint consumption in France.

The use of other approaches in the attempt to understand the recent past can often be misleading. A common practice, for instance, is to compare a particular month's outcome with its equivalent value from the preceding year. This procedure attempts to elicit a measure of past events that is unaffected by seasonality, but such an approach is both incomplete and unsound. For example, the previous year's results may have been affected by a high degree of randomness, or the figure might have been a high or low point in a short-lived cycle; similarly, the equivalent months of two consecutive years may not have the same number of working days; and so forth.

Another inadvisable approach, which is often used to avoid deseasonalization, is to prepare a 12-month moving average of, say, the monthly series to be analyzed. Such a procedure deseasonalizes the data but lags the actual data by about 6 months, since the moving average—by definition—refers to the middle value of the data.

The Trend

To complete the decomposition process, it is possible to separate the trend-cycle series into its two components: trend *and* cycle. The trend is usually calculated separately and plotted on the same graph along the trend-cycle curve. This is done in Chart 13-4 for the French printing paper industry. The trend curve indicates the prevailing direction of the series, and the cycle can then be seen more clearly.

Mathematically, many formulas can be used to represent theoretical trends. In practice, linear and exponential trends are, as far as business data are concerned, the most common. Exponential trend fitting is, in my experience, the most frequently used, as it is more natural to express growth in percentage terms to allow comparison between series. Great care should be

CHART 13-2. French Newsprint Consumption (Original Data)

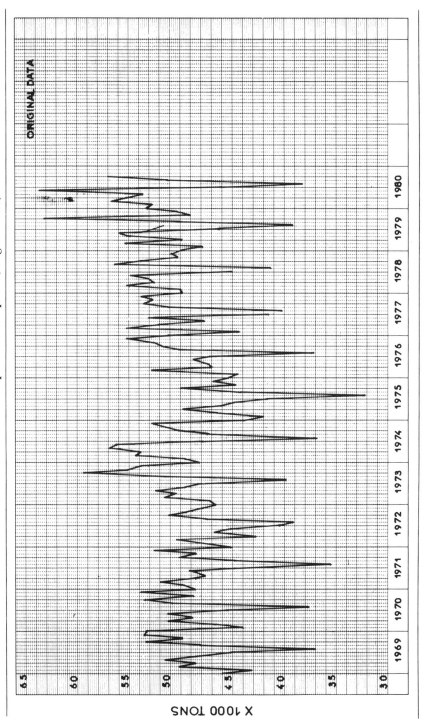

ORIGINAL DATA

X 1000 TONS

225

CHART 13-3. French Newsprint Consumption (Trend Cycle)

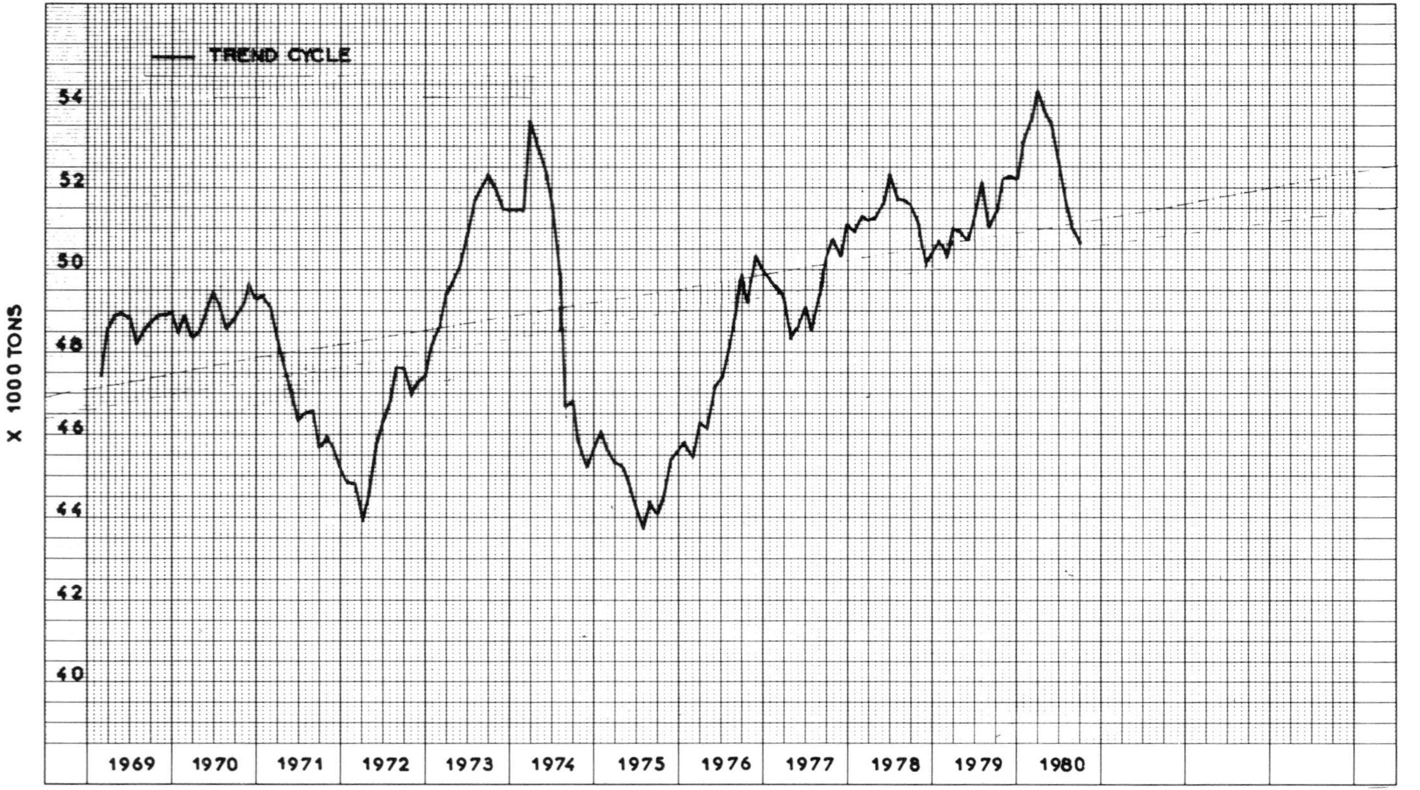

TREND CYCLE

X 1000 TONS

1969 1970 1971 1972 1973 1974 1975 1976 1977 1978 1979 1980

54 52 50 48 46 44 42 40

226

CHART 13-4. French Printing Paper Industry

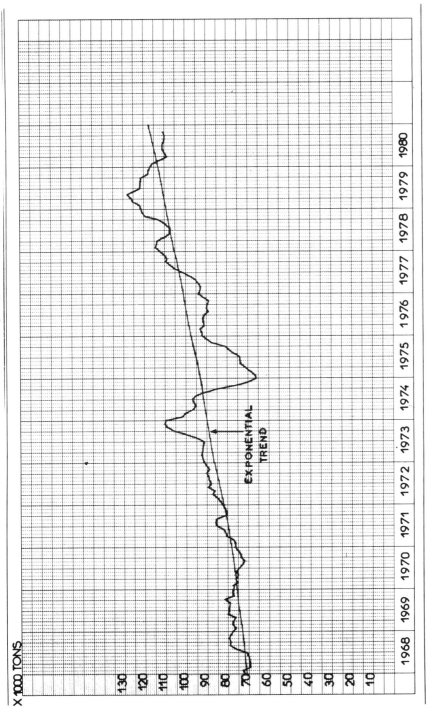

taken in calculating the trend of a series. Any error in this process will repeat itself from period to period, becoming increasingly prominent with exponential trends.

Chart 13-4 illustrates the monthly trend in the French printing paper industry. The exponential trend curve has been calculated over the 1964–1972 period and extrapolated thereafter.

It appears that the French printing paper business has experienced three recessions. The recession was mild in 1969, serious in 1974–1975, and just starting in 1980. In all cases recession was preceded by a boom comparable in intensity to the recession itself when assessed in terms of the area formed by the trend-cycle curve above and below the exponential trend. There is no mathematical principle that requires symmetry between the areas above and below the exponential trend each time there is a recession, or that states that a recession should follow a boom, and not vice versa. But this is nevertheless an economic fact, and it is believed that forecasters who acknowledge it will be in a much better position than those who do not take it into account.

It is up to the forecaster to choose the period that is most representative, in terms of calculating the trend. Obviously, to calculate the trend curve of Chart 13-4, both the boom and recession of 1974–1975 must be either included or, as was done, excluded altogether. Furthermore, if this trend curve is supposed to be representative of the whole 1968–1980 period, both boom and recession should fluctuate clearly above and below the trend curve. Otherwise a change in trend would be indicated.

Unfortunately, there can be no certainty that the trend will not change, and straight extrapolation may prove quite erroneous. On the other hand, the approach just described will allow the forecaster to detect when a change in trend is taking place—the earlier he or she can do so, the more effective the process will be.

Chart 13-5 presents the French gasoline consumption trend-cycle curve. Three very distinct trends were recorded between 1968 and 1980, the first of these being the old historical trend, which was very regular until the 1973 Yom Kippur War. The sharp price increase that followed this event had two results: an immediate and radical drop in gasoline consumption, and the evolution of a new lower trend. Before the Yom Kippur War, gasoline consumption in France achieved a growth of 7.7% per year. The new trend, right after the war, attained only 5.6%. After further price increases, in 1977, a third trend materialized, and gasoline consumption is now expanding at a rate of only 1.9% per year. Recent price increases indicate a further drop in rate of increase, between 0 and 1%. No mathematical means exists that could forecast this abrupt change in trend, unless one were able to forecast the price increase and the events leading up to it.

On the other hand, right from the start, the decomposition method was able to pick up the new trend fairly rapidly. It should be stressed that during 1974, many people continued to measure the growth of gasoline consumption on a monthly basis by comparing it with that of the previous year—a

CHART 13-5. French Gasoline Consumption

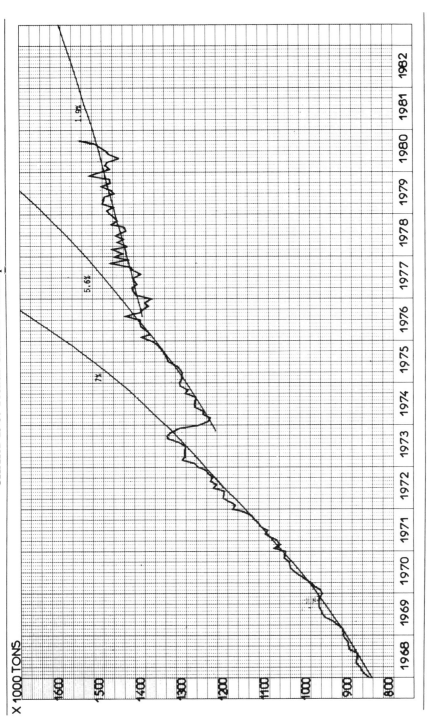

procedure that was argued to be incorrect. Each month they determined that the drop in consumption (see Chart 13-5) was increasing. This, of course, was incorrect, since most of the drop occurred during the last quarter of 1973; throughout the whole of 1974, gasoline consumption increased steadily at a yearly rate of 5.5%. This example demonstrates the importance of choosing the proper period to calculate the trend. Furthermore, it would be meaningless to calculate a trend of gasoline consumption in France for the entire 1972–1980 period.

CYCLE ANALYSIS

The phenomenon of the business cycle is well established. Between 1854 and 1945, 30 cycles were recorded in the United States, and since 1945 another eight have followed. There is no doubt as to the fact that they follow a recurrent pattern, but it has also been proven that no two business cycles are ever alike. For example, the expansion phase of the American economic cycle has been known to last from 25 to 105 months, and the contraction period from 7 to 65 months. During the postwar period, a full cycle covered from 34 to 117 months.

Business cycles do, however, exhibit some analogy. Chart 13-6 presents a reproduction from "Business Conditions Digest"[10] of the evolution of the 1975, 1958, 1954 business cycles, as measured by the Index of Industrial Production. The median behavior of all business cycles since the war has also been included. Their similarity may be used to analyze business cycles.

Cycles have been extensively studied in the areas of both macroeconomics and business. It has more recently been necessary to step up this research because of the staggering consequences for business life—from both human and profitability standpoints—that are brought about by the switch from expansion to contraction, and vice versa. A forecaster's primary objective is to forewarn the advent of a recession, and he or she should be looking out for signs of this throughout the whole expansion phase.

Even a sophisticated method, such as that of Box and Jenkins, is not able to predict turning points. Makridakis, Wheelwright, and McGee[1] have reported errors of 5.22% and 5.55% in the mean absolute percentage error (MAPE) of a monthly sales series connected with the French writing paper industry. These MAPEs were obtained with the Box–Jenkins and generalized adaptive filtering methods for the period prior to the 1974 recession.

When sales started to drop in September 1974, the MAPE increased considerably, as shown in the accompanying table on page 231.

Sophisticated methods did *not* pick up this change in the cycle, as is obvious from the large errors during the November–February recession period.

Five years afterward, a new recession came along; and the same method applied to the same series committed the same type of errors. These models were not able to forecast the major turning points of the series in 1974, and

CHART 13-6. Cycles of Industrial Production Index

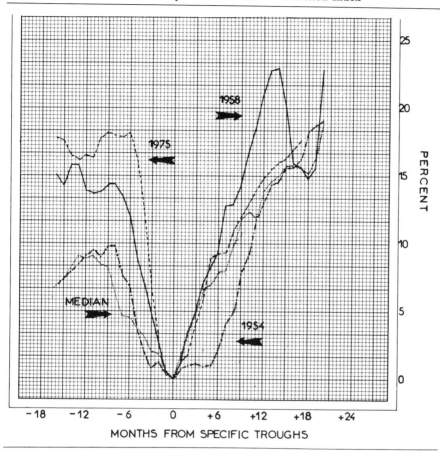

MONTHS FROM SPECIFIC TROUGHS

Time		Box–Jenkins %	Generalized Adaptive Filtering %
1974	September	+3.3	+4.4
	October	−7.9	−4.59
	November	−26.97	−19.13
	December	−41.08	−28.87
1975	January	−80.56	−72.42
	February	−88.39	−81.56

they were still unable to do so in 1980. This time the errors were smaller, but only because the recession was not as steep. They reached 40% with both models, which is much too high a level to allow managers to trust these methods.

To predict a turning point in a cycle, decomposition methods are useful—not so much because of their accuracy, but because of the trend-cycle curve derived from them. As has been shown, it is easy, using the graphs, to determine the position at any given time with regard to the trend and trend-cycle curves. In Chart 13-4, it was clear that in 1973 a boom had taken place, which should have been acknowledged as a warning of an impending recession. In 1979, the boom was less clearly defined, but the trend-cycle curve was well above the historical trend. Furthermore, the expansion phase in 1979 lasted for four years—a span of time long enough to provide some hint of a recession. Similar behavior has also been observed during the business cycles of the 1980s.

BUSINESS FORECASTING

It is well known that forecasting is not an exact science. This fact has escaped the attention of neither seasoned forecasters nor business managers. The sole reason for forecasting is to assist managers in making better decisions. It is not surprising that many businesspeople are reluctant to use a purely mathematical approach to forecasting, mainly because many managers do not fully understand the advantages and limitations involved.

Forecaster and Manager Symbiosis

Mintzberg[11] contended "that a great deal of the manager's inputs are soft and speculative—impressions and feelings about other people, hearsay, gossip and so on." Mintzberg further suggested that "the very analytical inputs, reports, documents, and hard data in general seem to be of relatively little importance to many managers."

If this assertion is correct, forecasters should actively look for methods that can be easily understood by managers. To be successful in a company, forecasters must be not only accurate but also convincing. The decomposition methods, and the forecasts based on them, have a strong appeal to executives. They are simple to understand and easy to interpret; furthermore, executives can relate their knowledge to past events as recorded in the trend-cycle curve. Finally, executives can incorporate their intuition and knowledge of forthcoming events into the extrapolation of the trend cycle. Thus, it is believed that the census method is capable of creating a true symbiosis between managers and forecasters. This is a most relevant factor, which should always be considered when choosing a forecasting method.

BUDGET FORECASTING

Forecasting plays a vital role in the formulation of budgets. Forecasting accuracy, however, is not necessarily the most important element in the budgeting process; management aspirations, optimism, and political concerns always enter the picture. It is therefore the task of the forecaster to introduce objectivity into the budgeting procedure, to the extent that this is possible.

A frequent ploy is to incorporate an optimistic element into a budget, which serves as a psychological driving force, motivating people to achieve better results. Forecasters, however, must resist the temptation to promote unwarranted optimism; their function is to *forecast* the future, not improve it.

In my opinion, the budgeting process should begin with the presentation of a forecast that takes the following into account:

National economy

International environment, when relevant to the company

Demand of the sectors in which the company is involved

Volume of sales

Market share

Price of goods sold

An elaboration of the information required for each of these points follows.

Many companies today regularly subscribe to forecasting services. At the same time, the forecasting department within the organization makes its own predictions for the most important company series. In the particular company with which I am concerned, the forecasting group produces trend-cycle curves and forecasts—on both a monthly and a quarterly basis—of all major series. The budget forecasting analysis includes a separate section for the incorporation of the forthcoming year into the current cycle, from which an attempt can be made to predict the next turning point, even if it is not expected to affect the forthcoming budget year.

This same approach is adopted when dealing with the international environment. A good trend-cycle analysis is generally produced by a combination of the forecaster's intuition and the scientific tools available. It should also incorporate the experience and judgment of the company managers, for it is they, rather than the forecasters, who have the most complete knowledge of the business.

It is often difficult to persuade managers to become involved with forecasting. They would perhaps be surprised to learn, however, how easily the problem can be overcome, with the simple use of a pencil, graph paper, and the trend-cycle curve. Forecasters can persuade management that quantitative forecasting is not mystical, nor is it something they cannot do.

The following example illustrates how the trend-cycle approach advocated in this chapter made a significant contribution to my company.

At the end of 1979, the forecasting department of Aussedat-Rey concluded that 1980 would be a negative growth year and predicted a 3.8% drop in the French printing paper industry. The preceding years' growth was as follows:

1979/1978	+9.1%
1978/1977	+12.9%
1977/1976	+9.0%
1976/1975	+22.0%
Average of the four years	13.0%

In early October, 1979, when the budget was under discussion, the sales department acknowledged a drop in growth. They suggested a 6% growth for 1979, based on an average obtained from regional sales managers. At that point, the forecasting department prepared the graph shown in Chart 13-7 (no 1980 data were available at the time). The two solid lines in the year 1980 show the average levels corresponding to the two forecasts (the upper line shows the 6% growth, while the lower one shows the 3.8% decline). On this evidence alone, it was argued that 6% growth was unattainable. It appeared also, in further discussion, that the sales department did not, in fact, anticipate a much better year in 1980 than the forecasting department. Their estimate was strongly influenced by the fact that during the previous four years the average growth had been about 13%. With regard to such a figure, 6% represented a sharp drop for 1980.

The forecasting department later sent the sales trend-cycle curve shown in Chart 13-7 (data for 1980 were still not included, as this was done in late 1979) to a dozen of their sales offices, asking managers simply to pencil in their own estimate of the curve for the coming year. From the resulting graphs, the forecasting department calculated an average curve. This Delphi-type approach proved very useful and resulted in an average estimated growth of −1%. The method has since been institutionalized, and in the opinion of all concerned, constitutes a considerable improvement in the forecasting of the company. (Incidentally, the actual decline for 1980 was a little more than 4%.)

Perhaps the most important advantage of this approach is that it brings together managers and forecasters. Both are now able to express their ideas in a vernacular language, to assimilate—with greater ease—each other's reasoning, and finally, to benefit from each other's intuition and knowledge. This factor is of great help in the endeavor to compensate for the less than perfect accuracy of available forecasting methods.

Trend-cycle analysis has also been effectively used in price forecasting. *Economie Papetière*,[12] a monthly French publication aimed at the paper industry, published the graph in Chart 13-8 showing the historical price movement of paper up until 1980. The 1981 forecast (prepared in 1980) is represented by the dotted lines. The bottom line retraces the classic behavior of paper prices during a recession, based on the many factors affecting them. Giving reasons for the decision, *Economie Papetière* forecast that

CHART 13-7. French Printing Paper Industry—1980 Forecast

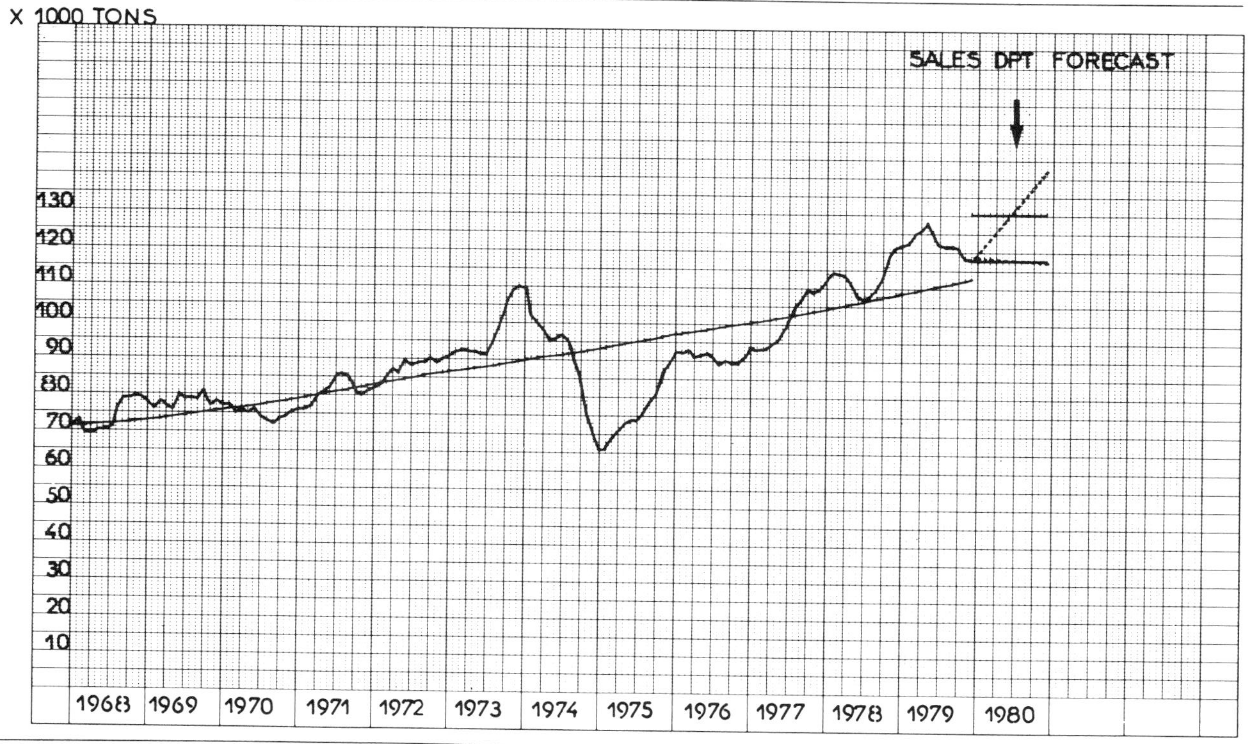

235

CHART 13-8. Paper Prices Forecast

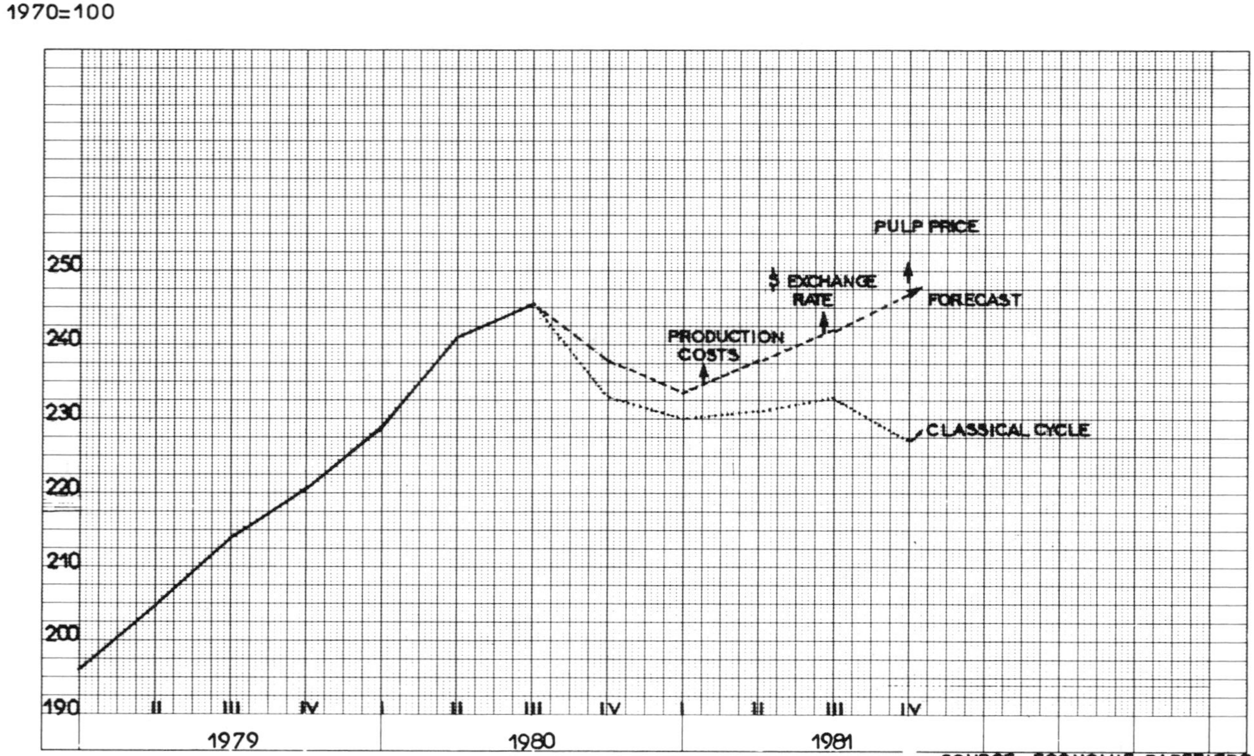
1970=100
250
240
230
220
210
200
190
II
III
IV
I
II
III
IV
I
II
III
IV
1979
1980
1981
PULP PRICE
$ EXCHANGE RATE
FORECAST
PRODUCTION COSTS
CLASSICAL CYCLE

SOURCE : ECONOMIE PAPETIERE
REPRINTED BY AUTHORIZATION

prices in 1981 would divert from their classic behavior pattern. This use of the trend-cycle curve clearly expresses the opinion of the editors in a visual form, and the reader can decide whether or not he or she wants to accept it.

Once budget and corporate plans are set, they must be monitored on a continuous basis, and time series decomposition is one of the best available methods for that purpose. Presenting the trend-cycle curves from the budget and the actual data on the same graph is the most striking way of measuring what has already been accomplished and what has still to be achieved.

SUMMARY

This chapter has presented decomposition methods and has argued that, as far as business forecasting is concerned, these methods are highly relevant and of extreme value. They are also simple to use, are intuitive, and can be used as a means to bring together managers and forecasters.

REFERENCES

1. Makridakis, S., S. C. Wheelwright, and V. E. McGee, *Forecasting Methods and Applications,* 2nd ed., John Wiley, New York, 1982.

2. Burman, J. P., "Seasonal Adjustment—A Survey," *TIMS Studies in the Management Sciences,* Vol. 12, 1979, pp. 45–57.

3. Nullau, B., *The Berlin Method—A New Approach to Time Series Analysis,* German Institute for Economic Research, Berlin, 1969.

4. McLaughlin, R. L., "Time Series Forecasting," *Marketing Research Technique,* Series No. 6, American Marketing Association, 1962.

5. McLaughlin, R. L., and J. J. Boyle, "Short-term Forecasting," American Marketing Association Booklet, 1968.

6. Organization for Economic Cooperation and Development (OECD), "The X-II Variant of U.S. Census Method II," *Sources and Methods,* no. 15, December 1972.

7. Shiskin, J., "Electronic Computers and Business Indicators," National Bureau of Economic Research, Occasional Paper 57, 1957.

8. Shiskin, J., "Tests and Revisions of Bureau of the Census Methods of Seasonal Adjustments," Bureau of the Census, Technical Paper No. 5, 1961.

9. Shiskin, J., A. H. Young, and J. C. Musgrave, "The X-II Variant of the Census II Method Seasonal Adjustment Program," Bureau of the Census, Technical Paper No. 15, 1967.

10. "Business Condition Digest," U.S. Government Printing Office, issued yearly.

11. Mintzberg, H., "Planning on the Left Side and Managing on the Right," *Harvard Business Review,* July–August, 1976, pp. 49–58.

12. Communication Conseil International (France), *Economie Papetière,* no. 4, 1980, pp. 8–11.

14

ECONOMETRIC METHODS FOR MANAGERIAL APPLICATIONS

HANS LEVENBACH
Core Analytic, Inc., Bridgewater, New Jersey

WILLIAM R. SCHULTZ
Intelsat, Washington, D.C.

INTRODUCTION

There has been a rapid expansion in the types of econometric methods applied to a multitude of studies in governments, corporations, and research institutions worldwide. Many of these quantitative measurements, involving the tools of probability and statistics, can be combined with the nonexperimental domain of economics to make up what is known as *econometric modeling*.

Econometric models range in size from a simple equation to models with literally thousands of *simultaneous equations*. Such a variety of uses has led to both misuses of the methodology and numerous documented successes for the practitioner. It is important for the manager to understand the basic features, uses, and interpretations of econometric methods so that maximum benefit can be derived from these techniques in a practical situation.

This chapter presents an overview of methods for econometric modeling for managerial use. We will stay with a perspective on applications of econometric methods for structural analysis, policy simulation analysis, and forecast modeling.

A section is devoted to development of an econometric model from the statement of the problem to data acquisition, model formulation, use of statistical estimators, and model evaluation and diagnosis. Also, discussion is directed to pitfalls in the econometric modeling process that will give a perspective of such modeling from a cost benefit perspective.

WHAT ARE ECONOMETRIC MODELS AND METHODS?

Initially, econometric methods were applied and gained notice as a way to model the macroeconomy. *Macroeconomics* deals with the macroaggregates of income, employment, and price levels.

Much use has also been made of econometric methods for forecasting of various problems. Arguments for and against the use of econometric methods to estimate quantitative economic models are continually being put forth. However incomplete, the advent of computer processing capability and the preferences of many managers nowadays for quantitative information have prompted the growing use of econometric methods for various business applications to economic problems.

Because the nature of the analysis is statistical and the models are mathematical approximations of reality, the various econometric methods are continually being refined to improve their ability to predict.

Essentially, in econometric methods statistical procedures are employed to estimate parameters of a mathematical model using data samples for variables in the model. Thus, we may start in a simplified way with a single-equation model having one variable endogenous to the system determined by several variables exogenous to the system. (In simultaneous-equation applications, those variables determined *within* the system are called *endogenous* variables, while those determined *outside* the system are called *exogenous*. Variables related to government expenditures, taxes, and interest rates are often considered exogenous.) We attempt to describe this relationship with allowance for uncertainty that shows up as a disturbance or error term in the relationship for each of the sample data points.

The usual direction is to develop more refined estimation procedures or detailed modeling systems with the end result that the analysis increases in complexity and cost. What is desired is a view and awareness of not only the types of econometric methods available but also their potential costs and benefits. Such consideration will be of much importance to the manager concerned with analyzing economic problems.

USES OF ECONOMETRIC MODELING

The nature of econometric modeling and the appropriate analysis methods can be classified according to the outputs desired. The outputs produce three classes of applications for econometric modeling.

The first and perhaps most widely used application is that of forecasting.

Forecasting is the activity of predicting change or the course of future events and conditions under uncertainty. Here the general focus is the development of a model with parameters estimated from data relevant to the problem at hand. The model is designed to provide predictive values for the variables outside the sample of data actually observed. This approach generally pertains to time series and the forecasting of future periods. In practice, input data or statistical estimation procedures are evaluated from the perspective of forecast performance.

A second application is that of structural analysis. *Structural analysis* relates to a process of deriving information concerning an underlying economic relationship through the specifications of a mathematical model. Parameters in the model have special meaning to the investigator.

For example, in an analysis for the demand of a product or service, a product manager requires estimates of price elasticities, which explain the responsiveness of changes in demand to changes in prices. For certain *demand functions* these price elasticities are found to be functions of the parameters in the model. These parameters are estimated using relevant historical or cross-sectional data.

Generally, attention is focused on the economic and theoretical aspects of the mathematical model rather than on the statistical niceties to approximate the relationship.

The general purpose of a structural analysis is to try and make sense of or to formulate a broad picture out of a phenomenon or relationship that is otherwise clouded by the interactions of numerous variables. Approximations are introduced by selecting observable information as proxy variables for the model. The results of such a model provide a basis for examining the *structure* of the system under consideration and then asking questions about the nature of the relationships.

Models formulated for structural analysis can be very simple or quite complex, and typically include many simultaneous equations. In general, it is possible and frequently necessary to segment the complex models so as to derive any essential information from a complex maze of activity.

A third application is *policy analysis,* in which models formulated for structural analysis or forecast purposes can be used to make scenarios using alternative assumptions about exogenous factors impacting the system. Thus, policy analysis will ask "what if" questions about the future state of a system or about alternative conditions in the system's recent past. The econometric model provides an approximation of the general structure of the system within the sample period of the data.

In many business applications it may be desirable to achieve certain targets to meet particular objectives. By employing an econometric model, we can simulate various alternative inputs (our controlling variables) to find the input that best achieves the desired target. The degree of accuracy will be directly dependent on the formulated model and appropriate use of econometric methods to estimate the model.

TYPES OF ECONOMETRIC MODELS

While we can view one classification of econometric models as their application, another classification can be their type. In this view, models are used to describe a particular system by observing its movement or time as measured by discrete, chronologically based values. The model is then estimated using sample data from the time period under question.

A second model can be estimated with similar but different data from another system. If the two sets of data come from the same statistical origins, we can expect the results of the estimated models to be similar statistically.

For each of these applications we can consider several types of econometric models that range from a time series regression model to simultaneous equation models. By a *regression model* we mean the statistical technique of predicting one variable from knowledge of one or more related variables. Within this context we address models that span the dimensions of time with a static and dynamic mathematical specification.

Alternatively, we can have models that employ cross-sectional data, in contrast to *time series* or chronologically dependent data. For example, suppose we are interested in the per capita consumption of electricity for a country and annual time series are available for 25 countries for 10 years. We can build 25 *regression* models, 10 *cross-sectional* models, or one *pooled* model. The latter integrates the two types of data by pooling or grouping together the individual time series for each of the cross sections. The sample data from the different cross sections may at the same or different time periods. What is relevant is the sampling, and analysis is done without regard to the time dimensions.

By combining each time series with the cross section of other systems, we are effectively pooling information to be used in the estimation process. Generally, we prefer to use as much information as possible for estimation purposes, so pooling of data can satisfy this need.

When time series of different cross sections have characteristics that would statistically alter our results, we must modify our econometric methods to assure model validity.

When using time series it is important to recognize that the estimation procedure may produce a static or dynamic response in the endogenous variables of the system. If the model is static, we essentially assume that the exogenous variables in the system impact the endogenous variables at the same time. This assumption may prove to be an adequate approximation of the process, particularly so when the measures cover large discrete periods such as a year.

On the other hand, a static model can be expected to be less accurate when data are monthly or quarterly. Here we can introduce dynamics into our approximation of the system process.

In general, we may expect the impact of the exogenous variables on the endogenous variables to be *distributed over time*. This type of distribution may not be known a priori, and thus will require the use of econometric methods to best describe and aproximate the dynamics of the system. There exist various "distributed-lag" procedures to help approximate and estimate such models.

Incorporating dynamics can substantially increase the cost of the analysis. When we need to analyze short-term changes in a system, the inclusion of dynamics may be well worth the effort.

Finally, econometric models can be developed in multiple levels of complexity. A simple-equation regression describing an economic process can represent the simplest form of an econometric model. Such a basic relationship may suffice for several reasons.

First, the dependent variable can be explained adequately by a simple equation of information when the determining information is outside the system. Endogenous information in the system can be ignored or has little impact on the variable of concern. Also, a single equation may suffice in that the cost of greater complexity outweighs the benefits to be derived from the analysis. Perhaps only limited information is desired and the levels of accuracy don't warrant inclusion of detailed interrelationships among a broader set of variables.

Many types of applications of econometric methods require modeling of several variables in a system simultaneously. We must then be able to develop a relationship for each of the variables to be explained in the system. However, each equation provides the means to explain only one variable in the system. Hence there must be as many equations as there are endogenous variables.

Econometric models of more than one equation can be nothing more than sets of single-equation models with little or no relation. They each can be explained by exogenous information. Other models can be more complex and simultaneous in that some endogenous variables are jointly determined by other variables within the system. In this situation, the estimation process becomes more complicated, because the statistical estimators employed assume that the explanatory variables in the model are independent of the model disturbance term. However, this unaccounted for portion of the model is correlated to variables within the system. Thus a more complex estimation process is required. The difficulties in estimating such models can be handled when the number of equations is kept small or when the system can be grouped into several independent blocks, known as *recursive systems*.

DEVELOPING AN ECONOMETRIC MODEL

In this section we go through the process of developing an econometric model and consider the alternative methods available for analysis. From the perspective of managerial applications, our interest will focus on the costs and benefits of all facets of econometric modeling.

We want to start with a statement of the problem and develop a mathematical model from a priori reasoning. Next, we must consider data acquisition and availability of appropriate proxy variables. Then the statistical estimation procedures are applied. Finally, model evaluation and diagnostics can be performed to assess the adequacy of the methods for the particular problem.

Statement of the Problem

An important part of an analysis is the statement of the problem. This should encompass not only identifying the critical issues but also determining what kind of information is desired. The latter point does not and should not imply a preconceived notion about actual numerical results, but rather should identify what we desire to achieve from a solution to the problem.

A second part of problem identification is the determination of an appropriate analytical approach. Does the problem lend itself to a statistical analysis that tries to draw inference from data information, or can the problem be adequately addressed through deductive reasoning?

If a problem lends itself to some empirical analysis, we want to develop a model that describes it in a simplified form. By properly specifying such a model we hope to be able to address issues that can yield useful answers to our problems. It is preferable to have the model-building process guided by a sound economic framework.

Limitations in economic theory may at times preclude very close adherence of the model to a theoretical framework. We may then need to consider a reformulation of the problem. Possible shortcomings in the analysis may need to be recognized before we proceed further.

In some cases a more comprehensive model can answer more questions than before. Therefore, we must assess in our problem statement the relative importance of the key issues before us. This will help to determine the direction and extent of an analysis to be undertaken.

Mathematical Model Formulation

A comprehensive statement of the problem gives us an idea about how we want to construct a model. The idea will include a course of direction in developing a theoretical framework plus a set of assumptions from which to determine the complexity of the model.

In practice, compromises must be made between the desire to extract more complete information and the limits of the analytical resources available to us. We want the model to provide a simplified framework that allows us to sort out the interrelationships in the system.

It is also desirable to keep the model simple in its mathematical form to facilitate the estimation of the parameters in the model. Typically, we proceed with a linear formulation of the structure to be modeled. Then we focus on a system of one to three equations. Modeling systems that are larger can usually be segmented into much smaller blocks. Any decision to model in a more complex fashion must be weighed against the value of the information to be derived.

Sometimes the modeling process does not start from a clear theoretical basis of economic thinking. Rather we have a measurement process that is assumed to have come from a subset of some other known factors. Here the modeling process can start with simplified assumptions and proceed with the evolution of different combinations of explanatory variables.

Data Selection

A critical component of econometric modeling is the appropriate use of data. Data are the quantitative measures of information in the modeling process. Such measurements can reflect monetary values, cardinal or ordinal measures of quantities, intervals of measures, or perhaps ratio scales. In all cases, data must be measured along a consistent interval scale to have meaning.

Several issues arise that require us to make choices about the type of data we select. First, there may not be any data that directly correspond to the variable considered in our model formulation. We may be forced to select a set of data that only provides a close approximation of the event we wish to observe. Our selection will be made in such a way as to minimize any misinformation conveyed.

Second, we may not be able to quantify explicitly some event that has significant impact on our system. Here we may have to construct a proxy variable that may be a "dummy" (or indicator) variable or perhaps some kind of trend variable. A *dummy variable* is constructed to have a value, say 1, when the event occurs and 0 otherwise. When quantitative data are not available, dummy variables are appropriate for representing one-time effects (strikes), fixed duration effects (war–peace), discontinuities related to changes in qualitative factors, differences in attributes (sex versus race), and seasonal variation. With time series data, models will often include a measure of the general seasonal variation.

Finally, we have to recognize that all data are subject to errors of measurement. Thus, we have the possibility of incorrectly specifying the relationships in the system.

Statistical Estimation of the Model

So far the discussion of the econometric modeling process has given us a mathematical model and shown us that data are available to relate explanatory variables to each of the dependent variables in the model. The *depen-*

dent variables are the factors that we would like to have the model predict. Moreover, the dependent variables are all subject to some small error.

What remains is to prescribe the relative impact of the explanatory variables on the system. This is accomplished through the role of *parameters* in the model. We must choose values for the parameters that will meet preselected criteria. In particular, we want to minimize the overall error or unexplained portion of the model for all data points.

Statistical estimation in econometric modeling is probably the most comprehensive and widely explored part of the modeling process. *Statistical estimators* provide the means to find estimates of model parameters using preselected criteria and information contained in the data.

Several key points must be made about the estimation process. First, all estimators are developed from a set of assumptions about the model structure, the statistical properties of the data, and the error term in the model. Violation of these assumptions can produce distortions in the estimated parameters.

Second, it is possible to use more generalized estimation procedures that have fewer restrictions and can overcome some of the potential problems, but only at greater expense. Fortunately, with growth in computation power, the cost of using more complicated estimators is substantially reduced.

Model Evaluation and Diagnostics

The final phase of a successful econometric modeling effort determines whether the model can be used in practice. This involves an examination of *residuals,* or forecast errors; validation of parameter estimates; and simulation of model and forecast performance.

A *residual analysis* is a statistical procedure for checking whether modeling assumptions can be supported by the data. In this process, we try to determine what the "unexplained" variation might tell us about the adequacy of the model. Quite often the inclusion of new factors is suggested by this procedure. At other times, variables with little correlation are deleted. Largely graphic, residual analysis is an effective tool for demonstrating departures from model assumptions.

Additional analyses into the nature of the parameters can suggest whether model coefficients have the "right sign." In relating sales to advertising expenditures, it makes sense that increasing advertising expenditures will lead to increased sales for the firm. The results of an econometric analysis of a firm's sales performance should point to a positive sign for the appropriate parameter if the sales history supports such a hypothesis.

Outliers are anomalies in the historical data that can at times give misleading results. Both the practitioner and the end user of the econometric analysis can benefit from being cognizant of the tools of residual diagnostics.

The ultimate value of an econometric model lies in its predictive ability, whether it is forecasting or structural in nature. There are many ways of measuring forecast accuracy and performance, none giving exclusively the best answer. In practice, development of a multimethod approach to econometric forecasting is recommended so that alternative approaches can be evaluated independently.

Multimethod approaches can be beneficial for isolating the estimation methodology or model form most appropriate for a given situation. Many times a simple, albeit incomplete, model specification yields more accurate forecasts because of lesser sensitivity to data inadequacies. At other times, estimation methodologies do not yield very stable parameter estimates because of limitations in the characteristics of the data.

There are special data problems in econometric applications that require specialized tools to handle them. Use of these tools, even when warranted from economic considerations, does not always yield corresponding improvements in forecast performance. Indeed, at times the opposite holds true.

While use of forecasts from econometric systems is widespread, there apparently is no universal acceptance that econometric systems produce consistently reliable and accurate forecasts. Simpler approaches often yield more accurate projections. However, the role of econometrics in forecasting is to provide an economic rationale for the process along with a mechanism for projecting numerical "forecasts."

PITFALLS IN ECONOMETRIC MODELING

The success of an econometric modeling effort lies in a number of factors related to quality of data, sensitivity of model specifications, and appropriateness of estimation methodology.

Quality of data is affected by measurement error and representativeness. Since data can be experimental or historical, quality cannot always be directly controlled by the investigator. In most econometric applications, historical data are gathered from various government or corporate sources where accuracy considerations cannot be effectively controlled. Most data go through various levels of aggregation and possible redefinition, so that their validity cannot always be assumed.

In demand analysis applications of econometrics, the "log-linear" formulation has practical appeal and is very commonly used for good reasons. In this situation elasticity coefficients are constant and thus have practical value. Empirical investigations do not always support this appealing formulation. At the same time, data limitations can preclude discovery of the dynamic nature of the elasticities. Thus, the practitioner might be inappropriately estimating and projecting constant elasticities for prices or income effects to management.

Statistical estimation techniques have complex algorithms and are not easily understood. As with any methodology, they have their limitations, not the least of which is the impact of unusual variation in the data on the precision of the estimates.

Even sophisticated techniques cannot overcome basic data problems. To offer some caution, a manager is well advised to complement a complex estimation process with a simpler but better understood methodology. Sometimes a heuristic guess can balance the overbearing impact that a sophisticated analysis can bring to a problem. A source of frustration in econometric modeling is the concern about the stability of the model over time. In forecasting applications, models need to be used over different forecast horizons. Their credibility is closely tied to the validity of the results over time.

Econometric models are expected to work best when the underlying assumptions change slowly. Then the practitioner has the opportunity to adjust model specifications without distorting results.

Lastly, the interaction of management, investigators, and available resources can introduce unexpected sources of error in the modeling process. Each provides special interests and constraints that may work to the detriment of all. Time constraints, budget cuts, and technical specializations have ways of affecting adversely the best intentions and project designs, especially in large projects. If objectives are clearly delineated, the chance of failure can be minimized.

SUMMARY

Modern econometric modeling techniques are finding increasing use in forecasting, structural analysis, and policy analysis throughout the world. Large econometric systems are available nowadays through commercial vendors and academic institutions for study of world, country, and regional economies. Their outputs are used by government agencies, corporate staffs, and academic researchers.

Managers need to be aware of the strengths and weaknesses of econometric modeling so that they can make the soundest decisions possible. This chapter has offered an overview, without technical detail, of methods, uses, and pitfalls of econometrics for managerial uses. With this background, a manager will possess the basic intelligence to offer support and direction to econometric modeling efforts.

CHAPTER

15

JUDGMENTAL AND BAYESIAN FORECASTING

ROBERT L. WINKLER

Fuqua School of Business, Duke University, Durham, North Carolina

INTRODUCTION

Forecasting is thought of by some as the development and application of various models and formulas to extrapolate into the future from a series of observed data, possibly including data on variables other than those being predicted. Examples of this approach include exponential smoothing, regression, Box–Jenkins models, and (allowing the incorporation of some theory from a substantive area of interest) econometric models. Indeed, a great deal of effort has gone into the study of such methods, which are quite useful and important. However, forecasting also includes the numerous forecasts that are made judgmentally or involve nontrivial judgmental input. The intent in forecasting should be for forecasts to reflect all relevant available information. In many cases some, most, or occasionally even all of this information is judgmental.

This chapter reviews judgmental and Bayesian forecasting. In *judgmental forecasting,* the final forecasts are made subjectively. Data or forecasts derived from nonjudgmental methods may be consulted, but the ultimate forecasts are judgmental. Topics covered in the discussion of judgmental forecasting include the importance of expert opinion in some forecasting situations, methods to aid in the formulation of judgmental forecasts, cognitive issues, and the combination of forecasts.

In *Bayesian forecasting,* a probability rule, called Bayes' theorem, is used

This work was supported in part by the National Science Foundation under Grant IST-8600788.

to generate forecasts and update the forecasts as new information becomes available. Some inputs to Bayesian procedures are often judgmental in nature, but they are combined mechanically rather than judgmentally. Basic notions of Bayesian forecasting are presented, and more sophisticated Bayesian models are mentioned briefly.

JUDGMENTAL FORECASTING

The Role of Expert Information

The study and use of sophisticated methods and models for forecasting is a relatively recent development when one considers that people have been making predictions, or forecasts, for many centuries. Of necessity, predictions in days past were judgmental in nature. With the data, methodology, and computing capabilities now available, forecasting systems can be created to generate forecasts from past series of observations and from empirical or theoretical relationships among variables. Yet there are still many forecasting situations in which expert judgment plays a very important role.

A setting in which expert information is obviously crucial is one with no directly relevant "hard data." An example might be the development of a new product quite different from anything currently on the market. At early stages in the development of the product, not only are historical data concerning the product completely lacking, but details are too vague to permit test marketing. However, experts could have valuable information about potential reactions of consumers to the product and about the chances of achieving various sales levels. Decisions to continue development of a product are not made in a vacuum; they rely on judgments concerning the likelihood of eventual success.

Another example involves the health risks associated with pollutants. In setting a standard for allowable concentrations of a pollutant in the air, a public environmental agency needs to forecast the possible health effects associated with different standards. If extensive experimental data were available concerning the reactions of humans to exposure to certain levels of the pollutant, forecasts could be based on these data. With potentially serious health effects, however, such experimentation poses serious ethical problems. As a result, available data are typically limited to human reactions to relatively low-level exposure and animal reactions to a wider range of concentrations. The judgment of experts is needed to evaluate indirectly relevant data like these and to come up with the forecasts needed in the standard-setting process. Judgmental forecasts are useful in many public policy decisions.

Even when extensive past data are available, judgment can play an important role. A lengthy history of sales of an established product might provide the basis for forecasts of future sales. In the absence of any changes in the environment surrounding the product, an extrapolation method might be used to provide forecasts. On the other hand, if anticipated changes in import tariffs or tax laws or the entry of a related product could influence sales, relying solely on extrapolation of past sales figures might not be wise. Expert judgment is important in consideration of the impact of factors such as these. Moreover, it should be noted that the decision as to whether a forecast should be generated via extrapolation or whether experts should be consulted to come up with a forecast is itself a judgmental call. Expert judgments clearly need to be considered, whether in selecting a mechanical forecasting method or in making the ultimate forecasts judgmentally.

A bit of reflection reveals that we are bombarded with judgmental forecasts all the time. Forecasts of economic variables such as interest rates, stock market averages, gross national product (GNP), and unemployment rates are made by economists, investment analysts, and a variety of other types of experts. Weather forecasters make subjective forecasts regarding the occurrence of rain, high and low temperatures, and other meteorological variables. Physicians observe symptoms and make judgments about whether a disease is present or whether a certain treatment will be effective on a particular patient. Political forecasters make predictions about the success of various pieces of legislation and about whether certain individuals will declare their candidacy for office. Sportswriters predict the outcomes of all sorts of sporting events, and bookies make predictions and stand behind them when they take bets. Global experts make forecasts about potential wars or agreements between countries.

In summary, everyone is exposed to many judgmental forecasts. Furthermore, the information of experts plays a very important role in forecasting. Often little information other than expert judgment is available. Even when large data bases exist, experts may have important information not considered in the data bases. Finally, in the use of mechanical forecasting methods and models, judgment plays a nontrivial role in the choice of a method or model and in the eventual use of the forecasts in decision making.

The Quantification of Judgments

Judgments can be expressed in many ways. Consider, for example, a weather forecaster predicting tomorrow's temperature. A quite informal forecast would be something like, "It will be hot tomorrow." This statement conveys some information, but it is vague, leaving its recipient wondering just *how* hot it will be. A more common type of temperature forecast is, "Tomorrow's high temperature will be about 30°C." A numerical forecast conveys information in a less ambiguous manner than a nonnumerical forecast. Of course, it is doubtful that the forecaster is absolutely certain that the high temperature will be *exactly* 30°C. Thus, the statement that the high temperature will be about 30°C might be accompanied by an indication of how much the high temperature might deviate from this value: "The high temperature will be between 27°C and 32°C," or, "With 95% probability the high temperature will be between 27°C and 32°C." Now the forecaster has not only conveyed a "best guess" (30°C) about tomorrow's high temperature but has also revealed the degree of uncertainty about that best guess.

The temperature example illustrates different types of judgmental forecasts. An informal verbal forecast conveys some information but is qualitative and may be interpreted differently by different users. An expression of the forecaster's judgments in quantitative terms provides additional information and is less subject to misinterpretation. The typical quantitative judgmental forecast is simply a point forecast ("Tomorrow's high temperature will be about 30°C"; "The unemployment rate for next year is predicted to be 8%"; "I forecast that this brand will have sales of $450,000 in the coming year"; "This patient's condition is improving and she should be ready to leave the hospital in another week").

A point forecast provides more information than an informal verbal forecast. Even more information is provided if the quantification is carried one step further to include a numerical expression of the forecaster's uncertainty. This might be expressed as a range of values ("The high temperature will be between 27°C and 32°C"). Better yet, an interval of values can be accompanied by a probability ("With probability .95 the high temperature will be between 27°C and 32°C"). Probability is the formal mathematical language of uncertainty; as such, it provides an appropriate vehicle to convey a forecaster's uncertainty about the event or variable that is being predicted. To represent this uncertainty completely, the forecaster could give an entire probability distribution; for instance, "Next year's unemployment rate is approximately normally distributed, with mean 8% and standard deviation 1.6%." From such a distribution, a user can generate point forecasts by considering summary measures such as the mean or median and can obtain interval forecasts for any desired probability level (50% intervals, 90% intervals, 99% intervals, etc.).

The quantification of judgments makes it easier to understand and to communicate an expert forecaster's subjective judgments. While "hot" has different meanings to different people, "30°C" is unambiguous. Furthermore, since forecasts can seldom be perfect, an interval forecast with a probability level associated with the interval provides a clearer indication of a forecaster's uncertainty than does a statement such as, "The high temperature will be near 30°C."

Assessment Issues

In judgmental forecasting, the term "assessment" refers to the process by which an expert arrives at forecasts. Given that it is desirable to quantify judgments to come up with numerical forecasts, the question is how the expert takes qualitative judgments and generates numerical forecasts. The assessment process should be structured to enable the expert to utilize any information and expertise that can be brought to bear on the issue of concern, forecasting some event or variable.

The design of the assessment process depends on the situation at hand. A weather forecaster who formulates judgmental forecasts regularly, has access to a myriad of weather maps and data, and receives regular feedback in the form of observed weather that can be compared with the forecasts probably needs no assistance in the form of explicit structuring of the forecasting process. On the other hand, a health expert making judgmental forecasts concerning health effects associated with exposure to a pollutant at various levels may not be used to making numerical forecasts judgmentally, may not have looked at some of the indirectly relevant experimental results for some time, and may not have directly relevant data to provide feedback on forecasts or information about the health effects. Careful structuring and assistance are valuable to the health expert.

One important aspect of the assessment process involves the information that is provided to the expert before the actual forecast is determined. At a minimum, this includes a careful definition of the events or variables of interest, including any conditions that are to be assumed, and the exact nature of the desired forecasts. In the case of health effects of pollutants, for instance, the variable of interest might be the proportion of a population that will suffer a certain health effect (such as a heart attack, an asthma attack, or an increase in blood pressure) if exposed to a given level of a pollutant for a specified amount of time. The health effect must be defined in an unambiguous manner, the level of the pollutant and the time of exposure must be specified, the population of interest (which could be the entire population of the United States or a certain city, or might be some subpopulation such as all individuals with heart disease) must be defined, and any other conditions (for instance, whether an individual is at rest or exercising when exposed, temperature and humidity conditions, levels of other pollutants) must be given. In addition, the type of forecast that is needed must be specified. Is the expert to provide a point forecast of the proportion of the population suffering the health effect, a point forecast together with an interval forecast, certain probabilities (say, the probability that at least 10% of the population suffers the adverse health effect), or an entire probability distribution for the proportion of the population suffering the health effect?

Other information might be provided to the expert. Presumably an expert is familiar with relevant studies involving the pollutant of interest. Nonetheless, it is helpful to summarize briefly some of the studies in case the expert has forgotten or is unaware of some findings. Usually the studies are only indirectly related to the forecasts of interest (for example, studies with animals instead of humans, studies with humans at very low exposure levels or under very restrictive conditions). Thus, the expert is not merely being asked to parrot results available from past data. The task at hand is the assimilation of such data and other information and the consideration of the implications for the expert's body of knowledge concerning the relationship between the level of exposure to the pollutant and the adverse health effects.

Another key aspect of the assessment process involves the methodology used to aid the expert in arriving at a numerical forecast. Suppose that a foreign exchange expert is trying to come up with a forecast for the exchange rate between the French franc and the United States dollar, expressed in terms of francs per dollar, as of one year from now. If a point estimate is wanted, it can be thought of informally as a "best guess," and the expert might simply come up with a number without further ado. Just as there are different kinds of summary measures of location in statistics, however, there are different types of point forecasts. Some possibilities are the most likely exchange rate, the expected or mean exchange rate, and the median exchange rate. Specifying a particular type of point forecast will influence the expert's thought process and the ultimate forecast. Asking questions in a manner consistent with the type of point forecast desired can be helpful. Consider the following question:

Do you think it is more likely that the exchange rate one year from now will be greater than 7.50 francs per dollar or less than 7.50 francs per dollar?

If the answer is "greater than 7.50 francs per dollar," the implication is that the expert's median forecast is above 7.50; if the answer is "less than 7.50 francs per dollar," the median is below 7.50; and if the answer is "the two options are equally likely," the median forecast is 7.50. If the rate given in the question is varied until it reaches a value at which the expert responds "the two options are equally likely," then that value can be taken as the median forecast. Note how this assessment method incorporates some structure that may help the expert think about the problem and come up with a forecast.

Probability forecasts are more difficult to assess than point forecasts. Although people deal with uncertainty every day and encounter probabilities in weather forecasts and other public statements, they often tend to feel a bit uncomfortable with the notion of probability. As a result, probability assessment often includes some discussion of uncertainty and probability, and assessment aids are particularly helpful. Instead of asking directly for a numerical probability, one can ask the expert to choose between two lotteries. Suppose that an economist is asked to choose between the following lotteries:

Lottery 1. You win $100 if the inflation rate in West Germany is less than 8% next year, and you win nothing if the inflation rate is 8% or greater.

Lottery 2. You win $100 with probability .50 and nothing with probability .50.

The payoffs are the same in the two lotteries. The expert's choice should therefore be based on whether the probability of an inflation rate of less than 8% is greater than, less than, or equal to .50. Choosing Lottery 1 implies that the expert's judgmental probability forecast is greater than one-half; choosing Lottery 2 implies that this probability is less than one-half; and being indifferent between the two lotteries implies that the probability is equal to one-half. The probability given in Lottery 2 can be varied until a point is reached at which the expert is indifferent, and the expert's probability forecast can then be taken as the value that results in indifference.

Some experts prefer to avoid dealing with numerical probabilities. Lottery 2 can be related to a device known as a "probability wheel." This is a circle divided into two portions of different colors. To have a probability of .75 in Lottery 2, the probability wheel can be set up so that three-quarters of the circle is blue and one-quarter is red, for example. Lottery 2 can then be expressed as follows:

> *Lottery 2.* The wheel will be spun; you win $100 if the wheel stops with the pointer in the blue sector, and you win nothing if the wheel stops with the pointer in the red sector.

The expert can look at the colors on the wheel instead of having to think in terms of numerical probabilities. This device is used often in probability assessment. Instead of making a numerical judgment, the expert makes a comparative judgment, comparing the event of interest (say, the inflation rate in West Germany being less than 8% next year) and a reference event (a certain color occurring on the spin of the probability wheel). It seems easier to make comparative judgments rather than absolute judgments, and in this sense a device such as the probability wheel can be a very useful aid to the expert in a probability forecasting task.

For a forecast consisting of an entire probability distribution for a variable of interest, the assessment process usually involves the consideration of a number of probabilities. For example, the lottery approach with the probability wheel can be used to assess the probability that the inflation rate in West Germany is less than 8% next year, as just discussed. Then the procedure can be repeated at different levels to find the probability that the inflation rate will be less than 3%, less than 5%, less than 10%, and so on. Alternatively, certain fractiles can be found. By dividing the range of possible values into two equally likely intervals, the forecaster can determine a judgmental median inflation rate. These two intervals can themselves be divided into two equally likely subintervals. For instance, if the median inflation rate is judged to be 6%, the expert can ponder the following questions. If the inflation rate in fact turns out to be below 6%, is it more likely to be below 4% or between 4% and 6%? Is it more likely to be below 3% or between 3% and 6%? What value divides the interval below 6% into two equally likely regions? This line of questioning is used to assess the .25

fractile, or the twenty-fifth percentile, of the expert's probability distribution for next year's rate of inflation in West Germany. Similarly, the expert can assess the .75 fractile, the .125 fractile, the .375 fractile, and so on. After a number of cumulative probabilities and/or fractiles are assessed, they can be plotted as points on a cumulative probability distribution and the expert can attempt to come up with a curve representing the cumulative probability distribution, which in turn represents the expert's forecast in the form of an entire probability distribution for the rate of inflation. The distribution provides a user of the forecast with not just a point forecast (which might be taken as the mean or median of the probability distribution) but a complete representation of the expert's uncertainty about next year's inflation rate.

Returning to the general discussion of assessment issues, another important factor concerns the structuring of the problem. Suppose that a sales manager wants to forecast future sales of a particular brand. One option, of course, is to work directly with possible future sales and generate a forecast. Another option is to consider other related events or variables. Suppose that a competitor might come out with a new brand in the near future. The sales manager might find it convenient to break down the problem by forecasting sales given that the new brand is introduced and given that it is not introduced. A forecast as to the likelihood that the new brand will be introduced can be made, and all of these forecasts can then be put together to determine a forecast for future sales. This is a simple example of how a problem can be broken down somewhat to make it easier for an expert to think about the problem and bring expertise to bear most effectively.

Through structuring or the desire for an entire probability distribution instead of just a point forecast, judgmental forecasting often involves multiple forecasts. The forecaster should be careful to check that the forecasts are not inconsistent with each other (for example, probability forecasts have to obey the rules of probability) and that forecasts made early in the process still seem reasonable at the end of the process. It is a good idea to use different assessment methods to guard against inconsistency and against simple slips in judgment. The results from different methods can then be reconciled to arrive at the expert's final judgmental forecast.

From this discussion of assessment issues, it can be seen that a carefully assessed judgmental forecast is not just a snap judgment. Every effort should be made to carefully define the forecast of interest, to review relevant available information, to structure the problem in a manner consistent with the expert's information, and to use assessment methods and aids to help the expert convert qualitative judgments into quantitative forecasts.

Cognitive Issues

A discussion of judgmental forecasting would be incomplete without some mention of psychological aspects of the process of acquiring information, processing it subjectively, and expressing it quantitatively in the form of forecasts. Individuals may have tendencies to misjudge the impact of pieces of information or to not utilize the information appropriately in forecasting under certain circumstances. Such tendencies, which are sometimes referred to as cognitive biases, can lead to forecasts that are not as good as they would be if the biases could be avoided. Awareness of cognitive biases can make it possible to design the assessment process so as to combat the biases and thereby reduce their impact.

An important consideration in terms of cognitive issues involves the order in which information is received. People naturally tend to recall recently seen information more clearly than older information. The most recent experimental study may be foremost in a health expert's mind in forecasting health effects of pollutants, even though earlier studies are equally informative. Thus, it is important to review all information and emphasize that older information should be given just as careful consideration as recent information. Of course, in some situations recent information may be more pertinent to the forecast. For forecasts of economic variables such as GNP, the current state of the economy would be expected to be more relevant than the state of the economy several years ago, and it would thus be reasonable for the forecaster to emphasize recent information. This emphasis should be a conscious decision, however, not simply a result of the ready availability of newer (or more-publicized) data and the forgetting of older data.

Another order-related cognitive issue pertains to the structuring of the assessment process. Suppose that a forecaster wants to determine a point forecast and an interval forecast for a variable. One option is to start out by thinking about the point forecast and then, once the point forecast is given, to move to an interval forecast by making judgments about the uncertainty surrounding the point forecast. For instance, a forecaster might first forecast that interest rates six months hence will be 9% and then indicate that interest rates will almost certainly be between 7% and 11%. A cognitive phenomenon called *anchoring* suggests that once the point forecast is set, it serves as an anchor for future judgments in the sense that such judgments may be closer to the anchor than they should be given the information that is available. This implies that it might be wise to think about extreme values *before* thinking about central, or most likely, values. The forecaster should be encouraged to think about a wide variety of scenarios. It is easy to think about scenarios that lead to "middle-of-the-road" results. Trying to imagine scenarios that could lead to surprisingly low interest rates or unusually high interest rates helps the forecaster realize the degree of uncertainty about interest rates. Given these extreme values and some idea of how likely they might be to occur, the forecaster can think about "middle values" to come up with a point forecast. If the forecaster is providing an entire probability distribution, probabilities in the tails of the distribution might be elicited before probabilities in the center of the distribution, to avoid anchoring on the central values.

Uncertainty is often a complicating factor in thinking about complex situations with several relevant variables. An easy way to simplify matters is to make "best guess" estimates of some variables and to treat these estimates as certainty equivalents (that is, to assume that in fact the variables are equal to these best guesses and that there is no uncertainty about the variables). This may, however, produce an unrealistic level of confidence and a systematic bias in the forecasts. It is important to evaluate all uncertainties and their implications for the forecast at hand. Some cognitive simplifications, such as thinking in terms of certainty equivalents, are necessary to prevent a cognitive overload, but they should not be used blindly.

A trap that is easy for forecasters to fall into is to let their forecasts be influenced by their preferences. For example, a sales manager may forecast high sales because high sales are desirable. On the other hand, a different sales manager may forecast a sales level lower than actually anticipated in order to have a low target that will be relatively easy to exceed. Both sales managers are basing their forecasts not just on their best judgments about likely sales levels, but also on their hopes or desires. The user of the forecasts may not share the forecaster's preferences and therefore would like to receive a forecast based on the forecaster's judgments but as value free as possible. This is a tricky problem, since the forecaster's preferences may be strong enough to intrude despite instructions to sort out such preferences and provide value-free forecasts. Incentive schemes to encourage honest forecasts may be helpful in this regard.

Cognitive issues should be given careful attention when the assessment process is structured. Attempts can be made to lead the forecaster to think in ways that will reduce the impact of potential cognitive biases. Also, since different cognitive biases may influence forecasts in different directions, a promising strategy is to use two or more approaches to generate a desired forecast and to reconcile differences among the results. Training forecasters to understand and attempt to overcome cognitive biases and encouraging them to use multiple approaches to consider and quantify their judgments seems likely to lead to forecasts that accurately represent the forecasters' information and expertise.

Combining Forecasts

As indicated earlier, in many forecasting situations the judgment of an expert can play a very important role in the forecasting process. But if one expert can provide valuable information, perhaps two or more experts can be even more valuable. Different experts may bring different approaches and somewhat different sets of information to a forecasting situation. Consulting several forecasters and combining their forecasts into a single forecast is directly analogous to taking a sample in statistics and combining the same observations via some summary statistic.

In line with the sampling analogy, the forecasts from several experts can be combined mechanically. Just as we take the sample mean of a set of observations, for example, we can take the simple average of the forecasts and treat it as a single combined forecast. The simple average has the advantage of being easy to use, and it treats the forecasts symmetrically. If we have no reason to believe that one forecaster is "better" than another, a symmetric rule seems appropriate. In addition, the simple average is quite robust, performing reasonably well even when the symmetry assumption is not suitable. In empirical studies, the simple average tends to outperform many more complicated procedures.

If there is good reason to believe that some forecasters are more accurate than others, the forecasts from the more accurate forecasters should be given more weight than those from the less accurate forecasters. The result is a weighted average instead of a simple average. If the forecasters are independent in the sense that their forecasting errors are independent, the weights are proportional to the reciprocals of the error variances. The larger the error variance, the smaller its reciprocal and thus the smaller the weight given to that forecast. When forecasters are dependent, the determination of the weights is a bit more complicated; with high dependence the weights are very sensitive to the exact nature and degree of dependence. In general, while simple averages are robust and easy to use, weighted averages have potential in situations in which a considerable amount of information is available about the relative accuracy of forecasters and about forecaster dependence. Combining rules more complex than the weighted averages are also available. The objective in any given situation is to combine forecasts to wind up with a single combined forecast that suitably reflects all of the information contained in the individual forecasts.

A direct mechanical combination of forecasts does not allow for any exchange of information. Another option is to provide forecasters with feedback and then allow them to revise their forecasts if they wish to do so. This feedback might consist merely of the complete set of individual forecasts (generally without an indication of who made which forecast or perhaps even who the other forecasters are). To convey a bit more information, each forecast might be accompanied by a short justification indicating the evidence that was considered and the reasoning used in coming up with the forecast. After the forecasts are revised by the forecasters, they can be combined mechanically or the process of feedback and reforecasting can be repeated. The forecasts might be expected to be more similar after each expert sees the forecasts and possibly the arguments of the other forecasters, since the exchange of information gives the experts more of a common base of information. However, the revised forecasts will probably still not be the same. Even with a relatively common base of information, the experts will generally have different opinions about what is most important and how it will influence the variable that is being forecast.

For more extensive exchange of information, the forecasters might actually get together to discuss their forecasts and the underlying data and theories. After the discussion, each forecaster can provide a revised forecast, and the revised forecasts can be combined mechanically. Note that as information is shared, either in writing or in a face-to-face discussion, the relative accuracy of the forecasts may become more similar. This shift strengthens the argument for a symmetric approach that treats the forecasters equally through a measure such as a simple average.

The possibility of group discussion can be extended to allow for a full behavioral approach to the combination of forecasts. In addition to discussing their initial individual forecasts and factors underlying these forecasts, the group can attempt to go one step further and come up with a single group forecast. That is, the forecasts might be combined behaviorally instead of mechanically. In such group decision making, questions concerning group dynamics become germane. The danger exists that when disagreements occur, the group forecast will be influenced more by debating skill and considerations of relative "power" in the group than by forecasting ability. Nonetheless, decisions are often made by committee, and the behavioral combination of forecasts should be considered as a viable alternative to mechanical combination, keeping potential shortcomings in mind.

A final note concerning combination of forecasts is that the forecasts being combined need not all be judgmental. For example, in economic forecasting, judgmental forecasts from economists might be combined with forecasts from econometric models and from extrapolation methods. When the forecasts being combined come from different types of sources, redundancy is likely to be reduced and the combined forecast is likely to be more informative. Even when forecasts are not combined formally, the availability of other forecasts can help in the formulation of a judgmental forecast. In many weather forecasting situations, the final forecasts are judgmental but the forecaster has access to forecasts generated using statistical methods and atmospheric models.

BAYESIAN FORECASTING

As new information becomes available, forecasters' opinions may change and forecasts may be updated. The previous discussion on combination of forecasts noted that a forecaster may revise forecasts on learning about the forecasts and arguments of other experts. Other types of new evidence may also lead to a reevaluation of judgments and forecasts. In general, it is desirable to base forecasts on any and all available information, including past data, informal observations, underlying theories, output from models, subjective judgments, and so on. It is therefore important to update forecasts as any type of new evidence is obtained.

Informally, the incorporation of new information is done judgmentally all the time. Everyone reconsiders opinions as new information is obtained. Strictly in terms of judgmental forecasts, then, updating becomes a matter of making subjective adjustments to forecasts. More formally, a result from probability theory known as Bayes' theorem can be used to assist in the updating process. Bayes' theorem serves to organize the revision process, considering separately the information previously available and the new evidence and then combining them in an appropriate manner. This separation may make it easier for a forecaster to think about the problem and may remove some of the cognitive burden by making it possible for the information to be combined formally via a mathematical formula.

Bayes' Theorem

Bayes' theorem, which is really nothing more than a simple formula for conditional probability, provides a general framework for updating quantitative forecasts. Since it involves probabilities, it is particularly useful when probability forecasts are of interest. However, it can also be used to revise point and interval forecasts.

To illustrate the simplest form of Bayes' theorem, suppose that a physician wants to forecast whether a patient has a particular disease. The forecast is to be a probability forecast. An extensive data bank is available concerning the disease in question, and the data bank indicates that among people with the symptoms exhibited by the patient, 5% have the disease. Thus, given the symptoms, the probability forecast is .05 that the patient has the disease. In Bayesian terms, this is called a *prior* probability, since it reflects the information available prior to the receipt of new evidence. Here the prior forecast is obtained from past data; in other cases, especially situations with limited past data, the prior forecast may be judgmental.

The physician can obtain new evidence in the form of one or more tests run on the patient. Suppose a particular test yields either a positive or a negative result. In the patient in question, the result turns out to be positive. This test has been used extensively, and its characteristics are well known: Among those with the particular disease, 99% show a positive reading and 1% show a negative reading, and among those without the disease, 6% show a positive reading and 94% show a negative reading. Another way of expressing the characteristics of the test is to say that the test has a 1% false-negative rate and a 6% false-positive rate.

Given that the patient has a positive result, the physician asks how likely such a result is if the patient has the disease and how likely it is if the patient does not have the disease. From the previous information about the test, the probability of a positive reading is .99 with the disease and .06 without the disease. These two probabilities are called *likelihoods,* since they measure how likely the new evidence is under the possible states of the world (the patient has the disease, the patient does not have the disease). The likelihoods serve to relate the new evidence to the events of concern.

The prior probabilities represent the information available before the test result is seen, and the likelihoods represent the information contained in the test result. The role of Bayes' theorem is to combine the prior probabilities and the likelihoods to arrive at revised probabilities reflecting both the prior information *and* the new evidence. In the medical example, Bayes' theorem can be expressed as follows:

$$P(\text{disease}|+) = \frac{P(\text{disease})P(+|\text{disease})}{P(\text{disease})P(+|\text{disease}) + P(\text{no disease})P(+|\text{no disease})}$$

where + denotes a positive reading. The prior probabilities are

$$P(\text{disease}) = .05$$

and

$$P(\text{no disease}) = .95.$$

The likelihoods are

$$P(+|\text{disease}) = .99$$

and

$$P(+|\text{no disease}) = .06.$$

Bayes' theorem therefore yields a revised probability forecast of

$$P(\text{disease}|+) = \frac{.05(.99)}{.05(.99) + .95(.06)} = .46.$$

After the positive reading on the test is observed, the revised probability is .46 that the patient has the disease (and $1 - .46$, or .54, that the patient does not have the disease).

As would be expected, a positive reading from the test results in an increase in the probability that the patient has the disease. Furthermore, Bayes' theorem indicates exactly how much the forecast should be increased, from .05 to .46. If, on the other hand, the test had provided a negative result, the Bayesian updating procedure would have given the revised probability forecast

$$P(\text{disease}|-) = \frac{P(\text{disease})P(-|\text{disease})}{P(\text{disease})P(-|\text{disease}) + P(\text{no disease})P(-|\text{no disease})}$$

$$= \frac{.05(.01)}{.05(.01) + .95(.94)} = .0006.$$

where " $-$ " denotes a negative reading. With a negative result, it is extremely unlikely that the patient has the disease.

A side benefit of the Bayesian framework is that it can provide forecasts in advance regarding the new evidence as well as revised forecasts for the event or variable of concern. The denominator of Bayes' theorem provides predictions for the new information. In the medical example, the denominator of Bayes' theorem, which can be calculated before the test is run, is a probability forecast for whether the test result will be positive:

$$P(+) = P(\text{disease})P(+|\text{disease})$$
$$+ P(\text{no disease})P(+|\text{no disease})$$
$$= .05(.99) + .95(.06) = .11.$$

Note that the denominator of the application of Bayes' theorem for a negative reading is

$$P(-) = P(\text{disease})P(-|\text{disease})$$
$$+ P(\text{no disease})P(-|\text{no disease})$$
$$= .05(.01) + .95(.94) = .89.$$

Thus, before the test is run it appears that the probability is .11 that the test reading will be positive and .89 that it will be negative.

Probability, Point and Interval Forecasts

Bayes' theorem deals in terms of probabilities or probability distributions. Thus, in Bayesian forecasting it is natural to think in terms of probability forecasts. The forecasts in the previous medical example, for instance, are probability forecasts for the patient having or not having the disease and probability forecasts for obtaining a positive or negative reading on the test. If the test resulted not just in a positive or negative reading but in a numerical measurement, such as a measurement of blood pressure or a cholesterol level, the Bayesian approach would generate an entire probability distribution. For example, a forecast might be that the patient's serum cholesterol level is normally distributed with a mean of 220 and a standard deviation of 10.

Point or interval forecasts, if desired, can always be obtained from a probability distribution. If a patient's serum cholesterol level is normally distributed with mean 220 and standard deviation 10, a reasonable point forecast for the serum cholesterol level would simply be the mean, 220. A 95% interval estimate would be approximately $220 \pm 2(10)$, which gives an interval from 200 to 240. If new information led to a revision of the probability distribution of serum cholesterol, the point and interval forecasts could be adjusted accordingly.

To illustrate the revision of probability distributions and the associated point and interval forecasts, suppose that a quality control expert is interested in forecasting the average weight in a shipment of parts that has just been received. Previous batches from the same supplier have averaged 235 grams per unit, and the sampling variability is such that the uncertainty about the average weight can be expressed by a variance of 12 grams^2. The quality control expert thinks that the average weight is approximately normally distributed. On the basis of this prior information, the point forecast for the average weight in the new shipment is 235 grams, and a 95% interval forecast is approximately $235 \pm 2 \sqrt{12}$, or from 228.1 to 241.9.

To obtain more information about the average weight in the new shipment, the quality control expert takes a sample of parts from the shipment and weighs them. The sample mean weight is 231 grams, and the variance of this estimate is 9 grams (that is, the standard error of the estimate is 3 grams). In a Bayesian revision for this situation, the mean of the posterior distribution is found by taking a weighted average of the prior mean and the sample mean. The weights are proportional to the reciprocals of the respective variances. Thus, the posterior mean is

$$\frac{(1/12)\,(235) + (1/9)\,(231)}{(1/12) + (1/9)} = 232.7.$$

The posterior variance is

$$\frac{1}{(1/12) + (1/9)} = 5.14.$$

After the sample is taken, the posterior distribution is approximately normally distributed with mean 232.7 and variance 5.14. Note that the revised mean is between the sample mean of 231 and the prior mean of 235. Also note that the revised variance of 5.14 is less than the prior variance of 12; the new information has reduced the uncertainty about the average weight in the shipment. A point forecast from the revised distribution is 232.7, and a 95% interval forecast is approximately $232.7 \pm 2 \sqrt{5.14}$, or from 228.2 to 237.2. The new information has caused the point forecast to shift toward the sample mean and has led to a narrower interval forecast.

Bayesian Model Building and Forecasting

At the heart of the Bayesian approach to statistics and forecasting is the notion of model building. Bayesian methodology does not begin by assuming that the forecast is of a certain form, such as a simple average or an exponentially smoothed average of past data. Instead, it begins with an attempt to model the underlying data-generating process. Questions such as whether observations are independent, whether period-to-period changes are independent, whether the process is changing over time, whether variables are normally distributed, whether variables are related in a linear or nonlinear fashion, and so on, are typically considered in the modeling process. The Bayesian approach is not unique in this regard, of course. Other approaches to statistics and forecasting also involve modeling of the data-generating process.

The modeling of the data-generating process focuses on the likelihood function. Another important aspect that *is* unique to the Bayesian approach is the formal inclusion of prior information. Thus, Bayesian model building refers to the determination not only of the likelihood function but also of the prior distribution. This distribution should reflect all available prior information, including both "hard data" and subjective judgments. The formal inclusion of judgmental information and the explicit recognition of the important role that judgment plays in all model building, including model building related to the likelihood function, are important features of the Bayesian approach. Another key feature is the fact that all uncertainties are represented directly through probabilities.

The examples of Bayesian forecasting given earlier represent very simple Bayesian models. In the medical example, a single event (the patient has the disease) is of interest, and the new information has to provide one of only two possible outcomes (a positive reading or a negative reading on the test). In the quality control example, a single sample of parts is taken at a given point in time, and the sampling distribution of interest is assumed to be approximately normal. The prior distribution is based directly on past data from previous shipments, with no changes over time being considered. This is illustrative of simple models involving processes such as the Bernoulli process, the Poisson process, and the independent normal process.

Bayesian models have also been developed and applied with more complex processes, such as Markov processes, normal autoregressive processes, and regression models with shifting parameters. Limited space and a desire to minimize technical detail prevent a full discussion of such complex models here. For an informal example, however, consider another quality control example. Suppose that a machine produces defective items at a certain average rate. Over time, the average rate changes in a stochastic fashion. One possibility is that the average rate during a given period is equal to the average rate during the previous period plus a term representing noise that is normally distributed. Samples of items from the process are taken regularly, and these samples can be used to revise the distribution of the current average defective rate. With this model, the point forecast of the current average defective rate is an exponentially weighted average of the observed defective rates in the samples, with the most recent sample being given the most weight. The exact weights depend on the various uncertainties (uncertainty about the initial defective rate, variability of the noise term, sampling variability in the individual samples) that should be examined in detail in the model-building process. This model is not overly complex, but the sketch does provide an indication of a model in which parameters shift over time.

Whether simple or more sophisticated models are involved, the basic notions of Bayesian model building are the same.

CONCLUSION

Interest in and emphasis on judgmental forecasting and Bayesian forecasting have been increasing recently. This reflects recognition that in many situations there is extensive subjective expertise and a paucity of "hard data." It also reflects recognition that models and forecasts need to be updated constantly to keep up with new information and with a changing environment. In this chapter, some basic notions pertaining to judgmental forecasting and Bayesian forecasting have been presented.

A brief chapter such as this can only begin to scratch the surface of topics such as judgmental and Bayesian forecasting. Detailed discussions of judgmental processes can be found in Hogarth[2] and in Kahneman, Slovic, and Tversky.[3] Assessment issues are studied in Winkler[5] and in Spetzler and Staël von Holstein.[4] An introductory presentation of Bayesian methods is given in Winkler.[6] More complex Bayesian models are covered in Zellner,[7] and a general approach to Bayesian forecasting is provided in Harrison and Stevens.[1] Most of these references themselves have extensive bibliographies for readers wanting to learn more about these topics.

REFERENCES

1. Harrison, P. J., and C. F. Stevens, "Bayesian Forecasting," *Journal of the Royal Statistical Society,* Series B, vol. 38, 1976, pp. 205–247.

2. Hogarth, R. M., *Judgement and Choice,* John Wiley, Chichester, 1980.

3. Kahneman, D., P. Slovic, and A. Tversky, *Judgment Under Uncertainty: Heuristics and Biases,* Cambridge University Press, Cambridge, MA, 1982.

4. Spetzler, C. S., and C.-A. S. Staël von Holstein, "Probability Encoding in Decision Analysis," *Management Science,* vol. 22, 1975, pp. 340–358.

5. Winkler, R. L., "The Assessment of Prior Distributions in Bayesian Analysis," *Journal of the American Statistical Association,* vol. 62, 1967, pp. 776–800.

6. Winkler, R. L., *An Introduction to Bayesian Inference and Decision,* Holt, Rinehart and Winston, New York, 1972.

7. Zellner, A., *An Introduction to Bayesian Inference in Econometrics,* John Wiley, New York, 1971.

CHAPTER

16

AN INTEGRATED APPROACH TO MEDIUM- AND LONG-TERM FORECASTING

The Marketing-Mix System

RUDOLF LEWANDOWSKI

Marketing Systems, Essen, Germany

INTRODUCTION

Forecasting methods in current use often suffer from three major deficiencies. First, they are too complex to be understood by the average user; second, they involve a number of unrealistic assumptions that greatly hinder practitioners who use them; and third, they do not integrate into a single model extrapolative and explicative variables.

The purpose of this chapter is to describe an approach to medium- and long-term forecasting that aims to correct these problems. This approach is now widely used in continental Europe but remains little known in the Anglo-Saxon world, since up to now it has been discussed mainly in German and French (see Lewandowski[2,3]).

The basic components of the marketing-mix approach to medium- and long-range forecasting, as will be described in this chapter, are (1) the combination of extrapolative and explicative variables into a single model; (2) the integration of the medium- and long-term elements into a single model; and (3) the development of a realistic system that can be used by practicing managers who have an interest in forecasting.

It should be emphasized that this approach is practice oriented and empirically developed, its main aim being to help practicing managers make forecasts in a more efficient and effective way. For this reason, it does not comprise highly sophisticated mathematical formulas, and as such it is hoped that the reader of this handbook will gain a clearer understanding of—and thus be able to improve on—his or her medium- and long-term forecasting functions.

THE INTEGRATED SETUP

There are two approaches to the study of the long term. The first of these is simply extrapolative, whereby some variable of interest is considered by itself and its trend is analyzed and then extrapolated in order to predict the future. Such an approach is both "blind" and "fatalistic"; however, in practice it has been found to produce satisfactory results. This has been observed for individual products as well as larger market segments, or even whole technologies. While such trends were initially thought to be linear, during the 1960s logistic or S-shaped curves were introduced to improve observation of the long-term behavior of the variable to be forecasted. It is today widely accepted that only nonlinear trends can adequately predict future patterns. The problem still to be solved, however, is which of the many existing nonlinear trends represents the best choice.

The second approach is to study the causal factors that influence certain events, and then make forecasts along the lines that if "a" happens, "b" will follow. This sort of causal approach, although it works very well in the physical and natural sciences, has severe limitations in the economic and business environments. On the other hand, it is imperative to establish a method of ascertaining how changes in one variable will affect the others; hence there is a need for the development of explanatory models that facilitate the interpretation of what actually happens in reality, and also help to provide more accurate forecasts. These models will be referred to as "explicative" in this chapter, meaning that their aim is to provide a clearer understanding of the factors affecting the future of a company, without necessarily going so far as to say that there may be causal relationships among the various elements comprising the explicative model.

A third alternative is to combine these two approaches into an integrated setup that includes both exploratory trends and explicative variables. Up to now, according to the forecasting literature, this procedure has not been successfully attempted, even though its potential benefit is obvious.

Another important element affecting the behavior of long-term trends is the influence of medium-term changes. In this respect, it is impossible to separate the medium and the long term; for example, a significant price increase forecasted for the medium term will inevitably affect long-term trends. Furthermore, cyclical fluctuations will affect longer-term developments and must therefore also be incorporated into the long-term model. Chart 16-1 shows the four possibilities of forecasting models.

CHART 16-1. The Four Types of Integrated (Long-Term and Medium-Term) Forecasting Models

Long Term	Medium Term	
	Extrapolative	Explicative
Extrapolative (e.g., time series)	Ld-Md	Ld-Mx
Explicative (e.g., causal)	Lx-Md	Lx-Mx

Key: Ld—Long-term extrapolative setup
Lx—Long-term explicative setup
Md—Medium-term extrapolative setup
Mx—Medium-term explicative setup

1. *Long-Term Extrapolative (Ld), Medium-Term Extrapolative (Md) Setup: Ld-Md.* This is a purely extrapolative setup, as both the long term and the medium term allow only for temporal developments that are not explained by incorporating explicative variables.

The analysis of such models is therefore automatic and is relatively simple to carry out, since it can be performed entirely with computer programs, particularly with regard to determining the extrapolative functions and their parameter optimization. The degree of explaining for the medium or long term with such functions can, however, only be mediocre.

The Ld-Md setup is of interest only when a large number of products have to be analyzed by a limited staff.

2. *Long-Term Extrapolative (Ld), Medium-Term Explicative (Mx) Setup: Ld-Mx.* The long-term setup here is of an extrapolative nature, while that of the medium term attempts an explicative explanation of medium-term development. When the law contained in Ld is well adapted to the market development, which is the case for time series with comprehensive material from the past and for products in the consumer goods sector, the medium-term analysis is not distorted and can provide excellent results. This setup concentrates more on an economic analysis and less on a long-term model construction.

3. *Long-Term Explicative (Lx), Medium-Term Extrapolative (Md) Setup: Lx-Md.* This setup aims at a comprehensive explanation of the medium- and long-term development using explicative models. However, the explicative part of the model is oriented mainly for the long term, while the medium term is defined by an extrapolative model.

4. *Long-Term Explicative (Lx), Medium-Term Explicative (Mx) Setup: Lx-Mx.* This setup aims to provide a comprehensive explanation of both the medium and the long term. However, due to its lack of extrapolative trends, it has not been adopted into the approach described in this chapter. A typical situation of this type would be a set of simultaneous equations, that is, an econometric model. Although the development of such models is extremely difficult, only this type of setup ensures the formation of actual explicative systems with satisfactory operational reliability.

The purpose of the integrated approach just described is (1) to separate medium- from long-term influences and to determine their specific consequences; (2) to forecast each of the consequences separately; and (3) to eliminate as far as possible economic distortions caused by fluctuations from long-term trends.

THE METHODOLOGY OF THE INTEGRATED SETUP

For a practical system to be developed, the approach must provide the possibility of combining the major elements of the medium and the long term, together with extrapolative and explicative characteristics. The purpose of this section is to illustrate how this can be achieved.

A series of nonlinear growth functions exists that can be used to describe long-term developments. These are the following:

Exponential function with saturation level

Symmetric-logistic function

Pyatt function

Gompertz function

Weblus function

Semilogarithmic function

von Boguslawski function

The choice of the most appropriate of these seven functions is, however, difficult. To avoid this problem, the functions have been classified into two groups (see Lewandowski[2]) known as "first and second order generalized logistic functions." The user is thereby able to let a computer program choose from these generalized logistic functions the one that best fits the data. The two classifications of functions are as follows:

Generalized logistic functions of the first order $\begin{cases} \text{Symmetric-logistic} \\ \text{Exponential} \\ \text{von Bertalanffy} \\ \text{Böhm} \end{cases}$

Generalized logistic functions of the second order $\begin{cases} \text{Gompertz} \\ \text{Johnson} \\ \text{Exponential} \end{cases}$

Some users may wish to look at long-term trends using one of the two generalized functions; such an approach, however, is somewhat simplistic in that it tends to disregard the medium term. My approach therefore provides for the integration of medium-term economic fluctuations with the generalized logistic functions. In addition, lag effects can be incorporated into the system so that the influence of the medium term can eventually be eliminated, in such a way that long-term trends can be studied and correctly extrapolated.

The advantage of a simple extrapolative approach is that it is easy to implement, being a more or less automatic procedure, and can be used when forecasts are required for large numbers of products. It does, however, fail to take into account explanatory variables, which have an undeniable influence on the medium and long term. In order for this important integration to be achieved, generalized logistic functions of the third, fourth, and fifth order (see Lewandowski[3]) can be introduced by the user.

Equation (16-1), for example, presents a third-order generalized logistic function (GLF3):

$$P_t = \frac{P_0^*}{1 + e^{a - bt - c \cdot Y_t + d \cdot Pr_t - f \cdot \Delta_t}} \tag{16-1}$$

where Y_t = private consumption at period t

Pr_t = relative market price at period t

Δ_t = economic variable that specifies price-income relation, which in turn is defined by

$$\Delta_t = \Delta Y_t - \Delta Pr_t$$

As can be seen, this model comprises both S-shaped curve-type trends and explicative variables such as private consumption, relative market prices, and price-income relations.

APPLICATION FOR THE CAR MARKET IN THE FEDERAL REPUBLIC OF GERMANY

The following description outlines the use of the generalized logistic function of the third order for determining the development of new automobile registrations in the Federal Republic of Germany. The model employs the following four explanatory variables:

$X1$ = Nominal wages and salaries

$X2$ = Inflation rate

$X3$ = Car repair costs

$X4$ = New models launched on the market in a period of six months

Taking into account these four variables and assuming a logistic trend-growth function model, Equation 16-2 was developed and empirically tested for new car registrations in the Federal Republic of Germany. We have

$$P_t = \frac{P^*}{1 + e^{a-bt+c\cdot Y_t+d\cdot\Delta Pr_t+e\Delta MP_t}} \tag{16-2}$$

where P^* = potential market level

P_t = current market performance

$Y_t = X1_t/X2_t$ (i.e., Y_t is inflation-adjusted index of wages and salaries)

$$\Delta Pr_t = \sum_{i=0}^{\infty} \lambda(1 - \lambda)^i Pr_{t-i}^* \text{ (i.e., changes in prices, allowing for time lags)}$$

where

$$\lambda = 0, 3$$

$$Pr_t^* = (X3_t - 3, 0)^2 + 9, 0$$

and

$$MP_t = \lambda \cdot X4_t + \lambda(1 - \lambda)X4_{t-1} + \lambda(1 - \lambda)^2 X4_{t-2} + \ldots$$

$$= \sum_{i=0}^{\infty} \lambda(1 - \lambda)^i MP_{t-i}$$

This type of model, therefore, allows market development to be followed with the aid of S-shaped functions, that is, with incorporation of saturation levels, as well as four economic variables. It has been found, however, that the model did not perform satisfactorily during the periods from 1963 to 1965, 1968 to 1970, and 1973 to 1976.

The first two periods represented a boom phase in the development of the car market in the Federal Republic of Germany, whereas the third phase was marked by a recessive development following the energy crisis. The model described here does not appear to be as suitable for the analysis of large cyclical fluctuations as for the description of "normal" business conditions.

A GENERALIZED LOGISTIC FUNCTION OF THE FOURTH ORDER (GLF4)

The fundamental idea of the GLF4 is based on the work proposed by Bonus.[1] The major difference of GLF4 is in the definition of the saturation level. Bonus has formulated the following model:

$$P_t^* = \frac{P_0^*}{1 + c \cdot Y_t^{-\alpha}} \tag{16-3}$$

that is, the potential market level P_t depends on the income level Y_t of private households.

If the Bonus model of the potential market evolution is incorporated into the definition of logistic growth, the following equation is obtained:

$$P_t' = b \cdot P_t(P_t^* - P_t) = b \cdot P_t \cdot \left(\frac{P_0^*}{1 + c \cdot Y_t^{-\alpha}} - P_t \right) \tag{16-4}$$

The solution of this equation is

$$P_t = \frac{P_0^*}{1 + e^{-b \cdot t} + d \cdot Y_t^{-\alpha}} = \frac{P_0^*}{1 + A_1 e^{-b \cdot t} + A_2 \cdot Y_t^{-\alpha}} \tag{16-5}$$

where $P_0^* = $ maximum saturation level of market, that is, maximum attainable level of P_t

$A_1 e^{-bt} = $ rate of logistic growth of market expansion

$A_2 Y_t^{-a} = $ influence of explicative variables Y_t

It is quite obvious, however, that market developments do not depend on a single variable. An application of the model with income and price variables will therefore now be considered.

The GLF4 can be modified as follows, to allow for the income and price variables:

$$P_t^* = \frac{P_0^*}{1 + CPr_t^\beta \cdot Y_t^{-\alpha}} \tag{16-6}$$

Thus, the influence of the price and income variables is accounted for in multiplicative form, which appears to be more appropriate than an additive representation of these two variables.

The solution of Equation 16-6 is

$$P_t = \frac{P_0^*}{1 + A_1 \cdot e^{-bt} + A_2 Y_t^{-\alpha} + A_3 Y^{-\alpha} Pr_t^\beta} \tag{16-7}$$

The term C can also represent an environmental variable for the medium term—for instance, the change in personal income (ΔX_t). This case is presented in Chart 16-2.

Although the differences between the fundamental structures of Equations 16-2 and 16-7 are relatively small, the growth hypotheses defined according to Equation 16-7 are more realistic and lead to a better description of actual market developments.

Although the ideas described in this and the preceding section had been applied for many years, it was found that in unfavorable situations (1966–1967, 1974–1975) the market development was only partially explained by

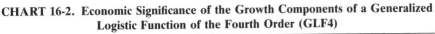

CHART 16-2. Economic Significance of the Growth Components of a Generalized Logistic Function of the Fourth Order (GLF4)

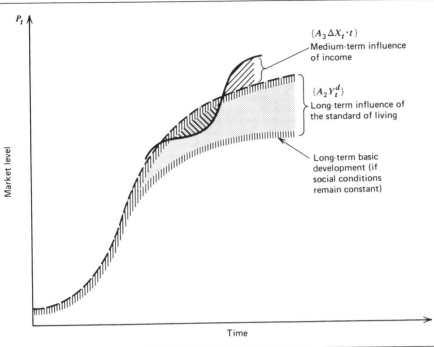

the models; this was also the case for the pronounced upswing in the years 1969–1970 and 1976–1977.

Thus, while a relatively high forecasting accuracy was achieved for the period from 1955 to 1965, with an average deviation of 3%, this was no longer the case from 1966 onward.

The generalized logistic function of the fourth order permits a better approximation of medium- and long-term analysis and forecasting by breaking down the most important factors influencing the market; but it does have several deficiencies. On the other hand, it was found that such functions exhibited a high degree of forecasting reliability, which became particularly clear when comparisons were made with purely extrapolative methods. For instance, forecasts made in 1975, using logistic functions, underestimated the actual demand level by about 25%. This underestimation will rise to about 35% for the year 1985, while the generalized logistic function of the fourth order will show a deviation of about 10%. Needless to say, however, an attempt to improve the GLF4 has been made, resulting in the GLF5 described in the next section.

A GENERALIZED LOGISTIC FUNCTION OF THE FIFTH ORDER (GLF5) AS A GENERAL FORECASTING SETUP

The GLF5 differs from the previously described generalized logistic functions of the third and fourth orders in that it has a more flexible structure, which applies not only to the long term but also to the medium-term component (see Lewandowski[3]). The GLF5 can be termed a function generator, incorporating all aspects and models of the medium and long term so far described. Chart 16-3 shows a schematic presentation of GLF5.

The application of the generalized logistic functions of the fifth order is vital within the framework of medium- and long-term forecasting. These functions describe not only generalized extrapolative models (with the aid of generalized logistic functions of the first and second orders), but also generalized explicative models of the GLF3 and GLF4; furthermore, they also can be expanded to incorporate even more diverse situations than those so far encountered.

Criticism has been raised concerning the considerable complexity involved with GLF5. However, in my opinion, the extraordinary possibilities of GLF5 have been overlooked. Its practical implementation by a large number of companies in recent years has proved that the technical difficulties arising from the application of specific systems of GLF5 can be kept to a minimum, while the quality of the analyses and forecasts could be considerably improved.

As applications have shown, the generalized logistic functions of the fifth order can become real explicative and operational systems that permit strategic corporate alternatives to be simulated and studied.

To easily generate these explicative models, the forecasting system *MARKET* was developed. This was done on behalf of about 20 international

CHART 16-3. Generation of a Generalized Logistic Function of the Fifth Order (GLF5)

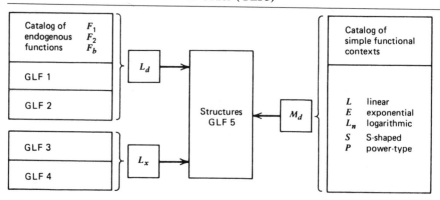

companies. The purpose of the system was to forecast the medium term and the long term for both sales and financial forecasting.

CONCLUSIONS

Even though there might be some difficulties with implementing the integrated setup described in this chapter, it is believed that it represents a unique and practical tool of market research for the analysis and forecasting of variables of interest.

The approach allows forecasters

To find the significant variables of market reactions

To determine the time lag effects for each variable

To define the explicative concepts that characterize market and consumer behavior

To describe the functional relationships among the explicative concepts and market and consumer behavior

To describe long-term trends by isolating medium-term influences

The term "integrated" is appropriate to the setup described here in that the various market and consumer reactions form an integrated relationship, both in the medium- and long-term sector.

It is believed that the integrated setup is currently the only one that enables the real explicative market structures to be determined, and as such it represents a real corporate model for simulating and forecasting market conditions.

It is important to emphasize that the generalized logistic function of the fifth order permits us to measure and understand changes in trend. This is extremely important and cannot be done by the "classic" forecasting methods.

The degree of accuracy of the approach depends on the requirements of the analysis, the amount of data available, and the specific industry or company. However, the division of the total market can be easily interpreted using the principal variables concerned. In this way, the user can go to a much greater depth if he or she so desires.

Because of the repeated use of the forecasting system *MARKET*, there have been several papers describing specific applications; for example, Lewandowski and Stöwsand,[7] Lewandowski and Faber,[4] Lewandowski and Faber,[5] Lewandowski and Rouas,[6] and Lewandowski.[3]

All of these models can incorporate both economic variables and internal factors related to marketing strategy dealing with the medium and long term.

REFERENCES

1. Bonus, H., *Die Ausbreitung des Fernsehens*, Diss. University of Bonn, 1967.

2. Lewandowski, R., *Prognose- und Informationssysteme, Band I*, de Gruyter Berlin, 1974.

3. Lewandowski, R., *Prognose- und Informationssysteme, Band II*, de Gruyter Berlin, 1980.

4. Lewandowski, R. and Faber, W., "An Analysis and Forecasting System for the Paper Market," in H. Dittner, ed., *Europa Birkner Marketing Report, Vol. 1: Paper Market Research*, Birkner & Co., Hamburg, 1978.

5. Lewandowski, R., and W. Faber, "Practical Setups of Market Modeling and Forecasting," *Journal of the European Society for Opinion and Marketing Research*, vol. 7, no. 5, September 1979, pp. 192–201.

6. Lewandowski, R., and J. Rouas, "The Application of Long and Medium Term MMIS at Colgate-Palmolive," paper presented at the Esomar Seminar on Information Systems in Action, Amsterdam, 1980.

7. Lewandowski, R., and H. Stöwsand, "Marketing Models for Use in Practice—A Criticism of Conventional Methods and a Practical Solution. It Won't Work Here," AMA/Esomar Conference, New York, 1979.

PART

3

FORECASTING CHALLENGES

17

FORECASTING AND THE ENVIRONMENT: THE CHALLENGES OF RAPID CHANGE

ALAN R. BECKENSTEIN

*The Colgate Darden Graduate School of Business Administration,
University of Virginia, Charlottesville*

Rapid changes in the economy and other elements of a firm's external environment occurred during the 1970s and 1980s. The impact of these events on standard forecasting techniques has been poorly understood. It is the purpose of this chapter to outline the impact of environmental change on forecasting techniques within the context of the total forecasting system of a corporation.

The relationship of environmental change to forecasting systems is addressed first. A survey of environmental factors and their impact is then presented. Performance measures are the subject of the third section. Finally, a general approach to incorporating environmental influences in forecasts is offered.

ENVIRONMENTAL CHANGE AND FORECASTING SYSTEMS

When managers forecast—and even when they choose not to do so formally—they make implicit hypotheses (assumptions) about the "environment" of their forecast. Consider the following example. Company X has decided to forecast its sales by relating them in a regression model to real gross national product (RGNP). Because the sales of the company are affected by the economy, and the business cycle in particular, a causal model has been chosen.

What is the "environment" of this forecasting system? The *environment of a forecast* is the set of factors not explicitly accounted for by the forecasting system itself. In the most general sense, the environment contains an infinite number of factors. More realistically, it contains all of the factors known in practice to influence the variable being forecast but not formally incorporated in the forecasting model. For company X, the environment includes those factors other than real GNP that affect sales.

Forecasting techniques tend to be quantitatively complex but qualitatively simple. Managers almost always employ a larger set of factors in thinking about how to forecast sales than do model builders in formal development of a forecasting system. Three obstacles exist to dissuade a model builder (or a manager) from incorporating all relevant environmental information in a formal model: (1) the cost of modeling, (2) a lack of (or high cost of) precise data, and (3) the absence of truly definitive historical experience from which the differential effects of separate variables can be isolated.

Forecasting experts are trained how to search for the most cost-effective model. They necessarily sacrifice realism for usefulness. They cannot work with too many variables or too much complexity, so they scientifically establish priorities. Where statistical indicators show that more complexity adds little value relative to cost, the forecaster stops.

Managers are trained to be sensitive to a wide range of factors in the business environment, an activity referred to as *environmental scanning*. While qualitatively complex, scanning lacks the rigor of statistical forecasting methods for calibrating precise effects. Usefulness is sacrificed for the realism and flexibility that broad-gauged scanning offers.

If scanning and formal model building were independent activities, we could combine the two and achieve an ideal balance of realism *and* usefulness. The balance is more complicated, however. When change in the environment is rapid—and the formal models encounter poor performance—scanning should be the basis for revamping the formal model to embrace the source of environmental change. This requires a two-pronged effort of more formalized scanning and more realistic models. Communication among scanners and model builders is essential. Each must understand the philosophy of the other to facilitate a meaningful contribution. Short of that, a communications gap arises which manifests itself (1) to managers as a failure of techniques and (2) to modelers as "noise" in the environment, which managers claim to understand only ex post facto.

The true state of affairs is that modelers make *premises* about the environment. Some of the premises are recognized explicitly, such as through explanatory variables that were either ignored or performed poorly at the margin during stable times. Others can be identified only by the managers/scanners. To the extent that early identification and continuous tracking of more promising environmental variables takes place, adaptation of forecasts to rapid change can be facilitated. The modelers' rigor must be applied to the scanners' ideas, and the scanners' ideas must be applied to the modeler's formal system.

Consider the following illustrative scenario about company X. Through 1971 a regression model explaining companywide sales with real GNP performed well both statistically and as a general guide to individual product line performance. During the 1973–1975 period, sales were affected by a number of unusual changes in the environment. The environmental changes and their impact on company X's model are summarized in Chart 17-1.

CHART 17-1. 1973–1975 Environmental Changes and Their Impact on Company X

Change	Impact
Accelerated inflation	Sales measured in dollars grew more rapidly than unit sales, causing former to be misleading Impact on model: Regression line tilted upward to account for inflation as inflationary experience was employed in reestimating regression Intelligence from management: Declining unit sales conflicted with forecasts of inflated dollar sales from model
Inventory cycle	Model underestimated sales during 1973 and early 1974 when customers were hoarding inventory; it overestimated sales during late 1974 and in 1975 when inventory levels were being reduced Intelligence from management: Sales force understood timing of inventory cycle but did not know how to adjust model's output to account for it
Business cycle	Explanatory variable (real GNP) accounted for cycle in crude way, but was imperfect for several reasons: 1. Real GNP was not as accurate an indicator as other more related components of GNP. Previously, there had been no improvement in model from paying attention to difference 2. Forecasts of real GNP became more inaccurate, causing sales forecast to become more unreliable 3. Sales of various products sold by company X were acyclical. Total sales forecast became inadequate for more specific decisions Intelligence from management: Impact of cycle was understood at product levels, but no ability to reconcile that information with total dollar sales forecast existed

Accelerated inflation, an inventory cycle, and the business cycle each affected the performance of forecasting models and the scanning of managers. The usefulness of the sales–RGNP relationship was lessened because the sacrifice in realism became too great. In other words, environmental change altered the choice of how much complexity to build into formal models while rendering some aspects of scanning efforts so useful as to demand more precise analysis.

The experience of company X was fairly typical during the 1970s.[1] The next section presents a broader survey of the impact of environmental change on forecasting.

ENVIRONMENTAL FACTORS IN FORECASTING

The remaining chapters in this third part of the handbook deal with how to forecast when particular environmental characteristics dominate. For example, business cycles present particular problems requiring technical solutions. Political risk might warrant the use of especially flexible methods. Consumer products, industrial products, and services have separate forecasting traditions based largely on different characterizations of environmental influences. The time horizon of forecasting is similarly affected by the nature of environmental change.

Environmental factors, which are common to most forecasting systems, can be classified as economic, organizational, competitive, technological, and demographic. Several are discussed here to provide an exposition of the impact of environmental factors in forecasting. While no attempt is made to be exhaustive, a number of prominent factors are discussed in each subsection that follows.

Economic Factors

Economic premises are often made in forecasts. For example, the fundamental choice of forecasting sales in units or dollars involves an assumption about *inflation*. Consider the contrast in the time series plots (in Chart 17-2) of the dollar and unit sales for company X. The entire difference between the two variables is inflation in the average selling price of X's products. Forecasting techniques would certainly diagnose the two time series differently, given no information about the specific form of the difference. It is reasonable to assume that the elimination of known causes—in this case inflation—from a time series will lead to greater forecasting accuracy.

Why does a simple point, such as adjusting for inflation, require explication? Forecasting models developed during periods of low inflation rates had no need to concern themselves with inflation. Historical fit was not improved by forecasting in units. A premise was therefore made about inflation when the dependent variable, dollar sales, was chosen. A manager who

CHART 17-2. Company X Sales in Dollars and Units (1965–1980)

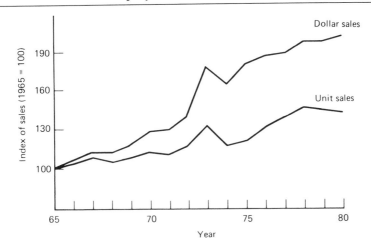

recognized that premise was in a better position to react to acceleration in inflation rates than if the role of inflation was ignored. The problems faced by company X (see Chart 17-1) could have been ameliorated by a company prepared to face the problem early.

Inflation does not affect all industries and all products in the same way. One problem this creates is that the variables chosen for forecasting may become inappropriate. The appropriate focus for forecasting may switch from the company's sales to the divisions' sales, the product line, the style, the geographic area, or the customer class. The level of specificity of variables to be forecast is commonly referred to as an *aggregation* problem.

Generally speaking, the desired level of aggregation decreases when inflation—and other environmental forces as well—changes more rapidly. This occurs for two reasons: (1) Management needs information for decisions that often differs for different disaggregated variables and (2) forecasting accuracy might be improved by focusing on the more specific behavior of disaggregated variables. The benefits of disaggregation must be weighed against the increased cost of forecasting more variables.

One of the most crucial economic premises made in forecasting models—especially those developed during the period from World War II through 1971—was that the *business cycle* did not exist. While most managers recognized the impact of a business cycle on their performance, there was rarely a premium to be paid for formal analysis of the impact of the business cycle. Relating variables blindly to time, without examining the true underlying phenomena, was sufficient for many purposes until the 1970s.

It is now understood that the practice of ignoring business cycles developed during a period that was a historical accident. In most industrialized nations, the period from 1946 to 1971 was characterized by expansion of both the economy and the population. Those nations strongly subject to the vagaries of international trade were more attentive to economic factors in forecasting. Countries such as the United States, with large and growing domestic markets, could afford to forecast with models accounting for only the major trends. The cost of more detail or precision in measurement was rarely worth the small incremental benefits.

How exactly does a business cycle affect the choice of what and how to forecast? The most important effect is in placing a premium on forecasting turning points. Managers who can more confidently predict a turning point in their sales can usually make anticipatory decisions that improve performance at the margin.

Managers can rely less on standard measures of forecasting accuracy when turning points become important. Mean squared errors or mean absolute deviations might become considerably less important than the profit improvement from anticipating turning points. The latter is much less definable and is less susceptible to being measured in a "quick and dirty" formula that an analyst can employ on the computer. Measurement problems do not relieve managers from the obligation to forecast even if that requires closer communication and understanding between manager and staff analyst/forecaster.

The differential effects of a business cycle on sectors of an economy are well documented.[1] Like inflation, more frequent and pronounced business cycles imply the need for more disaggregated forecasting. A natural corollary to this principle is that planning should focus on the differential impact of the business cycle on various business segments. If Detroit is affected differently than Atlanta, marketing strategies might be varied accordingly. If higher priced items are affected more or less than lower priced items, a number of tactical decisions are available to managers. Forecasts should be designed to aid the disaggregated decision making.

Products with different characteristics are affected differently by a business cycle. Consider two products sold by an automobile manufacturer: (1) passenger automobiles and (2) replacement parts for passenger automobiles. How might sales of autos and auto parts differ over a business cycle?

Automobiles are a durable consumer product. Their purchase can generally be postponed during an economic downturn. The logical consequence of a slump in auto sales is an increase in the sales rate of replacement parts. As the average age of the stock of autos in use increases, the demand for repair parts increases. The very same information about the state of automobile sales could be used to improve accuracy in forecasting replacement part sales.

Had we observed only the aggregate variable, sales of automobiles and parts, we would have observed a deceptively more stable variable. However, we would not have understood the true market phenomena. Also, we would have been denied the opportunity to enhance decision making about autos and parts separately.

Variable definition is a topic whose importance is enhanced by economic change. Most analysts pay little attention to the differences in forecasting orders, sales, production, and shipments. During a business cycle, important differences in these variables occur. Orders and sales tend to vary from historical relationships during an economic downturn when orders are canceled more frequently. In general, the more cyclical a product, the more advantageous it is for a producer to maintain a backlog of orders that can be managed to accommodate both cyclical and stochastic fluctuations.

Production and sales will also react differently during a cycle as optimal inventory levels change. Often rapid inflation will interact with this relationship as larger finished goods inventories (for producers) and raw material inventories (for purchasers) become desirable as a hedge against inflation.

During the 1973–1975 recession in the United States, an *inventory cycle* accompanied the business cycle and inflation. As related elsewhere,[1] an inventory cycle can cause traditionally strong relationships—such as sales and real GNP—to perform poorly in forecasting. The need to define variables accurately becomes critical (1) to avoid being deceived by the fluctuations observed, (2) to facilitate adjustment techniques that can compensate for the large errors of traditional models, and (3) to minimize the impact on forecasting during subsequent stable periods of the variations in historical data caused by the inventory cycle. During the 1980s, on the other hand, the business cycle was not accompanied by a pronounced inventory cycle. This made the forecasting somewhat easier.

Forecast variables that are affected by *international trade* face a very complex environment. Obviously sales to other nations belong in this category. Domestic products that face significant competition from imports are similarly affected. Market definition becomes more important when the international environment is dynamic. The difference between worldwide sales, domestic sales, apparent consumption, sales by domestic producers, import sales, and so on can spell the difference between successful and unsuccessful forecasting. As is the case with other economic changes, careful international variable definition is less important under stable conditions, but it becomes crucial when rapid change occurs.

Chart 17-3 lists some changes in the international economy during the last decade and their impact on forecasting in a company. It would be useful to be able to suggest accurate methods for forecasting the international economic phenomena themselves. There are world econometric forecasting models, and the large banks forecast important events qualitatively. But this is an area of forecasting subject to great inaccuracy. Therefore the exercise of responding to the impacts listed in Chart 17-3 is often one of reaction and flexibility rather than of precise accuracy.

Demographic Factors

One common premise implicit in many forecasts is the continuing growth of population. In the United States, as well as in most other industrialized

CHART 17-3. Recent Events in the International Economy and Their Impact on Forecasting

Event	Impact
Freely floating exchange rates, which have been volatile	Domestic and imported goods have had fluctuating costs relative to one another. In many cases, prices and profit margins of competing products have had large changes. Sales of individual manufacturers can therefore become more difficult to forecast. Sales by domestic manufacturers versus all sales can vary dramatically. Prices of raw materials traded become difficult to forecast.
Changes in timing of various national business cycles	When business cycles coincide, the impact on total sales of worldwide markets differs. When the cycles differ greatly, the problem of forecasting where sales will be strongest becomes important. (In 1974–1975 the cycles coincided in many countries.)
Changes in barriers to trade	When quotas or tariffs change, so does the environment for forecasting. Frequently, past observations have had limited value because of the environmental differences.

nations, population grew steadily during the post-World War II period. More important, the age distribution of the population shifted dramatically as the postwar "baby boom" segment matured, reached child-bearing age, and did not follow traditional patterns of when to bear children and how many to bear.

Many products and services are affected by the demographic shifts just mentioned. Some products, such as jeans, appeal primarily to only a segment of the population. As the postwar generation reaches middle age, will it continue to wear jeans? If not, jeans manufacturers will face a dwindling domestic market because of population shifts.

The shift of population geographically—to the "Sun Belt" in the United States, for example—is another environmental trend. This might affect sales of certain climate-related products. It might also alter the competitive positions of specific firms.

Forecasting models have typically ignored demographic factors for several reasons. First, the changes have manifested themselves slowly. In contrast, most time series models incorporate a relatively short history. Second, the improvement in forecasting performance from incorporating demographic factors is small for reasons related to the first point. Third, models already disaggregated by age class or geographic region are not common. Marketing research models are the major exception. It would be unusual to disaggregate only for demographic reasons unless radical shifts demanded such an approach. Therefore, the effects of disaggregated demographic changes could bear fruit in forecasting only if they could dominate a decision to disaggregate forecasts.

Organizational/Competitive Factors

The strategy of an organization, and therefore its approach to competition and the organizational implementation of that approach, can be considered part of a firm's forecasting environment. In a short- to intermediate-run forecast, changes in strategy can certainly affect variables to be forecasted. In a long-run forecast, the impact of corporation strategy on forecasting is less clear because the purpose of the forecast is to help shape strategic alternatives.

The effect of strategic variables on forecasting performance is as complex as the subject of corporate strategy itself. The purpose of this section is only to outline some common effects so as to sensitize the reader to the general issues. These effects can be broken down into two aspects of strategy: organizational and competitive.

Companies organize in such a manner as to implement their corporate strategy.[2] Differences in organizations—because they embody differences in strategy—create differences in how and what to forecast. As companies encounter environmental change, their strategies and hence their organizations frequently adapt. Predictable changes in the forecasting needs of managers are the likely result.

To illustrate, consider a company that is organized functionally, with the marketing function dominating management attention. Forecasting is typically related to the budgeting process and to the review of annual performance. A relatively short time horizon is employed. Goal setting frequently is the objective of forecasting. Top management obtains a forecast independent of the marketing managers and sales force to better evaluate their input to the goal-setting negotiation process and to allocate budgets.

The company later encounters a more hostile environment, which requires greater adaptation of individual business strategies. Decentralization occurs, and division general managers with profit responsibility replace marketing managers as the key decision makers. The purpose of forecasting changes. Accuracy becomes more important than goal setting. A longer time horizon becomes appropriate. Communication among general managers and forecasting specialists becomes more critical. Often the latter become expendable.

The overwhelming conclusion is that organizational change frequently changes the entire basis for forecasting. A system that churned out forecasts the same way in both environments would likely fail. It would either generate the wrong type of forecasts or the forecasts would not be used by managers. Forecasting systems must be tailored to the organization in which they are employed.[2] The organization is therefore a critical element of the forecasting environment.

Competitive factors can have equally profound effects on forecasting. Premises about competitors' responses are often implicit in forecasts. A sales forecast that ignores changes in the responses of competitors or in the marketing strategy of the subject company itself risks significant error. Changes in the nature of competition can occur due to changes in a number of factors. Some of these factors are the supply and demand balance, the number and size of competitors, the stage of the product life cycle, and technological change.

Frequently changes in competitive factors are not amenable to quantification in a forecasting system. They are nonetheless important premises that must be understood and checked as a source of error.

Other Factors

In particular industries, other sources of the environment can dominate forecasting. These include technological change, product characteristics (durable versus nondurable, luxury versus nonluxury), and the quantity and quality of information, among others. The factors discussed in this chapter are meant to exemplify, but not exhaust, the sources of environmental change. All important sources should be treated with the same care methodologically.

FORECASTING PERFORMANCE AND ENVIRONMENTAL CHANGE

One reason forecasting systems often fail is the employment of poor measures of performance. This statement is doubly true when environmental change is rapid. The well-known concept of a periodic audit[3] should be employed in all forecasting systems; it offers guidance to the rapid change situation. (See Chapter 32.) The costs and benefits of forecasting will, as always, be the basis for selecting criteria for the frequency of reestimating models or reselection of the best forecasting technique. Earlier it was established how environmental change alters those costs and benefits. More specifically, it was demonstrated how specific environmental changes could generate errors. It is the task of this section to offer specific error measurement techniques as a guide to periodic audit of the entire system.

The most common approach to forecasting performance measurement is *historical fit*. All historical data are employed in estimating the parameters of the forecasting model, and then such measures as mean squared error (MSE) or mean absolute percentage error (MAPE) are calculated. Error measures have no critical value greater than which a model is unacceptable. A situational analysis of the cost of errors, often performed qualitatively, is the only means of judging acceptable standards.

The task often ignored is to perform a *postaudit on forecasting errors* to judge their source. With a noncausal model, the postaudit is not very scientific. One can compare errors with past values, search for a pattern of error, or attempt to explain errors according to environmental change. With a causal model, the ability to ascertain the causes of errors becomes a more formal and necessary task.

How specifically is a postaudit to be performed? The major difference from historical fit is that a postaudit measures the accuracy of the true forecasts. The standard measures of error, such as MAPE and MSE, can be applied to true forecasts as readily as they are applied to historical fit. The error value associated with a forecast n months ahead is the typical measure.

When the environment is dynamic, true forecast measures will exceed their counterparts in historical fit. The MSE of a forecast will differ from the MSE of fit for two reasons: (1) The model itself is not a perfect predictor of the future and (2) the environmental premises of the model are invalid. For the example of company X, a regression model in which X's sales were regressed against RGNP had the following sources of error: (1) The sales–RGNP regression line did not have a perfect explanatory relationship, (2) the forecasts of RGNP were not accurate, and (3) many other forces in the environment affected sales.

An appropriate postaudit would compare fit error measures and forecast error measures and also attempt to explain each time period error qualitatively. Common sense and scanning should lead to some conclusions about the need for revising the model. If forecasts are more erroneous than fit, three alternatives exists:

1. If a systematic rationale for forecast error exists, the forecasting system should be augmented to account for that influence.
2. If the reasons for large errors are unusual nonrecurring events, no changes in models are necessary.
3. If the environmental change renders the forecasting system obsolete, wholesale redesign of the system is in order.

ADAPTING THE FORECASTING SYSTEM TO ENVIRONMENTAL CHANGE

Various aspects of environmental change and forecasting have been discussed in this chapter. Although the topic treated is very broad, it is nevertheless useful to offer general prescriptions for adapting forecasting systems to environmental change. Seven prescriptions, and examples of some, are offered in the following:

Prescription 1: Careful Variable Definition. Both the variables being forecast and any explanatory variables should be defined accurately so that environmental influences do not destroy their validity.

Example: Company X should forecast unit sales rather than dollars. It should not substitute data on orders or production for units sold. It might also consider whether a component of RGNP, such as disposable personal income, might be a better explanatory variable.

Prescription 2: Aggregation/Disaggregation Alternatives. The level of aggregation should be considered carefully. An investment in more disaggregated forecasting may yield premiums during turbulent periods. The sources of environmental change should be examined for disaggregation implications.

Example: Company X could consider replacing total corporate sales forecasts with product line forecasts, each perhaps broken down by customer class.

Prescription 3: Consideration of Causal Models. Where noncausal models have achieved poor results during rapid change periods, they should possibly be replaced by causal models that are better understood. That would facilitate the employment of scanning information when models require revision.

Example: Companies using simple time series models for forecasts of a time horizon longer than two months should consider regression models.

Prescription 4: Explicit Listing of Premises. The premises employed in a forecasting system should be listed explicitly. Both model builders and managers/scanners should participate in this process.

Example: The environmental factors listed in this chapter, among others, should be reviewed as candidates for premises.

Prescription 5: Premise Tracking System. A formal system of tracking the environmental factors deemed most important to the validity of forecasting system premises should be established.

Prescription 6: Broad Performance Measures. Performance measures of true forecasts should be employed. The various sources of error should be determined jointly by model builders and managers/scanners.

Example: For company X, the errors encountered in 1973–1975 should have been examined, and the environmental factors listed in Chart 17-1 should have been uncovered through that process.

Prescription 7: Periodic Audit/A Plan for Change. The periodic audit should explicitly evaluate environmental premises and encompass a contingency plan for the forecasting system when various environmental scenarios are experienced. Ideally, this activity should manage the balance between environmental scanning and formal models. It should be made explicit that premises are made deliberately and that scanners and modelers complement one another. Most important, a plan should exist detailing the roles of the various parties and recognizing the alternative shocks to the system that could occur and how they will lead to adaptations in the system.

REFERENCES

1. Beckenstein, A. R., "Forecasting Considerations in a Rapidly Changing Economy," in S. Makridakis and S. Wheelwright, eds., *Forecasting*, TIMS Stuides in Management Science, North-Holland, Amsterdam, 1979.

2. Lorange, P., and R. F. Vancil, *Strategic Planning Systems*, Prentice-Hall, Englewood Cliffs, NJ, 1977.

3. Wheelwright, S., and S. Makridakis, *Forecasting Methods for Management*, 4th ed., Wiley-Interscience, New York, 1984.

BIBLIOGRAPHY

Ascher, W., *Forecasting: An Appraisal for Policymakers and Planners*, Johns Hopkins University Press, Baltimore, 1978.

Houthakker, H. S., and L. D. Taylor, *Consumer Demand in the U.S., 1929–70: Analyses and Projections*, Harvard University Press, Cambridge, MA, 1966.

Kami, M. J., "Planning in Times of Unpredictability," *Columbia Journal of World Business*, Summer 1976, pp. 26–34.

Makridakis, S., "If We Cannot Forecast How Can We Plan?" *Long Range Planning* vol. 14, no. 3, 1981, pp. 10–20.

Pindyck, R. S., and D. L. Rubinfeld, *Econometric Models and Economic Forecasts*, McGraw-Hill, New York, 1976.

CHAPTER

18

PRICE FORECASTING USING EXPERIENCE CURVES AND THE PRODUCT LIFE-CYCLE CONCEPT

RICHARD N. DINO

The Center for Economic Analysis, Inc., Stamford, Connecticut

In recent years the markets for electronic products have experienced extremely aggressive price competition. Although advances in technology have provided some defense of profit margins, shortened product life cycles have exacerbated the financial risks of introducing new products. In such an environment, the financial viability of a proposed product for a new market demands reliable forecasts of the price evolution that may be expected over the product's life cycle. The central theme in this chapter is that prices in product markets change in a pattern related to the product life cycle. If in fact this is true, then the application of the product life-cycle concept and the factors that influence it can aid significantly in the development of a reliable projection of the evolution of price in a market.

THE PRODUCT LIFE-CYCLE CONCEPT

It is not the purpose of this chapter to critique or defend the product life-cycle concept; this is done extremely well in the literature, which at one extreme denies the very existence of the life cycle and at the other makes it the central theme in product marketing and planning. It is assumed here that the diffusion of a product into the marketplace follows an S-shaped path, allowing for the product's introduction and recognition, its growth, and finally its maturity. The time period necessary for complete diffusion can differ significantly among products. For example, a product in a rapidly changing technological environment could reach maturity much faster than

CHART 18-1. The Stages of Market Development

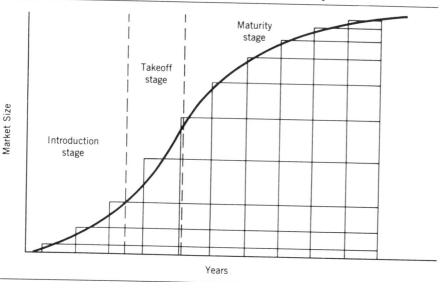

one in a stable never-changing structure or a nearly mature product for which innovation creates a new and explosive market. Furthermore, it is assumed that the product life-cycle concept can be modeled using state-of-the-art diffusion processes or those originally designed to help understand a biological life process, which have been accepted and utilized by product forecasters for a great many years.

Given these assumptions, shipments of a product are expected to follow an S-shaped path that initially exhibits a period of rapidly accelerating annual growth and low shipments volume (the introduction stage), followed by one of continued acceleration in growth coupled with increasing shipments volume (the takeoff and growth stage), and then finally by one with a decreasing growth rate (the maturity stage), which continues until growth ceases and the maximum size of the population is attained. As the product moves into this last stage of diffusion, its volume expands and contracts in dynamic equilibrium with its market environment during a period of variable length, after which product shipments begin to decline. One such process is pictured in Chart 18-1, which characterizes the stages of market development.

PRICE EVOLUTION AND THE PRODUCT LIFE CYCLE

The proposed link between a product's price evolution and its life cycle appeals to intuitive logic. Low shipments volume in the product's introduction stage is related to the period of customer learning and familiarization. During this time, the product is often considered a luxury item and is generally purchased only by the "leading-edge" of potential consumers. Leading-edge consumers like to experiment with new things, are innovators in their work and recreation, and are willing to pay a premium price to be among the early owners of a product. On the supply side, manufacturers of the product are few in number and often are protected by patents or copyrights. Initial manufacturing capacity is often limited, and production or technology standards may not yet be homogeneous. As a result of the conditions present at this stage of the product's evolution, price is often significantly greater than cost, profit margins can be very large, and pricing policy generally is monopolistic.

As more of the product is sold and information about it passes through the distribution channel, the market develops critical mass and moves into the second stage, the takeoff and growth stage. From the potential customer's viewpoint, the new product has been proven and is now considered to be highly desirable or even indispensable. Common production processes and technologies have been identified and adopted, research costs are being reclaimed, and potential producers become competitors and enter the market to lay their claim to a share of the huge profits enjoyed by the few producers who were present from the product's introduction. Manufacturing capacity increases and average costs decline with higher volume and production innovation. These conditions lead to aggressive price competition. As a result, price for the product moves in line with costs and the huge profit margins experienced by the few producers present in the early stage of the life cycle contract significantly.

By the time the maturity stage, the third phase of a product's evolution, is reached, diffusion or market penetration has been maximized and cumulative product shipments are approaching peak population. Most consumers who ever wanted to buy the product have done so; in fact, they may have been repeat customers on a replacement or a use basis. Low-cost producers survived the margin squeeze of takeoff and growth, and high-cost producers, unless they properly differentiated their product, were shaken out of the market. At this stage in the product cycle, technological innovation is slow, margins have narrowed, and the pricing strategies of the product's major producers are altered to reflect the dynamics of changes in the economic, market, and competitive environment.

In reality, the duration of one stage may be prolonged by appropriate marketing tactics. For example, it is not uncommon to find a period of transition between the takeoff and growth stage and the maturity stage of the product life cycle. As manufacturers perceive slowdown in the growth of their offering, models change, features are added, and new uses and applications are devised for products. Often, through the use of such strategies, the growth stage of the product's life cycle can be maintained and the peak population asymptote can be shifted outward and upward. Such phenomena can be identified easily for the products analyzed in this chapter.

THE EMPIRICAL TEST

Experience Curve Theory

To test the hypothesis that the price evolution of a product is linked structurally to stages of its life, experience curve theory is employed.

The concept of the experience curve rests on the premise that a producer's constant dollar costs decline over time as that producer gains experience in bringing the product to market. Unlike the learning curve, which is specifically associated with manufacturing and assembly operations, the experience curve is more general and incorporates efficiencies gained in *all* phases of the business, with each phase making some contribution to the final cost and, of course, price of the product. The inception of the product idea, the accompanying research and development, materials procurement, production, assembly, and distribution influence the ultimate cost and price of the product.

The use of an experience concept goes back many years, even before the Boston Consulting Group identified it as a major tool for tactical and strategic planning, It, like the product life-cycle concept, has been attacked as well as honored in the literature. A defense of its advantages or a documentation of its shortcomings is not intended here. The overwhelming evidence produced by the analysis of thousands of products, however, suggests that experience, and the efficiencies gained therefrom, reduce product costs in a nonlinear manner. It is this evidence that gives the experience curve methodology a place as an analytical tool in this chapter.

Experience curve models can be built through simple linear regression using logarithmically transformed data. The standard metric for experience is cumulative production volume. And although real cost declines can be calculated easily for any amount of increased experience, the analytical question usually asked is, "How much do constant dollar costs decline for every doubling of cumulative experience?" Chart 18-2 presents the results of estimation of a hypothetical experience curve and the calculation of its slope, A, with $(1 - A)$ indicating the amount constant dollar costs decrease for a doubling of cumulative volume.

Because of data restrictions, that is, because producers' costs spanning the history of the products analyzed here are not in the public domain, we make the assumption that real prices, in general, reflect the decline in real costs associated with increased experience. More specifically, prices in the industry, in general, follow the cost of the least-cost producer. This is a necessary condition for defense of market share, particularly when aggres-

CHART 18-2. Computation of an Experience Curve

$$\log C_N = \left[\frac{\log A}{\log E}\right] \log N + \log C_t$$

where C_N = constant dollar cost of electronic widgets
N = cumulative volume
A = estimated experience curve slope (%)
E = integer of doubling (= 2)
C_t = estimate of constant dollar cost of first (t) unit produced

Example: Electronic Widgets, 1975–1982
From regression

$$\log C_N = -0.599462 \log N + 14.1472$$

Calculating experience curve slope for doubling of cumulative volume

$$-0.599462 = \left[\frac{\log A}{\log 2}\right]$$

$$\log A = -0.41551544$$

$$A = [\exp(-0.41551544)] \times 100 = 66\%$$

This means that for a doubling of cumulative volume, constant-dollar cost
will decrease by 34% (1 − A).

---

sive price behavior is the order of the day. Through the use of experience curve analysis, we can measure price changes in response to cumulative volume increases during various stages of the product life cycle.

The Products

Despite its intuitive appeal, our hypothesis lies in the realm of the theoretical until tested for real products in real markets. So an empirical test for products in the electronics market, namely, radios, monochrome televisions, color televisions, and video cassette recorders, is included here. Each product analyzed is at a different stage in its diffusion process. Radios, first introduced 65 years ago, have the longest history of market penetration, while the video cassette recorder, introduced to consumers in 1974, has the shortest. Chart 18-3 presents the introduction years for each of these products.

The Data

Product history employed in the empirical test was developed using various annual versions of the Electronic Industries Association's (EIA) *Market Data Book* prepared by that organization's Marketing Statistics Committee.

CHART 18-3. Products/Markets in Empirical Test

Product/Market	Year Introduced
Radios	1922
Monochrome (b/w) TVs	1946
Color TVs	1954
Video Cassette Recorders	1974

Volume data for radios and video cassette recorders represent U.S. annual factory sales, and those for both monochrome and color televisions consist of U.S. annual factory production. Each series includes products produced or purchased by U.S. manufacturers plus those imported directly by distributors or dealers for resale. While it is true that, conceptually, a difference exists between factory sales and factory production, namely, producer's inventories, the difference in concept does not outweigh the importance of using a consistently measured series throughout the analytical time horizon. Every effort was undertaken to ensure the latter. Since this is a test of a *structural relationship,* it matters not whether production or sales data are employed.

Average prices were developed for each product using the same EIA sources by dividing annual dollar sales or production by the associated unit volume. Constant 1972 dollar prices were calculated by deflating the product's average price with the U.S. national income account deflator for consumer durable goods, excluding autos and auto parts.

Charts 18-4 through 18-7 contain the estimated experience curve equations referred to in the remainder of this chapter.

The Results

Radios

The product shipments and price history of radios goes back to 1922 when radios were first introduced to the public at large (see Charts 18-8 and 18-9, respectively). Data for the war years, 1943–1945, are not available. Cumulative shipments of radios had increased to 1.3 billion units in 1982 and constant dollar price, including mix shifts and technological impacts, had decreased to $22 from its highest level of $118 recorded in 1928. Increased numbers of broadcasting stations as well as technical innovation transformed the radio from a sit-around-the-fire, home entertainment medium in its early stages to a necessary and indispensable product for the beach and car.

The experience curve for the 1922–1982 history of radios has been estimated and a slope of roughly 83% calculated (see Chart 18-4). This translates to a 17% decline in constant dollar price for every doubling of cumulative

CHART 18-4. Experience Curve Equations: Radios

All Stages.   (Introduction to Present)
                                    1922–1982

ln(constant price) = 6.5̂77 − 0.2̂65 ln(cumulative volume)

SLOPE = 83.2%

Stage 1.   Introduction and Early Takeoff
                                    1922–1928

ln(constant price) = 3.9̂08 − 0.0̂73 ln(cumulative volume)

SLOPE = 105.2%

1928–1933

ln(constant price) = 14.2̂76 − 1.0̂07 ln(cumulative volume)

SLOPE = 49.8%

Stage 2.   Takeoff and Growth
                                    1928–1969

ln(constant price) = 8.9̂05 − 0.4̂60 ln(cumulative volume)

SLOPE = 72.7%

Stage 3.   Maturing
                                    1969–1982

ln(constant volume) = −4.0̂34 + 0.5̂04 ln(cumulative volume)

SLOPE = 141.8%

volume in the historical period. But, as can be seen in Chart 18-10, there is significant variation of the actual observations (●) around the conventional experience curve fit (line), an estimation procedure that incorporates all of the product's history. By dividing up the historical period into increments associated with the radio's product life cycle, a different picture emerges. From 1922–1928, the period representing the introduction stage of the product, a slope of 105% has been calculated (Charts 18-4, Stage 1, and 18-11) including the very high real $100 introductory price of 1922. Had this price been eliminated from the analysis as an outlier, the experience curve slope would have been even *higher* during this period. On a constant dollar basis, prices *rose* during this stage, consistent with the expectations of this chapter's hypothesis.

The 1928–1969 time frame represents the takeoff and growth stage of radio sales. During this period the experience curve slope dropped from the 105% of the introductory stage to 73% (Charts 18-4, Stage 2, and 18-12),

CHART 18-5. Experience Curve Equations:
Monochrome Televisions

All Stages.	(Introduction to Present) 1946–1982

$\ln(\text{constant price}) = 6.\hat{8}07 - 0.1\hat{8}5 \ \ln(\text{cumulative volume})$

SLOPE = 90.0%

Stage 1.	Introduction 1946–1949

$\ln(\text{constant price}) = 5.\hat{6}37 - 0.0\hat{0}7 \ \ln(\text{cumulative volume})$

SLOPE = 100.5%

1949–1953

$\ln(\text{constant price}) = 6.\hat{4}68 - 0.1\hat{1}0 \ \ln(\text{cumulative volume})$

SLOPE = 92.7%

Stage 2.	Early Takeoff 1953–1956

$\ln(\text{constant price}) = 10.\hat{5}15 - 0.5\hat{0}5 \ \ln(\text{cumulative volume})$

SLOPE = 70.5%

1956–1967

$\ln(\text{constant price}) = 9.\hat{6}40 - 0.4\hat{1}6 \ \ln(\text{cumulative volume})$

SLOPE = 74.5%

Stage 3.	Takeoff and Growth 1953–1967

$\ln(\text{constant price}) = 9.\hat{1}67 - 0.3\hat{7}5 \ \ln(\text{cumulative volume})$

SLOPE = 77.1%

1967–1970

$\ln(\text{constant price}) = 3\hat{0}.60 - 2.\hat{2}06 \ \ln(\text{cumulative volume})$

SLOPE = 21.7%

Stage 4.	Market Niche Adjustment 1970–1982

$\ln(\text{constant price}) = 1\hat{5}.645 - 0.\hat{9}40 \ \ln(\text{cumulative volume})$

SLOPE = 52.1%

CHART 18-6. Experience Curve Equations: Color Televisions

All Stages.

(Introduction to Present)
1954–1982

$$\ln(\text{constant price}) = 6.\hat{6}53 - 0.0\hat{8}6 \ \ln(\text{cumulative volume})$$

SLOPE = 94.2%

Stage 1.

Introduction
1954–1963

$$\ln(\text{constant price}) = 6.\hat{4}52 - 0.0\hat{5}0 \ \ln(\text{cumulative volume})$$

SLOPE = 96.6%

Stage 2.

Takeoff and Growth Stage
1966–1982

$$\ln(\text{constant price}) = 8.\hat{1}76 - 0.2\hat{2}5 \ \ln(\text{cumulative volume})$$

SLOPE = 85.6%

Stage 3.

Most Recent Period
1976–1982

$$\ln(\text{constant price}) = 10.\hat{1}85 - 0.3\hat{9}8 \ \ln(\text{cumulative volume})$$

SLOPE = 75.9%

indicating an average 27% decrease in constant dollar price for each doubling of cumulative experience.

This time period, however, involved an exogenous influence, which helped promote the price decline, in addition to the "experience effect." Prices of radios dropped precipitously during the early part of the takeoff and growth stage (Chart 18-11, right) but mostly due to the 1928–1933 price deflation in the U.S. economy as a whole. Therefore, the price drop during the takeoff and growth stage is not fully a function of manufacturing experience. But the experience phenomenon is very apparent during the latter part of the 1928–1969 time frame; mix shifts, quality improvements, and technological innovation, specifically the use of transistors, occurred during this time period and Japanese electronics imports began to dominate the market. As is very common during the takeoff and growth stage, these changes led to new applications and uses, prolonged the life of the product, and helped raise the peak population asymptote.

If the purpose of this research were to produce a forecasting equation to project future prices on the basis of this historical relationship, a *pure* estimate of the experience effect would only be assured with data adjusted for the depression.

The final period analyzed runs from 1969 to 1982. It is difficult to realisti-

**CHART 18-7. Experience Curve Equations: Video
Cassette Recorders**

All Stages.	Introduction to Present 1974–1982

$$\ln(\text{constant price}) = 7.\hat{6}78 - 0.1\hat{8}8 \ \ln(\text{cumulative volume})$$

SLOPE = 87.8%

Stage 1.	Introduction 1974–1976

$$\ln(\text{constant price}) = 7.\hat{2}28 - 0.1\hat{0}5 \ \ln(\text{cumulative volume})$$

SLOPE = 93.0%

Stage 2.	Takeoff and Growth 1976–1982

$$\ln(\text{constant price}) = 7.\hat{6}84 - 0.1\hat{8}8 \ \ln(\text{cumulative volume})$$

SLOPE = 87.8%

1977–1982

$$\ln(\text{constant price}) = 7.\hat{5}10 - 0.1\hat{6}6 \ \ln(\text{cumulative volume})$$

SLOPE = 89.1%

Stage 3.	Most Recent Period 1979–1982

$$\ln(\text{constant price}) = 8.\hat{3}10 - 0.2\hat{6}5 \ \ln(\text{cumulative volume})$$

SLOPE = 83.2%

cally label this time period for radios as the maturity stage, since maturity, and later decline, is associated with products that have nearly reached saturation. Whereas specific radio models may have come and gone, the generic radio has been transformed again and again, consistent with the intent of manufacturers to prolong the life of their individual product offerings. This behavior is common to enumerable products, particularly in the electronics industry. The 1969–1982 time frame for radios is a period when redesign and new applications and uses prolonged product life. During these years, a major impetus for the growth of radio shipments was the automobile.

The experience curve estimated for the 1969–1982 stage of the radio's life cycle has a slope of 142% (Charts 18-4, Stage 3, and 18-13), implying a 42% increase in constant dollar price for every doubling of cumulative experience. Just as the estimates made of the takeoff and growth stage were biased downward, the coefficients estimated for the latter part of the takeoff and growth stage are biased upward due to mix shifts, but still represent a change

CHART 18-8. Annual Factory Sales of Radios

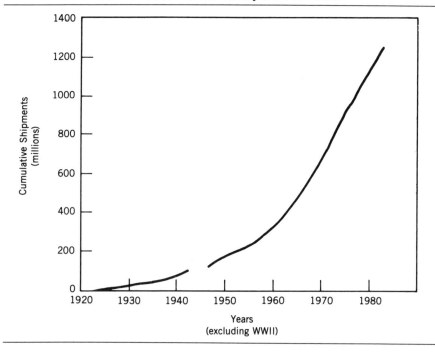

CHART 18-9. Radio Prices (Constant 1972 Dollars)

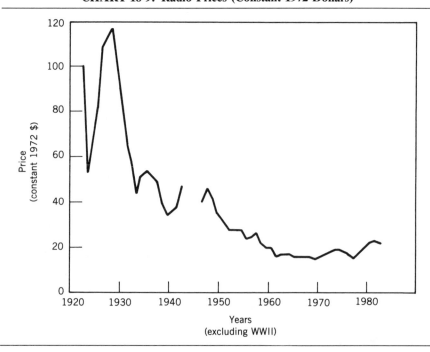

CHART 18-10. Experience Curve Analysis: Radios. Introduction to Present

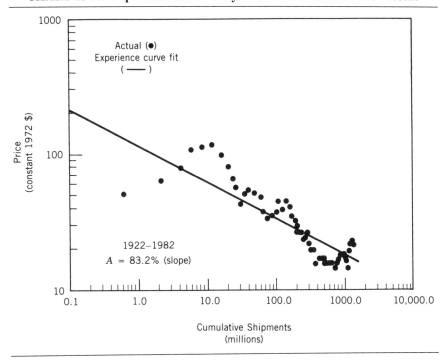

CHART 18-11. Experience Curve Analysis: Radios. Introduction and Early Takeoff Stage

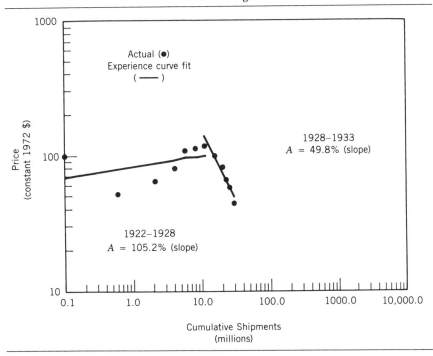

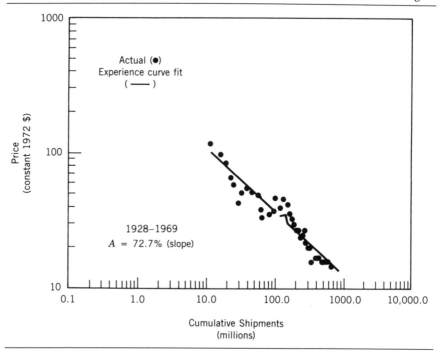

CHART 18-12. Experience Curve Analysis: Radios. Takeoff and Growth Stage

Actual (●)
Experience curve fit
(——)

Price
(constant 1972 $)

1928–1969
$A = 72.7\%$ (slope)

Cumulative Shipments
(millions)

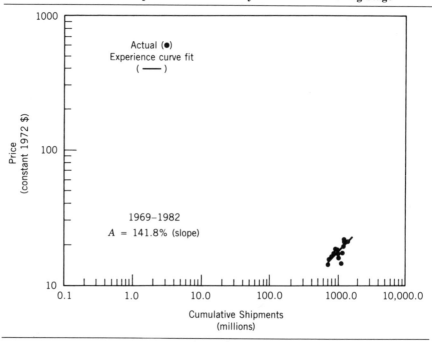

CHART 18-13. Experience Curve Analysis: Radios. Maturing Stage

Actual (●)
Experience curve fit
(——)

Price
(constant 1972 $)

1969–1982
$A = 141.8\%$ (slope)

Cumulative Shipments
(millions)

in the structure of the price/volume relationship as the product advances through its life cycle.

In 1969, the cumulative production of radios had reached 681 million units, and doubled only once in the 13 years to 1982, when cumulative volume was recorded at 1260 million units. The 42% constant price increase for every doubling of cumulative experience during this period, therefore, amounts to only 2.7% a year. Even if biased upward by a factor as high as 10, this estimate clearly indicates a much flatter slope than that calculated for the earlier 1928–1969 stage, a period during which cumulative volume doubled many times.

It is clear that the structural relationship does change in relative terms during this stage of the product's life, giving further support to the main hypothesis that price evolves in a manner related to a product's life cycle.

Monochrome Televisions

Chart 18-5 shows the time periods associated with various stages of the product life cycle of monochrome TVs. Time periods are easily identified for both the introduction and takeoff and growth stages. But around 1970, the product found a new market segment, which has since been providing a stimulus for continued and significant growth. This segment carved by monochrome TV manufacturers includes the potential buyer of a second or even third TV for use in the bedroom, kitchen, and/or workshop. Charts 18-14 and 18-15 present the cumulative experience of U.S. monochrome TV manufacturers and constant dollar price movement, respectively, over the 1946–1982 time horizon.

Experience curve analysis for the 1946–1982 time frame indicates a slope of 90% (Charts 18-5, all stages, and 18-16) implying a 10% decrease in constant dollar price for every doubling of cumulative volume. But, as was found during similar analysis of the radio market, actual (●) observations vary around the least squares fit of the experience curve. During the 1946–1949 introductory period, the experience curve slope was 101% (Charts 18-5, Stage 1, and 18-17). Technology and production had not yet been standardized, and the constant dollar prices charged by the small number of manufacturers increased.

By 1949, the TV market began to develop critical mass and the early squeaks in manufacturing processes had been greased. Production expanded with the entry of new producers, and constant dollar price began falling. The 1949–1953 period is also highlighted in Chart 18-17 to show the change in the price/volume relationship in the early years of takeoff and growth relative to that in the introduction period. The experience curve slope for 1949–1953 decreased to 93% (Chart 18-5, Stage 1). This period has been analyzed separately for another reason; in 1954, set manufacturers introduced color TVs. Monochrome price behavior adjusted accordingly in reaction to a fear of product share erosion. The experience curve of monochromes, estimated

CHART 18-14. Annual Factory Production of Monochrome Televisions

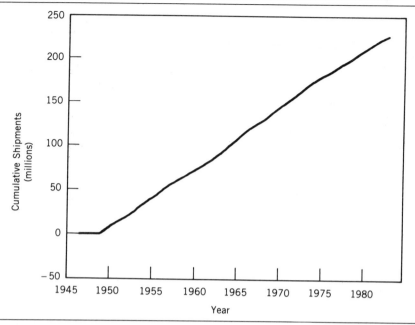

CHART 18-15. Monochrome Television Prices (Constant 1972 Dollars)

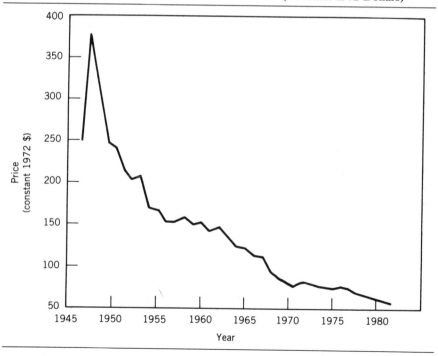

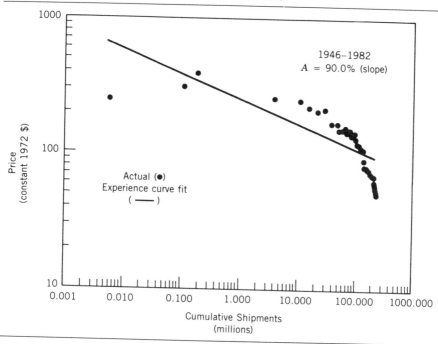

**CHART 18-16. Experience Curve Analysis: Monochrome Televisions.
Introduction to Present**

1946–1982
A = 90.0% (slope)

Price
(constant 1972 $)

Actual (●)
Experience curve fit
(——)

Cumulative Shipments
(millions)

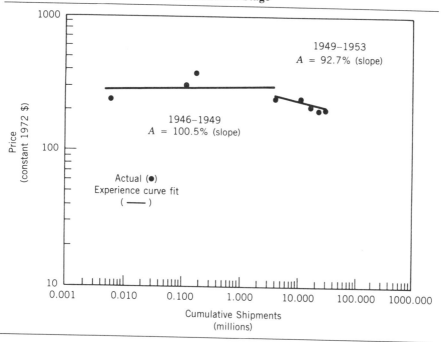

**CHART 18-17. Experience Curve Analysis: Monochrome Televisions.
Introduction Stage**

1949–1953
A = 92.7% (slope)

1946–1949
A = 100.5% (slope)

Price
(constant 1972 $)

Actual (●)
Experience curve fit
(——)

Cumulative Shipments
(millions)

for the period immediately following the introduction of color TVs, 1953–1956, resulted in a significant change in slope from 93% recorded before the introduction of color to 71% afterward (Charts 18-5, Stage 2, and 18-18).

In 1954, color TV prices were almost three times those of monochrome. And after three years from introduction, there had been only 125,000 color units shipped. This poorer than expected performance wiped out the immediate threat of market share erosion for monochrome TVs. An estimate of the monochrome experience curve for the 1956–1967 period (Charts 18-5, Stage 2, and 18-19) indicates continued downward adjustment in the constant dollar price of monochromes, but at a slope higher (75%) than that recorded during the initial reaction to the color TV threat (71%). The average experience curve slope during the entire 1953–1967 period was 77% (Charts 18-5, Stage 2, and 18-19). This period of constant dollar price decline is clearly associated with the takeoff and growth stage of monochrome TVs.

By 1967, 13 years after introduction, the color TV market entered the takeoff stage. As a result, monochrome TV prices fell through the floor. The estimated experience curve slope for 1967–1970 (Charts 18-5, Stage 3, and 18-19) indicates a precipitous constant dollar price drop in the monochrome market; one of nearly 80% for a doubling of cumulative volume. Although the direction of price movement is correct in relative terms, this estimate is biased downward by the significant adjustment in target market by monochrome manufacturers, a strategy employed to prolong the life of their product. Mix shifted away from the more expensive console model (replaced by the color set) toward the downsized and lower-priced models. By 1970, the initial and largest impacts of the downsize adjustment ran their course and from 1970–1982 prices continued to drop, almost 50% for every doubling of volume (Charts 18-5, Stage 4, and 18-20). During this 12-year period, monochrome products became smaller (currently available in Dick Tracy wrist-TV style) and new life blood was transfused into the market, extending the growth stage of monochrome TVs.

Color Televisions

The volume and constant price history for color TVs are presented in Charts 18-21 and 18-22, respectively.

The experience curve for the entire history of the product, 1954–1982, has been estimated and is presented in Charts 18-6, all stages, and 18-23. For every doubling of cumulative experience during this period, constant dollar color TV prices decreased 6%. But here, too, actual activity (●) varied from the least squares fit of the conventional experience curve (2). During the introductory period, the experience slope estimate of 97% indicates just a 3% reduction in constant dollar price for every volume doubling (Charts 18-6, Stage 1, and 18-24), while that measured for the takeoff and growth period (Charts 18-6, Stage 2, and 18-25) shows a sharp reduction to 86%, that is, a 14% decrease in real price for each volume doubling. This empirical evidence supports the main hypothesis.

CHART 18-18. Experience Curve Analysis: Monochrome Televisions. Early Takeoff Stage

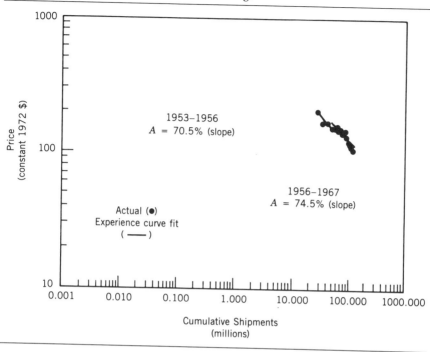

Price (constant 1972 $)

1953–1956
A = 70.5% (slope)

1956–1967
A = 74.5% (slope)

Actual (●)
Experience curve fit
(——)

Cumulative Shipments
(millions)

CHART 18-19. Experience Curve Analysis: Monochrome Televisions. Takeoff and Growth Stage

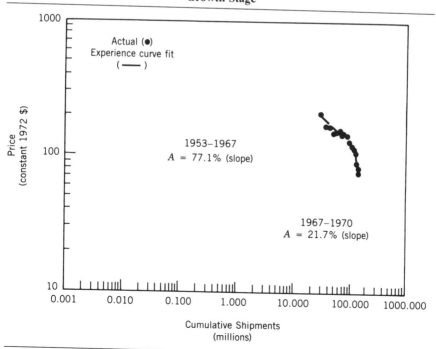

Price (constant 1972 $)

Actual (●)
Experience curve fit
(——)

1953–1967
A = 77.1% (slope)

1967–1970
A = 21.7% (slope)

Cumulative Shipments
(millions)

CHART 18-20. Experience Curve Analysis: Monochrome Televisions. Market Niche Adjustment Stage

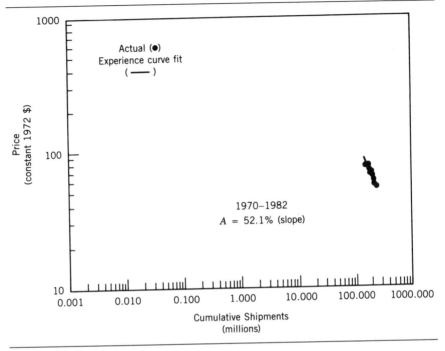

CHART 18-21. Annual Factory Production of Color Televisions

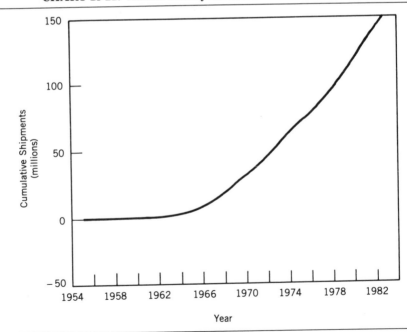

CHART 18-22. Color Television Prices (Constant 1972 Dollars)

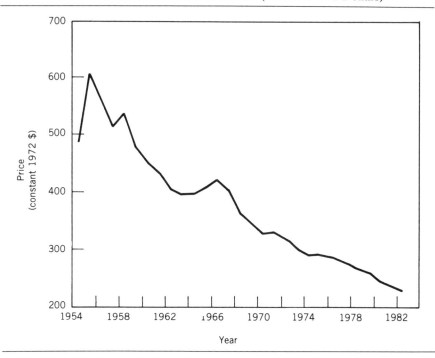

Year

CHART 18-23. Experience Curve Analysis: Color Televisions. Introduction to Present

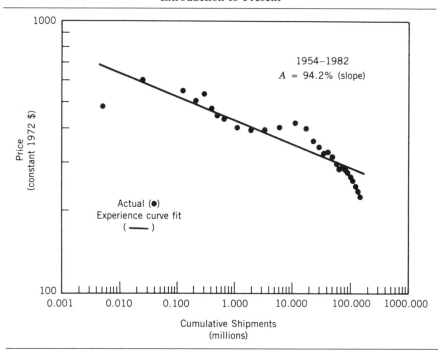

CHART 18-24. Experience Curve Analysis: Color Televisions. Introduction Stage

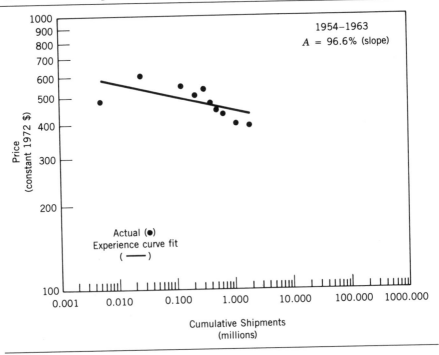

1954–1963

A = 96.6% (slope)

Price (constant 1972 $)

Actual (●)
Experience curve fit
(——)

Cumulative Shipments
(millions)

CHART 18-25. Experience Curve Analysis: Color Televisions. Takeoff and Growth Stage

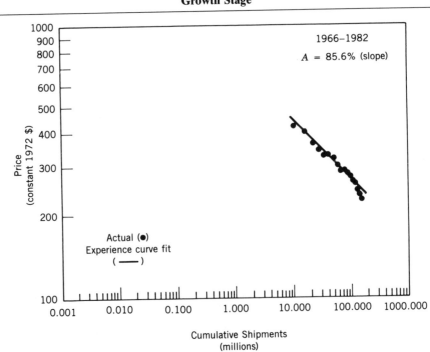

1966–1982

A = 85.6% (slope)

Price (constant 1972 $)

Actual (●)
Experience curve fit
(——)

Cumulative Shipments
(millions)

Video Cassette Recorders

Video cassette recorders were first introduced to U.S. consumers in 1974, and by 1976 the market reached critical mass and entered the takeoff and growth stage. Charts 18-26 and 18-27 present volume and price history for VCRs.

The experience curve for the 1974–1982 history of the video cassette recorder is depicted in Charts 18-7, all stages, and 18-28. The estimated slope over this time period was 88%, which translates to a 12% decrease in constant dollar price for every doubling of cumulative experience. But for the 1974–1976 Introductory period (Charts 18-7, Stage 1, and 18-29), the estimate of the experience curve slope was 93% compared with that of 88% measured for the takeoff and growth stage (Charts 18-7, Stage 2, and 18-30).

VALIDATION AND IMPLICATIONS FOR FORECASTING AND PLANNING

Empirical evidence supports the hypothesis that product prices change in a pattern related to product life cycle. While the data used here were not "pure" by any means, the evolution of price as a function of the product life cycle is clear. For all four products analyzed, price performance during the introductory stage was stable relative to that in the takeoff and growth stage.

CHART 18-26. Annual Factory Sales of Video Cassette Recorders

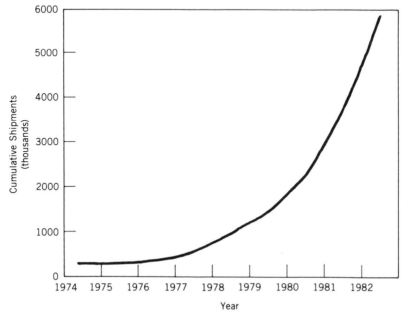

CHART 18-27. Video Cassette Recorder Prices (Constant 1972 Dollars)

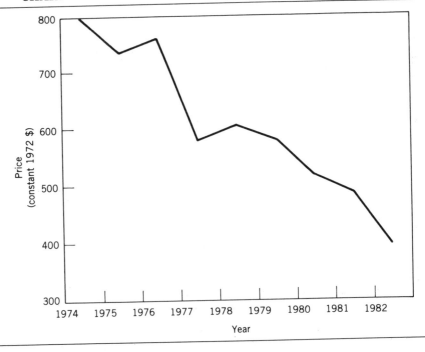

**CHART 18-28. Experience Curve Analysis: Video Cassette Recorders.
Introduction to Present**

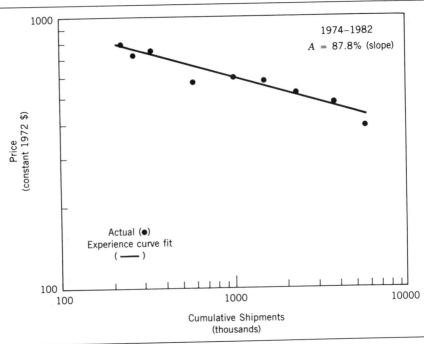

CHART 18-29. Experience Curve Analysis: Video Cassette Recorders. Introduction Stage

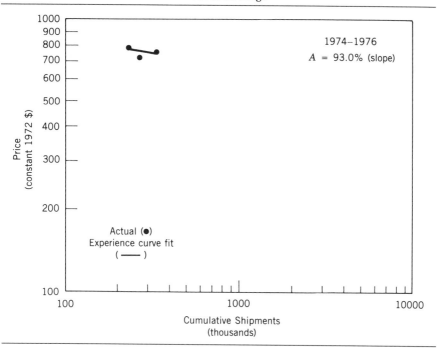

Cumulative Shipments
(thousands)

CHART 18-30. Experience Curve Analysis: Video Cassette Recorders. Takeoff and Growth Stage

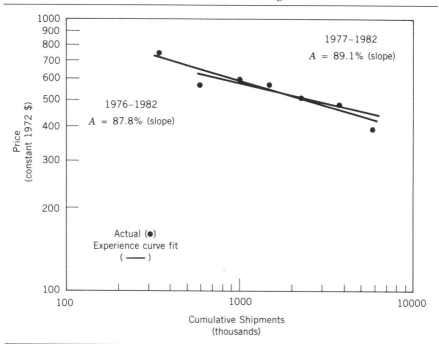

Cumulative Shipments
(thousands)

Two of the products analyzed in this study have only now begun to mature, as target markets have been changed in an attempt to prolong the growth stage and shift upward and outward the peak population asymptote. Even here, however, there is evidence, depicted in the overall product strategy of manufacturers, of a structural shift in the price/life-cycle relationship. Chart 18-31 summarizes the empirical results.

This analysis suggests that application of the stages of a product's life cycle to the forecasting of prices can aid significantly in the development of reliable price projections. The process is iterative and requires a successful integration of several tools of analysis. Pure market research, market and competitive analysis, and technology forecasting are but a few disciplines that will help the analyst determine the important factors that influence the life cycle of a product. Product and market knowledge become indispensable to the forecaster as he or she attempts to uncover product life-cycle influences.

The radio market is by far the most mature of the markets analyzed. And within the context of mix shift and the emphasis on autosound, the peak population asymptote for radios has shifted outward and upward over time. This has prolonged the life cycle of the generic radio but represents a protective strategy in a market beginning to mature. The estimates presented, then, indicate a change in the structure of price behavior during this period.

The television may rival the telephone as a means for information exchange. In the United States, 98% of households possess a TV set, compared with 97% having telephone service. Demand for television equipment is now determined mostly by upgrade and replacement needs and is therefore less sensitive to price considerations than it was in the product's early years, when every reduction in price brought TV within the reach of additional millions. Quality, features, general economic conditions, and the requirement for multiple TV sets generated by the spread of home computers and video games now play a more important role in determining the growth of this market.

Forecasting the Price of Color TVs

Note that in Chart 18-25 the experience curve slope for the 1966–1982 takeoff and growth stage of color televisions is 85.6%, implying a decrease of

CHART 18-31. Summary of Experience Curve Slopes for the Four Products Analyzed

Product	Introduction Stage	Takeoff and Growth Stage	Late Growth Stage
Radios	105.2%	72.7%	141.8%
Monochrome TVs	100.5%	77.1%	52.1%
Color TVs	96.6%	85.6%	—
VCRs	93.0%	87.8%	—

14.4% in constant dollar price for every doubling of cumulative color TV volume. Note also that the last seven observations representing the years 1976–1982 lie on a slope that is steeper than that measured in the entire takeoff and growth period. There is no doubt that changes along an experience curve slope represent concomitant changes in the stage of the product's life cycle. In the case of color TVs, the 1976–1982 period represents a time frame that is further along the S-shaped diffusion process than the earlier years of the takeoff and growth stage. As shown previously, these changes in experience curve slope are typical both within and between different stages of a product's life cycle. When developing a price forecasting model using experience curve methodology and the product life-cycle concept, it is good practice to allow the latest changes in the structural relationship between constant dollar price and cumulative volume to influence the forecasting equation. The experience curve estimate of the 1976–1982 period is 75.9% (Chart 18-6, Stage 3). Using the equation for this period from Chart 18-6, modified slightly to fit exactly through the constant dollar 1982 base price of $228, along with the exogenous input of actual history of cumulative shipments for the 1983–1986 time period, projections of the constant dollar

---

CHART 18-32. Forecasting the Price of Color Televisions

Experience curve base

1976–1981

$$\ln(\text{constant price}) = 10.185 - 0.398 \ln(\text{cumulative volume})$$
$$\text{SLOPE} = 75.9\%$$

Forecasting equation (Adjusted to constant price of $228 in 1982 base year)

Actual   1982 $\ln(\$228) = 10.\hat{1}68 - 0.3\hat{9}8 \ln(149{,}012)$

	Real price forecast	Actual cumulative volume
1983	$\ln(\$220) = 10.\hat{1}68 - 0.3\hat{9}8 \ln(162{,}998)$	
1984	$\ln(\$212) = 10.\hat{1}68 - 0.3\hat{9}8 \ln(179{,}081)$	
1985	$\ln(\$204) = 10.\hat{1}68 - 0.3\hat{9}8 \ln(195{,}981)$	
1986	$\ln(\$198) = 10.\hat{1}68 - 0.3\hat{9}8 \ln(212{,}681)$	

Comparison of forecast with actual

Year	Forecast	Actual	% Difference Forecast vs. Actual
1983	$220	$215	+2.3%
1984	$212	$207	+2.4%
1985	$204	$202	+1.0%
1986	$198	$199	−0.5%
		Average absolute error:	+/− 1.6%

price of color TVs can be made and compared with what actually occurred. Chart 18-32 contains the forecasting equation and these projections. While it is true that a forecast of cumulative volume would normally have been used as input to the price model, the *actual* volume data were used here to minimize any errors due to incorrect cumulative volume projections. By this means, the price model becomes the focus of attention in this phase of the analysis.

The average absolute error of the 1983–1986 price forecast of color TVs is just 1.6%.

Forecasting the Price of VCRs

In 1982, shipments of video cassette recorders grew almost twice as rapidly as in 1981. This behavior in the midst of an economic slump indicates the vast extent of the untapped potential market for VCRs. In 1982, only 1 household in 15 owned a video recorder, compared with 2.1 TVs in each household. Since then, continued price reductions have eroded consumer

CHART 18-33. Forecasting the Price of Video Cassette Recorders

Experience curve base

1979–1982

$$\ln(\text{constant price}) = 8.310 - 0.265 \ln(\text{cumulative volume})$$

$$\text{SLOPE} = 83.2\%$$

Forecasting equation (adjusted to constant price of $393 in 1982 base year)

Actual   1982 $\ln(\$393) = 8.\hat{2}72 - 0.2\hat{6}5 \ln(5,783)$

	Real price forecast	Actual cumulative volume
1983	$\ln(\$342) = 8.\hat{2}72 - 0.2\hat{6}5 \ln(9,874)$	
1984	$\ln(\$294) = 8.\hat{2}72 - 0.2\hat{6}5 \ln(17,490)$	
1985	$\ln(\$256) = 8.\hat{2}72 - 0.2\hat{6}5 \ln(29,340)$	
1986	$\ln(\$233) = 8.\hat{2}72 - 0.2\hat{6}5 \ln(41,840)$	

Comparison of forecast with actual

Year	Forecast	Actual	% Difference Forecast vs. Actual
1983	$342	$318	+7.5%
1984	$294	$274	+7.3%
1985	$256	$251	+2.0%
1986	$233	$237	+1.7%
		Average absolute error:	+/− 4.6%

resistance and increased the number of buyers by a proportion greater than the price cuts themselves.

Much like the recent trend in the color TV experience curve, for the 1979–1982 period Charts 18-7, Stage 3, and 18-33 (last four ●'s) display a steeper slope in VCRs than for either the 1976–1982 or 1977–1982 periods. Chart 18-33 provides not only the estimated experience curve of the 1979–1982 time frame but a comparison of the constant dollar price projections from the forecasting equation relative to actual history. Again, for the 1983–1986 projection period, actual cumulative VCR volume was used as exogenous input in order to focus attention on the price forecasting model, which was slightly modified to fit exactly through the constant price of $393 in the base year of 1982.

Conclusion

There is no set formula for determining the most important factors in every market and for every product therein. The analytical approach must be disciplined and structured. In a stand-alone process of estimating a product life-cycle curve, it will not be intuitively obvious when to expect a change from one stage of growth to another. Forecasting an inflection point in an S-shaped diffusion process is, at best, a qualitative judgment, and should be done only after a rigorous analysis of the product and the market it serves. This is where the integration of other disciplines and tools helps the analyst.

The marriage of experience curve theory and the product life-cycle concept provides one rigorous method for quantifying the impact of factors that influence product price. The ultimate goal of the process is to bound the uncertainty around a price forecast, so that better strategic decisions can be made today for tomorrow's markets.

BIBLIOGRAPHY

Abernathy, William J., and Kenneth Wayne, "Limits of the Learning Curve," *Harvard Business Review,* September/October 1974, pp. 109–119.

Bass, F. M., "A New Product Growth Model for Consumer Durables," *Management Science,* vol. 15, January 1969, pp. 215–227.

Boston Consulting Group, Inc., *Perspectives on Experience,* Boston, MA, 1967.

Clifford, D. Jr., "Managing the Product Life Cycle," *Dun's Review of Modern Management,* vol. 85, June 1965, pp. 34–38.

Cox, W. E., "Product Life Cycles as Marketing Models," *Journal of Business,* vol. 40, October 1967, pp. 375–384.

Dhalla, N. K., and S. Yuspeh, "Forget the Product Life Cycle Concept," *Harvard Business Review,* vol. 54, January/February 1976, pp. 102–112.

Gompertz, Benjamin, "On the Science Connected with Human Mortality," *Transactions of the Royal Society,* June 1825.

Harrell, Stephen G., and Elmer D. Taylor, "Modeling the Product Life Cycle for Consumer Durables," *Journal of Marketing,* vol. 45, Fall 1981, pp. 68–75.

Henderson, Bruce D., and Alan J. Zakon, "Pricing Strategy: How to Improve It (The Experience Curve)," in Kenneth J. Albert, ed., *Handbook of Business Problem Solving,* McGraw-Hill, New York, 1980, pp. 351–368.

Hirschmann, Winfred B., "Profit from the Learning Curve," *Harvard Business Review,* vol. 42, January/February 1964, pp. 125–139.

Kiechel III, Walter, "The Decline of the Experience Curve," *Fortune,* October 1981, pp. 139–146.

Mahajan, Vijay, and Eitan Muller, "Innovation Diffusion and New Product Growth Models in Marketing," *Journal of Marketing,* vol. 43, Fall 1979, pp. 55–68.

Mahajan, V., and Wind, Y. (eds) *Innovation Diffusion Models of New Product Acceptance,* Ballinger Publishing Company, Cambridge, MA, 1986.

Nielsen, Inc., "Identifying Phases in an Average Product 'Life Cycle,'" *Nielsen Researcher,* vol. 8, 1967, pp. 3–7.

Rink, D. R., and J. Swan, "Product Life Cycle Research: A Literature Review," *Journal of Business Research,* vol. 78, September 1979, pp. 219–242.

Smith, Ward C., "Product Life Cycle Strategy: How to Stay on the Growth Curve," *Management Review,* vol. 69, January 1980, pp. 8–13.

Thoreli, Hans B., and Stephen C. Burnett, "The Nature of Product Life Cycles for Industrial Goods Businesses," *Journal of Marketing,* vol. 45, Fall 1981, pp. 97–108.

Yelle, L. E., "The Learning Curve: Historical Review and Comprehensive Survey," *Decisions Sciences,* vol. 10, April 1979, pp. 302–328.

CHAPTER

19

LIFE-CYCLE FORECASTING

SATINDER K. MULLICK
GREGORY S. ANDERSON
ROBERT E. LEACH
WARD C. SMITH
Corning Glass Works, Corning, New York

Life-cycle analysis as a marketing tool has been steadily growing in importance over the last two decades. While early uses of the concept were qualitative, efforts have been made recently to quantify the life cycle for many product classes. Life-cycle terminology has been incorporated in planning matrices in many companies. "Embryonic," "growth," "mature," and "aging" are the most common classifications used by many corporations. Substantially more rapid growth has occurred through the use of mathematical modeling, particularly with the availability of simplified computer programming techniques. For example, observations of a medical instruments business over several years indicate that modeling life cycles for this activity could lead to a different business perspective, including some important insights into product management.

Misjudgment about life cycles can be extremely costly. For example, the light truck market took off like a hula hoop, and Dana Corporation, a manufacturer of frames and other steel component parts, paid a major price for misjudgment because it did not forecast the life cycle properly. The concept of the life cycle can be applied to a particular product model, to the product line that attempts to cover the spectrum of features and pricing to fit all the elements of a market segment, or to the market need itself. Each has a life cycle with longevity generally in the stated order. The study of each of the life-cycle elements of such a business is valid. The product life cycle offers a convenient focus for our purposes.

THE LIFE-CYCLE STAGES

Normally there are five stages in the life cycle of a successful product: product development, testing and introduction, rapid growth, steady state, and phasing out. However, to encompass another aspect of forecasting that relates indirectly to the product life cycle, we shall include another stage: the initial preproduct or technology development stage, which embraces the rapidly growing field of technological forecasting. Chart 19-1 summarizes these six stages, the typical decisions made, and the main forecasting techniques suitable at each stage. The remainder of this chapter contains a brief, introductory discussion of these six stages.

The typical decisions and shape of the life-cycle curve in Chart 19-1 are mainly representative of durable goods. While nondurable goods and services also have life-cycle curves that contain the same major phases, the shapes of the curves will differ, and the values (costs) of the decisions will change. Furthermore, the components of the curves are different: The durable goods life-cycle curve components consist of purchases represented by new orders, multiunit owners, and replacement sales; the nondurable goods and most services curves consist of initial buyers and repeat buyers. The values (costs) of the decisions will frequently be less for nondurable goods than for durable goods, although the ultimate costs of overstocking will be higher for nondurable goods because of the shorter phasing out period.

Some forecasting is required at all stages, but the amount and complexity are a function of the dollars involved in the decision.

FORM OF THE LIFE CYCLE

Chart 19-2 shows three distinct cycles in the dominant energy source—a wood-burning cycle, a coal-burning cycle, and a petroleum and natural gas cycle.

The form and the length of the life cycle are highly variable from industry to industry. They are a function of social, political, technological, and managerial influences.

For example, renewal, segmentation, innovation, and repositioning have been used successfully at Corning Glass Works to alter the life cycle of several products.

In late 1976, Pyrex® brand clear ovenware was a mature to aging business with heavy price competition. Consumers viewed it as a commodity, with no gift purchasing. The decision to market Pyrex® with attractive serving baskets created a gift image and an entirely new segment. The business was totally incremental, with no loss in the basic clear business.

In 1978, Corning Medical's Model 175 Blood Gas Analyzer was suffering price competition from a lower performance, lower cost product. Corning's Model 165/2 was nearing the end of its life cycle, with sales dropping off

CHART 19-1. Types of Decisions Made Over a Product's Life Cycle, with Related Forecasting Techniques

Stage of Life Cycle	Preproduct	Product Development	Market Testing and Early Introduction	Rapid Growth	Steady State	Phasing Out
Typical decisions	Allocation of R&D, Distribution system needs, Personnel needs, Acquisitions	Amount of development effort, Product design, Business strategies	Optimum facility size, Marketing strategies, including distribution and pricing	Facilities expansion, Marketing strategies, Production planning	Promotions specials, Pricing, Production planning, Inventories	Transfer of facilities, Marketing effort, Production planning
Forecasting techniques	Delphi method, Progress functions, Panel consensus, Trend analysis, Historical analogy, Technical monitoring, Sociopolitical monitoring	Delphi method, Historical analysis of comparable products, Priority pattern analysis, Input–Output analysis, Panel consensus, Technical monitoring, Learning curve	Consumer surveys, Tracking and warning systems, Market tests, Experimental designs, Analogy Sales	Statistical techniques for identifying turning points, Tracking and warning systems, Market surveys, Intention-to-buy surveys, Substitution theory, Trend analysis	Time series analysis and projection, Causal and econometric models, Market surveys for tracking and warning, Life-cycle analysis, Trend analysis, Technical monitoring, Sociopolitical monitoring	Slope characteristic, Statistical tracking and market research, Historical analogy and regression analysis

CHART 19-2. Life Cycle of Dominant Energy Source

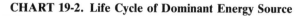

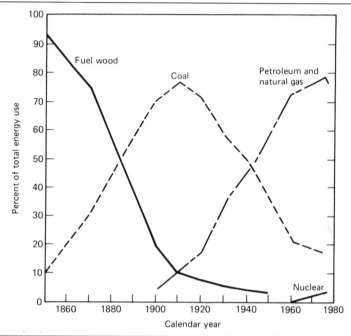

sharply. The new Corning Model 168, with features and price comparable to those of the competitor, was introduced in late 1978. This allowed the upward repositioning of the 175 and the downward repositioning of the 165/2. This move increased profitability in both the Model 175 and the Model 165/2, as well as providing a successful new product.

Stage 1. Preproduct Development

Before a specific new product concept emerges, there are usually sociological, political, or technological developments that make the new product possible or necessary. The forecasting objective, prior to product development, is to determine when a new product will be possible or needed or required by legislation and what the characteristics of the product will be.

Here are the major forecasting questions in the preproduct stage:

When is a particular technology most likely to be developed to the stage that products are feasible and marketable?

When will social and political pressures force a change in a product or require a new one?

What are the potential sales opportunities that will emerge from this technology or new product requirements?

What will the characteristics of these markets be?

What events must occur for technological breakthroughs or for legislation to force new products or changes in existing products?

A recent review of glass and competitive materials indicated the trend line of properties from various materials available since 1900. This information, with use of trend extrapolation, allows prediction of yet-to-be-invented properties. Corning's marketers can now anticipate new competition or envision new product concepts even before the inventions have been made.

The foregoing questions should be answered before the manager makes decisions relating to (1) how much R&D effort should be expended in technological development, (2) to what extent the company will participate in a new or expanding industry, (3) what type of distribution system will be needed to sell the new products and when it should be available, and (4) the personnel and facility requirements associated with the business. These are some of the same questions and decisions that arise during the product development stage. But they must be considered in at least a macro way at this stage so that preliminary work can be undertaken if long lead times are necessary in preparing for product introduction (e.g., obtaining a research capability and establishing a reputation in a business). Corning made many of these assessments in the 1960s when it decided to enter the medical business. More recently it assessed the impact of genetic engineering and related biotechnology in light of higher energy cost forecasts, and as a result has committed itself to building a technical and commercial capability in this area.

An analysis of technical and technoeconomic trends can frequently help identify a product opportunity long before the economic significance of a research accomplishment is seen. A rough idea of the technical or economic advantage of a new product can provide clues as to its viability while it is still at a concept stage. Once a product concept has been identified, qualitative techniques, such as the Delphi method or panel consensus, are often utilized.

The primary basis for such forecasts is expert opinion, although historical analogies should be used as cross-checks when possible. This type of forecasting will cover periods up to 20 years into the future.

The dramatic increase in social and political influence on the innovative process makes the consideration of these inputs an increasingly important task. Programs to systematically monitor social and political change can frequently spot new or radically changed product requirements while they are still on the horizon. Corning's ability to successfully market Celcor® automotive substrates was a direct result of recognizing coming automobile emission standards.

A common objection to much long-range forecasting is that it is virtually impossible to predict with accuracy what will happen several years into the future. We agree that uncertainty increases when a forecast is made for a period of more than two years. However, at the very least, the forecast and a measure of its accuracy enable the manager to know the risks and to choose an appropriate strategy from those available. As a minimum, it is also advisable to consider expert opinions and judgments in an objective rather than subjective way.

Stage 2. Product Development

In the early stages of product development, the manager wants answers to questions such as these:

What are the alternative growth opportunities to pursuing product X?

How have established products similar to product X fared?

Should we enter this business; if so, in what segments?

How should we allocate R&D efforts and funds?

How successful will different product concepts be?

How will product X fit into the markets 5 or 10 years from now?

Forecasts that help to answer these long-range questions must necessarily have long horizons themselves.

Systematic market research is, of course, a mainstay in this area. For example, priority pattern analysis can describe the consumer's preferences and the likelihood that he or she will buy a product; thus this can be of great value in forecasting (and updating) penetration levels and rates. But there are also other market research tools, which will be used according to the state of the market, the product concept, and whether the product will compete in a clearly defined and basically established market, or in an undefined and new market.

While there can be no direct data about a product that is still a gleam in the manufacturer's eye, information about its likely performance can be gathered in several ways, provided that the market in which it is to be sold is a known entity.

An examination of relevant technical parameters and their history can highlight the relative technical advantage of a new product. This advantage should be similar to that of other successful new products in the market.

Frequently, the most critical element of a new product is price. Knowing in advance the lowest price that can be offered while still coining satisfactory returns can be vital. An examination of the learning curve of a new product, even though still in development, can provide a good source of early price information.

Another approach is to compare a proposed product with competitive products and rank it on quantitative scales for different factors. This is called *product differences measurement*. Another and more formal approach is to construct disaggregate market models by splitting out different segments of a complex market for individual study and consideration. An alternative method of forecasting sales or profits for a new product in a defined market is to compare it with an "ancestor" that has similar characteristics, such as color television versus black and white television.

Even within a defined market, it will be necessary to determine whether the total market is elastic or inelastic, that is, will it continue its historic growth rate or will the new product expand the size of the total market?

When the market for a new product is weakly defined and the product concept may still be fluid, few data are available and history is not relevant. This has been true for modular housing, pollution measurement devices, time-shared computers, and educational learning devices. The Delphi method or other "expert opinion" techniques and market research are most applicable here, with input–output analysis in combination with other techniques occasionally being of value. As a caution, expert opinion can be very wrong. Many "experts" in the business machine market passed up the opportunity to commercialize the xerographic machine.

Stage 3. Product Testing and Introduction

Before a product can enter its (it is hoped) rapid growth stage, the market potential must be tested and the product introduced—and then more market testing may be advisable. At this stage, management needs answers to these questions:

> What shall our marketing plan be, that is, which markets should we enter and with what production quantities?
>
> How much manufacturing capacity will the early production stages require?
>
> As demand grows, where should we build this capacity?
>
> How shall we allocate our R&D resources over time?

Significant profits depend on finding the right answers to these questions. Therefore, it is economically feasible to expend large amounts of effort and money on obtaining good forecasts in the short, intermediate, and long range. Based on such a short- and long-term forecast for cancer research funding, Corning built a new plant to make tissue culture labware with the planned capability to double capacity in four increments. This meant Corning's profits were much higher than if the company had built a second plant several years later.

A sales forecast at this stage should provide three points of information:

(1) the date when rapid sales will begin, (2) the rate of market penetration during the rapid sales stage, and (3) the ultimate level of penetration or sales rate during the steady-state stage. The date when a product will enter the rapid growth stage is hard to predict three or four years in advance (the usual horizon). A company's main recourse is to use statistical tracking methods to check on how successfully the product is being introduced, along with routine market studies to determine if there have been any significant changes in the market and sales rate.

Although statistical tracking is a useful tool during the early introduction stages, there are rarely sufficient data for statistical forecasting. Market research studies can naturally be useful, as we have indicated. But, more commonly, the forecaster tries to identify a similar, older product whose penetration pattern should be similar to that of the new product, since overall markets can and do exhibit consistent patterns. As discussed earlier, the relative technical and economic advantage of the new product should be similar to those of other successful introductions.

When it is not possible to identify a similar product, a different approach must be used. For the purpose of initial introduction into the markets, it may only be necessary to determine the minimum sales rate required for a product venture to meet corporate objectives. Analyses like input–output, historical trend, and technological forecasting can provide a base for estimating this minimum. Also, the feasibility of not entering the market at all, or of continuing R&D right up to the rapid growth stage, can best be determined by sensitivity analysis of yearly profit and loss, income, and cash flow statements.

To estimate the date by which a product will enter the rapid growth stage is another matter. This date is a function of many factors: for example, the existence of a distribution system, customer acceptance of or familiarity with the product concept, the need met by the product, and significant events (such as color network programming).

Stage 4. Rapid Growth

When a product enters this stage, the most important decisions relate to facilities expansion. These decisions generally involve the largest expenditures in the life cycle (except major R&D decisions). Here commensurate forecasting and tracking efforts are justified.

Forecasting and tracking must provide the executive with three kinds of information at this juncture:

Firm verification of the rapid growth rate forecast made previously

A hard date when sales will level to "normal" steady-state growth

For component products, the deviation in the growth curve that may be caused by characteristic conditions along the pipeline such as inventory blockages, which results in an S-shaped curve with a "camel back hump"

Intermediate and long-range forecasting of the market growth rate and of the attainment of steady-state sales require detailed marketing studies, intention-to-buy surveys, and product comparisons.

When a product has entered rapid growth, there are generally sufficient data available to construct statistical and possibly even causal growth models, although the latter will necessarily contain assumptions that must be verified later.

The sales of most products follow some form of an S-shaped curve, and quantitative methods can help to establish the parameters of the curve. One of the most useful such techniques is substitution theory.* When a new product must displace an older one, it is possible to make a reliable prediction of the displacement rate with a small number of data (5% maximum penetration) and little mathematical rigor. However, special care must be used if adoption requires that a large capital investment be written off. Corning has applied this tool in looking at color TV's substitution for black and white TV. We expect this approach will apply as Corning's optical waveguides begin to replace copper cable in the decade ahead.

Simulation is also an excellent tool for these circumstances because it is essentially simpler than the alternative of building a more formal, more "mathematical" model. Simulation bypasses the need for analytical solution techniques and for mathematical duplication of a complex environment and allows experimentation. Simulation also indicates to the forecaster how the pipeline elements will behave and interact over time—knowledge that is very useful in forecasting, especially in constructing formal causal models at a later date.

This knowledge is not absolutely "hard," of course, and pipeline dynamics must be carefully tracked to determine if the various estimates and assumptions made were indeed correct. Statistical methods provide a good short-term basis for estimating and checking the growth rate and signaling when turning points occur.

One main activity during the rapid growth stage, then, is to check earlier estimates; if they appear incorrect, the forecaster should compute as accurately as possible the error in the forecast and obtain a revised estimate. In some instances, models developed earlier will include only "macroterms"; in such cases, market research can provide the information needed to break these terms down into their components.

Stage 5. Steady State

In planning production and establishing marketing strategy for the short and intermediate term, the manager's first considerations are usually accurate estimates of (1) the present sales level, and (2) the rate at which this level is

* J. C. Fisher and R. H. Pry, "A Simple Substitution Model of Technological Change," Report No. 70-C-215, General Electric Company, Schenectady, NY, June 1970.

changing. The forecaster thus must make two related contributions at this stage:

1. He or she should provide estimates of trends and seasonals, which obviously affect the sales level. Seasonals are particularly important for both overall production planning and inventory control. To do this, the forecaster needs to apply time series analysis and projection techniques, that is, statistical techniques.

2. He or she should relate the future sales level to factors that are more easily predictable, or have a "lead" relationship with sales, or both. Therefore, the forecaster needs to build causal models. Building permits are a good lead indicator for major appliances. At this point in the life cycle, sufficient time series data are available and enough causal relationships are known or suspected from direct experience and market studies so that the forecaster can indeed apply these two powerful sets of tools.

Also, important at this stage is the application of preproduct forecasting techniques to competing and technical alternatives. Predicting the rate at which a product will be displaced can provide important planning information and help to identify research goals. An often ignored alternative is to consider more aggressively altering the life-cycle pattern.

Traditional design strategy in the medical instruments market has been to approach each product model as an ultimate statement of the product need rather than as one of a series of statements that supports a changing need throughout a changing technology. It is easy to slip into project-oriented rather than need-maintenance-oriented management. This leads to a design philosophy that stresses a monolithic approach. It is a one-time statement with a maximum of features and state-of-the-art technology. It attempts to jump seven years ahead to allow time for other commitments and does not consider the customer's ability to absorb multiple new and simultaneous changes. In its attempt to be self-contained, this approach locks the user on the outside, both physically and in understanding. Such a design does not lend itself to the composite life-cycle strategy.

The composite life-cycle (or business maintenance) strategy requires a companion design strategy to be successful. It must seek the flexibility that allows replacement of a module containing rapidly changing technology. It must recognize that certain desirable features can be added later, perhaps when the customer is more receptive. It recognizes that design and marketing are interactive and dynamic over product life. Such a design strategy requires new disciplines and therefore is not easily accepted. If the need-maintenance approach described expands market share by adjusting to or even shaping a particular need, a second aggressive attack on the life-cycle pattern is the adaptation of the product to meet new needs. A screw compressor designed to compress and transport air and other gases can be adapted to transport confectionery sugar, even cement. With a change in its seals and addition of a bit of water, it becomes a vacuum pump. And where did it come from originally? Actually, it started life as an internal combustion engine. For each new market segment defined, the effective product life cycle is altered.

When one begins to creatively alter life cycles, two questions arise: "When does a product life cycle become a business life cycle?" and "What are the limits to the definition of a product?" Many products, by intent or good fortune, serve multiple needs. Another insight that would seem to contradict the multiple-need strategy is the observation that technologies survive products and that market needs survive technologies. The elegant complexity of business and markets is that activity expansion is practical in either or both directions. The expansion and pyramiding of life-cycle elements is descriptive of business growth. The key to profitability is maximizing the elements of synergy that exist for variations of the product, and at all functional levels of the business.

It is evident that a product life-cycle forecast is valid until someone makes a fundamental change. That change can be an image change, a feature addition, a price change, or even an alteration in accessibility. As creative as we are, we still forecast from past experience. When a company that dominated a particular instrument market went from distributor sales to direct sales, five competitors arrived to supply the distribution vacancy. The influx of new thought led to a new level of instrument design and performance. A decade later, when steady state was again reached, the unique image created by departure into a vertical dimension, as opposed to a horizontal dimension, again significantly altered market share. Each time this occurs, one is surprised at the significance of the departure from prediction. Equally surprising is what can constitute a fundamental change.

Stage 6. Phasing Out

Virtually all products go through a final phasing-out stage, whether it lasts only a few months, a few years, or extends for as long as 10 or 20 years. Most product analysis is concerned only with estimating or establishing the S-shaped curve and not in determining when the plateau or gradual growth will turn down. This can result in lost profits because of inventories that must eventually be scrapped, inability to phase in the excess capacity with new product requirements, and excessive marketing effort for a dying product.

The most important questions to answer in this stage are: "When will the decline or phasing out begin?" and "How long will it last?" Answers will aid in decisions relating to marketing strategies (promotion efforts, pricing, and when to withdraw the product), production scheduling and inventory control, and facilities planning. Three basic approaches are normally taken to answer the foregoing questions:

1. Trend projection techniques and primarily the slope characteristic method can help to make good forecasts for the entire life cycle, including prediction of the downturn point and duration of the phasing-out stage.

2. Historical analogies can be used to determine the overall pattern of the life cycle, and regression analysis (or some similar technique) can provide estimates of the parameters of the overall curve, product characteristics, and differences being used as the independent variables.

3. Good tracking and warning tools, such as the Census Bureau X-11 (Shiskin routine), can identify turning points, and market surveys and other techniques can then be employed to determine the reason for the turning point. That is, is it temporary because of competitive moves, or is it a long-term market trend? Tracking techniques can also be used in the first two approaches to determine the correctness of the assumptions and models.

Perhaps the least amount of effort in forecasting is normally expended in the phasing-out stage, although there are significant rewards for good forecasts here. Forecasts for phasing out products with short life cycles, such as cereals and apparel, are particularly crucial. One cannot discuss life-cycle forecasting and its relevant decision processes without observing that large established companies, which are most likely to apply such skills, have not distinguished themselves in the area of diversification into new products and businesses. Success seems more likely to favor the newcomer to the business scene. This phenomenon is associated with the inability of the established company to utilize forecasting techniques without applying the company's own interpretation—adjusting input and output data in ways that validate the status quo. Typical examples might be the defining of a market segment in terms of an existing product capability rather than in terms of market need. The result is a product activity that fits available resources, but one that is short lived.

Another variation of such selective forecasting involves the recognition that elements of the established business exist in a diversification product opportunity. Attempts to satisfy the market need are hopelessly bound up in the need to satisfy internal culture. In one such situation, a high-technology company purchased an exclusive position with a unique product. Two internal requirements took precedence. First, the product housing was an item manufacturable by the established company. Utilization of this part or some cost-reduced variation of it was mandatory and effectively limited more creative approaches in second-generation products. Second, development resources were directed at associated segments of the acquired market opportunity rather than at the optimization of the acquired business. This satisfied the need to bring into play the company's high-technology resources but proved irrelevant to market need. In such opportunities, the market may be correctly forecast, but cultural adjustments lead to product life cycles that are shortened prematurely. The forecasting techniques are not invalid, but the tendency for input–output data to pass through a "status quo" filter can create a disastrous result.

AN EXAMPLE: TV GLASS ENVELOPE DEMAND FORECASTING

When TV was being conceived in the 1940s, it was not clear whether the glass envelope in use today (glass panel and glass funnel) would be the final choice. There were alternative systems and materials. One system used a metal funnel and a sagged glass faceplate. This system was used for a while, and over a million black and white TV sets were actually sold. Corning Glass Works worked on the alternate system using glass panels and funnels for many years before convincing the industry to opt for that system. Corning Glass Works was not involved in the metal funnel system. If that system had prevailed, Corning Glass would not have enjoyed the worldwide growth opportunity and leadership in the TV industry.

When color TV was conceived, several forecasters assumed that black and white TV would fade away. In reality, the cost of small black and white TVs was reduced sharply, and a new multiple-set market was created. Thus the demand for glass envelopes has grown at a good rate for over three decades.

Of course, there were some who thought that color TV would replace black and white by 1960. They did not understand the dynamics involved in

CHART 19-3. Household Saturation (U.S. TV Sets)

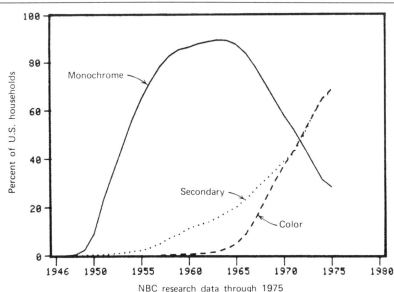

NBC research data through 1975

CHART 19-4. U.S. TV Set Sales to Dealers

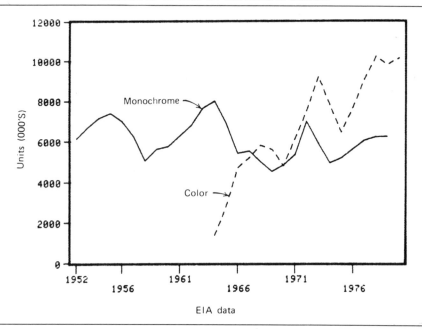

EIA data

solving all the problems. Color TV demand finally took off in 1965, and the major networks (NBC, CBS, ABC) went full blast to color programming to prevent losses in advertising income. (See Charts 19-3 and 19-4.)

Glass envelopes are now being used in video games and video terminals. The overall worldwide demand for glass envelopes has grown very well as new markets are identified. A couple of technologies or concepts have threatened the system using glass envelopes, but innovations and cost reductions have kept the competitive system from taking over. Projection TV systems remain a major threat.

AN EXAMPLE: LIFE-CYCLE FORECASTING OF MATERIALS/TECHNOLOGY

Over the years Corning Glass Works has invented materials with diverse cross-market applications. In the 1950s the company developed a thermal shock-resistant glass-based material ideal for missile nose cones. It was able to withstand the heat and stress of going from ground zero into space and back through atmospheric reentry, even at supersonic speeds. While this in itself was a major breakthrough, a different and unique application for this material (trademarked PYROCERAM®) resulted in CORNINGWARE® cookware in 1958. This versatile cookware could go directly from the freezer to the oven to the table. Some 20 years later, another property of this original nose cone material—its transparency to radio signals—permitted an extension of its consumer application as an ideal cookware for microwave ovens.

SUMMARY

The types of decisions made throughout the product life cycle vary considerably, according to payoff implications and the need for forecasting accuracy. It is, therefore, apparent that the types of techniques used throughout the product life cycle will change over time, and new methods should be introduced as the need for new forecasts arises. Since data availability also differs significantly over time and affects the selection of the forecasting technique, the value and effectiveness of a particular technique cannot be precisely stated without considering its specific application.

BIBLIOGRAPHY

Chambers, John C., Satinder K. Mullick, and Donald D. Smith, *An Executive Guide to Forecasting,* John Wiley, New York 1974 (original edition); Robert E. Krieger Publishing Company, Malabar, FL (reprint 1984). This book expands on the well-known *Harvard Business Review* article, "How To Choose The Right Forecasting Technique", (July–August 1971). It is full of interesting real world examples and applications. Well-known input–output models are compared. A bibliography for forecasting and market research techniques is also included for new practitioners.

Georgoff, David, and Robert G. Murdick, "Manager's Guide to Forecasting," *Harvard Business Review,* vol. 64, no. 1, January–February 1986, pp. 110–120. This article has compiled a chart that profiles the 20 most common forecasting techniques and rates their attributes against 16 important evaluative dimensions. The result is a practical guide that will help executives sort out their priorities when choosing a technique and enable them to combine methods to achieve the best possible results.

Levitt, Theodore, "The Globalization Of Markets," *Harvard Business Review,* vol. 61, no. 3, May–June 1983, pp. 92–102. This article adds an important dimension to life-cycle forecasting, since the diffusion of technology has an important implication for the globalization of markets—through reshaping of preferences with low prices and high quality. The process of world homogenization can lead to expanded markets and extended or shortened product life cycle. Coca-Cola and Pepsi-Cola, which are globally standardized products, are constantly expanding product life cycle. Digital watches, VCRs, video cameras, and food processors have shortened the product life cycles of many products.

Shanklin, William L., and John K. Ryans, Jr., "Organizing For High-Tech Marketing," *Harvard Business Review,* vol. 62, no. 6, November–December 1984, pp. 164–182. A stimulating article for those interested in life-cycle forecasting. The examples illustrated in this article are very interesting.

Smith, Ward D., "Product Life-Cycle Strategy: How To Stay On The Growth Curve," *Management Review* (publication of American Management Association), January 1980. This article relates sales growth to resource allocation for medical instruments. Executives and practitioners should find this article very stimulating.

20

FORECASTING RECESSIONS

ROBERT L. McLAUGHLIN

Turning Points, Cheshire, Connecticut

Every few years a severe shock, called "recession," strikes the economy. The minimum requirement for recession is at least two quarters of negative real GNP, although there are more important ways to measure. The most useful definition of recession is that the economy must meet three criteria, known as the three "D's": duration, diffusion, and depth. In effect, for the economy to be in recession, the decline must have (1) a *duration* long enough to be at least as long as the shortest past recession, (2) a wide *diffusion* through the economy, and (3) a *depth* at least as severe as the shallowest recession on record.

There have been 12 *slowdowns* in the U.S. economy since World War II. Eight of these were severe enough to become recessions. Four did not get that bad. During the postwar period from 1947 through 1986, the economy has grown an average of a little more than 3.0% per annum in real (i.e., excluding inflation) terms. We can generalize, then, that when we operate above 3.0% the economy is in a growth period. When growth is less than 3.0%, the economy is in a slowdown. If growth goes below zero (and fulfills the three D's), the economy is in recession.

RECESSION: ULTIMATE FORECAST CHALLENGE

Most of those who forecast do so because of the need to make decisions. And, if recessions represent an ultimate challenge to the forecaster, the truth is that one must forecast *any* time there is a decision to make. Decisions cannot be made for the past; they can only be made for the future. Consequently, whenever a decision must be made, a forecast—implicit or explicit—must also be made in support of that decision. Forecasting is decision support.

It is always difficult to forecast; it has never been easy. But the *maximum* problem of prediction is the forecasting of recession. And one of the most difficult recessions to forecast was that of 1980. In the fall of 1977 economists began predicting the end of the business cycle expansion that had begun in April 1975. It did not officially end until January 1980. In effect, forecasters—especially those who had to forecast in support of calendar year budgets—experienced three extremely difficult years, forecasting under the cloud of recession. One may think one only has to incorporate recession into the forecast every few years, but the period 1977 through 1986 proved how wrong is this insight.

The average peacetime business cycle from 1854 through 1986 (there have been 25 of them) has lasted 46 months—measured from peak to peak. Six peacetime cycles since World War II have averaged 44 months in duration. In the 65 years from 1854 through World War I, the average expansion was only 51% of the average business cycle. Between the two World Wars, this figure—in spite of the Great Depression—increased to 58%. Since World War II and the Keynesian revolution, the U.S. economy in peacetime has been in expansion over 75% of the time. Chart 20-1 records the distribution of quarterly percentage changes in the postwar period from the second quarter of 1947 through the third quarter of 1986. Note that 78% of the 158 quarters exhibited positive growth percentages. One is hard put to find bad news in these figures, particularly when we realize that the period prior to World War I is often described as the "good old days." The truth is that, back then, the U.S. economy was in recession half the time.

In March 1975, the severest recession of the postwar era troughed, and a new business cycle began the next month. It should not be surprising that in the fall of 1977, recession scenarios began to appear. Only 3 of 23 peacetime expansions since 1854 had lasted longer than 36 months, and only one of the three was postwar. So, with a strict statistical methodology, it was easy to predict a 1978 recession. If the expansion extended *beyond* June 1978, it would be the longest peacetime expansion since World War II—an event with a very low statistical probability. If ever a case has to be made that pure statistical inference cannot be used to forecast recession, the 1980 recession is probably the best example. (The business economist appears to be exonerated from this mistake, since a survey by the National Association of Business Economists in August 1977 produced a 1978 forecast for real GNP of +4.5%—the actual growth in that year turned out to be +4.4%. A year later, in August 1978, the survey produced a 1979 forecast of +2.5%—the actual growth in 1979 was +2.3%.)

Economists tend to agree that the monetary and fiscal policies of the federal government have an impact on production (i.e., GNP) about 6 to 12 months later and on prices about 18 to 24 months later. Though the time relationships may be imprecise, most of our economic forecasting methods are in some way dependent on this proposition. Economists continue to develop methods to forecast the economy, but events continue to increase

CHART 20-1. Quarterly Growth: Real GNP (Annual Rates) from 1947 (Second Quarter) Through 1986 (Third Quarter)

```
-10%
 -9   //                                               2
 -8
 -7   /                                                1
 -6
 -5   ///                                              3
 -4   /                                                1
 -3   /////                                            5
 -2   /////                                            5
 -1   /////   //                                       7
 -0
  0   /////   ////                                     9
  1   /////   ////                                     9
  2   /////   /////   ////                            14
  3   /////   /////   /////   /////                   20
  4   /////   ///                                      8
  5   /////   /////   //                              12
  6   /////   //                                       7
  7   /////   /////                                   10
  8   /////   //                                       7
  9   /////                                            5
 10   /////   /                                        6
 11   /                                                1
 12
 13   /                                                1
 14
 15
 16
 17
 18
 19   /                                                1
 20
                                                    ____
                                                     134
```

the problems. More and more, the U.S. economy is becoming interdependent with foreign economies and, inevitably, the forecasting problems grow more difficult.

The most popular methods of economic forecasting in recent years have included econometric models that have tended to accent Keynesian approaches (with particular reference to fiscal policies), monetarist methods in which the policies of the central bank have been most dominant, and the indicator approach, one of the oldest methods available. These can be briefly summarized.

1. The traditional *indicator approach* has employed a three-phase timing system—leaders, coinciders, and laggers—for analyzing, monitoring, and forecasting the national economy. The coinciders represent indicators whose timing at turning points tends to coincide with the timing of the economy itself. The leaders involve indicators whose timing at turning points tends to occur earlier than the timing of the economy, and the laggers occur later. The indicator approach has been particularly useful in monitoring where we *are* and in forecasting the short-term future (the next few months). The techniques of the indicator approach not only have been useful in monitoring and forecasting the economy, but also have been widely applied in the development of short-term *sales* forecasts.

2. The *econometric approach* is widely used by corporations in medium-term forecasts—those extending through the following year's budget period. This approach uses a system of equations to represent the whole economic process, beginning with government policy. (This approach is also very useful for long-term capacity forecasts that extend out 5 to 10 years. It is weak in short-term horizons—that is, weekly and monthly—though the indicator approach adequately serves here.)

3. The *monetarist approach* has been available for some time, but since the Roosevelt period Keynesian economics has flourished, putting monetarism into the shadows. About 15 years ago, when stagflation began to be prevalent in Keynesian societies, Milton Friedman led the "Chicago school" of monetarists to an alternative to Keynesian economics. The monetarists put primary emphasis on the monetary policies of the central bank, whereas the Keynesians put major emphasis on the fiscal policies (i.e., taxation and spending). Although monetarism results in different political results (conservative economics) than Keynesianism (liberal economics), it does *not* result in more "forecasting" techniques. The monetarists call for steady growth in the money supply, a tendency that results in limiting the amount of money in circulation. To put a lid on the amount of money fed into the economic system results in lower inflation, but also—it is claimed by nonmonetarists—lower employment. Although monetarists have not produced an elaborate forecasting technology, their political influence is great, and no economic forecast can be made without considering the monetarist view.

4. The *judgmental approach* is really the "all other" category. If we cannot clearly isolate an economic forecasting technique as emanating from one of the first three approaches, we can loosely include it in the judgmental category. The judgmental approach relies on the first three approaches (not to mention others such as surveys, anticipations, and time series analysis). In effect, then, it represents all the techniques—the three discussed and many, many more.

The many techniques of forecasting the economy, especially as they relate to forecasting recessions, can be summarized by use of a "five-phase" timing spectrum. The indicator, econometric, and monetarist approaches can all be viewed together here.

A FIVE-PHASE TIMING MODEL

An economic system can be viewed as a mass of indices that peak and trough at different times. These thousands of economic processes—for convenience—can be roughly organized into five time phases from "beginning to end." These are shown in Chart 20-2. All five lines are quarterly percentage rates of change (at annual rates). The top three lines are stripped of inflation. Since the fourth line is composed of costs, some of its elements do include inflation. The fifth, and last, line *is* inflation, as measured by the general price index used to deflate GNP. Each of the five lines is composed of many, many indices.

As a monitoring system, the top line represents a *first cause* indicator, whose effects trickle downward from upper left to lower right—finally ending in prices, the *final effect*. In between is the traditional "indicator" system comprising leading, coinciding, and lagging indicators. The trickle down effect can be seen best after the top line (the monetary fiscal policy index) troughed late in 1973. The shaded areas represent recessions, as defined by the National Bureau of Economic Research.

Although the timing of the various lines is hardly precise, the tendencies from upper left to lower right are clear and have been long established by econometric studies. Needless to say, the most interesting of these five rates of change is the first one, since it represents in a single line the summation of federal government economic policies. It is these fiscal and monetary policies that cause effects to trickle downward.

It is important to point out that policy does not direct all results. Many times the government is reacting to forces beyond its control, such as an OPEC oil price increase. It is not correct to imply that the government causes recession. Sometimes the policies do, but generally what happens to the economy, as depicted in the lower four lines, is a complex mixture of policy action and reaction.

The top line is composed of two components: fiscal policy and monetary policy. Each has equal weight in the index. The fiscal policy index is calculated by dividing government expenditures by government receipts (most of which are taxes). If in one period expenditures totaled $110 billion and receipts at the same time totaled $100 billion, the policy impact would be a 10% stimulus, with the government putting $10 billion more into the economy than it took out. In the U.S. form of representative government, fiscal policy is heavily influenced by Congress.

Monetary policy, on the other hand, is controlled by the Federal Reserve Board, a branch independent of the executive and legislative branches. Even so, the executive branch does appoint members to the Board. The intricate activities of the Federal Reserve are summarized in the policy line by the change in the money supply. It is well documented that a Federal Reserve policy action takes 6 to 12 months to have an impact on the economy—the middle of the five lines shown in Chart 20-2. It is also documented that the

CHART 20-2. A Five-Phase Timing Model of the U.S. Economy

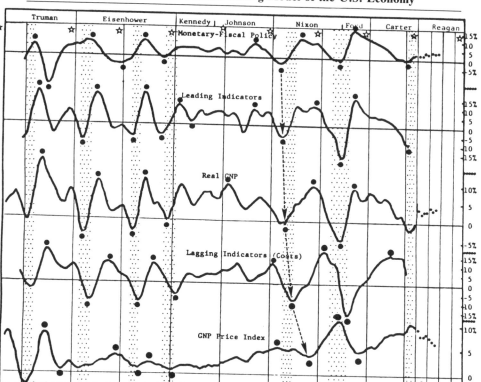

same policy action takes 18 to 24 months before finally affecting prices. This trickle down effect, with its imprecision and long time lags, cannot be fine tuned, and that is one reason why it is so difficult to manage the economic system.

Forecasting the behavior of the economy must start with trying to forecast government economic policy, with all its domestic politics and foreign influences on the system.

THE TRADITIONAL INDICATOR APPROACH

Back in the 1920s a method of forecasting the economy by timing indices was developed by the National Bureau of Economic Research; later, in the 1930s, the Bureau was requested by President Roosevelt to try to develop methods that would enable policymakers to *anticipate* economic activity. From these studies, the traditional "indicator" system was designed, and they are represented in the five-phase timing model by the three indices in the middle: (1) "Leading" indicators tend to peak and trough before the economy, (2) "coininciding" indicators—as represented by real GNP in the timing model—are those whose timing at peaks and troughs tends to roughly coincide with the timing of the general economy, and (3) "lagging" indicators tend to peak and trough after the general economy. Laggers perform the dual role of confirming turning points in the coinciders, as well as representing costs of doing business, such as interest rates and labor costs.

It is obvious that the so-called "leading" indicators lag the policy indicators in the top line. Consequently, in recent years, economists have considered both top lines as leaders. But the policy indicators have longer lead times. Long leaders are, inevitably, more difficult to handle. Leading indicators, representing the two top lines in the timing model, can be arrayed according to their timing at peaks and troughs. Such an array is known as an *indicator pyramid*.

INDICATOR PYRAMIDS

A device long used in logic is called a "straw man," in which a proposition or thesis is set up to see if it can be discredited. In economic forecasting, the straw man can be used to test for recession around business cycle peaks. (The opposite is the case *during* recession, in which the straw man idea is used to test for an impending trough.) Since an economy can be viewed as thousands of economic processes—which we usually see in the form of indices or indicators—we can arrange lists of indicators according to timing, just as was done with the five-phase timing model.

The indicator pyramid in Chart 20-3 is a list of leading indicators arrayed

CHART 20-3. An Indicator Pyramid

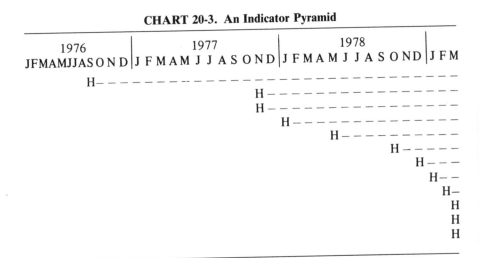

according to timing. It is called a pyramid for the simple reason that, if you tip your head to the right, it looks like one. In this pyramid, the Commerce Department's 12 official leading indicators are arrayed according to when they reached their highest levels (H) through March 1979, during the business cycle expansion that began in April 1975. Each minus sign represents a lower report issued since the high. The more minus signs that appear in the pyramid, the more pessimistic is the outlook. New highs at the right of a pyramid, then, represent optimism. (Note that the last three indices do not have any minus signs, signifying that the latest published figure *is* the high.) The indicator pyramid can be expanded into a much larger analytical model.

In Chart 20-4 there is an indicator pyramid containing 50 leading indicators. (These 50, along with others, are published each month in the govern-

---

CHART 20-4. A Recession Straw Man: Fifty Leading Indicators

A RECESSION STRAW MAN: FIFTY LEADING INDICATORS

Months Lead Time Before Past Recessions
-48 -42 -36 -30 -24 -18 -12 -6 0 +6

1975 1976 1977 1978 1979

Indicators	BCD#	Ave. Lead Time
Money Supply CHG (M2)	102	23.0
Money Supply CHG (M1)	85	18.3
Profits (with IVA & CCA)	80	18.3
Accession Rate	2	15.3
Housing Starts	28	12.8
Housing Permits	29+	12.8
Consumer Sentiment	58	12.7
Liquid Assets CHG	104+	12.3
Money Supply (M2: 1972$)	106+	12.0
Durable Unfilled Order CHG	25	11.8
Profitability % (Mfg.)	15	11.8
Money Supply (M1: 1972$)	105	11.3
Unemployment Claims	5	11.3
Price to Unit Labor Cost	17	11.3
Business Loans CHG	112	11.0
Stock Market	19+	11.0
Average Workweek	1+	10.8
Profitability % (Total)	22	10.8
Profits (1972$)	18	10.8
Cash Flow (1972$)	35	10.8
Sensitive Prices CHG	92+	10.8
Mortgage Debt CHG	33	10.5
Business Formation	12+	10.5
Overtime Hours	21	10.5
Quit Rate	4	10.3
New Businesses	13	10.0
Help Wanted Advertising	46	10.0
Layoff Rate	3+	9.8
Private Borrowing	110	9.3
Instalment Debt CHG	113	9.3
Capital Goods Orders	27	9.3
Residential Investment	89	9.0
Plant/Equipment Orders	20+	8.3
New Orders (Durables)	7	7.8
Inventories on Hand CHG	36+	7.8
Materials & Supplies CHG	38	7.7
Help Wanted Ads + Unemployed	60	7.5
Vendor Performance	32+	7.5
Instalment Loan Delinquency	39	7.3
Insured Unemployment Rate	45	6.8
New Orders (Consumers)	8+	6.0
Automobile Consumption	55	5.0
Inventories (Mfg/Trade)	31	4.8
Durable Unfilled Orders	96	4.8
Number Unemployed	37	4.8
Industrial Construction	9	4.8
Materials/Supplies on Hand	78	4.7
Business Inventories CHG	30	4.3
Goods Producing Employees	40	3.5
Unemployment Rate	43	3.5

0 = Traditional Lead Time Before Past Recessions
H = Most Recent High In This Business Cycle
- = Lower Reports Issued Since High Level (H)
+ = 12 Official Leading Indicators

Shade Assumes Economic Peak In September

ment magazine *Business Conditions Digest,* often called *BCD.*) We can use this form of the pyramid to compare the configuration of highs in the current business cycle expansion to their *average* lead times before past recessions. This straw man tested a recession to begin in September 1979. (Note that a shaded area appears on the graph starting in October 1979.) The "chain of circles" trickling downward from upper left to lower right represents the *average mean* lead times for each of the 50 indicators, as measured before the preceding six recessions. You will see that the minus signs extend to the right through January 1980—the month the U.S. economy peaked and started into its seventh postwar recession. So you see this pyramid set with data at the moment the recession officially began.

The basic premise behind this straw man is this: If the economy is to peak in September 1979, then a lot of leading indicators should reach highs before then—otherwise they are not "leading" indicators. In pure theory, for a recession to begin in September 1979, the highs of the 50 leading indicators ought to trickle randomly down the chain of circles—half plotted before the chain and half after. As you examine this pyramid, shown with actual data plotted through January 1980, note the configuration of the highs (H). Only 16 highs are to the left of the chain—32% of the total of 50 highs. The other 68% of the indicators continued to improve, and you will see that they are either on or to the right of the chain. When two thirds of the indicators go through to the right of the chain, the straw man is discredited. This pyramid discredits a September peak, because so many of the highs are to the right of the chain of circles.

All of this is easily said with 20-20 hindsight. It is quite another problem to deal with these events at the time they are occurring. The indicator pyramid, a relatively new analytical tool, was first used to test a trough in the U.S. recession of 1974–1975. One of the main problems with using this analytical tool at peaks is that the pyramid signals *slowdowns,* but some slowdowns do not become recessions. Since leading indicators have an average lead time of almost a year, it is obvious that they peak and turn down before slowdowns, just as clearly as they do before those slowdowns that later become recessions. Therefore, it is easy to be misled into forecasting a recession, if the pyramid is the only forecasting method used. But it certainly should not be the only one. (An important incident occurred in 1976, when the pyramid began to show highs—at one point almost half the indicators had at least one minus sign. Although there is no evidence that anyone began to forecast a recession at that time, the very mild slowdown still appears in the graphs—particularly in employment, construction, and durable good indices.)

Without doubt, the indicator pyramid is best used to analyze the current situation in light of periods before past business cycle peaks (or troughs, whichever the case may be). What the forecaster does is watch for patterns in the configuration of the highs that depart from normal (i.e., averages). When a situation develops that is out of the ordinary, the forecaster can separately analyze the key indicators in the list of 50.

The list of 50 leaders includes (1) government policy indicators, the longest leaders; (2) the conventional factory indicators ("smokestacks"), which respond to the policies; and then (3) inventory leaders, which lead by the least amount of time before recessions. In Chart 20-4 you will note that the long leader highs at the top were randomly distributed before and after the chain of circles, meaning that policies were not discrediting the September straw man thesis. But now look to the middle (smokestacks) and see the highs to the right of the chain. That contradiction was explained by the collapse of the dollar in the summer of 1978, an event that made American-made goods cheaper relative to goods imported into the United States. In effect, the domestic/import mix was changed in favor of the domestic manufacturers. Thus, the optimistic character of the middle of the pyramid.

A MODEL OF AN AVERAGE RECESSION

A rather simple recession model can be developed by averaging past recession behavior. In other words, the character of the ninth postwar business cycle can be evaluated in terms of the average of the preceding eight. In effect, the idea is to just add the eight cycles together and divide by eight. This yields an average recession/recovery model (ARRM) that enables one to analyze the current (ninth) situation. Once a recession is under way—a crucial assumption in the model—it is possible to track it by past standards.

As soon as the National Bureau of Economic Research announced (in June 1980) that the U.S. economy peaked in January 1980 and entered a recession, the first quarter of 1980 became the benchmark peak quarter and all six previous recessions were plotted together with a common peak. You see this in Chart 20-5, which shows an ARRM model for the Industrial Production Index. The solid line in the graph proxies as an average recession, assuming the first quarter of 1980 as its peak. The dotted line superimposed on it represents the current (seventh) situation, plotted through the fourth quarter of 1980. The vertical bars represent the two-in-three probability values (given the standard deviations of past recession experiences). The two large dots show the traditional timing for this index at peaks and troughs in the past six recessions. The small dot, plotted in February 1980, shows the highest point reached in the seventh (current) situation. The indexing calculations appear in the table below the graph.

As you can see, in the quarters following the peak, industrial production declined more sharply than average at first and then began to track closer to the average line. A forecaster monitoring this graph can keep close watch on the severity of the current situation, relative to the many past recessions that are included in the model (solid line). The ARRM model enables us to simulate some simple alternative forecasts quickly with a pencil and calculator. And the technique is so simple that it can easily be adapted to *any* index. All one needs is enough history to average a few past business cycles. It is a

CHART 20-5. Average Recession/Recovery Model: FRB Industrial Production Index

Assumption: that the first quarter of 1980 is the peak quarter of a business

	A	B	C	D	E	F
Peak:	48.4	53.3	57.3	60.2	68.4	73.4
Trough:	49.4	54.2	58.2	61.1	70.4	75.1
Recession ending:	1949	1954	1958	1961	1970	1975
-8	–	86.4	94.9H	83.1L	91.7	84.9
-7	95.1	86.9L	97.1H	87.4	93.3	87.9
-6	95.1	88.9L	97.4H	91.5	94.8	90.0
-5	95.4	87.6L	97.1H	95.4	95.7	91.8
-4	98.1	90.3L	96.5	100.0H	97.0	94.7
-3	99.0	96.6	100.0H	96.0L	98.7	97.0
-2	100.0	98.6	101.0H	96.4L	99.1	98.4
-1	101.0	100.0	99.7	102.2H	100.4	99.4L
Peak	100.0	100.0	100.0	100.0	100.0	100.0
+1	96.8	95.3L	95.8	98.4	97.5	98.8H
+2	93.7	92.3	90.5L	96.0	97.0	99.7H
+3	93.9	91.9	88.9L	94.6	96.8	100.3H
+4	93.4	92.5L	93.6	98.4H	94.7	94.8
+5	98.3	95.0	97.9	101.5H	96.7	86.1L
+6	106.6H	100.2	102.1	104.9	97.7	86.9L
+7	115.1H	104.5	107.1	106.6	98.2	91.7L
+8	117.0H	106.1	102.7	107.6	99.8	93.9L
+9	119.5H	108.6	103.2	108.7	103.4	97.1L
+10	119.7H	109.0	109.5	109.6	105.8	98.9L
+11	117.0H	108.6	107.1	111.7	108.0	100.1L

Six postwar recessions

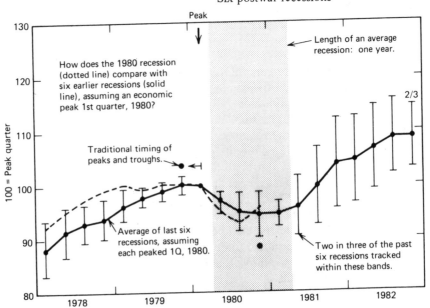

G 80.1 1980	H Average (4)	I Sigma (4)	J Average (6)	K Sigma (6)	L J + K Average Plus Hl	M J − K Average Minus Lo	N
			cycle expansion ending with the 1980 recession.				
92.5	87.7	3.6	88.2	4.9	93.1	83.3	
95.3	90.9	3.9	91.3	4.4	95.7	86.9	
97.2	92.9	2.5	93.0	3.3	96.3	89.7	
99.0	94.6	1.9	93.8	3.5	97.3	90.3	
100.0	96.6	1.4	96.1	3.3	99.4	92.8	
99.8	97.8	1.2	97.9	1.6	99.5	96.3	
100.1	99.0	.7	98.9	1.6	100.5	97.3	
100.0	99.8	1.4	100.1	1.5	101.6	98.6	
100.0	100.0	—	100.0	—	—	—	
95.1	97.1	1.1	97.1	1.4	98.5	95.7	
93.1	94.8	2.1	94.9	3.4	98.3	91.5	
95.7	94.3	2.0	94.4	3.9	98.3	90.5	
	94.1	.7	94.6	2.1	96.7	92.5	
	97.0	1.5	95.9	5.3	101.2	90.6	
	101.2	3.0	99.7	7.0	106.7	92.7	
	104.1	4.1	103.9	8.1	112.0	95.8	
	104.1	3.5	104.5	7.8	112.3	96.7	
	106.0	3.1	106.8	7.6	114.4	99.2	
	108.5	1.8	108.8	6.7	115.5	102.1	
	108.9	2.0	108.8	5.6	114.4	103.2	

Historical recession averages

decision-making tool for forecasting the microsectors of the economy, that is, industries, companies, divisions, and product lines.

The weakness of the ARRM model is that one must make an extremely important assumption: the choice of the peak quarter. It was first used in August 1979 after real GNP in the second quarter of 1979 plunged. The first simulation used the first quarter of 1979 as 100—the benchmark. That is fine if that is what the historians later say *was* the peak. But they did not. Whenever real GNP declines decisively, the forecaster should set up an ARRM model, as a simulation of events to come. But, as is always the case in virtually any economic model, such a simulation is based on assumptions. If the assumptions are correct, the model will probably behave well. If the assumptions are not correct, the model will not be faithful to actual events.

SUMMARY

Recession forecasting is one of the most difficult of all forecasting challenges. In recent years, the entry into recession has also caused problems for those forecasting it. It is no accident that the federal government—through its policies—is partly involved with recessions, and that most administrations try to prevent recessions. This has resulted in what has been called "gradualism," in which the economy is slowed down but not so much that it turns negative. In recent recessions, the economy has turned sideward toward the ends of the expansionary periods. The "horizontal" nature of these recent peaks has caused premature forecasts of recession. In particular, the 1980 recession exhibited this zero economic growth for over a year before finally plunging down in the sharpest quarterly drop since World War II.

21

FORECASTING MACROECONOMIC VARIABLES: AN ECLECTIC APPROACH

STEPHEN K. McNEES
Federal Reserve Bank of Boston

NICHOLAS S. PERNA
General Electric Co.

WHY FORECAST MACROECONOMIC VARIABLES?

Macroeconomic variables might appear irrelevant to an individual firm. After all, no one buys or sells total GNP and pays or receives the GNP implicit price deflator (IPD) or the Consumer Price Index (CPI) in exchange. Yet the probable future macroeconomic environment is critically important for any firm's planning and decisions:

- Macroeconomic variables describe the overall "economic climate" that shapes consumer psychology and business attitudes. They also affect government financial, expenditure, and tax policies, which in turn exert a powerful influence on business performance.

- In a highly integrated national and international economy, seemingly remote economic events spill over into individual markets of direct interest. For example, cost-of-living adjustments paid by the firm depend explicitly or implicitly on the internationally determined CPI. Sales depend not only on the firm's own prices, production, and marketing strategies, but on the income of all customers.

- Large, diversified organizations need a consistent, integrated view of the future for strategic planning and budgeting purposes. For example, in allocating funds for investment projects, it is important that the proposals share a common economic framework or benchmark in terms of inflation, interest rates, product demand projections, and so on. Internal consistency can be even more important for the firm's operations than the exact numerical accuracy of the macroeconomic forecast.

- Many forecasting techniques have been extensively applied to predicting macroeconomic variables. This experience can serve as a guide to which techniques will be most helpful in handling forecasting problems at the firm level.

This chapter explores the practical art of macroeconomic forecasting. It describes and assesses the variety of available forecasting techniques such as time series analysis, econometric models, and business cycle comparisons, and provides a catalog of information sources for forecasting the major macroeconomic variables. It outlines an eclectic approach to forecasting that permits the analyst to choose techniques that are most useful for the variables and forecast horizons of greatest interest. A number of concrete forecasting examples, such as consumer spending and inflation, are covered in considerable detail. Finally, it briefly assesses the eclectic approach to macroeconomic forecasting.

FORECASTING TECHNIQUES AND SOURCES

The best way to forecast depends on the interests of the forecast user and the resources at his or her disposal. The most appropriate technique depends on how many variables are to be forecasted, the specific variables, the forecast horizon, and the forecaster's budget.

Time Series Analysis

The simplest, least expensive way to forecast is with time series techniques.* There is evidence that this approach is useful for producing forecasts of some macroeconomic variables in many microeconomic applications. Nevertheless, the time series approach has some important limitations: First, the approach does not generally produce a rich, comprehensible, consistent *story* based on a theory of economic behavior to accompany the numerical prediction. Most users need to know not only *what* will happen, but *why* it will happen. Furthermore, the common practice of estimating separate time series equations does not assure that the standard

---

* See, for example, Charles R. Nelson, *Applied Time Series Analysis for Managerial Forecasting,* Holden-Day, San Francisco, 1973, or Robert S. Pindyck and Daniel L. Rubinfeld, *Econometric Models and Economic Forecasts,* McGraw-Hill, New York, 1976, part 3, pp. 421–550.

accounting identities are satisfied (for example, GNP must equal the sum of its components). The typical method of estimating a time series equation for inventory investment might require modification to ensure consistency between production and sales forecasts. In addition, time series results need not conform to a forecaster's economic "common sense" (for example, that unemployment rises when real GNP falls). Time series equations are not readily adaptable to hypothetical ("what if") experiments and therefore may not fully describe forecast risks and alternative outcomes. In short, even when the time series approach is relatively accurate, the informational content of a time series forecast is generally small.

Second, for many variables, the accuracy of time series forecasts tends to deteriorate relatively rapidly as the forecast horizon lengthens, because time series do not incorporate future (exogenous) influences that will affect future outcomes. A time series forecast would, for example, take into account only very slowly prospective drastic change in government spending or monetary policy. Time series forecasts can, however, provide a useful adjunct to the techniques next described, particularly if many "opinions" about the near term are desired.

Econometric Models

Because a well-constructed macroeconometric forecasting model can assure consistency, provide a rich description of the reasons for the forecast, and permit "what if" experiments, econometric models have become the primary tool of most macro forecasters today. Econometric relationships are an indispensable aid to predicting important macroeconomic variables, as illustrated in the following.

As a practical matter, constructing a satisfactory formal macroeconometric model is an extremely demanding and relatively expensive undertaking. Immense theoretical and statistical problems—problems for which no general consensus solutions exist—confront the forecaster. In addition, once a model is developed, considerable resources must be devoted to updating, reformulating, and reestimating. For example, toward the end of 1985 the Bureau of Economic Analysis completed a massive revision of the National Income and Products Accounts extending back to 1929. Among the changes were the incorporation of recent data from the Internal Revenue Service for corporate profits, dramatically different deflators for computer equipment, and the shifting of the base-year weights used in computing the price indices that convert nominal to real GNP. This necessitated the reexamination and reestimation of many equations in both large and small econometric models. For example, the revised data show net exports equal to −2.4% of real GNP in 1985 versus +0.9% in the earlier estimates.*

* See *Survey of Current Business,* Bureau of Economic Analysis, U.S. Department of Commerce, December 1985, pp. 1–19, and later issues for discussion and detailed data.

Econometric models do not forecast by themselves. At a minimum, the forecaster must provide projections of the future values of the exogenous variables required to solve the model (tax rates, the price of imported oil, federal spending programs, and monetary variables such as nonborrowed bank reserves, to name only a few). Even with this information, experience indicates that "first-pass" model runs do not produce the most accurate forecasts. Econometric model forecasters have found it necessary to adjust their model's initial forecast, at times quite extensively. Most judgmental adjustments are made for one of two reasons: The model has not been performing accurately or some external factor, not incorporated in the model, is expected to influence future events.

Cyclical Comparison

Economic theory may suggest that certain variables will influence the forecast but typically tells relatively little about the *timing* of their impact, for example, whether their influence will be immediate or spread out over time. Econometricians attempt to compensate for this by estimating lag patterns distributed over time. These estimated "distributed lags," however, represent *average* historical experience, combining recessions and booms.

Many forecasters find enough regularity in business cycle experience to segregate historical data by phases of the business cycle.* This seems most useful for highly cyclical variables such as expenditures on consumer durable goods, as will be illustrated later in Example 21-3. However, it can be difficult to match the phase of the current cycle with similar phases of previous cycles and to determine which previous cycle is most like the current one. As discussed in Examples 21-1 and 21-2, cyclical comparisons seem most useful for setting upper and lower limits during and shortly after a recession, or in constructing scenarios for alternative financial conditions. Cyclical comparisons have limited usefulness in pinpointing the onset of the next recession or the next downturn in housing or automobile sales.

A Role for Judgment: External Events and Past Errors

Virtually every important political, social, and economic event has some effect on macroeconomic variables. All forecasters, therefore, constantly survey current business conditions and prospective events that would influence the economy. A potentially valuable but often neglected source of information for improving forecasts is a forecaster's own recent errors, often

---

* A large number of economic series have been studied intensively and classified according to whether they lead, lag, or coincide with movements in the overall economy. See *Business Conditions Digest,* a monthly publication of the Bureau of Economic Analysis, U.S. Department of Commerce, for data, graphs, and descriptions of these series.

the first clue that a forecasting technique must be reassessed. By systematically comparing recent forecasts with actual outcomes, a forecaster can at times identify where the future forecast is likely to go off track. Analyzing the probable reasons for past errors will suggest how future forecasts should be modified. There are at least three different types of errors, each with different implications for modifying forecasts:

1. *Permanent Shifts.* At times the normal forecasting procedure will go off track, consistently underestimating or overestimating. This can occur, for example, when some important element has been omitted from the standard procedure. Even if this element is unknown, future forecasts can be adjusted to offset observed errors. Once the missing element has been identified, it can be included in the standard forecast procedure. However, the source of an error is often not evident. It is difficult to quantify the impact of important new phenomena until enough experience has accumulated to permit estimation of equations that include the phenomena. During the past decade, a number of major structural changes have taken place that affect both the macroeconomy and the interrelationships among its parts. The switch from fixed to flexible exchange rates in the early 1970s, the OPEC price explosions, and the spreading deregulation of financial markets in the late 1970s and early 1980s are only three examples of the many structural changes that have occurred.

2. *Reverse Shifts.* At other times an error can be traced to a disturbance that is likely to reverse itself. A strike or a supply shortage is a common example. Typically the output or sales loss due to a strike or a materials shortage is compensated for by a temporary, abnormally large increase once the disruption has ended.

3. *Transitory Shocks.* At still other times an abnormally large error will occur for no apparent reason. The forecaster can either ignore it or assume that it will decay gradually over time. Some forecasters tend to "overexplain" errors, to assume incorrectly that they are of the first or second type mentioned. Modifying the standard forecast procedure to incorporate some "instant theory" will destroy the information in the standard approach when the shock turns out to be only transitory.

Thus, recent error patterns can be used to modify future forecasts for better or for worse. The key is to try to understand the possible reasons for the error in order to decide whether and how to deal with it. Here the forecaster must rely on judgment, experience, and common sense.

External Information

Macroeconomic forecasters can draw on a large body of published information for help in formulating their own forecast. Among the most important sources (see Chart 21-1) are the following:

1. The median forecast of 11 variables from the *Business Outlook Survey* conducted quarterly by the American Statistical Association and the National Bureau of Economic Research.

2. Export and import forecasts published semiannually in the Organization for Economic Cooperation and Development's *Economic Outlook*.

3. Quarterly surveys of business capital spending plans, published quarterly in the *Survey of Current Business*.

4. Information on automobile sales, production, inventories, and pricing published weekly in *Ward's Automotive Reports* and reported in some newspapers.

5. The *Economic Report of the President,* the *Budget of the U.S. Government,* the *Mid-Session Review of the Budget,* and the reports of the Congressional Budget Office for projections of federal spending and tax policies and the underlying economic assumptions.

6. Periodic forecasts of food and energy prices issued by the U.S. Departments of Agriculture and Energy, reported in major newspapers.

7. In addition, many forecasters subscribe to at least one of the major commercial forecasting services.

An outside forecast can be used in a variety of ways to generate a "personal" forecast. The forecaster may want to use the outside forecast "as is" for variables in which he or she has no special interest or forecasting expertise. More commonly, the outside forecast can, as illustrated in the following, be used as a "first pass" or starting point for generating an independent view.

The following section outlines briefly an eclectic, judgmental approach to macroeconomic forecasting. The approach is eclectic in that it combines a variety of forecasting techniques—time series modeling, cyclical comparisons, econometric regularities, and external information sources. (The specific blend of approaches depends on the forecast variable and horizon.) It is judgmental in that it acknowledges at the outset that the forecaster will choose to override the "technique" whenever new information or intuition suggests that things are likely to turn out differently in the future than they have in the past. A primary advantage of this approach is that a forecast "story"—the reasons behind and risks surrounding the forecast—emerges from the interaction of the forecasting techniques and the forecaster's own judgment.

One disadvantage of this flexible approach is that it is hard to describe succinctly. Several features can only be learned from personal experience. The remainder of this chapter is devoted to concrete examples of how the eclectic, judgmental approach can be applied.

CHART 21-1. Forecasting Techniques and Information Sources, by Variable

Macroeconomic Variable	Techniques[a]	Sources[b]
Personal consumption		
Durable goods	3, 4, 2	ASA/NBER
Auto sales	3, 4	Ward's
Personal consumption, other	2	
Residential investment	3, 4	ASA/NBER
Housing starts	3, 4	ASA/NBER
Business fixed investment	4, 2	BEA, ASA/NBER
Federal government purchases	4	BEA, ASA/NBER
State and local government purchases	1	
Exports	4, 1	OECD
Imports	4, 2	OECD
Change in business inventories	1, 3	
Unemployment rate	2, 1, 4	CEA
Productivity	2, 3	
Compensation	2, 4, 3	BLS
GNP price deflator	4, 2	BLS, CEA
Consumer price index	4, 2	USDA

[a] Key to techniques: 1 = time series methods, 2 = econometric relationships, 3 = cyclical comparisons, 4 = external sources.

[b] *Sources:*

ASA/NBER: *Business Outlook Survey*. Published quarterly (March, June, September, December). Available from American Statistical Association, 806 15th St., N.W., Washington, DC 20005. (202) 393-3253.

OECD: *Economic Outlook*. Published semiannually (July and December). Available from OECD Publications and Information Center, Suite 1207, 1750 Pennsylvania Avenue, Washington, DC 20006. (202) 724-1857.

BEA: *Survey of Current Business*. Published montly by Bureau of Economic Analysis of U.S. Department of Commerce. Surveys of business capital spending plans for current and two subsequent quarters appear in March, June, September, and December issues. Budget information typically appears in February issue. Available from Superintendent of Documents, U.S. Government Printing Office, Washington, DC 20402.

Ward's: *Ward's Automotive Reports*. Published weekly. Available from Ward's Communications Inc., 28 W. Adams Street, Detroit, MI 48225. (313) 962-4433.

Budget of the U.S. Government. Published semiannually (January and July). Available from Superintendent of Documents, U.S. Government Printing Office, Washington, DC 20402.

BLS: *Monthly Labor Review*. Published monthly by Bureau of Labor Statistics of U.S. Department of Labor. Available from Superintendent of Documents, U.S. Government Printing Office, Washington, DC 20402.

CEA: *Annual Report*. Contained in *Economic Report of the President*. Published annually in January. Available from Superintendent of Documents, U.S. Government Printing Office, Washington, DC 20402.

Department of Agriculture: *Agricultural Outlook*. Published 10 times per year. Available from Superintendent of Documents, U.S. Government Printing Office, Washington, DC 20402.

AN ECLECTIC APPROACH TO FORECASTING: AN OVERVIEW

The accompanying flowchart (Chart 21-2) outlines an eclectic approach to forecasting GNP and other important macroeconomic variables. The task is divided into three stages: (1) real GNP and its components, (2) unemployment and productivity, and (3) compensation, profits, and prices. Each stage is described briefly here and several steps are illustrated in more detail in the following examples.

Components of Real GNP

It is helpful to start with the more "exogenous" components—those whose behavior is not closely tied to the current performance of the economy—and proceed toward the more "endogenous" variables, whose behavior depends heavily on "everything else." Begin (step 1A, Chart 21-2) with exports and federal government purchases, where initial estimates can be taken from external sources. In addition, the relatively accurate Commerce Department survey of capital spending plans provides a good initial estimate of nonresidential fixed investment. Experienced forecasters are aware that this capital spending survey has shown a tendency to overestimate spending for years in which the economy is weak and to underestimate spending for years in which the economy is strong. Next, (step 1B) time series or autoregressive equations can provide a good starting point for short-term estimates of state and local government purchases of goods and services and changes in business inventories. It is necessary to reestimate these equations frequently and to modify the longer-run forecasts with other information. Then, (step 1C) the ASA/NBER (American Statistical Association/National Bureau of Economic Research) median forecast of housing starts and personal consumption expenditures for durable goods (PCD) can be analyzed using the cyclical comparison technique (described in Example 21-3) to provide a rough guess about the frequency and amplitude of the phase of the current cycle. These forecasts must be revised again to reflect prospective financial conditions and institutional changes. Finally, (step 1D) an econometric relationship in conjunction with some external information can be used to produce a forecast of personal consumption expenditures for nondurable goods and services, as described in Example 21-2, and of expenditures for imports. Combining these steps produces an initial estimate of real GNP that should be used to go back and reassess the forecasts for its components, especially those for business fixed and inventory investment. If these prospects are changed significantly, the whole process may have to be repeated until a consistent view emerges.

This process of a continuing series of iterations to ensure consistency, both in the accounting and the economic sense of the word, is common to all the stages of the forecasting process. The eclectic approach forces the forecaster to obtain consistency, thus sharpening his or her original insights. A

CHART 21-2. Bare Bone Diagram of an Eclectic Approach to a Macroeconomic Forecast

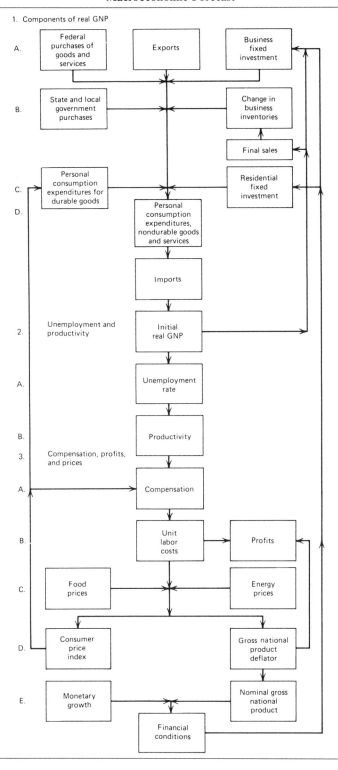

personal computer spreadsheet incorporating the equations, identities, and rules of thumb can greatly facilitate the use of the eclectic forecast technique.

Unemployment and Productivity

Compared with forecasting of real GNP, forecasting of unemployment and productivity is relatively straightforward, as explained in Examples 21-4 and 21-6 that follow. However, once again, this step may provide insights that will call into question some of the forecasts generated in step 1. No one promised that forecasting would be easy.

Compensation, Profits, and Prices

Integrating the "real" forecast with the "nominal" outlook for compensation, profits, and prices is the most challenging phase of forecasting. The procedure is illustrated for compensation and inflation in Examples 21-5 and 21-7. Since the real spending decisions forecast in step 1 are dependent on the rate of inflation, the results of step 3 will probably require another pass at the preliminary forecasts generated in the earlier steps. In particular, the nominal GNP forecast, combined with some assessment of the future course of monetary policy, provides an important clue to prospective financial conditions. These conditions heavily influence consumer spending on durable goods and housing.

The steps just outlined here and in Chart 21-2—starting with the *real* GNP and moving toward financial conditions—are probably the most appropriate approach for the production/sales decisions of nonfinancial businesses. Financial institutions and corporate treasurers would probably benefit from starting with the components of *nominal* GNP and combining these with monetary policy considerations to arrive at an impression of financial conditions, then turning to prices to arrive at real GNP as a residual. More generally, the obvious rule is: Focus your primary attention on what you care most (and know most) about!

EXAMPLE 21-1. REAL GNP: CYCLICAL COMPARISON AND "FORMULA" APPROACHES

As mentioned previously, the eclectic approach requires an initial real GNP forecast simply to "get the ball rolling." One could start with a consensus forecast, with a publicly available forecast such as that of the Council of Economic Advisers, or even with the naive assumption that economic growth will remain unchanged. This example develops two additional methods that can be applied to overall GNP as well as to other economic variables.

EXAMPLE 21-1. REAL GNP   359

Cyclical comparisons are useful because U.S. business fluctuations resemble each other in a number of important ways. In the seven recessions that have occurred since the end of the Korean War, all economic contractions have lasted from two to five quarters, with a mean duration of four quarters. The magnitude of decline has averaged about 2.5% from peak quarter to trough quarter but has ranged widely, from as little as 1.0% in 1960–1961 to as much as 4.3% in 1974–1975 (Chart 21-3). Thus, if one thought a recession was in the offing, the past 30 years' experience would suggest a "first guess" real GNP decline of 2.5% spread out over four quarters. As will be evident from looking at expansions, this technique does not provide as useful a clue to when the downturn might start. Yet it does give a feel for how long and deep the recession might be. The range of previous experience can be useful when forecasters find themselves in the midst of a recession with the need to project the rest of the cycle. It can also be helpful in constructing alternative outlooks. Forecast users often ask for a recession "scenario" to see how recession might affect them and to plan how they might soften its impact.

Duration of the recovery phase of the cycle has ranged much more widely than duration of recessions. Expansions have lasted as long as 35 quarters (1961:Q1 through 1969:Q4) and as short as four quarters (1980:Q3 through 1981:Q3). Thus, the average duration provides little guidance. In terms of magnitude of GNP rise, the first four quarters of recovery tend to fit a pattern. Steep downturns, that is, those in which the GNP fell more than 3%, were followed by sharp rebounds in the 6% to 8% range. Two of the three mild recessions were followed by mild recoveries, with the exception of the rapid rise following 1961:Q1. The second and third years have exhibited much wider diversity (Chart 21-3).

In a very real sense, Chart 21-4 emphasizes the regularity of recessions across business cycles, while Chart 21-3 underscores their rather unique individual personalities.

A "formula" provides yet another way of getting started. One such sim-

CHART 21-3. Real GNP During Seven Cycles

Total Decline (%)	Trough Quarter	Change Following Trough (%)		
		1st Year	2nd Year	3rd Year
−3.4	1982:Q4	6.3	4.7	2.5
−2.4	1980:Q3	3.3	−3.3	4.4
−4.3	1975:Q1	6.1	3.3	4.3
−1.1	1970:Q4	3.2	7.2	3.4
−1.0	1961:Q1	6.4	3.2	6.2
−3.5	1958:Q2	8.1	1.9	1.5
−3.0	1954:Q2	6.0	2.6	1.9

[a] Cumulative decline from peak to trough quarter. Troughs are those designated by the National Bureau of Economic Research.

CHART 21-4. Real GNP Before and After Trough

6 Quarters Before and After Trough

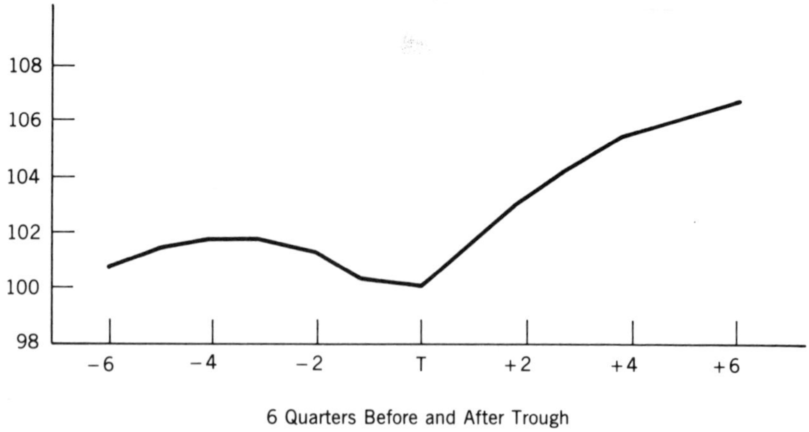

ple correlation projects the *year-ahead* real GNP change from the behavior of certain variables in previous years.*

For example

$$\%\Delta GNPC_t = 13.1 - 0.79\Delta TBill_{t-1} - 0.71\Delta TBill_{t-2}$$
$$- 0.12\Delta FXRate_{t-1} - 0.13CAPU_{t-1} \quad (21\text{-}1)$$

where $\Delta TBill$ = change in 30-day treasury bill rate during previous year and year before
$\Delta FXRate$ = change in trade-weighted exchange rate
$CAPU$ = manufacturing capacity utilization rate

This formula can be interpreted in the following manner: Falling interest rates and a falling exchange rate stimulate the economy, the latter by increasing exports and retarding the rise in imports. The capacity utilization rate serves as a measure of the extent to which changes in interest and exchange rates can be translated into real growth rather than inflationary pressures.

An advantage of this type of formula is that it requires no assumption by the forecaster of the explanatory variables to make a projection for the coming year. Its major disadvantage is that the equation reflects only a

---

* This particular equation is a modified version of one published periodically by Edward S. Hyman of Cyrus J. Lawrence Co. in his firm's newsletter, *Weekly Economic Data*.

EXAMPLE 21-2. PERSONAL CONSUMPTION EXPENDITURES   361

CHART 21-5.   Real GNP Growth "Model"

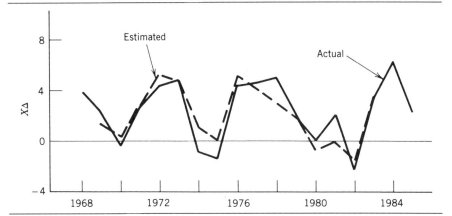

historical association or correlation and not an explicit theory of economic behavior. The user may thus be taking more forecast risk than with a carefully specified and estimated model with theoretical underpinnings. It is crucial, therefore, to resist the temptation to impute causality to this type of relationship by, for example, changing interest rates to see how these "affect" real GNP two or three years in the future.

Although the formula may well deteriorate in the future, it has tracked recent history quite well (Chart 21-5). Moreover, its current forecast for 1986 is fairly close to that obtained from more sophisticated but more time-consuming approaches.

EXAMPLE 21-2. PERSONAL CONSUMPTION EXPENDITURES: JUDGMENTALLY MODIFIED ECONOMETRICS AND CYCLICAL COMPARISON

The theory of consumer behavior is relatively well established. Most theories imply that consumer spending, especially that for nondurable goods and services (PCO), is related to its own past value and some measure of income. Even though economic theory does not establish whether the effect of inflation would be positive or negative, a number of empirical studies suggest that consumption has been influenced by inflation.

Theory also does not indicate which empirical measure of income is most appropriate. While several different measures have been used, each refinement of the income concept complicates the forecasting process. As is often the case in forecasting, it is preferable to use a measure that is already being forecast (in this case GNP) as a proxy for a theoretically ideal measure.

These considerations suggest the following econometric relationship:

$$PCO_t = -0.120 + 0.842\ PCO_{t-1} + 0.198\Delta GNP_t$$
$$+ 0.107\ GNP_{t-1} - 0.010\%\Delta CPI_t \quad (21\text{-}2)$$

where PCO and GNP are measured in constant dollars per capita.*

EXAMPLE 21-3. CONSUMER DURABLES

Consumer durables are the most cyclically volatile category of consumer spending. In 1984 automobiles and parts accounted for 46% of total real durables, furniture and household equipment represented 37%, and a catch-all category with jewelry, bicycles, and boats comprised the rest. Equations can be estimated for overall durables and for these components. However, true causal relationships rather than correlations require explanatory variables that include interest rates, relative prices, stocks of durables, population details, and the like. The cyclical comparison approach makes all this unnecessary. It also cannot answer such questions as, "What happens if interest rates rise?"

A quick glance at Chart 21-6 suggests that the cyclical comparison approach is more valuable in forecasting the first four quarters or so of recovery than the downturn phase. If one excludes the short-lived 1980 cycle and the strike-distorted 1970 episode, the average increase during the first four quarters of recovery has been 16%. This is very similar to the 15.3% rise over all the cycles shown in Chart 21-6. It is entirely possible that such "special factors" tend to cancel each other out over a large enough group of cycles. It is obvious from the data that not all cycles are alike. The behavior of automobile expenditures is an interesting example of this. Chart 21-6 shows that the "specific" cycle for consumer durables differs somewhat from what is called the "reference" cycle for the overall economy: consumer durables turned up earlier than the total economy in four of the seven cycles.

Production forecasts are often of considerable interest, particularly to supplier industries. *Ward's Automotive Reports* publishes U.S. automobile production scheduled by the major companies for the coming two quarters. As shown in Chart 21-7, from a recent study by the Federal Reserve Bank of New York,† these estimates tend to be overly optimistic. The study showed

---

* The equation was fitted to real per capita data for PCO and GNP. For a more complete discussion of the derivation and estimation of this form of consumption function, see E. Kuh and R. Schmalensee, *An Introduction to Applied Macroeconomics,* North-Holland/American Elsevier, New York, 1973, Ch. 3, pp. 31–49.

† Ethan S. Harris, "Forecasting Auto Output," *Quarterly Review,* Federal Reserve Bank of New York, vol. 10, no. 4, Winter 1985–1986, pp. 40–42.

CHART 21-6. Consumer Durables Spending (% Change from Trough) During Six Quarters Before and After Recession Trough (trough = 100)

	Quarter							
	1982:Q4	1980:Q3	1975:Q1	1970:Q4	1961:Q1	1958:Q2	1954:Q2	Average
Pre-trough								
6	94.8	110.8	113.7	108.7	109.0	108.2	96.4	105.9
5	97.5	108.3	110.5	108.3	104.6	110.9	101.1	105.9
4	91.8	111.6	107.6	107.7	106.2	108.2	99.6	104.7
3	94.5	108.5	108.5	105.6	109.5	106.4	99.6	104.7
2	95.1	107.4	109.4	107.0	108.2	106.5	102.5	105.2
1	96.1	95.6	98.0	107.4	105.7	100.8	99.0	100.4
Trough	100.0	100.0	100.0	100.0	100.0	100.0	100.0	100.0
Post-trough								
1	101.1	102.4	102.7	110.3	100.7	101.2	102.0	102.9
2	107.2	106.6	109.4	113.1	102.7	104.8	108.5	107.5
3	110.1	102.3	112.8	116.3	107.2	110.5	115.1	110.6
4	114.5	105.3	118.7	121.1	109.5	115.0	122.1	115.2
5	118.7	99.1	119.2	123.8	111.8	116.3	125.3	116.3
6	121.3	102.1	120.1	126.7	113.0	111.6	124.6	117.1

CHART 21-7. *Ward's* Projections and Actual Automobile Production[a]

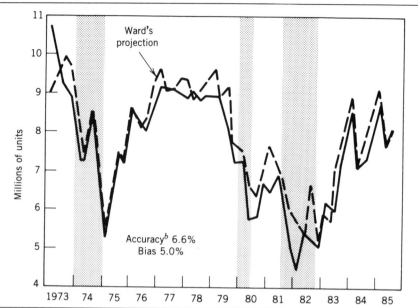

[a] Shaded areas represent periods of recession, as defined by the National Bureau of Economic Research.

[b] "Accuracy" is the mean absolute error and "bias" is the mean error, each as a percent of actual production.

Source: Various issues of *Ward's Automotive Reports* (1973–1985) and unpublished data from the Bureau of Economic Analysis.

how the accuracy of the production forecasts could be improved by incorporating the *Ward's* projection into a regression model along with other variables such as incomes, interest rates, inventories, and prices.

EXAMPLE 21-4. THE UNEMPLOYMENT RATE: OKUN'S LAW

The unemployment rate (RU) has been closely associated with the level of real economic activity. The statistical rule of thumb relating changes in the unemployment rate to the rate of real GNP growth has held up quite well since Arthur Okun pointed it out more than 20 years ago.* Nevertheless, the simplest version of "Okun's law" is modified to take into account three factors:

1. In sharp contrast to the last 30 years when the working-age population has grown at about a 1.75% annual rate, for the rest of the 1980s this popula-

---

* Arthur Okun, "Potential GNP: Its Measurement and Significance," *Proceedings of the American Statistical Association*, 1962.

EXAMPLE 21-5. COMPENSATION GROWTH   365

tion is projected to grow only about half as rapidly. To capture any impact of this change, growth of the working-age population has been added to the basic law ("POP").

2. The proportion of teenagers in the working-age population rose from 7.6% in 1954 to a peak of 10.9% in 1974, before declining to below 8% in 1986. This decline will continue throughout the 1980s. Teenagers' work experiences differ from those of other workers in several ways. For example, teenagers experience higher rates of unemployment than most other workers. They are more likely to change jobs, either voluntarily (as less experienced, lower paid workers they are more likely to seek better employment opportunities) or involuntarily (under last-hired first-fired seniority rules), and to enter or leave the work force to attend school. In light of these differences, the proportion of teenagers in the working-age population was also added to Okun's law ("TEEN").

3. Because the unemployment rate does not respond instantaneously to real economic growth, the previous year's as well as the current rate of economic growth was added to the law.

The resulting version of Okun's law is

$$RU_t = 0.86 - 0.44\%\Delta GNP_t - 0.08\%\Delta GNP_{t-1}$$
$$+ 0.48\%\Delta POP + 0.82\Delta\% \text{ TEEN} \quad (21\text{-}3)$$

This relationship has tracked the course of the unemployment rate since 1954 fairly closely. The large changes in the unemployment rate in the last six years were tracked especially well.

EXAMPLE 21-5. COMPENSATION GROWTH: THE PHILLIPS CURVE* VERSUS "BOTTOM UP"

Labor costs are by far the largest component of total costs, and unit labor cost increases usually represent the biggest single factor in price increases. The growth of labor compensation appears clearly linked to at least two factors: the degree of slack in labor markets and recent price experience.

It may sound circular to argue that price inflation depends on wage inflation, which in turn depends on price inflation. Yet this seems to be an accurate description of the wage-price (or price-wage-price) spiral in the U.S. economy. What breaks this process out of a completely simultaneous circle is the tendency of wage increases to *lag* behind price increases. Wage

---

* A. W. Phillips, "The Relation Between Unemployment and the Rate of Change of Money Wages in the United Kingdom, 1861–1957," *Economica*, vol. 25, 1958, pp. 238–299. The term "Phillips curve" is often used loosely to describe the "tradeoff" between inflation and the level or growth rate of economic activity.

increases reflect price *experience,* measured here as a weighted average of current inflation and that over the past two years. For example, although consumer price inflation in 1981 was down noticeably from its double-digit peak in 1979–1980, labor compensation increases were only marginally lower. Not until 1982 when inflation fell further and had therefore stayed down for two years did compensation increases slow dramatically. 1985 was the first year when compensation growth fell by more than consumer price inflation. This "wage stickiness," the slow adjustment of compensation growth to consumer prices, is what makes the transition from high to low rates of inflation so long and painful. On the other hand, this "wage stickiness" actually helps to moderate inflation increases when prices are on the way up. Between 1976 and 1979, price inflation increased dramatically, while wage inflation inched up relatively gradually.

Labor compensation growth also depends on the degree of demand pressure in labor markets. When these markets are "tight," employers bid up compensation growth rates to attract new workers. The clearest example of this was in the late 1960s when compensation growth rose more rapidly than price experience alone would have suggested. The Vietnam War boom drove the unemployment rate down to 3.5% and generated the greatest labor market demand pressure in the last 30 years. When labor markets are "slack," employers need not raise wages to attract new workers. The recent decline in compensation growth reflects both the more favorable price experience and the drop in labor market demand pressure.

Concretely, these considerations lead to the following statistical relationship:

$$\%\Delta COMP_t = 0.30 + 0.57\%\Delta P_t + 0.16\%\Delta P_{t-1} + 0.12\%\Delta P_{t-2} + \frac{12.18}{RU}$$

$$(21\text{-}4)$$

where COMP = worker compensation
           P = personal consumption price deflator
     RU = unemployment rate

The "bottom up" approach to compensation forecasting adds together the components of total compensation—union wages, nonunion wages, fringe benefits, and payroll taxes. *Caveat:* This approach requires a lot of judgment and much familiarity with the many different data sources and series.

Union Wages

Wages paid to workers covered by collective bargaining agreements consist of cost-of-living adjustments (COLAs), new settlements, and fixed (non-COLA) deferred increases. On average, COLA provisions have an "elasticity" of about 0.5% to 0.6% with respect to increases in the CPI: A 5%

EXAMPLE 21-5. COMPENSATION GROWTH 367

increase in the CPI produces a 2.5% to 3% increase in wages.* Escalator payments can be generated by combining this estimate with a forecast of the CPI. New settlements can be forecasted by examining the recent history of first-year fixed increases, taking into account the fact that the very low settlements of recent years have been heavily influenced by "give backs" or wage cuts in a number of industries. At the start of each year, the Bureau of Labor Statistics publishes estimates of the deferred fixed increases from previously negotiated major contracts. In 1985, this estimate was 3.7%.†

The weight for each of the three components of union wages indicates the proportion of workers under collective bargaining agreements receiving each kind of increase during the year. In 1985, for example, about 45% of union workers were scheduled for deferred increases from previously negotiated contracts. However, these weights can add to more than one because many workers receive more than one type of increase each year. 1985 also had a large fraction (about 25%) of workers who received no increase during the year. Moreover, the weights vary from year to year depending on the volume of negotiations taking place during that year. 1985 happened to be a "light year" compared with the previous two years so that the number of first-year settlements was small. Weights also vary depending on the proportion of new settlements calling for wage freezes and/or wage cuts.

Nonunion Wages

Until the past several years, the difference between the growth of union and nonunion wages was systematically related to labor market conditions as measured by the unemployment rate. When unemployment was high, union wages would rise faster than nonunion. However, deregulation and import competition have hit union wages harder than nonunion wages. On the basis of relationships that prevailed from the late 1950s to the late 1970s, one would have predicted that 1985's 7.3% unemployment rate would be associated with union wages rising about 1.5% faster than nonunion.‡ In fact, precisely the opposite occurred, with nonunion wages rising 1.5% faster than union wages. Lacking the ability to quantify the impact of such things as deregulation, import competition, and what appears to be a heightened management resistance to union wage demands, the best one can do is to try out some plausible union–nonunion patterns. For starters, one might assume

* See Nicholas S. Perna, "The Contractual Cost of Living Escalator," *Monthly Review,* Federal Reserve Bank of New York, June 1974, for one of the earliest estimates of this elasticity. See also "Major Collective Bargaining Settlements in Private Industry in 1984," *Current Wage Developments,* April 1985, p. 45, which mentions that COLA payouts averaged 50% of the CPI rise in 1984.

† Joan D. Borum and David Schlein, "Bargaining Activity Light in Private Industry in 1985," *Monthly Labor Review,* January 1985, p. 24.

‡ See p. 318 in the previous edition of this *Handbook.*

CHART 21-8. A "Bottom Up" Forecast of Labor Compensation in 1985

Compensation Variable	Percent Increase	Weight	Percent Contribution
Union wages			
COLAs[a]	2.1	.45	0.9
First year settlements[b]	3.0	.33	1.0
Deferred fixed increases[c]	3.7	.45	1.7
Union wage change			3.6
Nonunion wages (equals union plus/ minus adjustment)[d]			4.7
Average of union and nonunion wages			4.5
Further adjustments (for fringes, payroll taxes[d])			0.8
Employment cost per hour			5.3

[a] Cost of living adjustments, based on January 1985 CEA forecast.
[b] Same as previous year.
[c] *Monthly Labor Review*, January 1985, p. 24.
[d] Based on various components of the Employment Cost Index. See Bureau of Labor Statistics, U.S. Department of Labor, *Current Wage Developments*, Tables 9–14, various issues.

that union wages will continue to rise about 1.1% slower than nonunion wages, the same as in 1984.

Total Wages

Chart 21-8 illustrates how the three components can be weighted to estimate total union wages which, when combined with a guess about the union–nonunion differential, can generate an estimate of nonunion wages. This represents a judgmental but interesting way of trying to forecast the Bureau of Labor Statistics Employment Cost Index. In actuality, compensation as measured by the index rose 3.9%, a good deal slower than the 5.3% "bottom up" projection. The reasons for this overshoot were as follows. The CPI rose about half a point less than the CEA's (Council of Economic Advisers) 4.1% projection that was used in the example, thus triggering smaller COLAs. Newly negotiated first-year increases were even lower than the very low gains of 1984. While the difference between union and nonunion wages widened further, this was more than offset by a shrinkage of the "add-on" for fringes and payroll taxes.

EXAMPLE 21-6. PRODUCTIVITY GROWTH

Compensation growth does not increase output costs when it is matched by productivity growth. The sources of productivity growth are not fully under-

EXAMPLE 21-7. PRICE BEHAVIOR   369

stood. Before 1973, the secular or "trend" rate of productivity growth in the United States had been fairly stable in the postwar period. The rate of productivity growth from business cycle peak to the next peak ranged from 1.7% to 2.5%; during economic expansions, productivity growth ranged from 2.1% to 2.9%. In contrast, from the business cycle peak in 1973 to the one in 1980, productivity grew at only a 0.6% annual rate. In addition, from the 1975 cyclical trough to the 1980 cyclical peak, productivity growth averaged only 1.3% per year. The causes of this productivity slowdown remain a mystery. Energy shocks; government regulation; the training, experience, and composition of the work force; environmental investment—all of these factors and many others have been offered as reasons. Nevertheless, attempts to measure their influence on the slowdown have not succeeded in solving the puzzle.

Two facets of productivity growth are, however, fairly well established. First, the secular rate of productivity growth depends importantly on the size of the capital stock in relation to the number of hours worked. Labor is more productive when it has more plant and equipment to work with. Second, productivity growth is highly cyclical. Productivity grows rapidly early in economic expansions, when output increases rapidly and when much idle capacity is available. Similarly, productivity growth slows markedly near cyclical peaks when available capacity is most fully utilized and when output grows more slowly, or actually falls in recessions.

The following simple statistical relationship based on these two observations tracks the historical course of productivity fairly well:

$$\%\Delta PD_t = 10.2 + 0.29\%\Delta PD_{t-1} + 0.65\%\Delta \frac{K}{L}$$
$$- 0.16\ CAPU_t + 0.90\%\Delta GNP_t + 0.21\Delta\%GNP \quad (21\text{-}5)$$

where PD_t = productivity or output per hour
  K = capital stock
  L = hours worked
  CAPU = capacity utilization rate

EXAMPLE 21-7. PRICE BEHAVIOR

Prices are influenced by unit labor costs, that is, compensation per hour relative to output per hour, or productivity. Because productivity growth is highly volatile, especially over the business cycle, pricing policies are based on both current unit labor costs and "trend" or "standard" unit labor costs—compensation growth relative to the "trend" rate of productivity growth.

The 1970s have shown that understanding of the rate of inflation requires some attention to food and energy prices as well as to unit labor costs. Sharp increases in food and energy prices played a major role in the two bouts of double-digit inflation in 1974 and 1980. By the same token, the large drop in the inflation rate in recent years substantially exceeded the decline in unit labor costs; in 1983, energy prices increased only about 1.5% and food prices about 2.5%.

These considerations suggest the following price equation:

$$\%\Delta P_t = 0.46 + 0.17\%\Delta ULC_t + 0.53\%SULC_t$$
$$+ 0.08\%\Delta PE + 0.08\%\Delta PF \quad (21\text{-}6)$$

where P = price deflator, personal consumption expenditure
ULC = unit labor cost
SULC = standard unit labor costs, or compensation less "trend" productivity growth
PE = price of energy
PF = price of food

This relationship tracks both the accelerations of inflation in the 1970s and the major deceleration in the 1980s without appealing to hard-to-forecast variables like the exchange rate, import prices, or the rate of monetary growth.

EXAMPLE 21-8. PROFITS: GNP AND STANDARD & POOR'S

Corporate profits forecasts are an important input for many economic decisions. They are used by financial investors in selecting their portfolios. In addition, businesses use the macroeconomic profit outlook as a reference in setting internal earnings targets for their companies.

Their extreme volatility makes profits difficult to predict accurately. The most comprehensive but highly demanding approach would be to try to explain all the items on the corporate income statement. A useful alternative is to use an equation driven by the other variables in the macroeconomic outlook. For example, profits are related to the pace of economic activity and financial conditions. The former factor can be represented by nominal GNP growth, the current and lagged level of capacity utilization. The latter can be proxied by the trade-weighted dollar exchange rate, the change in the inflation rate, and a measure of interest rates.

This particular formulation could be used to predict the NIA (National Income Account) measure of profits or the Standard & Poor's measure of earnings per share. The two differ significantly. The S&P measure represents earnings as reported to share owners in annual and quarterly financial statements. NIA profits, on the other hand, are closer to what businesses report to the Internal Revenue Service. Thus, a change in the depreciation laws will affect NIA profits but usually not S&P earnings, because most firms tend to use straight-line depreciation in reporting earnings to their share owners. Since the GNP measures current production, NIA profits do *not* include capital gains and writeoffs for closed plants and the like, while the S&P series does include these. Numerically, these and other differences can get quite large. For instance, NIA profits rose 22% in 1983, while S&P 500 earnings rose only half as much.

When applied to the S&P 500 measure of earnings per share, this formulation yields the following empirical relationship:

$$\%\Delta S\&P = 70.05 - 0.48 \text{ interest}_t + 1.53 \text{ CAPU}_t - 2.12 \text{ CAPU}_{t-1}$$
$$- 0.13 \text{ EX}_t + 1.69\%\Delta CPI + 0.59\%\Delta GNP \quad (21\text{-}7)$$

where EX is the foreign exchange value of the dollar.

SUMMARY AND CONCLUSIONS

Business decisionmakers place increasing reliance on explicit, quantitative forecasts of the overall economic environment—the expected future paths of the most important macroeconomic variables. This chapter provides a brief description of the practical art of generating short-term forecasts of economywide variables. Its major points are:

- Among the major forecasting techniques—time series, econometric modeling, cyclical comparison, and "judgmental"—each has its own advantages and disadvantages. Consequently, most practitioners use at least a little of each technique to arrive at the "best guess" forecast.

- External information—from other forecasters and from government agencies—is important for formulating a "personal" view on where the economy is heading. Bits and pieces of current, actual data are combined to estimate the initial starting point for what may unfold over the next year or more. An outsider's forecast is often used as a "first pass" to get the forecasting process started.

- Errors are a source of both annoyance and information to the forecaster. Sometimes past errors provide the first clue of an emerging new development in the economy. Other times it is better to let bygones be bygones—creating an "instant theory" to "explain" past mistakes risks making future errors larger. Sometimes, as shown in the wage example, a forecast is "right for the wrong reasons."

- The most appropriate forecasting technique depends on the resources of the forecaster and the interests of the forecast user:

  For the financial market, current-dollar magnitudes are more important than real or constant-dollar components of GNP.

  For highly cyclical variables such as housing and consumer durables, the cyclical comparison approach lends insight to questions of timing, but careful attention to prospective financial developments is needed to gauge magnitudes and pinpoint turning points.

• Accuracy is of course the proof of the pudding in forecasting. However, most forecast users have additional requirements:

When "what if" questions must be answered, the forecaster will be drawn away from time series or even judgmental techniques toward concrete rules of thumb or formal econometric models.

In forecasting profits, the choice between Standard & Poor's measure of profits (earnings per share) and that of the National Income Account (profits reported to the Internal Revenue Service) depends very much on the needs of the forecast user.

Just as a road map cannot tell you where you want to go, this brief outline cannot teach you how to forecast. On the other hand, once your forecasting destination has been fixed and your available means of transport have been assessed, it may help you avoid some wrong turns in the black-box maze of macroeconomic forecasting.

22

FORECASTING POLITICAL RISKS FOR INTERNATIONAL OPERATIONS

JOSE DE LA TORRE
INSEAD, Fontainebleau, France

DAVID H. NECKAR
Michael J. Marchant Underwriting Agency, Ltd.
Lloyd's, London, England

The level of turmoil the world has experienced in the last 20 years has been considerable in spite of, or perhaps because of, the absence of large-scale wars. No region, no corner of the globe, has been untouched by one form or another of social and political conflict. Consider the following arbitrary list:

- War in the Middle East and in the Falklands
- Racial unrest in the Netherlands, France, and Sri Lanka
- Revolution in Iran and Nicaragua
- Labor strife in Poland, Italy, and Brazil
- Religious animosity in Ireland and India
- Military coups in Portugal, Ethiopia, and Turkey
- Guerrilla activity in Angola and Colombia
- Streaming of refugees into Miami, Thailand, and Hong Kong
- Political repression in Chile and South Africa
- Civil war in Lebanon and El Salvador

Ms. Dorothea Bensen provided valuable assistance in the preparation of this paper.

- Acerbic regionalism in Spain and Belgium
- Tribal animosity throughout Central Africa
- Inner-city clashes in Britain and the United States
- Repression of dissidents in the Soviet Union and Eastern Europe
- Political assassinations in Egypt and the Philippines
- Financial crisis in most of Latin America
- Drought and famine in Africa
- Antinuclear demonstrations in Western Europe
- Full-scale invasion in Cambodia and Afghanistan
- Unprecedented unemployment throughout the industrial world
- Separatist action in New Caledonia and Quebec
- Terrorist activities almost everywhere

Conflict of this nature can often lead to political or policy changes that, in turn, may have significant adverse consequences on the activities of multinational companies operating in these and neighboring areas. Furthermore, nonviolent changes in political regimes, such as the rise and fall from power of socialist governments in Chile, France, or Greece, or the transfer of power from colonial to nationalist administrations, as occurred in Zimbabwe and Papua New Guinea, may also result in drastic changes in the conditions under which foreign companies are allowed to continue domestic operations.

In 1985, the world's stock of foreign direct investment (FDI) (defined as situations in which 25% or more of the equity in a firm is in foreign hands) approached a value of $900 billion. If other assets owned abroad by nonfinancial corporations, such as bank deposits, securities, inventories, and minority (less than 25%) interests, were added to this figure, the total could well exceed $1500 billion. In addition, world trade in goods and services amounted to more than $2000 billion in 1984. Given that a significant proportion of these assets could be exposed to political risks at any time, the implications for the management of global operations are rather sobering.

Surely there is nothing new in this. Trade and investment have been exposed to political risks ever since the first caravans ventured across the Middle East several milennia ago. It is rather the magnitude of the exposure, and the much publicized losses associated with the nationalizations that followed regime changes in postcolonial Africa, Cuba, Iran, and Nicaragua, that have thrust the issue of political risks to the forefront of business and academic concern. Our aim in this chapter is to respond to Kobrin's[32] plea for greater conceptualization in the field of political risk analysis. The first section of the chapter attempts to clarify the meaning and scope of the term "political risk" and its area of application. Next, we review some of the major approaches proposed in recent years for the assessment of political and environmental risks, and develop from these a guide to the specification of relevant causal relationships between the sources of risk and corporate contingencies. We then elaborate a comprehensive model of general applicability that incorporates all major variables discussed. Finally, we conclude with a few comments on the dynamics of regime change and corporate strategy that make any such model subject to constant review and evaluation.

DEFINING THE ISSUE

The term "political risk" has been much overused and abused in both the academic and business press. There are probably as many definitions as there are authors and methodologies. We feel compelled nonetheless to add to this relative congestion in the interest of clarity. A useful starting point is to distinguish between the actual contingencies faced by the foreign firm operating in a developing or industrial country and the proximate sources of the risk.

What concerns the international investor is not political change or instability per se, but the impact that any externally induced shock may have on the value of its assets. For this we can distinguish two generally different contingency losses. The first we may define as the involuntary loss of control (generally meaning property rights) over specific assets located in a foreign country, typically without adequate compensation. Expropriation, nationalization, the ravages of civil war, and wanton destruction by terrorists are examples of such losses. In fact, much of the literature and analysis on political risks have focused on specific instances of these types of loss, and particularly on the frequency and extent of expropriations.* A second, perhaps more important yet less well understood, contingency concerns the loss in the expected value of a foreign-controlled affiliate due to discriminatory actions taken against it, either because of its foreign nature or as part and parcel of a general tightening on free-market prerogatives. Here we may include various forms of discriminatory controls and restrictions often imposed by governments in times of domestic crisis (including foreign exchange and remittance restrictions), limitations on access to factor markets

---

* There is no denying the importance of these losses. As summarized by Burton and Inoue,[6] the expropriation risk has been variously estimate to affect 1% per year of the number of foreign affiliates active in less developed countries (LDCs) during the 1960–1977 period; represent cumulatively over the 1956–1972 period a total of 18.8% of the stock of foreign direct investment in 1972 plus the value of the expropriated assets[61]; amount to 1.6% of the total value of U.S. foreign direct investment in LDCs during 1960–1974[25]; and account for a cumulative (1960–1976) 4.4% of the 1976 stock of wholly and partially owned firms in LDCs plus the value of the seized assets.[31]

(financial, labor, or raw materials) and on outputs (e.g., on prices or diversification possibilities), and changing rules on domestic value added, taxation, or export performance requirements. All of these have the effect of reducing the expected value of the affiliate to the parent company without any of the drama of expropriation.

The second dimension of the exposure to political risks concerns the proximate cause. One may want to distinguish between the actions undertaken by legitimate (if not necessarily representative or democratically elected) governments in the exercise of their national prerogatives, and those that are the result of actions undertaken by actors outside the direct control of governmental authorities.* Chart 22-1 summarizes this first level of classification. The only point that need be made at this state is that hitherto most attention has been concentrated on the upper left-hand cell, that is, on either massive or selective seizure of properties by established or revolutionary governments, while considerably more may be at risk in the gradual erosion of asset values implied by the other categories.†

A different approach is to define the horizontal dimension of the matrix, not in terms of the source of the risk, but based on the indiscriminate or selective nature of the actions. This difference between "macro" risks, that is, those that affect all foreign (or, for that matter, many national) operations in the country in question, and "micro" risks, defined as those that target a single or a few companies for intervention on the basis of specific arguments (which can be more or less rational depending on point of view), is one that has been made repeatedly in the literature[30,32,45,50] with apparent little effect in terms of the evolution of practice.

Consider the four types of risks illustrated in Chart 22-2. Type A consists of the potential for massive expropriations of foreign properties typically related to drastic changes in government, such as those following decolonialization or the triumph of a Marxist revolutionary rebel force. These are often associated with closed systems in developing countries, which explode after a long period of national frustration or discontent, followed by growing repression and a collapse of authority. All foreign investors are subject to the same treatment with few exceptions (e.g., the often-cited case of Gulf Oil in Angola), as they are closely identified with the previous regime and offer a ready source for the rebirth of national pride. Type B risks, on the other hand, can occur more gradually and in both industrial or developing economies. They consist of sector-specific or company-specific exposure, which can be traced to the particular characteristics of the industry in question (e.g., its degree of technological sophistication or its oligopolistic nature)

---

* Simon[50] made a similar distinction between "societal" forces (i.e., those that emerge from general social phenomena) and governmental actions.
† It is also important to make a distinction between sudden changes in governments, government policies, or externally induced events and gradual evolution along a more or less predictable sociopolitical pattern. For more on this see Kobrin.[30]

CHART 22-1. Exposure to Political Risks

	Loss may be the result of:	
Contingencies may include:	The actions of legitimate government authorities	Events caused by actors outside the control of government
Involuntary loss of control over specific assets without adequate compensation	• Total or partial expropriation • Forced divestiture • Confiscation • Cancellation or unfair calling of performance bonds	• War • Revolution • Terrorism • Strikes • Extortion
Reduction in the value of a stream of benefits expected from the foreign-controlled affiliate	• Nonapplicability of "national treatment" • Restrictions in access to financial, labor, or material markets • Controls on prices, outputs, or activities • Currency and remittance restrictions • Value-added and export performance requirements	• Nationalistic buyers or suppliers • Threats and disruption to operations by hostile groups • Externally induced financial constraints • Externally imposed limits on imports or exports

377

CHART 22-2. The Nature of Political Risks

	Macro risks	Micro risks
Loss contingencies Involuntary loss of control over specific assets without adequate compensation	Type A: Massive expropriations	Type B: Selective nationalizations
Value continencies Reduction in the expected value of the benefits to be derived from the foreign affiliate	Type C: General deterioration of the investment climate	Type D: Restrictions targeted to key sectors
	Macro risks Sudden convulsive chances that threaten most of the population of foreign direct investors within the country	*Micro risks* Interventions generally motivated by specific consideration closely related to the economic and social conditions prevailing at the time, and to specific industry and firm characteristics

and to the current situation in the host country with regard to the salience of the investment relative to national priorities and objectives. Thus, drastic changes in government may or may not result in massive expropriations, just as the gradual evolution of national goals and industry characteristics may bring certain sectors of economic activity under sudden scrutiny by nonradical government authorities eager to bring key economic sectors under national control.*

On a less dramatic level, type C risks may nonetheless have considerable implications for the real value of a subsidiary to the parent company. A change in government orientation, occurring either in the course of a freely held election or in response to external threats, can result in increases in taxation, new requirements in terms of domestic equity participation, lower remittance allowances, and so on, all or any of which can substantially alter the post-tax, home currency present value of the benefits realized by the affiliate. Similarly, type D risks entail considerable potential for loss. As LDC governments strive for a greater share of the fruits derived from foreign company operations in their territory, case-by-case analysis and lengthy negotiation on domestic value added, export performance, ownership limitations, and the like will be more and more the rule than the exception. Of course, the evaluation of the potential benefits of the investment and the split of the spoils will be greatly dependent on the sector and the company involved, and not only on what the country has to offer.[8]

We conclude this discussion, therefore, with a working definition of political risk as "the probability distribution that a real or potential loss will occur due to the exposure of a foreign affiliate to a set of contingencies that range from the total seizure of corporate assets without compensation to the unprovoked interference of external agents, with or without governmental sanction, with the normal operations and performance expected from the affiliate." Whether the loss is caused by legitimate government acts or is the result of forces acting internally within the host country or emanating from the home or global environment is a methodological problem. Similarly, whether these forces will affect the whole of foreign industry or simply the most salient (for whatever reasons) sectors are key questions to which we now turn.

MAJOR APPROACHES

A number of excellent reviews of the literature on political risk assessment exist already[30,33,46,50] and need not be duplicated here. It will suffice for our

---

* For a more elaborate approach that adds whether the actors' impacts on the firm are direct or indirect (that is, influence those who can impact directly), and whether they are caused by internal (within the host country) or external (home country or global) forces, see Simon.[51]

purposes to summarize the major findings and studies that can lend support to the conceptual framework presented here, and to review some of the major approaches tried to date in order to deal with the challenge of assessing political risks.

The Empirical Evidence

Empirical data on sociopolitical events and their impact on international business are hard to come by. First, the collection of data over long time periods and covering a sufficiently large number of countries presents substantial problems of accuracy, validity, and comparability. Second, while the most dramatic impacts are readily reported in the press (e.g., major nationalizations and confiscation of assets), the quality of the reporting is not always homogeneous or reliable. Third, there are no time series or data banks that report on the multitude of minor inconveniences and obstacles imposed on foreign companies on a daily basis by governments and other environmental actors. In fact, it is doubtful that this information exists within individual corporations, which limits the reliability of case studies. How many firms keep track of the opportunity losses they incur due to the discriminating credit policies followed by a country's central banking authorities? Fourth, the application of quantitative methodologies to political phenomena is a relatively new development.[1,7,18,24,50] Thus, there has been a general skepticism by the business community of any model or result using political variables. Finally, and perhaps most critically, there has not been sufficient theoretical work until recently that allowed for the specification of causal relationships between political, social, and economic data and the contingencies faced by firms.

Expropriation

A number of serious studies have attempted to explain the incidence of expropriation across countries, time, and industries. (For a complete set of references on studies of expropriation see Burton and Inoue.[6]) First among these was Truitt,[54,55] who considered the experience of British and U.S. investors in the post World War II era. He concluded, inter alia, that the extractive and service sectors were more vulnerable than other sectors to expropriation and that certain organizational characteristics, such as size and ownership structure, were associated with a higher frequency of takeover. Hawkins and colleagues[23] confirmed Truitt's sectoral findings and provided a breakdown of expropriations by regions and the nature of the takeover. They concluded, on the basis of a sample of 170 U.S. affiliates in 1946–1970, that economic motivations, and not the ideological rhetoric designed for public consumption, were paramount; most expropriations were directed at controlling an economic activity vital to the nation. Bradley[4] examined the characteristics common to a sample of 114 affiliates of U.S.

multinationals expropriated by foreign governments during the period 1960–1976. First, he cast doubts on the widely held belief that joint ventures reduced political risks. He also showed that very high and, surprisingly, very low levels of technological complexity seem to be a deterrent to expropriation. It seems that the lack of indigenous capacity and skills may block the former, while a lack of interest may protect the latter. Third, Bradley's data indicated that affiliates that were highly integrated into a multinational system were less likely to undergo expropriation, particularly if cutting them off from the parent company network would render them of little value. Finally, contrary to Truitt, he concluded that large visible firms appear to be more vulnerable.

Four more recent studies using larger data bases have covered some of the same ground and have tested for further hypothesized relationships among country, corporate, and contingency variables. Jodice[26] examined expropriation propensity in the extractive sector by studying 511 acts of forced divestment executed by 76 nations over the 1960–1976 period and involving 1535 firms. He found little evidence that willingness to expropriate was associated with the level of economic development of the host country, but instead confirmed that the "capacity" of the state [as measured by the ratio of central government revenue to gross domestic product (GDP)] was strongly correlated with the incidence of expropriation. In addition, failure to perform economically and the degree of foreign aid dependence of the host country were positively and negatively, respectively, related to the frequency of expropriation. Finally, Jodice established that governing elites tend to use expropriation as a means of distracting attention from their own shortcomings in times of increasing political turmoil.*

Kobrin,[31] using the same data base, focused on industry- and corporate-specific factors associated with the incidence of forced divestment. His "underlying hypothesis is that in the vast majority of countries where forced divestment is used selectively, its being chosen vis-à-vis alternative regulatory or administrative policies is, inter alia, a function of firm and industry-specific characteristics."† When countries were classified according to the

---

* The Jodice[26] and Kobrin[31] papers have a wealth of data on the history and regional distribution of expropriations in recent years. They show, among other things, that some of the smaller countries, for example, Italy, the Netherlands, Belgium, and Canada, have a much higher ratio of share of expropriations to share of foreign direct investment (FDI) than does the United States, Britain, or France. Also, Africa and the Middle East show a greater propensity to expropriate than does Asia or (the lowest!) Latin America.

† An interesting divergence between the Kobrin[31] and Burton and Inoue[6] studies concerns this point. While the former argued that mass expropriations account for slightly over 10% of all takings in his sample, the latter, using essentially the same data base, concluded that large-scale nationalizations account for more than 70% of all firms taken. The discrepancy arises from the use of acts (by Kobrin) versus firms, although in both analyses it appears that selectivity is on the rise.

number of firms taken in a given act, the more "selective" takers acted mainly in the more highly sensitive sectors, that is, those such as agriculture, mining, and petroleum, in which national priorities and sensibilities were the greatest. He also confirmed that technological complexity and global integration of the subsidiary help reduce vulnerability to takeovers, while industry maturity encourages it, for manufacturing affiliates. Finally, his results concerning organizational structure verify that wholly owned subsidiaries and joint ventures with government partners increase vulnerability.

Burton and Inoue[6] examined an even larger data base consisting of 1857 cases of expropriation, which includes for the first time the experience of Japanese investors. They focused on a "stages of economic development" hypothesis by which countries in the early stages tend to expropriate agricultural, utilities, and banking affiliates (often associated with the decolonialization process), while manufacturing assumes greater importance in the later stages. They also confirmed regional patterns of expropriation, North Africa acting mainly on petroleum, Black Africa on basic industries and services, Latin American on manufacturing, and Asia on agriculture. Their analysis, however, is limited by the fact that no relative intensity of expropriation can be determined becasue of lack of base data on the stock of investment by region and sector, and by the distorting effect of several large-scale undertakings in Cuba and Africa. Finally, a study by Juhl,[27] whose sources and data base are not specified, supports most of these findings, particularly the view that vulnerability increases with the host country's capacity to assume responsibility for the affiliate (measured in this case by the percentage of secondary school students within their age group).

Bargaining Power

The dearth of evidence on contingencies other than expropriation makes it practically impossible to confirm the existence of causal relationships with the confidence of the aforementioned studies. The literature on foreign investment in developing countries, however, provides an ample basis for specifying hypothetical relationships.[6,35,41,44,57,58] Two basic models can be used to do this. First, there is the series of propositions deriving from the relative bargaining power model and its corollary, the obsolescent bargain paradigm. The second concerns the dependencia model and its assumptions about relative gains and losses to the host country from dependence on foreign investment. The former attempts to judge optimal policy on the basis of social cost–benefit analysis, subject to the existence of both firm- and country-specific advantages and to the opportunities for internalizing transactions within the firm. The latter, on the other hand, places a premium on noneconomic factors such as national identity and self-reliance.

Four recent studies focus some of these hypotheses on narrowly defined areas in the relationship between host country and multinational investor, and do so in a way that is consistent with the foregoing conclusions. Fagre and Wells[13] looked at the ownership policies of multinational companies in Latin America. Assuming that LDCs, ceteris paribus, will insist on minimum foreign ownership, the authors took the resulting ownership pattern (adjusted for both corporate and country preferences) as the proxy for bargaining power on the part of the multinational, and tested this against a series of propositions about the source of such power. They concluded that technology (R&D/sales), product differentiation (advertising/sales), and market access (both intracorporate transfers and export volume) are significantly correlated with corporate bargaining power. The relationships concerning size, product diversity, and competition are more complex, but equally interesting for our purposes.

Poynter[42] examined the characteristics common to a sample of 104 foreign subsidiaries operating in Tanzania, Zambia, Indonesia, and Kenya, which had experienced government intervention ranging from expropriation to minor forms of harassment between mid-1970 and mid-1975. His findings confirm the proposition that control over sourcing of production inputs and over sales to associated companies is a deterrent to host government intervention. A high level of operational and managerial complexity of the subsidiary also seems to provide insurance against interference. On the other hand, large firms operating in strategically important (to the host country) fields were found to experience above-average intervention. Finally, Poynter discovered that managers of foreign firms who pursue aggressive policies of lobbying for their causes not only were better informed of the political winds, but succeeded in lowering the level of intervention by the government.

A study by Lecraw,[36] based on data collected in the late 1970s on 153 subsidiaries of U.S., European, Japanese, and LDC parents operating in six manufacturing industries and in the five ASEAN countries (Thailand, Malaysia, Singapore, Indonesia, and the Philippines), tested the impact of firm-specific advantages (technology leadership, advertising intensity, asset size, and export intensity) as well as country-specific advantages (market attractiveness and industry competition) on three sets of dependent variables: actual equity ownership held by the foreign firm, bargaining success (a firm- and country-corrected ownership variable), and "effective control." Lecraw confirmed and extended previous findings on the impact of unique corporate resources on bargaining strength, but went further in concluding that the same firm-specific advantages are positively correlated with the exercise of effective control (that is, control by the parent over key aspects of the venture) even in the absence of majority ownership. Furthermore, he found a strong linear relationship between the success of the venture (a composite variable that included profitability, management satisfaction with results, and performance relative to other companies in the same industry and country) and the degree of effective control the parent exercised over the affiliate. In contrast, the relationship between ownership and success was J-shaped, with 50/50 arrangements faring the worst.

Finally, Kim[28] extended Poynter's[42] analysis with a detailed look at the level of industry competition and the "political responsiveness" of the subsidiary relative to the degree of government intervention in the firm's operations. His study, based on data on 147 U.S.-based subsidiaries in four manufacturing sectors in the ASEAN region, found a very marked increase in government intervention associated with rising levels of industry competition. He was also able to confirm the ability of firm-specific advantages to reduce government interference with local operations, independent of the strength of the competitive factor. And he supported Poynter's recommendation that an active political role (a willingness to seek out opportunities for discussion with local leaders on their political agenda and active promotion of the corporation's viewpoint) served to lower significantly the level of political intervention as perceived by the management of the sample firms.

Political Assessment Models

The practice of assessing political risks varies from the use of general surveys, followed perhaps by an inspection visit to the country in question, to highly sophisticated internal assessment systems employed by some of the major international corporations and financial institutions. Managerial attention to these issues is a fairly recent phenomenon* and thus few standards have as yet emerged in the profession. Two useful reviews of these models are presented by Kobrin[32] and Simon.[52] Kobrin identified four classes of models, as follows:

- Observational, generally those involving multivariate analysis of macro data along the lines of some of the empirical studies cited in this chapter
- Unstructured, characterized by implicit or intuitive relationships among environmental variables and the corporate contingencies under consideration, and carried out either systematically or unsystematically
- Structured, with detailed and explicit specification of the underlying relationships and the application of complex methodologies

Simon, on the other hand, used a classification scheme that groups all subjective methods into one of four categories—idiosyncratic/impressionistic, comprehensive qualitative, Bayesian, or Delphi—and the more objective methods into two categories—econometric models and cross-national political analyses. We shall use two broadly defined dimensions to review these models (see Chart 22-3): The first measures the extent to which the model deals with the specific industry and corporate characteristics relevant

---

* A recent survey by Blank and colleagues[3] revealed that by 1979, 55% of the firms surveyed had taken some steps to establish formal responsibility for political assessment.

CHART 22-3. Political Forecasting Models Classified by Their Orientation and Their Geographic Scope

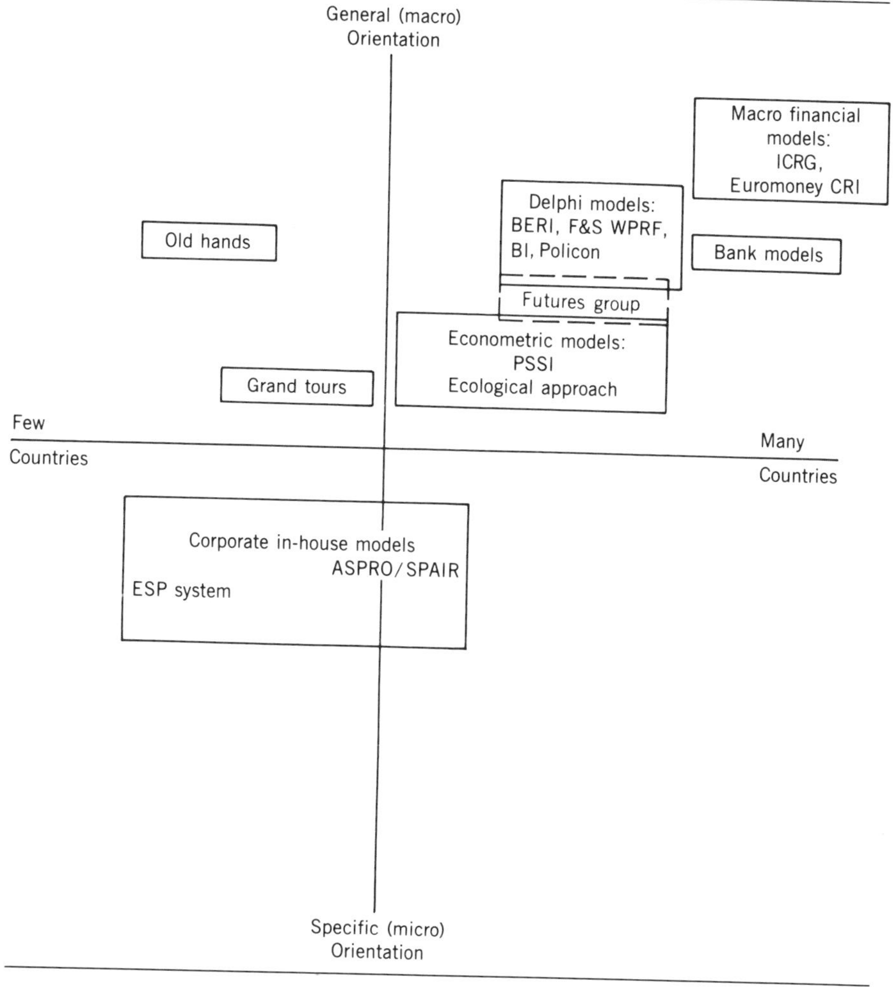

General (macro)
Orientation

Macro financial
models:
ICRG,
Euromoney CRI

Delphi models:
BERI, F&S WPRF,
BI, Policon

Old hands

Bank models

Futures group

Econometric models:
PSSI
Ecological approach

Grand tours

Few
Countries

Many
Countries

Corporate in-house models
ASPRO/SPAIR

ESP system

Specific (micro)
Orientation

to the individual investor (its specificity), while the second accounts for the breadth of its coverage (its range).

Idiosyncratic/Impressionistic Models

Until very recently, most international firms limited their analysis of the political climate in a country to casual observations by "local experts" or corporate "old hands" sent in for this purpose, and to such occasions when a particular new investment or financial commitment was being considered. If management perceived political risks to be high, the investment would be canceled or postponed, or a "risk premium" would be added to the calculations to account for the higher probability of loss. Seldom was this exercise conceived as an ongoing proposition; unless a major catastrophe occurred, the country's political rating was unlikely to be reassessed.

In one of the earliest surveys of corporate practice in this area, Stobaugh[53] reported a prevalence for the "go/no go" or "premium for risk" methods involving little quantification or sophistication. Root[47] also showed the lack of systematic approaches to risk assessment by U.S. multinationals, as did Marois[37] for French companies. Finally, Rummel and Heenan[48] confirmed the use of casual observation by trusted corporate officials as a preferred method of assessment. These idiosyncratic/impressionistic approaches suffer from excessive subjectivity that can be dangerous and misleading. Old stereotypes of foreign societies, rooted in either the corporate or individual mind, can play a vital and often distorting role in the decision-making process.

General/Broadly Based Models

Much formalization and modeling of macropolitical and macroeconomic risks has occurred in the last 15 years. The major international banks, spurred by dramatic increases in lending to less developed countries since 1974, were primarily concerned with what they called sovereign country risk, essentially the prospects for default or rescheduling of external debt by the borrowing nation. The specific nature of the risks involved allowed systematic analysis of macroeconomic data, although there was general recognition that some subjective or judgmental elements needed to be included as well. Van Agtmael[56] reported on early efforts in this direction in which, in addition to standard measures of debt-servicing capacity, foreign reserves, and the quality of the country's financial management, a complex political checklist was employed to introduce a systematic approach to an area where "qualitative judgment is unavoidable."[56] A more recent and extremely ambitious methodology, together with examples drawn from many banks' practices, can be found in Nagy.[40] He proposed a "structured qualitative approach to the quantification of country risk" that combines an assessment of the size of loss with the probability of occurrence for different types of borrowers over time in a discounted present value model. Krayenbuehl[34] suggested that the global assessment be divided into a political component (i.e., the will to honor external obligations) and a "transfer" risk, consisting of a solvency and a liquidity measure of the ability to pay. Finally, Mascarenhas and Sand,[38] in a comprehensive review of U.S. bank practices, identified four major organizational approaches to country risk assessment which varied in technical and structural sophistication and which produced significantly different results.

A second group of these general surveys consists of a number of "expert" assessments, typically obtained as the end product of a multistage consultation process that may or may not involve Delphi methods. Some of these reports might include econometric data as well, but their major characteristic is the progressive ranking of a large number of countries according to a more or less explicit logic of analysis. The BERI (Business Environment Risk Index) service is the oldest of these, and consists of a rating system that ranks countries on the basis of four subcategories highlighting political, operational, financial, and nationalistic factors. Judgments on 48 countries, made by a panel of experts located throughout the world, are processed and sent back for another iteration. BERI also produces detailed forecast reports for certain countries and a lending risk rating that evaluates a country's credit worthiness over the following five years.

Competing rating systems utilizing similar methodology have been developed by Frost & Sullivan (*World Political Risk Forecast*), Business International and Data Resources Inc. (*Policon*). Most of these are available to users on-line and, at least in the case of Policon, users may alter the weight of different variables or include their own judgmental information whenever it is considered superior to the model's. Two financially oriented rating systems worth noting are the *Institutional Investor's* Country Credit Rating and *Euromoney's* Country Risk Index covering 109 and 116 countries, respectively. The latest entry to the "expert" assessment rating field is by the Futures Group; their Political Stability Prospects reports combine observational data in formal models with expert-generated opinions to produce a stability index on a probabilistic distribution.

These and other similar techniques have the advantage of permitting rank ordering of different environments on a fairly comparative basis. They also allow, in some cases, for a significant degree of flexibility, since the weights associated with the various criteria can be modified to suit different circumstances. However, the rankings can be only as good as the judgments that go into their components, and several observers have noted the tendency to utilize "establishment" private sector experts who may not necessarily view events dispassionately. Furthermore, the ratings are static by definition; they represent a view of past events and conditions that may bear no relationship to the future. The most serious criticism in this sense is that as long as the relationship between socioeconomic factors and political risk remains implicit in the experts' minds, no evaluation of the rating's utility for a specific application can be made.

Two models developed in the 1970s are based on such explicit causal relationships and rely primarily on econometric and other objective data. Perhaps the best known of these is the Political System Stability Index first described by Haendel and colleagues[22] and later elaborated on.[21] Because it measures directly a series of discrete components of the political and social environment (e.g., number of riots, ethnolinguistic fragmentation, and legislative effectiveness, among others), the index is claimed to be free of judgmental inferences or distortions. One cannot escape, however, the model's implicit assumption that it accurately represents reality in both its structure and the choice of variables. Although tested historically (data were collected for 65 countries over the period 1960–1966), the issue of variability in the relevance of specific factors for all countries and over time remains largely unanswered. In this sense, a major innovation of the model was the addition of confidence estimates, which were assigned to the index scores for each component and each country. The second model, the Knudsen[22] "ecological" approach, is based on the notions first put forth by Gurr[20] that a high level of national frustration will exist whenever there is a gap between the aspirations of a people and their welfare, both dynamic concepts. If combined with a visible foreign-owned sector, such frustration may lead to intervention or expropriation, since foreign firms serve as useful scapegoats for failure of the existing political order to satisfy the economic and political yearnings of the people. Knudsen tested his model on data for 1968–1971 and developed a classification of Latin American countries according to their propensity to expropriate, which corresponds closely to later studies in the area (e.g., see the previous discussion in this chapter on Jodice's findings).

Regardless of the thoroughness of the model's specifications or the accuracy of its measures, all of these methods of estimating environmental risk share two unavoidable drawbacks. First, they are macro-risk oriented and largely ignore the need of the individual firm for custom-tailored measurement of project-specific risks. Although they are useful as a first-order indicator of the potential dangers threatening a given investment (a "red flag" function, as Kobrin called it), these broad measures of risk tend to overstate the threat to specific projects that may be immune to intervention under most circumstances, and they may fail to anticipate the partial losses that would result from a gradual tightening of operating freedom facing foreign firms in many developing and developed countries.

Second, these models are based on historical data that may be totally or partially irrelevant for future conditions. For example, recent high levels of political turmoil leading to a radical change in government may appear under the various quantitative indices as evidence of a high degree of political instability. While this may be undeniable for the immediate past, does it signify that instability will continue into the future? Or is the new government more likely to address the root causes of past instability and lead the nation to a new era of prosperity and tranquility? Obviously, no time series analysis can answer these questions adequately. Furthermore, to the extent that the data fed into the analysis are not entirely current, there will be a potentially significant gap between the last period for which data are available and current conditions. Given the rate of change of political and social phenomena in the less developed countries, and the difficulties and commensurate delays in generating reliable data in many of them, this is not a trivial problem.

In-House Models

The environmental turbulence that characterized most of the 1970s, culminating with the fall of the Iranian monarchy in 1979, gave extraordinary impetus to the development of in-house capabilities in political and economic assessment among the world's largest international corporations. A survey conducted on behalf of the U.S. Conference Board[3] confirmed the rise in corporate interest in political risk analysis during the decade. It concluded, however, that most of these efforts consisted of intuitive and unsystematic attempts to translate vague notions of the "quality of the investment climate" into recommendations for investment policy. Reliance on unstructured field visits and studies made by "old hands" and outside "experts" (usually meaning ex-secret service or foreign office operatives) was commonly reported. While some of these studies could be extremely thorough, there was typically little specification of the implied relationships, and each analyst was free to draw his or her own conclusions as to which factors were most important, how they were likely to evolve in the future, and what consequences this could imply for the firm or the particular project.

A good example of an extensive corporate model is the ESP (for economic, social, and political) system developed by Dow Chemical for its Latin American operations.[39] Following considerable background research into the country's current economic and political situation, a team is formed of members drawn from the highest management levels of the local affiliate, the regional headquarters, and the corporate political affairs staff. This team then carries out extensive interviews in the country in question with the aid of an instrument that has been developed specifically to meet the requirements of that country and of the local investment in it. The results are used to develop four scenarios covering key economic, social, and political events having potential impact on the development of the local business. Probabilities are assigned independently to each of the four scenarios (labeled, respectively, "realistic," "optimistic," "pessimistic," and "crisis"), they are reviewed in a Delphi process, and a summary of the conclusions is prepared for top management. Dow's approach has the advantages that it is specifically tailored to the company's needs and that it involves line and senior corporate officials in the assessment, thus assuring that the results will be taken relatively seriously. It does not deal, however, with the need for clear specification of causality, relying instead on the experience of the leaders of the team to interpret events correctly and consistently. It also implies high costs and, particularly, high time commitments, thus limiting its applicability to a few countries per year at best.

Other companies have made use of scenario methodologies in an attempt to deal with sociopolitical projections. Most of these experiences do not deal specifically with foreign political risks, but intend instead to cover a broad spectrum of phenomena affecting the firm, its technologies, and its markets.* The cost and complexity of this technique would appear to limit its

---

* For a review of the use of scenario techniques in corporate planning, see Raubitschek.[43] Wack[59] offered a detailed description of the same methodology as applied at Shell Oil International during the 1970s.

application except in cases of very large investments such as oil and mineral extraction.

A related methodology, much cited in the literature, is that developed by Shell Oil to assess the probability that contracts for the exploration, development, and production of oil in a certain country will be maintained on an equitable basis for a period of up to 10 years. As described by Bunn and Mustafaoglu[5] and by Gebelein and colleagues,[15] the Shell approach and its subsequent variants (e.g., the models developed by Risk Insights, Inc., of New York) include a formal specification of the relationships involved, expert opinions constrained in a fashion designed to limit judgment errors, and a sophisticated statistical algorithm to combine the results of both aggregate econometric data and individual assessments. As Kobrin[32] viewed it, this was one of ''the most sophisticated and effective approaches to political risk assessment'' that existed at that time. Its major limitation is again cost. To apply the methodology to a large number of countries, or for that matter to a number of industries with different characteristics and risk profiles, would be extremely costly and cumbersome.

Summary

The multitude of studies and models described in this section are indicative of the complexity and multidimensionality implied in measurement of political risks specific to the foreign activities of individual firms across many countries. The various analyses of the expropriation experience of foreign investors have yielded significant evidence of the importance of considerations rooted in both the national environment (cultural, political, social, and economic) and in industry, firm, and project (structural) characteristics. The latter have been confirmed by more recent studies on the determinants of bargaining power. The general thrust of practice in the field, however, tends to be polarized between those models and techniques aimed at measuring macropolitical risks on a comparative basis for a large number of subject countries, and those that are specific to a firm's needs but limited in their geographic scope. Chart 22-3 illustrates this dichotomy. The search for the ideal approach obviously leads to the bottom right-hand corner of the chart, and this area is where considerable efforts have been spent recently.

Macro models must play an important role in this search. While it is true that political stability is no guarantee of the absence of potential exposure to loss, nor is instability necessarily associated with the probability of loss, the fact remains that 75% of all instances of expropriation have been linked to regime changes. The preferred approach must therefore have the capability of measuring macro risks and the ability to interpret them in terms of project-specific considerations.

Methodologically, all existing models have certain strengths and limitations. Expert-based systems can be criticized for not always making causal relationships explicit and for their potential bias in the judgments of the experts. Econometric models often suffer from the difficulty of securing current sources of data for many of the important independent variables necessary for the analysis. In-house methods can be expensive, time consuming, and of limited geographic coverage.

It follows that what is needed is an eclectic approach that combines the best each method has to offer and includes both macro and micro judgments on the risks faced by specific foreign affiliates. The next section outlines the elements that should be included in such an approach. It incorporates the lessons derived from the model-building efforts of the last 15 years and the broad experience of a major underwriter of political risk insurance in assessing the potential for loss in hundreds of projects from many firms and industries throughout the world.

MODELING POLITICAL RISKS

Since risk is both a country- and a project-dependent concept, any model designed to forecast the probability of loss must encompass both elements. It should also not be limited to assessing the likelihood of expropriation, that is, the compulsory takeover of foreign assets by the host government without the "prompt, adequate, and effective" compensation called for by international law, but should include other contingencies that can result from changes in national policy. A firm operating in a given country needs to go beyond an assessment of the probability of expropriation; it must be prepared to deal with whatever change in political conditions may be forthcoming. It is this ability to predict an emerging situation before it is fully manifested, in order to circumvent the crisis, that is essential for survival and prosperity in many foreign operations.

Chart 22-4 summarizes the structure of the recommended framework for analysis. Its logic is rather simple and straightforward; its implementation is another matter. It begins by examining a series of national characteristics— economic, social, and political forces at work—that may or may not be critical to the issue of political stability. Whether such is the case will depend on the importance of the particular factor, on its relationship to others, and on the magnitude of any changes or discontinuities involved. Furthermore, the source of trouble could be internal (e.g., political repression) or external (e.g., a drastic fall in commodity export prices). It is important to note, however, that these forces may, when activated, have dramatically different impacts depending, to a large extent, on the maturity and absorptive capacity of national institutions. A country in which political parties, the press, the educational establishment, the financial system, and so on have achieved high levels of development should be able to withstand greater shocks, so that shock does not easily precipitate drastic change in the social fabric or in the institutions themselves. The institutional framework, therefore, acts as a filter and softens the impact of environmental forces on events. An accurate

CHART 22-4. A Conceptual Model for Project-Specific Political Risk Analysis

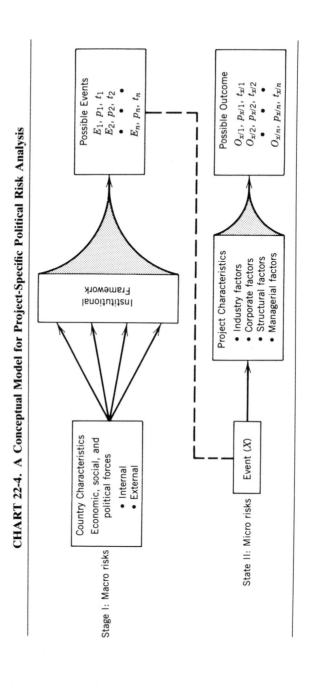

Stage I: Macro risks

Country Characteristics
Economic, social, and political forces
- Internal
- External

Institutional Framework

Possible Events
E_1, p_1, t_1
E_2, p_2, t_2
$\bullet$
$\bullet$
$\bullet$
E_n, p_n, t_n

State II: Micro risks

Event (X)

Project Characteristics
- Industry factors
- Corporate factors
- Structural factors
- Managerial factors

Possible Outcome
$O_{x/1}, p_{x/1}, t_{x/1}$
$O_{x/2}, p_{x/2}, t_{x/2}$
$\bullet$
$\bullet$
$\bullet$
$O_{x/n}, p_{x/n}, t_{x/n}$

judgment on the qualities of this filter is then as necessary to good political risk forecasting as an understanding of the underlying forces themselves. In the end, any number of political events can be the result of these conditions, each with its own probability distribution and probable timetable.

Stage I of political risk forecasting consists, therefore, of an assessment of the forces at work in the nation and without, the institutions tempering the effectiveness of these forces, and the likely events that they may precipitate. This is the realm of "country" risk analysis. Much of it is amenable to econometric modeling and to the use of expert methods similar to those described earlier. In the corresponding section that follows we shall illustrate the variables that ought to be included in this analysis. The output should establish some basic measures of reference comparable across countries, it should identify current trends and any potential breaks in them, and it should delimit the areas of concern that may harbor the seeds of potential threats to foreign investors.

Not all events, however, will have similar consequences for different projects. As established in the preceding review, industry and corporate factors as well as a number of characteristics of the structure of the investment will play a determinant role in the likelihood and probable extent of any potential losses. Thus, for each project or affiliate, every possible event can be seen as having a set of outcomes or consequences that are unique to it. These alternative outcomes have themselves a certain probability distribution and time horizon. Stage II of political risk forecasting consists of bringing into sharper relief the features of the project that either increase or diminish the possible negative consequences of each event. In this sense it is akin to estimating the conditional probabilities of various contingencies given a number of possible events. Since these events may or may not be mutually exclusive, final estimates of the likelihood of loss can be arrived at by the proper mathematical manipulation of the probability estimates.

What follows is not a specification of such a comprehensive model, since obviously that would require considerably more space than is available here and an intimate knowledge of the circumstances applicable to a specific investment project. Instead, we present a brief description of all the elements we believe must be included in the analysis. Chart 22-5 summarizes our approach. The country-associated risk analysis involves a total of 22 variables or composite factors that must be monitored on an ongoing basis, yielding estimates of possible events, their probability of occurrence, and the expected timetable. The project-associated risk examines an additional 16 variables that are likely to have a major impact on the consequences of political change on a foreign affiliate.

Country-Associated Risk

Two arbitrary but useful distinctions are made between economic and sociopolitical factors on the one hand and internal and external sources of risk on

CHART 22-5. Major Variables (Factors) for Assessing Project Specific Political Risk

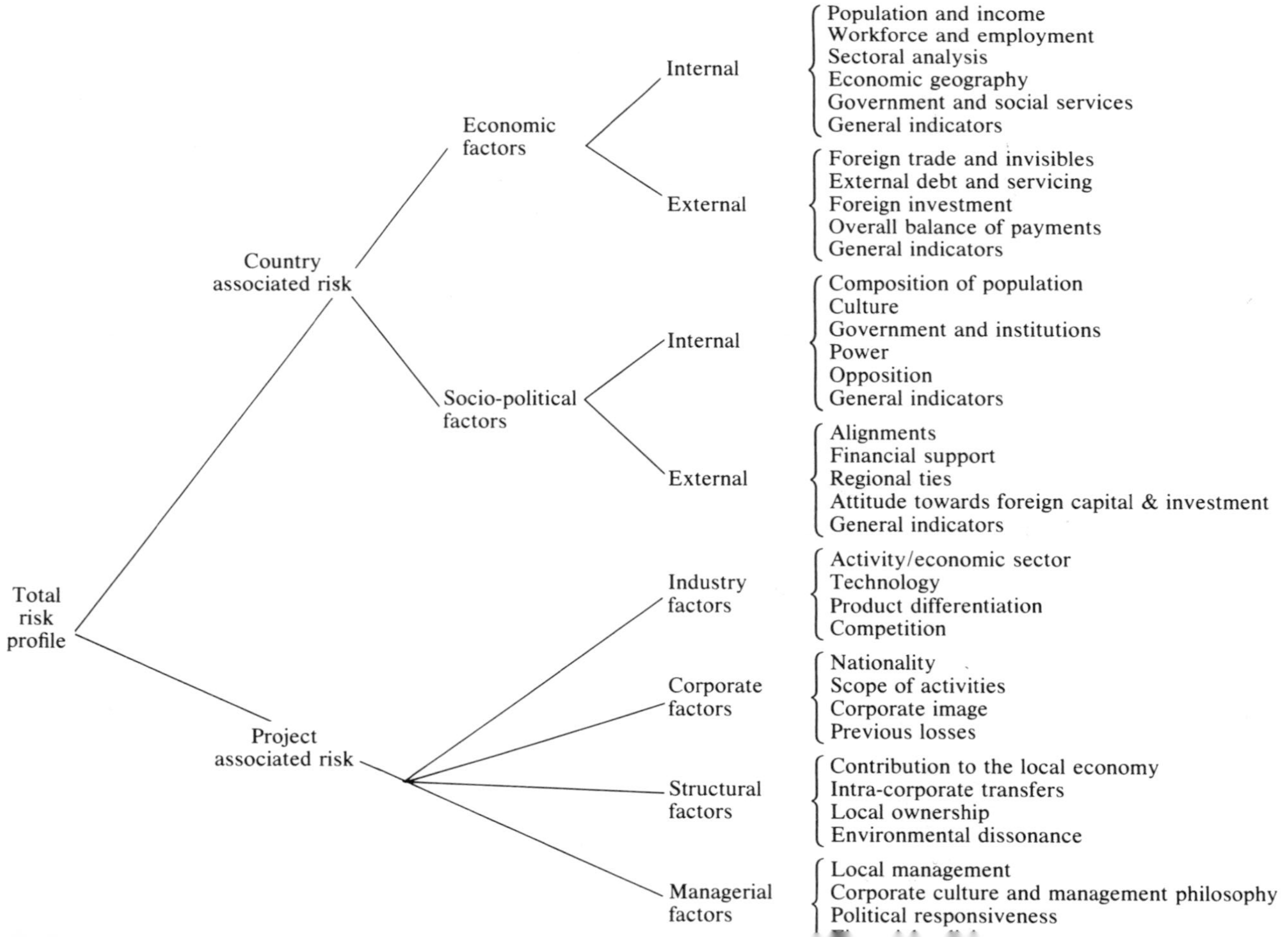

Total risk profile

Country associated risk

- Economic factors
  - Internal
    - Population and income
    - Workforce and employment
    - Sectoral analysis
    - Economic geography
    - Government and social services
    - General indicators
  - External
    - Foreign trade and invisibles
    - External debt and servicing
    - Foreign investment
    - Overall balance of payments
    - General indicators
- Socio-political factors
  - Internal
    - Composition of population
    - Culture
    - Government and institutions
    - Power
    - Opposition
    - General indicators
  - External
    - Alignments
    - Financial support
    - Regional ties
    - Attitude towards foreign capital & investment
    - General indicators

Project associated risk

- Industry factors
  - Activity/economic sector
  - Technology
  - Product differentiation
  - Competition
- Corporate factors
  - Nationality
  - Scope of activities
  - Corporate image
  - Previous losses
- Structural factors
  - Contribution to the local economy
  - Intra-corporate transfers
  - Local ownership
  - Environmental dissonance
- Managerial factors
  - Local management
  - Corporate culture and management philosophy
  - Political responsiveness

394

the other. The division is arbitrary because developments in all four areas have interactive effects on the other variables under scrutiny. It is important for the analyst to be sensitized to this web of hidden relationships and to not follow the simple structure blindly. Also, it should be noted that many external influences, particularly in the economic sphere, can be systemic to the whole world. It is in such cases that the institutional elements of the analysis can serve to distinguish among countries in terms of expected impacts. In the discussion that follows, the institutional issues are covered in various categories, both explicitly and implicitly.

Economic Factors: Internal

One must understand the basic components of the host nation's economy, its rate of development, and its vulnerability in order to anticipate factors that can affect the general business environment. A critical point is the state of the country's agricultural sector against a background of the rate of urbanization and the level of unemployment and underemployment. We may wish to carry out this analysis under six separate headings.

1. *Population and Income.* Historical trends in the size of the country's population, its economic growth, and its per capita income provide a first approximation of national welfare. When viewed against the recent past, public pronouncements about expected growth rates indicate the potential disparity between the countries aspirations and its capacity to provide for its future. Efforts at controlling population growth are worth observing. In contrast to governments of many nations in Africa and Latin America, the Chinese government, aware of the need to reduce this gap between expectations and its capacity to deliver on them, has instituted severe sanctions for families with more than one child. Similar programs in India and Mexico have met with considerably less success. Income distribution figures over time provide useful clues to potential trouble. In Mexico, for example, the percentage of national income going to the poorest 70% of the population has declined steadily since the late 1940s, when it oscillated around 34%, to less than 27% in recent years. The implications for social discontent are evident, even in a high-growth economy, which was the case in Mexico through the late 1970s. But when growth slows or turns negative, as it did in Mexico after 1982, the consequences can be worrisome. Nonetheless, one has to relate perceived inequalities in income distribution to cultural attitudes toward wealth. In Hong Kong, where income distribution is extremely uneven, the wealthy are admired by lower and middle class Chinese and inspire emulation.

2. *Work Force and Employment.* Analysis of the size and composition of the country's work force, its sectoral and geographic distribution, and its productivity aids understanding of the nature of the human resource pool and its deployment. Disturbing trends in real productivity, migration, or urban unemployment, for example, should be carefully noted. Social instability and political risk in developing countries can easily result from the polarization of the population into urban and rural camps with different problems and priorities. Two significant series are the rate of economic growth necessary to absorb population increases, particularly in depressed areas, and the tendency by foreign companies to capture scarce managerial talent so critical for development.

3. *Sectoral Analysis.* The stage of development of the host country's economy will guide this section of the analysis. In the less developed countries one should address issues such as:

- What is the strength and diversity of the agricultural sector, and is the country self-sufficient in foodstuffs?
- How significant is the industrial sector—can it respond to the need to generate jobs and foreign exchange?
- What are considered strategic sectors, and who controls them?
- How large is the public sector, and how efficient?

The emphasis among more industrialized countries may shift to

- How competitive is the industrial sector, in costs and technology; are lame-duck industries artificially kept alive?
- How rapid is the shift to services, and what is its impact on employment?
- What are the strategic sectors, and how is government control over them exercised?
- Is there a discernible trend toward greater government involvement in the economy, and with what results?

4. *Economic Geography.* Natural resources provide opportunities for growth and capital accumulation that can be a significant force for stability. Yet when controlled by foreign enterprises, subject to wide price fluctuations, vulnerable to natural disasters, or the source of national complacency and waste, natural wealth can be a major source of danger. In general, the more dependent the economy on a single source of wealth, the less stable it is, as recent history amply corroborates.

5. *Government and Social Services.* The sources and structure of government revenues and the sectoral and geographic pattern of expenditures are critical items. Are basic needs (e.g., health services, education, economic infrastructure, defense, etc.) adequately covered? Is the budget in deficit, and if so, how is it financed? The rigidity of government programs to economic conditions is also a fundamental question. If revenues are highly volatile while expenditures consist of inflexible social programs (e.g., food subsidies in many African countries, defense expenditures in South Korea and El Salvador), any disturbance to the revenue stream could have severe political consequences. Finally, the dependence of regional agencies on central revenue sources can be a constant bone of contention in countries where demands for regional autonomy are strong.

6. *General Indicators.* Time series on price indices, wage rates, interest rate levels, money supply, and so on should be monitored for any major breaks or discontinuities.

At this stage of the process, the analyst should have a reasonable picture of which economic variables are critical for continuity in the country's current economic development strategy, the vulnerability of the strategy to failure in any of these critical links, the likelihood of such failures, and as a result, the probability that performance will fall short of expectations. The objective is not economic analysis per se, but a search for what one might call the potential for trouble. If "what is likely to go wrong. . . " follow Murphy's perverse dictum, it is the political consequences that interest us, as these are ultimately the ones that may affect the safety and profitability of the investment.

Economic Factors: External

To complete our understanding of the nation's economic conditions, we turn to its external payments position. What are its international obligations, the extent of its foreign indebtedness and servicing requirements, its level of diversification of export earnings, its exposure to commodity price fluctuations, the rigidity of its import requirements, and so on? Five headings would be helpful in organizing the analysis of these issues.

1. *Foreign Trade and Invisibles.* In addition to examining the evolution of the country's current account balance and its composition, it is important to assess the relative income and price elasticity of both imports and exports. To the extent that imports consist of essential items (e.g., food, raw materials, energy), the degree to which the country can compress imports in times of crisis is limited. The last decade has shown how vulnerable most countries are to sudden price changes in certain commodities, both as they increase (the 1970s for the oil importers) and decrease (the mid-1980s for the oil exporters). Time series of the nation's terms of trade are most useful for tracking these changes in external purchasing power. Finally, the relative importance of trading partners may change as an indication of evolving competitive conditions, or trade in invisibles (tourism, services, etc.) may increase in importance, each of which has critical implications for the stability of export earnings over time.

2. *External Debt and Servicing.* The following three series of data should be first considered:

- The level of outstanding foreign debt, public and private, in absolute terms and relative to GNP and export earnings
- Its maturity profile
- The level of debt service (including dividend payments on foreign investments) relative to national income and exports

If difficulties in servicing foreign obligations are expected, the impact on the transfer risk and import controls must be assessed, just as effects on the domestic economy and political pressures are likely to emerge in parallel. One needs only to recall the recent experience of Argentina, Mexico, and Peru, to name a few, to dramatize the importance of this analysis.

3. *Foreign Investment.* Countries that often shun external indebtedness as a solution to their exchange difficulties turn instead to foreign investment on the twin assumptions that more real income is thereby generated to pay future claims and that dividend payments are cyclical and not likely to fall due in hard times. This, history has taught us, is not always the case. The size and importance of the foreign sector, its distribution by branches of economic activity, its diversification by country of origin, and so on are all critical elements in the analysis. They affect the probability that when all else fails, a nationalistic government will point to the spectre of foreign ownership as the root of all evil. Not that expropriation need be wholesale, but that the probability of any intervention is a function of the salience of the foreign-controlled sector and, as such, needs to be monitored.

4. *Overall Balance of Payments.* A general review of the overall payments position should complete this analysis. Emphasis should be placed on the capital account and on the level and changes in the country's reserves, that is, the country's liquidity situation. Lack of confidence in the government in power can manifest itself in various ways, such as a drop in remittances by foreign workers (Portugal after 1974) or in sudden moves of short-term capital flows and "errors and omissions."

5. *General Indicators.* The official and unofficial exchange rates, their movements over time (particularly relative to inflation differentials), and the spread and terms that national borrowers can obtain in international capital markets are all further clues as to how solid is the country's external position.

This set of questions serves to determine to what extent external constraints will dictate domestic economic policy. A high degree of dependence and instability, together with external debt servicing difficulties, will substantially increase the risk of host government interference with foreign investors in the country, both in terms of expropriation and convertibility. Shortly after the revolution in Mozambique, the government, faced with severe external payment difficulties, nationalized those enterprises that consumed significant amounts of foreign exchange. Likewise in Nicaragua, the grave shortage of foreign exchange after Somoza's ouster prompted the new government to take control of the main sources of foreign earnings. And the frequent use of "temporary" suspensions of dividend convertibility during difficult times in countries like Brazil underscore the need for such analysis.

Sociopolitical Factors: Internal

To understand the political situation of the host country and its potential for inspiring change, one needs to begin with the cohesiveness of the social structure, the disparity between people's beliefs and aspirations on the one hand and the quality of leadership on the other, the relative power of government and opposition groups, and the strength and traditions of national institutions. Again, six major headings will guide the analysis.

1. *Composition of Population.* The homogeneity of the local population in terms of ethnolinguistic groups, religious persuasion, or tribal and class components needs to be examined as a guide to the cohesiveness of the social structure. The political and social status of these different groups, their participation in key governing institutions, their political activism, and the distribution of wealth and power among them are key components of the analysis. Recent examples of countries plagued by these differences abound. Belgium with its struggle between Flemish and Walloons and North Ireland with its religious wars are sources of instability in their regions. Equally, in many Arab countries minority sects (e.g., the Wahabites in Saudi Arabia and the Alawites in Syria) hold the reins of power against a background of religious fundamentalism stimulated by the Iranian revolution, ethnic separatism, and the presence of large numbers of foreign workers. The Tamil uprisings in Sri Lanka have been a cause of major concern in recent months, while in the Far East resentment of Chinese minorities has already brought about reactions such as Malaysia's program for increasing the share of economic activity in Malay hands.

2. *Culture.* An analysis of the underlying cultural values and beliefs of the host society may also hold the key to an understanding, not so much of the potential for instability, although this may be the case, but of the likelihood that foreign influences (e.g., the local affiliates of multinational corporations) will be the first to suffer the consequences of any potential disruption to the established regime. The concept of cultural risk is familiar to investors in tourism projects in many developing countries. The picture of half-naked wealthy foreigners being served hand and foot in the midst of abject poverty is one that has given rise to considerable resentment and opposition, particularly in countries with strict religious and moral values. Similarly, foreign-induced industrialization has led to the loss of traditional norms and values in many primitive areas of the world and may result in a level of cultural alienation that will heighten conflict and identify the foreign enterprise (and not the process of modernization) as the source of evil. The experience of Iran throughout the late years of the Shah's regime is a good example of this process.

3. *Government and Institutions.* Understanding of how the country's system of government and its sociopolitical institutions work, or are meant to work, is a crucial point in the analysis. There is a formal aspect to this which consists of establishing the principal characteristics of the constitutional order; the relative functions of the head of state, the government (prime minister, cabinet officers, agency directors, and other appointed officials), the legislative bodies, and the legal system; and the nature and structure of bodies such as the law enforcement agencies, the armed forces, and the political parties and similar organizations. For example, constitutional issues were paramount in the recent passage from military to civilian rule in Brazil, as the matter of direct election of the President and the right of the incumbent to appoint state governors were in direct conflict. Finally, the resilience of national institutions, the role and stability of the civil service, the capacity of political parties to incorporate vastly different interest groups under a common banner (as the PRI had done in Mexico for many generations), the ability of the press or the educational establishment to serve as legitimate outlets for venting pressure, and so on, are critical to the analysis, for they will help in assessment of the severity of any reaction to domestic or foreign forces calling for change.

4. *Power.* The effective structure of power, and not only the formal trappings of government and institutions, will determine the question of political risk. Who are the key decision makers, what are their background and education, what are their attitudes to critical issues and their relationship to each other; what are the role and power of the internal security apparatus; who are the main beneficiaries of the status quo; and what is the influence of pressure groups such as the trade associations, labor unions, army, and media, are all part of the agenda. This is a particularly critical and difficult area of analysis, since almost by definition the data are obscure or concealed. More than any other in the process, this analysis calls for careful judgment and a great deal of skill in inferring from external observations (or interviews whenever possible) the real intentions of the players. No wonder, for example, that many heads of large multinational companies have been rushing to talk at length with representatives of the outlawed African National Congress concerning their intentions for South Africa should they come to exercise or share power.

5. *Opposition.* The basic problem in assessing the strength of opposition groups, their sources of support, and their effectiveness is again access to reliable and balanced information. Official sources must be treated with great skepticism. Authoritarian regimes in particular have a major stake in concealing the truth about instances of rebellious actions. The reaction of the Saudi Arabian government to the Great Mosque incident is typical of this tendency to obfuscate potentially serious evidence of internal dissention and present it to the outside world as an isolated minor incident involving a few religious fanatics. Equally, it would have been difficult to gauge the extent of opposition to the Marcos regime in the Philippines had it not been for the interest of the world's media.

6. *General Indicators.* In addition to the preceding items, data to be monitored include the level and frequency of strikes, riots, or terrorist acts; the number and treatment of political prisoners; and the extent of official corruption.

It should be evident that most of the information sought under these various headings is highly judgmental and difficult to evaluate objectively. Sources intimately familiar with local conditions are essential to the analysis. Therefore, it is advisable that external expert opinion be obtained and that these views be cross-examined by on-the-field assessments carried out to a large extent by the firm's own local staff.

Sociopolitical Factors: External

Political instability is often externally induced. At best, external influences can exacerbate internal conditions by playing on the fears or frustrations of the local population or by lending moral, financial, or ideological support to opposition groups. We now turn our attention to five such problem sources.

1. *Alignments.* The first feature to establish is the country's international alignment, its principal political allies, its public positions on key global issues (e.g., apartheid, the Middle East, etc.), and its mutual dependencies. In this context, an examination of the country's voting record in the United Nations may be useful. Historically, one should examine how treaties of friendship have been established and what is the scope of the country's sovereign freedom (e.g., the case of Afghanistan and the Soviet Union). Recent events in Poland suggest that the aspirations of the people may not always be in line with the country's external alignment. The discrepancy may result in manifest expressions of dissatisfaction and internal unrest.

2. *Financial Support.* This includes both direct sources of economic support, such as the provision of financial aid, food, and military assistance, and instances of de facto support by virtue of important economic and trade linkages. Many of the U.S. programs in Israel, El Salvador, and Saudi Arabia, among others, are clear examples of the first kind. The position of France in Africa is also noteworthy: By virtue of the CFA (Communauté

Française Africaine) franc system, the French government and treasury exercise considerable de facto influence over many states in the region, while also being engaged in direct military assistance programs such as in Chad and the Central African Republic. More complex, but not less critical, are the myriad of relationships that characterize Saudi Arabia's influence over many of its Arab neighbors. Recent events in the Iraq–Iran and Lebanese conflicts illustrate the latter.

3. *Regional Ties.* Irrespective of the country's global alignment, its relations with its immediate neighbors is often of paramount importance to its political stability. Border disputes, external military threats, the spillover effect of nearby revolutionary activities, and so on can have a profound impact on domestic tranquility and on government priorities. The activities of Qaddafi with respect to his neighbors in Egypt, Tunisia, and Chad; his support of guerrilla activities in Western Sahara, the Gambia, Senegal, and the Central African Republic; plus his backing of terrorist movements in many other Mediterranean countries is certainly one of the most extreme cases of regional destabilization in recent history. Central America, where Nicaragua (with Cuban support) exercises a major influence on events in El Salvador and Costa Rica, while the United States encourages Honduras to serve as haven for the American-backed "contra" forces attacking Nicaragua, is a case in point for careful evaluation of regional domino effects. The current situation in southern Africa is also illustrative of the importance of regional ties. Countries like Lesotho, Mozambique, and Swaziland have to temper their inclination to support the struggle for black power in South Africa with the realities of their economic dependence on Pretoria. Finally, regional proximity and conflict may result in a flow of refugees, political or otherwise, that can tax the financial capability of the host nation or result in civil unrest, riots, or increased delinquency, as has been the case in Thailand, Sudan, and even southern Florida.

4. *Attitude Toward Foreign Capital and Investment.* More and more countries are codifying their attitudes and expectations with respect to foreign investment. Simultaneously, one can observe a general trend toward more liberal foreign investment policies among developing countries in the first half of the 1980s, often achieved by a generous interpretation of such codes as might exist. In 1974, Zaire nationalized a number of enterprises, some of which were "protected" by its investment code; a decade later the Mexican government approved a series of foreign investment proposals that would have been unthinkable a few years earlier. National codes of investment, therefore, serve only as guide to the scope for legal protection normally afforded foreigners in the country, and must be supplemented by other information on recent practice. Fortunately, many of the rating services (e.g., Business International's Investment, Licensing and Trading Conditions Abroad) maintain up-to-date records on foreign investment flows and decisions by local authorities, and local chambers of commerce or similar groups conduct regular polls on local attitudes toward foreign investors, both of which can be very valuable in assessing trends in this area. The record of local courts in dealing with conflicts involving foreign subsidiaries, particularly questions of compensation for expropriated assets, can also contribute to this aspect of the analysis.

5. *General Indicators.* Other indicators that should be monitored might include human rights' records as published by international organizations such as Amnesty International, the existence of formal and active opposition groups in exile, signs of diplomatic stress between host and home country, and terrorist acts committed in other countries against citizens or assets of the host nation.

As with the preceding section, the knowledge and data sources required to complete this part of the analysis are highly specialized. A similar conclusion is thus warranted as to the utility of seeking expert advice supplemented by the views of those in the field.

Project-Associated Risks

Having specified the range of variables related to the level of risk associated with the country, we now turn our attention to those characteristics of the project or the foreign subsidiary that can alter significantly the potential for loss faced by the parent company. Four major categories facilitate the analysis. As noted in the literature review and as we have gleaned from practice, industry and corporate characteristics have a major influence on the level of risk. Both of these sets of factors are generally exogenously determined and can be altered only over long periods of time, if at all. Structural and managerial factors, however, are subject to management action and can be tailored to meet local circumstances in such a way that the risk/return tradeoff is optimized for the foreign investor. It is in the context of these two sets of variables that the concept of managing political risks takes a realistic meaning.

Industry Factors

It has been obvious from the early days of political risk analysis that different economic sectors experience different propensity to expropriation and government intervention in general. Four industry characteristics seem to be closely associated with this:

1. *Activity/Economic Sector.* The historical evidence is that foreign companies involved in primary activities (extractive or agricultural) and public infrastructure (transportation or utilities) have been relatively more exposed to political risks, subject to regional variations. There is a widely shared conviction among third world countries that natural resource endowments should be exploited for the national welfare rather than for private or foreign profit. More recently, financial institutions have been subject to increasing rates of interference as issues of capital flow have gained in importance. Brazil provides a good example of the shift in national priorities from primary to high-technology sectors among the more advanced developing countries. Foreign investors in the electronics, information, and telecommunication industries have been progressively squeezed out of many activities and forced to license their technology to local firms or abandon the Brazilian market altogether. The level of foreign capital, the size of the enterprise, and its relative monopoly power may also contribute to make it a more attractive target for intervention. There are occasions when the foreign investor is the only agent capable of deploying the technology or capital resources required for a given project. However, it is usually only a matter of time before the government (or its successor) begins to question the value of the foreign monopoly. Thus it seems that while sectoral factors remain important, there will be critical variations in risk profiles based on the level of development and local priorities of the country as these relate to the political and economic salience of the project.

2. *Technology.* The conventional wisdom, as well as the evidence just cited, point to the relative immunity of high-technology projects from political interference. The higher the R&D intensity or the technological complexity of the business, the less likely that it will be expropriated and the higher the relative bargaining power of the foreign investor. Similarly, the more rapid the rate of change of the technology, the greater the protection enjoyed by the foreign subsidiary from arbitrary discrimination. The reasons are obvious: Not only are local firms unable to assume the role of the foreign multinational in such cases, but also if they were to attempt it they risk falling rapidly behind a constantly changing technological frontier. This argument is considerably less valid among the most advanced developing countries and in the industrial world. The experience of the information technology industries in some European countries, Brazil, and Korea are indicative of the need to moderate the value of technological superiority on the basis of local conditions.

3. *Product Differentiation.* Highly differentiated goods require specialized inputs for their sale or service, which are often exclusively provided by multinational corporations. The capacity of local firms to assume these functions is less in the case of differentiated products than for commodity goods. Therefore, ceteris paribus, producers of specialized, highly advertised, or otherwise differentiated goods will be less subject to government intervention, because they are more capable of exercising their bargaining power.

4. *Competition.* The bargaining power model would also support the proposition that as the level of competition (and therefore alternative sources of capital and technology) increases, the foreign firm is more exposed to political intervention. The evidence cited earlier seems to confirm this view, notwithstanding the fact that monopoly power will also attract opposition and, subsequently, higher risk. Thus, one emerges with a U-shaped configuration of the risk profile, largest whenever competition is either nonexistent or very active.

Corporate Factors

A number of characteristics of the investor are in themselves associated with the level of risk, and can be represented by the four factors that follow.

1. *Nationality.* The nationality of the foreign investor is relevant to the risk factor inasmuch as it is subject to the quality of the relations that the host country has or has had with the investor's home country. Difficulties can arise from the vestiges of a colonial relationship or from previous support for an earlier government. The memories of its bitter struggle for independence still complicate Algeria's dealings with France, and the question of compensation for nationalized French interests has never been properly settled. The Nigerian nationalization of British oil interests in 1979 had more to do with the two countries' position on the Rhodesian issue than with the sector or companies involved. U.S. corporations in Latin American tend to be exposed to relatively higher risks than their European counterparts since they have inherited, undeservedly for the most part, an historical role as symbols of support for repressive military regimes. British companies in Argentina underwent a rough period during and following the Falklands war.

2. *Scope of Activities.* The nature of the company's activities and the geographic location of its affiliates may have a material influence on the level of risk. The Arab countries' boycott of firms doing business with Israel, China's attempt to boycott Japanese companies engaged in trade and investment in Taiwan, and the current exposure to risk of companies with operations in South Africa are examples of this. Similarly, diversified corporations with sensitive activities in defense sectors may find as a result that the level of risk for their nondefense investments in other countries increases.

3. *Corporate Image.* Corrupt payments scandals or a history of involvement in the financing of political subversion have left lasting scars on certain U.S. corporations, which are still viewed by local governments and opposition groups with mistrust. ITT's activities in Chile and United Fruit's actions in Central America are notorious in this sense. The disaster at Union Carbide's Bhopal, India, subsidiary has deeply affected the company's image. Plans to open a new industrial ceramics plant in Allgau, West Germany, were canceled after the local villagers rejected the proposed investment and the resulting jobs. On the other hand, stated corporate policies on disclosure and joint ventures, for example, can contribute to a better world climate for the company's investments.

4. *Previous Losses.* Careful scrutiny of circumstances that have led to politically motivated losses is essential. Not only can predictable patterns be derived from such analysis, but the relative bargaining strength of the company may be assessed from those instances in which it avoided losses while most other firms did not. The classic example is how Gulf Oil managed to survive the transition from Portuguese colonial rule, through bitter civil war, to Marxist revolution and triumph in Angola, and emerge in a privileged position.

Structural Factors

Irrespective of the quality of its industrial and corporate characteristics, how the project or investment is structured will have a major impact on its risk profile. Again, four aspects of the structure should be analyzed.

1. *Contribution to the Local Economy.* It is essential to attempt to quantify the perceived net benefits to the local economy resulting from the foreign firm's participation. Generally, transfers of foreign capital, employment creation, the generation of income and tax revenues, reinvested earnings, savings of foreign exchange due to import substitution effects, technology transfer, and the development of local suppliers and export sales are viewed positively. These may be partially offset by costs such as dividend and capital repatriation, the payment of license and management fees and royalties, transfer pricing losses, additional imports, and the potential elimination of local competitors. It should be noted that the view the local authorities will have on the relative merit of these costs and benefits will differ from the firm's, and that it is the former that counts.* While more acute in the case of investments in developing countries, the same reasoning applies in sensitive sectors between industrial nations. Witness, for example, the West German government's unenthusiastic reaction to repeated attempts by the French Thomson-Brandt group to rationalize the consumer electronics industry in Europe by acquiring such German companies as Saba, Nordmende, Grundig, and Telefunken. Lastly, one needs to examine any special agreements concluded between the investor and the host country to ascertain whether these agreements increase the risk. To its consternation, the investor may find that contracts are not morally or legally binding if the situation has changed, and that the contracts may be modified by unilateral acts. As the foreign firm's bargaining power deteriorates with time, initial attractive investment concessions by the host government may be subject to renegotiation or withdrawal once capital and other commitments have been made. Only by assuring that social and economic benefits accrue to the host nation over the life of the project, and that these benefits are evident to all major

---

* Wells[60] summarized the arguments for a rigorous analysis of social costs and benefits on the part of multinational corporations.

political forces in government or opposition, can the foreign investor have a major impact on how it is perceived and therefore on the likelihood that changes in economic or political factors will result in a lower probability of intervention.

2. *Intracorporate Transfers.* The more closely the affiliate or project is tied to the global network of the parent company, the lower the risk of expropriation or interference. If the local operation is managed as one more cog in the multinational's global wheel, with large intracorporate transfers of products, intermediate goods, technology, and management, little purpose is served in taking it over; one inherits an empty shell. On the other hand, a self-sufficient, local-for-local type of operation is considerably more exposed to local pressures for divestiture, regulation, and eventually, nationalization. Chrysler managed to salvage its Peruvian assembly operation in the face of widespread industry nationalization by keeping a stranglehold on the supply of key auto and truck components from plants in Brazil, Argentina, and the United States while simultaneously threatening the loss of export revenues in the event of nationalization. IBM's recent experience in Mexico shows the willingness of the government to make significant concessions (e.g., 100% ownership, reduced local content requirements, etc.) for a globally integrated subsidiary, while long-established foreign producers of micro-computers (Hewlett-Packard and Apple), which operated strictly local-for-local subsidiaries, had to face more stringent performance requirements.

3. *Local Ownership.* The degree of local ownership in the foreign subsidiary is both the result of the bargaining process and a major influence on the risk. In local-for-local operations, the presence of domestic partners is almost an immutable requirement. Otherwise, if at all permitted, chances are that the affiliate will be under considerable pressure for local integration in the medium term. Not all partners, however, are equally safe. Government agencies and members of the ruling classes may be in fact more dangerous than no local partners at all, as recent experiences in Nicaragua have amply demonstrated. Joint ventures in fields in which technological superiority or product differentiation value has eroded may actually hasten the day when total control of such affiliates passes into local hands, as has been suggested was the case in many extractive sectors.

4. *Environmental Dissonance.* Various factors can be considered under this heading. The actual location of the affiliate can have an influence on the risk factor, because it affects the perceived contribution to national development goals and it exposes the firm to varying levels of population, ethnic, environmental, unionization, or guerrilla risks. Cultural compatibility can also be managed as a function of location or in the project's structural design. Environmental impact has gained in importance, especially following the recent disasters in Mexico and India. The renegotiation of RTZ's investment in Bougainville Island in the mid-1970s, for example, was made more difficult by the company's lack of sensitivity to traditional values of land tenure severely affected by the mine's operation and by the environmental impact of such a large project on the land and rivers of the area.

Managerial Factors

In the end, it is up to management to reduce the level of risk associated with foreign operations by pursuing prudent policies of limiting exposure while attending to the national and corporate interest. While conflict is unavoidable, the four policy areas outlined hereafter offer significant latitude for reducing risks consistent with minimum sacrifice in profitability.

1. *Local Management.* The use of local managers to the largest extent possible can serve to reduce risks in at least three ways. First, local managers are likely to be better attuned to local conditions and better connected to the sources of power and influence than expatriates, and are thus in a better position to anticipate change and evaluate its impact on the firm. Second, their presence alone offers the government a guarantee that the national interest is represented in the highest councils of the firm. Finally, local managers, by the training they receive and experience they acquire, come to represent a valuable asset to both the firm and the nation. In fact, to the extent that technology is embodied in people and these are local nationals, the state can be assured of continued access to key technologies without the need to control foreign enterprises directly or to interfere with their operations.

2. *Corporate Culture and Management Philosophy.* Expatriates will continue to play a key role in the management structure of multinational companies. In fact, the more complex and diversified the operations of the parent company, the more likely that it will have to rely on the judgment and skills of an international cadre of executives. The experience and training of these managers, and their sensitivity to the political and social reality of the countries in which they are called to serve, will play a critical role in anticipating and preventing potential trouble as well as in dealing with the consequences of local turmoil when it arrives. Whether the point of view of the man (or woman) in the field will be accepted at headquarters depends largely on the quality of the management development function in the organization and on the corporation's value system. While little hard evidence exists on this point, there seems to be abundant anecdotal support for the view that many a situation fraught with danger can be resolved satisfactorily by having good managers at hand whose voices are heard and respected at home.

3. *Political Responsiveness.* As cited earlier, there appears to be strong support for the view that an activist political role on the part of local management reduces risk. Frequent contact with national social and political forces, active lobbying for industrial issues, time spent on understanding the local environment, and significant investment in public affairs and in promoting a local corporate image have been shown to be positively correlated to low levels of government intervention. Obviously, any efforts in this direction must be carefully monitored lest they be interpreted as meddling in internal affairs. But the foreign corporation has a role to play in the host country's political life; if it is well played, it can lead to a better relationship over the long term.

4. *Financial Policies.* Finally, there are a host of financial policies that any multinational enterprise can put into effect to either reduce or avoid the risks associated with political change. While this is not the place to describe these (see references 4, 10–12, 16, 17, 19, 49), it should be noted that many of the policies that reduce the magnitude of the loss in the case of intervention (e.g., the excessive use of local sources of finance) may unwittingly hasten such an intervention.

Summary

It is obvious from the preceding discussion that the cost in time and money of carrying out a detailed analysis for each country and each operation throughout the world would be prohibitive for any moderately large multinational corporation. Thus, any corporate system of forecasting political risks ought to strive for a compromise between the general and broadly based information available from multicountry rating and evaluation services and the provision of case-by-case specific inputs from internal and contractual sources.

The macro, or country, risk component of the analysis is particularly suited to standardization and the systematic manipulation of large time series data bases. No individual firm, except perhaps the very large, can hope to duplicate the resources available to specialized agencies for collecting, processing, and analyzing macroeconomic and sociopolitical data on a global basis. Significant economies of scale are possible in this endeavor when operating across multiple countries. Most important, specialized agencies can amortize the cost of developing and constantly updating such a system over a large customer base. Both econometric models and expert-based systems would appear to be more cost efficient and preferable when developed and constructed outside the firm. Yet they need to be understood and applied in the context of very specific conditions.

It follows that there remains a genuine requirement for an internal function in assessing macro risks, that is, second-guessing of the results of any external inputs within the corporation by those familiar with the content of the models used in the analysis (i.e., its internal logic, sources of data, assumptions, and specifications). These corporate executives would benefit from their knowledge of the specific circumstances of the firm's investments in various areas and the reality of history and conditions in the field. They can then perform a control function, different from that of persons responsible for the generation of data and output, and thus be free from any loyalty or commitment to the model itself or to its component parts. Their task is to make sure that the externally supplied assessments are suitable to the company's needs and acceptable to those who have to act on the basis of the information provided.

The second part of the analysis, that is, once the probability and time horizon of certain events have been established, can only be performed by those intimately familiar with the company's operations. How certain events will affect the profitability of, or the capacity to repatriate funds from, a given project or subsidiary needs to be determined on the basis of data available only to management. Therefore, a second role for the function of political risk assessment within the corporation consists of interpreting the results of the country risk forecasts in terms of the realities of industry, corporate, structural, and managerial factors only known internally.

There is, however, an important qualitative difference between these two roles. Monitoring the quality and accuracy of country risk forecasts provided by external services and adapting them to the corporate reality should be functions performed and coordinated centrally. While operational management can and should have an input to the process, the modification of the model's specifications and the interpretation of their biases can only be appropriately conducted after considerable experience with such a system over relatively long time periods. Given the value of corporate memory in this process, it would be logical to centralize responsibility accordingly. The second role, that of evaluating micro risks from a given set of country risk forecasts, can only be done at the local level. Obviously, corporate involvement may be desirable to assure impartiality and comparability across countries and projects, but since local management will be called on to act on the results of the analysis, such management must be party to the conclusions. Besides, such management is often the only point where both the corporate and national vision converge on many of the key issues on which actual events and consequences will hinge.

CONCLUSIONS

In assessing whether to set up, expand, or contract operations in a given country, one should distinguish between two sets of issues. The first has to do with the contribution the project or the affiliate is likely to make to the corporation's global strategy, including the returns from the venture proper as well as any synergistic or competitive contributions to other units in the corporate system. Such an assessment of "strategic attractiveness" will be based on a number of factors such as the degree of global competition (vs. fragmented national markets) prevalent in the industry, the size and importance of the market, the fit with the company's long-term strategic priorities, and so forth. It should result in a differentiated approach to global opportunities. The more attractive a particular location and the more critical to the achievement of corporate objectives, the more willing the company should be to undertake a high level of risk and commit the necessary resources to achieve these objectives. It follows that the higher the priority accorded to a particular subsidiary in the company's global strategy, the greater the firm's need for management integration and control. This typically means either control through majority ownership or effective managerial control over all aspects of the project critical to its success.

These views ought to be tempered by a second set of assessments concerning the quality of the "investment climate" in the country in question. To the extent that the risk of political upheaval and intervention is high, the expected returns may not materialize or may be significantly reduced, irrespective of the market's attractiveness. As the investment climate deteriorates, the foreign investor will attempt to reduce its financial, technological, and human resource commitments (and exposure) while still attempting to retain the maximum market performance allowable under the circumstances. This may call for unorthodox approaches to ownership and control, which take into account the need to minimize exposure consistent with market presence. In contrast, an excellent investment climate is no substitute for market potential, and thus a joint venture or independent arms-length transaction may be the preferred vehicle to gain a foothold in such a market without undue commitment of scarce corporate resources. Where poor market prospects coexist with a bad investment climate, it is clear that the firm will tend to limit both its commitments and exposure. Chart 22-6 summarizes these choices.

Multinational corporations are accustomed to making the first set of assessments as part and parcel of their normal strategic planning process. This chapter has dealt with the need to make the second set of assessments in such a manner that it can be incorporated into the global strategic review process.

This chapter also should have made clear that so many diverse factors impinge on an evaluation of the risk profile of a particular corporate project that the construction of a single model that faithfully and accurately represents the interaction and complexity of all these factors is a monumental challenge. Yet the importance of adequate political intelligence cannot be underestimated as a greater proportion of corporate decisions and assets are exposed to political change and intervention in a multitude of national environments. The difficulties inherent in the analysis do not make the task any less urgent.

No mechanical system could be expected to deal with the subtleties required for political risk analysis. Rough rankings of countries in terms of their relative political stability have limited use as predictors of potential losses in specific situations. That causality is not easily determined in political phenomena, that up-to-date information is difficult to obtain, and that stability in itself is not necessarily a good measure of risk all contribute to the

CHART 22-6. Preferred Strategic Posture in Foreign Markets According to Strategic Attraction and Political Climate

Market Attractiveness or Degree of Fit With Corporate Strategy	Assessment of Political/Investment Climate		
	Good	Unstable	Poor
High	Maximum commitment of human and financial resources and high tolerance for commercial risks; wholly-owned affiliates preferred	Limit financial exposure while sustaining market and human investments; accept normal commercial risks; majority-owned affiliate preferred	Minimize financial exposure consistent with market presence; aim for minority position with licensing as long-term hedge
Medium	Maintain high resource commitment and risk tolerance subject to better alternative investment opportunities	Unwilling to commit significant resources; prefer to act through joint venture if necessary or appropriate	Little interest in market presence; pursue only if possible without financial exposure of any consequence
Low	Indifferent to market opportunities; token financial or human commitment possible; independent distributor or joint venture preferred	Little if any resource commitment desirable; export sales agents preferred vehicle for any market activity; licensing possible	No interest except for occasional exports or limited licensing agreements

412

many doubts often expressed about such methods. Furthermore, we have argued that the nature of the industry and investor, and the timing and characteristics of the project, are critical variables that alter significantly the risk profile within the same set of economic and political conditions.

Yet no human being could possibly master this complexity for more than just a handful of countries. Unaided by standardized quantitative tools, the political risk analyst would drown in a sea of information. Judgment can best be applied when the range of variables to consider has been reduced to a manageable set. Here lies the challenge of true modeling of political risk at the corporate level. It must make use of good measures of quantifiable variables and systematic analysis that can reduce large quantities of data, according to accepted causal models, to probabilistic estimates of possible events in an efficient fashion. Second, it must call for many qualitative assessments of elusive trends, such as levels of national aspirations and frustrations, that can only be obtained through intimate knowledge of the terrain. Third, it must make all of this relevant to the particular project at hand. And finally, it demands good judgment above all, to mix the many inputs in a coherent manner so as to spot, as did Sherlock Holmes, the dog that did not bark in the night.

A final question that may be asked is how best to incorporate this analysis into the strategic planning process. Various sources confirm the confusion that reigns in corporate headquarters about the proper scope and role of political analyses in evaluating foreign investment opportunities. This is partly due to lack of accepted standards, and has resulted in significant disenchantment and skepticism with the concept. Is political risk forecasting one more short-lived corporate fad? Most executives would readily agree with the desirability of having such an input available to the planning function, but not many firms have made the necessary investment in terms of both staff and administrative systems to generate the information and incorporate it into the decision-making process. As existing models are perfected, one might predict that the required commitment and organizational linkages will emerge.

REFERENCES

1. Armstrong, J. Scott, *Long Range Forecasting,* John Wiley, New York, 1978.
2. Bassiry, G. R., and R. Hrair Dekmejian, "MNCs and the Iranian Revolution: An Empirical Study," *Management International Review,* vol. 25, no. 2, 1985, pp. 67–75.
3. Blank, Stephen, et al., *Assessing the Political Environment: An Emerging Function in International Companies,* Conference Board Report No. 794, New York, 1980.
4. Bradley, David G., "Managing Against Expropriation," *Harvard Business Review,* July–August 1977, pp. 75–83.
5. Bunn, D. W., and M. M. Mustafaoglu, "Forecasting Political Risk," *Management Science,* November 1978, pp. 1557–1567.
6. Burton, F. N., and Hisashi Inoue, "Expropriations of Foreign-Owned Firms in Developing

Countries: A Cross-National Analysis," *Journal of World Trade Law,* September–October 1984, pp. 396–414.

7. Chourcri, Nazli, and Thomas W. Robinson, eds., *Forecasting in International Relations: Theory, Methods, Problems, Prospects,* W. H. Freeman, San Francisco, 1978.

8. de la Torre, Jose, "Foreign Investment and Economic Development: Conflict and Negotiation," *Journal of International Business Studies,* Fall 1981, pp. 9–32.

9. De St. Jorre, J., "IRIS: A Study of How to Fail in Business," *The International Herald Tribune,* April 20, 1983.

10. Doz, Yves, and C. K. Prahalad, "How MNCs Cope with Host Government Intervention," *Harvard Business Review,* March–April 1980, pp. 149–157.

11. Eiteman, David K., and Arthur I. Stonehill, "Reacting to Political Risk," chap. 6 in J. de la Torre, ed., *Multinational Business Finance,* Addison-Wesley, Reading, MA, 1982.

12. Encarnation, Dennis J., and Sushil Vachani, "Foreign Ownership: When Hosts Change the Rules," *Harvard Business Review,* September–October 1985, pp. 152–160.

13. Fagre, Nathan, and Louis T. Wells Jr., "Bargaining Power of Multinationals and Host Governments," *Journal of International Business Studies,* Fall 1982, pp. 9–23.

14. Frank, Isaiah, *Foreign Enterprise in Developing Countries,* Johns Hopkins University Press, Baltimore, 1980.

15. Gebelein, C. A., C. E. Pearson, and M. Silbergh, "Assessing Political Risk of Oil Investment Ventures," *Journal of Petroleum Technology,* May 1978, pp. 725–730.

16. Ghadar, Fariborz, Stephen J. Kobrin, and Theodore H. Moran, eds., *Managing International Political Risk: Strategies and Techniques,* Georgetown University Press, Washington, DC, 1983.

17. Ghadar, Fariborz, and Theordore H. Moran, eds., *International Political Risk Management: New Dimensions,* Georgetown University Press, Washington, DC, 1984.

18. Gillespie, John V., and Betty A. Nesvold, eds., *Macro Quantitative Analysis: Conflict, Development and Democratization,* Sage, Beverly Hills, CA, 1971.

19. Gladwin, Thomas N., and Ingo Walter, *Multinationals Under Fire: Lessons in the Management of Conflict,* John Wiley, New York, 1980.

20. Gurr, Ted Robert, *Why Men Rebel,* Princeton University Press, Princeton, NJ, 1971.

21. Haendel, Dan, *Foreign Investments and the Management of Political Risk,* Westview, Boulder, CO, 1979.

22. Haendel, Dan, Gerald T. West, and Robert G. Meadow, *Overseas Investment and Political Risk,* Monograph Series No. 21, Foreign Policy Research Institute, Philadelphia, 1975.

23. Hawkins, Robert G., Norman Mintz, and Michael Provissiero, "Government Takeovers of U.S. Foreign Affiliates," *Journal of International Business Studies,* Spring 1976, pp. 3–15.

24. Heuer, Richard J. Jr., ed., *Quantitative Approaches to Political Intelligence: The CIA Experience,* Westview, Boulder, CO, 1978.

25. Hufbauer, Gary C., and P. H. Briggs, "Expropriation Losses and Tax Policy," *Harvard International Law Journal,* Summer 1975, pp. 533–564.

26. Jodice, David A., "Sources of Change in Third World Regimes for Foreign Direct Investment: 1968–1976," *International Organization,* Spring 1980, pp. 177–206.

27. Juhl, P., "Economically Rational Design of Developing Countries' Expropriation Policies Towards Foreign Investment," *Management International Review,* vol. 25, no. 2, 1985, pp. 45–52.

28. Kim, W. Chan, "The Dynamic Bargaining Power Position of Multinationals: Managing Competition and Host Government Intervention in Developing Countries," Working Paper, The University of Michigan, Ann Arbor, December 1985.

29. Knudsen, Harald, "Explaining the National Propensity to Expropriate: An Ecological Approach," *Journal of International Business Studies,* Spring 1974, pp. 51–71.

30. Kobrin, Stephen J., "Political Risk: A Review and Reconsideration," *Journal of International Business Studies,* Spring/Summer 1979, pp. 67–80.

31. Kobrin, Stephen J., "Foreign Enterprise and Forced Divestment in LDCs," *International Organization,* Winter 1980, pp. 65–88.

32. Kobrin, Stephen J., "Political Assessment by International Firms: Models or Methodologies?," *Journal of Policy Modeling,* vol. 3, no. 2, 1981, pp. 251–270.

33. Kobrin, Stephen J., *Managing Political Risk Assessment: Strategic Response to Environmental Change,* University of California Press, Berkeley, 1982.

34. Krayenbuehl, Thomas E., *Country Risk: Assessment and Monitoring,* Woodhead-Faulkner, Cambridge, MA, 1985.

35. Lall, Sanjaya, and Paul Streeten, *Foreign Investment, Transnationals, and Developing Countries,* Macmillan, London, 1977.

36. Lecraw, Donald J., "Bargaining Power, Ownership, and Profitability of Transnational Corporations in Developing Countries," *Journal of International Business Studies,* Spring/Summer 1984, pp. 27–43.

37. Marois, Bernard, "Comment les Entreprises Francaises Gerent le Risque Politique," *Revue Francaise de Gestion,* Mai–Aout 1981, pp. 4–9.

38. Mascarenhas, Briance, and Ole Christian Sand, "Country-Risk Assessment Systems in Banks: Patterns and Performance," *Journal of International Business Studies,* Spring 1985, pp. 19–35.

39. Miquel, Rafael, "The Case for ESP Studies" and "Some Comments on ESP Analysis and Its Uses by Management," Dow Chemical manuscripts, June 1978 and February 1980.

40. Nagy, Pancras, *Country Risk,* Euromoney, London 1979 and 1984.

41. Penrose, Edith, "Ownership and Control: Multinational Firms in Less Developed Countries," in G. K. Helleiner, ed., *A World Divided—The Less Developed Countries in the International Economy,* Cambridge University Press, Cambridge, MA, 1976, pp. 147–174.

42. Poynter, Thomas A., "Government Intervention in Less Developed Countries: The Experience of Multinational Companies," *Journal of International Business Studies,* Spring/Summer 1982, pp. 9–23.

43. Raubitschek, Ruth S., "Scenarios and Strategy Formulation," Research Paper, Harvard Business School, June 2, 1983.

44. Reuber, Grant L., *Private Foreign Investment in Development,* Clarendon, Oxford, 1973.

45. Robock, Stefan H., "Political Risk: Identification and Assessment," *Columbia Journal of World Business,* July–August 1971, pp. 6–20.

46. Robock, Stefan H., and Kenneth Simmonds, "Assessing Political Risk and National Controls," *International Business and Multinational Enterprises,* Irwin, New York, 1983, Ch. 15.

47. Root, Franklyn R., "U.S. Business Abroad and Political Risk," *MSU Business Topics,* Winter 1968, pp. 73–80.

48. Rummel, R. J., and David R. Heenan, "How Multinationals Analyze Political Risk," *Harvard Business Review,* January–February 1978, pp. 67–76.

49. Shapiro, Alan C., "Managing Political Risk: A Policy Approach," *Columbia Journal of World Business,* Fall 1981, pp. 63–70.

50. Simon, Jeffrey D., "Political Risk Assessment: Past Trends and Future Prospects," *Columbia Journal of World Business,* Fall 1982, pp. 62–71.

51. Simon, Jeffrey D., "A Theoretical Perspective on Political Risk," *Journal of International Business Studies,* Winter 1984, 123–143.

52. Simon, Jeffrey D., "Political Risk Forecasting," *Futures*, April 1985, pp. 133–147.

53. Stobaugh, Robert B. Jr., "How to Analyze Foreign Investment Climates," *Harvard Business Review*, September–October 1969, pp. 100–108.

54. Truitt, J. Frederick, "Expropriation of Foreign Investment: Summary of the Post World War II Experience of American and British Investors in Less Developed Countries," *Journal of International Business Studies*, Fall 1970, pp. 21–34.

55. Truitt, J. Frederick, *Expropriation of Private Foreign Investment*, Indiana University Press, Bloomington, IN, 1974.

56. van Agtmael, Antoine W., "Evaluating the Risks of Lending to Developing Countries," *Euromoney*, April 1976, pp. 16–30.

57. Vernon, Raymond, *Sovereignty at Bay*, Basic Books, New York, 1971.

58. Vernon, Raymond, *Storm Over the Multinationals: The Real Issues*, Harvard University Press, Cambridge, MA, 1977.

59. Wack, Pierre, "Scenarios: Uncharted Waters Ahead" and "Scenarios: Shooting the Rapids," *Harvard Business Review*, September–October 1985, pp. 72–89, and November–December 1985, pp. 139–150.

60. Wells, Louis T. Jr., "Social Cost/Benefit Analysis for MNCs," *Harvard Business Review*, March–April 1975, pp. 40–50.

61. Williams, M. I., "The Extent and Significance of the Nationalization of Foreign-Owned Assets in Developing Countries," *Oxford Economic Papers*, July 1975, pp. 268–273.

23

ING THE LONG-RUN
RAW MATERIAL
ILABILITY

AN L. SIMON

Business and Management
of Maryland, College Park

Will raw materials be more scarce, or less scarce, in future decades than at present? The actual outcome will have important consequences for our economic lives. And our *expectations* about the outcome will probably have even greater consequences than the outcome itself. Yet there are large and violent disagreements between two points of view, the "doomsayers" who expect us to "run out" and who therefore forecast higher prices, and the "cornucopias" expect prices to be progressively lower as raw materials come to be more available rather than less available. My own forecast is simply stated: I am quite sure that prices of all natural resources will go down indefinitely.

The aim of this chapter is to set forth the basis for such a forecast. The nature of this particular forecasting situation forces us to consider the very foundations of long-run economic forecasting, and indeed, of all forecasting.

My forecasting "method" may be summarized as follows:

1. Ask, "Is there any convincing reason not to consider the percentage changes from year to year in the longest available data series on a resource's price to be a representative sample of the universe from which the past, present, and future prices of this resource are drawn?" That is, is there some convincing reason not to generalize from the sample already drawn to samples that will be drawn in the future?

If the observations had been those of secular constancy in the past, rather than secular decline, the sample-universe logic would seem more straightforward. But the constancy of an amount of change, or of a percentage rate of change, is based on the same foundation; predictions about a spacecraft circling the earth and about a spacecraft traveling away from the earth toward the stars are on much the same footing.

Many persons assert we are now at a turning point in history with regard to resources, which implies that the past is *not* a representative sample of the universe from which the next set of years will be drawn. If their reasoning is convincing to you, then my predictions will not be credited by you. (One of my arguments against such a turning point now is that such has usually been the assertion in the past.)

2. If you do not reject the past as a sample of the universe from which the next set of observations will be drawn, we next ask if there is a reasonable "theoretical" explanation for the observed trend. Such an explanation is not necessary for one to believe that the trend will continue. Few of us could explain why a spacecraft circles the earth or travels away from it, and people prudently did not await an explanation for the transmission of cholera before acting on the information that there was a geographic pattern of disease connected with certain wells in London. But a theoretical explanation increases belief that the observed trend is not just caused by chance.

The explanation that the trend of decreasing cost results from market feedbacks causing new discoveries, substitutes, and so on, accompanied by externalities that leave us better off than before shortages arose, is persuasive to me. Of course one can never be sure that a theoretical explanation is sound; the test is your general wisdom and judgment.

3. If the answer to question 1 is "no" and to question 2 is "yes"—or even if the answer to 2 is "no" but the data in 1 are so many and so consistent that your statistical sense tells you that they are overwhelming—then you will extrapolate the observed trend with a monotonic function that seems to fit the data relatively well. That is the nature of my forecasting method. As I read Barnett and Morse,[3] the source of my general point of view on the history and future of raw material availability, this also is the forecasting method implicitly used by them. And it is the forecasting method used by many—but certainly not all—other makers of forecasts throughout the ages.

I will proceed as follows. First I will discuss appropriate ways to measure economic scarcity of raw materials. Then I'll provide a long-run history of raw material scarcity. Next I'll set forth the Malthusian theory, which is at the heart of pessimistic forecasts of raw material scarcity, and explain why I do not find that line of thinking persuasive; I offer another way of thinking instead. Then I'll discuss the appropriate weights to put on long-ago data versus more recent information, which is much the same as discussing whether the longest-run trend should be believed rather than more recent "reversals."

MEASUREMENT OF SCARCITY TRENDS

Economists generally view the expenditures in physical or money terms necessary to obtain a good, relative to some other quantity of expenditures, as the appropriate measure of scarcity. This is in contrast to measuring scarcity with an actual or hypothetical estimate of physical quantities that are thought to "exist," as technologists are wont to do.

Two measures of cost are of particular interest here: the price of the raw material relative to consumer goods, and the price relative to wages. Each measure needs a further few words.

The price relative to consumer goods is the most popular measure, perhaps largely because of its similarity to an inflation deflator. But the average cost of all consumer goods taken together—an index of consumer prices—has fallen over the years in more-developed countries, measured in terms of what an unskilled worker can buy; this is shown by the long-run increase in the standard of living. Therefore, if a raw material has remained at least level in price compared with the average of all (or of consumer) goods, its "real" cost has fallen. Therefore, even if raw material prices had *not* fallen as fast as the prices of consumer goods (as in fact they have), this would *not* be ground for alarm about resources exerting a braking effect on economic growth, or becoming an increasingly serious constraint.

The price of natural resources *relative to wages* is, in my view, the best measure of scarcity with respect to human welfare. This measure tells us how much of our most valuable resource, our own lives, we must give up in order to obtain the resources. This bears considerable relationship to the measure of labor input time per unit of output that Barnett and Morse used, but it is easier to obtain, and is more comprehensive.

We should note that it is not really the natural resource itself that is of interest to us, but rather the services that we get from the resource. Just as it is not a computer itself, but the computing services we get from it, and then the use of those computing services in the production of other goods, that affects us, it is not copper or land or oil that matters to us, but rather the services that each renders in the creation of final products. Therefore the relevant measure of the available resource is the cost of the services that we get from the resource.

TRENDS IN RESOURCE SCARCITY

Now that we have arrived at some operational measures of scarcity, let's look at the record, in accord with the first step in my forecasting method. The historical cost record of raw materials is easy to summarize. Following on Barnett and Morse,[3] I have written at length elsewhere[4] about this matter, so I'll be brief here: Scarcity has been *decreasing rather than increasing* in the long run for all raw materials except lumber and oil, and even they have recently shown signs of becoming less exceptional. Charts 23-1 and 23-2

CHART 23-1. Scarcity of Copper as Measured by Its Price Relative to Wages

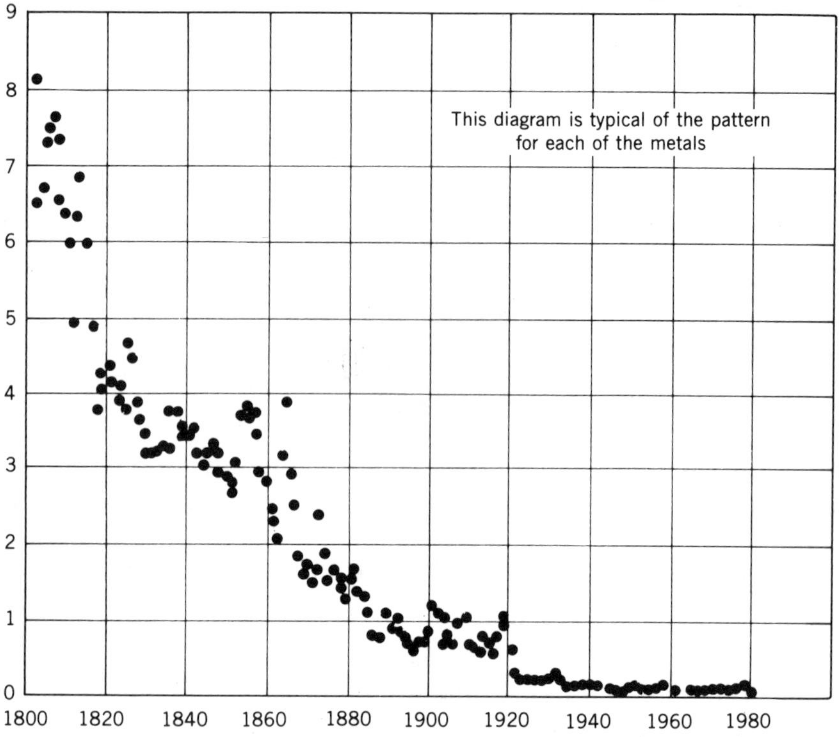

This diagram is typical of the pattern for each of the metals

show this effect for copper, which is representative of all the metals. And this trend of falling prices of copper has been going on a very long time. The price of copper in labor time in the year 1 A.D. was about 120 times as great as it is in the United States now. The price of iron was about 240 times as great then as now; in 800 B.C. it was 360 times as great; while in 1800 B.C. it was 1620 times as great. Food is an especially important resource, and the evidence is especially strong that we are on a benign trend despite rising population.

MALTHUSIAN AND OTHER THEORIES

Now let us move to the second step in my forecasting method, the theory. First let us consider contrary theories, because they cast light on the credibility of the theory I offer. The question that we wish to address theoretically must be kept firmly in mind: Must the cost of one or more important raw materials rise in the long run? The doomsayers assert that there is theoretical reason to answer the question in the affirmative, that there is no escaping a

CHART 23-2. Scarcity of Copper as Measured by Its Price Relative to the Consumer Price Index

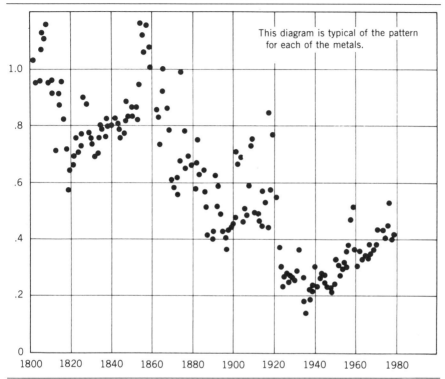

This diagram is typical of the pattern for each of the metals.

rise in raw material cost in the very long run. Their reasoning is as follows: The reservoir of some raw material X is fixed, meaning that the reservoir cannot be increased, just as the reservoir of authentic Mona Lisa paintings cannot be increased. (They have in mind, however, generic materials such as, say, copper and land and energy rather than one-of-a-kinds such as the Mona Lisa; about those one-of-a-kinds there is no dispute.) Next they assume that (1) the demand for the use of the material will increase due to population growth or income growth or both, (2) the reservoir will decline due to some of it being lost or otherwise unavailable, or (3) there will be both increased demand and decreased reservoir. If humankind first exploits the richest lodes and ores, successive mining operations will be successively more expensive. Implicitly, these writers are also assuming that eventually there will be either stationarity of technology or a growth in technology slower than the rate of decrease in richness of lode. Under those assumed conditions, cost must indeed increase.

Certainly costs do increase during some periods, as reflected in real price rises at some times in history. And it is reasonable to suppose that during those periods the doomsday conditions hold (though price rises may sometimes be due to nonphysical causes such as the formation of OPEC).

If the Malthusian concept of diminishing returns is given content by specifying a period of the order of a human life expectation, give or take an expected length of life, the "theory" fails completely in its predictive record; as we have seen, the trends in scarcity have been downward throughout history despite forecasters having made dire predictions implicitly based on the Malthusian concept since the beginning of recorded history and surely before.

If instead of testing the Malthusian theory on the past, one looks to the future, but if one does not specify an observable (or even identifiable) time period during which prices will rise permanently to levels above what they are now, instead simply says increased scarcity will happen and "sometime," then the Malthusian theory is meaningless scientifically, according to the standard canon of scientific meaning; a theory about "sometime" cannot be tested, even in principle.

A very different theoretical viewpoint sees the process by which resources have become progressively more available as part of the broader story of the creation and adoption of new technology largely in response to increased demand and/or increased prices for the resources due to population growth. The relationship between technology and demand assuredly is not that which is suggested by the idea of a "race" between them. Greater population certainly implies increased demand, and therefore higher costs, in the short run. But in this case the long run is not just a sequence of short runs, and it is fallacious to draw any conclusions from this short-run analysis. In the longer run, technology's advance comes from people, and technological advance is the sole factor responsible for the long-run declines in material costs.

The process by which increased demand due to more people and higher income causes advances in resource technology is only a special case of the general relationship between demand and technical advance. Here are two famous natural resource cases that illustrate the process:

1. Ivory used for billiard balls threatened to run out in the nineteenth century. As a result of a prize offered for a replacement material, celluloid was developed, and that discovery led directly to the wide range of plastics that now give us an astonishing variety of products (including billiard balls) at prices so low as to boggle the nineteenth century mind.

2. England was full of alarm in the 1600s at an impending shortage of energy due to the deforestation of the country for firewood. People feared a scarcity of fuel for both heating and for the iron industry. This impending scarcity led to the use of coal.

Then in the mid-1800s the English worried about an impending coal crisis. The great English economist Jevons calculated that a shortage of coal would bring England's industry to a standstill by 1900; he carefully assessed that oil could never make a decisive difference. Triggered by the impending scarcity of coal (and of whale oil, whose story comes next), ingenious profit-minded people developed oil into a more desirable fuel than coal ever was. And now in 1986 we find England exporting both coal and oil!

Another element in the story: Because of increased demand due to population growth and increased income, the price of whale oil for lamps jumped in the 1840s, and the American Civil War pushed it even higher, leading to a whale oil "crisis." This provided incentive for enterprising people to discover and produce substitutes. First came oil from rapeseed, olives, and linseed, and camphene oil from pine trees. Then inventors learned how to get coal oil from coal, a flourishing industry in 1859. About then, other ingenious persons produced kerosene from the rock oil that seeped to the surface, a product so desirable that its price rose from $0.75 to $2.00 a gallon. This stimulated enterprisers to increase the supply of oil, and finally Edwin L. Drake brought in his famous well in Titusville, Pennsylvania. Learning how to refine the oil took a while. But in a few years there were hundreds of small refiners in the United States, and soon the bottom fell out of the whale oil market, the price falling from $2.50 or more per gallon at its peak around 1866 to well below a dollar.

A forecast seems even more convincing if the future of the relevant variables is predicted as a function of an independent variable whose future magnitude is itself predicted with some confidence. Increases in natural resource availability have accompanied (and in my view, have been caused by) increases in population and total demand. It seems reasonable to forecast continued increases for population and total demand in the future. Hence this constitutes additional grounds for forecasting continued increases in natural resource availability.

So, I believe that the first two steps of my forecasting method—examination of the experiential data, and analysis of theoretical arguments (and especially inquiry into a theoretical mechanism that explains the observed data)—lead solidly to the third-step conclusion that it is reasonable to forecast a continuation of the observed trend, continued decline in resource prices and increase in availability.

HOW LONG SHOULD THE BASE PERIOD BE FOR A LONG-RUN FORECAST?

If you find that there has indeed been a trend during the relevant past, then it is often reasonable to extend that trend as the basis of your prediction. But the pattern of the past is often not consistent, in which case you must decide which parts of the past to pay most attention to.

In my view, the most important element in making sound long-run predictions from trends is to examine the sweep of history as far back in the past as possible, to ensure that what you think is a trend is not just a blip in history. For example, notice in Chart 23-2 how differently one would predict the course of future copper prices from 1970's evidence alone than from the evidence going back to 1800.

The main reason for looking at a longer rather than a shorter period is because the longer period contains more information. But the relevance of the information from various periods in the past is, of course, a most difficult question. It is generally reasonable to weight the recent past more heavily than the distant past, though never completely forgetting the distant past. The most common source of error is to extend an apparent trend during a short period of time—an uptrend in copper prices within the last three years, say—into a prediction for the long-run future—say, prices two decades from now. One of the many examples of fallacious short-trend extension was the conclusion by individuals and governments that the raw material scarcity that appeared in 1973–1974 would continue to get worse into the indefinite future. That conclusion was very costly in waste of social and personal resources. (For an excellent discussion of the accuracy of forecasts, see Ascher[2] and Armstrong.[1])

SUMMARY

To summarize: I forecast that prices of all natural resources will go down. My forecasting "method" is as follows:

1. Ask, "Is there any convincing reason not to consider the percentage changes from year to year in the longest data series on a resource's cost to be a representative sample of the "universe" from which past, present, and future costs are drawn?" That is, is there some convincing reason not to generalize from the sample already drawn to samples that will be drawn in the future?

2. If you do not reject the past as a sample of the universe from which the next set of observations will be drawn, then we next ask if there is a reasonable "theoretical" explanation for the observed trend. Such an explanation is not necessary for one to believe that the trend will continue. But a theoretical explanation increases belief that the observed trend is not just caused by chance.

The explanation I accept for the trend of decreasing cost is a set of market feedbacks resulting in new discoveries, substitutes, and so on, with externalities that leave us better off than before shortages arose.

3. If the answer to question 1 is "no" and to question 2 is "yes"—or even if the answer to 2 is "no" but the data in 1 are so many and so consistent that your statistical sense tells you that they are overwhelming— then it seems reasonable to extrapolate the observed trend with a monotonic function that seems to fit the data relatively well.

The appropriate economic measurement of raw-material scarcity is cost or price. The very longest trends throughout humankind's history exhibit decreasing rather than increasing scarcity for all raw materials except sawlogs and oil, and there are persuasive reasons to think that they, too, will show decreasing scarcity in the future. Malthusian diminishing returns theory does not fit these observed facts and is not compelling intellectually; a theory of endogenous invention is more persuasive, in my view. An explanation of the persistence and predictive power of trends was offered, and it is argued that, ceteris paribus, longer trends are a preferable basis than are shorter trends where the two conflict, because the longer trends contain more information.

REFERENCES

1. Armstrong, J. Scott, *Long Range Forecasting,* John Wiley, New York, 1978.
2. Ascher, William, *Forecasting,* Johns Hopkins University Press, Baltimore, 1978.
3. Barnett, Harold J., and Chandler Morse, *Scarcity and Growth: The Economics of Natural Resource Availability,* Johns Hopkins University Press, Baltimore, 1953.
4. Simon, Julian L., *The Ultimate Resource,* Princeton University Press, Princeton, MA, 1981.

CHAPTER

24

ANTICIPATORY ANALYSIS FOR NEW ENTRY STRATEGIES

JEAN-CLAUDE LARRÉCHÉ
INSEAD, Fontainebleau, France

INTRODUCTION

The long-term survival of a corporation depends on its ability to expand and renew its activities over time. Its two main axes for renewal and growth include primarily the introduction of new products and the penetration of new markets. These two types of actions are globally called *new entries*.

In a recent survey of 148 companies, Hopkins[16] found that on average 15% of the current sales volume of these companies was attributable to new products introduced in the past five years. Moreover, two thirds of the executives responding in the survey stated that the dependence on new products would increase in the future. In terms of performance, the median failure rate was 33% indicating that, for half of the companies surveyed, more than one out of three new products did not meet management's expectations.*

Because of their importance for business and their inherent risks, new entry activities represent an area where the need for forecasting is critical. It is also, unfortunately, an area where the applicability of classic forecasting techniques is limited. One obvious difficulty in using classic forecasting techniques for a new entry is the lack of historical data. Another is that a new entry creates a disruption of the existing market equilibrium, thus invalidating the historical market or competitive patterns.

One can distinguish three types of new entry failures. A type 1 failure corresponds to a potential risk that had been anticipated, but was accepted

---

* Several other studies are reviewed in two excellent books on new product planning: Urban and Hauser[32] and Choffray and Lilien.[8]

as a reasonable business undertaking. A type 2 failure results from an event that could not be reasonably anticipated before the new entry. A type 3 failure is due to factors that were not correctly analyzed by management, although they could have reasonably been anticipated.

The third type of failure is the one that is most controllable and should be systematically reduced. It can be decomposed into two elements: an unsatisfactory breadth of analysis or an unsatisfactory depth of analysis, and these two sources of error call for different corrective actions. To minimize the risk of not considering an influent factor, management should follow a comprehensive framework to review all facets of a new entry. On the other hand, a number of models are available or can be developed to analyze in depth critical problem areas.

The use of a comprehensive framework to systematically investigate the strategic implications of the future evolution of a market situation is termed an *anticipatory analysis.** Although an anticipatory analysis may be performed in various circumstances, this chapter concentrates more specifically on the evaluation of new entry strategies. It will be assumed that a product-market opportunity has already been identified as being economically attractive. The issues of opportunity identification as well as preliminary technological and commercial feasibility studies will not be covered here.

A typology of new entry situations will first be described to put into perspective the various managerial problems that are regrouped under this generic title. A framework will then be presented that identifies the main aspects of an anticipatory analysis for new entries. Finally, some representative models more specifically used for new product planning will be discussed.

A TYPOLOGY OF NEW ENTRY SITUATIONS

Research results on new entries are plagued with definitional problems. A new entry may at one extreme represent a major venture for a corporation and at the other extreme only a minor product line extension. In one case it may open a completely new industry based on a revolutionary technology, and in another case it may only be an imitation of well-established and fully tested competitive products. It is obvious that the resources and risks involved will be considerably different for these various types of new entries.

---

* A similar concept is the "prospective" approach.[11] The prospective approach tends, however, to be associated with a specific procedure, while the expression "anticipatory analysis" is used to represent a general philosophy. This philosophy implies that one analyzes systematically the elements of a dynamic situation to anticipate its evolution, irrespective of the availability, form, or quality of available data. Instead of being constrained by existing quantitative data, as is the case in classical forecasting, anticipatory analysis encourages the extraction of information from the organization by raising appropriate questions.

CHART 24-1. Typology of New Entries

Market	For firm	Product for market	Product: For industry New / For firm New	Product: For industry Exist / For firm New	Product: For industry Exist / For firm Exist
New	New	New	1	4	9
New	New	New	2	5	10
Exist	Exist	Exist New	6	11	
Exist	Exist	New	3	7	12
Exist	Exist	Exist	8	13	

The know-how of a corporation will also vary widely in these different cases, and a typology of new entry situations should illustrate the varying levels of information available for anticipatory analysis.

The concept of new entry can be classified by specifying *what* is new (a product or a market) and *for whom* it is new (for the industry at large or for a specific firm, market, or product). One can consequently organize new entries around five classifications*:

1. Is the product new for the industry?
2. Is the product new for the firm?
3. Is the market new for the industry?
4. Is the market new for the firm?
5. Is the product new for the market?

These five dichotomies would provide 32 types of new entries if they were totally independent. Some of them are, however, redundant: A product that is new for an industry must a fortiori be new for the firm and for the market. The 13 remaining feasible and mutually exclusive types of new entries are represented in Chart 24-1. At one extreme is the complete innovation corresponding to cell 1. A firm develops a product that is new for the industry and

* In this discussion, a market is considered a specific consumer group. An industry is a set of firms that have a similar technological basis or compete in some markets, although they may not always manufacture similar products or be systematically present in the same markets.

introduces it in a market from which the industry was absent. This is extremely rare, as a single firm is usually unlikely to create a product *and* a market that are simultaneously new for an industry. The entries of Univac into computers, Xerox into reprography, and Polaroid into instantaneous photography are examples of a type 1 new entry.

At the other extreme, the firm is launching in a market in which it already operates a product that it has already introduced in other markets. Competition has already introduced a similar product in this market. The firm may have delayed its introduction by oversight or to avoid cannibalization with its current product line. In this situation, the firm has a great deal of information: It knows the product, it knows the market, and it has already benefited from observing the market's reaction to competitive offerings. An example of such a new entry is the delayed introduction of a product in a less developed country.

The amount of information available varies significantly according to the type of new entry considered, and the typology provides a guide to systematically search for possible data sources: from other products of the firm in similar markets, from the same product of the firm in other markets, from similar competitive products in similar or other markets, and from similar markets served by competition with different products. Even in the best case, however, the information available to anticipate the outcome of a new entry will be less than when forecasting the sales of a given product already established in a specific market. It is thus particularly important to isolate all available information and to exploit it as much as possible, and this is the purpose of anticipatory analysis.

KEY ELEMENTS OF ANTICIPATORY ANALYSIS

Marketing is one of the major interfaces of the firm with its environment, and it requires consideration of a broad range of elements internal as well as external to the firm. A systematic analysis of these elements is becoming increasingly important as growth opportunities become less obvious and competition intensifies. This represents an irreversible evolution from perceptions inherited from the 1960s in which free spending was more characteristic of marketing than careful analyses. A marketing audit represents the integration of such systematic analyses.[19,23] Its purpose is to provide a diagnosis of a firm's market posture based mainly on historical data.

An anticipatory analysis, on the other hand, is primarily concerned with the future. This future will be affected by uncertain external factors and also by the actions of the firm, which makes anticipatory analysis more difficult than a historical marketing audit. The impact of a new entry strategy may be considerable. For instance, launching a new product at a low price may develop new segments of the market and result in a growth rate higher than the one that could have been projected on the basis of historical data. Furthermore, a strategy may result in competitive reactions, the effects of which are difficult to predict.

These different factors influencing the success of a new entry strategy lead to the definition of three components of anticipatory analysis:

1. *Projective Analysis.* The purpose of projective analysis is to determine one, or several, probable schemes of the evolution of the situation, assuming a simple extrapolation of past strategies. This projection would not consider a new entry contemplated by the firm.

2. *Proactive Analysis.* Assuming that competitors do not change their strategies, proactive analysis tries to anticipate the evolution of the situation for alternative strategies of the firm.

3. *Reaction Analysis.* The highest level of sophistication in anticipatory analysis consists in taking into account the reaction of competitors to the actions of the firm.*

The process of anticipatory analysis is represented schematically in Chart 24-2. Projective analysis is a direct extension of the marketing audit in the future. On the basis of the resulting projections, alternative strategies are formulated and their effects are evaluated assuming an unchanged behavior of competitors. This may lead to the cancellation, modification, or addition of alternative strategies. The remaining set of strategies is then evaluated taking into account possible reactions from competitors. This may again result in deletion, modification, and addition of alternative strategies. The end result of the anticipatory analysis is a systematic investigation of alternative strategies.

In each of the steps in the anticipatory analysis, the investigation involves four basic components: the firm, the environment, the market, and the competition. The relative importance of each varies over the phases of the analysis. Firm and market considerations are relatively important all through the analysis, as they constitute the key components of the exchange relationship. Environmental factors will be considered mainly in the projective phase, while the relative importance of competitive issues will increase in the proactive and reaction analysis phases.

The key elements of an anticipatory analysis for new entries will now be briefly presented (see Chart 24-3). The resulting framework is not exhaus-

* The economists have in particular used reaction functions to study imperfect competition as in the Cournot and Stackelberg solutions (Henderson and Quandt,[15] pp. 223–231). Urban and Hauser[32] used the expressions "proactive" and "reactive strategies" to reflect the degree of initiative of the firm compared with its competitors (pp. 572–574). Here, proactive and reaction analyses represent two different stages of an anticipatory analysis.

CHART 24-2. Marketing Audit and Anticipatory Analysis

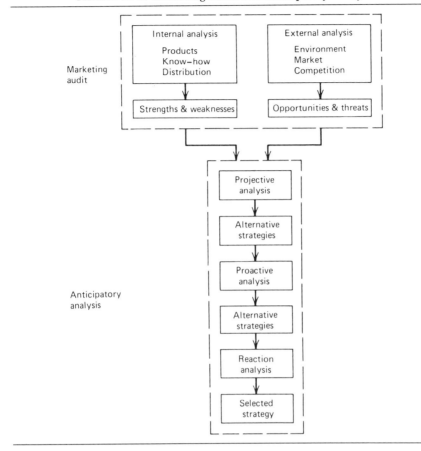

tive, but it does isolate issues determining the success or failure of new entries.

Anticipatory Environmental Analysis

The importance of correctly anticipating the evolution of the environment is well illustrated by the diverging strategies followed by Sears, Roebuck and Company and Montgomery Ward between 1945 and 1955. After World War II, Montgomery Ward anticipated another great depression and consequently decided to limit its growth. On the opposite side, Sears anticipated a long period of prosperity and consequently decided to expand rapidly in metropolitan centers. While the two merchandisers were of somewhat similar size before the war, Sears was three times bigger than Montgomery Ward in 1955 and in a much better strategic posture. Had an important depression

CHART 24-3. Key Elements of an Anticipatory Analysis for New Entries

Environmental Analysis

Evolution of economic, sociocultural, technological, and legal environments
Impact of new entry or other firm's actions on the environment

Internal Analysis

Coherence with distinctive competence
Cost estimates: reliability and evolution
Resources available
Capacity to monitor and adapt

Market Analysis

Market projection
Market stability
Direct market posture elements
  Awareness
  Market positioning
  Product availability
Impact on primary demand
  New consumers
  New applications
  Increased usage
  Increased added value
Impact on selective demand

Competitive Analysis

Projection of current competitors' actions
  Competitors' objectives
  Competitors' resources
  Market gaps
  Competition intensity
New sources of competition
Impact of entry strategy on competitors
  Sales
  Market share
  Profits
  Emotional impact
Potential competitive reactions
  Marketing mix element level
  Product market level
  Product market portfolio level

---

occurred, the relative performances of the two firms probably would have been inverted.

The issues to be covered in an anticipatory analysis include:

1. *Economic Environment.* What is the expected evolution of inflation, GNP growth, purchasing power, raw material costs and availability, interest rates, and demographics?

2. *Sociocultural Environment.* What is the expected evolution of life styles, values, and reference groups?

3. *Technological Environment.* What improvements can be anticipated in the design or manufacturing of existing products? What substitute products could emerge in the future?

4. *Legal Environment.* What laws are likely to be adopted in the future, especially in the areas of product safety, advertising, pollution, or energy conservation?

The main emphasis in anticipating the future evolution of the environment is undoubtedly on projective analysis. Although usually less significant, the proactive and reaction analyses should not be neglected, as they may isolate important issues in some specific situations. In the proactive analysis, for instance, a strategy to penetrate a new country based on local manufacturing and job creations could develop goodwill with the local government and facilitate the entry. In the reaction analysis, potential unsolicited reactions to the new entry from various elements such as antitrust agencies or consumerist, religious, and cultural groups should be investigated.

Anticipatory Internal Analysis

Anticipatory internal analysis is primarily concerned with factors that could create changes in the firm's competitive advantage.

1. *Coherence of an Entry Strategy with the Firm's Distinctive Competence.* An ideal entry strategy is one that simultaneously fully satisfies market needs, provides a clear and defendable competitive advantage, and is based on the distinctive competence of the firm. This ideal strategy is seldom feasible, and the decision is usually more one of degree: How far should the firm move from its area of competence to adequately satisfy market needs and keep a competitive advantage? The real issue is to explicitly consider this deviation in anticipating the outcome of the corresponding entry strategy.

In a projective phase, coherence of the entry strategy with the firm's current distinctive competence should be explicitly considered to systematically identify potential risks and the uncertainties that may exist in various estimates. In a proactive phase, the actions that the firm has taken, or could take, to decrease the risks associated with a deviation from its current distinctive competence should be explicitly analyzed. Such actions include, for instance, extensive product testing, market research, hiring of managerial talent with experience in the new area, consultancy, and appropriate selection of an advertising agency.

2. *Cost Behavior.* Cost estimates are crucial in the selection of an entry strategy. In a projective phase, one should consider possible changes in cost estimates due to environmental factors such as inflation on labor or raw materials, or stricter legal norms on product reliability or pollution standards. In a proactive phase, one should investigate the behavior of cost for alternative strategies and, in particular, the so-called experience effects. The Boston Consulting Group[4] has brought empirical evidence that in a wide range of products, unit costs tend to decline by 20% to 30% every time cumulative production of the product is doubled. This shows that substantial cost variations may result from different production levels and that these potential variations are particularly important at the time of the new entry.

3. *Resources Available.* In planning a new entry, resources are allocated according to the objectives set. More ambitious objectives will necessitate higher resources to be reached and may entail a higher perceived financial risk. In a study of 37 entries, Biggadike[2] has, however, found that projects with higher market share objectives tend to be more successful (see Chart 24-4). The percentage of entrants achieving their objective was 50% for those with market share objectives above 10% and only 32% for others. Entry on a large scale will result in lower costs and a higher efficiency, which may in part explain these findings. Another reason is that a project to which higher resources have been committed will draw more management attention and care. Resources should consequently be concentrated on key entries, and one should systematically question the desirability of minor projects creating unnecessary dispersion.

The anticipatory analysis should also investigate why resources can become inadequate and whether their level of allocation can be adjusted when required. A new entry plan that is already extending the financial capabilities of the firm is less likely to succeed if disfavorable, unexpected events occur. An analysis of the business portfolio provides an anticipation of future cash flows,[10] and the role of the new entry within this portfolio gives an indication of its priority in obtaining extra resources when required.

4. *Capacity to Monitor and Adapt.* A new entry creates a disturbance in a competitive market. To monitor market changes closely, an information system needs to be set up where timeliness is more important than minute accuracy. A flexible organization, clear procedures, easy communications, and clear responsibilities are also essential to success.

CHART 24.4 Market Objectives and Achievement in First Two Years of Entry

Share Objective	Number of Entrants	Achieved Objective	Missed Objective
Up to 5%	16	4	12
6–10%	3	2	1
11–15%	7	2	5
16–20%	5	4	1
More than 20%	6	3	3
	37	15	22

Source: Biggadike.[2]

Anticipatory Market Analysis

In an anticipatory analysis for a new entry, attention will be concentrated on the factors influencing the evolution of the market. A desirable step-by-step approach consists in making a projection of the market without the new entry, then considering the impact of alternative strategies for the new entry, and finally taking into account the full dynamics of the situation with reactions from, and counterreactions to, competition.

1. *Market Projection.* In the case of an entry into an existing market, a projection can be made of the market's evolution in the absence of the new entry as a basis for analysis. Such projection can in part be done through classical forecasting techniques, although it should not be limited to a forecast of market size only. It also should include basic market elements such as the relative importance of the sources of growth, including new users, new applications, or more usage of the product; the relative growth of alternative market segments; the evolution of the needs of these market segments; and the impact of these factors on the evolution of the market shares and profitability of the main competitors in the market, assuming a continuation of their current strategies.

2. *Market Stability.* The more stable a market is, the more robust one can expect a projection of that market to be. On the other hand, the more unstable a market is, the more opportunities that exist for new entries. The evaluation of the stability of a market is an important aspect of anticipating the outcome of a new entry strategy. It should consider consumers' and distributors' satisfaction and loyalty, potential technological changes, strengths of competitive postures, and entry costs.

3. *Direct Market Posture Elements.* The market posture of a product is ultimately determined by market share, sales, and profits. To anticipate the impact of a given entry strategy one should, however, first consider in depth the factors that are more directly under the influence of the firm: the brand and features awareness that the new entry will achieve; the market positioning of the new entry relative to consumer needs and competitive offerings; and the availability of the new product in distribution channels.

4. *Impact of Entry Strategy on Primary Demand.* *Primary demand* is the total demand for a product class. A new entry can in some circumstances develop this primary demand. This may in some cases be easier than gaining consumers away from the competition and will generate a less intensive competitive reaction. In the case of a completely new product creating a new product class, the development of primary demand is indeed the only avenue of expansion. There are, however, two broad issues to be considered in developing primary demand. The first is to identify the sources of primary demand that can be tapped with a new entry. The main sources to consider are new consumers, new applications, increased usage on existing applications, and increased added value per usage.

The second issue is the ability of the new entrant to keep the benefits of the additional primary demand that it has developed. There is ample evidence that efforts made by the smaller firms to develop the primary demand tend to benefit proportionally more to the market leader. This is obvious, for instance, when a firm makes potential consumers aware of the existence and benefits of a given product class; the consumers then discover that within this product class another firm provides a product better adapted to their need. The capability of the firm to retain the expansion of primary demand brought by its new entry will depend to a large extent on the three direct market posture elements previously discussed: awareness, market positioning, and product availability.

5. *Impact of Entry Strategy on Selective Demand. Selective demand* is the demand for a specific brand in a product class. An obvious objective of a new entry strategy is to gain selective demand. The demand for the new entry will be gained, at least partly, on competitors, unless it is obtained entirely from a development of the primary demand. Even in this unlikely case, competitors may not lose sales but will lose market share. All competitors will not be equally affected by the new entrant, and this will influence their individual reactions. It is consequently important to anticipate not only the level of selective demand for the new entrant but also how much market share has been transferred from each of the competitors and from cannibalization of existing offerings of the firm. The new entry will gain market share mainly from the brands that are positioned close to it, that is, those most similar to it in terms of product characteristics, price, or distribution outlets. It can consequently be said that through market positioning a firm does, to a large extent, choose its competition. For each alternative entry strategy, it is thus essential to anticipate the market position that will be achieved and the resulting pattern of competition.

Anticipatory Competitive Analysis

In the high market growth situation of the 1960s, a strategy formulated in the "absolute" to satisfy simultaneously the needs of the market and the objectives of the firm was to a large extent a sufficient condition of success. In the more competitive contemporary situation, the satisfaction of market needs is more than ever a necessary condition, but not a sufficient one. A market strategy will be effective only if it is also adequate relative to competitive actions, and competitive analysis has become increasingly important.[24,26]

Following a systematic approach, an anticipatory competitive analysis should contain a projective phase investigating probable actions of existing and potential competitors in the absence of a new entry by the firm; a proactive phase considering the impact of new entry strategies on competitors; and a reaction phase analyzing potential reactions of competitors to new entry strategies.

1. *Projection of Current Competitors' Actions.* When planning a new entry into an existing market, one should anticipate that current competitors, even if they do not expect the new entry, are also in the process of planning their own future actions. A failure in anticipating actions simultaneously prepared by competitors may result in a reduced competitive advantage for the new entrant compared with what it expected, in excessive competition in some market areas, and at the extreme in a possible market obsolescence of the new entry before it is even introduced. Some of the factors to consider in order to anticipate the actions currently planned by competitors are their objectives and resources, the market gaps they may try to fill, and current competition intensity.

2. *New Sources of Competition.* The new entry contemplated by the firm may also be exposed to the competition of other corporations that plan to enter the market in the future. These are firms that can base this new entry on a distinct competitive advantage and have the resources required to exploit it. They include, for instance, firms that: already have similar products in other markets, such as foreign competitors; already serve the market with other types of products; could penetrate the market by forward or backward vertical integration of their activities; could acquire an existing competitor in the market and provide it with additional resources or a new distinctive advantage.

3. *Impact of Entry Strategy on Competitors.* The impact of the new entry on competitors will depend on the relative importance of their increased sales due to the development of primary demand and of their current sales lost to the new entrant. The importance of this impact can be analyzed at four levels: sales, profits, market share, and emotions.

A new entry will result in a loss of market share for some competitors, even if their sales or profits increase due to the development of primary demand. A firm that is primarily concerned with its sales or profit level may not realize in the short run that its market share is declining. As a result, its competitors may gain a cost advantage which may considerably weaken its posture in the long run. This is one of the reasons why market share is increasingly seen as one of the most critical performance measures of the marketing-oriented firm.[5] A new entry that gains its market share from less marketing-oriented competitors is consequently less likely to generate strong reactions, especially if it does not reduce their sales or profits.

When a firm enters a market, it will also have an impact on competitors beyond sales, market share, and profits. This is an emotional impact due to the interpretation by the competitors of the firm's intentions and of their implications for the industry. For instance, the new entry of a specific firm in a market may be interpreted as a signal that this market has high potential, that prices are going to decline, that technology is going to be renewed, or that marketing investments should be expected to increase significantly. These interpretations may lead some firms to join the market, others to suspend additional investments in this market, and still others to fight off the new entrant beyond an economically reasonable level.

4. *Potential Competitive Reactions.* The analysis of the impact of the new entrant on the market and on the competition provides a number of indications of the possible retaliatory moves that the competition could undertake. To anticipate the main scenarios, these competitive moves can be systematically analyzed at three levels:

a. *The Marketing Mix Element Level.* Competitors may react directly against the distinctive advantage that the new entrant is capitalizing on. They may, for instance, respond to an improved product by their own product enhancement, to a cheaper product by price cuts, and to high promotional investments by increasing their own promotional budgets.

b. *The Product Market Level.* Instead of responding to the new entrant on its own terms, competitors may choose to keep the initiative and react on other elements of the marketing mix. They may, for instance, react to an improved product by price cuts and to high promotional investments by increased allowances to distributors.

c. *The Product Market Portfolio Level.* Competitors may also be able to counterattack in another product market where the new entrant is more vulnerable. The existence of such a possibility depends on the interrelationships of competitors across product markets, but it should be anticipated by the new entrant.

MODELS FOR NEW ENTRIES

Given the strategic importance of new entries, it is not surprising that a large number of models have been developed to assist managers in this area. The more representative of these models are presented here, and the emphasis is placed on the issues that they address in the context of a systematic anticipatory analysis. The progressive coverage of various elements can be illustrated by looking at the classes of models that have emerged over time: stochastic models, process models, aggregate models, and product positioning models.

Stochastic Models

Stochastic models attempt to estimate the long-term equilibrium market share of a product from the past purchasing behavior of consumers. This behavior is represented by a probabilistic process that is the combined outcome of all factors influencing purchasing decisions. The nature and parameters of this probabilistic process are determined from data gathered in a market test or in the first months of introduction of the new product. This approach cannot consequently be of help in the early stages of the new entry planning process. Furthermore, it requires that successive purchases made by a representative group of consumers be observed over a relatively short period of time, and this limits its use to frequently purchased packaged consumer goods.

In this case, stochastic models are perfectly adapted to the type of data provided by consumer panels and are useful in forecasting the equilibrium market share on the basis of early sales results. Equilibrium market share is particularly difficult to anticipate judgmentally from early sales results of frequently purchased packaged consumer goods, as sales will usually go through a peak and stabilize later at a lower level. This is due to the fact that the early growth comes from new triers of the product, and then new triers and repeat buyers combine to produce a high level of sales which declines as sales come from only repeat buyers. Stochastic models attempt to represent this phenomenon by operationalizing in different ways the general concept of brand loyalty. This can be achieved by separating explicitly repeat buyers from new triers, by distinguishing between different repeat classes, or by estimating the purchase probability of a brand given a purchase history for one individual.

Different types of stochastic models have been developed since the late 1950s.* The stochastic modeling approach is illustrated here by a brief description of STEAM, one of the most complete stochastic models.[20,21] It uses data gathered from a consumer panel in the first months following the launching of a new product to estimate the sales volume after the introductory period. The households belonging to the panel are divided into "depth of trial" (DOT) classes according to the number of times they have purchased the new product. Those who have never bought the product are in DOT class zero, those who have bought it once are in DOT class one, those who have bought it twice are in DOT class two, and so on. This separation of the population into DOT classes provides a higher homogeneity within each class in terms of experience and brand loyalty.

In each of these DOT classes, and on the basis of consumer panel data, the STEAM model determines the probability distribution of inter-purchase times. This distribution can be used to compute the probability that a household in a given DOT class will buy the new brand within one week, two weeks, and so on. From these probability distributions, the STEAM model simulates the behavior of individual households and provides an estimate of future brand sales.

The results of one application of the STEAM model are shown in Chart 24-5. In this example, the model has been used on the basis of the consumer panel data gathered in the first six months after the launching of a new brand. Probability distributions were estimated from these data, which allowed a

---

* For an excellent review of stochastic models, see Massy et al.[21] and Montgomery and Ryans,[22] from which this section draws.

CHART 24-5. Example of Application of the STEAM Model

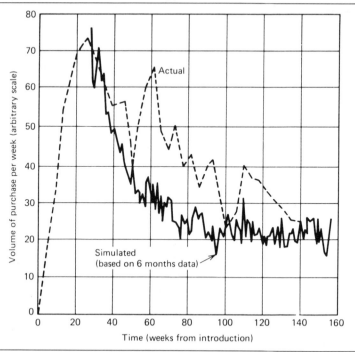

Source: Massy et al.[21] (p. 412).

simulation of individual households in order to forecast sales from six months to three years after the introduction of the new brand. While sales have increased regularly over the first six months, the model forecasts a decline and a stabilization of sales at a much lower level. Starting around week 50, the firm tried to stop the sales decline with an intensive promotional campaign. This was obviously not taken into account in the projections of the model and results in higher actual than predicted sales. Despite these additional marketing efforts, the sales of the new brand appear to decline inexorably toward the predicted equilibrium level. The analysis of repeat sales by the STEAM model has successfully detected the basic response to the product by the market, which seems to be only temporarily affected by increased promotional investment.

By analyzing market dynamics in detail over a period of time, stochastic models can project the long-run sales equilibrium level of a new brand as long as these dynamics do not change. Stochastic models require that data be available either from a market test or from the beginning of the introduction period. Consequently, they cannot contribute to the early phases of the new entry planning process and are mainly limited to frequently purchased consumer packaged goods. With some exceptions,[13,14,17] they merely provide a projection of market dynamics but do not make any provision for the influence that a change in the brand strategy would have on these dynamics.

Process Models

Process models explicitly consider that after the introduction of a new product, consumers go through different stages, from total ignorance of the product to its repeated purchase and strong brand loyalty. At a given point in time, different consumers will be in different stages in the consumption process. The transfer of consumers from one stage to the next is influenced by the marketing elements of the new entry strategy. This influence can be explicitly represented in the model, and the impact of alternative strategies on predicted sales can consequently be tested.

The best-known process models for new products are DEMON,[7] NEWS,[6] SPRINTER,[31] NEWPROD,[1] and TRACKER[3]. The process modeling approach is illustrated here by a brief description of SPRINTER. This model has been designed to assist in the formulation of marketing strategies for new frequently purchased consumer products. It is based on the process of diffusion of innovation and decomposes the population of consumers into five classes according to the nature of their purchases. Consumers are considered to move from one class to another according to the process represented in Chart 24-6. For instance, consumers buying the new brand for the first time will move from the potential trial class to the preference class. When buying the new brand a second time, they will move to the loyalty I class, and so on.

In each of these classes, the consumer behavior process is composed of five stages:

Awareness process

↓

Purchase intent process

↓

Search process

↓

Choice process

↓

Postpurchase process

CHART 24-6. General Structure of the SPRINTER Model

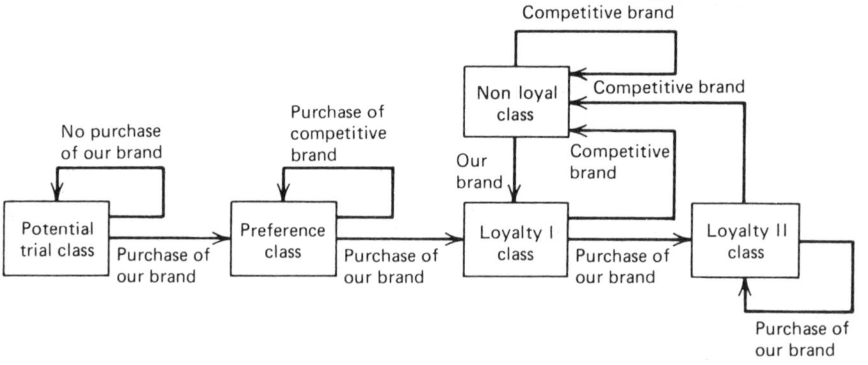

Source: Urban[31] (p. 311).

The number of potential consumers moving from one stage to the next is a function of the marketing activities of the firm, which include advertising, sampling, couponing, pricing, and distribution. The representation of this diffusion process is different for each class. For instance, advertising and promotion are particularly important in bringing a consumer to her or his first purchase of the new product, and their effects are modeled in detail in the potential trial class. After several purchases, consumers have a better knowledge of the product. Promotional activities are consequently represented in a more global fashion in the loyalty classes, while the effects of price on the purchase decision receive more attention.

Consumers are not simulated individually, and the "movement" of consumers just referred to is only figurative. The process is modeled at the level of the total number of consumers in each class. More than 500 equations represent the phenomena which ultimately determine the number of consumers buying the product in a time period and the resulting changes in the number of consumers in each class. The critical elements in these equations are response functions that describe the effects of marketing decisions. The estimation of these response functions, as well as of other parameters, requires an important data gathering program. For the introduction of a new brand, data are gathered in a market test through: a store audit; a consumers panel; awareness, attitudes, purchase intent, and product usage surveys; salesmen's reports; and advertising audits.

The SPRINTER model can be used to test alternative marketing strategies for a new product. In addition, the risk associated with the new brand can be evaluated by giving probability distributions for the input parameters and running a Monte Carlo analysis. Finally, the model provides an option to search automatically for the best strategy within a range of feasible decisions specified by the user.

The strength of process models is to explicitly consider the impact of marketing strategies on the outcome of a new entry. In addition, the detailed representation of the diffusion process provides a better understanding of market dynamics and a better diagnosis of potential problems at various levels: awareness, purchase intent, product availability, sales, profits, and so on. A potential drawback of process models lies in their strong data requirements. This is in part alleviated, however, by the fact that the modeled process can be represented in such a way that the model can accept judgmental inputs formulated by managers on the basis of their experience and of their knowledge of the new entry situation (see, e.g., Assmus[1]).

Aggregate Models

Aggregate models represent a situation at a global level in a single equation, or at least in a very limited number of equations. This is in fact the case with most classical forecasting techniques. The main purpose of such aggregate models is prediction, rather than explanation, and their explanatory power tends to be poor.

In the area of new entry planning, aggregate models are difficult to develop because of the lack of historical data. When an entry is planned in an existing market, classical forecasting techniques can obviously be used to predict the evolution of the total market size, assuming it will not be significantly affected by the new entry. However, aggregate models to predict sales or market share of a new entry are difficult to develop because of the lack of historical data. A notable exception, however, is the new product model developed at the N. W. Ayer advertising agency.[9] The purpose of this model was to predict product performance before market introduction. A data base has been built by the advertising agency of N. W. Ayer from the introduction of 60 food products, household supplies, and personal care items. These data were gathered from consumer surveys, retail audits, commercial data services, and a panel of experienced marketing and advertising executives. The principle of this approach was to develop a model from this data base in order to draw lessons from past introductions and to forecast the performance of new brands in similar product classes. The missing history of a new brand was in a sense replaced by observations made on past introductions of similar products.

The general structure of the model is composed of three stages, as illustrated in Chart 24-7: advertising recall, initial purchase, and repeat purchase. The marketing variables that have a major influence vary from one stage to the next. Advertising recall is mainly a function of the general product positioning and advertising. The initial purchase is mainly influenced by advertising recall, distribution, packaging, promotion, and consumer satisfaction with the product samples. At the repeat purchase level, price, product satisfaction, and purchase frequency become the critical factors. The response functions describing the influence of these marketing variables on advertising recall, initial purchase, and repeat purchase have been estimated

CHART 24-7. General Structure of the AYER Model

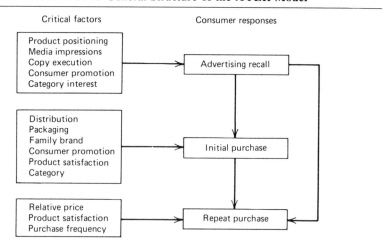

Source: Claycamp and Liddy[9] (p. 415).

from the data base. For instance, initial purchase of a new brand 13 weeks after introduction has been found to be best represented by:

$$
\begin{aligned}
\text{Initial purchase} = {} & -16 + 0.36 \text{ (advertising recall)} \\
& + 0.19 \text{ (distribution} \times \text{packaging)} \\
& + 9.25 \text{ (family brand)} \\
& + 0.09 \text{ (consumer promotion)} \\
& + 0.02 \text{ (product satisfaction)} \\
& + 0.07 \text{ (category usage)}
\end{aligned}
$$

The model is used before the introduction of a new brand by first asking a group of experts from the agency and the firm to estimate the values of the independent variables (product positioning, media impressions, etc.) for a given new entry strategy. The expected values of advertising recall, initial purchase, and repeat purchase are then computed by replacing the independent variables by their estimated values in the three response functions.

This model has been tested on eight new entries to predict initial purchase 13 weeks after introduction. For seven out of eight entries, the actual initial purchases were within ±10% of the predicted levels, and for five of them the predictive accuracy was within ±5%. The eighth entry had achieved better than anticipated retail distribution, and its actual initial purchases were 13% higher than the predicted level.

This aggregate model takes into account a number of market factors that are under the direct influence of elements of the marketing mix, and consequently it can be used to test alternative marketing strategies. Its use is limited, however, to new frequently purchased packaged consumer brands that are similar to the products in the data base.

CHART 24-8. Example of a Perceptual Map

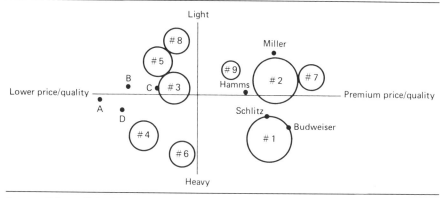

Source: Johnson[18] (p. 16)

Product Positioning Models

None of the previous models explicitly takes into account the characteristics of the new product. The impact of product characteristics is considered only globally, through variables representing product positioning and product satisfaction in the Ayer model, or implicitly in consumers' responses in other models.

More recently, a number of techniques have been developed that explicitly take into account the influence of product characteristics on consumer choice.* The purpose of these techniques is to guide market research and to provide a representation of the tradeoffs made by consumers in choosing a specific brand in a product class. An example of such a representation is given in Chart 24-8 for a beer market. It indicates that the two most determining characteristics for consumers in choosing between beer brands are perceived price/quality and lightness. In addition, it gives the position on these dimensions of four national brands and four regional brands (A–D). Finally, the numbers 1 through 9 correspond to the most preferred combinations of the two characteristics (or "ideal points") for nine market segments; the radius of the circle around each number is proportional to the size of the corresponding segment. For instance, the Miller and Hamms brands seem to be most preferred by segment 2, while Schlitz and Budweiser seem to be closer to the preferences of segment 1.

These techniques are the basis of some new product models such as LINMAP,[27] PERCEPTOR,[30] STRATOP,[25] and ASSESSOR.[29]

For instance, the purpose of the PERCEPTOR model is to help managers in the design, evaluation, and refinement of new frequently purchased consumer products. It is based on a series of market surveys that provide

---

* For an excellent review of these techniques, see Green and Srinivasan[12] and Shocker and Srinivasan.[28]

perceptual maps such as the one represented in Chart 24-8, but at different levels. In a first stage, a perceptual map is obtained representing the positions of existing brands and the ideal points of homogeneous market segments. This study provides a basis to analyze the current situation and to generate new product concepts. In a second stage, a new product concept is shown to a sample of consumers, and data are gathered to provide a new perceptual map that includes the perceived position of the new product concept. If the new concept appears to have a market potential, a third survey is made where the physical product is given to a consumer sample for actual use; this provides another perceptual map including the perceived position of the new product after usage.

In estimating the long-run market share of a new product, the PERCEPTOR model uses a classic decomposition between the effects of first trials and repeat purchases. The probabilities of trial and of repeat purchase are postulated to be a function of the squared distance between the positions of an ideal point and of the new brand. They are, however, estimated from perceptual maps gathered at different stages. The probability of trial function is estimated from the perceptual map obtained from consumers exposed to the new concept and from their stated purchase intentions. The probability of repeat purchase is estimated from the perceptual map obtained from consumers having actually used the product and from their stated intentions to repurchase the new product.

Like most new product models, PERCEPTOR provides an estimate of the expected market share of a new product. Being based on the positioning of the new brand relative to existing offerings and to the market needs, it also gives two critical inputs to the formulation of an entry strategy. First, it gives an estimation of the market share obtained by the new entry from each of the existing brands. This estimation of market share transfers is based on relative positions, and the closer the new brand is positioned to an existing offering the more impact it should be expected to have on its market share.

Second, the market share corresponding to alternative positioning strategies can be estimated. When the expected outcome of a positioning strategy is found acceptable, the product characteristics and marketing mix corresponding to this strategy can be determined. In this fashion, the model can guide the modification and improvement of a new product before its introduction.

CONCLUSIONS

New product or market entries are essential to preserve the long-term competitiveness and survival of a firm. The development of adequate entry strategies is also one of the most difficult areas of management, as illustrated by the high failure rates reported in the literature. To reduce this risk of failure, a complete anticipatory analysis should be systematically performed with the following objectives:

1. Evaluating the factors influencing the future performance of an entry strategy

2. Identifying improved entry strategies

3. Providing a detailed knowledge of the situation and of potential threats so that strategies may be more readily modified after entry according to the course of events

An anticipatory analysis for a new entry should systematically investigate the future evolution of the environment, the firm, the market, and the competition. This investigation should be performed at three levels. In an initial projective phase, the expected evolution of these key areas is determined, assuming that the firm will not undertake a new entry. In a proactive phase, the impact of alternative new entry strategies on the environment, the firm, the market, and the competition is evaluated. Finally, in a reaction analysis phase, the possible reactions of these elements are investigated. Such a systematic approach is necessary to avoid two major pitfalls. The first one is a basic implicit assumption that there is a predetermined evolution of the firm, the environment, the market, and the competition and that a new entry will insert itself naturally in this evolution. This reflects a total reliance on projective analysis and underestimates the direct impact or the reactions that a new entry may generate in a given situation. The second pitfall is the human tendency to select elements of the analysis that support a preconceived position on a particular problem. This is particularly likely in new entry decisions that may have significant organizational implications, and some aspects of the problem may remain hidden by default. Not only may this bias the decisions but, in addition, it may leave management unprepared when new events develop during the entry period.

Models have been developed over the last 20 years to assist managers in new entry decisions, and representative examples of these models have been presented. They differ widely in terms of the techniques that they use and the points in the planning process where they can make a contribution. What is more important, however, is to realize for which areas of an anticipatory analysis they can be most valuable and what are their current limitations. The purpose of a new entry model is to assist management in investigating in detail a subcomponent of the situation and in testing alternative strategies, given some simplifying assumptions. The responsibility of the manager lies in having a complete view of the elements influencing the new entry, through a systematic anticipatory analysis, and in exploiting models to get a better understanding of some aspects of the situation when feasible. Not only will this allow him or her to better appreciate the likely performance of a new entry strategy, but also, and maybe more importantly, it will help in facing new events when they emerge.

REFERENCES

1. Assmus, Gert, "NEWPROD: The Design and Implementation of a New Product Model," *Journal of Marketing,* vol. 39, January 1975, pp. 16–23.

2. Biggadike, Ralph, *Entering New Markets: Strategies and Performance,* Report No. 77–108, Marketing Science Institute, Cambridge, MA, September 1977.

3. Blattberg, Robert, and John Golanty, "TRACKER: An Early Test Market Forecasting and Diagnostic Model for New Product Planning," *Journal of Marketing Research,* vol. 15, May 1978, pp. 192–202.

4. Boston Consulting Group, *Perspectives on Experience,* Boston Consulting Group, Boston, 1970.

5. Buzzell, Robert D., Bradley T. Gale, and Ralph C. Sultan, "Market Share: A Key to Profitability," *Harvard Business Review,* vol. 53, no. 1, January–February 1975, pp. 97–106.

6. Charnes, A., W. W. Cooper, J. K. Devoe, D. B. Learner, L. Light, L. Pringle, and E. F. Snow, "NEWS Report: A Discussion of the Theory and Application of the Planning Portion of Demon," in Jagdish N. Sheth, ed. *Models of Buyer Behavior.* Harper & Row, New York, 1974, pp. 296–309.

7. Charnes, A., W. W. Cooper, J. K. Devoe, and D. B. Learner, "DEMON: A Management Model for Marketing New Products," *California Management Review,* vol. 11, no. 1, Fall 1968, pp. 31–46.

8. Choffray, Jean-Marie, and Gary L. Lilien, *Market Planning for New Industrial Products,* John Wiley, New York, 1980.

9. Claycamp, Henry J., and Lucien E. Liddy, "Prediction of New Product Performance: An Analytical Approach," *Journal of Marketing Research,* vol. 6, November 1969, pp. 414–420.

10. Day, George S., "Diagnosing the Product Portfolio," *Journal of Marketing,* vol. 41, no. 2, April 1977, pp. 29–38.

11. Godet, Michel, *The Crisis in Forecasting and the Emergence of the "Prospective" Approach,* Pergamon Press, New York, 1979.

12. Green, Paul E., and V. Srinivasan, "Conjoint Analysis in Consumer Research: Issues and Outlook," *Journal of Consumer Research,* vol. 5, no. 2, September 1978, pp. 103–123.

13. Harary, Frank, and Benjamin Lipstein, "The Dynamics of Brand Loyalty: A Market Approach," *Operations Research,* vol. 10, January–February 1962, pp. 19–40.

14. Hartung, Philip H., and James L. Fisher, "Brand Switching and Mathematical Programming in Market Expansion," *Management Science,* vol. 11, August 1965, pp. 231–243.

15. Henderson, James M., and Richard E. Quandt, *Microeconomic Theory,* 2nd ed., McGraw-Hill, New York, 1971.

16. Hopkins, David S., *New Product Winners and Losers,* The Conference Board, New York, 1979.

17. Horsky, Dan, "An Empirical Analysis of the Optimal Advertising Policy," *Management Science,* vol. 23, 1977, pp. 1037–1049.

18. Johnson, Richard M., "Market Segmentation: A Strategic Management Tool," *Journal of Marketing Research,* vol. 8, February 1971, pp.13–18.

19. Kotler, Philip, William Gregor, and William Rodgers, "The Marketing Audit Comes of Age," *Sloan Management Review,* vol. 18, no. 2, Winter 1977, pp. 25–43.

20. Massy, William F., "Forecasting the Demand for a New Convenience Product," *Journal of Marketing Research,* vol. 6, no. 4, November 1969, pp. 405–413.

21. Massy, William F., David B. Montgomery, and David G. Morrison, *Stochastic Models of Buying Behavior,* The M.I.T. Press, Cambridge, MA, 1970.

22. Montgomery, David B., and Adrian B. Ryans, "Stochastic Models of Consumer Choice Behavior, in Scott Ward and Thomas S. Robertson, eds., *Consumer Behavior: Theoretical Sources,* Prentice-Hall, Englewood Cliffs, NJ, 1973, pp. 521–576.

23. Naylor, John, and Alan Wood, *Practical Marketing Audits,* Associated Business Programmes, London, 1978.

24. Oxenfeldt, Alfred R., and William L. Moore, "Customer or Competitor, Which Guideline for Marketing?" *Management Review,* August 1978, pp. 43–48.

25. Pessemier, Edgar A., *Product Management: Strategy and Organization,* John Wiley, New York, 1977, Ch. 5.

26. Porter, Michael E., *Competitive Strategy,* Free Press, New York, 1980.

27. Shocker, Allan D., and V. Srinivasan, "A Consumer-Based Methodology for the Identification of New Product Ideas," *Management Science,* vol. 20, February 1974, pp. 921–937.

28. Shocker, Allan D., and V. Srinivasan, "Multiattribute Approaches to Product-Concept Evaluation and Generation: A Critical Review," *Journal of Marketing Research,* vol. 16, May 1979, pp. 159–180.

29. Silk, Alvin J., and Glen L. Urban, "Pre-Test-Market Evaluation of New Packaged Goods: A Model and Measurement Methodology," *Journal of Marketing Research,* vol. 15, May 1978, pp. 171–191.

30. Urban, Glen L., "PERCEPTOR: A Model for Product Positioning," *Management Science,* vol. 21, April, 1975, pp. 858–871.

31. Urban, Glen L., "SPRINTER Mod III: A Model for the Analysis of New Frequently Purchased Consumer Products," *Operations Research,* vol. 18, no. 5, 1970.

32. Urban, Glen L., and John R. Hauser, *Design and Marketing of New Products,* Prentice-Hall, Englewood Cliffs, NJ, 1980.

25

FORECASTING FOR INDUSTRIAL PRODUCTS

DAVID WEINSTEIN
INSEAD, Fontainebleau, France

INTRODUCTION

Forecasting the sales of industrial goods is critically important for a great many organizations. Within the firm, the sales forecast serves as a basis for the allocation of departmental resources in sales, production, finance, personnel, research and development (R&D), and so on. Outside it, this same forecast will affect suppliers, major customers, and others whose activities depend on the particular industrial product. Even though, in theory at least, industrial sales forecasting is no different from any other type of prediction, the use of statistical forecasting methods is not widespread in this field. The majority of industrial sales forecasting remains intuitive, complex, and, quite often, highly political.

A review of the relevant literature and extensive field research involving interviews with numerous managers show that the chances of changing present methods of industrial forecasting are small. There are several reasons for this. First, market structures change, and with them the premises for the forecast. Second, since personal objectives, and in turn rewards for achievement, are derived from their forecasts, salespeople and executives are reluctant to "formalize" and reveal their forecasting methods. Moreover, the present forecasting procedure involves discussions and performance reviews at various hierarchical levels. This exchange of information up and down the organization is regarded as a vital by-product of the forecasting process, since it helps the organization remain alert to changes both in the marketplace and within the company. Thus, the process itself is as important as the forecast, which explains why the managers interviewed felt that drastic changes in industrial forecasting practices were inconceivable.

Managers are not insensitive to the dangers of bias and gamesmanship in their present practices. But although a changeover to statistical methods might result in greater forecasting accuracy, the costs of doing so—in terms of existing benefits that would be lost by a change—are prohibitive. Thus, rather than drastically change their approach, most managers prefer merely to identify weaknesses and make improvements wherever possible using the present system. The challenge, then, is to help preserve the strengths of current practices and find remedies for issues that are problematic.

The purpose of this chapter is to identify these issues and propose practical solutions. In the following section, the industrial sales forecasting process is described in more detail to help the reader understand both the concepts proposed and how they may be applied. The problems of the process that are general to most industrial situations—the "universal weaknesses"—are then discussed. Next, a framework for analysis is provided, which is designed to identify and assess specific sources of bias in a given sales forecasting system. Last, some recent developments aimed at improving industrial sales forecasting are considered.

THE TYPICAL FORECASTING SYSTEM

The typical forecasting system for industrial products has three major components: a salesforce composite subsystem, a headquarters subsystem, and a reconciliation subsystem.[8] The first two subsystems feed into the third, which then assesses both vantage points and combines them to make a forecast. As can be seen from the solid lines in Chart 25-1, the process may be iterative: If the reconciliation subsystem fails to yield a forecast (whether by consent or by decree), further rounds of discussion will take place until a forecast is finally obtained. The solid lines represent explicit information; the dotted lines show informal flows of information and feedback. Explicit information flowing from headquarters staff to the sales force, for example, would probably include economic and industrial statistics, likely competitive developments, constraints on capacity, new product information, and promotional plans. Explicit information flowing from the sales force to headquarters might include developments observed at the level of end users, suggestions for tactical moves to overcome competition (e.g., lowering prices, increasing promotion, etc.), and constraints on manpower. A great deal of implicit information also flows between the three subsystems, including both formal and informal feedback; an example is the perceptual impressions from past experience of working members of other subsystems.

A distinction should be made, however, between two types of forecast—the strategic and the tactical—in which the subsystems in Chart 25-1 play rather different relative roles. The former involves new projects (e.g., the introduction of a new product or the exploration of a new territory), whereas the latter relates to a current activity. Another distinction is that a strategic

CHART 25-1. Typical Forecasting System for Industrial Products

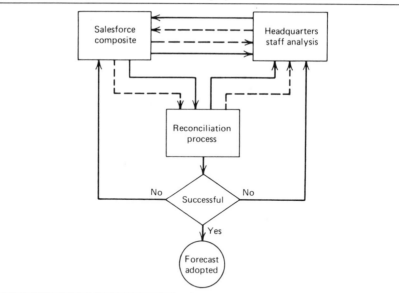

forecast usually implies a change in the allocation of resources (e.g., making investments or divestments) and is long term in orientation, whereas tactical forecasting is done on a shorter-term basis.

Strategic forecasting is generally under the control of headquarters and is derived from such information as (1) selected salesperson and executive opinion, (2) macrostatistical projection of useful variables (e.g., regional surveys of buying power or sales, by Standard Industrial Classification[2]), and (3) feedback from local test markets. More detailed discussion of the analytical approaches adopted in this kind of forecasting is given elsewhere in this handbook and in other literature.[16,21]

The role of the sales force, then, is rather limited as far as strategic forecasting is concerned. Tactical forecasting, on the other hand, is based on the combined opinions of headquarters and sales force, and it is this type of forecasting, the more problematic, that will concern us for the rest of this chapter. The most important ingredient of the tactical forecast is the intuitive judgment of the sales force—the "sales force composite." A brief discussion of the salesperson's role may help explain his or her preeminence in this type of forecasting.

The determinants of the salesperson's role are, first, the product, and second, the market. The typical industrial salesperson deals with a mix of complex products and a restricted number of clients. The clients require not only different technical specifications and logistical services, but also a deep understanding of their business and organization. Thus the salesperson should be technically competent and have a good personal rapport with members of the customer organization. Salespeople's intimate knowledge of their territory is indispensable in industrial marketing; because of their invaluable experience, their judgment is very influential.

There is evidence that the performance of statistical forecasting routines is superior to that of human judgment.[6,15,16,30] However, while the former can only detect and evaluate structural changes a posteriori, the salesperson may be able to identify such changes as they occur, or at least once enough evidence of impending change has been accumulated. More important, the salesperson's credibility vis-à-vis his or her superior is high, for the former is held personally responsible for his or her actions.

For these reasons, the sales forecasting process for industrial products has resulted in a "bottom-up" procedure which is firmly rooted and difficult to change. One obvious strength of such a system is the benefit of the salesperson's alertness and ability to interpret phenomena encountered in the field. Another advantage of the sales force composite is the scrutiny to which the information is subjected as it travels through the system via different parties, each with a personal vantage point. These two strengths are the basic reasons for the longevity of sales force composites in the forecasting of industrial sales.

The discussions that follow are based on an investigation of numerous sales force composites in a cross section of industries and countries.[8] The research method involved a careful analysis of the systems, based on three waves of interviews across numerous organizations.[12]

ISSUES OF CONCERN

The sales force composite is a product of human judgment. While Chapters 30, 31 and 32 discuss in detail the problems it entails, here our primary concern is with the interaction among the individuals responsible for this judgment. Such interaction includes an exchange of information, on the one hand, but also negotiation and gamesmanship on the other. An obvious weakness is the danger of bias inherent in this system. The sales forecast, as has been said, is used not only for plans in production scheduling and so on, but also for the personal objectives of the sales force—that is, their sales quota. Achievement of the latter brings financial bonus and stature in the organization. However, since the forecast on which the quota is based depends largely on the salesperson's own opinion, it is highly likely that biases will come into play. The nature of such biases depends on the particular business, its reward system, the individuals involved, and the way they interact. A systematic framework of analysis to help the manager identify and assess the problems of bias specific to his or her own situation will be discussed later. Three universal weaknesses of industrial sales forecasting systems, all of them involving bias of one kind or another, must be considered first. These are (1) expertise and contagion errors, (2) loss and distortion of valuable information, and (3) confusion of forecasts with objectives.

Expertise and Contagion Errors

The cornerstone of the forecasting process is the individual salesperson's experience and insight into his or her client's territory. The salesperson prepares a forecast on this basis, and discusses it with his or her superior, who then prepares a more aggregate forecast, as a function of personal experience and observations of past forecasting errors by subordinates. The individual errors of judgment at every level are called "expertise" errors. Staelin and Turner[23] have shown that the smaller the "building blocks" of the forecast, the smaller the aggregate error, for at the territory level errors in different directions will mutually cancel.

The assumption here is that every salesperson prepares a forecast independently. However, this is not always the case, since salespeople communicate with each other and are also exposed to common information provided by staff at headquarters and other sources. In particular, data on the macroeconomic outlook, capacity constraints, and promotional plans might be disseminated by corporate planners. This could cause a "contagion" error,[23] that is, a common forecasting error at individual territory level by all salespeople receiving the same information.

Since the design of sales territories is subject to other concerns, treatment of expertise errors by disaggregation is not always possible. Thus the salesperson's analysis can only be improved by training and consulting activities. The isolation of systematic individual biases, as will be described later, is also of considerable importance. These activities may be carried out on a continuous basis, within the interaction of the salesperson and his or her superior, in the form of evaluation of past forecasts. Furthermore, headquarters staff may provide periodic training programs or conferences that are aimed at reducing expertise errors.

Contagion errors should be considered in light of the common information that is disseminated. Consider, for example, the case of production capacity constraints when communicated to the sales force. A common reaction by the salesperson is to try to change his or her sales mix in order to avoid negotiations with those responsible for allocation and possibly disappointing clients. Thus, the communication of capacity constraints may eventually cause overcapacity and restrict previous expansion plans based on strategic market potential. Contagion errors may be caused by pessimistic industry and economic forecasts, thereby creating self-fulfilling prophecies. A similar effect may be caused by the "reputation" of other parties to the sale. For example, past problems of quality control or customer service may be extrapolated by the sales force, causing a downward bias in the forecasts of the affected products.

Sensitivity to formal and informal information that might cause contagion error is essential. In discussing this problem with managers, it was noticed that the amount of formal attention to contagion errors varies. One practical approach is for every manager who collects subordinates' forecasts to aggregate them and communicate his or her perception of percentage contagion error and possible causes. As the process moves up the system, increasing evidence may thus be accumulated regarding contagion errors.

Another approach to the problem involves sequencing and experimentation. Corporations have been studied that require every salesperson and manager to provide an independent forecast before being exposed to common information; after exposure the person is allowed to correct his or her forecast. In one case, at a time when contagion errors were suspected to be serious, an organization withheld information from a sample of salespeople and managers in order to provide a "control" for these errors. This approach is clearly extreme, but it does show the amount of concern and effort that some firms are willing to invest.

Loss and Distortion of Information

A system in which humans collect, transmit, transform, and interpret information is expected to filter and distort information. Senior executives, when interviewed, were content to "live with the problem," since too much information flowing directly to them would clutter their overview. However, the same executives complained that there are some data that sales force composites lose. Retention of these data, they say, would improve decisions that are based on the sales forecast. More specifically, these concerns may be divided into three categories: absorption of uncertainty, loss of data for segmentation analysis, and loss of timely strategic information.

Absorption of Uncertainty

The end result of a sales force composite forecast is usually a predicted value for future sales. Since this is the outcome of numerous deliberations, it is considered by the users (i.e., senior executives) to be fairly reliable. However, they also know that uncertainty is associated with the forecast, and awareness of the extent of such uncertainty is invaluable, because it is this factor that represents the risk of the strategy being pursued. This is important in two ways, for both overestimates and underestimates result in either real or opportunity costs, which management has to take into consideration.

Three different approaches may be used to conserve risk information within the system: conditional forecasting, three-point forecasting, and key account reporting. Under the first approach, rather than submit forecasts, salespeople and their superiors present scenarios in which explicit assumptions are made about customer behavior and needs, competitive activity, environmental forces, and internal company resources. The combination of these variables into several possible scenarios allows management to assess the upside and downside risk involved. The second approach requires the submission of three estimates (pessimistic, most likely, and optimistic), rather than a single sales figure prediction. There are two benefits to this approach, the immediate one being that the possible risk is determined by the range of variation. The second is the possibility of simulating various scenarios and obtaining the "risk profile" of the periods' sales using the Monte Carlo simulation. This profile would allow management to trade off reward and risk according to their risk preference.[11]

Finally, a "key account" approach could also help ascertain the possible risk. Under this method, certain accounts are monitored closely, and their unexpected behavior is "flagged." Accounts in this category may be opinion-leading companies or disproportionately large customers whose behavior may considerably influence sales. To utilize the information from such accounts, past experience must be accumulated before explicit extrapolations can be made.

Lack of Data for Segmentation Analysis

The forecasting system is generally segmented according to past strategies (e.g. by product, geographic region, or end use). Due to the ever-changing nature of the competitive environment, it is in the interest of product managers to study alternative segmentation schemes (e.g. in terms of the account size, purchasing organization types, technology, etc.). As shown in Chart 25-2, the salesperson prepares a forecast by aggregating forecasts of individual accounts. In turn, his or her manager aggregates the forecast across the sales territories. Concern has been expressed, particularly by product managers, that after this aggregation they no longer have access to the raw data at a disaggregate level. Thus, unless they undertake a special research project, a study of the consequences of alternative segmentation schemes is impossible. If raw data by accounts were available on a timely basis, management could anticipate the emergence of new segments and act on it earlier than is presently the case. This problem may be solved by retention of account characteristics, sales records, and forecasts in a data bank accessible to management. The data would be collected from forecasting forms, call reports, and purchase orders that are periodically filled out by individual salespeople.

Although the principles behind such data bank are simple, its successful utilization has several prerequisites. The notion of segmentation analysis and periodic forecasting by various segmentation schemes should be a "way of life" for managers, so that demand for the service will persist. Also, the sales force should be motivated to provide the information periodically, since the resulting analysis would eventually be to its benefit. Finally, the proper infrastructure for building and maintaining this computer-based system should be available.

CHART 25-2. Steel Products Company: Annual Sales Forecast

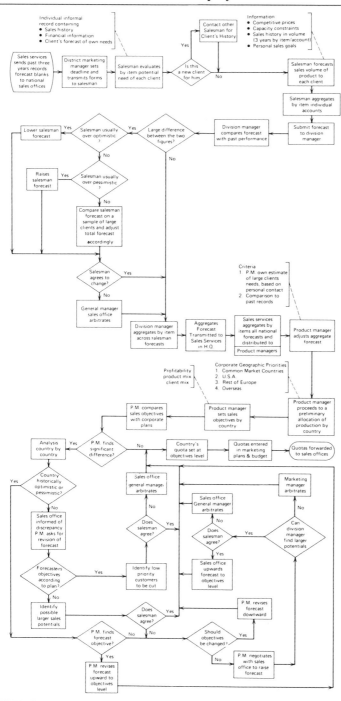

Loss of Strategic Information

Because industrial marketers rely heavily on sales force composite forecasts, they take the risk of failing to detect certain strategic changes that might be taking place in the field. Two research experiments may be cited here. In one, the appearance of a new, significant, and competitive product was not reported by many salespeople who had been formally trained to do so.[20] In the other, information that salespeople obtained from their customers was not correct, and in fact, systematic changes in client perception had been taking place, with salespeople being unable to detect them.[9]

The measures companies may take to correct these flaws are mainly in the form of positive and constructive feedback to the sales force, coupled with periodic training. Whereas rewards for especially valuable information may be offered, a system could also be designed to provide for the flow of qualitative information alongside quantitative forecasts. In other words, a "strategic observation" section may be required as an appendix to each quantitative forecast. This section would include the manager's observations and also significant observations made by subordinates.

Clearly, some information will always be suppressed or distorted; however, the importance of this problem can be minimized by providing the format for reporting strategic observations and giving positive feedback when such information is actually transmitted. The more isolated and helpless the salesperson feels, the less motivated he or she will be to help the organization change in the face of phenomena the salesperson can actually observe in the field.

Confusion Between Forecasts and Objectives

An important function of the forecast in a management system is to set targets and objectives for the individuals concerned. Forecasts and objectives are thus always linked to each other. However, as the literature shows, the setting of objectives is a rather complex process.[18,19] The more related the objectives are to the forecast, the more difficult it is to avoid bias.[5,15] Furthermore, the greater the role of the individual in setting his or her own objectives, the higher the likelihood of bias.[29] The amount of bias and its direction depend on the way objectives are used by the organization. In practice, then, a manager's understanding of his or her use of objectives would help identify the bias introduced by subordinates into their forecasts. The following represents a brief discussion of the three purposes of setting objectives, that is, to reduce fluctuations, to determine performance norms, and to provide motivation.[4]

Reduction of Fluctuation. Fluctuation is likely to be reduced when a superior delegates and a subordinate commits himself or herself to a prespecified achievement. Fluctuation in forecasting follows the same rules: as the forecasting process makes its way up the system, more aspects of the external and internal environment are considered, and possible responses are given to various uncertainties. The process of aggregation should cause a mutual cancellation of "expertise effect" errors, thus smoothing out the forecast. Objective setting and forecasting thus both entail useful opportunities for sharing opinions about the business, evaluation, and feedback.[5] However, this process of aggregation to avoid fluctuation may instead aggregate bias, depending on the mix of individuals involved.

Determination of Norms of Performance. When both the subordinate and his or her superior know what is expected of them—at their respective levels—they can reduce their role ambiguity. Since in many cases good performance is rewarded whereas failure may entail penalties, there is a need to determine precisely what is meant by "good performance."[7,25,26] Because of this, however, a wish to impress superiors may bias a subordinate's forecast.

Provision of Motivation. The level at which an objective is set is in itself of motivating value. For example, a sales quota just above a salesperson's own estimation might stimulate him or her to work harder, whereas one set far beyond the person's abilities might be demoralizing. Likewise, given a progressive bonus structure, a target just under the salesperson's capability might be stimulating, whereas one set too low might result in complacency. Setting too high an objective can also result in salespeople giving an unrealistically low forecast next time around.

The response of individuals to the process of setting of objectives also depends on their culture and individual profile.[3,4] Furthermore, their forecasts will be affected by the nature of their interaction with others. In other words, the sales force composite process is one of "rolling negotiations" (the salesperson with his or her superior, and the superior with his or her own superior). The next section provides a framework for assessing some of the biases involved in the process.

FRAMEWORK FOR ANALYZING BIAS

The "bottom-up" nature of the process of industrial sales forecasting, coupled with the inseparability of forecasts and objectives, makes negotiation necessary at every stage in the company hierarchy. Replications of studies of sales force composite systems in the United States, Europe, and South America show that at every subordinate–superior interface, the process follows five steps (see Chart 25-3).[27]

1. Benchmark Forecast Preparation

The "benchmark forecast" is the forecast of the individual at each level of the forecasting hierarchy. The benchmark is based on four types of input: (1)

CHART 25-3. Rolling Negotiation Concept

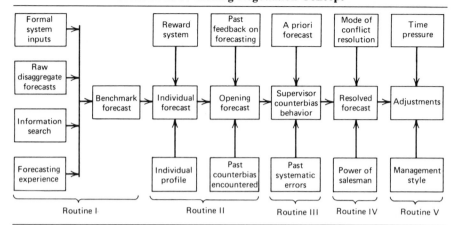

formal system inputs, (2) raw disaggregated forecasts, (3) information search, and (4) past forecasting experience. Once such a benchmark is determined, bias behavior and negotiation tactics enter the process.

Formal System Inputs. The individual communicates on a continuous basis with parties in and out of the organization who assimilate, transmit, and manipulate information.[22] The routing of this information, and its content, will depend on the organization's structure and the strategy it pursues. For example, multiproduct- and multimarket-oriented businesses usually use some form of matrix organization, with managers communicating laterally with the salespeople, providing them with strategic information.

Raw Disaggregate Forecasts. At every level there is input of disaggregate data that were complied at an earlier stage. Salespeople will first obtain or perform forecasts for their largest clients or key accounts. Similarly, a sales manager will obtain forecasts for the salesperson reporting to him or her, as well as for the accounts the manager handles directly. The reason this category should be distinguished from the previous one is that it is used as a filter for the former, as shown in Chart 25-3.

Information Search. Interviews with numerous salespeople and their managers reveal that each individual searches for information beyond these formal organizational interfaces. The more experience an individual has, the larger his or her informal network of information. This may include colleagues in competing firms, professional associations, trade publications, and so on. The more uncertainty the individual faces, the more he or she will rely on such an informal search.

Past Forecasting Experience. The way the individual processes information also depends on his or her past experience with the procedure. On the one hand, past forecasting performance bears on the process in terms of the size of past errors and their direction (however, "error" in this case is the difference between the benchmark forecast in the previous period and the actual results, rather than the formally agreed forecast). On the other hand, the individual's formal training is also a part of the experience. Salespeople who receive formal education may utilize certain information and methods quite differently from those who do not. This variance may be observed across different companies, as well as within the same organization.

2. Individual Bias Behavior

As previously discussed, three factors contribute to the individual bias that is applied to the benchmark forecast: the need for reducing fluctuations, norms of performance, and motivation. Individual bias may be divided into two types: income maximizing[24] and approval seeking.[5] Obviously the profile and experience of the salesperson will influence his or her behavior. Our investigations show that younger, inexperienced salespeople display greater optimism than their more mature and weathered counterparts.[13] Similarly, within multinational corporations, Italian forecasters, for example, were found to be more optimistic than their French colleagues. Finally, the initial forecast may be used as an "opening position" in a negotiation process whose end result may be influenced by many nonmarket or customer-oriented factors.

3. Superior Counterbias Behavior

When a subordinate or an executive submits a forecast to his or her superior, the latter will naturally evaluate the prediction. The criteria that he or she will inevitably use are personal observations on the territory or product in question. Variation between the subordinate's and the superior's forecast will trigger a comparison of analyses and attempts to reach a concensus on "what will happen." However, the superior also inspects the submitted forecast from another vantage point: in terms of past forecasts from the subordinate. Thus, if the subordinate has shown signs of overoptimism in the past, the superior will try to temper it, and vice versa.

4. Resolution

How the gap is bridged between a supervisor's and a subordinate's forecast differs across companies and cultures. Some companies insist on a concensus; others, however, use downward imposition. Moreover, a systematic difference emerges according to the role of the salesperson. As has been said, the salesperson in industrial marketing is a "boundary person" with his or her role extending to the organizations of both employer and clients.[29] This role gives the salesperson power over the performance of his or her function. The more important the role of the salesperson in the mix of marketing activities, the more complex is his or her task and hence the greater is the power the person possesses.

5. Authorization and Adjustment

Following the resolution, any changes in objectives must be disaggregated down to the individual salesperson level. Most companies interviewed felt that concensus seeking is desirable; however, because the forecasting process is rather time consuming, downward imposition may sometimes have to take place. Some companies, once they impose forecasts from the "top down," take steps to explain the forecasts provided and offer formal qualitative feedback, while others do nothing of the sort.

This model of the interface between a subordinate and superior during the forecasting process is of a "rolling" nature. It applies to all interfaces as the process flows up the hierarchical system. The framework is useful for analysis of the interface in relation to past forecasting performance. Thus, certain systematic deviations may be identified as a function of untempered pessimism or optimism. Similarly, the analysis may identify good quota negotiators (who minimize sales quotas in order to maximize their bonus) as a source of variance between sales forecasts and actual performance. Clearly, different sources of bias will play different roles in various industries, companies, cultures, and times. The role of this framework is to help both the superior and subordinate to analyze their past forecasting (either separately or together) with the help of a systematic agenda. Efforts to implement this model in quantitative estimation of bias for various individual situations are under way.

THE FORECASTING MANAGER

Rather than consider the issues in isolation, the forecasting process may be seen as a clear organizational responsibility. Since forecasting errors, especially those caused by "contagion," are somewhat costly, minimizing them justifies an organizational investment. One corporation with which I am familiar has appointed a "forecasting manager." The task of this executive is to improve the system, information flow, and training of salespeople, as well as to train managers in the use of forecasting methods—both statistical and intuitive. A major side benefit that has occurred in this case is the provision of feedback to individual forecasters on the quality of their forecasts, which can thus point to personal biases.

INCENTIVE TO SALESFORCE FOR BETTER FORECASTING

An interesting attempt by management to heighten the interest of salespeople in the forecasting process was reported in the literature involving IBM's subsidiary in Brazil.[10] The management of this organization decided to financially reward salespeople for better forecasts. In addition to the reward that the individual received for outdoing his or her objective for the period, a bonus was provided for forecasting performance. The method, called the "OFA system," requires the individual to commit himself or herself to the period's sales objective, but also to state what his or her forecast is with respect to attaining it. As a result, with the increasing reward for better sales performance in relation to the objective, the ratio of forecast/objective enables the person to receive an additional bonus as the ratio approaches 1 (see Chart 25-4).

FUTURE DIRECTIONS

Analytical Developments

The gap between process-based sales force composite forecasting and analytical methods has, fortunately, started to close as a result of two trends. On the one hand, more and more managers are now exposed through business schools and executive education to analytical forecasting methods. Certainly, the result has not been a mass conversion to analytical methods. However, those who are analytically "literate" in the forecasting process have been able to compare their intuitive forecast with their judgmental one without the contaminating effect of organizational politics and performance pressures.

Concurrent with this educational phenomenon is the use of microcomputers, which has spread at an unprecedented pace, especially use of user-friendly spreadsheet software packages. The ability to manipulate numbers easily and efficiently has considerably improved the quantitative skills of many managers, who traditionally had shied away from such analysis. This environment has facilitated efforts to provide a more analytical basis for the individual's forecasts.[21]

These changes have resulted in a trend toward the integration of analytical forecasting methods in individual manager's forecasts. At present, this integration is subject to each person's initiative and intellectual curiosity, and thus its depth and quality are uneven across companies and even within individual firms. The next stage in the process will occur when senior managers in those organizations in which some such integration has been seen realize that this haphazard change has been useful and that analytical forecasting methods should be systematically adopted throughout the corpora-

CHART 25-4. The OFA System[a] Grid and Formulas[b]

A/O × 100 (Actual results divided by objective, then multiplied by 100)	F/O (Forecast divided by objective)										
	0	0.5	1.0	1.5	2.0	2.5	3.0	3.5	4.0	4.5	5.0
0	—	—	—	—	—	—	—	—	—	—	—
50	30	60	—	—	—	—	—	—	—	—	—
100	60	90	120	90	60	30	—	—	—	—	—
150	90	120	150	180	150	120	90	60	30	—	—
200	120	150	180	210	240	210	180	150	120	90	60
250	150	180	210	240	270	300	270	240	210	180	150
300	180	210	240	270	300	330	360	330	300	270	240
350	210	240	270	300	330	360	390	420	390	360	330
400	240	270	300	330	360	390	420	450	480	450	420
450	270	300	330	360	390	420	450	480	510	540	510
500	300	330	360	390	420	450	480	510	540	570	600

[a] O = objective, F = forecast, A = actual results.

[b] Calculation of grid numbers: If F is equal to A, then OFA = $120 \times F/O$; if F is smaller than A, then OFA = $60 \times (A + F)$; if F is bigger than A, then OFA = $60 \times (3A - F)/O$.

Source: Gonick.[10]

tion. When qualified users and adequate hardware and software become available, it will be interesting to monitor the effect on corporate performance.

Another approach that has stirred considerable interest in academic and managerial circles has been the use of artificial intelligence and expert systems. The marketing field has always respected intuitive experience and striven to incorporate it in managerial decision making, as this chapter has shown.[20,22] It is clearly realized that the intuitive experience that marketing managers and salespeople accumulate during their career improves the quality of their sales forecasts. The emergence of standard tools and procedures able to extract such expertise and enable others to use it thus holds great promise for industrial sales forecasting. If intuitive experience could be transmitted to others, these persons could start from this experience base and perhaps could improve on it.

Researchers, too, have now grown to respect managers' intuitive judgment. Rather than viewing analytical methods as opposed to judgmental ones, they have in recent years sought to integrate the two. Two fields of research activity should be mentioned here. One is the combination of diverse forecasts to improve a given forecast.[4,20,28] The other, one step more advanced than this, is concerned with the actual combination of the analytical and intuitive components of these diverse forecasts to make a whole.[1,14]

CONCLUSION

This chapter has shown that due to the importance of forecasting for industrial products, statistical forecasting methods have not been attractive to management of companies making industrial products. The sales force composite system, which has been the dominant method, contains numerous situation-specific biases as well as some universal weaknesses. Several ways of treating the weaknesses to minimize their effects have been proposed, together with a framework that models the interface, occurring at various levels, between the forecaster and his or her superior. This framework should help in the analysis of a particular situation and in the assessment of some of the biases present. Not all biases and weaknesses have been captured by the analysis presented. However, since the advantages of the sales force composite forecasting practice override its weaknesses, it is felt that industrial companies will continue the struggle with this double-edged sword. If the company attempts to correct the weaknesses and to treat biases systematically, further ways to improve the system will emerge and the "faults" of using humans rather than statistical routines will be minimized.

Finally, encouraging changes have been taking place in both management and research communities. On the one hand, management is more and more willing and able to incorporate analytical methods because of business education and the growing use of microcomputers. On the other hand, more and more researchers recognize that the ultimate forecasting model is probably a myth and that a diversity of methods must be utilized, including using the know-how of the experienced salesperson or manager who is close to the scene. This must lead to the conclusion that analytical methods and the sales force composite method used in industrial sales forecasting are starting to draw nearer.

REFERENCES

1. Ashton, Alison H., and Robert H. Ashton, "Aggregating Subjective Forecasts: Some Empirical Results," *Management Science,* vol. 31, no. 12, December 1985, pp. 1499–1508.
2. Barr, J. J., "SIC: A Basic Tool For Marketers," in Donald E. Vinson and Donald Sumplinpaglia, eds., *The Environment of Industrial Marketing,* Grid, Inc., Columbia, OH, pp. 114–119.
3. Churchill, Gilbert A., Neil M. Ford, and Orville C. Walker Jr., "Organizational Climate and Job Satisfaction in the Salesforce," *Journal of Marketing Research,* no. 13, November 1976, pp. 323–332.
4. Churchill, Gilbert A., Neil M. Ford, and Orville C. Walker Jr., "Personal Characteristics of Salespeople and the Attractiveness of Alternative Rewards," *Journal of Business Research,* 1979, pp. 25–50.
5. Cyert, Richard M., and James G. Morih, *A Behavioral Theory of the Firm,* Prentice Hall, Englewood Cliffs, NJ, 1963.
6. Dalrymple, Douglas J., "Sales Forecasting Methods and Accuracy," *Business Horizons,* December 1975, pp. 69–73.
7. Donnelly, James H. Jr., and John M. Ivanovich, "Role Clarity and the Salesman," *Journal of Marketing,* no. 39, 1975, pp. 71–74.
8. Farley, John U., James M. Hulbert, and David Weinstein, "Price Setting and Volume Planning by Two European Industrial Companies: A Study and Comparison of Decision Processes," *Journal of Marketing,* vol. 44, Winter 1980, pp. 46–54.
9. Fouss, James H., and Elaine Solomon, "Salespeople as Researchers: Help or Hazard?" *Journal of Marketing,* vol. 44, Summer 1980, pp. 36–39.
10. Gonick, Jacob, "Tie Salesmen's Bonuses to Their Forecasts," *Harvard Business Review,* May–June 1978, pp. 116–123.
11. Hertz, David, *New Power for Management,* McGraw-Hill, New York, 1969.
12. Hulbert, James M., John U. Farley, and John A. Howard, "Information Processing and Decision Making in Marketing Organizations," *Journal of Marketing Research,* no. 9, February 1972, pp. 75–77.
13. Jolson, Marvin A., "The Salesman's Career Cycle," *Journal of Marketing,* no. 38, July 1974, pp. 39–46.
14. Laurence, M. J., R. H. Edmundson, and M. J. O'Connor, "The Accuracy of Combining Judgemental and Statistical Forecasts," unpublished manuscript, The University of New South Wales, 1986.
15. Lowe, E. A., and R. W. Shaw, "An Analysis on Managerial Biasing: Evidence from a Company's Budgeting Process," *The Journal of Management Studies,* vol. 5, February 1968, pp. 304–315.
16. Mabert, Vincent A., "Statistical Versus Salesforce Executive Opinion Short Range Forecasts: A Time Series Analysis Case Study," *Decision Sciences,* vol. 7, 1976, pp. 315–318.

17. Makridakis, Spyros, and Steven C. Wheelwright, *Forecasting: Methods and Applications*, John Wiley, New York, 1986.

18. Modig, Jan-Eric, "Forecasting Gamesmanship," *Managerial Planning*, September–October 1976, pp. 24–26.

19. Oliver, Richard L., "Alternative Conceptions of the Motivation Component in Expectancy Theory," in Richard P. Bagozi, ed., *Sales Management: New Developments from Behavioral and Decision Model Research*, Marketing Science Institute, Cambridge, MA, 1978, pp. 40–63.

20. Robertson, Don H., "Sales Feedback on Competitors' Activity," *Journal of Marketing*, no. 38, April 1974, pp. 69–71.

21. Scott, Jerome E., and Stephen K. Keiser, "Forecasting Acceptance of New Industrial Products with Judgemental Modeling," *Journal of Marketing*, vol. 18, no. 2, Spring 1981, pp. 51–67.

22. Simon, Herbert A., "Applying Information Technology to Organization Design," *Public Administration Review*, May–June 1973, pp. 268–278.

23. Staelin, Richard, and Ronald E. Turner, "Error in Judgmental Sales Forecasts Theory and Results," *Journal of Marketing Research*, vol. 10, February 1973, pp. 10–16.

24. Steinbrink, John P., "How to Pay Your Salesforce," *Harvard Business Review*, July–August 1978, pp. 111-122.

25. Teas, Kenneth R., John G. Wacker, and R. Eugene Hughes, "Path Analysis of Causes and Consequences of Salespeople's Perceptions of Role Clarity," *Journal of Marketing Research*, no. 16, August 1979, pp. 355–369.

26. Walker, Orvill C., Gilbert A. Churchill Jr., and Neil M. Ford, "Organizational Determinants of the Industrial Salesman's Role Conflict and Ambiguity," *Journal of Marketing*, no. 30, January 1975, pp. 32–39.

27. Weinstein, David, *Analysis of Salesforce Composite Systems*, paper presented at TIMS International Conference, Athens, July 1977.

28. Winkler, Robert L., and Spyros Makridakis, "The Combination of Forecasts: Some Empirical Results," *Journal of the Royal Statistical Society*, ser. A, vol. 146, 1983, pp. 150–157.

29. Wotruba, Thomas R., and Michael L. Ludlow, "Salesforce Participation in Quota Setting and Sales Forecasting," *Journal of Marketing*, vol. 40, April 1976, pp. 11–16.

CHAPTER

26

FORECASTING FOR SERVICE PRODUCTS: CONCEPTS AND SYSTEMS

VINCENT A. MABERT

Graduate School of Business, Indiana University, Bloomington

MICHAEL J. SHOWALTER

Florida State University, Tallahassee

INTRODUCTION

In 1986 the service sector of the United States economy accounted for more than 70% of the work force and more than 66% of the GNP.[5] This growth is largely a result of changes in the economy that have led to a more affluent middle class. In many service industries growth should continue to increase into the twenty-first century. Government, communications, leisure/entertainment, and finance are four areas in which significant growth has occurred and should continue.

From all indications, a startling transformation has taken place in consumer markets. Services now account for over two fifths of the average consumer expenditure. Changing consumer demand patterns have not only increased the demand for existing services but also fostered the introduction of many new services. Important trends in consumer services include a growing emphasis on security, which has expanded the market for such services as insurance, banking, and investment; greater stress on health, which has led to an increasing demand for dental, medical, and hospital services; and growth in the number of working women, which has led to greater demand for the services provided by restaurants, clothiers, and day-care centers.

Increased spending for business service has been even more impressive. Business service firms offer the twin advantages of low overhead and expert assistance. Except for the largest companies, it is impossible to duplicate efficiently the service provided by such firms as A.C. Nielsen, Dun & Bradstreet, or Booz, Allen, and Hamilton.

Significant growth for services puts tremendous pressure on firms to better predict the future to position their services and resources adequately. In this chapter we will discuss the unique features of services, concepts in service forecasting, techniques for long- and short-range prediction, and forecast system objectives.

SERVICE CHARACTERISTICS AND DEMAND FORECASTING

Forecasting of service demand differs substantially from forecasting of (physical) product demand, due to the unique characteristics of services. The most important characteristic is the fact that consumption and production of services occur simultaneously. Unlike products, which may be produced and inventoried to satisfy future demand, services must be provided whenever the customer contacts the service organization or shortly thereafter. If customer demand has not been anticipated (forecasted), adequate resources may not be available to satisfy demand. On the other hand, anticipated demand may not materialize, resulting in underutilized resources. Thus, demand forecasting accuracy has an impact on the organization's ability to provide customer service and at the same time effectively utilize productive resources.

The intangible nature of a service creates technical problems in developing demand forecasts. Whereas a product has a physical presence that can be accurately measured along several dimensions, a "unit of service" is far more difficult to quantify. The "quantity" of service received by a customer depends on the customer's expectations and needs. Due to the vagary of consumer behavior, provision of the same set of activities to two customers can result in different service (benefit) being received.

Much of the service demand in forecasts must be specified in units of critical input to the service system rather than in units of output. For example, a hospital may forecast demand for service in terms of number of patients admitted, with the knowledge that each patient will require differing amounts of medical care and will receive differing levels of service; or the U.S. Postal Service may forecast service demand in terms of number of letters to be received, knowing that some will require more sorting than others and differing levels of service (time interval until delivery) will be provided each letter. Thus, the emphasis on *what* must be forecast has changed. For products, the emphasis is on forecasting demand in terms of dollars or volume of *output* required from the manufacturing system; with services the forecast is of the dollars or volume of *input* that initiates the service output. These surrogate forecasts of service demand must be considered cautiously whenever management decisions are based on them, because they may not accurately reflect the levels of productive resources or service output actually required.

The product life-cycle concept applies to services as well as products. For those services that have a simple technology base and/or require minimal capital investment, the product life cycle becomes an important element in developing short- and intermediate-term forecasts of service demand. Most services are not patentable (although some services can be copyrighted) and are subject to copying by competitors. If the operating system to provide the service requires no new technology, competitors can quickly and easily provide the same service, or if the underlying technology is labor intensive, new service organizations can easily enter the industry (i.e., real estate firms, business consulting services). Services with either of these characteristics tend to experience a life cycle significantly shorter than the average life cycle for other services and most products. For such services, short- and intermediate-term demand forecasts must explicitly account for dominance of the life-cycle pattern on demand.

A final characteristic of services that may affect the forecasting of demand is the need for customer contact with the service system. If the customer must interact with the productive system to receive the service, the proximity of the productive system to the customer becomes important. The potential demand for service is a function of the location of the service facility relative to a particular customer market. This results in demand forecasting activity that is service-facility specific. If customers in a market area cannot be attracted to a service facility, there is no need to forecast potential customer demand. A *product* can be expanded into other market areas on a regional or national basis simply by expanding the distribution system for that product. To expand the market area for a *service* that requires customer interaction, however, necessitates the addition of service facility in the new market area. Thus, demand forecasting for service tends to be service/facility focused, and total demand forecasts will be aggregated from the individual facility forecasts.

DEMAND FORECASTING REQUIREMENTS FOR DECISION MAKING

Managerial decision making in service organizations is concerned primarily with the relationship between demand and capacity. As already mentioned, services cannot be inventoried in advance of demand; therefore, management seeks to make decisions that maintain an equilibrium between demand and capacity. Any imbalance between the two is undesirable from an efficiency perspective, because imbalance results in either unsatisfied (lost) demand or underutilization of capacity. Thus, management centers its attention on the problems of (1) managing the demand for services, (2) managing the capacity of the service organization, or (3) managing both demand and capacity. Although management could most effectively achieve balance by modifying both demand and capacity simultaneously, it is unlikely to be able to influence both equally. Generally, management has greater control over capacity level in both the long range and the short range. The degree of control exercised over demand for services may vary considerably from one organization to another, depending on the strength of the marketing program and the nature of the market environment. Similar to that for "physical" products, demand for services may be viewed as controllable by the organization over the long range but relatively uncontrollable in the short range (the latter being the period when it is most difficult to achieve balance in service products organizations).

Solving this balance problem generally requires considerable information input. One type of input is forecast of future demand. It should be expected that the same form of forecasted demand data would not be suitable for each problem situation. In reality, the forecasted demand information requirements differ substantially from one setting to another. Each forecast must emphasize different *components* of demand to facilitate good decision making.

Problems relating to the management of demand for services can be classified as either *demand identification* or *demand manipulation* problems. Demand identification problems focus on the determination of market opportunities for the service organization. Market opportunities include unsatisfied demands for existing services as well as unsatisfied demands for services the organization currently does not provide. Chart 26-1 presents a matrix of components of forecasted demand information required to analyze each of these demand identification problems.

The second category of demand problems relates to the need for demand manipulation. It is likely that there may not be sufficient demand to operate the service organization's productive capacity efficiently. A variety of techniques could be used by management to modify market demand in the short run, such as service mix packaging, pricing, backordering, advertising/promotion, and service substitution. The problem facing management is to determine the potential for these techniques to modify demand. Chart 26-1 identifies the components of forecast demand information considered essential to determine the relative impact of each demand manipulation technique.

Decision making regarding capacity management in a service organization can be similarly classified as either *capacity identification* or *capacity manipulation*. Capacity identification problems focus on determining what capacity additions, deletions, and/or modifications are required to satisfy future market requirements. These capacity identification problems focus on determination of the facility(s) size (in terms of input–output rate), the location of the facility(s), and the process technology(s) to be utilized at each facility. Chart 26-2 presents a matrix of the components of forecast demand

CHART 26-1. Components of Forecast Demand Information For Decision Making[a]

	Service Life Cycle	Market Share	Location of Demand	Average Demand	Maximum Demand	Minimum Demand	Trend of Demand	Seasonality of Demand	Pattern of Demand Variability
I. Demand identification									
A. Market opportunities									
1. New markets		X[a]		X			X		
2. Existing markets	X	X			X				
B. Service opportunities									
1. New services	X	X		X	X				
2. Existing services	X	X		X	X				
II. Demand manipulation									
A. Services mix packaging		X		X	X				
B. Services pricing	X	X		X	X	X			
C. Services backordering					X			X	
D. Services adv./promo.		X				X	X		
E. Services substitutibility		X		X		X			X

[a] The marked categories specify those components of forecasted demand information that must be explicitly recognized and measured.

CHART 26-2. Components of Forecast Demand Information for Capacity Decision Making[a]

	Service Life Cycle	Market Share	Location of Demand	Average Demand	Maximum Demand	Minimum Demand	Trend of Demand	Seasonality of Demand	Pattern of Demand Variability
I. Capacity identification									
A. Facility(s) size	X[a]		X		X		X		
B. Facility(s) location		X	X	X					
C. Facility(s) technology	X			X				X	
II. Capacity manipulation									
A. Labor force size				X			X	X	X
B. Labor force composition			X	X		X		X	X
C. Labor force task reassignment flexibility									X
D. Labor force overtime					X			X	
E. Subcontracting					X		X	X	X

[a] The marked categories specify those components of forecasted demand information that must be explicitly recognized and measured.

information required to analyze each of these capacity identification problems.

If management is not able to manipulate demand to maximize efficiency of the service organization, it may have to modify capacity of the productive system in order to balance demand and capacity for optimal efficiency. The capacity manipulation classification includes techniques management can use to modify capacity in the short run, such as hiring/firing employees; employing full-time, part-time, and/or temporary employees; reassigning employees among different tasks; using overtime/undertime; and subcontracting another service organization's capacity. The problem for management is to determine the potential of these techniques to modify capacity to achieve a balance of demand and capacity. Chart 26-2 identifies the critical components of forecast demand necessary to determine the relative value of each capacity manipulation technique.

No attempt has been made to identify what specific forecasting techniques should be used to generate forecast demand information for use in evaluating each problem. For a given problem, a number of forecasting methodologies may be equally acceptable. By definition, an acceptable forecasting methodology is one that adequately represents the *components* of demand necessary to provide analysis of the specific area of interest to management.

In the next sections, a forecasting structure is presented and illustrated with case study examples. At this point, you will see how various techniques can assist in the forecasting problem.

FORECASTING SERVICE PRODUCTS

Structuring Forecasts

The prediction of future events requires that a structure be formulated to depict the forecasting occasion. Two terms need to be clearly defined: market demand and sales forecast. These two concepts are not the same and have unique implications. Kotler[7,p.99] defined them as:

> *Market demand* for a product/service class is the total volume which would be bought by a defined customer group in a defined location in a defined time period under defined environmental conditions and marketing effort.
>
> *Sales forecast* is the expected level of company sales based on a chosen marketing plan and assumed environmental conditions.

In a macro sense, market demand forecasting attempts to measure all potential sales, while company sales forecasting represents a micro activity. Whether an analyst views a forecasting problem from a macro or micro perspective may depend on his or her assigned mission. For example, Mc-

Donald's Corporation's planners are concerned about the trends (demand identification) in consumer eating patterns and would attempt to forecast market demand for different types of food service that might be implemented (demand manipulation). However, a unit manager would execute a micro sales forecast to determine material and work force requirements on a day-to-day basis (capacity manipulation). This would involve both demand identification and manipulation. Identification would recognize the normal daily traffic, while manipulation could reflect the presence of a coupon promotion program currently in effect.

This example highlights another issue in forecasting, and that is the appropriate forecast horizon. In many situations, long-range forecasts deal with company or division/unit sales forecasts. The long-range versus short-range forecasts reflect two extremes on the forecasting continuum. Generally, the long-range forecast attempts to account for the actions of many market forces, such as competition, consumer awareness, political and economic conditions, and technological trends. In the short range, the forecasting problem focuses mainly on the marketing efforts of the organization and does not account, in an explicit way, for macro factors like technology and political conditions.

Forecasting procedures range from simple approaches to highly sophisticated statistical methods. There are three data base sources for systematic forecasting:

1. Past behavior or historical data
2. Current behavior
3. Future intentions

The development and implementation of a good forecasting system may rely on a combination of all three of these items rather than on just one. Also, the system may rely on a number of techniques such as regression, exponential smoothing, and consumer surveys.

Forecasting Practice

A small survey was conducted of 17 service organizations in Indiana to determine the techniques and data sources utilized in forecasting a variety of requirements. Ten of the respondents were financial institutions (banks and savings and loans), the others were academic institutions.

Chart 26-3 presents the information collected for the financial institutions. The sample covers large to small organizations, judged by assets and number of employees. The chart indicates that a variety of data sources are used, mostly relating to business and economic activity. All use their forecasts for budgeting, while the larger institutions also use forecasts for portfolio management. Larger institutions use computers for forecasting, with no pattern

CHART 26-3. Techniques and Data Sources Used by Financial Institutions for Forecasting

Size Assets (Millions $)/ Employees	Techniques Used	Input Variables	Forecast Uses	Time Range	Computerized	Number of People
2296/2480	Simulation Regression External sources	Prime rate Economic indicators	Portfolio management Budget	3–5 years Yearly Quarterly	Yes	4
1900/2135	Regression External sources	Prime rate Economic indicators	Portfolio Budget	Yearly Quarterly	Yes	3
320/240	Regression External sources	Prime rate Economic indicators	Portfolio Budget	Yearly Quarterly	Yes	5
280/280	Time series	Historical economic indicators	Budget	3 years	Yes	2–3
270/300	Regression Time series	Prime rate Economic indicators	Portfolio Budget	Yearly Monthly	Yes	2–3
225/275	Time series	Historical data Economic indicators	Portfolio Budget	5 years Yearly	—	5
175/170	Time series	Historical data Economic indicators	Budget	3–5 years Yearly	—	2–6
104/130	Time series	Historical data Economic indicators	Budget	Yearly Quarterly	—	5
70/170	Time series	Historical data Economic indicators	Budget	Yearly Quarterly	—	5
20/45	Time series	Historical data Economic indicators	Budget	Yearly Quarterly	—	5

apparent as to the number of individuals involved in the forecasting function. Most forecasting is on an annual and/or a quarterly basis. Some longer-range forecasting is present for 4 of the 10 surveyed.

Chart 26-4 presents the results for the academic institutions. The size of the schools varied from 32,000 to 1,100 students, and a variety of data sources were used. Most data relate to demographic information on population, with time series analysis being a popular analysis technique in this area. A broad range of uses are presented such as facility planning, budgeting, curriculum design, placement, and faculty sizing.

This group of 17 organizations may not be a representative sample, but it does illustrate a number of aspects that we have discussed. First, there is no single technique that can be universally applied to the forecasting needs of service organizations. Second, data base requirements vary substantially, some firms being sensitive to economic activity while others react to population factors. Third, forecasts are used for a variety of functions, from budgeting to work force sizing. And fourth, the organizational commitment has no pattern. In some cases it is highly centralized, with a well-defined group responsible for forecast creation. In other cases it is decentralized, with major departments/divisions executing this function.

Forecasting is a unique activity for each organization, and any attempt to provide an optimal approach would be foolish. Rather, a broad structure based on forecast horizon and demand dynamics is suggested. The next two sections illustrate the complexity of forecasting service products with a number of case examples taken from various service firms.

LONG-RANGE FORECASTING

Long-range forecasts are critical input for strategic planning in any organization. Very few services lend themselves to easy forecasting. In some cases, demand may be rather stable in pattern and competitive relationships may be nonexistent, as in public utilities. However, in the vast majority of markets, demand is not stable from year to year and sales forecasting becomes a critical factor in the firm's success.

The long-run forecast helps chart the course an organization will take in positioning itself in the marketplace. Major decisions on new service products, equipment, and facility acquisitions and on manpower planning evolve from the long-run forecasts. For example, electric utilities now require a 10-year lead time to bring generating capacity on-line. This long lead time requires extensive advance planning if enough capacity is to be available without overbuilding.

Long-run forecasting can be executed in highly dynamic or relatively stable markets. *Highly dynamic* market forecasting involves identifying a market need/want (segmentation), matching the service delivery system to

CHART 26-4. Techniques and Data Sources Used by Academic Institutions for Forecasting

Enrollment	Employee(s)	Techniques Used	Input Variables	Forecast Uses	Time Range	Computerized	Number of People Involved
32,000	5,400	Time series Some regression	No. of H.S. grads. Individual trends Retention rates	Budgeting Facility plan	10 years 2 years Yearly	Yes	All admin.
30,000	10,000	Regression Executive opinion	Birth rates College going rates Economic data	Facility plan Budgeting Faculty planning	10 years 2 years Monthly	Yes	All admin.
17,108	2,500	Time series Trend analysis	Census figures Live births	Financial & facility plan.	10 years 5 years 2 years	Yes	6-12
11,000	4,000	Time series Regression	Census data, Number of H.S. graduates	Facility plan. Budgeting Cash flow plan.	5 years 2 years	Yes	4
6,500	3,000	Time series Jury Planned size	Census data National trends Private education costs	Faculty plan. Curriculum Size/facility	4-8 years facilities 2-3 years budget	For control only	All admin.
4,300	700	Time series	Birth rates Proj. number of 18-year-olds Government stats.	Income-budget Faculty plan Curriculum	10 years 3 years Yearly	No	7-10
1,100	150	Time series Company representatives	Govt. statistics (from Center for Technical Assessment)	Faculty plan. Recruitment Academic prog./ placement Budget	10 years 5 years	Yes	9

478

the need/want (competitive edge), and then making the market aware of the available service (advertising/education). One quickly sees that this forecasting situation is intimately involved with the market planning effort of the firm and that it emphasizes demand manipulation.

On the other hand, *stable* market forecasting implies little or limited effort expended to influence/educate the market about the service. Rather, stable market forecasting assumes that fundamental demand already exists for the service (i.e., electric power, waste disposal, health care, etc.), little service differentiation is present, and advertising/education has minimum impact on consumer behavior. Thus, demand identification becomes an input to capacity manipulation. Let us look at two case studies of long-range forecasting that involves both identification and manipulation of demand and capacity.

The Ministry of Tourism of the Turks and Caicos Islands wanted to know the potential of the islands as a vacation spot and how to attract more visitors in the highly dynamic leisure-time market. A six-phase program was conducted.[15] First, a task force gathered all available data on previous visitors to the island, studying the embarkation and disembarkation documents completed by every nonresident visitor to the island during the most recent 18-month period. Second, the information was analyzed to determine the geographic and demographic composition of previous visitors. A profile of previous visitors was established and was used to determine travel behavior with reference to geographic origin, sex, time of year, average length of stay, purpose of visit, and method of transportation. These facts were analyzed to establish an 18-month pattern, with particular emphasis placed on identifying patterns within the peak or off-peak seasons. Third, historical visitor profiles were developed to target the prospective audience. Three potential markets were identified: seasonal island travelers, owners and operators of private aircraft, and scuba divers. Fourth, advertising campaigns were targeted in eight metropolitan markets, four determined to be highly seasonal (New York, Detroit, Boston, and Washington, DC) and four determined to be relatively nonseasonal (Miami, Tampa, Jacksonville, and Orlando). Markets with additional potential were then identified for similarities in the profile. Fifth, results of the program were measured through a continuing arrival survey. Finally, the results of the research are being used to modify existing efforts in charting future programs with the greatest potential. The results of this program have been quite successful. Since the program was introduced in 1977, the number of nonresident visitors to the islands has increased by approximately 85%, from 6,500 in 1977 to approximately 12,000 in 1978.

Thus, one quickly sees that the success of forecasting market potential for services is intimately involved in the nature of the service and the identification of the target market. The forecasting function is clearly linked with identifying customers' wants (demand identification), making the customer aware of available service (demand manipulation), and delivering quality service (capacity management).

The second case study involves a more mature market. Stable market forecasting occurs in markets in which the service is homogeneous, is well established, and experiences little volatility. Utilities (electric, gas, water, waste disposal, phone, etc.) are examples of a stable market service. In most cases the forecasting task should focus on demand identification rather than on manipulating demand through an extensive marketing plan. This is not to say that market planning does not exist. The market plan, however, has minimal influence in changing consumer behavior, since stable markets are generally saturated and exhibit little basis for predicting future behavior for capacity decisions. Often statistical procedures like regression and time series analysis are used to analyze historical data to determine patterns, relationships, and trends.

The forecasting of peak power consumption for Duke Power[4] illustrates the stable market forecasting system, in which decisions on long-range capacity are critical. The historical total power consumption is divided into two parts: base load (BL) and weather-response (WR) usage. The base load represents the system requirements influenced by general public and economic activities, but excluding weather effects. The weather-response usage in the summer represents a tremendous increase in demand due to air conditioning. However, this weather-response effect lasts for a short period. Knowing the base load and weather-response consumption is important in capacity planning so "brownouts" are minimized.

The daily summer consumption data were analyzed. Scatter plots of degree-hours between noon and 4:00 p.m. were examined to identify unusual characteristics and outliers. With the data screening completed, regression was used to estimate the relationship of power consumption and weather effects. The model is

$$MW = B_0 + B_1 \text{ (dHr)} \tag{26-1}$$

where MW is the actual peak power consumption for the particular summer afternoon and dHr is the weighted difference from 67° F between 12:00 noon and 4:00 p.m.

Using Equation 26-1, B_0 was interpreted as the base load for that year. The weather-related component was the product of B_1 times the 20-year average value of degree-hours for a particular day. This approach was applied on the summer months data for 12 years (1963–1974) to obtain the base load and weather-effect relationships over that period. These data became the basis for projecting future levels of each component. A trend line was fitted to each component to reflect the appropriate growth rate to obtain a forecast. Chart 26-5 illustrates the overall approach.

However, blindly using the trend projections may be inappropriate. At this point the forecaster must use judgment, because future behavior does not always mimic past behavior. With energy conservation becoming an

CHART 26-5. Long Range Forecasting of Load Requirements at Duke Power Company

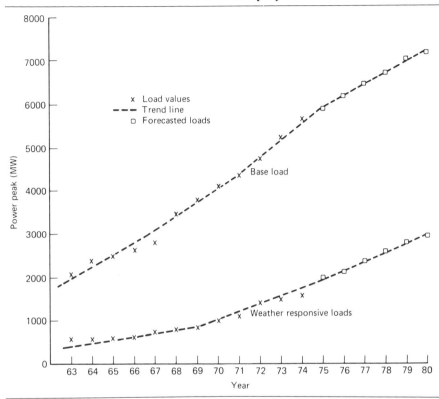

important issue in the early 1970s, Duke Power forecasters recognized that some adjustment was necessary. To account for this trend, all future forecasts were modified by the ratio of actual 1974 to forecasted 1974 consumption. This modification reflects the conservation activities taking place at that time.

These case studies illustrate two different approaches to long-range forecasting. The forecasting of tourism business required both demand identification and manipulation. Identification in this case involved profiling vacationer characteristics and island services. With identification completed, manipulation involved promotional activities in user markets to attract vacationers. On the other hand, Duke Power's approach was to identify demand and forecast future consumption levels with regression. No attempt was made to explicitly manipulate demand in planning for coming years. Duke will then manipulate capacity to satisfy expected demand.

SHORT-RANGE FORECASTING

The short-range forecasting problem presents an extremely challenging area for services. Since services cannot be readily inventoried, the service delivery system must match supply and demand. In those situations where an appointment system or customer backlogging is possible, the matching problem becomes easier. However, the appointment system is the exception rather than the rule. With demand randomly occurring, the service delivery system must intentionally overstaff to provide a reasonable level of service. Determining the appropriate level of staff influences the service level, operating costs, and profitability of the organization.

Short-range forecasting occurs at the operating unit level. Generally, capacity manipulation is the primary focus, like determining expected traffic for staffing needs for a branch bank or fast food establishment. At this point, the forecast horizon may range from a day to a month and the forecast interval may be an hour or less. Telephone operator scheduling[3,6] and flight crew scheduling[1] are just two decision areas that utilize very short planning horizons.

Again, the market forces present may yield either a dynamic or stable forecasting situation. The dynamic situation requires that the forecasting system respond to rapidly changing events like promotional programs and new service introductions. In such a setting, there is less reliance on historical information and more weighting of managerial judgment for forecast generation. The Burger Chef FAST system (forecasting and labor scheduling technique) illustrates the dynamic short-range forecasting activity in the fast food industry.

FAST is a transaction-based (as opposed to sales dollar-based) forecasting system that relies on a moving average of customer transactions for the past 10 weeks (excluding exceptional days) to forecast transactions for the week, day, and hour. This forecast is then converted to a work force schedule by day and hour.

A forecast of total expected transactions for the week is determined by the unit manager. Historical transaction levels are reviewed with a major concern for transaction one year ago on the same week and last week's transactions. This provides an indication of seasonal swings and current trends. A third factor considered by the unit manager is exceptional events occurring during the week near the unit. Such things as special coupon programs, fairs (county and state), school activities, and so on, all can have an impact on demand. The weekly forecast is entered into the FAST program and an hourly labor schedule for the entire week is produced.

Chart 26-6 illustrates one day (Thursday) of the weekly report for one unit. In the upper left corner, management's expected weekly transactions are displayed. On the basis of historical daily patterns, using the 10-week moving average model, this figure is broken down into expected transactions by day, and percent of total weekly demands for Thursday. The remainder of

CHART 26-6. Daily Forecast Prepared by Burger Chef FAST System

REPORT ID 8771501 DIST : 32 AREA : 030 BURGER CHEF SYSTEMS INC. AREA MGR : J.D. HAYMAN DAY
RUN DATE 07/06/79 FOR PERIOD 04 WEEK 4 HOURLY LABOR SCHEDULE WESTERN INDIANA DIST. 5

RESTAURANT 0875   WALNUT STREET   THURSDAY   GRILL

WK FORECAST TRAN 4,229
DAILY TRANS 660
DAILY % OF WK 15.6%
AVG DAILY TRANS 625

	07	08	09	10	11	12	01	02	03	04	05	06	07	08	09	10	11	12	01
TRANS PER HR	0	0	0	1	29	109	149	74	38	32	34	43	46	32	31	31	11	0	0
% PER HR	.0	.0	.0	.1	4.4	16.5	22.6	11.2	5.8	4.9	5.1	6.5	7.0	4.8	4.7	4.7	1.7	.0	.0
UNITS/TRANS	.0	.0	.0	.8	2.9	3.1	3.1	3.0	2.5	2.3	3.0	3.6	3.2	3.0	3.0	2.8	2.4	.0	.0
TOTAL UNITS/HR	0	0	0	1	84	338	462	222	95	74	102	155	147	96	93	87	26	0	0
CREWING:																			
FRONTLINE	.0	.0	.0	.0	1.1	2.9	3.7	2.0	1.3	1.2	1.2	1.4	1.5	1.2	1.1	1.1	.5	.0	.0
DINING ROOM ATTEND	.0	.0	.0	.0	.0	.0	.0	.0	.0	.0	.0	.0	.0	.0	.0	.0	.0	.0	.0
DRIVE THRU	.0	.0	.0	.0	.0	.0	.0	.0	.0	.0	.0	.00	.0	.0	.0	.0	.0	.0	.0
DRINK DRAWER	.0	.0	.0	.0	.0	.0	.0	.0	.0	.0	.0	.0	.0	.0	.0	.0	.0	.0	.0
COORDINATOR	.0	.0	.0	.0	.0	.0	.0	.0	.0	.0	.0	.0	.0	.0	.0	.0	.0	.0	.0
BACKLINE	.0	.0	.0	.0	.9	3.0	3.5	2.0	1.0	.8	1.1	1.5	1.4	1.0	1.0	1.0	.3	.0	.0
HRLY TOTAL	.0	.0	.0	.0	2.0	5.9	7.2	4.0	2.3	2.0	2.3	2.9	2.9	2.2	2.1	2.1	.8	.0	.0

DAILY TOTALS:

TOTAL HRS	38.7/50.0
FOOD PREP	2.7
OPEN/PORTER	3.5
CLOSE	3.0
SCHEDULED HRS	47.9/60.0
ALLOWED MANHRS	66.0
STO MGMT ADJ HRS	8.0 PER

this report provides information regarding expected hourly transactions, the work force needed, and a summary of labor standards.

A similar man/system approach is utilized by Indiana Bell for operator scheduling. Management develops weekly estimates of phone call work loads based on history and judgment of future events for the upcoming week. This estimate is then broken down using historical between-day and within-day patterns. These data are maintained and processed by a system called FMS/FRPS, which is provided by the McDonnell Douglas Automation Company (McAUTO). The system ultimately takes the weekly forecasts and converts them into quarter-hour staff requirements, which can range from 2 to 35 operators.

At Burger Chef and Indiana Bell, the manager is an integral part of the forecasting function. He or she reviews historical demand to provide a base estimate. This base may then be modified to reflect exceptional conditions that may be present during the coming week. In this situation the manager accounts for the dynamics of the fast food market or special communication events when making the forecast. Other service industries experience more stable demand patterns which influence the type of forecasting system. In such a setting, greater reliance on a mechanical system is possible, as illustrated by the following Chemical Bank case study.

At Chemical Bank,[2] the short-range forecasting system concentrates on the paper flow problem of the back office. The operations group is under pressure to meet deadlines for transit checks—checks drawn on other banks and cashed at Chemical Bank. Before checks can be sent to the Federal Reserve Bank or correspondent banks for collection, they must be encoded, proofed, microfilmed, sorted, and bundled. Transit checks missing the appropriate dispatch time mean lost funds availability to the bank. Therefore, the determination of the appropriate staffing level (capacity manipulation) requires good forecasts.

A variety of projection methods, such as three-parameter exponential smoothing and the Box–Jenkins approach, were investigated as predictors of daily volumes and proved inadequate. Projection techniques assume that the time series behavior is equally spaced over time, that is, all changes in the work load occur at equally spaced intervals. For example, those individuals conducting weekly or biweekly transactions have behavior patterns that are equally spaced in time because they occur every 5 or 10 operating days. However, the banking environment is more complex, since many individuals' transactions are controlled by calendar dates, which are not equally spaced over time due to the unequal number of days in a month. Also, holidays provide additional influences that affect daily volumes. To overcome the deficiencies of the projection techniques, an alternative approach using regression was investigated and subsequently implemented for management's use.

An initial investigation indicated that week day, calendar day, month, and holidays all had an impact on work loads. These four classifications of variables were identified as potentially important in predicting daily volumes at Chemical Bank. They were obtained through data analysis and experience. Boyd and Mabert[2] stressed that experience and familiarity with the banking industry were important in identifying the potential variables in the model. This was especially true with the new holiday variables. For example, the presence of a federal holiday caused increased work loads before and after .the holiday.

A multiple variable regression model was developed as the most appropriate method to model daily volumes for the variables identified. The identified variables represented temporal effects that reflected behavior shifts between one period and another. Therefore, a series of dummy zero-one variables were required that were turned on and off for the appropriate day being predicted. Two years of daily data were used to estimate the model, given by

$$V_t = B_0 + B_1X_1 + B_2X_2 + \cdots + B_nX_n \qquad (26\text{-}2)$$

where V_t = volume forecast for day t, measured in pounds of checks

B_0 = estimated constant

B_i = estimated coefficient for impact of event type i

X_i = a zero-one variable indicating absence or presence of event i (i.e., Monday, third month, day after Christmas, etc.)

To keep the model current, it is updated once a month. The most recent month's data are added to the master data set, while the oldest are removed. The coefficients are then reestimated. The model utilizes approximately 30 of the 54 variables identified. In general, the model has provided R^2s around .85, with only minor shifts from that value.

The daily forecasts are then converted to expected half-hour arrivals at the bank using historical arrival percentages. The half-hour forecasts are used as input to a mathematical programming model to determine the appropriate full- and part-time staff. Chart 26-7 illustrates a typical report, showing the number of workers, work hours, work flow, and productivity.[10]

The Indianapolis Police Department (IPD) was faced with a similar daily staff forecasting problem for the communication area at its headquarters facility.[8] It needed to improve cost performance by better matching emergency phone call demand and dispatch operator staff. The following model was implemented:

$$F_{tdmh} = C_tI_dI_m + S_h + \text{DEL}_{m-1} \qquad (26\text{-}3)$$

where F_{tdmh} = forecast for weekday d during month m with event h present from time origin t

C_t = daily calls (run) average for last 365 days from origin

I_d = seasonal index for weekday d

I_m = seasonal index for month m

S_h = impact of special event h

DEL_{m-1} = weight adjustment factor given by $(C_k - F_k)/K$
C_k = Actual number of calls (runs) for day k.
F_k = Base forecast for day k using Equation 26-3 without adjustment factor DEL_{m-1}
K = Number of days in month $m - 1$

This forecasting model is a combined multiplicative/additive approach, using seasonal indices to estimate systematic daily and monthly patterns. Special effects (unique events like Christmas, New Year's Eve, July Fourth, Halloween) are measured by the variable S_h. Future predictions are adjusted by DEL_{m-1}, which represents a tracking signal on the prior month's average daily error. The adjustment process reflects the need for short-run corrections because of changing work load patterns. The daily forecasts are then broken down by hour of the day, based on the particular day of the week. Historical call distributions per hour provide the data necessary for this step.

CHART 26-7. Shift Scheduler Output

Shift Schedule for 77/12/5

Shift Start–Stop	Type of Employee	No. of Employees	Empl. Hrs.	Hrs. Avail. for Work	Machine Hrs.
3:00–10:30	Part-time	4	30.0	25.4	24.4
4:00–10:30	Part-time	47	305.5	254.0	243.9
4:00–9:00	Part-time	33	165.0	147.3	141.5
Total		84	500.5	426.8	409.7

Time Period	Work Left from Prev. Per.	New Work Avail.	Total Work	Total No. Exp.	Capacity	Work Left Over	Capacity Excess or Shortage
1:00–1:30	0	24,090	24,090	0	0	24,090	-24,090
1:30–2:00	24,090	4,087	28,177	0	0	28,177	-28,177
2:00–2:30	28,177	5,884	34,061	0	0	34,061	-34,061
2:30–3:00	34,061	15,451	49,512	0	0	49,512	-49,512
3:00–3:30	49,512	16,408	65,920	4	2,096	63,824	-63,824
3:30–4:00	63,824	21,046	84,870	4	2,088	82,782	-82,782
4:00–4:30	82,782	3,855	86,637	84	43,092	43,545	-43,545
4:30–5:00	43,545	3,623	47,168	84	48,216	0	1,048
5:00–5:30	0	44,992	44,992	84	44,100	892	-892
5:30–6:00	892	41,832	42,724	84	44,436	0	1,712
6:00–6:30	0	26,815	26,815	84	44,100	0	17,285
6:30–7:00	0	51,515	51,515	84	44,016	7,499	-7,499
7:00–7:30	7,499	70,213	77,712	84	43,848	33,864	-33,864
7:30–8:00	33,864	54,676	98,540	84	42,168	56,372	-56,372
8:00–8:30	56,372	22,380	78,752	84	41,412	37,340	-37,340
8:30–9:00	37,340	20,350	57,690	84	40,740	16,950	-16,950
9:00–9:30	16,950	10,349	27,299	51	23,919	3,380	-3,380
9:30–10:00	3,380	7,450	10,830	51	24,123	0	13,293
10:00–10:30	0	6,349	6,348	51	24,684	0	18,336

Total volume predicted (in pounds): 1,421
Total volume predicted (in items): 461,364
Total cost: 2,359.61

The approach in Equation 26-3 was compared with five other techniques.[9] The other approaches utilized regression analysis and complex intervention ARIMA (autoregressive integrated moving average) models. The implemented approach was found to perform as well as or better than all other approaches tested.

For these case studies, demand identification and capacity manipulation are the primary concerns of management. The studies illustrate that forecasting at the operating unit level utilizes a short horizon and interval for planning requirements. When demand is relatively stable, greater reliance on mechanical techniques is possible, as shown at Chemical Bank and IPD. Changes do occur over time, and monitoring procedures need to be established. For example, several procedures are used at Chemical Bank to measure forecast error and are reviewed monthly for possible corrective action.[11] However, when demand dynamics are great, more human judgment is present in generating the forecasts of demand.

FORECASTING SYSTEMS

Many of the forecasting procedures developed for services focus on specific products within the service organization. For example, if a bank is viewed as a representative service firm, over 100 service products are provided by that organization. These service products range from consumer services of savings accounts, checking accounts, and so on to the commercial department for seasonal loans, wire transfer, and lockbox services. The traditional approach taken by the service organization has been to forecast each of these products individually and determine appropriate staffing levels for each.

This traditional approach results in a variety of individuals within the organization developing forecasts and making decisions based on the estimates. Some estimates may be expressed as end-item services (i.e., deposit slips, lockbox letters, stock transfers, etc.) that are provided and delivered by the operating personnel. As shown here, such forecasts can be based on statistical projections of historical data. Elsewhere in the organization top management may utilize forecasts of overall service activity, often expressed in dollar terms, to plan business operations and prepare financial budgets. Similarly, middle managers frequently prepare forecasts that involve divisions or unit groups for promotion, advertising, hiring, and so on.

The facts that forecasts are used for so many different decision-making purposes and are based on such varied sources (i.e., economic data, managerial judgment) present a significant coordinating problem to many service firms to take advantage of these information sources. More often than not these individual forecasts are never brought together within the organization to ensure that the whole equals the sum of the parts. As a result, the overall business plan for the organization, and the different promotional, operational, and financial plans made by top management, may never be implemented in a coordinated way. The implications for uncoordinated activities are tremendous for the service firm.

With the advent of computer technology, approaches are now available to reduce the magnitude of the coordination problem present in large service organizations. *Pyramid* or *constrained* forecasting is one approach that can provide for many of the forecasting needs just discussed. It provides a means of coordinating, integrating, and forcing consistency in the service product demand forecasts prepared by individual parts of the organization using different levels of aggregation. This approach is a routine, automatic method for preparing forecasts that are consistent among the various groups in the organization. The basic notion in any application, however, is one of forcing the forecasts produced at lower levels to agree in total, by time period, with those produced at higher levels.

Pyramid forecasting uses as its primary input forecasts that are prepared independently at each level of the firm's service structure. These data are then available for use in a software package capable of performing, first, an upward implosion of independent service product forecasts and, second, a downward explosion of forecasts that have been modified by top management input. The upward implosion process consists of aggregating the forecasts from individual operating units into product group forecasts, and then aggregating the product group forecasts into total forecasts for the organization. These aggregated forecasts are then compared with the overall forecasts prepared by top management and an adjustment is made, if necessary. Next, the finalized total forecast is exploded back into management—constrained forecasts for product groups and divisions, and operating forecasts are developed for individual departments. The results of the pyramid forecasting approach is a consolidated forecast that forces agreement among the various levels within the organization.

This approach, which has been implemented in a number of manufacturing organizations, should be equally applicable in service firms to help coordinate their activities. American Software is one firm currently marketing a package to perform this coordination effort.[12] It involves a significant data base to drive the system and a major commitment of staff and funding to keep it operational.

An alternative approach to achieving coordination of demand forecasts for different services within an organization is disaggregation. Top management develops an aggregate forecast of demand that is used as the basis for disaggregation into demand forecasts for individual services over the same, or shorter, time horizon. Since all of the individual service forecasts are derived from the same source, coordination presumably occurs within all units and levels of the organization. Because the aggregate demand forecast is subject to top management control and approval, there will be some degree of overall direction for the organization.

The selection of the "unit of measure" constituting aggregate demand for the organization is a crucial decision. This unit must be readily convertible into a demand forecast for every service offered by the organization. Quite often the unit of measure will be a surrogate of services demand. The greater the variety of services offered, the more likely the unit of measure will be expressed in terms of some key (common) input resource. For example, in a hospital the unit of measure is patient census or its corollary, the number/percent of beds occupied. On the basis of top management's forecast of census over the long term and short term, each of the departmental units in the hospital, such as nursing, laboratory, pharmacy, food services, and materials, can prepare demand forecasts for the services it offers. These individual demand forecasts become the primary input into all financial and operational planning within the units. Any variation in the census forecast is reflected in the individual disaggregated demand forecasts. In addition, management-dictated revisions (upward/downward) of demand forecasts can easily be used to coordinate replanning throughout the organization.

A well-known disaggregating system that has existed in the manufacturing field for many years and may be applicable to a number of service organizations is materials requirements planning (MRP). This approach involves looking at the service firm as a multilevel structure in which higher level forecasts/goals are communicated down to lower levels for service scheduling purposes. MRP in a manufacturing firm can be viewed as a procedure for forecasting lower level requirements for materials, staff, and services. For example, hospital services involve a broad spectrum of requirements ranging from personnel services to material supply items. Forecasting what to have available and when can be a challenging problem to the materials/purchasing managers of a large hospital. In many cases, bed census information can be broken down with reasonable accuracy to predict the need for various supply items. This breakdown process by period in the future can be easily accomplished by a materials requirements software package. In this way, material managers will know when to place replenishment orders and for how much.

The scheduling of specific supply items for surgical areas can also be assisted by requirements planning logic.[13] Many hospitals utilize an elective surgery scheduling system that allows administrators significant advanced information on the number of patients and the kinds of surgery to be performed. This information becomes part of a bill of materials and bill of labor required for input into the MRP system. On the basis of this information, administrators can better predict the need for specific materials, facilities, and medical personnel.

Forecasting within service organizations needs to be viewed as a systems concept. This systems concept reflects the rather complex and diverse nature of most service organizations. Historical approaches to service forecasting often focused only on individual operating units or products. Future improvement in productivity for service firms will come from implementing a coordinated approach to forecasting, and converting the forecasts to useful decision-making information in the areas of staff, materials, and facilities.

The decision support systems will offer management useful planning tools for the future.

CONCLUSIONS

This chapter has focused on the forecasting of service products, describing the demand and capacity interaction present in service organizations and the wide variety of approaches that can be taken to generate the forecasted demand. In stable market environments, formalized techniques such as regression are used for both long- and short-range forecasting. The forecast focus in stable markets is on demand identification, with management prepared to manipulate capacity. In dynamic markets, demand manipulation and human judgment become more important for forecasting.

It is clear that no single technique or set of rules will guarantee good forecast performance. Computing technology (hardware and software) should continue to improve, simplifying the capturing, storing, editing, analyzing, and manipulating of significant amounts of data. This information will be the critical element in future forecasting systems, which systems can be tailored to the specific setting and linked into other organizational activities like marketing plans and the data collection system. In this way the forecasting system can adapt and provide useful information.

REFERENCES

1. Baker, E., L. Bodin, W. Finnegan, and R. Ponder, "Efficient Heuristic Solutions to an Airline Crew Scheduling Problem," *AIIE Transactions,* vol. 11, no. 1, March 1979, pp. 37–41.

2. Boyd, K., and V. A. Mabert, "A Two Stage Forecasting Approach at Chemical Bank of New York for Check Processing," *Journal of Bank Research,* vol. 8, no. 2, Summer 1977, pp. 101–107.

3. Buffa, E., M. J. Cosgrove, and B. J. Luce, "An Integrated Work Shift Scheduling System," *Decision Sciences,* vol. 7, no. 4, October 1976, pp. 620–630.

4. "Duke Power Company—Revised," Intercollegiate Case Clearing House, Case #9-677-147, Soldiers Field, Boston, MA, 1977.

5. Joint Economic Committee, "Economic Indicators," U.S. Government, Washington, DC, 1982.

6. Keith, E., "Operator Scheduling," *AIIE Transactions,* vol. 11, no. 1, March 1979, pp. 37–41.

7. Kotler, P., *Marketing Management,* Prentice Hall, Englewood Cliffs, NJ, 1967.

8. Mabert, V. A., "Planning Police Communications Support," *IIE Transactions,* vol. 15, no. 4, December 1983.

9. Mabert, V. A., "Short Interval Forecasting of Emergency Phone Call (911) Work Loads," *Journal of Operations Management,* vol. 5, no. 3, May 1985, pp. 259–272.

10. Mabert, V. A., R. Fairhurst, and M. A. Kilpatrick, "An Encoder Daily Shift Scheduling System at Chemical Bank," *Journal of Bank Research,* vol. 9, no. 3, Fall 1979, pp. 173–180.

11. Mabert, V. A., and R. L. Stocco, "Managing and Monitoring a Forecasting System: The Chemical Bank Experience," *Journal of Bank Research,* vol. 13, no. 3, Autumn 1982, pp. 195–201.

12. Newberry, T. L., and C. D. Bhane, "How Management Should Use and Interact with Sales Forecast," *Inventories and Production,* July/August 1981.

13. Steinberg, E., B. Khumawala, and R. Scamell, "Requirements Planning Systems in the Health Care Environment," *Journal of Operations Management,* vol. 2, no. 4, August 1982, pp. 251–260.

14. U.S. Department of Commerce, "U.S. Service Industries in World Markets," U.S. Government, Washington, DC, 1976.

15. Yesavich, P. C., "Where on Earth are the Turks and Caicos Islands?" *Resort Management,* vol. 33, September 1979, pp. 22–24.

27

THE EMERGING LONG TERM: APPRAISING NEW TECHNOLOGIES AND THEIR IMPLICATIONS FOR MANAGEMENT

SPYROS MAKRIDAKIS

INSEAD, Fontainebleau, France

Traditional forecasting methods are appropriate for discovering and extrapolating established patterns or relationships. Technological innovation, however, can substantially alter these established trends. The steam engine allowed the emergence of new technologies and brought the industrial revolution. The car, the airplane, the telephone, and the computer are all products of new technologies that have made a substantial impact on our lives.

How will developing new technologies modify existing patterns and relationships? This chapter describes emerging technologies with the aim of assessing and providing a better understanding of their impact on the future. Of course, many things may happen (not excluding a nuclear holocaust) that could slow down or reverse these emerging technologies. Alternative, completely new technologies may appear, rendering obsolete those emerging at present. For the purposes of this chapter, however, the impact of emerging technologies on society and organizations will be explored under the assumption that there will be no reversals.

Often long-term forecasting does not have to involve fancy methods or science fiction-type speculation. Several trends have been establishing themselves which, if analyzed and properly assessed, can help us understand the shape of the future and the impact of future events on ourselves and our organizations. As has been said, many more things may happen in the meantime that may change the trends being currently established or, alternatively, new trends may emerge. This does not mean, however, that we should not carefully study the implications of environmental trends that have already become apparent and attempt to determine their effects on society and our organizations.

All of us as individuals, employees of organizations, and members of society, will be greatly affected by the emerging new technologies. An analysis of trends in these technologies indicates that they will bring a period of social and organizational change. During such a period the importance of forecasting and forward thinking may become critical. This raises important questions for organizations. How will their particular business be affected? How will the structure of competition change? What will be the effect of new technologies on unemployment and job satisfaction? How will the new technologies be financed? How can they best be introduced into the organization?

This chapter first describes the major technological changes that will affect organizations and society and then discuss their implications for business.

THE "MICRO" REVOLUTION

There is a good deal of talk about the "information revolution." It is said that this revolution will be similar in scope and impact to the industrial revolution that brought sweeping changes in the late eighteenth and early nineteenth centuries. "Micro revolution" is a more appropriate name than information revolution, since several other aspects besides information seem to be involved. The technologies of the micro revolution are already established. It is only a matter of time until they are applied on a widespread basis. What is not yet clear, however, is their impact on organizations and society.

The industrial revolution brought about huge environmental changes by substituting mechanical energy for manual labor. The enormous technical and social transformations that followed greatly affected the nature and size of organizations and the task of management. We can say, in fact, that it was during the industrial revolution that the professional manager was born. This new type of manager had to deal with the more complex problems facing organizations, achieve a more efficient and effective transformation of resources, and deal with the diverse needs of the large numbers of people employed by new companies.

The origins of the micro revolution can be found in various fields including computers, physics, biology, chemistry, and engineering. Already some of its products can be seen. For example, there has been a huge reduction in the components used to process information (e.g., in computers), and we now have the technological ability to deal with minuscule elements (e.g., a living cell).

Further developments in the micro revolution will greatly influence all aspects of business organizations and will affect the management of both businesses and society.

There are three main aspects of the micro revolution: microchips, biochemistry and genetic engineering, and lasers. A fourth aspect, telecommunications, must also be included, since though it is not directly related to micro technology it is both a beneficiary and an integral part of it.

Microchips

Microchips are tiny electronic elements currently about the size of a thumbnail on which huge amounts of information can be stored. At present, microchips that can hold up to 1,024,000 bits of information—the equivalent of about 100 pages of an average book—are readily available. Obviously, this is a huge amount of information to store, in particular when storage is not "passive," in contrast to, say, a microfiche film. With a microfiche, information once stored can be retrieved only by looking at the film sequentially and reading its contents. With a microchip, information can be retrieved in any desired form or quantity. For example, if a microchip contains information about sales figures, amounts and prices referring to the sales of any particular product can be found within seconds and can be retrieved in any desired form. Correlations, for instance, can be obtained. The data can be graphed or the impact of price on quantities sold can be measured. Clearly such an ability to retrieve and process information has important implications for management.

The mass production of microchips has reduced their cost and made them economical for an ever greater variety of applications. Furthermore, with new technical developments, the capacity of microchips is increasing. For instance, microchips that can store up to 2 million bits of information are now in the development stage.

At present microchips are being used for the following major applications.

Microprocessors

Microprocessors are small units that, in addition to storing information, can also process it (e.g., calculate, perform logical functions, make decisions, and store intermediate results for subsequent use). They are presently used for numerous tasks such as automatic control in engineering, guidance systems, real-time processing of information, regulating the functioning of mechanical devices, (e.g., cars, washing machines, airplane engines), precision apparatus, medical devices, and all types of computer applications. As microchips become smaller, so do microprocessors. And as they decrease in size, the speed of storing, retrieving, and processing information increases.

In addition, as microchips become cheaper, so do microprocessors. The result is more possibilities for applications. Finally, as the number of applications involving microprocessors increases, demand allows their mass production, which further decreases costs and makes their use economically more feasible. The areas in which microprocessors can be used are potentially enormous. This means that their cost will become extremely low if, in the future, they realize this potential.

Data Banks

Data banks allow the storage of huge amounts of information. Obviously, as microchips become more widely available, cheaper, and capable of storing ever larger volumes of information, the creation of ever larger data banks will also become possible. Moreover, public data bases (accessed through regular telephone lines) are now becoming commercially economical. Such data banks make useful information easily accessible to various users without the users having the tedious and expensive task of collecting data on their own. It is not farfetched to say that conventional book libraries could become an antiquity before the end of the century, being replaced by data banks accessible to all in their homes through personal computers and regular telephone lines.

Computers

Computers (a rather unfortunate name, since they can perform many more tasks than just computing; a better name would have been information processors) have been with us for less than 50 years. Yet they have revolutionized the way information is stored, retrieved, and processed. Microchips and microprocessors have revolutionized computers. As microchips and microprocessors become smaller, more efficient, and cheaper, so do computers. The speed of computers is constantly increasing, as the basis of a computer is many sophisticated microprocessors assembled together.

Computers can store and retrieve large amounts of information and perform a great variety of tasks. The same machine (hardware) can be made to perform many tasks by changing the instructions given to the computer through a program (software). Computers allow a two-way interaction between machine and user through a language that can be learned by the user in a few hours to a few days (depending on the particular language). Efficient and easy-to-use languages exist at present and new ones will obviously be developed. Such languages are interactive and close to natural languages, such as English, French, and Greek. Furthermore, user-oriented, interactive computer systems that are accessible to many users at once are already available.

Computers are used today for almost anything. As they become smaller and cheaper, the areas of application increase. Personal computers selling for less than $600 today are more powerful and can store more data in their main memory than computers that were selling for more than $100,000 in 1970. Moreover, the flexibility and versatility of programming has allowed the development of programs that can perform tasks once thought to be the exclusive prerogative of the human mind. For instance, 10 years ago even the most sophisticated computer could not beat an average chess player. Today, small computers that can be held in the hand can beat the majority of good chess players. It is estimated that by the year 2000 a computer will be the world champion, beating the best human player.

Robots

Cheap and tiny microchips built into microprocessors, which in turn are programmed into a computer, can be incorporated in mechanical-electronic systems capable of performing simple manual tasks. Such machines have been named "robots" and are being used to replace unskilled and semi-skilled labor. Not all mechanical devices that use microprocessors can be classified as robots. Washing machines, for example, are not robots because they can do only one task. Robots, on the other hand, are "programmable, multi-functional manipulators designed to move materials, parts, tools or specialized components through a variable programmed motion, thus achieving the requirements of a variety of tasks" (Robot Institute of America). Robots were first used to perform heavy or dangerous jobs. Recently, however, their use has been enlarged to almost any kind of repetitive task. The determinant of using robots is not necessarily the difficulty/complexity of the task, but rather the economics (cost of designing and building the robot versus the benefits involved) of substituting capital for labor. At present, the cost of designing and building robots is rather high, which limits their application to simple, mass-production processes in large, high-volume industries. However, as labor costs increase and microchips, microprocessors, and computers become cheaper, robots will be used in a wide variety of repetitive manual tasks.

Lately, robots have been equipped with sensing devices that considerably increase their capabilities of performing a diverse variety of tasks, but they are still in a primitive stage compared with humans. They are unable to do many things humans can take for granted. A robot, for instance, has great difficulties in walking through a crowded corridor, or getting down a flight of stairs. On the other hand, robots can lift heavy weights, do dangerous or unhealthy tasks, and be obedient and productive day and night, seven days a week, with no demands for holidays, sick leave, or wage increases.

Biochemistry and Genetic Engineering

The concept of biotechnology is not a new one. The same basic principle— that of manufacturing products by the use of strains (microorganisms) that affect the raw material through a biological process—is used in wine or cheesemaking. The present breakthrough in biotechnology, however, is that the strains can be made to act at will, much faster and cheaper than the natural processes that occur with ageing. Biotechnology is becoming more efficient and effective as improved processes make possible the production of enzymes, vaccines, and similar products on an industrial scale.

Advances in electronic microscopes and lasers (discussed later) have allowed the development of a technology closely related to biochemistry called "genetic engineering," which is capable of identifying and operating on single living cells (splicing the cell). Such operations permit modifications of cells to achieve desirable characteristics or eliminate unwanted traits. This type of engineering on living cells holds tremendous potential, since it makes it conceivable that in the future we will be able to obtain, say, cows that produce 10 or 20 times more milk than usual, or chickens that lay eggs more than once a day. In addition, intermediate processes (e.g., those produced by enzymes) can be speeded up or made more efficient; new plants or animals can be produced by varying or combining parts of the cells of existing plants or animals, and so on.

The combination of biochemistry and genetic engineering will increase the economic usefulness of both over traditional technologies. The benefits from these technologies will be in the following directions:

1. Improve production yields
2. Decrease production cost
3. Produce chemical alternatives for natural products that are in short supply or expensive to obtain
4. Produce new chemicals or materials
5. Produce new species of plants
6. Achieve certain desired characteristics in existing plants
7. Produce new microorganisms
8. Alter the makeup of cells to achieve desired characteristics in living animals

The implications of biochemistry and genetic engineering are immense as far as the production of food, drugs, fertilizers, and all types of synthetic materials are concerned. At present, genetic engineering and biochemistry are still in their early stages, but by the year 2000 they will play some part in most aspects of food, agricultural, chemical, and drug production. Japan, the United States, and several western European countries are currently spending considerable sums of money on basic and applied research and development in these areas.

Biochemistry and genetic engineering have already been used with considerable success in the following areas:

- Health
- Agriculture and related industries
- Chemical production
- Fishing and sea farming
- Raw material production
- Waste treatment and pollution control
- Mineral extraction and treatment
- Development of energy from organic or synthetic sources

Further improvements in these areas will help alleviate food shortages and undernourishment and allow resources to be concentrated on solving social problems. Furthermore, the pollution of the environment could be eliminated through bioprocesses that separate pollutants and collect the materials involved as by-products for other industrial or agricultural uses. This is likely to take place as the efficient use of waste materials provides a good economic motive. Finally, energy could be obtained through biochemistry by using appropriate processes on natural products, thus increasing energy sources. Fuel, for instance, can be obtained from sugarcane.

Laser Technology

Laser technology owes its origin to physics; however, its areas of application are very widespread. Lasers provide the means for extremely efficient and highly precise operations, such as cutting of diamonds or strong metals, medical operations on the eye (without surgical cuts), mass transfer of information between distant points, transformation of heavy materials, and many others in physics, biology, medicine, telecommunications, engineering, manufacturing, and space. As the cost of utilizing lasers decreases, the areas of application increase.

The growing applications of laser technology are further enhanced by the advancements in microprocessors, which can be coupled with laser systems to guide them in performing a large variety of tasks requiring delicacy, high precision, and/or powerful energy requirements.

Though older and more advanced than genetic engineering or biochemistry, laser technology is still young. However, its potential is also huge, extending to almost anything that requires precise operations, the transformation of matter, communications, sound and light manipulations, or scanning. In the not too distant future all transformation of matter could be done more efficiently, more cheaply, and with a much higher precision through laser technology.

Telecommunications

In addition to traditional forms of communication, such as the telephone, radio, and television, the computer has provided the possibility of two-way telecommunication between one or more users. This can be done through a central computer accessible by telephone line to many users.

Computer telecommunications offer new and exciting possibilities that might fundamentally change patterns of communication. One has only to think that computer communication can combine the advantages of microprocessors, data banks, computers, and lasers. For example, a local doctor in a village could use a microprocessor to monitor the heart functioning and blood pressure of a patient, send this information by telephone to a computer in the city that is capable of processing it, and in turn be connected to a medical data bank to determine whether the patient has a heart illness, and if so, what kind of treatment is required. Alternatively, grammer school children in, say, India, could learn English or mathematics by having a small computer terminal connected, through a satellite, to a large computer in New York or Moscow.

IMPLICATIONS OF THE MICRO REVOLUTION IN MANAGEMENT

In the remainder of this chapter, the effects of the micro revolution on management are discussed. Management must realize that the micro revolution will affect all aspects of business operations. Managers will, therefore, have to understand and concentrate their attention on the consequences of the new technologies. Automation will be a central outcome; the ability to deal with people and change, to mobilize resources, and to manage uncertainty will also be important elements whose influence will be discussed.

The Management of Automation

Through the micro revolution, the possibilities for automation are limitless. The running of business or nonprofit organizations (whether manufacturing or service) will be automated to a great extent. The main questions are how fast and to what extent this automation will take place. The science fiction vision of completely automated factories operated by a few white-collar workers might not be too far in the future.

In manufacturing organizations, highly computerized operations will become commonplace. The present use of computer-aided design (CAD), computer-aided manufacturing (CAM), and flexible manufacturing systems (FMS) will be greatly extended as more powerful and cheaper computers become available and more resources are devoted to developing appropriate computer programs. In addition, robotics will replace unskilled and semi-skilled labor, further automating manufacturing. Furthermore, more material will be obtained through biochemical processes and such material will be processed more efficiently through lasers and new, more efficient technologies based on computer-developed and -operated systems.

The consequence of more automation in these forms will be cheaper operating costs and an abundance of materials, finished products, and computer-related services. Simon's concept (see Chapter 23) of exponentially decreasing prices for raw materials will also extend to manufacturing goods, thus creating an abundance of material things. Finally, scheduling, production planning, production control, and the handling of inventories will be completely computerized and carried out automatically. Human interference will be mainly confined to dealing with exceptions.

In service organizations, all aspects of information handling and financing will be centralized and computerized. Through on-line, real-time computers, interconnected nationally or globally, efficient and highly automated services will be available on a worldwide basis. Services for the stock market, banking, financial, and exchange markets will be available through home computers.

How can management deal with micro automation? What will be the major problems and challenges facing managers in the last part of the twentieth century? What social problems might be created by automation, and what financing will be necessary to implement the major changes? A major concern for managers must be to have a clear understanding of the new technologies and their implications so that they can apply them as efficiently and effectively as possible within their organizations.

Learning about the new technologies and mastering the necessary resources to implement them while avoiding internal resistance to change will be critical aspects of the job of managing. In addition, the rate of obsolescence as new technologies and systems become available (including more efficient computers and robots) will create new challenges and risks for management.

The Management of People

Even though existing management practices are concerned to a great extent with the human aspect of organizations, it is believed that much more will have to be done in this direction in the future. "Managing people" will include more than just dealing with the psychological or welfare aspects of those working in the organization. In addition, social concerns may require a longer commitment toward employees and workers (this is already what is happening in Japan and to some extent in most European countries) than is the practice at present. This "marriage" of employees and workers to the enterprise may reduce flexibility and increase the need for better selection and motivation of people, when few rewards and fewer punishments can be applied.

During the transition period at least, it may be hard to find and/or keep well-trained, professional employees, as they will be much in demand and will have wider mobility on an international basis. Most probably labor costs will increase (this would be one of the factors leading to automation) and effective ways will therefore be needed to efficiently manage and motivate the labor force to advance organizational goals.

The Management of Change

The industrial revolution caused huge dislocations of labor and resulted in big social problems. The micro revolution may bring similar results. What can be done, for instance, for the workers replaced by robots, or the white-collar workers currently doing paperwork when such work is computerized? Unions and governments, concerned with unemployment, will probably resist automation, since most likely it will mean fewer jobs. On the other hand, the need to stay competitive will force organizations to use automation and make cost savings that would entail fewer workers.

Management's ability to introduce change will be a major determinant of success in the future. Without substantial automation, the ability of Western industrialized businesses to compete with the third world countries, whose labor costs are considerably lower, will be diminished.

Finally, workers and employees will increasingly demand more control over their working environment and more participation in the decision making affecting their future. This may require more management by consensus, which may further complicate the problems associated with change. Implementing change will no doubt be more difficult when those making the decision to implement it are to be directly affected by such change.

The Management of Mobilizing Resources

Discovering and/or implementing new technologies is usually expensive. It requires large research and development expenditures, large capital outlays, long lead times, and often high risks. Moreover, as time passes and technology becomes more complex and sophisticated, ever larger sums must be invested to make new technological discoveries and/or to implement existing ones. This means that conventional financing may require fundamental changes. Internal financing through equities, bonds, or other similar instruments, bank borrowings, syndicated loans, and so on, may not be adequate, since large sums of money will be needed. Alternative schemes of financing will have to be contemplated. These might require the government to become involved in stimulating financing, securing the money required for such financing, or sharing the risks involved. This could be done either directly—as is already the case in France, where the governmental budget specifies money in the nationalized companies for investment in desired areas—or as in Japan, where the government guarantees bank loans intended for R&D or investment in certain highly promising areas. Alternatively, joint agreements among firms, interfirm alliances, semipublic (or nationalized) organizations, new forms of capital with appropriate tax incentives, and so forth, may become necessary to allow companies to compete internationally.

Successful managers will be those who can secure the required financing to automate their organizations and invent, or keep up, with the new micro technologies. Furthermore, organizations will require ways of securing financing for R&D and the mass production and distribution of the products of the new technologies. Such tasks required of managers will call for inventiveness: Novel schemes will have to be devised for financing the huge cash outlays necessary to automate, finance new projects, and implement new technologies.

The Management of Uncertainty

Humans exhibit a strong psychological need to master and control the environment, and are not fond of surprises and uncertainty. Long-term forecasting is well known to be inaccurate, holding many surprises. Future uncertainty will always be present and must be dealt with. Thus, the problem of risk associated with future decision making is brought to the forefront of management. If the future is uncertain, how can risk be managed? This becomes particularly relevant when large sums of money are involved, as in the case of financing new and sophisticated technologies. How long will the proposed new technology last before a new one is invented? How profitable will the technology be? How much money will it take to implement it? Should money be invested in R&D for developing new technologies? Should joint R&D projects be undertaken? Should technologies be licensed? These are obviously important questions that must be answered correctly, since their influence on organizations will be critical.

Predicting environmental and technological change becomes more difficult as product life cycles become shorter, and this further increases future uncertainty. In addition, competition becomes keener as worldwide communications increase and the earth becomes a global village. The choices left, therefore, become more limited. A country can isolate itself (as for example, Communist China has done to a great extent), but such an alternative is not very realistic for industrialized countries, as it would mean lower standards of living for their inhabitants. Alternatively, a country and its businesses can become part of a global network, which means competing with everyone on a worldwide basis. Obviously, in such a case (even if some regional or national barriers exist) businesses will have to keep up with the newest of technological developments and invest in them in order to be competitive. However, because it is impossible to forecast accurately the high rate of technological obsolescence, strong competition will make future uncertainty and risks high. New forms of management will be needed to cope realistically with high uncertainty and risk. The importance of strategy will become critical as a way of assessing uncertainty and determining acceptable levels of risk within which organizations can comfortably operate.

CONCLUSIONS

This chapter has discussed some new technologies that have already emerged on the horizon. The application of these technologies is not as yet widespread; however, before too long their impact will be felt by almost all businesses and other organizations. The "micro" revolution will without doubt produce substantial changes in business organizations and society in general. Managers must start thinking seriously and taking concrete steps *now* to face the consequences of the forthcoming micro revolution.

Micro automation will require managers capable of understanding its various aspects and of dealing with its ramifications. Furthermore, it will require managers who are proficient (or whose background and training are suitable for the task) in the micro technologies. The manager of the last part of the twentieth century will have to be the innovator and driving force in applying the micro revolution, just as the manager of the beginning of the nineteenth century had to understand and apply mechanical automation during the industrial revolution.

BIBLIOGRAPHY

Argote, A., P. S. Goodman and D. Schkade, "The Human Side of Robotics: How Workers React to a Robot," *Sloan Management Review,* Spring 1983, pp. 31–42.

Armstrong, J. S., *Long Range Forecasting: From Crystal Ball to Computer,* 2nd Ed., John Wiley, New York, 1985.

Cantley, M. F., "Boning Up on Biotechnology, Part 1," book review article, *Long Range Planning Journal,* 1982, vol. 15, no. 1, pp. 110–114.

Naisbitt, J., *Megatrends: Ten New Directions Transforming Our Lives,* Warner Books, New York, 1982.

Simon, J. L., *The Ultimate Resource,* Princeton University Press, Princeton, NJ, 1981.

The Management of Automation, Proceedings of British Management Data Foundation Conference, April 14, 1981.

28

THE EVALUATION OF FORECASTS

ESSAM MAHMOUD
University of Michigan-Flint, Flint, Michigan

INTRODUCTION

Many forecasters and decision makers such as executive managers, planners, production managers, sales managers, and inventory managers have different needs in terms of the following:

- The timing of an event (e.g., when the next recession will start)
- The magnitude of a variable (e.g., sales volume next month)
- The timing and quantities of some variable (e.g., when and how much raw material to order)
- The monitoring of some quantity (e.g., market share)

Managers need the foregoing predictions and are faced with the problem of having to select forecasting techniques from the many that are available. Forecasting techniques range from naive models, moving average, exponential smoothing (single, double, etc.), adaptive techniques, and econometric models to sophisticated techniques (Box–Jenkins, Parzen method, etc.). In addition, forecasts can be made judgmentally. The obvious question is, what is the best way of predicting the future?

This chapter deals with the evaluation of forecasts. The discussion will

Professors Hossein Shalchi and Gillian Rice provided useful comments, and Rochelle Moleski and Lonnie Miller gave invaluable help.

focus on a number of issues that are directly related to the process of fore-casting evaluation. These issues are

1. Research in the area of forecasting evaluation
2. The reliability of the data sources available
3. The accuracy measures available
4. The range of forecasting alternatives
5. The adjustment of forecasts through monitoring of forecast accuracy on a continuous basis

RESEARCH IN FORECAST EVALUATION

Many research studies summarize the accuracy and performance of quanti-tative and qualitative forecasting techniques. For example, numerous stud-ies have indicated that quantitative techniques perform better than qualita-tive techniques, while others have found the opposite result or that performance of both is about the same. Other research has evaluated the performance of a particular model relative to that of other models. Many studies have indicated that simple forecasting techniques do as well as so-phisticated techniques, and in some cases they do better. Others have shown the importance of using combining forecasting techniques and the improve-ment in accuracy whether using a simple combining approach or a weighted approach. Detailed information on many of the findings is summarized in an article by Mahmoud.[9] Chart 28-1 summarizes briefly some of the most im-portant findings.

On the whole, past research suggests that quantitative methods outper-form qualitative methods. This is of obvious significance to practitioners wishing to improve their forecasting accuracy. Forecasters or practitioners must, however, be aware of the particular circumstances under which empir-ical research has demonstrated the superiority of quantitative methods. Only when the circumstances are similar in practice can more accurate forecasts using quantitative techniques be expected. For instance, when the forecaster is dealing with a limited number of observations, qualitative methods might be more appropriate. Armstrong[1] suggested that it is advantageous to experi-ment with more than one qualitative method, as some are more accurate than others.

Another interesting conclusion from the practitioner's point of view is that simple forecasting methods have been found to perform equally as accurately as do sophisticated methods.[14,15] These findings encourage practi-tioners to view forecasting methodologies as a set of methods within their ability to understand and to use. This is especially true in the case of man-agers who wish to predict and cope with future uncertainties but do not have the training or expertise to deal with very complex forecasting techniques.

CHART 28-1. Research Results in Comparison of Forecasting Techniques

Area of Application	Main Results	Literature Source(s)
Quantitative methods vs. judgmental methods	Quantitative methods provided better forecasts than judgmental methods	Armstrong,[1] Fildes and Fitzgerald[3]
Box–Jenkins vs. exponential smoothing	Box–Jenkins models were less accurate than moving average and smoothing methods	Makridakis and Hibon[14]
Combining forecasts using simple or weighted average	Combining methods provided good forecast which resulted in total overall better performance on average than individual methods	Makridakis et al.,[15] Winkler and Makridakis[25]
Combining corresponding sets of individual forecasts	Forecast users reap gains from combining predictions from different sources	Zarnowitz[28]
Forecasting systems for reducing bias in forecasts	Design features of forecasting systems that can be used to improve performance of any forecasting method	Moriarty[19]
Assessment of state of the art of forecasting	Overall assessment of state of art of forecasting and guidelines for forecasters	Makridakis[13]

For theorists, these findings encourage concentration of efforts on the development and refining of simpler forecasting models and on the simplification of the more complex techniques.

RELIABILITY OF DATA SOURCES

A major consideration in the selection of a forecasting method for a particular application is the type of pattern in the data. Normally there are four different data patterns: horizontal, seasonal, cyclical, and trend. However, more than one of these patterns could exist in a particular time series. Identifying the type of data enables the forecaster to concentrate on methods that are suitable to the particular data pattern.

Before a data pattern is identified, it is important that the forecaster recognize the dependence of any forecasting method on a reliable data base.[10,21] Proper operation and maintenance of an accurate and timely data system give the forecaster an instrument with which to control and minimize the shortcomings of various forecasting methods. It is, therefore, essential to evaluate the data bases available to verify the reliability of the data before analyzing the data pattern.

Finally, from a practical standpoint, if valuable results are to be obtained from applying forecasting models, managers and forecasters must remember that a forecast is only as accurate as the data set on which it is based.

MEASURES OF FORECASTING ACCURACY

Accuracy plays an important role in evaluating forecasting methods. Accuracy can refer to "goodness of fit," which in turn measures how well the forecasting model is able to reproduce the data that were used to develop the forecasting model. Most important, however, it should refer to the future (postsample), that is, to data that have not been used to develop the forecasting model. Perceived accuracy varies from one application to another and from one decision maker to another.[26] For some decision situations, plus or minus 10% may be sufficient; in others, a variation of as little as 5% could spell disaster. Thus, being familiar with the different accuracy measures and their pros and cons enables decision makers to achieve more accurate forecasts.

While accuracy is a significant factor in evaluating forecasts, its definition is difficult. Difficulty is associated with the absence of a single universally accepted measure of accuracy[7,9,16,18]: Specific accuracy measures are different for different types of forecasting applications. In this section some of the most widely applied measures will be discussed to show their advantages and disadvantages.

It should be noted that one common goal is to minimize the error in the forecast. Thus, the error is defined as

$$\text{Error} = \text{actual} - \text{forecast}$$

or

$$e_t = A_t - F_t$$

where

$$e_t = \text{error at period } t$$

$$A_t = \text{actual value at period } t$$

$$F_t = \text{forecasted value at period } t$$

For a time series of a variable such as sales of product A, Chart 28-2 represents the actual value of the monthly sales of product A from January 1980 to December 1985, that is, 72 periods. By identifying the data pattern

CHART 28-2. Monthly Sales of Product A

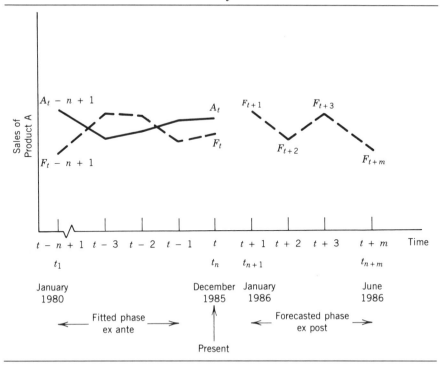

and choosing the appropriate model, the forecaster can measure the performance of the model by calculating the total errors from January 1980 to December 1985 (fitted phase). The difference between the two values (actual−forecast) is a measure of the error in forecasting this variable for each period. In this fashion, t_1 = January 1980 and t_n = December 1985. Remember that December 1985 represents the current period. In Chart 28-2, it should also be noted that the forecaster can consider the fitted phase as starting from January 1980 and represented by periods t_1 through t_n, and the forecasted phase is from period t_{n+1} to period t_{n+m}. The forecaster would like to forecast sales for the first six months of 1986. These periods are defined as $t+1, t+2$, to $t+m$, where $m = 6$. In other words, F_{t+1} represents the sales forecast for January 1986, F_{t+2} for February 1986, and F_{t+m} for June 1986. A clear distinction is needed between the errors of fitting the model to the data from January 1980 to December 1985 (the fitted phase) and the errors of forecasting from January 1986 to June 1986 (the forecasted phase). Total errors (TE) from January 1980 to December 1985 (fitted phase):

$$\text{TE} = \sum_{t=1}^{n}(A_t - F_t)$$

or

$$TE = \sum_{t=1}^{n} e_t$$

where $t = 1, 2, \cdots, n$, from January 1980 to December 1985. The right-hand side is known as "the sum of the error term."

The total errors of the forecast for January 1986 to June 1986 (TE) can be calculated as follows, after the actual sales values for those months are known:

$$TE = \sum_{t=n+1}^{m} e_t$$

where e_{n+1} is the error of January 1986 and e_m represents the error of June 1986 in our example.

Summary of Measures

A summary of accuracy measures is presented in the following based on sources such as Makridakis and colleagues,[15] Armstrong,[1] Steece,[22] and Mahmoud.[10] Some of these measures are more widely used than others. However, it is important to know what types of measures are available. Some of these measures are here summarized and discussed.

Error = Actual − Forecast

$$e_t = A_t - F_t$$

This represents an individual error for a given time t.

Mean Error (ME)

$$ME = \frac{\sum_{t=1}^{n} (A_t - F_t)}{n}$$

Mean Absolute Error (MAE)

$$MAE = \frac{\sum_{t=1}^{n} |e_t|}{n} = \frac{\sum_{t=1}^{n} |(A_t - F_t)|}{n}$$

This measure is also known as mean absolute deviation (MAD). The measure gives an equal weight to the individual error of each period, while not offsetting the positive and negative values of the individual error. MAE is an appropriate measure whenever the loss function is linear and symmetric. In the case of a linear cost function, the MAE of 10 units is twice as costly as an error of 5 units.

Percentage Error (PE$_t$)

$$PE_t = \frac{A_t - F_t}{A_t} (100)$$

The error is determined based on a weighted value that is the actual value of each period.

Mean Percentage Error (MPE)

$$MPE = \frac{\sum_{t=1}^{n} PE_t}{n}$$

or

$$MPE = \left[\frac{\sum_{t=1}^{n} (A_t - F_t)/A_t}{n} \right] 100$$

If the percentage errors are simply added together, positive values will offset negative values and the average percentage error will be small, even though the individual errors may be substantial. MPE assumes a linear cost function.

An alternative approach to MPE is the mean absolute percentage error (MAPE), which combines the individual percentage errors without offsetting the negative and positive values.

Mean Absolute Percentage Error (MAPE)

$$MAPE = \frac{\sum_{t=1}^{n} |PE_t|}{n}$$

This measure is similar to the mean absolute error (MAE) or to MAD. However, MAPE treats each error equally without taking account of the sign. It is useful in comparing different forecasting models. MAPE assumes that the cost of errors is more closely related to the percentage error than to the unit error.

Adjusted Mean Absolute Percentage Error

$$\overline{MAPE} = \left[\frac{\sum_{t=1}^{n} (|A_t - E_t|)/[1/2(A_t + F_t)]}{n} \right] 100$$

The $\overline{\text{MAPE}}$ is similar to the MAPE. It does not weigh the error on the basis of the actual value only but on both the actual and forecasted values for the same period.

Mean Squared Error (MSE)

$$\text{MSE} = \frac{\sum_{t=1}^{n} (A_t - F_t)^2}{n}$$

MSE is one of the most commonly used measures of accuracy. Forecasters usually choose models that minimize MSE. However, there are two short-comings of using MSE as a measurement of accuracy.[17] First, an examination of the MSE developed during the fitted phase may give little indication of the accuracy of the model at the forecasting phase. Second, MSE as a measure of forecasting accuracy is limited by the fact that different methods use different procedures in the fitting phase. For example, smoothing methods are highly dependent on initial forecasting estimates, whereas regression methods minimize the MSE by giving equal weight to all observations. Furthermore, Box–Jenkins minimizes the MSE of a nonlinear optimization procedure. Thus, comparisons are difficult and highly dependent on absolute units, which makes comparisons among series practically impossible.

Root Mean Squared Error (RMSE)

$$\text{RMSE} = \sqrt{\frac{\sum_{t=1}^{n} (A_t - F_t)^2}{n}}$$

This is similar to the MSE measure, but the associated cost function is quadratic. The disadvantage of using the RMSE, as with MSE, is that it is an absolute measure of the errors.

Standard Deviation of Error (SDE)

$$\text{SDE} = \sqrt{\frac{\sum_{t=1}^{n} (A_t - F_t)^2}{n - 1}}$$

The SDE is similar to the RMSE. The only difference is that the total sum squared of the errors is divided by $n - 1$ instead of by n.

Coefficient of Variation (CV)

CV is similar to the statistical inference coefficient of variation. It relates either SDE or RMSE to the average of the actual data. The smaller the value, the better the performance of the model.

$$CV = \frac{SDE}{(\sum_{t=1}^{n} A_t)/n} \, 100$$

or

$$CV = \frac{RMSE}{(\sum_{t=1}^{n} A_t)/n}$$

Coefficient of Determination (R^2)

$$R^2 = 1 - \frac{\sum_{t=1}^{n} [(F_t - \bar{F})(A_t - \bar{A})]^2}{[\sum_{t=1}^{n} (F_t - \bar{F})^2][\sum_{t=1}^{n} (A_t - \bar{A})^2]}$$

where $\bar{A}$ is the average of A_t and $\bar{F}$ is the average of F_t. It is commonly used in regression analysis. It can also be used as a measure of accuracy for time series models. R^2 ranges from 0 to 1. The closer the value of R^2 to 1, the better the forecast of the model. However, one should be familiar with the interpretation and the use of R^2. Armstrong[1] and Nelson[20] discussed its use.

Theil's U Statistic

$$U = \sqrt{\frac{\sum_{t=1}^{n-1} [(F_{t+1} - A_{t+1})/A_t]^2}{\sum_{t=1}^{n-1} [(A_{t+1} - A_t)/A_t]^2}}$$

Theil[23] explained in detail the use of the U statistic as a relative accuracy measure. U as a measure of accuracy allows a relative comparison of formal forecasting methods with naive approaches and also squares the error involved so that large errors are given much more weight than small errors.

When the accuracies of a naive method and the formal forecasting model are compared, the interpretation of the U statistic is as follows:

If $U = 1$, the naive method is as good as the forecasting model being evaluated.

If $U < 1$, the forecasting model being used is better than the naive method.

If $U > 1$, the naive method produces better results than the forecasting model.

Durbin–Watson Statistic (D-W)

$$\text{D-W} = \frac{\sum_{t=2}^{n} (e_t - e_{t-1})^2}{\sum_{t=1}^{n} e_t^2}$$

Makridakis and colleagues[17] detailed the computation and its use. As a rule of thumb, a good fitted forecasted model would reveal a value of D-W statistic around 2.

Dollar-Based Accuracy Measures

To facilitate managerial decision making, it is preferable to evaluate the performance of forecasting methods in terms of dollars. Mahmoud[10] and Mahmoud and colleagues[11] have developed several accuracy measures that managers can use in measuring the opportunity cost of an inaccurate prediction in terms of dollars. The different measures are applicable in various practical situations, depending on the inventory and production policies implemented. One of these dollar-based accuracy measures can be implemented under the following assumption, for example. This assumption is that management requires the amount to be produced to be equal to the amount of the forecast minus the amount of inventory available at the beginning of each period. Thus, the forecast is defined as F_t, and A_t represents the actual value at the same period. The cost of forecasting error, C_t at period t, can be defined as

$$C_t = h \, Z_t(F_t - A_t) + s \, (1 - Z_t)(A_t - F_t)$$

where h = stock-holding cost per item per period
$\quad s$ = shortage cost per item
$\quad Z_t$ = 1 if $F_t \geq A_t$, otherwise Z_t = zero
The total loss-cost function over the n forecasting periods is determined as follows:

$$TC = \Sigma_{t=1}^{n} [h \, Z_t(F_t - A_t) + s \, (1 - Z_t)(A_t - F_t)]$$

Thus, managers can evaluate the performance of a forecasting model or models in terms of dollars. This measure would be useful in determining the best alternative when the cost of implementing a particular forecasting method is important. There are often tradeoffs between the accuracy achieved by using a particular forecasting method and the costs involved in using this method. If both the costs of use and the costs associated with accuracy can be measured in dollar terms, it is easier to select the best forecasting method. The costs of using a forecasting method consist of development costs, data storage costs, maintenance costs, and the cost of repeated applications. For more details see Makridakis and colleagues[17] and Mahmoud.[10]

Determining the total cost (cost of implementing the method and the cost of its accuracy) of different forecasting methods in terms of dollars enables managers to choose the method that provides them with the accuracy they would like to achieve within given financial constraints and according to the level of technology and forecasting abilities available. A model can be chosen based on the tradeoff between the amount of money that could be saved and the extra money required to consider implementing a more sophisticated model. This accuracy measure is also useful when comparing the performance of combining two or more simple forecasting models with use of a sophisticated method.

Relative Accuracy Measures

A comparison of two or more models is often needed to be able to select the most accurate model. Managers can judge the performance of a model relative to a naive method or to some other model(s). In the naive method, the forecast of the next period is equal to the actual value of the current period. One would expect the forecasting model to perform better than the naive model.

The performance of the forecasting model relative to the naive model can be determined by applying the following ratio:

$$\frac{\text{Accuracy measure of forecasting method}}{\text{Accuracy measure of naive method}} \left(\text{e.g.,} \ \frac{\text{MSE}_S}{\text{MSE}_N} \ \text{or} \ \frac{\text{MAPE}_S}{\text{MAPE}_N}, \text{etc.} \right)$$

where MSE_S represents the mean squared error of the forecasting technique and MSE_N represents the mean squared error of the naive method (MAPE_S represents the mean absolute percentage error of the forecasting technique and MAPE_N represents the mean absolute percentage error of the naive method). Managers can judge if the forecasting model is worth considering by comparing the accuracy measures of the two methods:

1. If the accuracy measure of the forecasting method (e.g., MSE_S or MAPE_S) is less than the accuracy measure of the naive method (e.g., MSE_N or MAPE_N), the ratio is less than 1 and the forecasting method is worth considering.

2. If the MSE_S or MAPE_S is greater than the MSE_N or MAPE_N, respectively, the ratio is greater than 1 and the naive method is better than the forecasting method.

3. If the MSE_S or MAPE_S is equal to the MSE_N or MAPE_N, respectively, the ratio is equal to 1 and the forecasting method performs no better nor worse than the naive method.

It should be clear that in situations where the data are very stable and do not fluctuate, the naive method would be appropriate.

In the case of evaluating any two forecasting methods, the same rules can be followed. For example, if a manager would like to determine the relative performance of two methods, such as single exponential smoothing and

Box–Jenkins, he or she would define the ratio as follows:

$$\frac{\text{MSE}_S}{\text{MSE}_{B\text{-}J}} \quad \text{or} \quad \frac{\text{MSE}_1}{\text{MSE}_2}$$

If the MSE_S or MSE_1 (mean squared error using single exponential smoothing) is less than $\text{MSE}_{B\text{-}J}$ or MSE_2 (mean squared error using Box–Jenkins method), the ratio is less than 1 and the exponential smoothing model is more accurate than the Box–Jenkins model. Other conclusions follow the same pattern as in the naive method comparison.

The foregoing do not represent an exhaustive list of accuracy measures. More such measures are discussed by Armstrong[1] and by Makridakis and colleagues.[17]

Structural Change and Bias

Forecasters should find systematic methods that improve the forecast performance. It is desirable for a forecasting system to correct potential biases before the forecast is integrated into the organization. Thus, an approach is needed that helps forecasters detect bias and measure it. Once bias is measured, it can be corrected. This could be achieved either by applying a test of structural stability, as explained by Tiao and colleagues,[24] or by determining bias decomposition, as discussed by Theil.[23]

It is important to realize that almost all forecasts can be expected to contain some error. However, one would select the model that minimizes the errors.

Theil[23] showed the usefulness of using three different bias attributes, the mean difference error, U^M; the regression pattern error, U^R; and the random error expressed in terms of population parameters, U^D. Expected squared error can be decomposed into three components as follows:

$$\begin{aligned}
\text{MSE} &= E(A_t - F_t)^2 \\
&= (\mu_A - \mu_F)^2 + (\sigma_F - \rho\sigma_A)^2 + (1 - \rho^2)\sigma_A^2
\end{aligned}$$

where μ_A and μ_F = population means of actual value A_t and forecasted value F_t

σ_A and σ_F = population standard deviations

ρ = population correlation between A_t and F_t

Dividing the previous equation by MSE provides the following:

$$1 = \underbrace{\frac{(\mu_A - \mu_F)^2}{\text{MSE}}}_{\substack{\text{mean} \\ \text{difference} \\ \text{error}}} + \underbrace{\frac{(\sigma_F - \rho\sigma_A)^2}{\text{MSE}}}_{\substack{\text{regression} \\ \text{pattern} \\ \text{error}}} + \underbrace{\frac{(1 - \rho^2)\sigma_A^2}{\text{MSE}}}_{\substack{\text{random} \\ \text{error}}}$$

Thus, the three components derived by Theil can be defined as follows:

$$\text{Mean difference error} = U^M = \frac{(\bar{A} - \bar{F})^2}{\text{MSE}}$$

$$\text{Regression pattern error} = U^R = \frac{(S_F - rS_A)^2}{\text{MSE}}$$

$$\text{Random error} = U^D = \frac{(1 - r^2)S_A^2}{\text{MSE}}$$

where S is the standard deviation and r the correlation coefficient

The bias attributed to differences in sample average levels of actual values A_t and forecasted values F_t is measured by U^M. In a regression of the form

$$A_t = F_t + \varepsilon_t$$

U^R measures the deviation of the sample regression slope from 1 and U^D measures the sample variance of the regression error term ε_t. To achieve perfect forecasts, $U^M = U^R = 0$ and $U^D = 1$. Thus, one could conclude in practice that if both values U^M and U^R are close to 0 and U^D is close to 1, the forecaster has achieved an unbiased forecast. For more detailed information related to the use and application of different cases, readers refer to Theil[23] and Moriarty.[19]

FORECASTING ALTERNATIVES

The issue of considering alternative models, measures, or approaches is an important one. The work of Makridakis and colleagues,[15] known as the M-competition, indicated the importance of three factors (time horizon, type of data, and accuracy measure) that affect the forecasting accuracy of various methods.

Accuracy depends on the application considered. Managers should consider alternative accuracy measures when these are to be used for a variety of forecasting applications. For example, Makridakis[12] indicated that in the case of forecasting inventories, large errors are undesirable, and thus the use of the MSE accuracy measure would be appropriate. In budget forecasting, the MAPE accuracy measure is commonly used. In situations requiring a single forecast (e.g., in bidding for a large contract in the futures market), average rankings of a particular accuracy measure must be used. Where only two methods are considered and the size of the error is not important, the percentage-better method should be employed.

Some forecasting techniques require a minimum number of data points. For example, applying Census II and decomposition forecasting methods using some computer packages requires a minimum of 78 data points. If the data base does not include the minimum number of data points that a particular model requires, the model cannot be used.

Different models also are appropriate for different time horizons. For example, it is advisable to consider deseasonalizing single exponential smoothing and Holt's method when forecasting for one period ahead. When forecasting for four or six periods ahead, sophisticated methods such as Parzen's and Lewandowski's methods are recommended.[15]

Fildes[2] indicated the importance of considering alternative variables to be included in econometric or regression models. The inclusion of different variables affects the explanatory power and predictive accuracy of such models. By considering a checklist of variables and their likely impact on the decision being contemplated, variables that most require attention can be identified. The availability of such alternatives depends on the information available and the number of data points needed.

It is important to consider the alternative of combining two or more forecasting methods instead of relying on only one method. Several studies have shown how combining forecasts can improve accuracy.[10,15,18,28] Users can consider one of three methods of combining forecasting techniques (see Makridakis and Winkler[18]). The first form takes a simple average of two or more forecasts. The second approach is known as historical weighting, in which each forecast generated from each model is weighted by the ratio of one minus individual mean squared error to total mean squared error for all forecasts. The third method uses subjective weighting, in which managers apply weights to the forecasts on the basis of personal judgments as to which methods more closely reflect the changing reality.

Even the first method, the simple average of two or more forecasting models, can improve accuracy.

In conclusion, being aware of the conditions under which some techniques perform better than others enables managers to prepare for different alternatives. By monitoring which alternative works best, managers are better able to achieve their goals effectively.

MONITORING THE PERFORMANCE OF FORECASTING METHODS

The manager should monitor the environment closely and constantly attempt to adjust the parameters of the forecasting model to incorporate any environmental changes. This would provide a predicted figure that would be closer to the actual value. Makridakis[13] and Gardner[6] indicated that monitoring changes is an extremely important task, ensuring that the system remains in control. Thus, quantitative forecasts can be modified to account for nonrandom changes. The constant monitoring of forecasting methods can be achieved easily through a good forecasting system. Since computers and many good forecasting packages are now widely available, managers (or forecasters) have the responsibility to select the best program(s) or the system that provides them with many of these guidelines.

It is crucial to detect errors as quickly as possible. The forecasting model can then be refitted to the data or changed to a more appropriate model to prevent serious production or inventory problems. In inventory control, for example, forecast monitoring is essential because of the need to take action when there is a significant change in demand. If the forecast model suggests an increase in demand, new orders should be placed on a priority basis. If demand is expected to fall, unneeded orders must be canceled promptly to prevent excess inventory investment.

Monitoring devices (tracking signals) are used to keep watch for signs of bias in the forecast errors. Gardner[5] also discussed three warning signs that can be used to show when a forecasting system goes out of control:

1. *Simple Cumulative Sum (Cusum) of Forecast Errors.* This can be computed and tested in several different ways. The cumulative sum of the errors at the end of each period is compared with the smoothed mean absolute deviation (MAD). Cusum is determined as follows:

$$e_t = A_t - F_t$$

$$\text{SUM}_t = e_t + \text{SUM}_{t-1}$$

$$\text{MAD}_t = \alpha \, |e_t| + (1 - \alpha) \, \text{MAD}_{t-1}$$

$$C_t = \left| \frac{\text{SUM}_t}{\text{MAD}_t} \right|$$

where e_t = error for period t

$\quad A_t$ = actual value

$\quad F_t$ = forecast value

SUM_t = sum of error at period t

MAD_t = smoothed mean absolute deviation at period t

The smoothing parameter α should have a value between 0 and 1. C_t is the tracking signal (cusum) for period t. Cusum should fluctuate around 0 when the system is in control. Biased errors occur when the cusum departs from 0 or the system is out of control if the C_t exceeds the value of the smoothed MAD_t.

2. *Smoothed-Error Tracking Signal.* The tracking signal T_t is measured by using the following set of equations:

$$E_t = \alpha \, |e_t| + (1 - \alpha) \, E_{t-1}$$

$$\text{MAD}_t = \alpha \, |e_t| + (1 - \alpha) \, \text{MAD}_{t-1}$$

$$T_t = \left| \frac{E_t}{\text{MAD}_t} \right|$$

where E_t represents the updated value of the error e_t.

3. *First-Order Autocorrelation in Forecast Errors.* This is more complex than the previous two indicators. The existence of any significant positive autocorrelation indicates lack of control. For more details and signals, see Gardner.[5]

Applying any of the three methods is recommended. All are easy to use. The only problem is determining the starting values, for example, MAD_{t-1} and SUM_{t-1}, which represent the values at the starting point for the previous period $t - 1$. SUM_{t-1} can start with a value of zero. MAD_{t-1} can be set equal to its expected value.

Monitoring forecasts constantly by using one of the tracking signals discussed previously alerts the manager to any problems in the forecasting system. An action such as refitting the model or searching for another model or a combination of models may be necessary. Also, monitoring the error and adjusting the forecast constantly enable the manager to take courses of action related to the decisions affected by the forecast, such as adjusting inventory or production.

IMPLICATIONS

This chapter has outlined some of the important issues related to forecasting evaluation. Organizations or individuals implement the process of evaluation differently, depending on knowledge of forecasting, forecasting training facilities, time available, data available, the computer system used, the degree of integration, and the software used.

The level of knowledge that a particular forecaster has will reflect on his or her forecasting performance, given a forecasting situation. Having more knowledge enables the forecaster to use more techniques and more tests to check the accuracy and the basic assumptions under which a particular method can be implemented. However, it does not take a great deal of time or effort to gain the needed knowledge. Once a particular person (or team) starts, he or she (or it) will gain knowledge, especially with the help of the many forecasting software packages available for a variety of computers.

Time is an important factor, especially for those who handle many forecasts in a given time period and for those who forecast a limited number of variables during the same time. Obviously the latter would be able to apply more accuracy measures and set different alternatives and check thoroughly for model specification, performance, and so on.

Integrating forecasting applications into the organizational planning process would help forecasters to monitor closely any changes and their impact on forecasting. Wright[27] showed the importance of considering forecasting as part of the decision support system and not as a self-contained activity.

Finally, the availability of a good forecasting system will have a great impact on the forecaster or the decision maker. The forecaster would be able to address many of the issues discussed in this chapter. For example, to achieve a better accuracy performance, the forecaster applies more than one accuracy measure to ensure thorough evaluation. This can be achieved either by including more accuracy measures in the forecasting package being used or by buying a package that already includes several such measures. Furthermore, a package that includes comprehensive forecasting methods would enable the forecaster to test the performance of a variety of models. A package or system that provides the forecaster with different tools for diagnostic checking, model specification, and monitoring of the forecast error, as was mentioned earlier, would be more useful. For example, Wheelwright and Makridakis[26] described in detail two comprehensive forecasting systems, SIBYL-RUNNER and FUTURCAST. The latter system consists of a wide range of forecasting techniques which allow the forecaster to use at least five different accuracy measures and different techniques for model structure such as autocorrelation. It also permits combining more than one forecasting technique. The system allows the forecaster to monitor the environmental change and include the change in the model. However, even forecasters with limited programs or packages can implement many of the different issues discussed in this chapter.

CONCLUSIONS

Managers or forecasters face a great deal of difficulty in evaluating their forecasts. A systematic evaluation procedure should be integrated into the organizational planning activities and made a part of the decision support system. However, understanding of the state of the art of forecasting techniques, awareness of the most important findings, the availability of different accuracy measures and their uses, the availability of reliable data bases, the contribution of different alternatives, knowledge about monitoring environmental changes, and the availability of good computer forecasting systems are important criteria to be considered when evaluating forecasts. The value and the outcome of the evaluation process depend on the organization's data bases and the forecaster's experience, the forecaster's knowledge of certain forecasting models, and his or her ability to understand past and current changes.

REFERENCES

1. Armstrong, J. S., *Long-Range Forecasting: From Crystal Ball to Computer*, 2nd ed., John Wiley, New York, 1985.

2. Fildes, Robert, "Forecasting: The Issues," in S. Makridakis and S. Wheelwright, eds., *The Handbook of Forecasting: A Manager's Guide*, John Wiley, New York, 1982, pp. 83–104.

3. Fildes, R., and D. Fitzgerald, "The Use of Information in Balance of Payments Forecasting," paper presented at First International Symposium on Forecasting, Quebec, Canada, May 1981.

4. Gardenfors, P., "On the Information Provided by Forecasting Models," *Technological Forecasting and Social Change*, vol. 16, 1980, pp. 351–361.

5. Gardner, E. S., "Automatic Monitoring of Forecast Errors," *Journal of Forecasting*, vol. 2, no. 1, 1983, pp. 1–21.

6. Gardner, E. S., "Exponential Smoothing: The State of the Art," *Journal of Forecasting*, vol. 4, no. 1, 1985, pp. 1–28.

7. Gardner, E. S., and D. G. Dannenbring, "Forecasting with Exponential Smoothing: Some Guidelines for Model Selection," *Decision Science*, vol. 11, 1980, pp. 370–383.

8. Granger, C. W. J., "Prediction With a Generalized Cost of Error Function," *Operation Research Quarterly*, vol. 20, no. 2, 1969, pp. 199–207.

9. Mahmoud, Essam, "Accuracy in Forecasting: A Survey," *Journal of Forecasting*, vol. 3, 1984, pp. 139–159.

10. Mahmoud, Essam, "Short-Term Forecasting: Matching Techniques to Tasks. An Integrated Framework and Empirical Investigation," Ph.D Dissertation, State University of New York at Buffalo, June 1982.

11. Mahmoud, Essam, Suresh K. Goyal, and H. Shalchi, Loss-Cost Functions for Measuring the Accuracy of Sales Forecasting Methods, working paper, University of Michigan at Flint, 1986.

12. Makridakis, Spyros, "Empirical Evidence Versus Personal Experience," *Journal of Forecasting*, vol. 2, no. 3, 1983, pp. 295–311.

13. Makridakis, Spyros, "The Art and Science of Forecasting: An Assessment and Future Directions," *International Journal of Forecasting*, vol. 2, no. 1, 1986, pp. 15–40.

14. Makridakis, S., and M. Hibon, "Accuracy of Forecasting: An Empirical Investigation," *Journal of the Royal Statistical Society*, vol. 142, part 2, 1979, pp. 97–145.

15. Makridakis, S., A. Anderson, R. Carbone, R. Fildes, M. Hibon, R. Lewandowski, E. Parzen, and R. Winkler, "The Accuracy of Extrapolation (Time Series) Methods: Results of a Forecasting Competition," *Journal of Forecasting*, vol. 1, 1982, pp. 111–153.

16. Makridakis, S., and S. C. Wheelwright, "Forecasting: Framework and Overview," in S. Makridakis and S. C. Wheelwright, eds., *Forecasting TIMS Studies in Management Science*, vol. 12, North-Holland, Amsterdam, 1979.

17. Makridakis, S., S. C. Wheelwright, and V. E. McGee, *Forecasting: Methods and Applications*, 2nd ed., John Wiley, New York, 1983.

18. Makridakis, S., and R. Winkler, "Averages of Forecasts: Some Empirical Results," *Management Science*, vol. 29, no. 9, 1983, pp. 987–996.

19. Moriarty, Mark M., "Design Features of Forecasting Systems Involving Management Judgements," *Journal of Marketing Research*, vol. 22, November 1985, pp. 353–364.

20. Nelson, C. R., "The First Order Moving Average Process Identification, Estimation and Prediction," *Journal of Econometrics*, vol. 2, 1974, pp. 121–141.

21. Rice, G., and Essam Mahmoud, "Forecasting and the Database: An Analysis of Databases for International Business," *Journal of Forecasting,* vol. 4, 1985, pp. 89–97.

22. Steece, Bert, "Evaluation of Forecasts," in Spyros Makridakis and Steven C. Wheelwright, eds., *The Handbook of Forecasting: A Manager's Guide,* John Wiley, New York, 1982, pp. 457–468.

23. Theil, H., *Applied Economic Forecasting,* North-Holland Publishing Co., Amsterdam, 1971.

24. Tiao, G. C., G. E. P. Box, and W. J. Hamming, "Analysis of Los Angeles Photochemical Smog Data: A Statistical Overview," *Journal of the Air Pollution Control Association,* vol. 25, 1975.

25. Winkler, R. L., and S. Makridakis, "The Combination of Forecasts," *Journal of the Royal Statistical Society,* Series A, vol. 145, 1983, pp. 150–157.

26. Wheelwright, S., and S. Makridakis, *Forecasting Methods for Management,* 4th ed., John Wiley, New York, 1985.

27. Wright, David J., et al., "Evaluation of Forecasting Methods for Decision Support," *International Journal of Forecasting,* vol. 2, no. 2, 1986, pp. 131–256.

28. Zarnowitz, V., "The Accuracy of Individual and Group Forecasts From Business Outlook Surveys," *Journal of Forecasting,* vol. 3, 1984, pp. 10–27.

CHAPTER

29

SELECTING AND USING EXTERNAL DATA SOURCES AND FORECASTING SERVICES TO SUPPORT A FORECASTING STRATEGY

TIMOTHY A. DAVIDSON
LAURENCE PRUSAK
Temple, Barker & Sloane, Inc., Lexington, Massachusetts

INTRODUCTION

Once an organization has recognized that quantitative forecasts are needed to serve as a baseline foundation to the planning and control process, attention often turns to the acquisition of external data and expert forecasting services. Only the largest organizations attempt to rely solely on in-house staff dedicated to data collection and mathematical modeling. It is difficult to imagine an industry in today's economy whose destiny is self-contained—a microeconomy whose dynamics are not in the least influenced by events, strategies, and evolutionary trends emanating from the outside. If such a condition existed, long-term sales and market forecasts could be accurately determined without outside help. Because the dynamics of one industry are affected by (and affect) those of others, the forecasting task cannot be treated parochially. The economic forecasting industry and many syndicated data services have emerged in answer to this need.

In 1963, a handful of major American firms in quite dissimilar markets (Esso, GE, IBM, Bethlehem Steel, and John Deere) recognized the advantages of working with a national economic model and engaged Lawrence

Klein and the Wharton Economic Forecasting Associates (WEFA) to provide such a service. Klein's model was based on the pioneering work of Paul Samuelson in the 1940s. These early patrons were among the first to draw practical benefit from a series of mathematical equations that represented an input–output model of the U.S. economy. By the mid-1970s, Data Resources Incorporated, Chase Econometrics, and WEFA had established a profitable practice providing services to large American industrial organizations. Each of these firms had its own complex national economic model as its raison d'être, and each produced notably different projections.

Significant advances in economic modeling techniques and in survey methods coupled with the utilization of the computer have contributed to the growth of this industry since the early 1970s. Several newly formed forecasting service firms are directing products and services toward the small- and medium-sized organization. Competition and wide-scale use of computerized data delivery systems via time-sharing networks promise to provide forecasting services to firms who could not afford such luxuries in the 1970s.

This chapter illustrates the multiplicity of data and forecasting services available to large and small organizations having recognized needs for better planning. It provides guidelines for choosing and using such products and services effectively.

DEVELOPING A FORECASTING STRATEGY

Normally, organizations will decide they want a forecasting system when they observe large deviations from plan, year after year. They observe that some items are out of stock while others are hopelessly overstocked. The short-range production schedule contains more last-minute changes than not. Inventories and service staff are at the wrong geographic location for the demand. The cost of poor planning becomes very evident to the financial controller, to the operations manager, and to the marketing/sales director, often resulting in the establishment of a task force to suggest some systematic changes.

After cursory examination of an organization's planning/scheduling process, the task force often finds that different parts of the organization are using forecasts for demand that

Have been prepared informally and independently

Are heavily laced with judgment

Have little relationship with past patterns of demand

Have not received consensus approval by a managerial committee

Are not periodically reviewed and modified when conditions change

Many of these deficiencies can be resolved with procedural improvements such as the establishment of a single company forecast and a permanent forecast review committee. Such a committee's responsibilities include the production, review, and distribution of one demand forecast to be used in marketing, manufacturing, and financial planning throughout the organization.

It soon becomes evident that the periodic production of forecast values for each key item is a greater challenge than the procedural deficiencies. It is at this point that the task force recognizes the need to examine both quantitative and judgmental forecasting approaches.

Quantitative forecasting is based on a mathematical model of the patterns of demand for an item and/or the relationships between explanatory variables and the demand. In the consumer goods industry, manufacturers can sometimes develop sales forecasts based solely on the patterns of trend, seasonality, and cycle that are evidenced in a product's shipment history. These period-to-period changes reflect the purchase behavior of the wholesaler and/or the consumer. More accurate forecasts of a product's sales can often result from the examination of the mathematical relationship between causal (or explanatory) variables such as price, advertising expenditures, and trade promotion discounts.

PREREQUISITES FOR QUANTITATIVE FORECASTING

Before long, the forecasting task force realizes that to proceed with quantitative forecast model development the organization will need

Historical data for the items under study

Forecast data for the causal model inputs

Technical know-how in statistical forecasting

Computer programs for time series analysis or for causal model building

Computer terminals or micro computers

If forecasts are to be systematically generated on a regular basis over a long time, and if the aforementioned requisites are available with existing resources, the organization can proceed to develop an in-house system. Such a solution approach minimizes out-of-pocket costs and provides greater control. More frequently, firms look to outside services to provide one or more of the prerequisites and continue to use those services until equivalent in-house resources are provided. The extent to which company resources are expended on the development of a forecasting system should be proportional to the savings derived from the use of better forecasts. That is, successful forecasting should lead to lower costs or greater profits.

The benefits clearly depend on what is being forecasted. For example, reducing inventory safety stocks due to better forecasts can free capital that can then be invested elsewhere. Better forecasts of receipts and disbursements may reduce the need to borrow short-term funds and thus reduce interest expense. If the benefits of forecasting can be expressed in monetary terms, the future stream of benefits and costs can be discounted to obtain the present value of the project. The expected benefits should also be weighted by the probability that they will be achieved. Even precise forecasts will not assure a company a benefit such as cost savings or greater profits. They only have the potential to do so providing that management responds wisely to their signals. When the benefits are nonmonetary, a subjective estimate of benefit values is necessary.

Similarly, the cost of producing forecasts depends on what is being forecast and the accuracy required. In general, the costs include the expense of developing models and computer systems, the costs of data acquisition and storage, and the computer (time-sharing) costs. New users of forecasting systems often underestimate the data acquisition costs and the costs of administering and maintaining the effectiveness of a forecasting system.

With the problem identified and the potential benefits quantified, the task force needs to draw up specifications that define the extent of the forecasting effort.

The level of detail (e.g., regional versus national forecasts), the time horizon, the desired accuracy needed to return the expected benefits, the speed of forecast production, and its frequency all need to be specified prior to the development of quantitative models or data systems employing the forecasts.

PUBLISHED FORECAST DATA

Forecasts of macroeconomic variables like population, GNP, personal income, and so on are produced and published by government and private data sources to help organizations in long-term planning. The following U.S. government sources provide macroeconomic forecasts free to the public:

U.S. Bureau of The Census, *Current Population Reports* (Series P-25): Contains demographic projections such as population by age, sex, race, and income

Bureau of Labor Statistics, *Monthly Labor Review:* Provides yearly national, industry, and occupational projections of the labor force

OBERS Area Economic Projections (1985): Contains projections of population, employment, personal income, and earnings by industry for states and regions, Bureau of Economic Advisors (BEA) economic areas, Standard Metropolitan Statistical Areas (SMSAs) and non-SMSA portions of BEA areas

U.S. Industrial Outlook: Contains trends and short- and long-term outlooks for over 350 industries

Some private organizations produce macroeconomic forecasts of demographic and economic trends at reasonable cost:

American Demographics: Each monthly issue has some demographic
projections, as well as analytical articles

Conference Board: This private business association provides statistics
and graphs on consumer behavior in the marketplace. Projections of consumer attitudes and buying plans are also provided

National Planning Association, *National and Regional Economic Projection Series,* Washington, DC: This long-range forecasting service analyzes and projects population, employment, personal income, and personal consumption expenditures for the United States, states, and
SMSAs

Sales and Marketing Management, *Survey of Buying Power:* Contains
short-range projections and growth rates for population, households, effective buying income, and retail sales for states, counties, and SMSAs

Business International's *Forecasting Studies:* Cover trends and key indicators; contain some non-U.S. forecasts

Commodity Research Bureau: Publishes demand, supply, and price level
forecasts of all major commodities

Business Week, Fortune: Feature forecasts projecting major industry
trends

Trade journals: Produce short-term and some long-term forecasts for their
industry focus such as *Electronics'* "World Market Forecasts," *Oil and
Gas Journal's* "Forecast/Review," and *Iron Age's* (Chiltons) "Annual
Metalworking Forecast" (see Periodical section in this chapter)

Many university, public, and corporate libraries have the capacity to do
literature searches. They can effectively scan hundreds of journals for published forecasts.

The major advantage of using published sources is the low cost. However, the labor required to search, transcribe, and validate the forecast data
often offsets that low cost. More important is the fact that these macrofore-
casts are at times not specific enough for an organization's routine forecasting needs.

DATA SOURCES

All quantitative modeling is based on the examination of historical data
collected and arranged in time sequence with the oldest first and the most

recent last. Such data are called time series data. Good quality time series data contain no inconsistencies, gaps, or errors. The published forecast data discussed earlier can be thought of as the extrapolations of historical data series into the future. The major premise of all quantitative modeling is that the patterns and relationships that have occurred in the past will remain in the future.

Most organizations require microeconomic forecasting models specific to their industry segment, their company, or their own product/service. The first and foremost data source needed for microeconomic modeling is the organization's own record-keeping system. Company records of shipments, financial records of manufacturing, distribution, and selling costs, and other data (such as price discounts, advertising expenditures, etc.) form the core of the management information data base that underlies a forecasting system. The validity, the span, and the consistency of the company source data will have a definite bearing on their utility in the development of forecasting models.

When causal modeling is found to be important (e.g., multiple regression modeling of sales demand), then data from external sources are likely to be used for the independent variables. The major sources of external data are the U.S. government, periodicals and journals, trade associations, syndicated data sources, and forecasting service organizations. Of these, the government is the largest source of both demographic and economic information.

Perhaps the most important tools for a forecaster are the various indices to government publications. The most comprehensive index to U.S. government source data is the *American Statistics Index: A Comprehensive Guide and Index to the Statistical Publications of the United States Government,* a Congressional Information Service annual with monthly supplements. This publication indexes every statistic put out by the federal government. It covers social, economic, demographic, and natural resources and some technical/scientific data. Publications are indexed by subject and name, by economic, demographic, and geographic category, by title, and by agency report number. A list of other important indices is in the bibliography to this chapter. Another convenient source of data is the monthly GPO catalog, available as a data base for quick and accurate searching. Major sources of governmental data the forecaster will find useful include

U.S. Bureau of the Census: Conducts extensive dicennial census studies of the population, housing characteristics, social phenomena, and other subjects. Some of these series are updated by *Current Population Reports.*

Census Bureau: Every five years the Bureau does very comprehensive economic censuses. These reports are the most extensive statistical sources available for almost every industry and service in the United

States, and are available from 12-page handouts to multivolume sets, depending on the level of detail required. They are classified as:

Census of Agriculture

Census of Mineral Industries

Census of Manufacturing

Census of Retail Trade

Census of Wholesale Trade

Census of Transportation

Census of Governments

Census of Construction Industries

Census of Service Industries

Each of these has detailed production, consumption, employment, payroll, value added, and geographic information.

County Business Patterns: This 51-volume set (one volume for each state, and a volume for the total United States) lists, by county, the number of business establishments, sorted by SIC code. The volumes also break out the number of establishments by employee size.

Foreign trade statistics: i.e., Imports and exports by commodity, value, and countries of origin, also provided by the Census Bureau. (Much of the Bureau data is available on computer tapes.)

U.S. Bureau of Labor Statistics: Collects, processes, analyzes, and disseminates data relating to employment, unemployment, the labor force, productivity, prices, family expenditures, wages, industrial relations, and occupational safety and health. The two most useful publications are the monthlies *Employment & Earnings* and *Monthly Labor Review*.

Bureau of Economic Analysis: Produces estimates of national income, gross national product, and related series; estimates of income distribution, input–output accounts, and anticipated business investment; analyses of business trends, balance of international payments, and foreign investments and transactions of the U.S. government.

Federal Reserve System, the *Department of the Treasury,* and the *Internal Revenue Service:* Provide financial and business statistics such as money supply; interest rates; federal finance; securities; credit; corporate, partnership, and individual expenditures; and bank and savings institution statistics. The 11 regional Federal Reserve Banks often publish useful regional, state, and local data, frequently with forecasts.

Other useful government publications are detailed in the bibliography to this chapter.

International Sources

The source with the most diverse macroeconomic data is the United Nations, although its data are often one to two years old. Published sources include:

U.N. Yearbook of International Trade Statistics

U.N. Demographic Yearbook

UNESCO Statistical Yearbook

These can be supplemented with the

Monthly Bulletin of Statistics

The International Monetary Fund publishes some excellent statistical sources for almost every country. Some are

Government Finance Statistics Yearbook

Balance of Payments Statistics

Direction of Trade Statistics

The World Bank, through Johns Hopkins Press, publishes two (economic and social) volumes of *World Tables,* and the OECD has several good statistical publications available.

An excellent commercial source for data is *The Economist,* both the weekly issues and in other publications, which publishes the quarterly *EIU* reports with data and trends for over 140 countries, as well as two good hardcover volumes, *World Business Cycles* and *The World in Figures* (with a good summation for every nation).

The Economist also has an *Economic Outlook* that has short-term forecasts for every nation, as does the IMF, *World Economic Outlook.* The World Bank publishes the *World Development Report,* which has short- and long-term world and regional forecasts. PREDICAST's *WORLDCASTS* is a yearly eight-volume set that gives abstracts of many international forecasts in print.

Periodicals and Journals

In addition to periodicals such as *The Wall Street Journal, Business Week, Forbes, Fortune,* and so on, which keep managers abreast of the most current data and trends, many trade journals such as *Chain Store Age, National*

Petroleum News, and *Datamation* publish annual statistical surveys, which are often valuable data sources for the subject industry. To find names of trade journals arranged by industry, check the *Standard Periodical Directory* or Ulrich's *International Periodical Directory.*

Two good indices to "special" issues of trade journals, that is, annual issues with special statistical or directory features, are

Guide to Special Issues, Special Libraries Association

Special Issues Index Greenwood Press

Trade Associations

Most industries and markets have some sort of trade association representing them. These associations often act as data collection agencies and publish an assortment of macrostatistics covering the trade or industry as a whole. Access to these data may be restricted, however, to association members. Two good directories of these associations are

National Trade & Professional Associations in US, Columbia Books

Encyclopedia of Associations, Gale Research Company (also international and regional editions)

They include the following kinds of publications:

Department Store and Specialty Store Merchandising and Operating Results, National Retail Merchants Association

Annual Statistical Report from the American Iron and Steel Institute

Syndicated Sources

Statistics are also published by commercial organizations. Fairchild Publications is one example of a firm that publishes a variety of books containing data on such industries as clothing, appliances, and textiles. Financial data such as stock prices, trading volumes, dividends, company earnings ratios, bond yields, and information relating to credit can be obtained from

Standard & Poor's *Statistical Service, Stock Guide, Stock Reports, Bond Guide,* and *Industry Surveys*

Dun & Bradstreet's *Marketing Services* and *Credit Services*

Moody's manuals

Much of these data can be accessed from computerized data bases such as Dun's *Market Identifiers,* Standard & Poor's *Compustat, Value Line,* and

Dow-Jones' *News Retrieval Service*. A complete list of data base suppliers for all kinds of data, historical as well as forecast, can be found in

Directory of Online Databases (quarterly), Cuadra Associates, Inc., Santa Monica, California

Database Directory (yearly), Knowledge Industry, Inc.

Many market research firms sell data on a subscription basis. The data provided by these organizations are sometimes subjective when dealing with consumer preferences. Other syndicated data suppliers report product movement in specific market areas or through certain channels of distribution (outlets). Much of this market research is based on a sampling (versus a census) of the population and therefore requires certain demographic adjustments to project full market size. Prominent syndicated data firms include:

Market Facts, Inc., NPD Research, Inc., National Family Opinion (NFO), and Market Research Corporation of America (MRCA) for consumer panels and mail survey

A. C. Nielsen Company and Audits and Surveys, Inc. for retail store audits and product-tracking services

Selling Areas-Marketing, Inc. (SAMI) and Pipeline for audit services covering warehouse withdrawals

Predicasts, Inc., which abstracts short- and long-range forecast statistics for basic economic indicators and industry forecasts from the news media, periodicals, and journals

Information Resources Inc., A. C. Nielsen, SAMI/Burke and Burgoyne are among a growing number of syndicated data suppliers that offer measures of point-of-sale retail grocery and drug store activity. This new data source results from the use of optical scanners and computer-based cash registers. Over 50% of the U.S. grocery store volume in 1985 was audited by such scanners. Although mass merchandisers, discount houses and catalog showrooms often use scanners as well, no syndicated data supplier has begun to consolidate such retail sales activity for re-sale to business planners. To keep abreast of the evolution of syndicated data products and suppliers in the United States, contact the American Marketing Association, Chicago, Illinois

FORECASTING SERVICE ORGANIZATIONS

When in-house statistical forecasting, economic modeling, and system development staff talent are not available, an organization may turn to forecasting service firms for help in establishing forecasting models and a forecasting system. Certain of these organizations maintain large macroeconomic models of the U.S. economy and provide historical data and forecasts to their clients for a fee.

There are many advantages to using such services. They often forecast variables that are not available from other sources. Their forecasting specialists produce unbiased forecasts of variables that may have already been forecast by the government or trade associations. Many of these organizations will carry on specific research and micro forecasting work for a client firm. Considerable energy is spent on providing data that are current, correct, and easy to access by the client via time-sharing computer terminals. The major disadvantage is that these services are often expensive. They may involve an annual subscription fee as well as time-sharing computer charges.

By the end of the 1970s, three firms emerged as leaders in economic forecasting: Data Resources, Inc. (DRI), Chase Econometrics, and Wharton Economic Forecasting Associates, Inc. (See Chapter 21 for examples of this approach.) Each uses an input–output (econometric) model of the U.S. economy consisting of from 800 to 1000 equations. Included are factors such as interest rates, housing starts, consumer debt burden, auto sales, plant utilization rates, and business investment. The differences in their macro forecasts are largely due to judgmental input of certain exogenous factors such as the Federal Reserve Board's monetary policy, the possibility of legislative changes in taxes or industry regulations, or the possibility of foreign actions such as war or OPEC price changes. Frequently the results of their models are published for several scenarios; the user then decides which one he or she will adopt as most likely.

Merrill-Lynch Economics Inc., a subsidiary of the big brokerage firm, is a newer and smaller player in the economic forecasting industry. The Merrill-Lynch approach creates a macro model of the economy by aggregating the effects of individual industry macro models.

On average, no forecasting service firm does any better or worse in forecasting than the others. Most client firms believe that they do better than their own in-house staff. It is wise to conduct a rigorous comparative analysis when considering the use of these agencies, as some do far better than others in dealing with the dynamics of a particular industry. For an interesting comparison of the accuracy of the forecasts produced by the major services, see Stephen McNees, "The Forecasting Record for the 1970s," published in the September/October 1980 issue of the *New England Economic Review*. This article would help a financial organization select Wharton due to its track record in projecting interest rates in the turbulent late 1970s.

The major difference in the four services is their ancillary products. Wharton, for example, is known for its international model, Chase for its metals service, and DRI for its model of the chemical industry. Thus, managers may well base their decision on what service to engage on the basis of the special products and services they need. However, to obtain the specialized services, a client must subscribe to the use of the basic macro model offered.

Other economic consulting firms offer more tailor-made services to organizations in need of forecasting know-how. These specialized services include

Developing and programming computerized forecasting systems for materials requirements planning (MRP)

Doing one-time forecast modeling projects

Providing a complete corporate forecasting system on a continuous basis with computer-to-computer linkages

Providing computer software, hardware facilities, and technical support staff to provide a "turnkey" solution to company forecasting needs

Economies of scale and staff specialization in devising and implementing forecasting models gives economic consulting firms the ability to develop forecasting systems in less time and at lower costs than if the same-quality job were done by in-house staff. This is especially true for small- or medium-sized firms that cannot afford the staffing costs for a forecasting department. Arthur D. Little, Booz, Allen & Hamilton, and Temple, Barker & Sloane, Inc. are examples of consulting organizations that provide microeconomic modeling and forecasting system development services. Several directories for business consultants are listed in the bibliography to this chapter.

The most important factors in choosing among alternative consulting firms include their forecasting experience in the particular industry, their responsiveness to client needs, the quality of peripheral support services (like computer programs and their availability on time-sharing computers), their educational programs, and their ability to communicate with management on technical subjects without losing sight of practical solutions.

SOFTWARE AND SERVICE BUREAUS

Most recognized forecasting approaches are in the public domain. The theory behind them is published in numerous texts and papers. If an organization chose to, it could commission its programming staff to reproduce promising forecasting approaches for use on in-house computers. Over 90% of U.S. manufacturers find it more economical to use software products containing one or more forecasting modeling methods on their in-house computer to develop models. The following are examples of such software products: SIBYL/RUNNER and the ADDATA Sales Forecasting System from the Applied Decision Systems division of Temple, Barker & Sloane, Inc.; BETA from the Econo-scope Group Inc.; Futurcast from Futurion Associates; FLEXICAST from Health Products Research, Incl.; LAECON from

Lochrie and Associates; and EPS from Data Resources, Inc.; SmartForecasts from SmartSoftware Inc.; ESP from Economica and the Sales Forecaster from American Software.

CONCLUSIONS

Forecasting services will continue to expand to serve a market of medium- to small-sized firms in the 1990s, resulting in the integration of macroeconomic-, industry-, corporate-, and product-level models. Managers will have the ability to measure the impact of industry outlook models on their own marketing mix models. They will be able to utilize pro forma financial planning devices to determine the impact of a given macro forecast scenario on their own balance sheet and income statements. The development of regional and localized data and forecasts, and improved international forecasting, will allow the assessment of business strategy at local, national, and worldwide levels.

Economic demography will become a primary forecast tool. With the 1980 census, it is possible to show maps of population distribution on office terminals. Managers will be able to examine county-by-county breakdowns by income, age distribution, population density, and rate of growth. The question that remains to be answered is whether, with more accurate and timely information made available to them, managers will be able to make better (more profitable) decisions.

BIBLIOGRAPHY

Indices and Guides to Data Sources

National

Androit, John, ed., *Guide to U.S. Government Publications,* McLean, VA. Documents index (every 18 months). Indexes statistical publications of the U.S. government by title and originating agency.

Daniels, Lorna, ed., *Business Information Sources,* University of California Press, Berkeley, CA, 1985. Best general book on the subject.

Wasserman, Paul, ed., *Encyclopedia of Business Information Sources,* 5th ed., Gale Research Company, Detroit, MI, 1983. Listing of information services on detailed subjects and industries arranged alphabetically by subject.

Wasserman, Paul, ed., *Statistical Sources: A Subject Guide to Data on Industrial, Business, Social, Educational, Financial and Other Topics for the United States and Internationally,* 9th ed., Gale Research Company, Detroit, MI, 1984. Updated periodically. Provides a selected listing of key statistical sources organized by subject or country.

U.S. Bureau of the Census, *Bureau of the Census Catalog,* U.S. Bureau of the Census, Washington, DC. Published yearly, this contains a descriptive list of Census Bureau publications arranged by subject.

Directories of Business Consultants

These two directories cover most consulting firms and have some information on them:

Consultants and Consulting Organizations Directory, 6th ed., Gale Research Company, Detroit, 1984.

Directory of Management Consultants, 1985 ed., Consultants News, Fitzwilliam, NH.

Resources: Useful Data Sources

Bureau of the Census

Statistical Abstract of the United States: Annual

Historical Statistics of the United States: 1780–1970

Social Indicators: Provide a comprehensive compilation of industrial, social, political, and economic statistics in the United States. Published every three years

County Business Patterns: Yearly, 51 volumes

Enterprise Statistics: Every five years

Foreign Trade Series on Imports and Exports: Monthly

Current Industrial Reports: Monthly and annually

County and City Data Book: Every five years

Bureau of Labor Statistics (BLS)

Handbook of Labor Statistics: One of the most useful government tools for forecasters. It makes available in one volume all the major series done by the BLS including such topics as GNP, national income, labor force, employment, productivity prices, and unions

Monthly Labor Review

Survey of Consumer Expenditures

CPI Detailed Report

PPI Detailed Report

Bureau of Economic Analysis (BEA)

Survey of Current Business: Monthly

Business Statistics: Biyearly; supplement to *Survey of Current Business*

U.S. Industrial Outlook: Yearly

Business Conditions Digest: Monthly

Other Government Sources

Economic Report of the President: Yearly; extensive statistical appendixes

Federal Reserve Bulletin: Monthly

Economic indicators, Council of Economic Advisers: Monthly

The Budget of the U.S. Government: Yearly

Social Security Bulletin: Monthly

Statistics of Income Bulletin: Quarterly & Yearly. From Internatl Revenue Service

MANAGING THE
FORECASTING FUNCTION

CHAPTER

30

FORECASTING AND PLANNING: AN EVALUATION*

ROBIN M. HOGARTH
Graduate School of Business, University of Chicago

SPYROS MAKRIDAKIS
INSEAD, Fontainebleau, France

INTRODUCTION

Intuitive forecasting and planning are not new phenomena. On the other hand, *formal* forecasting and planning (F & P) activities have risen to prominence in business, nonprofit, and public organizations within only a few decades. Furthermore, annual expenditure related to F & P now involves billions of dollars.

The utility of these activities has, however, been questioned.[56,173] The purpose of this paper, therefore, is to assess forecasting accuracy and planning effectiveness in organizations and to provide guidelines to calibrate expectations. There are three sections. First, since F & P concern future decisions, we explicitly recognize their dependence on human judgment by reviewing findings from psychology. In the second section we assess current approaches to F & P and in the third we summarize strengths and weaknesses of F & P and propose alternative conceptualizations.

The following persons provided comments on earlier drafts: Scott Armstrong, Claude Faucheux, Robert Fildes, Dominique Héau, Bob Kenmore, Larry Nadler, Edith Penrose and Heinz Thanheiser. Lindsey Hill handled many drafts admirably and aided considerably in documentation.

* This chapter is reprinted with permission from *Management Science*, vol. 27, no. 2, February 1981, pp. 115–138.

HUMAN JUDGMENTAL ABILITIES: IMPLICATIONS FOR F & P

Although there is no generally accepted definition of planning, most writers agree that it involves attempts at purposeful, future-oriented decision making. The distinction between formal and informal planning in organizations can, however, be defined operationally by the degree of specificity of the former, as for example when plans are committed to writing (see Thune and House[160]).

As a decision-making activity, planning requires[1]: (1) The existence of values and goals, (2) the generation of alternative courses of action, (3) the assessment of alternatives, and (4) the implementation of the alternative selected. (5) Forecasts are also needed in both the generation and assessment of alternatives and the prediction of future states of the environment. (6) In addition, monitoring and control are often mentioned as integral elements of planning.

For problems of any complexity, planning clearly necessitates a wide variety of inputs and skills. Values and goals are difficult to communicate and often must be sensed by planners rather than directly obtained from policymakers.[19] The generation of alternatives and many other aspects of forecasting require much imagination and creative thinking. On the other hand, the assessment of alternatives and certain aspects of forecasting call for high analytical competence and facility with the tools of management science. Implementation, monitoring, and control require managerial skills, not the least of which is the ability to handle political processes within organizations.

The evaluation of planning is problematic in that so many components contribute to its relative effectiveness. Good plans can fail through poor implementation. Erroneous forecasts can kill the best of plans, and accurate forecasts can be offset through poor planning. Furthermore, goals and values can be neither "right" nor "wrong," although one could question their coherence.

Judgment necessarily plays a crucial role in F & P. Consider, for example, the specification of goals, intuitive predictions, choices concerning data sources, forecasting methodologies, adjustments to model-derived forecasts, and the assessment of the feasibility of implementation strategies.

There are two key findings from cognitive psychology relating to human judgment: (1) ability to process information is limited and (2) people are adaptive. Thus, to understand the process of judgment it is necessary to specify the context in which it occurs.[23,145] The importance of a person's cognitive system can be gauged by noting that the efficiency of purposeful behavior depends on an understanding of the environment in which it occurs. *People are strongly motivated to understand, and thus control the environment in which they live.*[172] This search for understanding and control is, we maintain, the raison d'être of F & P activities, and when coupled with human cognitive limitations is the cause of many false expectations and failures in these areas.

The actual outcomes people experience, however, depend not only on their own actions, but on events outside their control (i.e., chance). This statement can be illuminated by considering Chart 30-1, which provides a conceptual diagram of stages of information processing.

The model implicit in this chart conceives of judgment taking place within a system involving three elements in mutual interaction.[81] First, there is the person; second, the task environment within which the person makes judgments; and third, actions that result from judgment and that can subsequently affect both the person and the task environment. In Chart 30-1, the person is represented by his or her "schema," by which is meant the person's belief and value system relative to the judgmental task. The operations of judgment are decomposed into (a) *acquisition* of information, (b) *processing* of the information accessed, and (c) *output*. Output implies *action*, which together with external factors, yields an *outcome*. The outcome then feeds back into the person's schema and can also affect the task environ-

CHART 30-1. Conceptual Model of Judgment (Based on Hogarth[80])

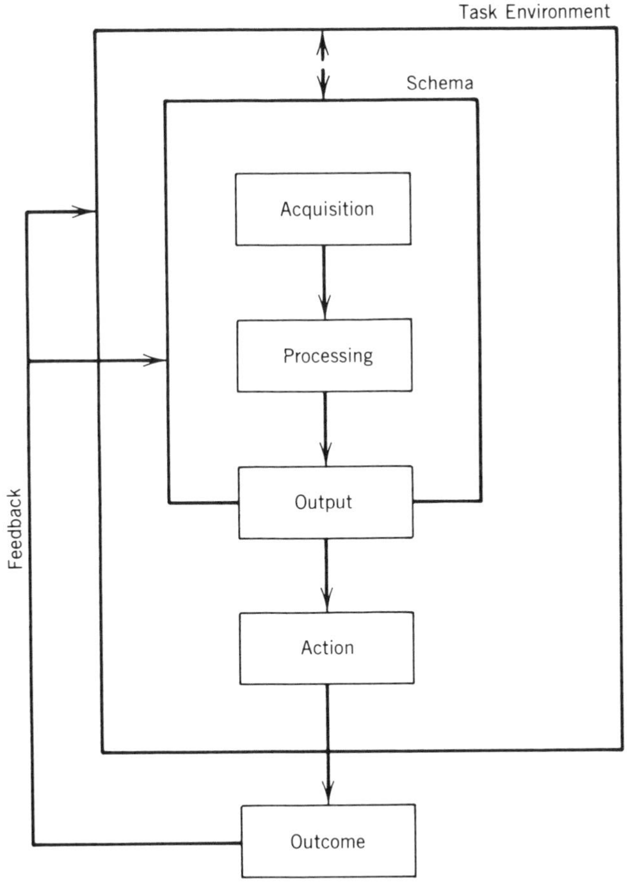

ment. At the same time, the person's schema affects the perception of the environment and its complexity, the problem identification, the tasks involved, the type of action required, the objectives, and so forth.

Much evidence indicates that superficial information search and processing biases cause gross errors in human decision making.[78,83,101,152,155] To relate this evidence to F & P, Chart 30-2 summarizes the main sources of bias organized by the stages of information processing indicated in Chart 30-1. It

CHART 30-2. Information Processing Biases (Organized by Stages of Processing, Chart 30-1)

	Bias/Source of Bias	Description	Example	Literature sources[a]
Acquisition of Information	Availability	—Ease with which specific instances can be recalled from memory affects judgments of frequency	—Frequency of well-publicized events are overestimated (e.g., deaths due to homicide, cancer); frequency of less well-publicized events are underestimated (e.g., deaths due to asthma and diabetes)	106, 154, 163
		—Chance "availability" of particular "cues" in the immediate environment affects judgment	—Problem solving can be hindered/facilitated by cues perceived by chance in a particular setting (hints set up cognitive "direction")	113
	Selective Perception	—People structure problems on the basis of their own experience	—The same problem can be seen by a marketing manager as a marketing problem, as a financial problem by a finance manager, etc.	42
		—Anticipation of what one expects to see bias what one does see	—Identification of incongruent objects, e.g., playing cards with *red* spades, is either inaccurately reported or causes discomfort	22
		—People seek information consistent with their own views/hypotheses	—Interviewers seek information about candidates consistent with first impressions rather than information that could refute those impressions	170, 171
		—People downplay/disregard conflicting evidence	—In forming impressions, people underweight information that does not yield to a consistent profile	3

CHART 30-2 (*Continued*)

Bias/Source of Bias	Description	Example	Literature sources[a]
Frequency	—Cue used to judge strength of predictive relationships is observed frequency rather than observed relative frequency. Information on "non-occurrences" of an event is unavailable and ignored	—When considering relative performance (of say, two persons), the absolute number of successes is given greater weight than the relative number of successes to successes *and* failures (i.e., the denominator is ignored). Note, the number of failures is frequently unavailable	57, 156, 169
Concrete information (ignoring base-rate, or prior information)	—*Concrete* information (i.e., vivid, or based on experience/incidents) dominates *abstract* information (e.g., summaries, statistical base-rates, etc.)	—When purchasing a car, the positive or negative experience of a *single* acquaintance is liable to weigh more heavily in judgment than available and more valid statistical information, e.g., in *Consumer Reports*	13, 17, 73, 89, 111, 125, 126
Illusory correlation	—Belief that two variables covary when in fact they do not. (Possibly related to "Frequency" above)	—Selection of an inappropriate variable to make a prediction	26, 67, 144, 156, 169
Data presentation	—Order effects (primacy/recency)	—Sometimes the first items in a sequential presentation assume undue importance (primacy), sometimes the last items (recency)	155
	—Mode of presentation	—Sequential vs. intact data displays can affect what people are able to access. Contrast, for example, complete listed unit-price shopping vs. own sequential information search	44, 85, 138, 141
	—Mixture of types of information, e.g., qualitative and quantitative	—Concentration on quantitative data, exclusion of qualitative, or vice versa	149
	—Logical data displays	—Apparently complete "logical" data displays can blind people to critical omissions	62
	—Context effects on perceived variability	—Assessments of variability, of say a series of numbers, is affected by the absolute size (e.g., mean level) of the numbers	98

Acquisition of Information (vertical row label spanning all rows)

CHART 30-2 (*Continued*)

Bias/Source of Bias	Description	Example	Literature sources[a]
Inconsistency	—Inability to apply a consistent judgmental strategy over a repetitive set of cases	—Judgments involving selections, e.g., personnel/graduate school admissions	20, 39, 41, 65, 74, 120, 143
Conservatism	—Failure to revise opinion on receipt of new information to the same extent as Bayes' theorem (may be counterbalanced by "best-guess" strategy and produce near optimal performance in the presence of unreliable data sources)	—Opinion revision in many applied settings, e.g., military, business, medicine, law	45, 48
Non-linear extrapolation	—Inability to extrapolate growth processes (e.g., exponential) and tendency to underestimate joint probabilities of several events	—Gross underestimation of outcomes of exponentially increasing processes and overestimation of joint probabilities of several events	12, 29, 30, 167, 168
"Heuristics" used to reduce mental effort:			
—Habit/"rules of thumb"	—Choosing an alternative because it has previously been satisfactory	—Consumer shopping; "rules of thumb" adopted in certain professions	93
—Anchoring and adjustment	—Prediction made by anchoring on a cue or value and then adjusting to allow for the circumstances of the present case	—Making a sales forecast by taking last year's sales and adding, say, 5%	164
—Representativeness	—Judgments of likelihood of an event by estimating degree of *similarity* to the class of events of which it is supposed to be an exemplar	—Stereotyping, e.g., imagining that someone is a lawyer because she exhibits characteristics typical of a lawyer	88, 89
—Law of *small* numbers	—Characteristics of small samples are deemed to be representative of the populations from which they are drawn	—Interpretation of data, too much weight given to small sample results (which are quite likely to be atypical)	16, 165
—Justifiability	—A "processing" rule can be used if the individual finds a rationale to "justify" it	—When provided with an apparently rational argument, people tend to follow a decision rule even if it is really inappropriate	150, 162

Processing of Information (vertical label spanning rows)

CHART 30-2 (*Continued*)

	Bias/Source of Bias	Description	Example	Literature sources[a]
Processing of Information	—Regression bias	—Extreme values of a variable are used to predict extreme values of the next observation of the variable (thus failing to allow for regression to the mean)	—Following observation of bad performance by an employee, a manager could attribute subsequent improvement to his intervention (e.g., warning to the employee). However, due to regression effects, improvement (performance closer to the mean level), is likely *without* intervention	25, 89
	—"Best-guess" strategy	—Under conditions involving several sources of uncertainty, simplification is made by ignoring some uncertainties and basing judgment on the "most likely" hypothesis. (Note, people simplify by ignoring uncertainty). More generally, tendency to discount uncertainty	—Ignoring the fact that information sources are unreliable	63
	The decision environment:			
	—Complexity	—Complexity induced by time pressure, information overload, distractions, lead to reduced consistency of judgment	—In decisions taken under time pressure, information processing may be quite superficial	50, 131, 134, 175
	—Emotional stress	—Emotional stress reduces care with which people select and process information	—Panic judgment	83
	—Social pressures	—Social pressures, e.g., of a group, cause people to distort their judgments	—The majority in a group can unduly influence judgment of minority members	9
	Information sources:			
	—Consistency of information sources	—Consistency of information sources can lead to increases in confidence in judgment but not to increased predictive accuracy	—People often like to have more information, even though it is redundant with what they already have	89, 130, 151, 152
	—Data presentation	See items under the ACQUISITION section		

CHART 30-2 (*Continued*)

	Bias/Source of Bias	Description	Example	Literature sources[a]
Output	*Response mode:*			
	—Question format	—The way a person is required or chooses to make a judgment can affect the outcome	—Preferences for risky prospects have been found to be inconsistent with the prices for which people are willing to sell them	69, 104, 105, 150, 161
	—Scale effects	—The scale on which responses are recorded can affect responses	—Estimates of probabilities can vary when estimated directly on a scale from zero to one, or when "odds" or even "log-odds" are used	78, 155
	Wishful thinking	—People's preferences for outcomes of events affect their assessment of the events	—People sometimes assess the probability of outcomes they desire higher than their state of knowledge justifies	38, 122, 148 7 (pp. 79, 80)
	Illusion of control	—Activity concerning an uncertain outcome can by itself induce in a person feelings of control over the uncertain event	—Activities such as planning, or even the making of forecasts, can induce feelings of control over the uncertain future	96, 97, 132
Feedback	Outcome irrelevant learning structures	—Outcomes observed yield inaccurate or incomplete information concerning predictive relationships. This can lead, inter alia, to irrealistic confidence in one's own judgment	—In personnel selection you can learn how good your judgment is concerning candidates selected, but you usually have no information concerning subsequent performance of rejected candidates	46, 52, 53, 129 For 'overconfidence' see 61, 103
	Misperception of chance fluctuations (e.g., gambler's fallacy)	—Observation of an unexpected number of similar chance outcomes leads to expectation that the probability of the appearance of an event not recently seen increases	—So-called "gambler's fallacy"—after observing, say, 9 successive reds in roulette, people tend to believe that black is more likely on the next throw	84, 166
	Success/failure attributions	—Tendency to attribute success to skill and failure to chance (related to "Illusion of Control" — see above).	—Successes in one's job, e.g., making a difficult sale, are attributed to one's skill; failures to "bad luck"	82,97,121. For a review of "Attribution theory," see 139

CHART 30-2 (*Continued*)

	Bias/Source of Bias	Description	Example	Literature sources[a]
Feedback	Logical fallacies in recall	—Inability to recall details of an event leads to "logical" reconstruction, which can be inaccurate	—Eyewitness testimony	24, 108, 157
	Hindsight bias	—In retrospect, people are not "surprised" about what has happened in the past. They can easily find plausible explanations	—"Monday morning quarterback" phenomenon	59, 60, 61

[a] The references provided here cannot claim to be comprehensive; however, review papers are cited in which readers will be able to find additional references. It should also be added that individuals may vary on their susceptibility to different forms of bias. A large literature exists, for example, concerning "cognitive styles."[133]

also provides brief definitions, descriptions, illustrations, and references to the source literature.

Of crucial concern here are the conditions under which the biases described in Chart 30-2 occur, and their consequent effects on F & P. Chart 30-1 indicates that understanding of a judgmental task—as represented in the person's schema—is mediated by several stages of information processing and links with the environment. In particular, links between the person's schema, actions, outcomes, and feedback to the schema are crucial. If the action–outcome–feedback links are *short* and *frequent*, the individual is in a good position to learn about, and thus comprehend, the probable effects of actions on outcomes: short links enhance the ability to improve decision making by taking corrective actions. The opposite is true when the links are infrequent, long (in time) and subject to distortion. This suggests that people will have difficulty in providing adequate inputs in many F & P activities in which the action–outcome–feedback links are neither short nor clear.

On the other hand, the judgmental performances people exhibit through motor skills are considerable. Imagine, for example, the series of complex judgmental tasks accomplished when driving a car, or skiing. However, note that these situations can be characterized by short and frequent action–outcome–feedback loops. Whereas evolution has provided humans with considerable facility for making judgments that meet the characteristics of motor tasks, this is not true of many conceptual judgments.[81,149] Indeed, most of the biases documented in Chart 30-2 have been demonstrated in situations where short feedback loops have either been lacking or, when present, have not necessarily been readily interpretable by the individual.[52] Interestingly enough, experiments that have examined intuitive decision-making skills in dynamic environments involving interdependent, sequential judgmental tasks coupled with feedback on performance show people to be quite efficient.[81]

A further point concerning the results summarized in Chart 30-2 is the criticism that many biases found to operate in the unfamiliar circumstances of the psychological laboratory might not generalize to more naturalistic environments. However, in a rapidly changing world it is uncertain to what environment laboratory experiments should and can generalize. Lack of ability to handle unfamiliar tasks is clearly no cause for optimism.[54,152]

A benchmark of judgmental ability is provided by numerous studies that have compared the relative predictive performance of experts and simple quantitative models. Almost all indicate the superiority of models.[40,66,102,143] (For a review see ref. 7, pp. 251–259 and pp. 363–372.) Although difficult to accept emotionally, such evidence must be considered seriously. Decision makers and policymakers should become aware of the nature of their inherent judgmental limitations.

What implications do these findings have for F & P? First, to avoid information *acquisition* biases it is necessary to sample deliberately from as wide a base as possible, to avoid accepting forecasts and plans in haste, and to strive to find information that could *disconfirm* hypotheses and forecasts. Too often people seek information to confirm their existing ideas, and often redundantly, rather than more potentially valid disconfirming evidence.[170] Institutionalizing procedures using counterattitudinal role playing, dialectics, or "devil's advocates" could be helpful in this respect.[34] Second, since people are inefficient at aggregating information, this should be done mechanically where possible.[51] Third, greater care needs to be exercised in interpreting the apparent *causes of outcomes*. Consider, for example, the so-called "illusion of control." Langer[96] has documented how even in chance-determined situations (e.g., lotteries), observing an early sequence of "successes" can lead people to believe they have some control over outcomes. Similarly, if people are allowed to engage in cognitive activity about the outcome prior to its occurrence (e.g., by choosing a ticket number), they are also inclined to believe they gain some control. These findings are entirely consistent with the need *to master and control the environment*.

Detecting patterns to control outcomes is functional. F & P activities fall precisely into the types of situation studied by Langer.[96] People spend time on forecasting and elaborating plans with expectations of increasing control. Furthermore, in judging the effectiveness of F & P, it does not seem unreasonable to attribute successful outcomes to accurate forecasting and good planning, but to discount failures (see also ref. 97). The use of F & P to reduce uncertainty and gain control is both functional for organizations and understandable given human needs. The "illusion," however, consists of failing to attribute to outcomes the appropriate relative contributions of skill (including use of F & P) and chance.

Suggestions for overcoming some important judgmental biases enumerated in Chart 30-2 have been provided by Kahneman and Tversky[90] and Spetzler and Staël von Holstein.[158] In particular, these papers provide procedures to guard against over-confidence in judgment, and the tendencies to ignore both regression effects and relevant base-rate data.

FORECASTING AND PLANNING: EMPIRICAL EVIDENCE

The separation of forecasting accuracy and planning effectiveness in the overall assessment of F & P is problematic. This section examines the predictive accuracy of F & P divided into activities concerning long-, medium- and short-term horizons. We also make some general observations. In the subsequent section, other factors are considered.

Long-Range Forecasting and Planning

Long-range forecasting (two years or longer) is notoriously inaccurate. Ascher[10] has examined the predictive accuracy of forecasting (and indirectly, planning) in the fields of population, economics, energy, transportation, and technology. His conclusions are pessimistic. Ascher found errors varying from a few to a few hundred percentage points, as well as systematic biases. He also stated that one could not specify beforehand which forecasting approach, or forecaster, would have been right or wrong. Furthermore, because policymakers are supplied with so many, varying forecasts, the problem of "choosing" a forecast can be as difficult as making one's own. Parenthetically, it should be noted that the fields examined by Ascher are characterized by much experience and expertise in making forecasts as well as by readily available data. One can therefore imagine the situation in other fields with data less "suitable" for forecasting (i.e., with less aggregation and greater fluctuations).

Ascher's conclusions are echoed by opinions expressed in the long-term forecasting literature (e.g., ref. 64). It is difficult to assess the size of forecasting errors; unforeseen changes in trends can occur; discontinuities are possible; and new events or conditions emerge. Moreover, past data can provide contradictory clues to future trends.[43] For instance, while growth of some products in an industry can occur in one way, growth of others follows different patterns.[43] As we argue below in the following, planning activities must accept the inaccuracy inherent in long-term forecasts. Even in the early 1970s, for example, how many imagined the possibility of an oil embargo, a quadrupling of oil prices, severe shortage of raw materials, stagflation, high unemployment together with high inflation and interest rates, a near collapse of the stock market, and two recessions in a period of less than five years?

Despite many fervent proponents, there is concurrently much disappointment in long-range planning as presently practiced.[43,56,76,137,159,173] Long-range planning, it is claimed, has fallen short of its promises, and fundamental changes are necessary both in conception and execution. This has given rise to "strategic planning."[5,72] In practice, however, "many managers use the phrases "strategic planning" and "long-range planning" interchangeably.[72,p.24] Long-range planning, it should be noted, grew and flourished in the 1960s,[110] a period characterized by relative stability and high growth rates. Furthermore, forecasting errors tended to be positive (i.e., actual values exceeded forecasts). Thus, even if plans proved to be "wrong," few complained of the direction of the errors. However, this did not occur in the 1970s when forecasting was on occasion grossly in error in the opposite direction.

Medium-Term Forecasting and Planning

Medium-term plans (three months to two years) are theoretically derived from long-term plans and incorporate medium-term forecasts, estimates of available resources, constraints, and competitive considerations. The most common forms are operational budgets, which also serve the important function of control mechanisms.

Considerable misconceptions exist concerning the ability of economists and business forecasters to predict important changes either in the general level of economic activity or for a given industry, firm, or product. Cyclical turning points, in particular, are notoriously difficult to forecast.[114,119] The problem faced by economists and planners is twofold: first, unanticipated recessions occur; second, predicted recessions fail to materialize. Furthermore, the timing of economic recessions and accelerations is frequently missed. Finally, as with long-term forecasts, there are many different forecasts available from which people can chose those that best fit their preconceptions.

How well have forecasters and planners performed in medium-term F & P situations? Chart 30-3 summarizes empirical findings and provides detailed references. *Mirroring the findings documented in Chart 30-2,* it should be noted that in these applied studies, forecasters and planners have shown systematic deficiencies in their predictions and plans for the future; furthermore, in a majority of cases their estimates are less accurate than those of simple quantitative models (however, for exceptions see the finance literature, e.g., ref. 21).

An important question concerns that extent to which operational plans are met either because forecasts were correct and plans appropriate or because forecasts and plans became the targets of self-fulfilling or self-defeating prophecies. In other words, could any reasonable forecasts and plans be attained without commitment and corrective actions? Alternatively, is it possible that *effective* forecasting and planning can invalidate the original forecasts (e.g., consider actions taken by a government to avoid a predicted recession)?

Short-Term Forecasting and Planning

There is considerable inertia in most economic and natural phenomena. Thus the present states of many variables are predictive of the short-term future (i.e., three months or less). Rather simple, mechanistic methods, such as those used in time series forecasting, can often make accurate short-term forecasts and even outperform more theoretically elegant and elaborate approaches used in econometric forecasting.[6,114]

Short-term planning is characterized by several operations essential to basic business function, for example, establishment of schedules for production, distribution and employment, cash management and so on. It is the only form of F & P for which forecasts can be reasonably accurate and real

CHART 30-3. Empirical Studies of Forecasting (F) and Planning (P)

Subject Study	Area of Application	Description	Main Finding(s)	Literature sources
Forecasting Services	F	—Extensive attempt to determine the validity of "expert" forecasting in the stock market	—Recommendations made by the major financial services— between 1928 and 1932—had an average record 1.4% worse than the "average" common stock annually —Recommendations made by *Wall Street Journal* between 1904 and 1929 achieved a result poorer than a representative sample of the average of the market	35
	F	—Examination of forecasts published in the *Wall Street Journal*	—Average absolute percentage error of the forecasts was 20.1%, with a range of 0 to 218.2%	33
	F	—Follow-up study of Cowles[35]	—Financial services did not forecast better than the average of the market. Furthermore, 80% of all forecasts were optimistic	36
	F	—Examination of earning projections, of 185 companies, made by five forecasting services	—Correlation between predicted and actual earnings was very low. The careful and painstaking efforts of analysts to forecast companies' earnings did very slightly better than simple projections of past trends	37

CHART 30-3 (*Continued*)

Subject Study	Area of Application	Description	Main Finding(s)	Literature sources
Forecasting Services	F	—Examination of reliability of published predictions of future earnings	—The errors occurred over a wide range (for 1966–1970 period of study they ranged from −395.6 to 108.5%). Mean error was negative and overprediction of earnings were much more frequent than underpredictions	117
Security Analysis	F	—Analysis and examination of forecasts made by security analysts	—Forecasts made by the analysts were not more accurate than simple projection	136
	F	—Analysis and comparison of forecasts of earnings made by analysts and companies	—On average, analysts overestimated earnings by nearly 9% (with range of −25 to +150%), while corporate forecasts were overestimated by 6% (with range from −37.5 to 126.4%)	14
	F	—Comparisons were made between analysts and a regression model (estimating future returns of 35 securities)	—Results of analysts were worse than those of regression model	47
	F	—Forecasts of earnings per share made by analysts were compared with those of time series quantitative models	—Quantitative models do as well as, or better than, forecasts provided by analysts	55, 68
			—Analysts show bias toward overestimating actual earnings performance. Analysts forecast better than random walk model in 68 of 100 companies	11
	F & P	—Study of judgmental processes of stockbrokers	—The longer a stockbroker had been in the business, the less insight he/she had concerning own judgmental policy	153

CHART 30-3 (*Continued*)

Subject Study	Area of Application	Description	Main Finding(s)	Literature sources
Mutual Funds	F & P	—Evaluation of performance of mutual funds to random selected portfolio, or average of market	—Mutual funds have performed the same, or worse than, the average of the market	15, 58, 86
Management Forecasts	F	—Comparison of management forecasts of earnings and those of Box–Jenkins method.	—In cases in which management forecasts proved reasonably accurate, overall they were not more so than those generated from Box–Jenkins. Where management forecasts proved relatively inaccurate, those from Box–Jenkins models were significantly less so	109
	F	—Comparison between sales forecasts made by management and those made by three quantitative models	—Sales forecasts of corporate executives gave less accurate results than those of quantitative models over five-year period of comparison	112
Subjective Probability Forecasts (For Additional References, See Exhibit 2).	F	—Subjective probabilities from 23 participants were collected in experiment involving forecasting F.T. Share Index, dollar-sterling rate, and three oil prices	—There was common tendency to underestimate probability of extreme values, and there were substantial differences between individuals. Thus, some participants reported distribution that were realistic and informative, but unfortunately there was no obvious means of identifying those individuals in advance. Performance does not appear to be associated with experience or academic training, and it is not noticeably correlated with performance in single-point forecasting	128

CHART 30-3 (*Continued*)

Subject Study	Area of Application	Description	Main Finding(s)	Literature sources
Bowman's Theory of Managerial Decision Making	P	—Development of decision rules for managerial decision making	—Simple decision rules may result in more accurate decisions than experienced managers. Averaging past decisions of managers may result in better performance than individual managerial decisions	18, 46
	P	—Testing or expanding Bowman's theory on managerial decision making[22]	—All findings have been consistent with Bowman's original findings that decision rules or averaging of past decisions of managers produces better results than individual managerial decisions.	49, 95, 135
Miscellaneous	F	—Experimental design to test accuracy of intuitive judgment versus exponential smoothing models	—Winters' exponential smoothing produced forecasts statistically more accurate than those of human forecasters	2
	F	—Comparative study of methods for long-range market forecasting	—"Objective" methods more accurate than intuitive ones; casual methods more accurate than naive ones; and superiority of objective over intuitive increases as "amount of change" in environment increases	8
	P	—Testing how planning affects performance	—Amount of planning and objective measures of financial performance are not positively correlated; however, number of informal channels of communication used, percentage of relevant items of information received that are used in reaching decisions, and financial performance are positively correlated	70

CHART 30-3 (*Continued*)

Subject Study	Area of Application	Description	Main Finding(s)	Literature sources
Miscellaneous	P	—Simulation of portfolio selection process of investment officer in bank	—Investment officer's "intuitions" captured as witnessed by similarity between portfolios selected by simulation model and by investment officer.	28

gains made consistently. However, it typically receives less attention than it merits.

Some comparisons in Chart 30-3 involve short-term F & P. These indicate both systematic biases and large errors; quantitative models outperform judgmental forecasts; in addition, simpler models are often at least as accurate as sophisticated ones; even random walk models sometimes outpredict the alternative formulations. Moreover, simple decision rules can often be as effective as elaborate F & P procedures (see also the following).

General Examination of Forecasting and Planning

Comments in this section have concerned different time horizons. Other evidence, however, bears on F & P irrespective of horizon length.

In an important study, Grinyer and Norburn[70] attempted to relate measures of corporate financial and management performance to planning activities. They examined 21 companies in a variety of industries. No significant relationship was found between extent of planning and financial and management measures. Indeed, the only significant relationship detected was "between the number of items of information used in reaching decisions on appropriate action and financial performance." Further studies have also indicated lack of relationships between planning and various measures of financial performance.[94,99] On the other hand, studies by Karger and Malik,[91] Herold,[77] and Thune and House[60] concluded that formal planning was positively related to financial performance; in addition, a study by Ansoff and colleagues[4] indicates that mergers are managed more effectively with explicit planning. The evidence is unclear and was recently well summarized by Wood and LaForce[174]: "the review of the available empirical studies disclosed conflicting findings in the planning evaluation area" (p. 517). More studies are, therefore, urgently needed despite the inherent methodological problems of isolating the effects of formal planning systems from other variables.

Weaker and more difficult comparisons could also be made between organizations at different time periods. Is current performance better than in the past? It is difficult to state that there has been marked improvement because of planning per se. Indeed, some even claim the opposite.[173] Other possible comparisons concern countries with different levels of commitment to planning. Do, for instance, Eastern European countries with their planned, centralized economies fare better than their Western counterparts? Similarly, has a country like France, with its heavy commitment to planning, performed better (or have people been more satisfied) than countries with lower planned inputs, such as West Germany or the United States?

Marquand,[116] a planning official in the English government, summarized precisely the essence of the dilemma between more or less planning activities:

> U.K. economic performance was inferior to that of, on the one hand, France with its formal 5 year plans and its dirigiste politics, and on the other to that of Germany where Chancellor Erhard's economic miracle had produced similar effects by opposite means. How far were the methods adopted in each country a source of their success, and in which direction should the United Kingdom move? (p. 3)

There are so many factors involved that F & P can only play a secondary role in accounting for the relative performance of organizations and governments. Thus, it cannot be said that F & P are *not* useful tools for decision makers and policymakers. On the other hand, empirical evidence of effects of F & P on objective performance measures can be seriously questioned.

FORECASTING AND PLANNING: IMPLICATIONS AND RECONCEPTUALIZATION

We first emphasize the principal similarities between findings in the psychology of judgment and evidence and observations on F & P. Subsequently we draw implications and make suggestions for reconceptualizing these activities.

Similarities Between Psychological Findings and Evidence on F & P

The human need to master and control the environment is evident in F & P. Furthermore, there is uncanny similarity between the history of F & P and experiments concerning the "illusion of control"[96,97] discussed previously. Observation of successes in predicting the outcomes of known random processes (e.g., coin tossing) can lead to unfounded beliefs of control in experimental situations. Similarly, the successes met by F & P in the 1960s caused by underprediction as opposed to overprediction seem to have led to analogous real-world illusions of control which have been shattered by subsequent events. Nonetheless, people have a tendency to attribute success to their own efforts and failure to external factors.[82] Indeed, both animals and humans have sometimes been shown to develop more effective decisions if they do have "illusions of control"—the illusion leads to more proactive and self-fulfilling behavior.[132] The issue that is not clear, however, is the extent to which such illusions are functional.

Linked to the illusion of control are tendencies to see patterns where none exist.[146] These are further related to extensive findings indicating that intuitive notions of probabilistic concepts are deficient. Experiments show that people often lack the concepts of independence between random events and sampling variability[88]; in addition, they frequently underestimate the uncertainty inherent in the environment,[78] which leads, inter alia, to mistaken confidence in judgment.[103] For F & P, the implications involve the all too frequent surprises by unforeseen events, which in turn discredit F & P.

Paul Samuelson has probably best captured the inability of forecasters and planners to understand the full extent of uncertainty: "I think that the greatest error in forecasting is not realizing how important are the probabilities of events other than those everyone is agreeing upon."[142]

A further important psychological finding is that although the availability of additional information increases confidence in judgment, it does not necessarily increase predictive accuracy.[129,130,151] This has serious implications for F & P, given the tendencies to consult and subscribe to many forecasting services and to create huge data banks. Furthermore, since people have a tendency to retain information selectively in accord with their prejudices, and to reject possible disconfirming evidence, the potential dysfunctional consequences of collecting data from many, often differing sources is disturbing. As more information becomes available, it is increasingly easier to "prove" what one wishes. Emshoff and Mitroff[56] emphasized this point in relation to problems engendered by large, strategic MIS: "Access to more information results in its selective use to support preconceived positions. . . . They (managers) assume that the quality of decisions has improved because of the amount of information that support it" (p. 50).

Finally, as can be verified by comparing Charts 30-2 and 30-3, there are many other similarities between the literatures on information-processing biases and F & P.

Suggestions for Reconceptualizing F & P

We preface our suggestions by considering human conceptual skills from an evolutionary perspective. Skills have been developed over millenia for dealing with a relatively slowly changing environment. Furthermore, such skills were necessarily first developed to ensure *physical* survival. Since humans adapted to the environment, it is environmental demands that preceded human development. However, within this century there has been dramatic acceleration in the rate of environmental change. Paradoxically, it is human conceptual development that has triggered these changes through technological breakthroughs.

This emphasis on evolutionary processes stresses the need for organizations to have an adaptive approach to F & P. This, we argue, involves (1) acknowledging human limitations and possibilities, (2) explicitly recognizing the functions F & P can serve within organizations, (3) issues concerning the precision of both goals and forecasts and the time frame within which F & P are considered, and (4) evaluating the benefits and costs of the often conflicting goals that F & P attempt to meet.

1. We have already said much about human limitations. Of particular importance is the need to develop appropriate attitudes for facing the uncertainty inherent in the future. People should heed Russell's[140] admonition to learn "how to live without certainty, and yet without being paralysed by hesitation" (p. 14). Forecasting must therefore be used to identify sources of uncertainty in the environment. Planning should concern itself with developing policies that acknowledge the uncertainties and are on the efficient frontier. Planning cannot assume forecast accuracy.

2. Some argue that executives and policymakers do admit the inherent deficiencies of planning but recognize functional side effects such as improvements in communication and coordination, educating people to think explicitly about the future, and the use of planning as a mechanism for motivation and control. However, the question that should be raised is whether these side effects could not be achieved more effectively through direct means. Consider, for example, specific programs to improve coordination. Two programs we believe planners should consider concern the cognitive biases enumerated in Chart 30-2 and training in imagination and creativity. Furthermore, there are many advantages to helping people make explicit the causal chains (and thus assumptions) they use in confronting the future (for an appropriate methodology and example, see ref. 75).

Both the manifest and latent functions of F & P need to be specified and, in the case of the latter, compared with other procedures that could meet the same goals.

3. The specificity of goals and forecasts should be linked to the time frame. Long- and medium-term plans involve periods for which action–outcome–feedback loops (see Chart 30-1) are necessarily deficient and where learning is problematic. However, objectives that define direction are necessary. The precision with which such direction is specified should, we argue, be an inverse function of the length of the planning horizon. Whereas textbooks advocate precise goals, there are many advantages to deliberate ambiguity. March[115] has made a penetrating analysis of this issue. He pointed out that the formulation of and adherence to specific goals at a particular point in time can hamper learning and adaptation, since both experience and environmental changes modify values. Specific goals can be interpreted too narrowly, leading to so-called goal displacement (where the objective to attain indicators of goals becomes more important than the actual goals); furthermore, the creative interpretation of ambiguous goals can be most important.

Note that March does not state simplistically that goals should be fuzzy; rather there is what he calls and "optimal clarity problem."

Analogous points can be made about the precision of medium- and long-term forecasts. One should *use* such forecasts (as aids to contemplate possible trends for example), but not *believe* them.

In the context of economic planning, Bray[19] suggested a model that implies selecting a trajectory over time which can be adjusted en route. Taking the position that forecasts are necessarily inaccurate in noisy systems, he argued that planning should be based on the principle of setting control parameters to maintain the trajectory of the system within certain limits, as opposed to basing periodic actions on predictions. In a simulation study, Bray compared this principle to the "stop-go" policies followed by successive U.K. governments in the post-World War II period; results indicated that the United Kingdom would be considerably better off today had she followed Bray's principles. Although this approach can be criticized—it assumes an excellent model of the underlying process—we believe it deserves further development.

Given the limitations of F & P, what should be done from a practical viewpoint? Would it be better, for example, to abandon formal F & P and rely solely on intuitive procedures? We do not think so.

First, intuitive procedures do not have an impressive record (recall Charts 30-2 and 30-3). Second, in the short term "traditional" F & P are not only feasible but can be accurate. Indeed, we believe that few organizations avail themselves of the considerable benefits to be had in this domain. For instance, evidence has been cited that quantitative, and particularly simple, models can outperform humans in a wide range of situations (see Chart 30-3). In Chart 30-4 we further summarize studies, showing that quite simple models can provide comparable and often better results than more sophisticated models. Formal F & P can and should be used in "traditional" mode for short-term situations. On the other hand, more careful analysis is needed concerning longer F & P horizons.

4. It should be recognized that the choice of an F & P system for the medium and long term is itself a decision. That is, organizations face an "optimal planning" problem and thus decision-theoretic principles are in order. At a conceptual level, it is convenient to distinguish between two kinds of costs and benefits of F & P: (a) dollar gains/losses from accurate/inaccurate F & P per se, and (b) effects of F & P procedures on the organization (e.g., on motivation and commitment). The operational decision-theoretic concepts we believe relevant to these issues are (a) sensitivity analysis, (b) assessing the value of information, and (c) the use of multiattribute utility analysis as an aid to both planning and organizational design.

First, whereas organizations must accept the inaccuracy of forecasts, the fact that losses from forecasting errors are often not symmetric also needs to be explicitly recognized. Planning alternatives have different risk profiles

CHART 30-4. Studies Indicating Robust Performance of "Simple" Versus "Sophisticated" Models

Area of Application	Main Results	Literature Sources
—Time series forecasting	—"Simple" time series models often predict as well as or better than more sophisticated versions.	27, 71, 114, 123
—Time series vs. econometric models	—Mechanistic time series models predict well in comparison with "causal" econometric models.	6, 31, 32, 118, 124, 147
—Anticipatory surveys vs. econometric models	—Anticipatory surveys seem to be more accurate than econometric models in predicting expenditures in investment in United States.	87, 107
—Complexity and accuracy	—Added complexity in models does not tend to increase predictive accuracy (review of 16 studies). Furthermore, no single econometric model is consistently superior to others.	6
—Group forecasting	—Simple averages of group opinions can be remarkably predictive compared with other combination schemes.	79[a]
—Linear weighting schemes	—Equal weighting of independent variables can often outpredict "optimally" derived least squares regression weights. Furthermore, simple weighting procedures are often to be preferred to more sophisticated models in studies of multiattribute decision making.	100

[a] Review papers.

and *sensitivity analysis* can and should be used to test the relative robustness of alternative strategies to forecasting errors. Because the judgment literature indicates that people often lack imagination and are confronted by too many "surprises" even when attempting to think probabilistically, we strongly recommend varying subjective inputs to simulation models and sensitivity analysis to a far greater extent than is currently done. Furthermore, one should also question whether the structure of the models used, and not just the values of some variables, is appropriate. That is, sensitivity analysis also needs to be applied to the manner in which planning problems are formulated. The "illusion of control," it should be recalled, tends to restrict one's beliefs to considering only certain scenarios as possible, and people often fail to search actively for possible disconfirming evidence.[62] However, when one aggregates across many possibilities, seemingly isolated and rare events can and do occur with alarming frequency (as witnessed, for example, by recent events on both the national and geopolitical scenes).

Second, although it may be comforting to seek additional information to improve specific forecasts, the possibility of increasing forecast accuracy and the corresponding costs and benefits should be assessed. The *value of information* is, paradoxically, often overestimated by unaided intuition with the result that the search for additional information brings no more than false psychological comfort. For example, a recent case that came to our attention was the expenditure of $20 million to plan and forecast a $160 million investment. However, a detailed analysis of the situation and possible errors in forecasts indicated that even perfectly accurate forecasts would not be worth anything like $20 million. In some situations, even perfect knowledge of the future has relatively little value!

Third, and as noted earlier, it is important to recognize and specify the manifest and latent functions of F & P (i.e., what the F & P system is *supposed* to be doing and what it *is* doing). Furthermore, whereas both the inaccuracy of forecasts and the ambiguity of organizational goals must be accepted, one can and should be specific about the goals of F & P activities, the extent to which they are compatible, and/or one's willingness to make tradeoffs. Consider, for example, the desire to have "flexible" plans but to use the F & P system as a motivational device. Could a flexible plan advocating a growth rate between 2% and 8% really provide an adequate springboard for motivation? On the other hand, say, a 10% growth rate could also have dysfunctional consequences. Imagine, for instance, a manager under pressure offering discounts to meet targets in the short term, but in so doing affecting the stability of prices in the medium term and profitability in the long term.

Both the design of F & P systems and the assessment of organizational and strategic consequences can be considerably facilitated by using the framework of *multiattribute utility analysis*. Using this framework as a conceptual tool, different F & P systems and plans can be considered as decision alternatives where the dimensions of evaluation (i.e., attributes) are both organizational consequences (e.g., flexibility, motivation, control) and the more traditional F & P measures (e.g., relative expected performance in dollar consequences). Whereas one should clearly not expect precise answers from multiattribute models, the wide range of situations to which they have been applied attests to their ability to provide insights into complex problems. Consider, for example, reports in this area that have covered complex issues such as the evaluation of social programs,[49] air pollution control programs, the selection of computer systems, determining corporate strategy, and the siting of airports and nuclear power facilities,[92] to name but a few. Advantages to be had by conceptualizing F & P within the multiattribute framework include (a) a synthetic, evaluative overview of the issues, (b) recognition that explicit tradeoffs need to be made between attributes of F & P systems (e.g., organizational flexibility vs. profits from the realization of particular projects), (c) greater possibilities of detecting weaknesses in existing plans, which in turn can lead to designing new plans and procedures; (d) recognition that specific knowledge about both organizational processes and the effects of F & P systems is deficient (this can be significant in leading to more precise and relevant questions about these issues, some of which could be amenable to research[127]), and most important (e) monitoring the F & P system itself by updating the multiattribute analysis over time on a continuing basis, that is, by refining data inputs and considering new criteria and alternatives as information is received and situations evolve. Although the difficulties of achieving an adequate multiattribute representation of the F & P problem should not be underestimated, we stress (a) the choice of the best system available is relative rather than absolute, (b) although many subjective inputs to such analyses are necessarily of dubious precision, rough orders of magnitude are to be preferred to none. Furthermore, there are less illusions if one knows which inputs are based on questionable data, (c) the multiattribute procedure can raise questions that are currently obfuscated, and (d) like long-term forecasts, this methodology should be *used* as a cognitive aid to overcome human limitations rather than *believed* to be an optimal model. Finally, although multiattribute analysis is no panacea, what better alternatives have been suggested?

One of our major arguments is for realism in F & P. Illusions and limitations need to be recognized; the use of F & P for control, motivation and communication accepted for what they are; and the extent of future uncertainties both appreciated and appropriately incorporated in plans. F & P can be useful, but current practices need to be changed. A systematic balancing of the benefits and costs of F & P within the decision-theoretic framework discussed is, we believe, one way of approaching these important issues.

REFERENCES

1. Ackoff, R. L., *A Concept of Corporate Planning,* John Wiley, New York, 1970.
2. Adam, E. E., and R. J. Ebert, "A Comparison of Human and Statistical Forecasting," *AIEEE Transactions,* vol. 8, 1976, pp. 120–127.
3. Anderson, N. H., and A. Jacobson, "Effect of Stimulus Inconsistency and Discounting Instructions in Personality Impression Formation," *Journal of Personality and Social Psychology,* vol. 2, no. 4, 1965, pp. 531–539.
4. Ansoff, H. I., "The State of Practice in Planning Systems," *Sloan Management Review,* vol. 18, Winter 1977, pp. 1–24.
5. Ansoff, H. I., J. Avner, R. G. Brandenburg, F. E. Portner, and R. Radosevich, "Does Planning Pay? The Effect of Planning on Success of Acquisitions in American Firms," *Long Range Planning,* vol. 3, no. 2, 1970, pp. 2–7.

6. Armstrong, J. S., "Forecasting with Econometric Methods: Folklore Versus Fact," *Journal of Business,* vol. 51, no. 4, 1978, pp. 549–564.

7. Armstrong, J. S., *"Long-Range Forecasting: From Crystal Ball to Computer,* John Wiley, New York, 1978.

8. Armstrong, J. S., and M. C. Grohman, "A Comparative Study of Methods for Long-Range Market Forecasting," *Management Science,* vol. 19, no. 2, 1972, pp. 211-221.

9. Asch, S. E., "Effects of Group Pressure on the Modification and Distortion of Judgments," in H. Geutzkow, ed., *Groups, Leadership and Men,* Carnegie Institute of Technology Press, Pittsburgh, 1951.

10. Ascher, W., *Forecasting: An Appraisal for Policy Makers and Planners,* The Johns Hopkins University Press, Baltimore, 1978.

11. Barefield, R. M., and E. E. Comisky, "The Accuracy of Analysts' Forecasts of Earnings Per Share," *Journal of Business Research,* vol. 3, no. 3, 1975, pp. 247–252.

12. Bar-Hillel, M., "On the Subjective Probability of Compound Events," *Organizational Behavior and Human Performance,* vol. 9, no. 3, 1973, pp. 396–406.

13. Bar-Hillel, M. "The Base-Rate Fallacy in Probability Judgments," *Acta Psychologica,* vol. 44, no. 3, 1980, pp. 211–233.

14. Basi, B. A., R. J. Carey, and R. D. Twark, "A Comparison of the Accuracy of Corporate and Security Analysts' Forecasts of Earnings," *Accounting Review,* vol. 51, no. 2, 1976, pp. 244–254.

15. Bauman, W. S., "The Less Popular Stocks Versus the Most Popular Stocks," *Financial Analysts Journal,* vol. 21, no. 1, 1965, pp. 61–69.

16. J. Berkson, T. B. Magath, and M. Hurn, "The Error of Estimate of the Blood Cell Count As Made with the Hemocytometer," *American Journal of Physiology,* vol. 128, 1940, pp. 309–323.

17. Borgida, E., and R. E. Nisbett, "The Differential Impact of Abstract vs. Concrete Information on Decisions," *Journal of Applied Social Psychology,* vol. 7, no. 3, 1977, pp. 258–271.

18. Bowman, E. H., "Consistency and Optimality in Managerial Decision Making," *Management Science,* vol. 10, no. 1, 1963, pp. 310–321.

19. Bray, J., "Optimal Control of a Noisy Economy with the U.K. as an Example," *Journal of the Royal Statistical Society A,* vol. 138, part 3, 1975, pp. 339–366.

20. Brehmer, B., "Social Judgment Theory and the Analysis of Interpersonal Conflict," *Psychological Bulletin,* vol. 83, no. 6, 1976, pp. 985–1003.

21. Brown, L. D., and M. S. Rozeff, "The Superiority of Analyst Forecasts as Measures of Expectations: Evidence from Earnings," *Journal of Finance,* vol. 33, no. 1, 1978, pp. 1–16.

22. Bruner, J. S., and L. J. Postman, "On the Perception of Incongruity: A Paradigm," *Journal of Personality,* vol. 18, 1949, pp. 206–223.

23. Brunswik, E., "Organismic Achievement and Environmental Probability," *Psychological Review,* vol. 50, no. 3, 1943, pp. 255–272.

24. Buckhout, R., "Eyewitness Testimony," *Scientific American,* vol. 231, no. 6, 1974, pp. 23–31.

25. Campbell, D. T., "Reforms as Experiments," *American Psychologist,* vol. 24, no. 4, 1969, pp. 409–429.

26. Chapman, L. J., and J. P. Chapman, "Illusory Correlation as an Obstacle to the Use of Valid Psychodiagnostic Signs," *Journal of Abnormal Psychology,* vol. 74, no. 3, 1969, pp. 271–280.

27. Chatfield, C., and D. L. Prothero, "Box–Jenkins Seasonal Forecasting Problems in a

Case Study," *Journal of Royal Statistical Society,* Series A, vol. 136, part 3, 1973, pp. 295–315.

28. Clarkson, G. P. E., *Portfolio Selection: A Simulation of Trust Investment,* Prentice-Hall, Englewood Cliffs, NJ, 1962.

29. Cohen, J., E. I. Chesnick, and D. Haran, "Evaluation of Compound Probabilities in Sequential Choice," *Nature,* vol. 232, no. 5310, 1971, pp. 414–416.

30. Cohen, J., E. I. Chesnick, and D. Haran, "A Confirmation of the Inertial ψ-Effect in Sequential Choice and Decision," *British Journal of Psychology,* vol. 63, no. 1, 1972, pp. 41–46.

31. Cooper, J. P., and C. R. Nelson, "The Ex-ante Prediction Performance of the St. Louis and FRB-MIT-PENN Econometric Models and Some Results on Composite Predictors," *Journal of Money, Credit and Banking,* vol. 7, no. 1, 1975, pp. 1–32.

32. Cooper, R., "The Predictive Performance of Quarterly Econometric Models of the United States," in Bert G. Hickman, ed., *Econometric Models of Cyclical Behavior,* vol. 2, *Studies in Income and Wealth,* no. 36, Columbia University Press, New York, pp. 813–926 (discussion on pp. 926–947).

33. Copeland, R. M., and R. J. Marioni, "Executives Forecasts of Earnings per Share Versus Forecasts of Naive Models," *Journal of Business,* vol. 45, no. 4, 1972, pp. 497–512.

34. Cosier, R. A., "The Effects of Three Potential Aids for Making Strategic Decisions on Prediction Accuracy," *Organizational Behavior and Human Performance,* vol. 22, no. 2, 1978, pp. 295–306.

35. Cowles, A., "Can Stock Market Forecasters Forecast?" *Econometricia,* vol. 1, no. 3, 1933, pp. 309–324.

36. Cowles, A., "Stock Market Forecasting," *Econometricia,* vol. 12, nos. 3 & 4, 1944, pp. 67–84.

37. Cragg, J. G., and B. G. Malkiel, "The Consensus and Accuracy of Some Predictions of the Growth of Corporate Earnings," *Journal of Finance,* vol. 23, no. 1, 1968, pp. 67–84.

38. Cyert, R. M., W. R. Dill, and J. G. March, "The Role of Expectations in Business Decision Making," *Administrative Science Quarterly,* vol. 3, 1958, pp. 307–340.

39. Dawes, R. M., "A Case Study of Graduate Admissions: Applications of Three Principles of Human Decision Making," *American Psychologist,* vol. 26, no. 2, 1971, pp. 180–188.

40. Dawes, R. M., "Shallow Psychology," in J. S. Carroll and J. W. Payne, eds., *Cognition and Social Behavior,* Erlbaum, Hillsdale, NJ, 1976.

41. Dawes, R. M., and B. Corrigan, "Linear Models in Decision Making," *Psychological Bulletin,* vol. 81, no. 2, 1974, pp. 95–106.

42. Dearborn, D. C., and H. A. Simon, "Selective Perception: A Note on the Departmental Identification of Executives," *Sociometry,* vol. 21, no. 2, 1958, pp. 140–144.

43. Dhalla, N. K., and S. Yuspeh, "Forget the Product Life Cycle Concept," *Harvard Business Review,* vol. 54, no. 1, 1976, pp. 102–112.

44. Dickson, G. W., J. A. Senn, and N. L. Chervany, "Research in Management Information Systems: The Minnesota Experiments," *Management Science,* vol. 23, no. 9, 1977, pp. 913–923.

45. DuCharme, W. M., "A Response Bias Explanation of Conservative Human Inference," *Journal of Experimental Psychology,* vol. 85, 1970, pp. 66–74.

46. Ebert, R. J., "Environmental Structure and Programmed Decision Effectiveness," *Management Science,* vol. 19, no. 4, 1972, pp. 435–445.

47. Ebert, R. J. and T. E. Kruse, "Bootstrapping the Security Analyst," *Journal of Applied Psychology,* vol. 63, no. 1, 1978, pp. 110–119.

48. Edwards, W., "Conservatism in Human Information Processing," in B. Kleinmuntz, ed., *Formal Representation of Human Judgment,* John Wiley, New York, 1968.

49. Edwards, W., M. Guttentag, and K. Snapper, "Effective Evaluation: A Decision Theoretic Approach," in E. L. Struening and M. Guttentag, eds., *Handbook of Evaluation Research*, vol. 1, Sage, Beverly Hills, CA, 1975.

50. Einhorn, H. J., "Use of Nonlinear, Noncompensatory Models as a Function of Task and Amount of Information," *Organizational Behavior and Human Performance*, vol. 6, no. 1, 1971, pp. 1–27.

51. Einhorn, H. J., "Expert Measurement and Mechanical Combination," *Organizational Behavior and Human Performance*, vol. 7, no. 1, 1972, pp. 86–106.

52. Einhorn, H. J., "Learning from Experience and Suboptimal Rules in Decision Making," in T. Wallsten, ed., *Cognitive Processes in Choice and Decision Behavior*, Erlbaum, Hillsdale, NJ, 1980.

53. Einhorn, H. J., and R. M. Hogarth, "Confidence in Judgment: Persistence of the Illusion of Validity," *Psychological Review*, vol. 85, no. 5, 1978, pp. 395–476.

54. Einhorn, H. J., and R. M. Hogarth, "Behavioral Decision Theory: Processes of Judgment and Choice," *Annual Review of Psychology*, vol. 32, 1981, pp. 53–88.

55. Elton, E. J., and M. J. Gruber, "Earnings Estimates and the Accuracy of Expectational Data," *Management Society*, vol. 18, no. 8, 1972, pp. 409–424.

56. Emshoff, J. R., and I. I. Mitroff, "Improving the Effectiveness of Corporate Planning," *Business Horizons*, vol. 21, no. 5, 1978, pp. 49–60.

57. Estes, W. K., "The Cognitive Side of Probability Learning," *Psychological Review*, vol. 83, no. 1, 1976, pp. 37–64.

58. Fama, E. F., "The Behavior of Stock Market Prices," *Journal of Business*, vol. 38, no. 1, 1965, pp. 34–105.

59. Fischhoff, B., "Hindsight ≠ Foresight: The Effect of Outcome Knowledge on Judgment under Uncertainty," *Journal of Experimental Psychology: Human Perception and Performance*, vol. 1, no. 2, 1975, pp. 288–299.

60. Fischhoff, B., "Perceived Informativeness of Facts," *Journal of Experimental Psychology: Human Perception and Performance*, vol. 3, no. 2, 1977, pp. 349–358.

61. Fischhoff, B., P. Slovic, and S. Lichtenstein, "Knowing with Certainty: The Appropriateness of Extreme Confidence," *Journal of Experimental Psychology: Human Perception and Performance*, vol. 3, no. 4, 1977, pp. 552–564.

62. Fischhoff, B., P. Slovic, and S. Lichtenstein, "Fault Trees: Sensitivity of Estimated Failure Probabilities to Problem Representation," *Journal of Experimental Psychology: Human Perception and Performance*, vol. 4, no. 2, 1978, pp. 330–344.

63. Gettys, C. F., C. W. Kelly, and C. R. Peterson, "The Best Guess Hypothesis in Multistage Inference," *Organizational Behavior and Human Performance*, vol. 10, no. 3, 1973, pp. 364–373.

64. Gold, B., "The Shaky Foundations of Capital Budgeting," *California Management Review*, vol. 19, no. 2, Winter 1976, pp. 51–60.

65. Goldberg, L. R., "Man Versus Model of Man: A Rationale, Plus Some Evidence for a Method of Improving on Clinical Inferences," *Psychological Bulletin*, vol. 73, no. 6, 1970, pp. 422–432.

66. Goldberg, L. R., "Man Versus Model of Man: Just How Conflicting Is That Evidence?," *Organizational Behavior and Human Performance*, vol. 16, no. 1, 1976, pp. 13–22.

67. Golding, S. L., and L. G. Rorer, "Illusory Correlation and Subjective Judgment," *Journal of Abnormal Psychology*, vol. 80, no. 3, 1972, pp. 249–260.

68. Green D., and J. Segall, "The Predictive Power of First Quarter Earnings Reports," *Journal of Business*, vol. 40, no. 1, 1967, pp. 44–45.

69. Grether, D. M., and C. R. Plott, "Economic Theory of Choice and the Preference Reversal Phenomenon," *American Economic Review*, vol. 69, no. 4, 1979, pp. 623–638.

70. Grinyer, P. H., and D. Norburn, "Planning for Existing Markets: Perceptions of Executives and Financial Performance," *Journal of Royal Statistical Society*, Series A, vol. 138, part 1, 1975, pp. 70–98.

71. Groff, G. K., "Empirical Comparison of Models for Short-Range Forecasting," *Management Science*, vol. 20, no. 1, 1973, pp. 22–31.

72. Guth, W. D., "Formulating Organizational Objectives and Strategy: A Systematic Approach," *Journal of Business Policy*, Fall 1971, pp. 24–31.

73. Hammerton, M., "A Case of Radical Probability Estimation," *Journal of Experimental Psychology*, vol. 101, no. 2, 1973, pp. 252–254.

74. Hammond, K. R., and B. Brehmer, "Quasi-Rationality and Distrust: Implications for International Conflict," in L. Rappoport and D. A. Summers, eds., *Human Judgment and Social Interaction*, Holt, Rinehart & Winston, New York, 1973.

75. Hammond, K. R., J. L. Mumpower, and T. H. Smith, "Linking Environmental Models with Models of Human Judgment: A Symmetrical Decision Aid," *IEEE Transactions of Systems, Man, and Cybernetics*, vol. SMC-7, no. 5, 1977, pp. 358–367.

76. Hayashi, K. K., "Corporate Planning Practices in Japanese Multinationals," *Academic Management Journal*, vol. 21, no. 2, 1978, pp. 211–226.

77. Herold, D. M., "Long-range Planning and Organizational Performance," *Academic Management Journal*, vol. 15, no. 1, 1972, pp. 91–102.

78. Hogarth, R. M., "Cognitive Processes and the Assessment of Subjective Probability Distributions," *Journal of American Statistical Association*, vol. 70, no. 350, 1975, pp. 271–289.

79. Hogarth, R. M., "Methods for Aggregating Opinions," in H. Jungermann and G. de Zeeuw, eds., *Decision Making and Change in Human Affairs*, Reidel, Dordrecht, The Netherlands, 1977, pp. 231–255.

80. Hogarth, R. M. *Judgement and Choice: The Psychology of Decision*, John Wiley, Chichester, England, 1980.

81. Hogarth, R. M., "Beyond Discrete Biases: Functional and Dysfunctional Aspects of Judgmental Heuristics," unpublished manuscript, University of Chicago, Graduate School of Business, Center for Decision Research, 1980.

82. Hogarth, R. M., and S. Makridakis, "Decision Making in a Dynamic, Competitive Environment: Random Strategies and Causal Attributions," unpublished manuscript, University of Chicago, Graduate School of Business, Center for Decision Research, 1979.

83. Janis, I. L., and L. Mann, *Decision Making: A Psychological Analysis of Conflict, Choice and Commitment*, The Free Press, New York, 1977.

84. Jarvik, M. E., "Probability Learning and a Negative Recency Effect in the Serial Anticipation of Alternative Symbols," *Journal of Experimental Psychology*, vol. 41, 1951, pp. 291–297.

85. Jenkins, M. H., and W. C. Ward, "Judgment of Contingency between Responses and Outcomes," *Psychological Monographs: General and Applied*, vol. 79, no. 1 (whole No. 594), 1965, pp. 1–17.

86. Jensen, M. C., "The Performance of Mutual Funds in the Period 1945–1964," *Journal of Finance*, vol. 23, no. 2, 1968, pp. 389–416.

87. Jorgenson, D. W., J. Hunter, and M. I. Nadiri, "The Predictive Performance of Econometric Models of Quarterly Investment Behavior," *Econometricia*, vol. 38, no. 2, 1970, pp. 213–224.

88. Kahneman, D., and A. Tversky, "Subjective Probability: A Judgment of Representativeness," *Cognitive Psychology*, vol. 3, no. 3, 1972, pp. 430–454.

89. Kahneman, D., and A. Tversky, "On the Psychology of Prediction," *Psychological Review*, vol. 80, no. 4, 1973, pp. 237–251.

90. Kahneman, D., and A. Tversky, "Intuitive Prediction: Biases and corrective Procedures," in *TIMS Studies in Management Science,* vol. 12, 1979, pp. 313–327.

91. Karger, D. W., and Z. A. Malik, "Long Range Planning and Organizational Performance," *Long Range Planning,* vol. 8, no. 6, 1975, pp. 60–64.

92. Keeney, R. L., and H. Raiffa, *Decisions with Multiple Objectives: Preferences and Value Tradeoffs,* John Wiley, New York, 1976.

93. Knafl, K., and G. Burkett, "Professional Socialization in a Surgical Specialty: Acquiring Medical Judgment," *Social Science of Medicine,* vol. 9, 1975, pp. 397–404.

94. Kudla, R. J., "The Effects of Strategic Planning on Common Stock Returns," *Academic Management Journal,* vol. 23, no. 1, 1980, pp. 5–20.

95. Kunreuther, H., "Extensions of Bowman's Theory of Managerial Decision Making," *Management Science,* vol. 15, no. 8, 1969, pp. B-415–439.

96. Langer, E. J., "The Illusion of Control," *Journal of Personality and Social Psychology,* vol. 32, no. 2, 1979, pp. 311–328.

97. Langer, E. J., and J. Roth, "The Effect of Sequence of Outcomes in a Chance Task on the Illusion of Control," *Journal of Personality and Social Psychology,* vol. 32, no. 6, 1975, pp. 951–955.

98. Lathrop, R. G., "Perceived Variability," *Journal of Experimental Psychology,* vol. 73, no. 4, 1967, pp. 498–502.

99. Leontiades, M., and A. Tezel, "Planning Perceptions and Planning Results," *Strategic Management Journal,* vol. 1, 1980, p⌐. 65–75.

100. Leung, P., "Sensitivity Analysis of the Effect of variations in the Form and Parameters of a Multiattribute Utility Model: A Survey, *Behavioral Science,* vol. 23, no. 6, 1978, pp. 478–485.

101. Lewin, K., "Group Decision and Social Change," in T. Newcomb and E. Hartley, eds., *Readings in Social Psychology,* Holt, New York, 1947.

102. Libby, R., "Man Versus Model of Man: Some Conflicting Evidence," *Organizational Behavior and Human Performance,* vol. 16, no. 1, 1976, pp. 1–12.

103. Lichtenstein, S., B. Fischhoff, and L. D. Phillips, "Calibration of Probabilities: The State of the Art," in H. Jungermann and G. de Zeeuw, eds., *Decision Making and Change in Human Affairs,* Reidel, Dordrecht, The Netherlands, 1977.

104. Lichtenstein, S., and P. Slovic, "Reversals of Preference between bids and Choices in Gambling Decisions," *Journal of Experimental Psychology,* vol. 89, no. 1, 1971, pp. 46–55.

105. Lichtenstein, S., and P. Slovic, "Response-Induced Reversals of Preference in Gambling: An Extended Replication in Las Vegas," *Journal of Experimental Psychology,* vol. 101, no. 1, 1973, pp. 16–20.

106. Lichtenstein, S., P. Slovic, B. Fischhoff, M. Layman, and B. Combs, "Judged Frequency of Lethal Events," *Journal of Experimental Psychology: Human Learning and Memory,* vol. 4, no. 6, 1978, pp. 551–578.

107. Liebling, H. I., P. T. Bidwell and K. E. Hall, "The Recent Performance of Anticipations Surveys and Econometric Model Projections of Investment Spending in the United States," *Journal of Business,* vol. 49, no. 4, 1976, pp. 451–477.

108. Loftus, E. F., "Leading Questions and the Eyewitness Report," *Cognitive Psychology,* vol. 7, no. 4, 1975, pp. 560–572.

109. Lorek, R. S., C. L. McDonald, and D. H. Patz, "A Comparative Examination of Management Forecasts and Box–Jenkins Forecasts of Earnings," *Accounting Review,* vol. 51, no. 2, 1976, pp. 321–330.

110. Lucado, W. E., "Corporate Planning—A Current Status Report," *Management Planning,* November/December 1974, pp. 27–34.

111. Lyon, D., and P. Slovic, "Dominance of Accuracy Information and Neglect of Base Rates in Probability Estimation," *Acta Psychologica*, vol. 40, 1976, pp. 287–298.

112. Mabert, V. A., "Statistical Versus Sales Force–Executive Opinion Short-Range Forecasts: A Time-Series Analysis Case Study," *Decision Science*, vol. 7, 1976, pp. 310–318.

113. Maier, N. R. F., "Reasoning in Humans: II. The Solution of a Problem and Its Appearance in Consciousness," *Journal of Comparative Psychology*, vol. 12, no. 2, 1931, pp. 181–194.

114. Makridakis, S., and M. Hibon, "Accuracy of Forecasting: An Empirical Investigation," *Journal of the Royal Statistical Society, A*, vol. 142, part 2, 1979, pp. 97–125.

115. March, J. G., "Bounded Rationality, Ambiguity, and the Engineering of Choice," *Bell Journal of Economics*, vol. 9, no. 2, 1978, pp. 587–608.

116. Marquand, J., "Government Economic Planning in the United Kingdom," *Long Range Planning*, vol. 11, no. 6, 1978, pp. 2–8.

117. McDonald, C. L., "An Empirical Examination of the Reliability of Published Predictions of Future Earnings," *Accounting Review*, vol. 48, no. 3, 1973, pp. 502–510.

118. McNees, S. K., "An Evaluation of Economic Forecasts," *New England Economic Review*, November/December 1975.

119. McNees, S. K., "Forecasting Performance in the 1970's," in *TIMS Studies in Management Science*, vol. 12, 1979.

120. Meehl, P. E., *Clinical Versus Statistical Prediction: A Theoretical Analysis and Review of the Literature*, University of Minnesota Press, Minneapolis, 1954.

121. Miller, D. T., "Ego Involvement and Attributions for Success and Failure," *Journal of Personality and Social Psychology*, vol. 34, no. 5, 1976, pp. 901–906.

122. Morlock, H., "The Effect of Outcome Desirability on Information Required for Decisions," *Behavioral Science*, vol. 12, no. 4, 1967, pp. 296–300.

123. Mullins, D. W., and R. B. Homonoff, "Applications of Inventory Cash Management Models," in S. C. Myers, ed., *Modern Developments in Financial Management*, Praeger, New York, 1976.

124. Naylor, T. H., T. G. Seaks, and D. W. Wichern, "Box–Jenkins Methods: An Alternative to Econometric Models," *International Statistical Review*, vol. 40, no. 2, 1972, pp. 123–137.

125. Nisbett, R. E., and E. Borgida, "Attribution and the Psychology of Prediction," *Journal of Personality and Social Psychology*, vol. 32, no. 5, 1975, pp. 932–943.

126. Nisbett, R. E., E. Borgida, R. Crandall, and H. Reed, "Popular Induction: Information Is Not Necessarily Informative," in J. S. Carroll and J. W. Payne, eds., *Cognition and Social Behavior*, Erlbaum, Hillsdale, N.J., 1976.

127. Nutt, P. C., "An Experimental Comparison of the Effectiveness of Three Planning Methods," *Management Science*, vol. 23, no. 5, 1977, pp. 499–511.

128. O'Carroll, F. M., "Subjective Probabilities and Short-Term Economic Forecasts: An Empirical Investigation," *Journal of Applied Statistics*, vol. 26, no. 3, 1977, pp. 269–278.

129. Oskamp, S., "The Relationship of Clinical Experience and Training Methods to Several criteria of Clinical Prediction," *Psychological Monographs: General and Applied*, vol. 76, no. 28, whole No. 5477, 1962.

130. Oskamp, S., "Overconfidence in case-Study Judgments," *Journal of Consulting Psychology*, vol. 29, no. 3, 1965, pp. 261–265.

131. Payne, J. W., "Task Complexity and Contingent Processing in Decision Making: An Information Search and Protocol Analysis," *Organizational Behavior and Human Performance*, vol. 16, no. 2, 1976, pp. 366–387.

132. Perlmutter, L. C., and R. A. Monty, "The Importance of Perceived Control: Fact or Fantasy?," *American Scientist*, vol. 65, November/December 1977, pp. 759–765.

133. Pinson, C., "Consumer Cognitive Styles: Review and Implications for Marketers," in E. Topritzhofer, ed., *Marketing, Neue Ergebnisse aus Forschung und Praxis,* Gabler, Wiesbaden, West Germany, 1978.

134. Pollay, R. W., "The Structure of Executive Decisions and Decision Times," Administrative Science Quarterly, vol. 15, no. 4, 1970, pp. 459–471.

135. Remus, W. E. "Testing Bowman's Managerial Coefficient Theory Using a Competitive Gaming Environment," *Management Science,* vol. 24, no. 8, 1978, pp. 827–835.

136. Richards, R. M., "Analsts' Performance and the Accuracy of Corporate Earnings Forecasts," *Journal of Business,* vol. 49, no. 3, 1976, pp. 350–357.

137. Ringbakk, K. A., "Organised Planning in Major U.S. Companies," *Long Range Planning,* vol. 2, no. 2, 1969, pp. 46–57.

138. Ronen, J. "Effects of Some Probability Displays on Choices," *Organizational Behavior and Human Performance,* vol. 9, no. 1, 1973, pp. 1–15.

139. Ross, L., "The Intuitive Psychologist and His Shortcomings: Distortions in the Attribution Process," in L. Berkowitz, ed., *Advances in Experimental Social Psychology,* vol. 10, Academic Press, New York, 1977.

140. Russell, B., *History of Western Philosophy,* 2nd ed., George Allen & Unwin, London, 1961.

141. Russo, J. E., "The Value of Unit Price Information," *Journal of Marketing Research,* vol. 14, no. 2, 1977, pp. 193–201.

142. Samuelson, P., Quoted in *Business Week,* December 21, 1974, p. 51.

143. Sawyer, J., "Measurement *and* Prediction, Clinical *and* Statistical," *Psychological Bulletin,* vol. 66, no. 3, 1966, pp. 178–200.

144. Shweder, R. A., "Likeness and Likelihood in Everyday Thought: Magical Thinking in Judgments about Personality," *Current Anthropology,* vol. 18, no. 4, 1977, pp. 637–658.

145. Simon, H. A., and A. Newell, "Human Problem Solving: The State of the Theory in 1970," *American Psychologist,* vol. 26, no. 2, 1971, pp. 145–159.

146. Simon, H. A., and R. K. Sumner, "Patterns in Music," in B. Kleinmuntz, ed., *Formal Representation of Human Judgment,* John Wiley, New York, 1968.

147. Sims, C. A., "Evaluating Short-Term Macroeconomic Forecasts: The Dutch Performance," *Review of Economics and Statistics,* vol. 49, no. 2, 1967, pp. 225–236.

148. Slovic, P., "Value as a Determiner of Subjective Probability," *IEEE Tranactions on Human Factors in Electronics,* vol. HFE-7, no. 1, 1966, pp. 22–28.

149. Slovic, P., "From Shakespeare to Simon: Speculations—and Some Evidence—About Man's Ability to Process Information," *Oregon Research Institute Research Monograph,* vol. 12, no. 2, 1972, Oregon Research Institute, Eugene.

150. Slovic, P., "Choice Between Equally-Valued Alternatives," *Journal of Experimental Psychology: Human Perception and Performance,* vol. 1, no. 3, 1975, pp. 280—287.

151. Slovic, P., "Toward Understanding and Improving Decisions," in W. Howell, ed., *Human Performance and Productivity,* Erlbaum, Hillsdale, NJ, 1980.

152. Slovic, P., B. Fischhoff, and S. Lichtenstein, "Behavioral Decision Theory," *Annual Review of Psychology,* vol. 28, 1977, pp. 1–39.

153. Slovic, P., D. Fleissner, and W. S. Bauman, "Analyzing the Use of Information in Investment Decision Making: A Methodological Proposal," *Journal of Business,* vol. 45, no. 2, 1972, pp. 283–301.

154. Slovic, P., H. Kunreuther, and G. F. White, "Decision Processes, Rationality and Adjustment to Natural Hazards," in G. F. White, ed., *Natural Hazards, Local, National and Global,* Oxford University Press, New York, 1974.

155. Slovic, P., and S. Lichtenstein, "Comparison of Bayesian and Regression Approaches to

the Study of Information Processing in Judgment," *Organizational Behavior and Human Performance,* vol. 6, no. 6, 1971, pp. 649–744.

156. Smedslund, J., "The Concept of Correlation in Adults," *Scandinavian Journal of Psychology,* vol. 4, no. 3, 1963, pp. 165–173.

157. Snyder, M., and S. W. Uranowitz, "Reconstructing the Past: Some Cognitive Consequences of Person Perception," *Journal of Personality and Social Psychology,* vol. 36, no. 9, 1978, pp. 941–950.

158. Spetzler, C. S., and C.-A. S. Staël von Holstein, "Probability Encoding in Decision Analysis," *Management Science,* vol. 22, no. 3, 1975, pp. 340–358.

159. Stonich, P. J., "Formal Planning Pitfalls and How to Avoid Them," *Management Review,* vol. 64, no. 6, 1975, pp. 4–11.

160. Thune, S. S., and R. J. House, "Where Long-Range Planning Pays Off," *Business Horizons,* vol. 13, no. 4, 1970, pp. 81–87.

161. Tversky, A., "Intransitivity of Preferences," *Psychological Review,* vol. 76, no. 1, 1969, pp. 31–48.

162. Tversky, A., "Elimination by Aspects: A Theory of Choice," *Psychological Review,* vol. 79, no. 4, 1972, pp. 281–299.

163. Tversky, A., "Availability: A Heuristic for Judging Frequency and Probability," *Cognitive Psychology,* vol. 5, no. 2, 1973, pp. 207–232.

164. Tversky, A., "Judgment under Uncertainty: Heuristics and Biases," *Science,* vol. 185, 27 September 1974, pp. 1124–1131.

165. Tversky, A., and D. Kahneman, "The Belief in the 'Law of Small Numbers'," *Psychological Bulletin,* vol. 76, no. 2, 1971, pp. 105–110.

166. Wagenaar, W. A., "Appreciation of Conditional Probabilities in Binary Sequences," *Acta Psychologica,* vol. 34, nos. 2 & 3, 1970, pp. 348–356.

167. Wagenaar, W. A., "The Pond-and-Duckweek Problem: Three Experiments on the Misperception of Exponential Growth," *Acta Psychologica,* vol. 43, no. 3, 1979, 239–251.

168. Wagenaar, W. A., and H. Timmers, "Intuitive Prediction of Growth," in D. F. Burkhardt and W. H. Ittelson, eds., *Environmental Assessment of Socio-Economic Systems,* Plenum, New York, 1978.

169. Ward, W. C., and H. M. Jenkins, "The Display of Information and the Judgment of Contingency," *Canadian Journal of Psychology,* vol. 19, no. 3, 1965, pp. 231–241.

170. Wason, P. C., "On the Failure to Eliminate Hypotheses in a Conceptual Task," *Quarterly Journal of Experimental Psychology,* vol. 12, no. 3, 1960, pp. 129–140.

171. Webster, E. C., *Decision Making in the Employment Interview,* Industrial Relations Centre, McGill University, Montreal, 1964.

172. White, R. W., "Motivation Reconsidered, The Concept of Competence," *Psychological Review,* vol. 66, no. 5, 1959, pp. 297–333.

173. Wildavsky, A., "If Planning is Everything, Maybe It's Nothing," *Policy Science,* vol. 4, no. 2, 1973, pp. 127–153.

174. Wood, D. R., Jr., and R. L. LaForce, "The Impact of Comprehensive Planning on Financial Performance," *Academic Management Journal,* vol. 22, no. 3, 1979, pp. 516–526.

175. Wright, P., "The Harassed Decision Maker: Time Pressures, Distractions and the Use of Evidence," *Journal of Applied Psychology,* vol. 59, no. 5, 1974, pp. 555–561.

——————— 31 ———————
INTEGRATING FORECASTING AND DECISION MAKING

WILLIAM REMUS
College of Business Administration
University of Hawaii, Honolulu

MARK G. SIMKIN
College of Business Administration
University of Nevada, Reno

INTRODUCTION

All organizations must monitor and respond to the environment. Some variables in the organization's environment need only be monitored, but crucial environmental variables need both to be monitored and their future values predicted. Forecasting these crucial variables gives management the lead time to make decisions and plan. A good forecast allows an organization to take advantage of opportunities and avoid pitfalls in the environment through timely decision making.

The purpose of this chapter is to identify those characteristics of forecasts that make them useful for decision-making purposes and to illustrate the role that these characteristics play in common forecasting/decision-making settings. To illustrate characteristics, consider the following story.

Freddie Falsepoint was the statistical analyst for the telephone company in Metro City. It was November. When his boss, Pete "Piles-It-On" Hardgrove, asked for a sales forecast for the coming year, Freddie thought to himself: "Just what I need—another project." Thus, Freddie delayed the

The following persons provided assistance in preparing this chapter: John Dobra, Milton Tsuda, and Robert Schmitt.

CHART 31-1. Freddie Falsepoint's Memo to Peter Hardgrove

Date: December 15, 1985

Memo To: Mr. Peter Hardgrove, Manager
           Marketing Services

From: Frederick Falsepoint, Analyst
Re: Sales Forecast for 1986

Demand for telephone products has been strong during the last few years, and it is expected that this trend will continue into the future, at least for the near term. Undoubtedly, the strength of this demand is in large part attributable to the excellent work of our customer representatives and the ability of our inventory staff to keep our installers supplied with equipment. In view of the large number of items carried by our company, this is no small achievement.

Given the items identified above and the present inflationary experience of the country, total sales next year are projected to be $X.Y million. Naturally, this projection is subject to statistical error which makes this forecast uncertain. Thus, an updated forecast will be provided at a later date.

---

project with the excuse that he "needed more data" to make a good forecast. As the end-of-the-year deadline approached, however, the marketing vice president began to ask for the forecast. With the vice president on his back, Pete finally ordered Freddie to prepare the forecast and have it to him by the next morning.

Freddie had less than eight hours and even fewer ideas. Thus, in the end Freddie took last year's sales figure, multiplied it by the inflation rate, added a small 4% upward adjustment, and called this result his forecast of corporate sales. Completing his forecast, Freddie drafted the memo illustrated in Chart 31-1. Freddie chuckled over the last phrase since he knew that the earliest he would probably get around to the next update was sometime next December—if that early! However, the forecast was finished, the boss was satisfied, and the only thing that remained was the Christmas shopping. . . .

THE GUIDELINES

What did Freddie do wrong? Just about everything! Even common sense would identify a number of pitfalls in the preceding story. However, to be specific, consider the guidelines for preparing decision-oriented forecasts outlined in Chart 31-2. From a review of these guidelines, it is apparent that Freddie Falsepoint did a miserable job. Let us examine these guidelines point by point.

1. *Prepare Forecasts in a Timely Fashion.* The first point is that the forecast be timely. Although it would appear that Freddie's work satisfies

CHART 31-2. Guidelines for Integrating Forecasting and Decision Making

Preparation

1. Forecasts must be timely.
2. Forecasts must be in the units appropriate for the decision.
3. Forecasts must be disaggregated to the degree required by the decision makers.
4. Forecasts should be detailed enough to show seasonal or other cyclical variations. Forecasts of quarters or even months are generally more useful than a simple annual forecast.
5. Forecasts should include not only the most likely value but also best-case and worst-case values.
6. Forecasting assumptions and limitations should be clearly spelled out in an appendix.
7. Forecasts should be documented in an easily understandable report.

Distribution

8. Forecasts should be "blessed" by top management.
9. Forecasts should be distributed to all appropriate managers.
10. Forecasts should be regularly updated and distributed.

---

this criterion, just the opposite is probably the case. Often, a manager must make a decision well in advance of the forecast period. For example, inventory reordering must be planned with enough lead time to allow for shipment. Similarly, budgets must be prepared for supervisory reviews long before the fiscal year in which they will be used. Since Freddie's forecast is just two weeks short of the planning year, it is unlikely that it will be of much use for the near term.

2. *Express Forecasts in Appropriate Units.* The second guideline is that the forecast be expressed in the dimensional units needed by the decision maker. Freddie's work does not do this. If the telephone sales forecast is used by inventory control staff, for example, the forecast should be in *units of equipment* rather than *dollars*. If the sales forecast will be used by both inventory staff and, say, cash planners, the forecast should be expressed in both units of equipment and dollar terms.

3. *Disaggregate Forecasts to the Decision-Making Level.* Freddie failed to provide any breakdown of sales in his forecast, but both telephone installers and the inventory control staff will want to know how many units of each type of telephone equipment will be sold in the coming year. For a forecast to be useful for decision-making purposes, the translation of dollars into disaggregated units should be done by the forecaster as a natural part of the forecasting process.

4. *Show Seasonal or Cyclical Variations.* The fourth guideline points out that many forecasted variables have seasonal patterns. When forecasts are made on a quarterly or monthly basis, these patterns become apparent and can be used to improve the decision-making process. In Freddie's case, the pattern of sales may be used to set the best times to order equipment and the pattern of orders over the year. Also, the pattern of sales may predict cash flow surpluses or times when additional financing may be needed. Freddie's forecast fails to help with these crucial problems.

5. *Include Best-Case and Worst-Case Values.* The fifth guideline suggests that forecasts should indicate not only the most likely value, but also the best-case value and the worst-case value. Freddie's forecast is only a point estimate and therefore does not follow this suggestion. One reason why the inclusion of best-case and worst-case values is desirable is because forecasting itself is an inexact art rather than a precise science. A forecast that includes a range of potential values calls attention to this property and gives the decision maker an indication of how much uncertainty the forecaster attaches to the forecast. Often, this range is computed statistically as a confidence interval, in which the range includes, say, 95% of all likely forecast outcomes. If a 95% figure is chosen, the range is said to be a *95% confidence interval.* When forecasts are developed using mathematical models, this confidence interval can be computed using statistics developed from sample data or a simulation procedure. However, even (reasonable) subjective forecast ranges are better than none at all. If a 95% confidence interval results in too wide a range (e.g., a sales forecast between −1000 and +4000 units), it is possible to compute a narrower range at lower probability.

Another reason why it is desirable to provide forecast ranges rather than point estimates is because many decision-making processes are not based on the most likely outcome, but rather on best-case or worst-case expectations. For example, to assure adequate supplies of telephone equipment, the inventory control staff of the company may want to purchase enough equipment for the high-order sales projections. On the other hand, where large investments in plant and equipment are involved, a conservative decision maker may want to base the decision on the worst-case portion of the forecasting range. Finally, the best, worst, and most likely projections permit a manager to devise strategies that are flexible enough to take advantage of the best case if it arises while preparing the company to survive the worst case.

When forecasting ranges are not provided to management but the decision-making process calls for them, it is reasonable to expect managers to create their own. Often, this creative process is subverbal and perhaps even subconscious. There is nothing inherently wrong with such creative processes as long as the resultant range estimates are reasonable. When judgmental methods result in unreasonable ranges, however, suboptimal decisions may result. For example, this may mean overstocking inventory because management was overly optimistic in its sales estimates, or it may mean a failure to capitalize on a given opportunity because management's worst-case projections of the project's potential were too low. In either case, bad decisions result from a lack of vital forecasting information. The provision of forecasting intervals may help avoid such trauma.

Looking back to Freddie Falsepoint's memo, we see that he failed to provide any forecasting intervals, although he did state that his projection was "subject to statistical error." For the situation at hand, however, the uncertainty in the forecast is not attributable to the (naive) statistical method that was used to create the forecast, but rather to the natural doubt surrounding any projection about future business behavior. The use of the word "statistical" in Freddie's memo has been used for sheer subterfuge. Because most managers are not particularly conversant with statistical methods and are therefore not prepared to discuss the drawbacks of statistical methodology, there is little doubt that Freddie will get away with his statement despite the fact that it is nonsense.

6. *Identify Forecasting Assumptions and Limitations.* The sixth guideline advises the forecaster to provide background information about his or her forecast(s). Managers tend to distrust forecasts that magically appear and that provide little in the way of explanation about how the forecast was constructed or the crucial assumption made by the forecaster. Forecasts increase in usefulness when managers are informed about the limits of the forecast—especially the conditions under which the forecast would no longer be valid. Thus, our sixth guide-line suggests that the forecaster explain assumptions, limiting conditions, and so forth in a straightforward way.

Freddie's memo failed to provide explanations about his forecast, but we are not required to make the same mistake. Perhaps the easiest way to make critical information available to the decision maker regarding the forecast is to summarize it in an appendix. This appendix is more desirable than footnotes because (1) the appendix can more fully document the forecasting assumptions and procedures and (2) the appendix can state more clearly what a decision maker needs to know in order to use the forecast(s) intelligently. Thus, the appendix should briefly explain in easy-to-understand terms how the forecasts were derived, what assumptions were made in the course of their construction, and what conditions limit their use. Just having this information in some obscure, jargon-filled, technical memorandum will not overcome managerial resistance, and certainly will not support the decision-making activities for which the forecast was intended.

7. *Document Forecasts in an Easy-to-Understand Report.* Managers would rather live with problems they cannot solve than implement solutions they do not understand. Thus, forecasts are of little value if they are unintelligible. Freddie's report is understandable owing to its simplicity rather than its detail.

Forecasts can be made more meaningful in at least three ways: (1) by limiting technical jargon, (2) by using consistent, easily understood formats, and (3) by employing graphs to depict data relationships. Technical jargon can be minimized by describing forecasting methodology in an appendix. Even here, however, descriptions should emphasize those assumptions that limit the usefulness of the forecast and not dwell on the technical details of data preparation or computer executions.

A second way of making forecasts more understandable is to use consistent, easily understood formats. For example, the forecast should use common names and abbreviations for inventory equipment or accounting values and use columns rather than rows for years or months if this is standard on other business reports. Spreadsheet templates of the type discussed in this chapter can be used to standardize forecast presentations if desired.

Finally, it is often useful to present both forecast values and (perhaps later) realized values in graphs. As explained in detail later in this chapter, graphs further understanding, increase awareness of relationships, and can be powerful tools for convincing managers of both the accuracy and/or usefulness of forecast elements.

8. *Obtain the "Blessings" of Top Management.* In spite of the many talents of the forecaster(s) and the many hours of work that might have been spent on a particular forecast, there is no assurance that the decision makers receiving the forecast will use it. Where the forecaster is employed in a little-understood corporate staff department, for example, there may be a tendency for the manager to dismiss the forecast as "uninformed" or "unofficial." For this reason, it is desirable that forecasts be "blessed" by top management in order to lend credibility to the forecast and encourage its use for planning purposes. In a similar light, broader participation in the development of a forecast, including users, can strengthen the organization's commitment to it. Finally, forecasting credibility can be enhanced by its appearance in a document signed by one or more high-ranking executives. In Freddie's case, for example, the memo should have been written by the marketing vice president, not Freddie.

The mechanisms for obtaining the blessings of top management will differ from situation to situation and from company to company. The price for the blessing may be adjustments to the forecast or it may be formal review by a committee. Armstrong[2] pointed out that adjustments to a forecast usually do not improve the accuracy of the forecast. In fact, he found some evidence that the adjusted forecasts are less accurate.[1] But the bottom line is that adjustments to forecasts are often essential if the forecasts are to be used.

9. *Distribute the Forecast to Those Who Need Them.* When a forecast is formally approved and released for use, there is still the danger that it will not be distributed to those who need it. To overcome this problem, the forecaster(s) should take the time to find out who might require the forecast and make sure that these individuals receive copies of all relevant reports. Our friend, Freddie, has washed his hands of this problem by simply directing his memo to his immediate boss. Such action is irresponsible.

10. *Update the Forecasts as Necessary.* At last we come to the problem of updating forecasts. Bad forecasting methodology is much worse than an inaccurate forecast, because the former is controllable whereas the latter usually is not. Updating a forecast is a vital part of the forecasting function. Thus, as new data become available, the forecast must be updated and redistributed. Presumably, the updated forecast will be more accurate and therefore more useful to the decision makers. Freddie is not planning on updating his forecast until he is told to do so. We all lose by such an attitude because valuable information will not be communicated and a vital task will go unfinished.

THE GUIDELINES APPLIED TO A PROTOTYPE PROBLEM

To illustrate the foregoing forecasting guidelines in a practical application, let us reexamine the forecasting problem of Freddie Falsepoint at the Metro City Telephone Company. A one-year forecast of product demand is required in order to project corporate revenues, hire training staff, schedule installation crews, and stock spare parts. Thus, the forecast must be prepared early enough for these subsequent activities to be executed in a timely fashion. A minimum would be three months lead time, that is, Freddie should complete his forecast by October 1 for the coming year.

Chart 31-3 illustrates a possible format. Here, the forecast has been prepared in units of equipment rather than in dollars because these are the relevant units to the decision makers—not dollar sales. Also note that (1) the forecast is disaggregated by product and (2) the forecast has been prepared by quarters. Disaggregation of the product forecast into different product lines is important because not all telephone installers will be familiar with all types of equipment and, of course, spare parts requirements will vary with the type of equipment installed. Similarly, the forecast has been prepared by quarters to aid decision makers—in this case because the installation of commercial phone equipment follows construction cycles and is not uniform throughout the year.

For each quarter, a range of possible demand values is shown in parentheses. These represent worst-case and best-case projections whose statistical properties are explained in an appendix. The inclusion of worst-case and best-cast values is important here because training and spare parts decisions may depend on these extremes rather than on the norms. This format (using parentheses) is not the only one possible but it is systematic, easily readable, and allows the listing of products along the left-hand margin and the listing of quarters across the top of the page. This data arrangement parallels the format of Metro's budgetary reports and is therefore convenient to managers.

After the forecast has been prepared, Freddie should obtain the formal approval of top management and draft a memo for vice-presidential signature. As noted previously, this will lend credibility to the forecast and make

CHART 31-3. The Telephone Forecast of Chart 31-1 Revised

Metro City Telephone Company
forecast demand for switchboard products
for fiscal year 19XX

	Quarter 1	Quarter 2	Quarter 3	Quarter 4	Year Total
Key Systems					
Product A	10	15	7	10	42
	(8–12)	(10–20)	(5–9)	(8–12)	(31–53)
Product B	2	9	5	4	20
	(0–3)	(7–11)	(2–8)	(0–7)	(9–29)
⋮	⋮	⋮	⋮	⋮	⋮
Product K	8	12	6	7	33
	(7–9)	(5–14)	(3–10)	(4–10)	(19–43)
Subtotals	XXX	XXX	XXX	XXX	XXX
	(X–Y)	(X–Y)	(X–Y)	(X–Y)	(X–Y)
PBXs					
Product M	0	0	1	2	3
	(0–1)	(0–2)	(0–3)	(0–3)	(0–9)
Product N	3	4	2	1	10
	(0–4)	(1–5)	(0–3)	(0–2)	(1–14)
⋮	⋮	⋮	⋮	⋮	⋮
Product Z	0	2	0	0	2
	(0–1)	(0–3)	(0–1)	(0–1)	(0–6)
Subtotals	XXX	XXX	XXX	XXX	XXX
	(X–Y)	(X–Y)	(X–Y)	(X–Y)	(X–Y)
Grand totals	XXX	XXX	XXX	XXX	XXX
	(X–Y)	(X–Y)	(X–Y)	(X–Y)	(X–Y)

it "official." This will probably not assure greater accuracy in the forecast, but it will enable managers to plan in unison.

After the forecast has been "blessed" by top management, Freddie should distribute it to the appropriate decision makers. These tasks will take time, again emphasizing the need for advanced planning and long lead times in forecast preparation. Although a written memo is the most common medium with which to distribute the forecast, such alternatives as the creation of data-base files or customized floppy disks for use with microcomputers can also be explored.

Finally, the forecast should be updated periodically to permit adjustments to inventory, training, or installation decisions. In general, the need to update forecasts will vary with the application. In this case, quarterly revisions would be advisable.

MICROCOMPUTER-ASSISTED FORECASTING

Both the developers and the users of decision-oriented forecasts may make good uses of microcomputers and related software. One possibility, of course, is to use microcomputer software packages for developing the forecasts themselves. Examples of such software would include statistical packages, data-reduction routines, and the newly emerging decision-support tools now available for microcomputer usage.[9] Some of these packages permit the user to download data from corporate data bases stored on mainframe computers, thereby facilitating access to current data and freeing the user from laborious data-entry chores.

Perhaps the most valuable software tool currently available on microcomputers is the electronic spreadsheet. A spreadsheet can assist managers by (1) organizing and formating data downloaded from mainframe data bases, (2) allowing decision makers to design custom forecasting models, (3) enabling managers to examine the implications of alternate forecast magnitudes or combinations of magnitudes, and (4) graphing data using integrated graphics routines.

From a decision-making standpoint, spreadsheets are perhaps most important for their ability to perform "what-if" analyses using custom models and forecast values as starting points. For example, the user can examine best-case and worst-case projections of future demand to assess their cash-planning implications.

Although it is not the purpose of this chapter to examine spreadsheet modeling techniques in detail, it should be clear that good models facilitate "what-if" simulation processes and therefore enhance the user's decision-making capability. Useful tips on the construction of such models may be found in Simkin[6] and a list of important documentation techniques may be found in Grupe.[3]

Finally, microcomputers can be used to create graphic output. Of course, graphic output is not limited to microcomputers, but because of integrated graphics routines in spreadsheet software, microcomputers are often the most convenient way of creating such output.

In forecasting and decision-making, graphs are often used to depict the past and to suggest the future. An example of such a graph is the sales forecast shown in Chart 31-4. However, care must always be taken when preparing a graph, because graphs can mislead managers. For example, the graph in Chart 31-4 uses a vertical axis running from 450,000 to 500,000. This exaggerates the variation in sales and can cause managers to overreact to the random variation in the data.[4,5] When the data are plotted (as in Chart 31-5) with an axis of 0 to 500,000 the variation is put in perspective.

With data such as those in Chart 31-4, managers often see patterns even when the data are random.[8,10,12] The best way to avoid this misinterpretation is to properly plot the data (as in Chart 31-5) and explicitly state on the graph

CHART 31-4. Graph Forecasting Sales in 1987 and 1988

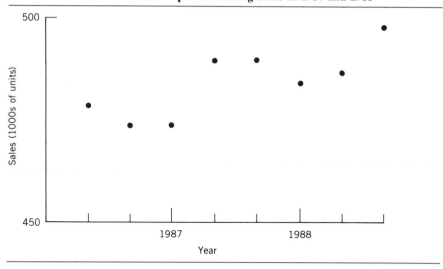

CHART 31-5. Chart 31-4 Revised to Show Complete Vertical Axis and Confidence Interval. Note: There is no statistically significant pattern in the data.

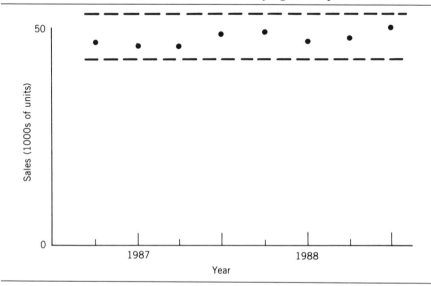

that there is no statistically significant pattern. Naturally, tests will need to be conducted prior to making that statement. Proper graphs also avoid a second problem. When, due to randomness, a new observation is other than expected, the manager may believe that there is a change in the pattern and infer a cause for that random variation.[4,12]

When managers make intuitive forecasts, they "anchor" on past data, forecast the next point, and then "adjust" that point to reflect their beliefs about what will really happen.[7,11] Such a process yields a point estimate that is one of many reasonable forecasts. To reflect the range of forecast, the forecaster should depict the range as a confidence interval on the graph. While this will not stop the intuitive point estimating, it will prompt the manager to also consider the worst and best cases (that is, the extremes of the confidence interval).

Even though graphic displays can mislead managers, they also can help managers understand forecasts and the forecast's limitations. Graphs are also very useful in helping to convince others of the best course of action to take. For the latter reason alone, graphic displays are increasingly used in forecasting and decision making.

SUMMARY

When forecasts are used as inputs to aid decision-making activities, it is important that the forecast be oriented to this purpose. In this chapter we have identified 10 characteristics of forecasts that make them useful for managerial decision making. These characteristics deal with the dimensions of (1) timeliness, (2) decision-making units. (3) level of aggregation, (4) seasonality, (5) forecast ranging, (6) explanatory appendices, (7) understandability, (8) top management approval, (9) distribution, and (10) updating. The closer a forecast adheres to the guidelines involving these items, the more useful the forecast is likely to be for decision-making purposes.

A second part of this chapter illustrated the application of the guidelines to a product–demand forecast. The purpose of this section was to demonstrate how the guidelines might be applied to a typical prototype problem and might improve the usefulness of the forecast for decision making.

The final part of this chapter discussed the usefulness of microcomputers to the twin processes of forecasting and decision making. It was noted that microcomputers can be used (1) to create forecasts using a wide variety of currently available software packages, (2) to download data from corporate data bases, (3) to distribute forecasts from a central computer, (4) to design customized forecasting models—for example, on spreadsheets, (5) to explore the implications of forecasts to individual departments—for example, again using spreadsheets or other simulation packages, and (6) to create graphs.

REFERENCES

1. Armstrong, J. Scott, *Long Range Forecasting,* John Wiley, New York, 1978.

2. Armstrong, J. Scott, "Evidence on the Value of Experts in Forecasting: The Seer-Sucker Theory," Working Paper No. 79-035, Wharton School, University of Pennsylvania, Philadelphia, 1979.

3. Grupe, F., "Tops for Better Worksheet Documentation," *LOTUS,* August, 1985, pp. 68–70.

4. Langer, E. J., "The Psychology of Chance," *Journal for the Theory of Social Behaviour,* vol. 7, no. 2, 1977, pp. 185–207.

5. Lathrop, R. G., "Perceived Variability," *Journal of Experimental Psychology,* vol. 73, 1967, pp. 498–502.

6. Simkin, M. G., "Nonfinancial Modeling Techniques on Electronic Spreadsheets," *Collegiate Microcomputer,* November, 1985.

7. Slovic, P., and S. Lichtenstein, "Comparison of Bayesian and Regression Approaches to the Study of Information Processing in Judgment," *Organization Behavior and Human Performance,* vol. 6, 1971, pp. 649–744.

8. Smedslund, J., "The Concept of Correlation in Adults," *Scandinavian Journal of Psychology,* vol. 4, 1963, pp. 165–173.

9. Spezzano, C., "Decision Support Software," *Popular Computing,* October, 1985, pp. 56+.

10. Tversky, A., and D. Kahneman, "Availability: A Heuristic for Judging Frequency and Probability," *Cognitive Psychology,* vol. 5, 1973, pp. 207–232.

11. Tversky, A., and D. Kahneman, "Judgment under Uncertainty: Heuristics and Biases," *Science,* vol. 185, 1974, pp. 1124–1131.

12. Ward, W. C., and H. M. Jenkins, "The Display of Information and the Judgment of Contingency," *Canadian Journal of Psychology,* vol. 19, 1965, pp. 231–241.

BIBLIOGRAPHY

Delbecq, Andre L., Andrew H. Van de Ven, and David H. Gustafson, *Group Techniques for Program Planning,* Scott, Foresman, Glenview, IL, 1975.

Ewing, D. E., *The Human Side of Planning,* Macmillan, Toronto, 1969.

MacCrimmon, Kenneth R., and Ronald N. Taylor, "Decision Making and Problem Solving," in Marvin D. Dunnette, ed., *Handbook of Industrial and Organizational Psychology* Rand-McNally, Chicago, 1976, pp. 1397–453.

Mockler, R. J., *Business Planning and Policy Formulation,* Appleton- Century-Crofts, New York, 1972.

Murphy, Alan H., and Robert L. Winkler, "Subjective Probability Forecasting: Some Real World Experiments," in Dirk Wendt and Charles Vlek, eds., *Utility, Probability, and Human Decision Making,* D. Reidel, Dordrecht, 1975.

Sackman, H., *Delphi Critique: Expert Opinion, Forecasting, and Group Processes,* Lexington Books, Washington, DC, 1975.

Slovic, Paul, Baruch Fischhoff, and Sara Lichtenstein, "Behavioral Decision Theory," *Annual Review of Psychology,* Annual Reviews, Inc., 1977, pp. 1–39.

Spetzler, C. S., and Carl A. S. Stael von Holstein, "Probability Encoding in Decision Analysis," *Management Science,* vol. 22, 1975, pp. 279–300.

Swalm, Ralph O., "Utility Theory: Insights into Risk Taking," *Harvard Business Review,* vol. 44, 1966, pp. 123–131.

Vroom, Victor H., and Philip W. Yetton, *Leadership and Decision-Making,* University of Pittsburg Press, Pittsburg, 1973.

Wheelwright, Steven C., and Darral G. Clarke, "Corporate Forecasting: Promise and Reality," *Harvard Business Review,* November-December 1976, p. 40.

Winkler, Robert L., "Probabilistic Prediction: Some Experimental Results," *Journal of the American Statistical Association,* vol. 66, 1971, pp. 675–685.

Woods, Donald H., "Improving Estimates that Involve Uncertainty," *Harvard Business Review,* vol. 44, 1966, pp. 91–98.

CHAPTER

32

THE FORECASTING AUDIT

J. SCOTT ARMSTRONG
Wharton School,
University of Pennsylvania,
Philadelphia

How do you know the forecasting procedures in an organization are reasonable? This chapter provides a checklist to conduct an audit of such procedures. The checklist should also help identify ways to improve forecasting within the organization. Although the discussion is presented in the context of sales forecasting, many of the principles are relevant to other forecasting situations.

THE SALES FORECAST

Imagine the following scene in the boardroom of a large corporation called Ajax:

Chairperson: The next thing on the agenda is a description of the sales forecasts for our company, provided by Mr. Raft, our chief executive officer.

Raft: Today I present to you the annual forecasts for our firm, covering the next five years. We take this forecasting task seriously. Top management was actively involved. As these managers are the ones who use the forecasts, it was appropriate that they also be involved in making the forecasts. Our industry is characterized by rapid change and a turbulent environment, and thus we realize that historical data provide

William Ascher, Robin Hogarth, Robert Fildes, Spyros Makridakis, and Kranti Toraskar provided useful comments on earlier versions of this chapter.

a poor guide to the future. Rather, we must be forward looking and use judgment. As a result, the members of our top management team spent many hours in meetings with me to prepare these forecasts.

In the final analysis, forecasting is more of an art than a science; nothing can currently replace experience and good judgment. Therefore, we sought the best experts. We hired one of the top economic consultants and obtained his opinions on the economic future of our firm.

We used the best possible method to prepare the forecasts. As I mentioned, it was essentially a judgmental procedure. But we also examined output from some highly sophisticated computer models. Of course, we used our judgment to modify the forecasts from these computer models.

The judgmental procedure we used with our management team also helped to achieve commitment to the forecasts. Since all those concerned have agreed to these forecasts, we intend to meet these forecasts!

Our most important need was to obtain more information. We spent much time and money this year to seek out whatever data were needed. This required that we obtain data from all areas of the company. In addition, we subscribed to one of the most prestigious econometric services so that we would have early access to their short-range macroeconomic forecasts.

Before I present the forecasts, some comment about last year's forecast is in order. Sales and profits at Ajax were lower than we had forecasted. Actually, we had been optimistic when we made last year's forecast. Also, the growth in the economy leveled off due to government policies. So the results were not surprising, after all.

The forecasts for the next five years are provided in the tables of the report before you. Overall, we have forecasted a growth in dollar sales of 12.5% for next year with an increase in profits of 16%. We believe that these figures will improve in years 2 through 5. For that time we are forecasting annual growth of 15% in sales and 20% in profits. Roughly half of the increase will be due to inflation and half to growth in unit sales. These forecasts provide our best assessment of the future. We are confident of them.

For the rest of the meeting, I suggest that you examine the forecasts. They cover in detail our eight major product areas for our three major geographic markets for each of the next five years. We believe you will find these forecasts reasonable and realistic.

A long discussion of the forecasts followed. Numerous questions were raised and answered. The board concluded unanimously that the forecasts were reasonable.

What is wrong with the Ajax meeting? Many things. My study of forecasting problems over the past 25 years has led to some guidelines for a reasonable forecasting process. I tried to violate as many guidelines as I could in the Ajax case. Perhaps you would like to reread the Ajax description to see how many things you believe to be wrong with it.

PITFALLS IN FORECASTING . . . AND SOLUTIONS

The Ajax case provides examples of forecasting pitfalls. These are listed in the following, and suggestions are made for corrective actions. Some of the solutions will seem counterintuitive. When possible, I have tried to base the recommendations on empirical studies. A set of references is provided in case you would like additional information.

Pitfall 1: Involvement of Top Management in Preparing Forecasts

Top management should be involved with forecasting, but not in the actual preparation of the forecasts. This is because of numerous problems, most notably that top management is likely to be biased toward a favorable view of the future (e.g., Larwood and Whittaker[27]). Managers find it difficult to use evidence that is contradictory to their own view. Also, the reward system in the company could bias their forecasts. Furthermore, their success over the years has given them too much confidence in their own judgment. Top management's time is also expensive. [This conclusion that top management should not prepare forecasts must be tempered by findings related to short-term financial forecasting; here, management forecasts of annual corporate earnings are more accurate than those by analysts or extrapolations (Armstrong[4]).]

Solutions: Management should decide what forecasts are needed. Managers' plans and opinions should be used as inputs in developing forecasts. They should also be involved in ensuring that the forecasting process is reasonable and that the proper data has been used. However, they should generally not be involved in analyzing the data to produce forecasts.

Pitfall 2: Excessive Use of Judgment

Numerous surveys of corporate forecasting practices agree with what most of us suspect: The most important forecasts usually are made judgmentally.

Opinion-based techniques are the most popular of the forecasting methods in firms (e.g., Dalrymple[9]). The use of judgment is especially prevalent in forecasting for long-range planning.

Although experts are good at telling how things are now, they are not good at forecasting *changes*. Objective methods are typically more accurate. The further one goes into the future, the less emphasis one should place on judgment and the more one should place on objective methods. This recommendation contradicts common sense; however, the limited research to date supports such a conclusion (Armstrong,[6] Chapter 15).

Solutions: If possible, decrease the use of judgmental methods for long-range forecasting. Judgment can be used as a source of data, but it should not be used to analyze the data. For analysis of data, reliance should be placed on methods such as extrapolation or econometrics. These methods are more accurate and, because they are easier to replicate, are less prone to tampering.

If elimination of judgmental methods is not possible, much can be done to improve them. The use of data banks and presentation techniques is helpful (for more on this, see solutions to Pitfall 10). Structured procedures for collecting and analyzing subjective forecasts provide another approach.

Judgment is useful for certain aspects of forecasting, such as in assessing the current situation. Experts can estimate current sales and can identify where changes have occurred and where forecasting assumptions are no longer valid. When judgment is used, the judgmental procedures should be carefully recorded. For example, how was the forecast question posed, who provided the forecasts, and when were they made? These procedures should also be examined against evidence on good practice as represented by the literature on judgmental forecasting. Stewart and Glantz[43] used such a procedure to audit a weather forecasting study by the U.S. National Defense University.

Pitfall 3: Unstructured Meetings

Organizations frequently develop their forecasts in unstructured meetings. When using experts to make forecasts or to provide inputs to forecasts, use at least three experts, or better yet, use 6 to 10; seldom would you need more than 20.[21,30] Larger groups are helpful when the experts have relevant knowledge yet differ among one another, when uncertainty is great, and when the cost of errors is high. Lack of structure during the meeting of experts can lead to conformity among the group members, however. You can get "one opinion six times" when you have a six-person meeting with the boss present.

Solutions: Obtain independent contributions from each expert. Structured techniques, such as the developmental discussion, can be used to reduce conformity in group meetings. For developmental discussions, the group leader prepares for the meeting by decomposing the problem so the group can work on it. During the meeting the leader provides an opportunity for all group members to participate, especially those with minority opinions; helps the group avoid evaluation; and does not add his or her own ideas. Consensus-seeking techniques have also helped to improve group forecasts.[22] Alternatively, you can simply eliminate the meeting by using questionnaires or the Delphi technique.

The Delphi technique calls for distributing more than one round of questionnaires to the same group of experts. They receive an anonymous summary of the group responses from their previous round, and they answer the same question a second time. Johnson[23] presented an example of the use of Delphi for a long-range market forecast at Corning Glass Works. Martino[32] provided descriptions of Delphi. Sackman[39] presented a skeptic's viewpoint, and Armstrong[6] reviewed the empirical evidence. As with other aspects of judgmental forecasting, detailed records should be kept on how the group made the forecasts. This can be important for demonstrating the integrity of the forecast. It will also aid in determining how to improve the process.

Pitfall 4: Use of the Most Expensive Expert

The use of the most expensive expert provides reassurance to top management. The more prestigious and more expensive the expert, the greater is the reassurance. Unfortunately, this reassurance is unjustified. Findings from extensive research on expert forecasts have led to a surprising conclusion: We do not know how to identify experts who will provide the best forecasts of change. This applies whether expertise is based on self-assessments, education, experience, or previous accuracy.[6]

Solutions: Some minimum level of expertise is required in the subject area of the forecast. Typically, however, this minimum is achieved quickly. These results have been obtained through research findings in psychology, finance, medicine, sociology, and other areas. The implication is interesting and valuable: Select inexpensive experts. Use the savings to hire *additional* experts.

In addition to reducing costs, it is also important to avoid bias. Specify the criteria for expertise in advance of expert selection. These specifications should be retained, along with a list of the experts considered and of those used.

Pitfall 5: Reliance on a Single Method

Typically, uncertainty exists about which forecasting method to use. Despite this, management often feels that one method must be best. The selection of the one best method is risky. For one thing, you might choose incorrectly.

Furthermore, even though a method may be best in principle, mistakes may occur in the use of the method.

Solutions: Be eclectic. Instead of devoting the budget to the presumably one best method, spread it among two or three reasonable methods. Preferably these methods should differ substantially from one another. That is, they should use different information, and they should process the information in different ways. This procedure means that you spend less on any one method and thus reduce its *reliability*. However, if the final forecast is based on an average of the forecasts from each method, it will gain modestly in accuracy because of compensating errors.[7] More important, combining helps to avoid large errors due to mistakes.

A variety of forecasting methods are available. Most methods can be described in terms of five categories: judgment, expert systems, extrapolation, econometrics, and segmentation. These categories are based not on the type of data but on *the way in which the data are analyzed:*

1. *Judgment.* The data are analyzed in the head. This category includes structured judgmental techniques such as questionnaires or Delphi.

2. *Expert systems* (also called "bootstrapping"). The judgmental rules have been formalized into an objective process. This can be done either by asking the forecaster to describe the forecasting procedure or by inferring the rules from a statistical examination of a set of forecasts.

3. *Extrapolation.* These methods use only the data on the variable to be forecast. They do not assess causality, but merely project the data using a mechanized procedure. Typical ways to extrapolate include the use of regression of the variable against time, of moving averages, and of exponential smoothing.

4. *Econometrics.* These methods use causal relationships in a formal way. The relationships can be estimated by a variety of techniques, but most common is the use of regression analysis.

5. *Segmentation.* These methods try to identify segments of similar decision-making units. Separate forecasts are then made of the population and behavior of each segment and the segment forecasts are added. (When using segmentation, one would draw on methods 1, 2, 3, or 4 to obtain forecasts within each segment.)

Numerous sources provide detailed descriptions of forecasting methods, especially methods 2, 3, and 4 (e.g., Levenbach and Cleary[29]). Guidelines on which methods are most appropriate for which situation are provided in Armstrong.[6,Ch. 15] Evidence on which methods are most accurate in different situations is provided in Armstrong[6] and Fildes.[13]

Pitfall 6: Highly Sophisticated Methods

Surprisingly, relatively simple methods are as accurate as highly sophisticated methods. For example, Armstrong,[1,2] in a review of published studies, found simple econometric methods to be as accurate as complex econometric methods. Similar results were obtained also for extrapolation methods.[5] Simple methods are also easier to understand, less expensive, and less prone to errors.

Solutions: A good rule of thumb is that the model should be simple enough so it can be understood by the user. As one test of understanding, users should be able to calculate the forecasts by hand. Another less stringent test is that the user should be able to describe the method to someone else.

Records should be maintained on what methods were considered, what criteria were used to select methods, and what forecasts were obtained from each of these methods. To support the use of these methods, one can rely on the published literature. For example, one guideline for econometric models is that they should only include variables that have a causal relationship with the variable being forecasted.

Pitfall 7: Judgmental Revision of Forecasts

Forecasters, and sometimes users of forecasts, make subjective adjustments to forecasts derived from objective methods. Early research suggested that subjective adjustments often make the forecasts less accurate.[19,25] Subjective adjustments are most detrimental where change is large. Research in economic forecasting has yielded different results: Subjective adjustments have yielded mixed results. It appears that for short-range economic forecasts, subjective adjustments have often helped, but they have not done so in long-range forecasting. My hypothesis is that the gain from judgment in improving the estimate of the *current situation* may outweigh the poorer forecasts of *changes*. Thus, in the short run, where changes are small, subjective adjustments should improve accuracy. Support for this is provided in McNees.[35]

Financial auditors,[10] psychologists, and weather forecasters[36] have concluded that subjective revisions are undesirable. The problem is particularly serious if the revisions are made by people who may be biased. Even if unbiased, the forecasters may lose credibility by making revisions. Glantz[16] described the forecast of a drought by the U.S. Bureau of Reclamation in 1977. This forecast led farmers to take expensive actions to save crops. (As one farmer put it, "Drought is when the government sends you a report telling you there's no water.") The forecast was not accurate and the government was sued for malpractice in forecasting. The key point in the suit was that while the objective forecast was somewhat on target, judgmental revisions caused the big error. The suit claimed that the revision procedure represented poor practice.

Solutions: Experts often have useful information to contribute. In particular, they have good information about the current situation and about plans for the future. One way to use this information is to make subjective estimates of current status. Another approach is to make subjective *inputs* to the model that forecasts change. Still another approach is to obtain expert forecasts and then to average these with objective forecasts. It seems risky, however, to make subjective revisions of forecasts after they have been obtained by an objective method; this often reduces accuracy.

In the event that judgment is used, it should be identified. A record should be made of the size of the adjustment and of the forecast errors with and without the adjustments. This audit trail is one of the most important steps in substantiating the integrity of the forecast. Without this, how can one assess why the forecast was in error? This tracking also allows one to see where the plan departs from the forecast.

Pitfall 8: Confusion Between the Plan and the Forecast

Management often fails to distinguish between the plan and the forecast. The plan is a formal description of objectives, the strategies that the organization intends to use in pursuing these goals, and the scheme used to monitor progress. These terms are also confused in the literature. For example, Vancil's article[45] in the *Harvard Business Review* was entitled "The Accuracy of Long-Range Planning"!

People in an organization should work to meet their plan, that is, to carry out their various marketing, production, and financial strategies. It is the plan, not the forecast, that should provide motivation for action. The forecast tells what is likely to happen, given the organization's environment, capabilities, and plan. The company should try to meet the plan, not to meet the forecast.

Solutions: Two separate reports should be prepared, one to describe the plan and the other to provide forecasts for each set of plans. The forecasting and planning processes interact, but they should each be treated separately. Certainly management can change plans to better achieve the organization's objectives. But the forecasts should be independently prepared for each plan. These forecasts should be easy to replicate, which again emphasizes the desirability of using objective methods.

Said another way, if the forecast is not satisfactory to management, the plan should be changed, not the forecast. Changing the forecast is analogous to changing the weather forecast to make a picnic a success. It can lead to charges of malpractice in forecasting.

Pitfall 9: Collection of Too Much Data

Obviously, we need information to make good forecasts. Surprisingly, however, we quickly reach the point where "more information" adds little value. This is especially true with judgmental forecasts, because the human mind is not capable of handling large amounts of data.[17] Also, it is likely that the forecaster will use irrelevant information if it is provided.[24] Objective methods make better use of large amounts of data, but even here additional data produce only modest gains.[6]

I suspect that the attempt to get more information is often a way to avoid making a forecast. Furthermore, one can avoid responsibility for the forecast by claiming that the data were inadequate.

The situation is not much different if "better" rather than "more" information is being sought. Improvements in the quality of the data beyond a modest level have not been shown to produce more accurate forecasts. This holds true even for econometric models.[11,33] For example, the accuracy of ex ante short-range forecasts, those in which the causal variables were forecasted, is not better than the accuracy of ex post short-range forecasts, in which the values used for the causal variables were known.[6] The explanation for this is not known, although some question whether the studies were designed so as to allow for a conclusion on the issue. In many of the studies, a subjective adjustment occurred for the ex ante but not for the ex post forecasting.

Solutions: It is popular to say that we want more information. This often leads to an expensive search and it delays decisions. Often, we make poor use of information already available. Forecasters should limit the budget for information and allocate more to methods for analyzing and using the existing information. Records should be kept on what data were sought and which were used, and, the expenditures on data collection and analysis should be tracked.

Pitfall 10: Selection of Data to Support Management's Beliefs

Management often seeks the data it needs in making its forecast. The danger in this approach is that the search for data may be structured to support management's beliefs. In other words, there is selective use of data. This search for "confirming evidence" is common even among scientists, who are presumably trained to look for disconfirming evidence.[3]

Solutions: The creation of a central data bank will help to overcome the biased use of data. The organization should decide in advance what types of data might possibly be relevant for each type of strategic decision. One way to do this would be to ask managers to specify what information is needed to make better forecasts. Another approach is to take an inventory of the information that is currently being used by the company in preparing forecasts. Still another approach is for the forecaster to decide what information would be useful. The important information would be collected routinely and stored in a central data bank (which could be a computer, a chart room, or a notebook). Unfortunately, one defect of this approach is that, for any given decision, the data bank will also contain many irrelevant data. This suggests that the central data bank should not be large; otherwise managers can find irrelevant data to confirm their beliefs.

Failure to monitor and use relevant data on a timely basis could lead to charges of malpractice. For example, the National Weather Service was sued by relatives of three fishermen who died in a storm at sea. The charge was that the Weather Service was negligent in repairing a damaged weather buoy that could have helped to predict the storm (*Philadelphia Inquirer*, 20 May 1984).

The presentation of the historical data may also be important if the data are used as an aid to judgmental forecasts. Tables can present data in simple ways. Even better, it would seem, are graphs. The graphs can display long historical trends to help overcome the problems that arise when experts weight the latest information too heavily. This advice to prepare graphs would seem to be common sense. Unfortunately, it is not so simple. An extensive review by deSantics[12] found much empirical evidence on the topic, but little of this evidence supported the value of graphic presentation for decision making. More directly related to forecasting, Lawrence and colleagues[28] found that subjects given graphs of historical time series data did not make more accurate extrapolations from the data then did those given tables.

Caution is needed when situations involve rapid exponential growth (growth by a constant percentage per year). Recent research suggests that judgmental forecasts greatly underestimate such growth. The suggestions for dealing with such problems are counterintuitive:

1. Observe the data at less frequent intervals.[47]

2. If possible, use an inverse representation of growth (e.g., to forecast population density, use square miles per person rather than people per square mile). People are better able to forecast exponential growth when it is expressed as a decreasing function.[44]

Here again, graphic presentation was not superior to tables.[46]

Pitfall 11: Use of an Econometric Service for Short-Range Forecasting

Ajax subscribed to an econometric service. It was not alone in its belief that econometrics provided more accurate short-range forecasts. Conclusions on this topic have varied over the years. For example, a recent review of the evidence[13] concluded that econometric methods are a bit more accurate. My own view based on a meta-analysis of the evidence, is that econometric methods have not produced significant improvements in accuracy in comparison with judgmental or extrapolation for *short-range* forecasting methods.[2,3,6] Furthermore, no significant differences in accuracy have been found among the various econometric forecasting services.[20,34]

Solutions: Reduce or eliminate expenditures for short-range forecasts from econometric services. Some econometric forecasts are available at no cost. Alternative sources of macroeconomic forecasts, such as extrapolations from surveys of business economists, are available at low cost.

Econometric models are useful for long-range forecasting. When outside services are used, keep track of the accuracy of each method along with its cost.

Pitfall 12: No Estimates of Uncertainty

According to Winston Churchill, "The most essential qualification for a politician is the ability to foretell what will happen tomorrow, next month, and next year, and to explain afterwards why it did not happen." This qualification is also useful to forecasters.

We deceive ourselves when we look back at our forecasts. Our subconscious is largely responsible. We are seldom surprised by the actual outcome, no matter how different it is from our prediction. To demonstrate this, Fischhoff and Beyth[14] asked people to make predictions of political and social events. After the events occurred, the people were asked to recall what predictions they had made. Often they remembered incorrectly what they had predicted: They remembered predicting the actual outcome even when they had predicted otherwise. When a subject had *written* the prediction and could see that it was incorrect, he or she would rationalize, claiming: "Yes, I wrote that, but I really knew it would happen the way it did."

Unfortunately, forecasters must contend with decision makers who would rather not hear about the uncertainties. As a result, uncertainty is often ignored. In a study on long-range metals forecasts, Rush and Page[38] found that only 22% of the 27 forecasts published from 1910 to 1940 made explicit references to uncertainty. From 1940 to 1964 the situation became worse, as only 8% of the 63 studies estimated uncertainty.

Solutions: Rationalizing that "we knew it would happen" may help us to survive in organizations, and it helps us to get through life without changing our beliefs. Nevertheless, we can take steps to deal with this habit of discarding conflicting information. One procedure is to determine in advance what forecasts would be "surprising." The simplest way to do this is to ask management to provide upper and lower bounds.

If politically feasible, uncertainty estimates should be presented along with the forecasts. At the very least, they should be offered, and they should be recorded by the forecaster. Upper and lower bounds can be calculated from objective methods. Williams and Goodman[49] showed how statistical confidence intervals, calculated from short-range forecasts of changes in the number of telephones in service, provided good estimates of the precision of the forecasts (90% of the outcomes were within the 95% confidence intervals).

Much care should be exercised if subjective estimates are used to obtain the upper and lower bounds. Estimates by a single expert are unlikely to be accurate.[31] This has been demonstrated in a study of one-year-ahead sales forecasts by Schreuder and Klaassen.[41] Management was asked to specify limits outside of which they were *sure* the actual value would not fall (100% confidence intervals!). In fact, 35% of the sales forecasts fell outside these limits. Furthermore, the use of confidence estimates has come under challenge in courtrooms; Wells and Murray[48] have shown that eyewitness confidence has little relationship to accuracy. However, if a number of experts are used, their average confidence levels will have some validity.

If upper and lower bounds have not been previously established, all is not lost. False outcomes can be prepared and presented to unsuspecting experts, who can be asked if the outcomes are surprising. The true outcomes can then be provided. A similar approach helped to reduce "hindsight bias."[42]

Pitfall 13: No Analysis of Previous Accuracy

Companies often fail to provide a quantitative appraisal of the accuracy of previous forecasts. In Dalrymple's survey,[9] half of the firms reported that they did not keep a good track record. A formal assessment might be useful in identifying the most appropriate forecasting methods. It can also be useful in identifying whether forecasts are being used properly. For example, Griffith and Wellman,[18] in a retrospective study of forecasts for six hospitals, found that when the forecast disagreed with management's prior beliefs, the forecast was ignored.

Solution: Summarize the accuracy of the methods that were used to make forecasts for the past year as well as for previous years. Examine the forecasts from the various methods to determine whether the differences among them are statistically significant. An analysis of ex ante and ex post forecasting errors may help identify the reasons for errors.

Pitfall 14: No Analysis of Alternative Futures

Companies often make their "best assessment of the future." However, much uncertainty often exists about the future. Changes might occur in the environment (e.g., the government imposes tariffs on the company's products) or in the organization's capabilities (e.g., the factory burns down). Alternatively, the company may fail to meet its plan (e.g., people in the organization were not committed to the plan, or the plan might not have been within the capability of the organization).

Solutions: Rather than providing *the* forecast, provide forecasts for a set of alternative futures. These forecasts should cover different possibilities for the organization's:

- environment,
- capabilities, and
- plans

Especially important are forecasts dealing with unfavorable environments. Management can then make contingency plans in light of these forecasts for alternative environments. This helps keep the organization open to change.

Forecasts of alternative futures can be presented as scenarios (short stories). This focuses attention on the forecast, and it also allows the organization to decide on plans appropriate for each scenario. (Much useful research has been published on scenarios in the past few years; see the review in Armstrong.[6]) These scenarios should *not* be used to assess the likelihood of occurrence. Rather, they are used after the forecasts have been made to draw attention to these possibilities.

Pitfall 15: Overconfidence

Read the following sentence:

FINISHED FILES ARE THE RESULT OF YEARS OF SCIENTIFIC STUDY COMBINED WITH THE EXPERIENCE OF YEARS.

Count aloud the number of times the letter "F" appears in the sentence. Count only once; do not go back and count again. Record your answer here: __. Now state your confidence in your answer on a scale from 0, meaning that you are sure you are incorrect, to 100%, meaning that you are sure you are correct. Record your answer here: __.

Most people feel confident of their answers. A convenience sample of 50 Wharton MBA students reported an average confidence level of about 91% for the letter-F test. But these confidence levels were *not* related to accuracy. For the 34% who had the correct answer (which is 6), the average confidence level was 87%. For the 66% who had incorrect answers (which ranged from 2 to 5), the average confidence level was 93%. The letter-F test illustrates that ratings of self-confidence by individuals are of such poor validity that one should assume them to be worthless for predictions of a single event (for evidence on this, see Fischhoff and MacGregor[15]). When experts work on forecasts, they typically gain confidence in those forecasts. This gain in confidence has little relationship to accuracy, especially when the task itself provides little feedback. Confidence by forecasters falsely reduces anxiety among those who use the forecasts.

Solutions: Be skeptical of subjective assessments of confidence made by an expert—or by yourself. Look for objective assessments (Armstrong[6] describes ways to obtain these). As mentioned previously, the best way to assess confidence is to see how well a given forecasting method has done in previous forecasts.

Interestingly, a better assessment of confidence can be made if the forecaster concentrates on reasons why the forecast would be incorrect. As shown,[8,26] the examination of contradictory reasons for a given prediction will lead to a better assessment of the uncertainty surrounding that prediction. This procedure helps to remove the optimistic bias. It also provides some evidence that an unbiased forecasting process was used. Records should be kept that describe the procedure actually used.

Pitfall 16: Poor Accounting of Costs and Benefits

No mention was made of the cost of the forecast. Quite often firms spend too little on forecasting; at other times they spend too much. According to a survey of 52 firms by Rothe,[37] few firms keep track of expenditures on forecasting.

Solutions: Ideally, firms should continue to increase expenditures on forecasting as long as they obtain a good rate of return on this investment. In practice, the benefit is not easy to determine. On the other hand, large departures from good practice might be spotted. Schnee,[40] for example, concluded that spending on weather forecasts in the United States is much larger than the savings that might result even if the forecasts were perfect.

Keep a separate record for the cost of forecasting. Also, though it is usually difficult to assess, it is helpful to estimate the cost/benefit ratio for each forecasting method.

Some general guidelines on expenditures might be established. One rule of thumb[6] is that expenditures for forecasting should not exceed 1% of dollar sales volume. This might be adjusted in light of the situation (e.g., lower budgets for large companies).

Of course, one must be diplomatic when presenting data on costs. Costs are firm, while benefits are speculative. This puts the forecaster in a tough position, especially when profits are low.

USING THE CHECKLIST

Managers are often asked to examine the forecasts. But are they experts at judging whether the forecasts are reasonable? Perhaps managers judge how "favorable" the forecasts are, rather than how reasonable they are.

Rather than giving extensive concern to the forecasts, the manager should concentrate on the *forecasting process*. Is this process reasonable in this situation? Forecasters can help in forecast auditing if they keep good records. The use of a notebook can be especially helpful in documenting the process used. People often differ on what is a reasonable forecasting method

CHART 32-1. Forecasting Audit Checklist

Forecasting Methods	No	?	Yes
1. Forecast independent of top management?	____	____	____
2. Forecast used objective methods?	____	____	____
3. Structured techniques used to obtain judgments?	____	____	____
4. Least expensive experts used?	____	____	____
5. More than one method used to obtain forecasts?	____	____	____
6. Users understand the forecasting methods?	____	____	____
7. Forecasts free of judgmental revisions?	____	____	____
8. Separate documents prepared for plans and forecasts?	____	____	____
Assumptions and Data			
9. Ample budget for analysis and presentation of data?	____	____	____
10. Central data bank exists?	____	____	____
11. Least expensive macroeconomic forecasts used?	____	____	____
Uncertainty			
12. Upper and lower bounds provided?	____	____	____
13. Quantitative analysis of previous accuracy provided?	____	____	____
14. Forecasts prepared for alternative futures?	____	____	____
15. Arguments listed against each forecast?	____	____	____
Costs and Benefits			
16. Amount spent on forecasting reasonable?	____	____	____

to use. The forecaster might be accused of being biased if he or she has no record of the process. The "Forecaster's Notebook" or diary can protect the forecaster as well as the organization. Failure to have a documented and replicable forecasting process for important forecasts might be used as evidence of malpractice.

The Forecasting Audit Checklist (Chart 32-1) can help in the examination of the forecasting process. (The numbers in the checklist correspond to the pitfalls discussed in this chapter.) An advantage of concentrating on the forecasting process rather than on the forecast is that the process can be improved over time. This will help to improve accuracy and reduce costs. When one looks only at the forecast, there is little hope for progress. An old Chinese proverb says, "Give a man a fish, and you feed him for a day. Teach a man to fish, and you feed him for a lifetime."

Management should agree on an auditing process well in advance of the forecast review. For example, the Forecasting Audit Checklist could be provided to the forecasters so they will know what questions the management would like to address. I suggest a four-step procedure for the audit meeting. These steps are listed here with reference to the checklist:

> **1.** *Assess the methods without the forecasts.* Most of the discussion should focus on the methods. Which forecasting methods were considered, which ones were used, and why were they used? The auditor can

examine whether the methods are reasonable. (See checklist items 1 through 8.)

2. Given that the methods are judged reasonable, *what assumptions and data were used in the forecast?* (This step may be difficult to separate from the previous step.) The auditor should judge whether all relevant factors have been examined. (See items 9 through 11.)

3. *Assess the uncertainty of the forecast.* Include upper and lower bounds for each forecast, contingency forecasts, previous accuracy, and the arguments against each forecast. (See items 12 through 15.)

4. Finally, *assess the costs of the forecast* (See item 16.)

Management could use this four-step procedure as the agenda for the audit meeting.

SUMMARY

The Ajax case illustrated forecasting pitfalls in an organization. Numerous steps can be taken to improve on this approach. Some of these steps, not intuitively obvious, were drawn from research. Other steps were obvious and were included because they are sometimes forgotten.

The "Forecast Audit Checklist" consists of 16 questions about the forecasting process, assumptions and data, uncertainty, and costs. These questions can be answered by "yes" or "no." A score of 16 yes's indicates that reasonable steps are being taken to obtain good forecasts for the organization; it provides an ideal to work toward. A score of 16 no's indicates negligence. The Ajax Corporation scored 16 no's. In other words, Ajax was as bleak a picture as I could imagine in terms of forecasting procedures.

The use of a formal checklist, such as the one presented here, should improve the assessment of forecast uncertainty by pointing out shortcomings in the current process. More important, it should provide ideas on how to improve the process.

REFERENCES

1. Armstrong, J. Scott, "Forecasting with Econometric Methods: Folklore vs. Fact," *Journal of Business,* vol. 51, 1978, pp. 549–64.

2. Armstrong, J. Scott, "Econometric Methods and the Science Court," *Journal of Business,* vol. 51, 1978, pp. 595–600.

3. Armstrong, J. Scott, "Advocacy and Objectivity in Science," *Management Science,* vol. 25, 1979, pp. 423–428.

4. Armstrong, J. Scott, "Relative Accuracy of Judgmental and Extrapolative Methods in Forecasting Annual Earnings," *Journal of Forecasting,* vol. 2, 1983, pp. 437–447.

5. Armstrong, J. Scott, "Forecasting by Extrapolation," *Interfaces,* vol. 14, no. 6, 1984, 52–61.

6. Armstrong, J. Scott, *Long-Range Forecasting: From Crystal Ball to Computer,* Wiley-Interscience, New York, 1985.

7. Armstrong, J. Scott, "Research on Forecasting: A Quarter-Century Review, 1960–1984," *Interfaces,* vol. 16, no. 1, 1986, pp. 89–109.

8. Cosier, Richard A., "The Effects of Three Potential Aids for Making Strategic Decisions on Predictive Accuracy," *Organizational Behavior and Human Performance,* vol. 22, 1978, pp. 295–306.

9. Dalrymple, Douglas J., "Sales Forecasting Practices: Results from a United States Survey," *International Journal of Forecasting,* in press.

10. Danos, Paul, and Eugene A. Imhoff, "Factors Affecting Auditors' Evaluations of Forecasts," *Journal of Accounting Research,* vol. 21, 1983, pp. 473–494.

11. Denton, Frank T., and E. H. Oksanen, "A Multi-Country Analysis of the Effects of Data Revisions on an Economic Model," *Journal of American Statistical Association,* vol. 67, 1972, pp. 286–291.

12. DeSanctis, Geraldine, "Computer Graphics as Decision Aids: Directions for Research," *Decision Sciences,* vol. 15, 1984, pp. 463–487.

13. Fildes, Robert, "Quantitative Forecasting—The State of the Art: Econometric Models," *Journal of the Operational Research Society,* vol. 36, 1985, pp. 549–580.

14. Fischhoff, Baruch, and Ruth Beyth, "I Knew It Would Happen: Remembered Probabilities of the Once-Future Things," *Organizational Behavior and Human Performance,* vol. 13, 1975, pp. 1–16.

15. Fischhoff, Baruch, and Don MacGregor, "Subjective Confidence in Forecasts," *Journal of Forecasting,* vol. 1, 1982, pp. 155–172.

16. Glantz, Michael H. "Consequences and Responsibilities in Drought Forecasting: The Case of Yakima," 1977, *Water Resources Research,* vol. 18, 1982, pp. 3–13.

17. Goldberg, Lewis R., "Simple Models or Simple Processes? Some Research on Clinical Judgments," *American Psychologist,* vol. 23, 1968, pp. 483–496.

18. Griffith, J. R., and B. T. Wellman, "Forecasting Bed Needs and Recommending Facilities Plans for Community Hospitals: A Review of Past Performance," *Medical Care,* vol. 17, 1979, pp. 293–303.

19. Harris, J. G. Jr., "Judgmental versus Mathematical Prediction: An Investigation by Analogy of the Clinical vs. Statistical Controversy," *Behavioral Science,* vol. 8, 1963, pp. 324–335.

20. Hatjoullis, G., and D. Wood, "Economic Forecasts—An Analysis of Performance," *Business Economist,* vol. 10, Spring 1979, pp. 6–21.

21. Hogarth, Robin M., "A Note on Aggregating Opinions," *Organizational Behavior and Human Performance,* vol. 21, 1978, pp. 40–46.

22. Holloman, Charles R., and Hal W. Hendrick, "Adequacy of Group Decisions as a Function of the Decision-Making Process," *Academy of Management Journal,* vol. 15, 1972, pp. 175–184.

23. Johnson, Jeffrey L., "A Ten-Year Delphi Forecast in the Electronics Industry," *Industrial Marketing Management,* vol. 5, March 1976, pp. 45–55.

24. Kahneman, Daniel, and A. Tversky, "On the Psychology of Prediction," *Psychological Review,* vol. 80, 1973, pp. 237–251.

25. Kelly, E. Lowell, and D. W. Fiske, "The Prediction of Success in the VA Training Program in Clinical Psychology," *American Psychologist,* vol. 5, 1950, pp. 395–406.

26. Koriat, Asher, Sarah Lichtenstein, and Baruch Fischhoff, "Reasons for Confidence,"

Journal of Experimental Psychology: Human Learning and Memory, vol. 6, 1980, pp. 107–118.

27. Larwood, Laurie, and William Whittaker, "Managerial Myopia: Self-Serving Biases in Organizational Planning," *Journal of Applied Psychology*, vol. 62, 1977, 194–198.

28. Lawrence, Michael J., R. H. Edmondson, and M. J. O'Connor, "An Examination of Judgmental Extrapolation of Time Series," *International Journal of Forecasting*, vol. 1, 1985, pp. 25–35.

29. Levenbach, Hans, and James P. Cleary, *The Modern Forecaster*, Lifetime Learning, Belmont, CA, 1984.

30. Libby, Robert, and Roger K. Blashfield, "Performance of a Composite as a Function of the Number of Judges," *Organizational Behavior and Human Performance*, vol. 21, 1978, pp. 121–129.

31. Lichtenstein, Sarah, B. Fischhoff, and L. D. Phillips, "Calibration of Probabilities: The State of the Art," in H. Jungermann and G. de Zeeuw, eds., *Decision Making and Change in Human Affairs*, Reidel, Dordrecht, Netherlands, 1977.

32. Martino, Joseph P., *Technological Forecasting for Decision Making*, American Elsevier, New York, 1983.

33. McDonald, John, "An Analysis of the Significance of Revisions to Some Quarterly U.K. National Income Time Series," *Journal of the Royal Statistical Society, Series A*, vol. 138, 1975, pp. 242–256.

34. McLaughlin, Robert L., "The Forecasters' Batting Averages," *Business Economics*, vol. 3, May 1973, pp. 58–59.

35. McNees, Stephen K., "An Evaluation of Economic Forecasts," *New England Economic Review*, November/December 1975, pp. 3–39.

36. Murphy, Allan H., and Barbara G. Brown, "A Comparative Evaluation of Objective and Subjective Weather Forecasts in the United States," *Journal of Forecasting*, vol. 3, 1984, pp. 369–393.

37. Rothe, James T., "Effectiveness of Sales Forecasting Methods," *Industrial Marketing Management*, vol. 7, 1978, pp. 114–118.

38. Rush, Howard, and William Page, "Long-Term Metals Forecasting: The Track Record 1910–1964," *Futures*, vol. 11, 1979, pp. 321–337.

39. Sackman, Harold, *Delphi Critique: Expert Opinion, Forecasting and Group Process*, Heath, Lexington, 1975.

40. Schnee, Jerome E., "Predicting the Unpredictable: The Impact of Meteorological Satellites on Weather Forecasting," *Technological Forecasting and Social Change*, vol. 10, 1977, pp. 299–307.

41. Schreuder, Hein, and Klaassen, Jan, "Confidential Revenue and Profit Forecasts by Management and Financial Analysts: Evidence from the Netherlands," *Accounting Review*, vol. 59, 1984, pp. 64–77.

42. Slovic, Paul, and B. Fischhoff, "On the Psychology of Experimental Surprises," *Journal of Experimental Psychology; Human Perception and Performance*, vol. 3, 1977, pp. 544–551.

43. Stewart, Thomas R., and Michael H. Glantz, "Expert Judgment and Climate Forecasting: A Methodological Critique of 'Climate Change to the Year 2000'," *Climatic Change*, vol. 7, no. 1, 1985, pp. 159–183.

44. Timmers, Han, and Willem A. Wagenaar, "Inverse Statistics and Misperception of Exponential Growth," *Perception and Psychophysics*, vol. 21, 1977, pp. 558–562.

45. Vancil, Richard F., "The Accuracy of Long-Range Planning," *Harvard Business Review*, vol. 10, 1970, pp. 98–101.

46. Wagenaar, Willem A., and Sabato D. Sagaria, "Misperception of Exponential Growth," *Perception and Psychophysics,* vol. 18, 1975, pp. 416–422.

47. Wagenaar, Willem A., and Han Timmers, "The Pond-and-Duckweed Problem: Three Experiments on the Misperception of Exponential Growth," *Acta Psychologica,* vol. 43, 1979, pp. 239–251.

48. Wells, Gary L., and Donna M. Murray, "Eyewitness Confidence," in Gary L. Wells and E. F. Loftus, eds., *Eyewitness Testimony: Psychological Perspectives,* Cambridge University Press, New York, 1984.

49. Williams, W. H., and M. L. Goodman, "A Simple Method for the Construction of Empirical Confidence Limits for Economic Forecasts," *Journal of the American Statistical Association,* vol. 66, 1971, pp. 752–754.

CHAPTER

33

THE FUTURE OF FORECASTING

SPYROS MAKRIDAKIS

INSEAD, Fontainebleau, France

No book on forecasting can avoid looking at the future of the forecasting field itself. As with any forecasting task, this requires examining the past, interpreting the present, and predicting the future. The chapters of this handbook have provided a wide variety of material dealing with the present state of the forecasting art, the areas in which forecasting can be successfully applied, the difficulties involved in such applications, and the challenges facing those who select a career in forecasting or participate in and manage aspects of the forecasting function. To complete our coverage of the field of forecasting, several questions need to be addressed concerning the future:

Where is forecasting going?

Where will new opportunities for improving the forecasting function come from?

How can the study of the future help executives improve planning and strategy and make better decisions in the present?

These and related questions are addressed in this concluding chapter, following a brief historical perspective on forecasting methods and practices.

FORECASTING: A HISTORICAL PERSPECTIVE

By the late 1930s the scientific foundations of what was to become the field of forecasting had been laid. The least squares estimation procedure proposed by Gauss and Legendre,[1] the work of Schuster[26] on hidden periodicities, the development of autoregressive[33] and moving average models,[29] the decomposition of time series,[19] and the application of regression techniques to real life data[11,25,30] laid the basis for all subsequent work.

World War II and a new breed of scientists introduced a solid theoretical vigor to the developing discipline,[31,32] and provided the means of integrating the work so far done in a sound theoretical framework. By 1950 the ground was prepared for the rapid growth in both the theory and practice of forecasting that has continued uninterrupted until today.

Between 1950 and 1970, five parallel and independent subfields were developed and utilized within the field of quantitative forecasting:

1. Econometric models, of increasing size and complexity, were used by economists to explain macroeconomic phenomena, answer "what if" types of questions, and forecast.

2. Filtering methods were used by engineers in their quest to filter "noise" out of an underlying pattern.

3. ARMA (Auto Regressive Moving Averages) schemes were used by statisticians to model the generating process of a wide class of time series and forecasts.

4. Decomposition techniques were used by governmental economists and forecasters to separate the components of economic time series in order to extract seasonality and trend cycles.

5. Exponential smoothing methods were used by operation researchers to forecast mainly for production scheduling and inventory demand.

In addition, human judgment, often needed to supplement quantitative methods, was studied to understand how people forecast. The work of management scientists[28] and psychologists[15] had direct relevance for forecasters.

During the late 1960s and 1970s, the field of forecasting started becoming popular. This was due partly to the appearance of commercial econometric services (DRI, Wharton Associates, Chase), partly to the work of Kalman[16] and Brown,[6] and partly to the influence of the Box and Jenkins[5] methodology.

A separate development during this time—the computer—brought badly needed computational power to the fingertips of researchers and practitioners. Computers provided the means to apply the theoretical knowledge of the new discipline to a wide variety of tasks in government,[27] economics,[17] business and military affairs,[6] and academia.[5] Forecasting applications quickly mushroomed and created a new industry and a professional forecasting body.

Popularity brought awareness, created demand, and resulted in commercial success as business and government organizations started using forecasting methods. At the same time, expectations of forecasting's capabilities began to run unrealistically high. Statistical methods and powerful computers were thought to be capable of always forecasting accurately, and of eliminating all future uncertainty. This did not happen. The benefits of forecasting have not included prophecy.

The 1970s and 1980s have been a learning ground. Initial forecasting successes were followed by large errors, including failures in predicting changes in economic activity (e.g., the 1973–1975 recession and the 1983 recovery) and their consequences on business revenues and costs. The complaints from users of forecasts were loud and had a sobering effect on those working in the field. It became obvious that a better understanding of the advantages and limitations of forecasting was necessary. As a consequence, the assessment of forecasting performance was brought into the forefront of research activities.

By 1970 a great number of different types of forecasts had already been made in such areas as population, transportation, energy, material prices, the economy, and business. It was natural, therefore, to study such predictions and evaluate their accuracy.[2,4,34] In addition, empirical studies scrutinized the relative performance of the various methods.[3,10,21,22] Finally, surveys among users in business and government provided a better knowledge of forecasting practices and of the usefulness of various methods.[7,24]

Evaluations of past forecasts, empirical studies, and surveys among forecasting users have provided the discipline of forecasting with information almost equivalent to that gained by laboratory experimentation. Theories and methods can now be evaluated in an objective manner, and the acceptability of methods among users can be discovered. Moreover, a realistic attitude toward the size of forecasting errors can be promoted, and the future uncertainty inherent in various forecasting tasks can be better understood.

FORECASTING: AN ASSESSMENT

Many forecasting methods are available at present, and guidelines are conflicting as to the most appropriate method, or the best way of forecasting. Although specific findings can be debated, the following six general conclusions can be drawn:

1. *Contradictory Results.* Different empirical studies have reached different conclusions as to the performance of various methods. No study has shown a clear superiority of one method over another. Moreover, no single method has, over time, consistently outperformed the remaining methods. This is true with economic and financial forecasting as well as with quantitative models.

2. *Judgmental Forecasting.* Humans possess unique knowledge and inside information that is not easy to include in quantitative methods. Surprisingly, however, empirical studies and laboratory experiments have shown that human judgmental forecasts are less accurate than those of quantitative methods. Humans tend to be optimistic and to underestimate future uncertainty. In addition, the cost of forecasting judgmentally is often considerably higher than the cost of using quantitative methods.

3. *Econometric Methods.* Empirical studies have shown that forecasts using econometric models are not necessarily more accurate than those employing time series methods.[10] However, econometric models are not used purely for forecasting. Instead, they attempt to explain economic or business phenomena and to increase our understanding of relationships between variables. In this area they provide unique information not obtainable by time series methods. Such information can indirectly contribute to improving forecasting accuracy.

4. *Sophisticated Methods.* Empirical evidence indicates that large, complex, or statistically sophisticated methods do not necessarily produce more accurate forecasts than smaller or relatively simple methods. This is true both in the area of econometric models and time series methods. Moreover, this conclusion is supported by evidence in other fields.[9]

5. *Adaptive Methods.* Adaptive methods are not more accurate than nonadaptive ones.[12] This finding holds true for short, medium, and long forecasting horizons.

6. *Least Squares Methods.* It has been found that methods that give equal weight to all data (ordinary least squares) are less accurate than discounted least squares, which weigh the most recent data more heavily.[22]

Implications of the Empirical Evidence

Judgmental forecasters are incapable of separating wishful thinking, politics, personal considerations, and their own emotional state from an objective evaluation of the past, present, or future. In addition, judgmental biases and limitations,[15] together with the human need to master and control the environment,[18] make for inaccurate forecasts, large errors, and underestimation of future uncertainty (see also Chapter 30).

Quantitative methods identify established patterns or existing relationships in a statistically optimal fashion, which is not the case with people, who can be influenced by illusory correlations.[13] The biggest advantage of quantitative methods is their objectivity. They predict the continuation of past patterns or relationships in a statistically unbiased way.

A major problem with quantitative models is that fitting a model to a set of data is a completely different task from that of forecasting beyond the historical data. Forecasting is concerned with the future, while fitting a model involves attempting to identify patterns or relationships that existed in the past. To make a forecast, established patterns and relationships must be extrapolated (relationships can also be interpolated). Chart 33-1 shows the percentage of data series in a forecasters' competition (the M-competition[22]) without and with pattern changes. The majority of the real-life series in this competition show a pattern change. Existing methods, however, assume

CHART 33-1. Series in M-Competition Without and With Pattern Changes

Type of Series	No Pattern Change	Small Pattern Change	Large Pattern Change
Monthly	55%	35%	10%
Quarterly	25%	50%	25%
Yearly	33.3%	33.3%	33.3%

CHART 33-2. Spearman's Rank Correlations Between Model Fitting and Various Forecasting Horizons

Forecasting Horizon	Correlation	
	Percent Errors	Square Error
1	.22	.25
2	.22	.22
3	.20	.21
4	.13	.13
6	.09	.07
8	.05	.05
12	.05	.06
15	−.01	.02
18	−.01	−.01

consistency[20] of patterns and relationships in order to forecast. Fitting the "best" model to historical data does not necessarily minimize postsample forecasting errors. Chart 33-2 shows the rank correlation between the accuracy of model fitting and that of forecasting (eight of the methods in the M-competition have been used). The rank correlations are initially small and become zero as the forecasting horizon increases. The relationship between model fitting and forecasting is small, suggesting that the accuracy of model fitting is a poor indicator of the accuracy of forecasts. Patterns seem to change frequently in the real world. Charts 33-1 and 33-2 suggest that alternative strategies to those presently used (i.e., fitting a model to past data) must be developed, if the objective is to improve the accuracy of forecasting beyond available historical data.

FUTURE DIRECTIONS

For academics, the major challenge ahead is the development of new methods, or the modification of existing ones, that are capable of accurately forecasting series whose patterns or relationships change over time. Practitioners, on the other hand, must understand and be more ready to accept the advantages and limitations of forecasting, and deal more effectively with issues of implementation.

Random Versus Systematic Changes

Data series are characterized by both random and systematic (i.e., nonrandom) changes that can, in turn, be of a temporary or permanent nature. Chart 33-3 outlines the ability of fixed model/parameter methods (using ordinary or discounted least squares) and adaptive model/parameter ones to predict under various conditions. Chart 33-4 illustrates the behavior of each of the forecasting methods in Chart 33-3 and shows the resulting forecasts using series from the M-Competition.[22] From these charts it appears that no method can deal with all three possibilities (random, systematic temporary, systematic permanent) of changes. An interesting possibility for future re-

CHART 33-3. Performance of Fixed Versus Adaptive Models Under Various Environmental Conditions

Type of Environment		Fixed Parameter/Model Methods		Adaptive Parameter/ Model Methods
		Ordinary Least Squares (OLS) Estimation	Discounted Least Squares (DLS) Estimation	
No change (random (fluctuations)		Optimal Changes ignored as they ought to be	Theorectically no problem Practically some recent random changes might influence forecasts	Theoretically no problem Practically some recent random changes might result in overreaction of model and its forecasts
Systematic Changes	Temporary (mostly cyclical fluctuations)	Problems for short term, since temporary changes are ignored Forecasts might be adequate for long-term	Best alternative Short-term forecasts will be slowly adjusted to changes Long-term forecasts will not be unduly influenced by temporary changes	Accurate short-term forecasts; serious problems for long term as changes are assumed to be permanent
	Permanent (mostly changes in trends)	Major problems for both short and long term as permanent changes are ignored	Forecasts will be slowly adjusted to take account of permanent changes as more weight is given to recent past	Optimal Model (or its parameters) adapts to permanent changes as it ought to

search is obviously the development of methods that can deal with all three types of changes in data.

Present forecasting methods use only part of the historical information available. Adaptive methods, for instance, have a short memory (they ignore all but recent information). Ordinary least squares methods, on the other hand, ignore systematic changes. This makes the forecasts they provide unresponsive to recent systematic changes and can result in large errors (they assume that all systematic changes around the basic pattern or relationship are random).

Past data contain information that can help forecasters identify the existence of future systematic changes and their nature. In the data of chart 33-5a there is no reason to suspect any kind of systematic change; the series is characterized by random fluctuations. Chart 33-5b, however, shows several temporary (cyclical) systematic changes. It could be assumed, therefore, that the most recent downturn is also cyclical. Finally, the information in Chart 33-5c indicates several changes in trend that might be permanent.

Various methods would provide different forecasts given each of the three series of Chart 33-5. All methods would forecast well from the data of Chart 33-5a, ordinary least squares probably doing best. It makes no sense, however, to extrapolate the most recent systematic change to make a forecast from the data of Chart 33-5b. The chance is high that the downturn is cyclical and that it will end soon. A way must be found, therefore, to predict the timing of the turning point. Moreover, if confidence intervals are to be constructed, they should not be symmetrical, since the chances of reaching a turning point increase as the time horizon of forecasting becomes longer. Ordinary least squares methods would do badly for the short term and better for the long term. Adaptive methods, assuming that the systematic change is permanent when in fact it is temporary, would do well for the short term (until the turning point) and badly for the long term. The performance of discounted least squares methods would be between those of ordinary least squares and adaptive methods.

It is not clear how to forecast from the data of Chart 33-5c. Although there seem to be several changes in trend, judgemental information is needed to decide whether the most recent change will continue. If no additional information is available, the long term could be forecasted by extrapolating the most recent change in trend. Alternatively, a more conservative forecast could be made by horizontally extrapolating the most recent value(s). When permanent systematic changes are involved, ordinary least squares methods will do extremely badly for both the short and the long term. The accuracy of adaptive methods will depend on the extent (intensity) of the changes and their permanence.

Another issue requiring further research is the combining of forecasts, which substantially improves forecasting accuracy.[23] Even further improvement might be possible by a better selection of the methods being combined. Theoretically, it is hard to explain the high accuracy obtained by combining.

CHART 33-4. Forecasts of Regression (OLS), Holt's Exponential Smoothing (DLS), and Bayesian Forecasting (Adaptive) Under Various Types of Changes

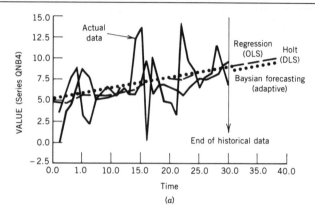

(a)

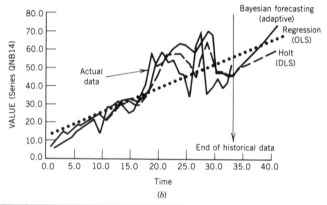

(b)

(a) Recurring changes around basic linear pattern. OLS, DLS, and adaptive methods provide similar forecasts. (All three methods extrapolate continuation of basic pattern)

(b) Systematic change in pattern. Short-term forecasts of methods different, long-term closer. (Adaptive method follows change of pattern and goes toward long-term linear trend faster than DLS.)

(c) Steep change in pattern. Forecasts of three methods very different. Difference becomes larger in long term. (Adaptive method assumes latest change to be permanent, OLS ignores it, DLS forecasts in between.)

(d) Exponential increase in trend. Forecasts of methods different in particular for long term. (Adaptive method follows the continuation of the pattern fastest, OLS method the slowest, DLS method in between.)

Assuming constancy of patterns or relationships, the best theoretical model should produce the most accurate forecasts.[14] But since patterns and relationships change, combining the forecasts of several models (some of them clearly inappropriate) produces an average that comes closer to reality than that of a theoretically correct model.

Several additional aspects need to be investigated through further research. How does one treat series with a permanent change in their pattern

CHART 33-4 (*Continued*)

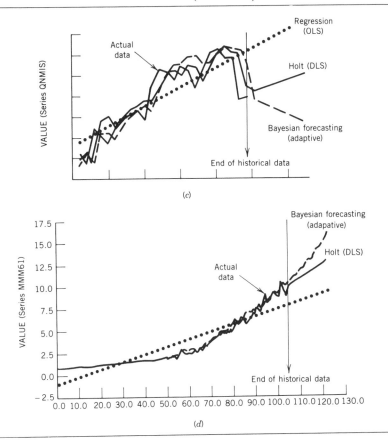

(c)

(d)

or relationship? Should the data before such a change be dropped, adjusted, or ignored? How should outliers be treated if the objective is not model fitting but forecasting (e.g., an outlier at the end of the data should not be ignored but should be given more weight if it indicates a permanent change).

Implementing Forecasting

To be useful, forecasting must improve planning, strategy, or decision making. There are three obstacles to its successful implementation, related to people, data, and systems. In addition, management must develop a more realistic view of forecasting's abilities and limitations.

People's Attitudes Toward Forecasting

People prefer making forecasts judgmentally. They believe that their knowledge of the product, market, and customers, as well as their insights and

CHART 33-5. Three Types of Series Requiring Different Forecasting Strategies

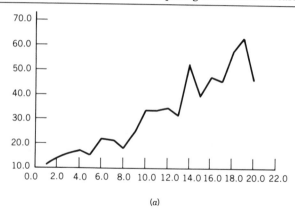

(a)

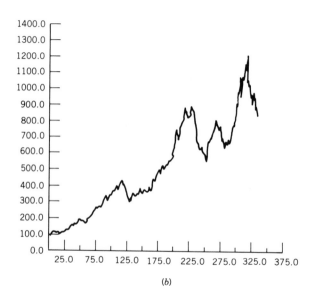

(b)

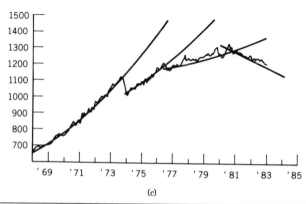

(c)

(a) Historical data suggest that latest downturn is random.
(b) Historical data suggest that latest downturn is cyclical.
(c) Historical data suggest that latest downturn might be permanent.

inside information, give them a unique ability to forecast judgmentally. They do not usually consider that quantitative methods can do an adequate job. As has been discussed, the empirical evidence shows otherwise. People should therefore concentrate their efforts on predicting systematic changes and dealing with important but specific parts of forecasting such as aggregating series, predicting sales to large customers, and figuring out the effect of special events or actions. It is not good practice to make judgmental forecasts when forecasts are required frequently and in large numbers. In such cases quantitative methods are more appropriate. Work in the judgmental psychology area suggests that formalizing the process of forecasting can considerably improve predictive accuracy.[8] Thus, instead of approaching each situation on an ad hoc basis, it is preferable to develop and systematically apply decision rules for dealing with similar forecasting tasks. People's efforts can then be concentrated on deciding what rule to apply, when existing rules are not valid any more and should be modified, or when new rules should be added.

Decision rules have three advantages. First, they save time: Instead of there being tens or hundreds of individualized situations, such situations are classified into categories that are dealt with in the same systematic way. Second, for discovery of decision rules, careful thinking and discussion are needed. Several people must be asked for the most appropriate factors influencing a forecasting situation. Moreover, the importance of such factors can then be tested and their influences measured, with use of a multiple regression model if quantitative inputs are available. Finally, the benefits from the decision rules, if any, can be determined so that logical improvements can be made if variations on them (or new rules) are employed.

A way of inducing people to consider quantitative forecasts and formalized decision rules is to suggest that such predictions be used as benchmarks, to be compared with judgmental forecasts. The comparison usually shows little or no difference, and can be used as a way of changing the forecasting process. After all, the objective is not to abolish judgment as a way of forecasting, but rather to shift the time spent on ad hoc work to the systematic handling of the various forecasting tasks.

Data and Information

Forecasting is not possible without historical data or judgmental information. Improving forecasting accuracy requires building an appropriate data base specifically for forecasting purposes. It also requires improving judgmental knowledge of the various forecasting tasks and the factors that affect them.

People forget and/or change jobs. Thus, finding ways of recording information can improve the handling of similar situations in the future. This means that information about the factors that affect sales, including special events or actions, should be classified and kept for future reference. Dealing with future situations can be facilitated if a catalog of similar past situations, and their impact, can be consulted.

Forecasting Systems

Computers provide storage and computational capabilities for dealing with the forecasting needs of organizations. As computers become bigger, cheaper, and more powerful, and as better programs are developed, the task of forecasting is accomplished more efficiently. Finding the right computer program and integrating it in an appropriate data base become critical for the successful implementation of forecasting methods. Forecasting systems should be selected for their friendliness and ease of interaction. Effective ways of incorporating human judgment in quantitative forecasts must be made available.

Realistic Expectations in Forecasting

The usefulness of forecasting can be improved if management adopts a more realistic attitude: Forecasting should not be viewed as a substitute for prophecy but rather as the best way of identifying and extrapolating established patterns or relationships to try to plan for the future. If such an attitude is accepted, forecasting errors must be considered inevitable and the circumstances that cause them investigated. If errors are viewed negatively, the preparers of forecasts attempt to hide them or to rationalize their occurrence. Accepting and understanding the size and nature of forecasting errors, on the other hand, facilitate learning and reduce the chances of making similar mistakes in the future. Users of forecasts must understand that the alternative of no forecasting will not improve their ability to cope with the future.

CONCLUSIONS

Forecasting will have an increasingly important role. This does not mean that forecasting accuracy will substantially increase—although significant improvements will be made—but rather that managers will understand better and accept the advantages and limitations of forecasting. Forecasting the future in a formal, systematic way is necessary, and although results can be inaccurate there is no alternative. Not doing so (see Chart 33-6) results in larger errors and worse results. Finally, future uncertainty cannot be eliminated, no matter how much money or effort is spent on forecasting. Instead, an important forecasting task is to assess such uncertainty in a realistic way. The advent of forecasting may have made managers feel more uncertain about the future, rather than less. Learning to live with uncertainty and figuring out its impact on planning and strategy will be a major challenge for both forecasters and managers.

CHART 33-6. The Don'ts of Forecasting

If Large Forecasting Errors or Other Problems Exist, Don't Attempt to Solve Them by:	Reasons
Abandoning forecasting	Dealing with planning and strategy will be even more problematic if no formal forecasting is done.
Substituting people	People do not necessarily produce more accurate forecasts than methods. At the same time, their forecasts are usually more expensive.
Using more sophisticated methods	Empirical evidence has shown that gains in accuracy from sophisticated methods are usually small.
Subscribing to more expensive newsletters or to several forecasting services	Empirical evidence has shown that forecasting accuracy is not improved by buying more expensive forecasts.
Assuming that present economic conditions will continue forever	History has shown that cyclical factors have always influenced business and economic series.

REFERENCES

1. Abbe, C., "Historical Note on the Method of Least Squares," *American Journal of Science and Arts.*, vol. 1, 1871, pp. 411–415.

2. Ahlers, D., and J. Lakonishok, "A Study of Economists' Consensus Forecasts," *Management Science*, vol. 29, no. 10, 1983, pp. 1113–1125.

3. Armstrong, J. S., "Forecasting with Econometric Methods: Folklore Versus Fact," *Journal of Business*, vol. 51, no. 4, 1978, pp. 549–564.

4. Ascher, W., *Forecasting: An Appraisal for Policy Makers and Planners*, Johns Hopkins University Press, Baltimore, 1978.

5. Box, G. E. P., and G. M. Jenkins, *Time Series Analysis: Forecasting and Control*, Holden-Day, San Francisco, 1970.

6. Brown, R. G., *Statistical Forecasting for Inventory Control*, Holden-Day, San Francisco, 1959.

7. Dalrymple, D. J., "Sales Forecasting Practices: Results from a United States Survey," *International Journal of Forecasting*, in press.

8. Dawes, R. M., "Forecasting One's Own Preferences," *International Journal of Forecasting*, vol. 2, 1986, pp. 5–15.

9. Einhorn, H. J., and R. M. Hogarth, "Unit Weighting Schemes For Decision Making," *Organizational Behaviour and Human Performance*, vol. 13, 1975, pp. 171–192.

10. Fildes, R., "Quantitative Forecasting the State of the Art: Econometric Models," *Journal of the Operational Research Society*, vol. 36, no. 7, 1985, pp. 549–580.

11. Galton, F., "Typical Laws of Heredity," *Proceedings of the Royal Institute*, vol. 8, 1877, pp. 282–301.

12. Gardner, E. S., and D. G. Dannenbring, "Forecasting with Exponential Smoothing: Some Guidelines for Model Selection," *Decision Sciences,* vol. 11, 1980, pp. 370–383.

13. Golding, S. L., and L. G. Roger, "Illusory Correlation and Subjective Judgement," *Journal of Abnormal Psychology,* vol. 80, no. 3, 1972, pp. 249–260.

14. Jenkins, G. M., "Discussion of Newbold and Granger," *Journal of the Royal Statistical Society,* Series A, vol. 137, 1974, pp. 148–150.

15. Kahneman, D., and A. Tversky, "On the Psychology of Prediction," *Psychological Review,* vol. 80, no. 4, 1973, pp. 237–251.

16. Kalman, R. E., "A New Approach to Linear Filtering and Prediction Problems," *Journal of Basic Engineering,* D, vol. 82, 1960, pp. 35–44.

17. Klein, L. R., *An Introduction to Econometrics,* Prentice-Hall, Englewood Cliffs, NJ, 1962.

18. Langer, E. J., "The Illusion of Control," *Journal of Personality and Social Psychology,* vol. 32, no. 2, 1975, pp. 311–328.

19. Macauley, F. R., "The Smoothing of Time Series," *National Bureau of Economic Research,* 1930, pp. 121–136.

20. Makridakis, S., "Forecasting Accuracy and the Assumption of Constancy," *OMEGA,* vol. 9, no. 3, 1981, pp. 307–311.

21. Makridakis, S., and M. Hibon, "Accuracy of Forecasting: An Empirical Investigation," *Journal of the Royal Statistical Society,* vol. 142, part 2, 1979, pp. 97–125.

22. Makridakis, S., et al, "The Accuracy of Extrapolation (Time Series) Methods: Results of a Forecasting Competition," *Journal of Forecasting,* vol. 1, 1982, pp. 111–153.

23. Makridakis, S., and R. Winkler, "Averages of Forecasts: Some Empirical Results," *Management Science,* vol. 29, no. 9, 1983, pp. 987–996.

24. Mentzer, J. T., and J. E. Cox, "Familiarity, Application, and Performance of Sales Forecasting Techniques," *Journal of Forecasting,* vol. 3, no. 1, 1984, pp. 27–36.

25. Pearson, K., "Regression, Heredity, and Panmixia," *Philosophical Transactions,* vol. A-187, 1896, pp. 253–318.

26. Schuster, A., "On the Periodicities of Sunspots," *Philosophical Transactions,* A, vol. 206, 1906, pp. 69–81.

27. Shiskin, J., et al., "The X-11 Variant of the Census II Method Seasonal Adjustment Program," Bureau of the Census, Technical Paper, No. 15, 1967.

28. Simon, H., "A Behavioral Model of Rational Choice," *Quarterly Journal of Economics,* vol. 69, 1955, pp. 99–118.

29. Slutsky, E., "The Summation of Random Causes as the Source of Cyclic Processes," *Econometricia,* vol. 5, 1937, pp. 105–146.

30. Snedecor, G. W., *Statistical Methods,* 1st ed., Iowa State Press, Ames, 1937.

31. Wiener, N., *Times Series,* MIT Press, Cambridge, MA, 1964, (1st ed. 1949).

32. Wold, H., *A Study in the Analysis of Stationary Time Series,* Almgrist and Wiksell, Stockholm, 1954, (1st ed. 1938).

33. Yule, G. U., "On the Method of Investigating Periodicities in Disturbed Series, with Special Reference to Wolfer's Sunspot Number," *Philosophical Transactions,* A, vol. 226, 1927, pp. 267–298.

34. Zarnowitz, V., "The Accuracy of Individual and Group Forecasts from Business Outlook Surveys," *Journal of Forecasting,* vol. 3, 1984, pp. 11–26.

INDEX

617